Ecclesiastical Memorials
by John Strype

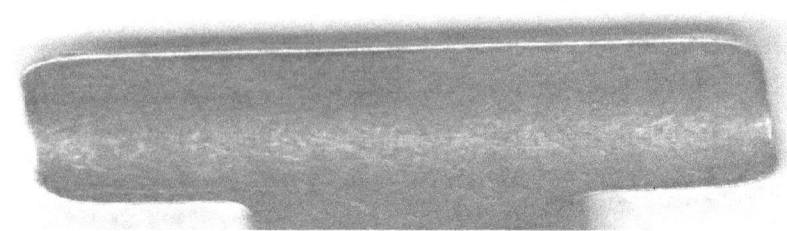

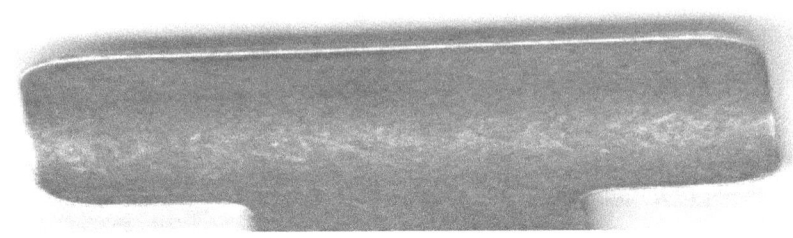

ECCLESIASTICAL MEMORIALS,

RELATING CHIEFLY TO

RELIGION,

AND

THE REFORMATION OF IT,

AND THE EMERGENCIES

OF THE

CHURCH OF ENGLAND,

UNDER

KING HENRY VIII. KING EDWARD VI.

AND

QUEEN MARY I.

WITH

LARGE APPENDIXES, CONTAINING ORIGINAL PAPERS, RECORDS, &c.

One generation shall praise thy works unto another, and declare thy power —The memorial of thine abundant kindness shall be shewed; and men shall sing of thy righteousness.

Psalm cxlv. 4, 7.

BY JOHN STRYPE, M.A.

VOL. III. PART II.

OXFORD,

AT THE CLARENDON PRESS.

MDCCCXXII.

HISTORICAL MEMORIALS,

ECCLESIASTICAL AND CIVIL,

OF

EVENTS

UNDER

THE REIGN OF QUEEN MARY I.

WHEREIN ARE BROUGHT TO LIGHT

VARIOUS THINGS CONCERNING THE MANAGEMENT OF AFFAIRS DURING THE FIVE YEARS OF HER GOVERNMENT:

AND, MORE PARTICULARLY,

The restoring of the Pope's authority and the Popish religion in this kingdom
and the rigorous methods of burning, and other severities, for the
replanting of it, used towards such as adhered to the
religion reformed under King Edward VI.

a 2

THE

CONTENTS OF THE CHAPTERS

IN THE

ECCLESIASTICAL MEMORIALS

OF

QUEEN MARY'S REIGN.

HISTORICAL MEMORIALS,

CHIEFLY

ECCLESIASTICAL,

IN A

REVIEW TAKEN OF THE REIGN

OF

QUEEN MARY I.

CHAP. XLIX.

Historical passages and occurrences in the months of March,
April, May, June, July, August.

WE are now come to the fifth year of the Queen. And Anno 1557.
therein these things may be worthy noting for posterity.

March 25, the Moscovy ambassador, (vulgarly called March.
the Duke of Moscovy,) lately come to London, went to The Mosco
Court, and about half a score aldermen, and a great com- goes to
pany of merchants, free of the Russia company, with him. Court.
He took barge at the Three Cranes, in the Vintry. His
garment was of cloth of tissue, and his hat and nightcap
were set with great pearls and rich stones, the finest that
ever were seen: and his men in cloth of gold and red damask, in side-gowns.

On the 31st he rode to dinner to the Lord Mayor, with Dines with
five knights, aldermen, and five other aldermen, and many the Lord
notable merchants of the Moscovy corporation. He rid in Mayor.
a gown of tissue, rich; his garment of purple velvet embroidered; the gard, and his hat, and the border of his

nightcap, set with ouches of pearl and stone. His horse trapped in crimson velvet, embroidered of gold; and the bridle gorgeously beseen. Seven of his men in gowns of crimson damask, and cloth of gold. After dinner he retired to his lodging, accompanied with the aldermen and merchants.

April.
Five burnt.

April 3, five persons (some of them sent out of Essex) were condemned for heresy at St. Paul's, *viz.* three men and two women, (one with a staff in her hand,) to be burnt in Smithfield: and on the twelfth day (which was the Monday in Passion-week) they were accordingly burnt there. One of them was a barber, dwelling in Lime-street; and one of the women was the wife of the Crane, [that is, she kept the inn known by that sign,] at the Crutched Friars, beside Tower-hill.

374
Bishop elect of Lincoln and Dr. Perryn preach.

April 4, it being the Sunday before Passion Sunday, Dr. Watson, bishop elect of Lincoln, preached at Alhallows the More, (or the Great,) in Thames-street, in the afternoon, a great audience of people being present. And the same afternoon, at Bow church, in Cheapside, did Dr. Perryn preach, master warden of the Black Friars, in St. Bartholomew, in Smithfield.

Lord Abbot preaches.

On the 11th day, being Passion Sunday, the Lord Abbot preached at Westminster a sermon that had the fame of being as goodly a sermon as had been heard in that time.

Maundy.

On the 15th the King and Queen made their maundy at Greenwich.

Good Friday sermon.

On the 16th day, being Good Friday, the preacher at Paul's Cross was Mr. Murryn; [*i. e.* Morwen, I suppose, a learned man of Oxford;] and made a godly sermon to a great audience.

Spittle sermon by Dr. Pendleton, and

The 19th day of April was Easter Monday: then Dr. Pendleton preached at St. Mary Spittle; whose sermon had praise. There were present the lord mayor, and twenty-three aldermen, and three judges, and all the masters of the hospital with green staves in their hands, and all the children of the hospital in blue garments, both men, children, and women; kept with certain lands, and the charity of the court of aldermen. And there were, by computation, above 20,000 people, old and young, to hear the sermon, according to the old custom.

On the 20th day, being Easter Tuesday, Dr. Yong preached at St. Mary Spittle; where were present the lord mayor and twenty-five aldermen; none being absent but Mr. Woodroff, upon account of sickness, as it seems. Present also Lord Broke, lord chief justice, Lord Justice Brown, Sir John Baker, chancellor of the Augmentations, and Sir Roger Cholmeley, recorder.

On the same day the Mosco ambassador resorted to Westminster abbey, and heard mass: and after went to the Lord Abbot's to dinner: and dinner ended, came into the monastery, and went up to see St. Edward's shrine, new set up; and then saw all the place through. And so took his leave of my Lord Abbot; and divers aldermen and many merchants met him: who together rode into the park, and so to London.

On the 21st, being Wednesday in Easter-week, Dr. Watson, bishop of Lincoln elect, preached at the Spittle.

On this day the King and Queen removed from Greenwich to Westminster, against St. George's day.

April 23, being St. George's day, the King's Grace went a procession at Whitehall, through the hall, and round about the court hard by the gate, certain of the knights of the Garter accompanying him; viz. the Lord Mountagu, the Lord Admiral, Sir Anthony St. Leger, the Lord Cobham, the Lord Dacre, Sir Thomas Cheyne, the Lord Paget, the Earl of Pembroke, the Earl of Arundel, the Lord Treasurer, and Secretary Petre, in a robe of crimson velvet, with the garter embroidered on his shoulder, [as chancellor of the Garter.] One bare a rod of black; and a doctor, the book of records. Then went all the heralds. And then the Lord Talbot bare the sword: after him, the sergeant at arms. And then came the King, the Queen's Grace looking out of a window beside the court, on the garden side. And 375 the Bishop of Winchester did execute the mass, wearing his mitre. The same afternoon were chosen three knights of

CHAP.
XLIX.

Anno 1557.
the Garter; *viz.* the Lord Fitz-Water, the deputy of Ireland; Lord Grey of Wilton, deputy of Guynes; and Sir
Robert Rochester, comptroller of the Queen's house. After,
the Duke of Muscovia (as that ambassador was usually
termed) came through the hall, and the guard stood on a
row, in their rich coats, with halberts; and so passed up to
the Queen's chamber, with divers aldermen and merchants.
And after came down again to the chapel to evensong, to
see the ceremonies. And immediately came the King, (the
Lord Strange bearing the sword,) and the knights of the
Garter, to evensong: which being done, they went all up to
the chamber of presence. After came the ambassador, and
took his barge to London.

Percy
created Earl
of North-
umberland.
The 30th of April, Mr. Percy was made a knight and a
baron: and the next day, that is, May 1, was created, at
Whitehall, Earl of Northumberland, with eight heralds and
a dozen trumpeters, going through the Queen's chamber,
and through the hall. And afore him went the Earl of
Pembroke and the Lord Mountagu; then the Earls of Arundel and Rutland, and himself walking in the midst, all in
crimson velvet, wearing their parliament robes. He wore
a hat of velvet, and a coronet of gold on his head.

May.
A Spaniard
killed.
May 1, the Spaniards gave an instance of their proud,
bloody, and revengeful natures: for, about noon, certain of
them fought at the court gates against one Spaniard, and
one of them thrust him through with his rapier, who died
immediately. Two of them that did this fact were brought
into the Court by one of the guard, who delivered them to
some of the King's servants, to have them to the Marshalsea.

Dr. Chad-
sey at Paul's
Cross.
May 2, Dr. Chadsey preached the Paul's Cross sermon;
and therein declared that certain traitors were taken at Scarborough castle.

Lord Shan-
dois buried.
May 3, the Lord Shandois, otherwise called Sir John of
Bridges, was buried with heralds, an hearse of wax, four
banners of images, and other appendages of funeral honour.

Certain
rebels
On that same day came five persons to the Tower, who

were the chief of those that came out of France, whither
they had fled afore, and had taken the castle of Scarborough in Yorkshire; *viz.* Stafford, Saunders, Staywel,
[sometimes named Straley, or Stretchley,] and Proctor, and
a Frenchman.

On the 4th of this instant May, a great horse-rider, named
Sir James Granado, rid before the King and Queen in the
privy garden: but the bridle-bit breaking, his horse ran
away, and threw him against the wall, whereby he brake
his neck, and his brains were dashed out. The 6th day he
was buried honourably at St. Dunstan's in the East.

On the 5th was the Lady Chamberlain, late wife of Sir
Leonard Chamberlain, of Oxfordshire, buried, with a fair
hearse of wax. At the mass preached Dr. Chadsey. A
great dole of money given at the church. And after, a
great dinner.

On the 14th was burnt in Cheapside, and other places of
London, certain meal that was not sweet. They said the
mealman had put in lime and sand to deceive the people.
And he himself was committed to the Counter.

The 22d, six prisoners were brought out of the Tower to
receive their trial, namely, Stafford, captain Saunders, Sey-
wel or Stowel, Prowter or Procter, a Frenchman, and one
other. They all, excepting the Frenchman, were cast, and
carried back to the Tower, through London, by land. On
the 25th, the Frenchman was arraigned and cast.

The 23d, Dr. White, bishop of Winchester, preached at
St. Mary Overy's: where an heretic was present to hear the
sermon, named Steven Gratwick, sent up some time before
by the Bishop of Chichester, his ordinary, and laid in the
Marshalsea. He was of Bright Hempson in Sussex. He
freely, in the face of the congregation, confuted the Bishop's
sermon.

The 27th, being Ascension-day, the King and Queen rode
unto Westminster abbey, accompanied with many lords,
knights, and gentlemen. There their Graces went a procession about the cloister, and so heard mass.

The 28th, was Thomas Stafford beheaded on Tower-hill,

by nine of the clock, Mr. Wode being his ghostly father. And after, three more, *viz.* Stowel, Procter, and Bradford, were drawn from the Tower, through London, unto Tyburn, and there hanged and quartered. And the morrow after was Stafford quartered, and his quarters hanged on a car, and carried to Newgate to boil.

Three burnt.

The same morning were burnt, beyond St. George's church, on this side Newington, three men for heresy ; namely, Gratwick above-said, who seemed to be a minister, Morant, and King.

Lady Gates buried.

On the same day, in the forenoon, was buried Mrs. Gates, widow, late wife, as it seems, to Sir John Gates, executed the first year of this Queen's reign. She gave seventeen fine black gowns, and fourteen of broad russet for poor men. There were carried two white branches, ten staff-torches, and four great tapers : and after mass, a great dinner.

Heads and quarters set up.

On the 29th were the heads of the four persons the day before executed, set up on London-bridge, and their sixteen quarters on every gate of London.

A May-game.

On the 30th was a goodly May-game in Fanchurch-street, with drums, and guns, and pikes, and the nine worthies, who rid : and each made his speech. There was also the morris-dance, and an elephant, with a castle ; and the lord and lady of this May appeared, to make up the show.

June.

War proclaimed with France.

June the 7th, proclamation of war with France was made in London : wherein it was shewn, that the late Duke of Northumberland was supported and furthered in his treason by Henry the French King, and his ministers ; and that they had secretly practised with Wyat and his treacherous band, and with Dudley, Asheton, &c. and gave them favour : as also he did to Stafford and the other rebels lately executed ; whom he had entertained in his realm, and other more yet untaken. This was proclaimed with trumpets blowing, and ten heralds of arms, the lord mayor and aldermen present.

377

A stageplay at the Grey Friars.

The same day began a stageplay at the Grey Friars, of the passion of Christ.

The same day was the Fishmongers' procession. The

mass kept at St. Peter's in Cornhill. Three crosses were
borne, and an hundred priests, in copes; and after, the
clerks, singing *Salve festa dies.* Then came the parish, with
white rods in their hands; and then the craft of the fish- The Fishmongers; and after, the lord mayor and aldermen, and all procession.
his officers, with white rods also in their hands. And so to
Paul's; where they offered at the high altar: and after, to
dinner to Fishmongers'-hall.

The same day came the inhabitants of St. Clement's pa- Procession
rish, without Temple-bar, in goodly procession unto Paul's, of St. Cle-
and did oblation at the high altar. This procession was ment.
made very pompous, with fourscore banners and streamers,
and the waits of the city playing; and threescore priests
and clerks in copes: and divers of the inns of court were
there, who went next the priests. Then came the parish,
with white rods in their hands. And so, after they had
made their offerings at St. Paul's, they marched back again,
with the waits playing, the priests and clerks singing, home-
wards.

.. On the 10th day of June the King and Queen took their The King
journey towards Hampton Court, with certain of the Coun- and Queen
cil, to hunt and to kill a great hart. The Council tarried Hampton
at Hampton Court till Saturday following, when they came Court.
again to Whitehall.

This day Sir John, a chantry priest, hung himself in A priest
his chamber with his own girdle. hangeth
himself.

The same day was the storehouse at Portsmouth burnt,
and much beer and victuals, and provisions for war, destroyed: a judgment, perhaps, for burning so many innocent persons.

The 14th of June certain gentlemen were carried to the Some sent
Tower, blindfold and muffled, [as Sir John Cheke and Sir to the
Peter Carow were served before: a Spanish trick.] Tower.

The 16th day, the young Duke of Norfolk rode abroad; Duke of
and at Stamford-hill, a dag, hanging at his saddle-bow, by Norfolk's
misfortune went off, and hit one of his men that rid before: with a
whereat his horse flung, and the man hanging by one of the horse.

stirrups, the horse kicked out his brains, by flinging out
with his legs.

Anno 1557.
The King
and Queen
in proces-
sion.

On the 17th the King and Queen went on procession at
Whitehall, on Corpus Christi day, through the hall and the
great court gate; the procession being attended with as
goodly singing as ever was heard.

Two burnt.

On the 18th two persons were carried beyond St. George's,
almost at Newington, to be burnt for heresy and other matters.   [Of whom Fox taketh no notice.]

Mrs. Hall
buried.

On the 19th was old Mrs. Hall buried in the parish of
St. Benet Sherehog. She gave certain good gowns both for
men and women, and twenty gowns to poor people. Several
ladies and others attended in mourning. She was memorable in being the mother of Mr. Edward Hall of Gray's Inn,
who set forth the chronicle called Hall's Chronicle. And I
conjecture she was that Mrs. Hall that was a great reliever
of such as were persecuted for religion in this reign, and to
whom several of the martyrs wrote letters, which are extant.

378

The Lord
Abbot
preacheth
at Paul's.

On the 20th day the Lord Abbot of Westminster preached at Paul's Cross. His sermon, which had much applause,
was upon Dives and Lazarus. The crosser holding his staff
at his preaching. The audience was great and solemn, consisting of the lord mayor, judges, aldermen, and divers worshipful persons, besides the common sort.

Sextons'
procession.

On the 21st was the sextons' procession, with standards
and staves, thirty and odd, and good singing, and waits
playing; and a canopy borne through Newgate and Old
Baily, and through Ludgate, and so to Paul's churchyard: thence through Cheap, along to Coopers'-hall to dinner.

Austin
Friars.

The 24th, St. John Baptist's day, at the Augustin Friars,
was as pleasing service celebrated as had been known, by the
merchant strangers, who, it seems, made use of this church
for their religious worship, after the Protestant strangers
were gone, and had left it.

A fair in
the church-

The 29th of June, being St. Peter's day, a small fair was

kept in St. Margaret's churchyard, Westminster: as, for CHAP.
wool, turners' ware, and such other small things. The same XLIX.
day was a goodly procession; in which the Lord Abbot Anno 1557.
went with his mitre and crosier, and a great number of copes yard at
of cloth of gold, with the vergers; and many worshipful ster.
gentlemen and women going also in procession in Westmin- A proces-
ster.

The same day, at afternoon, was the second year's mind The year's
[i. e. yearly obit] of good Master Lewyn, ironmonger. And mind of
at his dirge were all the livery: whereof the first was Mr.
Alderman Draper. After, they retired to the widow's place,
where they had a cake and wine; and, besides the parish,
all comers treated.

The last day of June was St. Powel's [Paul's] day; [i. e. The proces-
commemoration of a privilege] And at St. Paul's, London, Paul's with
was a goodly procession: for there was a priest of every the buck.
parish of the diocese [city, I suppose, he means] of London, with a cope; and the Bishop of London wearing his
mitre. And after, according to an old custom, came a fat
buck, and his head, with his horns, borne upon a banner-
pole; and forty persons, blowing with the horn, afore the
buck, and behind.

The same day was the Merchant Tailors' feast: at which Merchant
they had sixty bucks; and the master gave to divers parishes feast.
two bucks apiece to make merry. There dined the mayor,
sheriffs, and divers worshipful persons; and there the mayor
chose Mr. Mallory, alderman, sheriff for the King for the
year ensuing.

This same day the King's Grace rode on hunting into The King
the forest, and killed a great stag with guns.

July the 2d the Duke of Norfolk's son was christened July.
at Whitehall, in the afternoon; the King and the Lord Duke of
Chancellor godfathers, and the old Lady Duchess of Nor- son chris-
folk godmother: there were fourscore torches burning. This tened.
infant was he that was afterwards known by the name and
title of Philip Earl of Arundel.

The 3d day the King and Queen took their journey to- The King
wards Dover, and lay all night at Sittingborn; and on the departs.

CHAP.
XLIX.

Anno 1557.
Lady Tre-
sham bu-
ried.

379
The Queen
goes to
Richmond.

Sir Richard
Whitting-
ton buried
again.

Anne of
Cleves
dieth.

An English
army go
over sea.

A skirmish
between the
English and
French.

5th the King took shipping for Calais, on his journey towards Flanders.

The 10th, the Lady Tresham was buried at Peterborough, with four banners, and an hearse of wax, and
torches.

On the 15th the Queen dined at Lambeth with the Lord
Cardinal Pole, and after dinner removed to Richmond; and
there her Grace tarried her pleasure.

On the same day Whittington and the lady his wife was
coffined again, and leaded, at Whittington college, where
they had been buried; and had dirge said over night, and
the morrow-mass sung. He was the founder of the said
college, and built Newgate and other places, having been
mayor of London, annis 1397, 1406, 1419. [The reason of
this was, for that Whittington's corpse had been of late
taken up by one that was minister there, and the lead about
his body taken off, and the grave rifled, to search for treasure, which he supposed was buried with him.]

The 16th day of July died the Lady Anne of Cleve, at
Chelsey, sometime wife and queen unto King Henry VIII.
but never crowned. Her corpse was cered the night following.

In this month went a great army over sea after the King.
Among them went the Earl of Pembroke, chief captain of
the field, the Lord Mountagu, the Lord Clynton, and divers
other lords, knights, and gentlemen; some by shipping, and
some by land, from London towards Dover, arrayed in
goodly apparel, to the number of five hundred men, all in
blue cassocks, very goodly men, and the best be seen. And
on the 22d day came up a certain number of light horsemen, from the Lord Dacres of the north, beyond Carlisle,
to go over sea. And on the 23d of July, Sir George Paulet
and Sir William Courtnay took their barge at Tower-wharf
towards Dover, and divers captains.

On the 17th day of this month happened a skirmish at
Marguison, between the English and French; where our
men had the better, and took a good booty of cattle. There
were slain nine men of arms, and eighteen taken prisoners,

of the French; and of ours, three taken prisoners, and five CHAP.
hurt.   This was done by the help of the men of Guisnes, XLIX.
and Calais horsemen.

Anno 1557.

On the 29th, one Wakeham, who had broke out of the One fetched out of the sanctuary.
Tower, was fetched out of the sanctuary at Westminster,
by the constable of the Tower, and brought back again
through London.   On the 14th of August, this man broke
out again at midnight, and took sanctuary again.   He was
one of a company that had robbed Sir Edward Warner,
now, or late constable of the Tower.

On the same 29th of July, being St. Olave's day, was the St. Olave's day.
church holyday in Silver-street, the parish church whereof
was dedicated to that saint.   And at eight of the clock at
night began a stageplay, of a goodly matter, [relating, it is
like, to that saint,] that continued unto twelve at midnight;
and then they made an end with a good song.

On the same day began the hearse, at Westminster, for Anne of Cleves' hearse begun.
the Lady Anne of Cleves, consisting of carpenter's work
of seven principals; being as goodly an hearse as had been
seen.

August the 1st were the nuns of Sion enclosed in by the August. Nuns of Sion.
Bishop of London, and my Lord Abbot of Westminster,
certain of the Council, and certain friars of that order being
present: their habit of sheep's colour, and made of such
wool as the sheep beareth.   They had then a great charge
given them of their living, and warned that they were now 380
never more to go forth of those walls as long as they lived.

On the 3d of August, the body of the Lady Anne of Lady Anne of Cleves's funeral.
Cleves was brought from Chelsey, where her house was,
unto Westminster, to be buried; with all the children of
Westminster, and many priests and clerks.   Then the Grey
Amis of Paul's, and three crosses, and the monks of Westminster, and my Lord Bishop of London, and Lord Abbot
of Westminster, rode together next the monks.   Then the
two secretaries, Sir Edmund Peckham, and Sir Robert
Freston, cofferer to the Queen of England, my Lord Admiral, and Mr. Darcy of Essex, and many knights and gen-

tlemen. And before her corpse, her servants, her banner of arms. Then her gentlemen and her head officers. And then her chariot, with eight banners of arms, consisting of divers arms; and four banners of images of white taffeta, wrought with gold, and her arms. And so they passed by St. James's, and thence to Charing-cross, with an hundred torches burning, her servants bearing them. And the twelve beadmen of Westminster had new black gowns, bearing twelve torches, burning: there were four white branches, with arms. Then ladies and gentlewomen, all in black, with their horses. Eight heralds of arms, in black, and their horses. Arms set about the hearse, behind and before; and four heralds bearing the four white banners. At the church door, all did alight; and there the Lord Bishop of London, and the Lord Abbot, in their mitres and copes, did receive the good lady, censing her. Men bore her under a canopy of black velvet, with four black staves; and so brought her into the hearse, and there tarried dirge, remaining there all night, with lights burning.

Her mass of *requiem.*

On the 4th day, being the day after, was celebrated the mass of *requiem* for the said Lady Princess of Cleves. There the Lord Abbot of Westminster made a godly sermon, and the Bishop of London sung mass, in his mitre. And after mass, the said Bishop and Abbot, mitred, did cense the corpse; and afterwards she was carried to her tomb, where she lay, with an hearse-cloth of gold, the which lay over her: and there all head officers brake their staves, and all her housers [servants of her household] brake their rods; and all cast them into her tomb. All the lords and ladies, knights and gentlemen, and gentlewomen, did offer: and after mass was a great dinner at my Lord Marquis of Winchester; and my Lady of Winchester was the chief mourner. The Lord Admiral and the Lord Darcy went on each side of my said Lady of Winchester; and so they went in order to dinner.

Money for
Barwick.

On the 3d day of August, in the afternoon, came from the Chequer about seventeen horses, laden with money, towards

Barwick, and divers men riding with it with javelins and poleaxes, on horseback, and bows and sheaves of arrows, between eight and nine of the clock.

CHAP.
XLIX.

Anno 1557.

A seafight
between
the French
and Eng-
lish.

On the same 3d of August, the good ship called the Mary Rose, of London, accompanied with the Maudelyn Dryvers, and a small crayer of the west country, coming by south, chanced to meet with a French man of war, of the burden of ten score, or thereabouts, and had to the number of two hundred men.   In the Mary Rose was twenty-three men and a boy; in the Maudelyn eighteen; and in the bark of the west country twelve.   The Mary Rose sailing faster than the Frenchman, he presently set upon the two other ships: but the Mary Rose tacked about, and set upon the French ship, and boarded her, and slew to the number of an hundred men, with the captain, or ever the two other ships came to the fight.   There were slain in the Mary Rose two men, and one died a sevennight after, and six hurt, with the master, whose name was John Cowper.   Then came in the Maudelyn to the Mary Rose, and shot one piece of ordnance in at the French ship's stern, and going by her, shot arrows at the Frenchman.   The Maudelyn did no more hurt, the small bark nothing at all.   Thus they fought two hours; but at the length the Frenchmen were weary on their parts, and stood off, not having men to guide their sails. But if the Mary Rose had had men to enter the French ship, and a setter on, they had brought her away ere the other ships could have helped her.   Afterwards news was brought out of Dieppe, by a prisoner that had paid his ransom, that fifty men were carried out of the French ship in wheelbarrows to the chirurgeons, and the ship sore hurt and maimed.

381

On the 6th day came a new commandment, that the city of London should find a thousand men, with all manner of weapons, coats and harness, guns and morris pikes, and horsemen.

On the 7th, King Philip made answer to three letters, sent from the Queen's Privy Council, dated July 28, August the 1st and 3d: for they did continually acquaint him

CHAP.
XLIX.

Anno 1557.
with all the transactions and councils taken in England. He entitled his letter, *Prædilectis* [or rather *Perdilectis*] *et fidelibus nobis consanguineis nostris, et aliis Dominis, cœterisque selectis Consiliariis nostris in Anglia.* In this, as in all his letters, he subscribed his name at the bottom, and not at the beginning. Herein he treated the Council with much courtesy and good words, thanking them for their care of the Queen his wife, and of the State. *Agimusque vobis gratias pro amore et continuo studio, cura ac diligentia, quibus obsequio serenis. Reginæ conjugis nostræ charissimæ, beneficioque utilitati et tuitioni rerum istius regni, incumbitis. Est enim id nobis supra modum gratum, tantisque viris dignum, opinionique quam de vobis ingentem concepimus, admodum conveniens.* That is, " he thanked " them for their love, continual study, care, and diligence, " wherewith they laid out themselves in observance of his " most dear spouse the Queen, and for the benefit, profit, " and defence of the kingdom ; it being a thing beyond " measure grateful to him, and worthy of such men as they " were, and exactly agreeable to the great opinion which he " had conceived of them."

Proclamation for beer.
On the 13th, a proclamation was made for the price of beer and ale, and what should be paid the barrel and the kilderkin for either.

News of the taking of St. Quintin's.
On the 14th, tidings came from beyond sea, that the King had taken many noblemen of France, going to victual St. Quintin, besieged by his men ; as the constable of France for one ; and six thousand prisoners taken, and six carts and waggons, laden with treasure and victuals.

382

Procession for it.
On the 15th came commandment to all the churches in London to go a procession to St. Paul's ; and all priests in their copes. But before they went, they of Paul's sang *Te Deum laudamus.* And after that, down they went a procession into Cheap, round about the cross, singing *Salve festa dies.* And the lord mayor and aldermen, in scarlet, went round about St. Paul's, without ; and after, to Paul's Cross, to the sermon, where Dr. Harpsfield, archdeacon of London, preached, and made a godly sermon. In his said

sermon he declared how many were taken, and what noblemen. This was the day of the Assumption of our blessed
Lady the Virgin. The same day, at even, *Te Deum* was
sung in all churches in London, and ringing of bells; and
at night, bonfires and drinking in every street, in token of
thanks to God Almighty, that giveth victory.

On the 16th day of August, the hearse of the King of
Denmark was begun to be set up in a foursquare frame.

On the 17th day of August, Sir John Porte, of Darbyshire, knt. sat with the Bishop of the diocese, and the rest
of the commissioners, at Utcester in Staffordshire, to search
out heresies, and punish them. The commission was, *for
reformation of divers heresies.*

August 18, was the King of Denmark's hearse in St.
Paul's finished with wax, the like to which was never seen
in England, in regard of the fashion of square tapers.
Twenty-one banners and bannerols. The same night was
the dirge: the Lord Treasurer chief mourner. And after
him the Lord Darcy, Sir Robert Oxenbridge, Sir Edmund
Peckham, Sir Robert Freston, cofferer to the Queen, Sir
Richard Southwel, Sir Arthur Darcy, and many other noblemen and gentlemen, all in black. The Bishop of London began the dirge, with his mitre on all the dirge-while.
After the dirge, all the heralds and all the lords went into
the Bishop of London's place, and drank. In honour of
this King's obsequies were four goodly white branches, and
six dozen of torches; the choir hung with black and arms;
six pillars, covered with velvet; and a goodly hearse-cloth
of tinsel, the cross of cloth of silver: a majesty, and valance
fringe of gold, and ten dozen of pensils, and as many dozen
escutcheons of arms. The next day was the morrow-mass,
and a goodly sermon preached: and after, to my Lord of
London to dinner.

On the 22d, was the hearse of the Lady Anne of Cleves,
lately set up at Westminster abbey, taken down; which the
monks, by night, had spoiled of all the velvet cloth, arms,
banners, pensils, majesty, and valance, and all. The which
was never seen afore so done.

CHAP.
XLIX.

Anno 1557.

And that of the King of Denmark.

And on the 28d also was the King of Denmark's hearse, at Paul's, taken down by the waxchandlers and carpenters, (to whom this work pertained,) by order of Mr. Garter, and certain of the Lord Treasurer's servants.

Clarencieux buried.

On the 24th of this month of August, Mr. Tho. Halley, Clarencieux king at arms, was buried in St. Giles's parish, without Cripplegate, with coat, armour, and pennons of arms, and scutcheons of his arms, and two white branches, twelve staff-torches, and four great tapers, and a crown. And after dirge, the heralds repaired unto Mr. Greenhil, 383 the waxchandler, a man of note, (being waxchandler to Cardinal Pole,) living hard by: where they had spice-bread and cheese, and wine, great plenty. The morrow-mass also was celebrated, and a sermon preached. And after, followed a great dinner; whereat were all the heralds, together with the parishioners. There was a supper also as well as a dinner.

Merchant Tailors' feast.

The 29th day, being the decollation of St. John Baptist, was the Merchant Tailors' feast: when the lord mayor, Sir Tho. White, Mr. Harper, sheriff, Mr. Row, and all the clothing, and the four wardens of the yeomanry, and the company, heard mass at St. John's, in Smithfield, and offered every man a penny: and from thence to the hall, two and two together, to dinner.

The hearse of the Duchess of Norfolk.

The 31st, the young Duchess of Norfolk being lately deceased, and her hearse began to be set up on the 28th, in St. Clement's without Temple-bar, was this day finished, with banners, pensils, wax, and scutcheons.

CHAP. L.

A short journal of occurrences falling out in the months of September, October, November, December, and January.

September.

The Duchess's funeral.

THE noble wife of Thomas, the young Duke of Norfolk, daughter and heir of the Earl of Arundel, who seemed to have died in childbed, had her funerals solemnized on the

1st of September. At afternoon began the knell. The church, and the place, [*i. e.* Bath Place, now belonging to the Earl of Arundel,] and the street hanged with black and arms: by three of the clock she was brought to the church with an hundred mourners: her Grace had a canopy of black velvet, with four staves, borne over her, and many banners and bannerols borne about her; and the Bishop of London in his cope, and his mitre on his head, and all the choir of Paul's were present; two great white branches, and a twelve dozen staff torches; eight heralds of arms: the Lady Lumley chief mourner, and many lords, and knights, and gentlemen, ladies and gentlewomen attending the obsequies.

CHAP. L.

Anno 1557.

The 3d of September, at night, commandment came, that every church in London, and in every county and shire, should sing *Te Deum*, and make bonfires for the King's winning of St. Quintin's.

St. Quintin's.

Mention was made before, how in the month of July one Wakeham, a prisoner in the Tower, had twice broke prison, and taken sanctuary at Westminster; now, on the 10th day of September, he was the second time brought back to the Tower again by order of the Council. But on the 15th day following, he was restored unto Westminster again to sanctuary. This was a trial of skill for the privileges of this sanctuary. And we may observe what a power this new monastery had obtained, to prevail against an order of Council.

Sanctuary allowed to one that brake prison.

On the 12th day of this September came forth a commandment for matins and mass to be done every where by nine of the clock; and the parsons and curates to go to Paul's with surplices and copes; and to go a procession thence through London, and about Paul's, and *Te Deum laudamus* sung. This procession was accordingly performed. And there went the lord mayor and the aldermen in scarlet. And after, they went into the shrouds, and there Dr. Standish preached. And after evensong *Te Deum* was sung; and there was ringing of bells through London. And this for the good news that came from the English captains beyond the sea.

A procession for good news.

384

CHAP.
L.

Anno 1557.
Sir J. Cheke
dies.
A Spaniard
comes post
to the
Queen.
The 13th day concluded the life of Sir John Cheke, broke with grief, that had been King Edward's schoolmaster, till he died. And on the 16th he was buried privately in the church of St. Alban's, Wood-street, London.

The 15th day came out of Spain to the Queen's Court, in post, Monsieur Re Gomez, gorgeously appareled, with divers other Spaniards, with great chains, and their hats set with stones and pearls. They supped, and by seven of the clock were on horseback again; and so rode through Fleet-street, and at the Horn there they drank, and at the Greyhound. Thence through Cheapside; and so over the bridge, and rode all night towards Dover.

The Cardi-
nal's stew-
ard buried.
The 16th day of this September, Mr. Heyns, the Lord Cardinal's steward, was buried at Hampsted-heath with great solemnity.

Four burnt.
On the 17th, four persons, that is, three men and one woman, went out of Newgate unto Islington beyond the Butts in a valley, to be burnt for heresy. Two of them were man and wife, dwelling in St. Dunstan's in the East, on the east side of the churchyard, with Mr. Waters, sergeant at arms: their names were James and Margery Austoo. The two others were named Allerton and Roth.

A proces-
sion for
success in
France.
On the 20th of September a commandment came down to all parishes in London, that they should go on procession at Paul's, and *Te Deum* to be sung in all the churches in London; to sing and ring for the winning of other places in France.

Mrs. Finch
buried.
Ditto, Mrs. Finch, one of the privy chamber to the Queen, was buried in the Savoy.

Sir H. Hus-
sey buried,
and his
lady.
The 21st was the month mind of Sir Harry Hussey, knt. with a standard and pennon of arms; his coat-armour, target, helmet, and sword, and six dozen of escutcheons, and the heralds, attending. He had been carried to Slinfold in Sussex, and there buried September 3. And in the next month his lady deceased, and was there also buried.

Dr. Pendle-
ton buried.
The same day was Dr. Pendleton, a great preacher in this reign, and a great professor of religion in the former, but a backslider, was buried in St. Stephen's, in Walbroke,

where he was parson: being brought with all Paul's choir to be buried there.

The 29th, Mr. Dod, sergeant of the Queen's cellar, was buried in St. Botolph's parish without Aldersgate.

October the 5th, Sackfield, esquire, father unto Sir Richard Sackvile, knight, late chancellor of the augmentations, was honourably buried.

This day also Tho. Mildmay, esquire, and under-treasurer, and his wife, were buried at Chelmsford in Essex.

The 6th day a commandment came down, that forasmuch as the Pope and the Emperor were become friends and lovers, and the war ended between them, every parish priest in London should cause all expressions of joy to be shewn by bonfires and ringing of bells.

The 13th day a tailor was set on the pillory for heinous, seditious, and opprobrious words against the lord mayor and aldermen; and for being a common slanderer of people, and of his neighbours.

On the 21st, fifty great guns, newly made, were carried through Smithfield, Newgate, and Cheapside, to the Tower, and two hundred men accompanied, with guns, bows, and pikes, in harness and shirts of mail.

On the same day died the Countess of Arundel, at Bath Place, [afterwards called Arundel House,] in St. Clement's parish without Temple-bar.

On the 26th was a goodly hearse set up for her in the said parish church, with five principals, eight bannerols, &c. On the 27th she was brought to church, the Bishop of London, Paul's choir, and the clerks of London, going before: then came the corpse with five banners of arms borne: then came four heralds in their coats of arms, and bare four banners of images at the four corners: and then came the chief mourners, my Lady of Worcester, Lady Lumley, Lady North, and Lady Sentleger: then came an hundred mourners of men, and after as many ladies and gentlewomen, all in black; besides a great many poor women in black and rails, and four-and-twenty poor men, and many of her servants, in black, bearing of torchlights. On the

CHAP.
L.

Anno 1557.
Sergeant of
the Queen's
cellar
buried.
October.
Sackvile
buried.
Mildmay
buried, and
his wife.
385
Joy for
peace between the
Pope and
Emperor.
One set on
the pillory.
Fifty great
guns newly
made.
Countess of
Arundel
dies.
Her burial.

next day, being the 28th, was the mass of *requiem* sung, and a sermon preached, and after, her Grace was buried. And all her officers with white staves in their hands, and all the heralds waiting about her in their coat-armour. The Lord Abbot of Westminster was the preacher, and the Bishop of London sung the mass. A second mass was sung by another bishop, and a third by another priest. And after, all departed to my Lord's place to dinner.

November.
A man and his wife justly punished.

On the 5th day of November was an exemplary piece of justice done within the city. A man was carried on horseback with his face towards the horse's tail, having on a frieze gown, and a writing on his head, importing, that he let out his wife to divers men: his wife leading the horse, and a paper on her head for whoredom.

Master of the Rolls buried.

November the 8th, Sir Nicolas Hare, knt. master of the rolls, was buried honourably within the Temple.

Maynard buried.

On the 12th, Mr. Maynard, merchant, and sheriff of London in the sixth year of King Edward VI. was buried at Stepney with two white branches, and twelve torches, and four great tapers. And after, the company departed to his house at Poplar to a great dinner. This gentleman, when he was sheriff, kept a great house, and in the time of Christmas had a lord of misrule; and the King's lord of misrule came and dined with him. And at the Cross in Cheapside he made a great scaffold, and had a mock proclamation made there by his lord.

386

A post set up in Smithfield.

On the same day, a post was set up in Smithfield for three that should have been burnt for heresy, and both wood and coals brought ready: but the Lord Abbot of Westminster coming to Newgate, and talking with them, there was such hope of their abjuration, that they were stayed that day from burning; but on the next day, being St. Erkenwald's eve, they went out of Newgate thither to their burning. Their names were M. Gybson, Haleday, [or Halingdale, according to Fox,] and Sparrow. The first was the son of Gybson, esq. sergeant of arms, and of the revels, and of the King's tents. Of this Gybson more will be said hereafter.

Dorel buried.

On the 16th, was Mr. Dorel buried at St. Martin's,

Ludgate. He was a captain of the galleys, and knight of Rhodes.

CHAP. L.

On the 18th died the Lord Bray within the Blackfriars near Ludgate. He got his death at St. Quintin's. And on the 23d he was carried from Blackfriars to the Thames side; where were two great barges ready, covered with black and arms hanging. And so he went by water to Chelsey to be buried by his father, with four heralds of arms, and a standard, and a banner of arms, and two banners of images borne by two heralds of arms in their coat-armour; and so many noblemen mourners in black. And sixteen poor men had new gowns, and about sixteen coat torches, two white branches, and four great tapers; and a great armour, target, sword, and mantle, and an eight dozen of escutcheons: and many priests and clerks attended: they all came back from Chelsey to this lord's place at Blackfriars to dinner.

Anno 1557.
The Lord Bray dies.
His burial.

On the 18th day tidings came from the Earl of Northumberland in the borders of Scotland, that the Scots and the English met, and then fought: wherein many Scots were taken.

A fight with the Scots.

On the 21st the Lord Abbot of Westminster preached at Paul's Cross, and made a godly sermon.

Lord Abbot preaches.

The same day, the Queen set a crown on the head of Mr. Norroy king at arms, and created him Clarencieux with a cup of wine, at St. James's, her Grace's place.

Norroy created Clarencieux.

November 25, the Lady Hare, late wife of Sir Nic. Hare, late master of the rolls, buried soon after her husband.

Lady Hare buried.

The 30th, being St. Andrew's day, was a procession at Paul's, and a priest of every parish attending, each in his cope, and a goodly sermon preached; and after that, the procession, with *Salve festa dies.*

St. Andrew's procession.

The same day, the Queen and the Lord Cardinal came from Saint James's unto Whitehall: there they heard mass; and all the bishops, judges, and sergeants at law were present. After mass, Sir Thomas Tressham was created Lord of St. John's of Jerusalem, in England, and four knights of

Sir Thomas Tresham Lord of St. John's.

c 3

the said county. He buried his wife the last year.

Procession
at West-
minster.

The same day, my Lord Abbot went a procession in his mitre, and all the monks and clerks singing *Salve festa dies*, round about the abbey. And the Abbot sang the mass.

The Car-
dinal
preacheth.

This day also, after dinner, the Lord Cardinal made a godly sermon in the chapel. There were present, to honour the illustrious preacher, all the bishops and judges, 387 the lord mayor and all the aldermen; and many lords and knights, ladies and gentlewomen.

December.
Sir Rob.
Rochester
buried.

December 4, Sir Rob. Rochester, knt. comptroller of the Queen's house, and son of Robert Rochester, sergeant of the pantry to Henry VIII. was buried at the Charterhouse at Shene. He was chosen knight of the Garter, but never stalled at Windsor; and so was not buried with the garter, but after the manner of another knight. There was a goodly hearse of wax of five principals, with eight dozen of pensils, and eight dozen of escutcheons, and six dozen of torches, four banners of images, and a majesty and valance; Mr. Clarencieux and Mr. Lancaster, heralds, and many mourners, attending. The mass celebrated, and a sermon preached; and after, a great dinner.

St. Nicolas.

On the 5th, being St. Nicolas eve, St. Nicolas went abroad in most places, all people receiving him into their houses, and had good cheer after the old fashion.

Lady Row-
let buried.

On the 8th of December, the Lady Rowlet, one of the learned daughters of Sir Anthony Cook, and the youngest of five, wife of Sir Ralph Rowlet, knt. was buried in the parish of St. Mary Staining, London.

Dr. Weston
deprived.

On the 10th day, being Friday, was Doctor Weston deposed from his deanery of Windsor for uncleanness.

The guard
seize some
at Islington.

On the 12th, being Sunday, at Islington, there met certain persons that were gospellers, and some pretended players, and one Ruff, [Rough,] a Scot, formerly a friar. And under the pretence of a play, (which seemed indeed to be begun,) he was to have read a lecture to the assembly. And the communion was played, and should have been ad-

ministered; but the guards came too soon, or ever the chief
matter was begun. Of this Rough and his martyrdom something will be said in due place.

On the 13th, Sir William West, knt. [the same, I sup- *Sir William West buried.*
pose, with him that went over lately in the expedition to St.
Quintin's,] was buried in the parish church of St. Sepul-
chre's, without Newgate : three masses were sung, one of the
Trinity, another of our Lady, and the third of *requiem :* and
a trental of masses said; his standard, coat, helmet, and
sword offered ; and a sermon preached.

On the 17th a young man and a woman rode through *Some carted.*
London in a cart. And the bawd, the wife of John a Badoo,
was whipped at the said cart's tail; and the harlot did beat
her : and an old harlot of threescore did lead the horse.

December 20, Sir John Ruff, priest, before mentioned, *Rough burnt.*
and a woman named Mearing, were condemned to be burnt
in Smithfield. And on the 22d they were accordingly both
burnt.

December 25, the Lady Freston, the wife of Sir Richard *Lady Freston buried.*
Freston, knt. and cofferer unto Queen Mary, was buried in
Suffolk.

Ditto, divers courtiers were removed to higher rooms. *Advancements at Court.*
As Sir Ed. Hastings, master of the Queen's horse, was made
lord chamberlain; Sir Thomas Cornwallis, comptroller, in
the place of Sir Rob. Rochester deceased ; Sir Harry Jerningham, [or Jernegan,] master of the Queen's horse, and
Sir Harry Benefield, vice-chamberlain and captain of the
guards.

A gracious pardon from the King and Queen, dated De- 388
cember 5, was granted to one John Copstocke, late of Lon- *December.*
don, who had been indicted, for that he, after the first *One pardoned for words against King Philip.*
day of February, in the first and second years of their
reigns, and after a proclamation of a certain act of Parlia-
ment, the first and second of their said reigns, had imagined, *Acta publ. p. 48.*
and writ seditiously and maliciously, a certain malicious,
false, and scandalous book, entitled, *The Copy of John Bradford's Letter to the Queen : and to the Lords and Estates of
the Realm,* on the 27th of December, the 3d and 4th of

CHAP.
L.

Anno 1557.
A seditious
book.

1558.
January.
A lord of
misrule.

The French
come a-
gainst New-
nam, and
Calais.

The city
raises 500
men,

Who are
shipped for
Calais.

their reigns: the writer, perhaps, falsely using the name of the godly martyr of that name, the better to countenance his book. " In which book, among other false, malicious, " and scandalous clauses, (as the words of the pardon ran,) " was this sentence: Peradventure her Grace thinketh " (meaning the Queen) that the King will keep her more " company, and love her the better, if she will give him the " crown: yea, will crown him to make him live chaste, " and contrary to his nature. For peradventure after he " were crowned, he would be contented with one woman; " but in the mean space, he would have do of three or four " in one night, to prove which of them he liketh best: not " of ladies and gentlewomen, but of bakers' daughters, and " such other poor whores." Then followeth his pardon. *Pietatis motu de gra. nostra speciali—pardonavimus.*

January the 1st, new-year's-day eve, a lord of misrule came from Westminster with his heralds, trumpets, and drums, and many disguised in white. In this equipage he came into London; and was conducted into the Counter in the Poultry. And divers of his men lay there all night; and the rest went home to Westminster again by fours and sixes together, some on horseback, and some on foot.

January 3, tidings came to the Queen, that the French King was come to Newnam-bridge with a great host of men of war, and laid battering pieces unto it, and unto Ricebank by water, and unto Calais; and laid great battering pieces to it: and that there was great shooting.

This news was an unwelcome new-year's gift, and awakened the realm, too much lulled into security of affairs on that side, by the late success at St. Quintin's. For the very next day, *viz.* Jan. 4, the city of London raised 500 men pro-portionably out of every craft, to go to Calais: and found them harness, bows, morris-pikes, and guns, at their own cost and charges, and prest money, till they came to the Queen's navy, to take them on board. And in two days these men were raised and armed.

For January 6 they were brought to Leadenhall, and mustered before the lord mayor and aldermen: and in

the afternoon, by four of the clock, they took their way to
Tower-wharf; and there they took shipping for Calais.

And on the next day, *viz.* January 7, the merchants of
the staple of Calais took up an hundred and odd men to
go, on their cost, to Calais: and on the ensuing day they
took shipping also at Tower-wharf towards Calais: as did
other men of war. And also from other places were men
hastened away to the sea-ward.

On the 8th day were set up at Windsor the Earl of
Sussex, deputy of Ireland, his banner of arms, his helmet,
crest, mantle, and his sword, for his installation of the
Garter.

389
The insig-
nia of the
Earl of Sus-
sex set up at
Windsor.

On the 10th heavy tidings came to England, and particularly to London, that the French had won Calais:
which was the dolefullest news, and the heaviest taken,
that ever had happened: for traitor-like, it was said to be
sold and delivered unto them. The Duke of Guise was
chief captain. Every man was discharged the town, carry-
ing nothing with him.

On the 11th day the city took up a thousand men more,
of their own cost, and made them white coats with red
crosses. And every ward in London found certain men.

The 13th, the Lady Powis, daughter to Charles Bran-
don, lake Duke of Suffolk, was buried suitably to her
quality.

On the 16th, Sir Richard Freston (cofferer · unto the
Queen) was buried in Suffolk, living but a small time after
his lady.

The 17th was the month mind of Sir George Gifford
in Bucks; with a standard, a pennon of arms, coat-armour,
helmet, target, sword, and mantle, and two banners of
images.

The   of this month was buried Mr. Alsop, apothe-
cary unto King Henry VIII. and to King Edward VI.
and the sergeant of the confectionary unto Queen Mary.
He was buried very honourably with poor men and gowns,
and morrow-mass, and a great dinner.

On the 20th, the 5th of the Queen, began a Parliament.

CHAP.
L.

Anno 1557.

Her Grace took her chariot at the Whitehall, with her lords of the Parliament, the bishops and priests, and repaired all to the abbey to mass; and after that to the Parliament house.

The city commanded to get their men ready.

On the 21st came a commandment to the Lord Mayor, that he should make ready the raised men in harness, with white coats, welted with green, and red crosses, by the 23d of the same month; to be at Leadenhall, in order to their going away; that is, to try to recover Calais, or otherwise to annoy the French.

One pillorized.

The 22d, a man was set on the pillory for seditious words and rumours. For, no question, the mouths of the people would be open upon this great and shameful loss.

Dr. Barthelet buried.

Ditto, Doctor Barthelet, a physician in Blackfriars, was buried at St. Bartholomew's in Smithfield. For it was reckoned beneficial to the dead to be laid within the walls of a monastery.

The city soldiers take shipping.

On the 24th the raised soldiers appeared before the Lord Mayor in Leadenhall. There he took a view of all the men which each company delivered unto the Mayor, and the Mayor delivered them unto the captains at five at night; and at eight they took shipping.

Coiners.

Ditto, certain coiners taken in Cambridge went this day unto Westminster-hall.

A sermon at Paul's Cross.

On the 30th the Bishop of Winchester preached at Paul's Cross, and made a goodly sermon.

And now we will cast our eyes back again, and take some view of the affairs and transactions of the *spiritual estate*.

CHAP. LI.

390

New Bishops made. Commissions from the Cardinal. His orders to the Bishop of London. The Pope's displeasure against the Cardinal. His speech to the Londoners.

Pole, Watson, Christopherson, consecrated. Pole's Regist.

DOCTOR David Pole, the Cardinal's favourite, great officer in spirituals, was the beginning of the year, or rather the latter end of the last, elected Bishop of Peterborough;

who was sufficiently blessed and fortified with papal bulls.
One bull of provision from Pope Paul to David Pole, elect
of Peterborough, bare date April the 9th. There was another bull of absolution for the said elect of Peterborough,
and another to the Archbishop for the said election; and
yet another for his consecration. Accordingly the Cardinal-
Archbishop gave out his commission to Nicolas Archbishop
of York, to consecrate him, and Thomas Watson to be
bishop of Lincoln. And they both were consecrated on
Sunday, August 15, in the church of Cheswick, of the
diocese of London, by the said Nicolas, Thomas Bishop of
Ely, and William Bishop of Bangor, assisting. And November 21, John Christopherson, master of Trinity college
in Cambridge, a learned man in the Greek tongue, was
consecrated in a chapel of the Bishop of London's palace
in London, by the said Bishop of London, Thomas Bishop
of Ely, and Maurice Bishop of Rochester, assisting.

July the 20th, the Cardinal gave a mandate to the
Bishop of London, for making general processions at that
time, when almost all Christendom were miserably burning
in wars, " to beg of Him that sat at the right hand of the
" Father, to reduce Christian princes to concord, and to
" settle all Christendom in a desired tranquillity." And
these processions and public supplications to be used in
cathedral churches of his province thrice a week in cities,
and great towns twice, or at least once, together with singing of the Litany, and the mass, if it could be; otherwise
with three collects, one for the Church and others, the
second for peace, and the third for the King and Queen.

Other commissions went out to Henry Cole, LL. D.
dean of St. Paul's, to be the Cardinal's vicar-general in
spirituals: to take cognizance, and to proceed in all causes
in the Court of Audience; that is, to be auditor of causes in
the said court, and to be his commissary-general, and principal official; dated at St. James's, August 28: which offices
had lately become vacant, upon the preferment of David
Pole. This Cole was he that was sent down the year before
to Oxon, to have Cranmer despatched, and was privy to

CHAP.
LI. the secret reasons of it; and so might deserve to be preferred.

Anne 1557. Another commission to Maurice Clevocke, LL. B. the
To Cle-
vock;
Cardinal's chaplain, servant, and domestic, rector of Or-
pington, dean of Shoreham and Croiden; to visit the
churches of the said deaneries: dated at St. James's, August
ult.

391 Another commission to Henry Cole, LL. D. to be official
To Dr.
Cole;
of the Court of Canterbury, dated from Lambeth, October 1.
Another to him of the said date, constituting him dean of
the Arches; and to visit the churches in that deanery.

To Dr. Gef-
fry;
Another to William Geffry, LL. D. to be his official for
the diocese of Sarum, void upon the death of Capon, late
bishop there: dated October 18.

To Dr.
White;
Another to Thomas White, LL. D. to be his commissary,
or vice-chancellor in Oxford: dated from St. James's,
December 10.

And to
Chetham.
And finally, another to Thomas Chetham, *Dei et apostolicæ sedis gratia*, as the commission ran, *by the grace of
God and the apostolic see*, bishop of Sidon; to chrism children in the foreheads, to bless and consecrate altars, fixed
and portatile, cups, bells, vestments, &c. and to do all other
things belonging to the office of a bishop: dated March the
8th. Probably Thornden, bishop of Dover, might be dead;
P. 1706.
first edit.
who, as Fox writes, looking one Sunday upon his men at
bowls, fell suddenly into a palsy, and so was had to bed,
and died: and so this Chetham might be substituted for a
suffragan in his stead. The same Fox speaks of another
suffragan ordained by the Cardinal, that had been suffragan before to bishop Bonner; and that he brake his neck
down a pair of stairs in the Cardinal's house at Lambeth;
who, I suppose, must be this suffragan of Sidon.

The visita-
tion of both
Universities
by the Car-
dinal.
The Cardinal also this year [that is, reckoning the year
to begin in January] did visit both the Universities, by
certain commissioners, *viz.* a bishop for each, Scot of Chester,
for Cambridge, and Brooks of Glocester, for Oxon, and
some others, members of the respective Universities; and
Ormanet, an Italian, the Pope's datary, that came with the

Cardinal into England : both these visitations are related by
Fox, whereunto I refer the reader. The most remarkable
matters these visitors did in each University, were the severities used towards the bodies of some dead and buried
people, upon pretence that they were heretics when they
were alive; *viz.* Bucer and Fagius, of Cambridge, whose
bodies they digged out of their graves, and openly burnt ;
and Peter Martyr's wife, of Oxon, whose body they digged
up, and buried in a dunghill. Dr. Stokes made the oration
to the commissioners at Cambridge. The Cardinal's commissioners or visitors for Oxon, who, besides the Bishop
and Ormanet, were Cole, Wright, and Morwen, were at
their first coming entertained with an oration made by
Saunders, bachelor of the law ; the same who made himself
afterwards so famous for his slanderous accounts of the Reformation, and for his zeal in raising rebellions in Ireland
against Queen Elizabeth. In this speech he praised the
Cardinal most highly, and particularly for his good deserts
towards that University, in sending them two Spanish
readers of divinity ; first, the reverend father De Soto ;
whom he commended for going before the youth in good
life and learning, and thereby confirming their minds and
studies ; and a little after, John de Villa Garsya, whose wit,
learning, and good behaviour, the same orator also commended. And this, I suppose, was the friar John, that
persuaded Cranmer to recant as he was going to the stake.
Some part of this oration I have preserved in the Re-N°. LXIV.
pository.

Another thing the Cardinal now did was, that, being 392
sensible, I suppose, of burning daily such numbers of innocent people, he signified to Bonner, bishop of London, that
he would not have him to proceed to condemn the heretics,
at least not to deliver them to the secular power, until he
were first informed of them ; being angry with him for condemning some without giving him notice. For the Cardinal,
by his place of legate, had a control over the doings of the
bishops in their own respective dioceses. Bonner therefore
being at this time about to condemn two-and-twenty,

brought up together the latter end of August, from Colchester side, he sent a letter to the Cardinal concerning
this matter, which ran to this tenor : " That he thought to
" have had them all to Fulham, and to have given sentence
" against them, finding them desperate and obstinate, and
" nothing in them but pride and wilfulness; but perceiving
" by his last doings that his Grace was offended, he thought
" it his duty, before he any thing further proceeded against
" them, to advertise his Grace first thereof, and to know his
" good pleasure: which he desired he might do by the
" bearer." But by this seasonable stop of the Cardinal's
order, these two-and-twenty were sent home, and escaped for
this time by an easy subscription.

The Pope
cites Pole
to Rome.

Whether the interposing of the legate were out of clemency and pity, or out of policy, to lessen the odium of the
popish religion, which the people conceived against it for
these cruelties, I leave to others to judge. It is certain, not
long before this, he was accused by some Papists to the
Pope, as a bearer with heretics. Upon which partly, and
partly upon an old grudge against him, the Pope divested
him of his legatine authority; and sent his letters to him,
calling him to Rome: and sent one Peter Peto, a Franciscan friar, in his room, in quality of legate, made Cardinal
for that purpose. But the Queen, by fair entreaties, kept
her Cardinal at home, and, without his knowledge, commanded, that none that were sent by the Pope into England should be brought over in any English vessels, nor
suffered to come into any of her ports.

The reason
of his dis-
pleasure
against
him.

This anger of the Pope against Pole was twisted with
temporal matters: for he imagined he was of counsel to the
Queen, to make war upon France; and that he by his influence should and might have restrained her from aiding
Spain against the French; whom the Pope had provoked
to take up arms to revenge himself for former affronts offered him by the Spaniards, with whom he was highly offended, and hoped by the arms of France to recover the
kingdom of Naples. And therefore, as he told Ormanet,
whom Pole had sent to him, for this negligence and un-

worthy sufferance, he held him unworthy of the legatine
power. But the Queen sided with her Archbishop and relation.

But all this she carried with much seeming devotion and The Queen
submission to his Holiness; she and King Philip writing a writes to the
letter to him, dated May 21, setting forth how serviceable behalf.
Pole her cousin had been in restoring the nation to religion,
and directing her in the managery thereof, and what need
there was still of him. And therefore how affective it
was to her to hear that he should be recalled, and that the
legacy, which ever was annexed to the archbishopric, should 393
be now divided from it: and therefore prayed the Pope for
his favour. This letter, drawn up by the neat pen of
Ascham, her secretary for the Latin tongue, I have met
with, and they that please may read it in the Catalogue. N°. LXV.
Together with this letter, the Privy Council wrote an- And so
other very pressing one to the Pope, in July, in commenda- doth the
tion of the Cardinal; which was their answer to the Pope, Council.
upon the confirmation of the decree of revocation in the
consistory. It was writ, if I do not mistake the hand, by
that complete Latinist, Walter Haddon, doctor of the civil
law, and much employed under King Edward; but who, I
suppose, now only translated it into terse Latin. This letter
also is worthy preserving in the Catalogue. N°. LXVI.

Wherein they plainly told him, " that they could not be- The con-
" lieve a great while, that that counsel could possibly please tents of
" him, in a time when his legate's presence was so needful their letter.
" for the kingdom, to revoke him, having been sent from
" the apostolic see, and his mission confirmed by his Holi-
" ness himself. That they never heard, that a legate sent
" from the holy see was called home, when there was such
" need of him, without some great crime of prince or peo-
" ple. That the Queen had better deserved of his Holiness,
" and so had the people too; who, since they were recon-
" ciled, had laboured by all ways to shew their obedience to
" the apostolic see. That they reckoned this act of his pro-
" ceeded from his ignorance of the true state of the king-
" dom. Then they shewed him how fit a person Cardinal

" Pole was for the great work of uniting the kingdom to
" the Catholic Church; the high opinion the people had of
" him, for his noble birth and excellent qualities. They
" urged the great danger the nation would be in of a re-
" lapse, if the legate should go; as a man newly recovering
" out of a great sickness would be, if he should be then
" destitute of his physician. They wondered most of all, as
" being a thing never heard of, that the Pope should de-
" prive the see of Canterbury of a legacy, which was so
" joined to it, that it was never known to be divided from
" it: and that it looked as though he should have revoked
" an archbishop of Canterbury from the body of this
" Church; for there never was archbishop of Canterbury,
" but he was legate: and that this legatine power was a
" thing not proper only to the archbishop, but the nobi-
" lity, and the kings of England had an interest in that
" prerogative. And therefore they prayed his Holiness,
" that nothing of that power might be diminished; which,
" if it were, would be accompanied with so great a disturb-
" ance of right and orders, and with so great ignominy of
" the bishops, the clergy, nobility, and princes."

A former
letter writ
by them to
the Pope.
This was a second address of the nobility to the Pope
on this occasion: for, before this, and before the Pope's revocation came, (but the news thereof generally spread,) the
nobility wrote their letter to his Holiness, to prevent his
purpose, if it could be. Herein they expostulated the case
with him. They urged him with a breach of promise, given
them in the sacredest words, about two years before, when
the nation was restored to the unity of the Church; which
was, that the kingdom should enjoy all its old rights, privileges, and prerogatives, granted by any former popes, as
394 fully as ever it had done before. Among which, this prerogative was one of the chief, pertaining to the see of Canterbury, that the kings of England should always have the
Archbishop of Canterbury, for the time being, to be the
Pope's legate residing with them. And that this right, all the
kings of England, not only many years, but ages past, have
enjoyed: and that by the ancient laws of the land it was so

constituted. And they added, that they were driven, not by their will only, but by duty and necessity, to defend it: for they were bound by oath to preserve all the dignities, just privileges, and laws of the kingdom. This was a smart letter, and may be perused in the Catalogue.

After all, the Queen also addressed a letter from herself to his Holiness, to change his decree and sentence against the Cardinal. The messenger that carried the letter was ordered, in his way, to repair to King Philip, then at Cambray, that he might peruse the said letter, and, according to his approbation, despatch the courier forward with it. What his thoughts thereof were, will appear from his letter to the Privy Council, dated August 7. *Adeo nobis placuit consilium, responsio et expeditio facta super decreto de revocatione reverendissimi Cardinalis Reginaldi Poli a summo Pontifice in frequenti consistorio proposito et confirmato, ut visis literis, quas sereniss. Regina ad ejus sanctitatem scribebat, elegantes sane ac omni decentia, et quibus oportebat rationibus ornatas ; jussimus continuo ut cursor sine aliqua mora proficisceretur. Speramus enim tam placidis ac summissis literis, non posse summum Pontificem non moveri ; quinimo mutaturum sententiam ac decretum de dicta revocatione : quod nobis gratum admodum esset. Sed si id ab eo forsan non impetrabitur, vestra prudentia providendum, id erit quod magis consentaneum ac expediens esse judicabitis.* Importing, " that he was much pleased with the " counsel and answer that was made in the English Court, " in behalf of the Cardinal, upon the decree for the revoca- " tion of him, propounded and confirmed by the Pope in a " full consistory. That he read the Queen's letter, elegantly " writ, to his Holiness, backed with sufficient reasons, and " in such a style as became the person she writ to. And he " hoped such mild and submissive lines would move him " to alter the sentence : but if not, he left it to their pru- " dence that were of the Council, to take the course they " should judge most agreeable and expedient."

And as these applications were made to the Pope by others in Pole's behalf, so Pole, in his own, sent a messenger some months after, and a very sharp and close epistle to him: which shewed he did not much care for him.   I have seen it in one of Mr. Petyt's MS. volumes.   It is so very long, that it might be called a book rather than a letter ; so that it was not to be transcribed by me ; but I have extracted out of it many of the most material passages.

In the beginning he thus roundly bespake his Holiness : *Sanctitas vestra sic egit nobiscum, quo modo nullus unquam Pontifex cum ullo Cardinale.   Ita fit ut cum ipsa exemplo careat in iis quæ contra me fecit, ego et exemplo caream, quo pacto me erga Sanctitatem v. gerere debeam.   Nec enim ullum quod sciam extat exemplum summi Pontificis, qui Cardinali in suspicione hæresis a se vocato, cum is apostolici legati munere fungeretur, antequam ad causam dicendam accerseretur, legationem abrogaverit, atque in ejus locum, alterum substituerit.*   That is, " Your Holiness hath
395
" dealt with me after that manner as no Pope ever did with
" any Cardinal.   So that as you are without example in
" what you have done against me, I also shall be without
" an example how I ought to behave myself towards your
" Holiness : for there is no example extant, as I know
" of, of a Pope, who when himself had called a Cardinal
" into suspicion of heresy, should deprive him of his legacy,
" and put another in his place, and that even while he was
" performing the office of a legate, before he was cited to
" plead his own cause."

Conference
between
this Pope
and Pole
at his de-
parture for
England.
There had been an old enmity in this Pope towards Pole, while they were both Cardinals at Rome, arising, as it seems, from a report that went about, as though Pole favoured Lutheranism. But our Cardinal being to come away for England, they both had a meeting and serious communication together of this matter, at St. Paul's church in Rome : where Pole did so sufficiently vindicate himself, and give such full satisfaction to the other, that at parting he used these words unto Pole, (which in this his letter he put him in mind of :) " If God," said he, " grant us both such " a space of life, to meet together in another conclave, you " shall understand what this old man [pointing to himself]

" will do for your sake, [meaning that he would give his
" voice and interest for him, to make him Pope.] But if
" at this departure," said Pole, " this story were not at an
" end, I thought that when we gratulated the Pope, we
" were come to a *plaudite*. And if it were not then ended,
" certainly when I was made archbishop, I reckoned there
" would an end be put to these slanders of me." Again,

" If any one should so abuse the name of Catholic, as to
" accuse me in any wise of heresy, I am sufficiently armed
" against that by your Holiness's own testimony, which
" you gave of me, when, in a full consistory, you spake of
" conferring upon me the archbishopric.

" *Post tam honorificum testimonium*, After this so ho-
" nourable a testimony, and that your Holiness heareth no-
" thing since concerning me, but strifes and contentions
" with the remainders of the heretics and schismatics, and
" illustrious victories over them, to the great increase of
" Catholic religion, and the honour of the apostolic see, that
" you should now study to render me suspected of the
" crime of heresy and misbelief."

Again, " All that God hath in this realm done by me is
" most ingrateful to heretics; who rejoice in nothing so
" much as that this name [of *heretic*] is imposed upon me
" by your Holiness, as I hear many now do. But grant, I
" had sometime not only assented to the doctrine of the he-
" retics, (which is very far from the truth,) but combined
" with them against the Church, and had openly opposed
" it; yet, at this time, wherein all see such a glorious victory
" of Christ obtained for the unity and obedience of the
" Church against heretics, by me, a minister of the aposto-
" lic see, and of your Holiness, and the daily conflicts I
" have with them for their and others' salvation, and the
" glory of the apostolic see; he that were a truly godly and
" catholic man, would not object to me the impiety of the
" time past, or call me to answer for it, but rather would give
" God thanks, that it is with me as it was with Paul, that he
" that before opposed the Church, now most earnestly de- 396
" fended it, and reduced many to the bosom of the Church,

" and by all means convinced and restrained such as were
" rebellious and obstinate. But the course of my whole life
" is led in the obedience of the faith, and of the Roman
" Church; and those that most opposed it, chiefly sought
" me, and laid snares for me, and intended my ruin. My
" whole employment and labour is, that I may daily gain
" more to Christ and the Church, and to cut off those that
" are obstinate, as rotten members.

The legate's
service to
the see ill
requited.

*An potui ego suspicari fore, ut cujus pietatem ita defen-
derim, dignitati et honori ita faverim, qui Pontifex tantum
ex hac Christi et ecclesiæ victoria honoris fructum ceperit,
me ministro, quantum multis adhinc seculis nullus Pontifex
cujusquam legati sui opera; is mihi tam insignem contu-
meliam mercedis loco redderet? Vero quod ego suspicari non
potui, hoc tandem accidit, ut alia aliquando præter omnium
hominum opinionem et judicium accidunt.* That is, " Could
" I ever think it would happen, that he, whose piety I so
" defended, whose honour and dignity I bare such an incli-
" nation unto, who being Pope, from this victory of Christ
" and the Church reaped such respect and esteem by my
" service, as for many ages past no Pope ever did by any
" legate, should, instead of a reward, requite me with such
" a signal reproach? But what I, for my part, could not
" suspect, fell out, as other things sometimes happen beside
" the opinion and judgment of all men."

Again, " In vain I seem to strive against him, who being
" constituted by Christ supreme judge on earth, takes upon
" him the person of an accuser, and saith, he doth it not
" out of an ill-will. For what ill-will should he have to-
" wards me, by whom he never was offended? But rather
" he had many causes of love and friendship with Cardinal
" Pole and Cardinal Moron: but when God's cause was in
" hand, and the purity of faith, [these are the Pope's
" words,] all the bonds, even the straitest bonds of hu-
" man friendship, must be cast of."—*Se cogitare, collegium
ab omni suspicione hæresis purgatum successori relinquere.*
" That he was thinking of leaving the college of cardinals
" to his successor, purged of all suspicion of heresy. And

" because there were none of the whole college more sus-
" pected than those two, therefore he would begin his pur-
" gation with them; and therein he thought he should offer
" a grateful sacrifice to God."

Pole challenged any to shew particularly any fault of his.
The Pope, he said, specified none, but only that he suspected him, and that for many years.

In this letter he gave the Pope an account how the Queen
managed the matter; *viz.* that when the Queen went to the
sea-side to take her leave of the King her husband, the Cardinal being absent, she received there, by her ambassador,
letters from the Pope, concerning taking away the legacy
from Pole, but leaving him the other legacy of the archi-
episcopal see. Letters were also then sent to the Cardinal
to the same effect: of which, the letters being detained from
him, and not delivered, he was ignorant. But when he
knew some other way, he sent to the Secretary and the
Queen, to know if there were any letters to him from the
Pope. At first they dissembled: at last the Queen confessed it, that she had letters both to him and herself, concerning the embassy sent to his Holiness to Rome; but
that she would not deliver his letters to him, till she were
come to London, and saw him there. A few days after, she
told him all, with much grief of mind, which she shewed in
her countenance and words.

*How the
Queen ma-
naged this
affair.*

397

Whereas the Queen had forbid the Pope's nuncio, in this
transaction, to come over into England, but to tarry on the
other side of the sea; thus did Pole represent the matter to
the Pope. " The nuncio was commanded to tarry at Ca-
" lais, until the Queen's messenger, whom she would send
" to Rome, should come back again: which she said she
" did for just causes, and which she doubted not his Holi-
" ness would approve of. Which when our Cardinal un-
" derstood, he immediately went, he said, to the Queen,
" and moved her and the Council, that he should be per-
" mitted to come without any delay. But the Queen and
" Council began presently to contend with him, and tell
" him, that he should not interpose himself in this matter,

*The nuncio
commanded
to tarry at
Calais.*

D 3

" but leave the whole affair to the Queen ; and withal, they
" desired him to go forward with the office of the legacy, until
" he should receive the Pope's *breves* concerning it.   But
" Pole refused to do it.   But they told him, that the Pope
" had said to the Queen's ambassador, that he [the Cardi-
" nal] should be moved with no rumours, although all af-
" firmed the legacy were taken from him, nor should desist
" in performing this office, until he should receive a *breve*
" concerning it from the Pope.   To which Pole answered,
" (as he relates in his letter,) that if the Pope said so, that
" he did it when he suspected little less than that his nuncio
" that brought the *breve* should be forbid to come to him ;
" and that since he knew this, he would not long execute

Pole desists
his office :
and

" the office of the legate : but if they would permit his Holi-
" ness's nuncio to come, he would execute it until he came.
" But since he could not persuade the Queen nor her coun-
" sellors to suffer this, he would no longer perform that
" office.   And while things were in this state, he resolved

Ormanet
sent to the
Pope.

" to send to his Holiness his auditor, Nicolas Ormanet,
" who, in all that time of his legacy, performed his office
" with much faithfulness and praise of godly men, that he
" should give account of the Cardinal's doings."

The re-
proach Pole
suffered by
the Pope.

He said, " that he must be pardoned, though he said
" that his Holiness had so offended him, *ut nullus unquam*
" *Cardinalis ab ullo Pontifice majori contumelia sit affectus,*
" *cum majores illa [Sanctitas vestra] quidem, fructus hono-*
" *ris ex meis laboribus, quam multis jam seculis ullus Pon-*
" *tifex cujusquam legati sui opera ceperit.*   That never
" any Cardinal suffered more reproach from a Pope, though
" your Holiness hath reaped greater fruit of honour from
" my labours, than any Pope by any legate, for many ages,
" ever did."

And trouble
the Queen
underwent.

And speaking concerning the trouble this affair had
created the Queen, he subjoined, " Since these things are
" so, let your Holiness consider what that spirit is, that cast-
" eth this mother of obedience into so great sorrow and
" consternation : for so may the Queen be well called, whom
" God hath made a mother of sons rejoicing in the sight of

" the whole Church; joyful in sons which she hath begot-
" ten to the Church; joyful in the assistance of so noble a
" birth, which Christ had given her.——What a doleful
" spectacle doth your Holiness set before this holy woman, 398
" *cum Regem, ejus virum, fulmine vocis suæ schismaticum,*
" *me hæreticum vocat;* when, by the thunder of your
" voice, you call the King, her husband, schismatic, and
" me heretic."

The issue at length of this business was, that the Pope,
for the present, sent word by Ormanet, Pole's messenger,
that he might for a time still remain legate, as he was before. And soon after, his nominated legate, Peto, died on
the other side of the sea.

In fine, this matter between the Pope and Cardinal Pole,
doth the author of the book, entitled, *Execution for Trea-*
son, and not for Religion, thus set forth, and make his remark of: " Neither was Queen Mary (a person not little
" devoted to the Roman religion) so afraid of the Pope's
" cursings, but that both she and her whole Council, and
" that with the assent of all the judges of the realm, according
" to the ancient laws, in favour of Cardinal Pole, her kins-
" man, did forbid the entry of his bulls, and of a cardinal's
" hat at Calais, that was sent from the Pope to one Friar
" Peyto, whom the Pope did assign to be a Cardinal, in
" disgrace of Cardinal Pole. Neither did Cardinal Pole
" himself, at the same time, obey the Pope's command-
" ments, nor shewed himself afraid, being assisted by the
" Queen, when the Pope did threaten him with pain of ex-
" communication; but did still oppose himself against the
" Pope's commandment for the said pretended Cardinal
" Peyto: who, notwithstanding all the threatenings of the
" Pope, was forced to go up and down in the streets of
" London, like a begging friar. A stout resistance in a
" queen for a poor cardinal's hat."

I add only one thing more concerning this affair, that
upon occasion of the aforesaid revoking of the Cardinal from
being legate, and appointing the same office to Friar Peyto,
there were certain questions put to some of the learned law-

CHAP.
LI.

Anno 1557.

The Cardi-
nal's speech
to the Lon-
doners.

yers of this realm, touching the Pope's jurisdiction in England : which, together with their answers, are still extant in
the Paper House. This was like to prove somewhat dangerous to the Pope, had he not desisted.

I have one thing more to relate of our Cardinal, which I
find no footsteps of in any history. Great industry had been
used to get the old monkery restored, and the abbeys built
again. The Queen's conscience was so possessed with it,
that she had above two years ago, publicly before her treasurer, and several of her great officers, restored back the
abbey-lands that remained in the possession of the crown.
The Pope urged it excessively to the English ambassadors ;
and no question the Cardinal was often solicited from Rome
about it. This year, on St. Andrew's day, the great festival
of the reconciliation with Rome, yearly solemnized, he either
came in person into the city of London, or sent for the chief
magistrates thereof to him, and made to them a long ha-
rangue concerning the religious buildings, and the churches
demolished, and the revenues thereof seized ; exhorting the
citizens to launch out their purses towards religious buildings, and the endowments thereof : " calling them first to
" penance, as having their hands in that sacrilege ; and that
" they should do worthy fruits of penance : which partly
399 " consisted in rebuilding of those houses, which would be a
" noble act, and grateful to God, and profitable to the
" realm. But this being more than the city of itself could
" compass, he bade them begin with the repair of their pa-
" rish churches, now run into great decay of themselves,
" and spoiled of their revenues and goods, as the monaste-
" ries were. He took occasion hence to direct his speech to
" such citizens as had obtained the goods and lands of the
" Church into their hands. From them especially he re-
" quired a competent part thereof back again to the Church,
" for the repairing her ruins, as the Church had willingly
" yielded, that they should enjoy what they had got. He
" compared such to a child, to whom the mother gave an
" apple ; which she perceiving him feed much upon, and
" knowing it would do him hurt, asked a piece of him, but

" he would not part with any. In the mean time the father
" comes in, and in anger beats the child for his unkindness,
" and takes it all away, and throws it out of the window.
" This, as he applied it, might Christ, the Church's hus-
" band, do. [And that, as he, I suppose, secretly meant,
" by Christ's vicar, the Pope.] Then he exhorted them to
" this under the name of alms-deeds; praising Italy for this
" virtue, saying, there was more given in two cities in Italy
" to monasteries and poor folks in one month, than in this
" realm in one whole year. Another fruit of their penance
" should be to honour the Church and priesthood, as before
" it was so dishonoured, this nation being gone further
" therein, than any schismatical nation had done, that ever
" he read of. Not that he would have them be at any fur-
" ther charge, than to give them that part which God had
" reserved to himself; and those were the tithes of all kinds:
" which when they denied the priest, they denied to give
" God his part. Another worthy fruit of their penance
" would be their discovering of heretics: for there could
" not be a greater work of cruelty, he said, against the
" commonweal, than to nourish and favour any such: none
" so pernicious to the commonweal, no thieves, murderers,
" adulterers; and no kind of treason to be compared to
" theirs." And as for those many holy men, that now for
three years had been fried to death, and burnt most barba-
rously to ashes, he made no more of than, as he styled them,
" a multitude of brambles and briars cast into the fire.
" Then, to flatter the citizens, he ran out into the praises of
" Sir Thomas More, a citizen born, who parted with his
" life to maintain the Pope's authority; and added to him
" much speech of Bishop Fisher, and the other monks that
" sacrificed their lives to the Pope's cause. He descended
" to urge parents and masters to reduce the younger sort to
" the old religion; which sort was generally bent to heresy:
" which appeared in that when any heretic went to execu-
" tion, he wanted not encouragement to die in his opinion;
" and while in prison, so much cherishing. He proceeded
" to exhort them earnestly to the observation of the ceremo-

"nies, because men could not live without ceremonies : and
"that at the observation of them began the very education
"of the children of God, as the law shewed that they were
"the pedagogues to Christ.   The heretics made this the
"first part of schism and heresy, to destroy the unity of the
400 "Church by contempt or change of ceremonies, as God
"made it the beginning of his good education of his chil-
"dren the Jews.   That the observation of ceremonies gave
"more light than all the reading of Scripture, whereto the
"heretics did so cleave, could do, had the reader never so
"good a wit to understand what he read, and though he
"put as much diligence in reading as he could, with the
"contempt of ceremonies.   And that they were most apt to
"receive light, that were more obedient to follow ceremo-
"nies than to read.   That many fell into heresy by thinking
"no better way to come to the knowledge of God and his
"laws, than by reading of books : wherein, he said, they
"were sore deceived ; and that the principal way to come
"to the light of the knowledge of God and his ways, was
"not gotten by reading, but by taking away the impedi-
"ment of that light ; and they be our sins, which were
"taken away by the sacrament of penance.

"Lastly, he exhorted them to alms, that is, to that sort
"of alms that consisted in building monasteries, by the
"example of Italy, the country whence he came.   That in
"Venice there were above threescore monasteries, and in
"Florence above fourscore ; and the most part founded by
"the voluntary alms of the citizens.   And that this was a
"mighty reproach to the city of London, where were not
"ten places, neither hospitals nor monasteries, within the
"city, nor about it.   And as for the citizens themselves,
"the poor might die for hunger."   This is the sum of his
long discourse, which may be read by them that please in
No LXVIII. the Catalogue.

CHAP. LII.

Matters relating to the gospellers. Trudgeover, Rough,
and Richard Gibson, martyrs. Gibson's confession.

LET us now turn our eyes to the gospellers, and to their Anno 1557.
dealings with them: which may in part appear by this jour- Letters and orders of
nal following, which seems to have been an exscript out of Council for
the Council-Book. heretics.

" July 28. Sondrie letters to the sheriffs of Kent, Essex, Fox's MSS.
" Suffolk, and Stafford, the maior of Rochester, and bayliffs
" of Colchester, to signify to the Council, what moved
" them to stay from execution such persons as had bene
" condempned for religion, and delyvered to them by their
" ordinaryes."

" August 3. Where sondrie letters had bene before di- Letters to Browne
" rected to divers justices for the apprehension of one concerning
" Trudgeover, he being taken and executed by Mr. An- Trudge-over.
" thony Browne, serjeant at law, in Essex; a letter as this
" day was directed to the said Sergeant Browne, geving
" hym thanks for his diligent proceding against the said
" Trudge: willing hym to distribute his head and quarters
" according to his and his collegues former determinations,
" and to procede with his complices according to the quali-
" ties of their offences."

A word or two of this man by the way. His true name Some account of
was George Eagles, some time a tailor by occupation. He Trudge-over.
was called *Trudge*, and *Trudgeover*, and *Trudge over the*
world, because of his extraordinary and continual travels 401
about from place to place, to exhort and confirm the brethren. The Council had heard of him, and sent orders
to waylay him. But he and his company concealed themselves a great while in the northern parts of Essex, in privy
closets and barns, in holes and thickets, in fields and woods.
At length such a thirst there was for his blood, that a proclamation went out in four counties, where his chief haunts
were, *viz.* Essex, Suffolk, Norfolk, and Kent, to take him,
and promising twenty pounds as a reward: which encou-

raged more diligent search for him. And soon after he was taken in a field not far from Colchester, whence he had fled. At the sessions at Chelmsford, he was indicted of treason, because he had assembled companies together contrary to the laws of the realm; it being enacted not long before, to avoid sedition, that if men should flock together above six, it was made treason. In fine, he was cast, condemned, and cruelly hanged, drawn, and quartered as a traitor. And as though he were one of the worst sort of rebels, his four quarters were set up in four several great places, namely, Colchester, Harwich, St. Osith's, and Chelmsford, where on the market cross his head also was advanced, for a terror. In which service Sergeant Brown, living at North Weald, as he had the main hand, so in the aforesaid letter he had the Council's thanks. One of the reasons, I suppose, that made the Council so offended with this Trudgeover was, because he was accused in his meetings to pray to God, *to change the Queen's heart, or soon to take her away*: though at his trial he denied that he prayed any more, than that God would change her heart.

" Aug. 7. The lords understanding by Sir John Butler's
" letter, being sheriff of Essex, that his under-sheriff had re-
" spited a woman from execution, which should have been
" burned at Colchester, did set a fyne upon Sir John his
" head of ten pounds, for that he was to answer his depu-
" ties doings."

" Decemb. 27. A letter sent unto Boner, bishop of Lon-
" don, with the examination of a Scottish man, named John
" Rough, presently sent unto Newgate, willing him to pro-
" cede against the said Rough, according to the laws."

John Rough, the minister, martyr. This letter is extant in Fox, but the date there is not the 27th, but the 15th, which is the truer. This Rough was a considerable man. He had been twice at Rome. In his younger days he was a black friar in Sterling in Scotland; afterwards chaplain to Hamilton, Earl of Arran; and living at St. Andrews, had a yearly pension of twenty pounds from King Henry, being probably a promoter of that King's reputation and interest in those parts. In the beginning of King Edward's time, becoming known unto the Duke of Somerset, he had the same yearly pension allowed him, and was sent as a preacher to Carlisle, Barwick, and Newcastle. In this reign of King Edward, the Archbishop of York gave him a benefice near Hull. In Queen Mary's time he and his wife fled to Freezland, and dwelt at Norden there: and there got a poor living by knitting. In October 1557, coming into England for yarn, it so fell out, that he became minister to the congregation of gospellers at London, among whom he celebrated divine service by King Edward's communion book. At one of their meetings at Islington, December 12, he was taken and condemned, and burnt ten days after in Smithfield. This man wrote a letter to the congregation a little before his death, wherein he bade them " look up with their eyes of hope, " for the redemption was not far off: but my wickedness," as he added, " hath deserved that I shall not see it." Whose prophecy, if I may so call it, fell true; for within the year Queen Mary died, and the gospel was restored. Dr. Watson, now bishop of Lincoln, hastened his death. This man, once in King Edward's reign, preached a sermon in the north, (perhaps at York, or Hull,) wherein he vented such doctrine, that he was like to have been prosecuted for treason: but this Rough, by his interest, saved his life. Watson happened to be present once when Rough was brought before Bishop Boner, and, forgetting his former kindness, presently informed the said Bishop, that he had known Rough in the north, and that he was a pestilent heretic there, where he had done more harm than an hundred besides of his opinion. Whereat Rough asked him, " Why, sir, " is this the reward you give me, for saving your life in King " Edward's days, when you preached erroneous doctrine?"

By these letters and orders of Council, it appears how severely the State still went on against all that complied not with the old religion: and how ingrateful to the sheriffs and magistrates this burning work was: so that they ventured to stay these executions; and the Council was fain to quicken them by letters and fines.

402

CHAP.
LII.

Anno 1557.
Ric. Gib-
son, a pri-
soner, his
declaration.
Among those that suffered for religion under Queen Mary, Richard Gibson, a gentleman, was one, who being surety for a debt, had laid long in the Poultry-Counter, London. This man, upon suspicion of holding amiss in the points of the sacrament, and authority of the Church, was required by the Bishop to make a declaration of his mind in the doctrine of the sacrament, and to subscribe it, in order to his dismission. He therefore the last year, in the month of October, drew it up warily in words of Scripture, and submitted himself to the Church in general terms; *viz.*

" EMANUEL.

Fox's MSS.
" Forasmuch as my long imprisonment, as also the cause
" of the same, is not hyd, therefore have I thought my-
" self in conscience bownd, for the avoyding of offence, to
" make it known, that as what I hold for an infallible and an
" undoubted truth, I hold it not of presumption, nor yet of
" men, neyther for that men say so, and affirm it so to be,
" as is supposed, but of a pure and single conscience before
" God and man, as I am taught by the Word. By whose
" power men, and all things that ever wer made, have their
" being; and without whose power no man can speak the
" truth: and therefore without it, must nedes be lyers. And
" that it may appere that I so do, therfore thus I say:

" Because our Savior Jesus Christ at his last supper
" took bread, and when he had geven thanks brake it, and
" gave it to his disciples, and said, *Take, eat, this is my body,*
" *which is geven for you:* and in like maner took the cup,
" and gave it to his disciples, and said, *This is my bloud of*
403 " *the new testament, which is shed for many:* and sayd,
" *This do in remembrance of me:* therfore I do believe, that
" as the Church is authorized by the power of the Word to
" minister it, as they are taught by the same, so do I affirm,
" and believe as often, when and where I do receive it, that
" I do eat the flesh and drink the blood of my Lord God
" and Saviour Jesus Christ. And to this holy Catholic
" Church of Christ I humbly submit myself, promising

" therein to lyve to the uttermost of my knowledge, by the
" grace of God, as it shall become a good Christian man:
" and here in this realm to lyve as it becometh a true sub-
" ject unto the King and Queen's Majesty; and also to be
" obedient to all other their Majesties rulers and officers,
" and of them sent: so far as I may lawfully be without
" offence either to God or man. If I may not be permitted
" so to lyve, I am fully resolved, by the grace of God,
" without resistance, as I am tawght by the word, with
" patience to possess my soul.

" By me, Ric. Gybson, 27 of Octob. anno Dom. 1556."

Such general submissions as these the prisoners now and
then would make, and sometimes they escaped by them,
when they had to deal with ecclesiastical officers disposed to
mercy: but this declaration of Gybson would not now do.
And besides, he was suspected of disliking the mass, dis-
owning the seven sacraments, approving the English service
in King Edward's days, and for not coming to his parish
church, nor bearing tapers upon Candlemas-day, nor taking
ashes upon Ash-Wednesday; for being against confession
to a priest, and such like. Whereupon Bishop Boner sent
thirteen articles to him to purge him, requiring a direct
answer thereunto. Gybson was minded to subscribe for the
saving of his life, but yet would have done it in a more wary
style, and in expressions more qualified, for the better salving
of his own conscience. So he drew up his answer to the articles in this manner following.

" EMANUEL.

" Psal. 55. B. *In God's word will I rejoyce; in the Lord's
word will I comfort me.*

" First of all, I openly protest, before God and man, that
" I have both taught and believed, and do so think and
" believe, that the faith, religion, and service, used now in
" this realm of England, of them which are in part of the
" Church of Christ, and members of his body, is good and
" laudable, and not against God's holy word, but most

Another
confession
of Gybson.

"agreeable unto the same: and especially in the true use
"of baptisme, confirmation, penance, the supper of the
"Lord, (reverently called of the Grecians, *eucharistia*, and
"of the Latinians, *gratiarum actio*, and *sacrificium laudis*,)
"order, matrimony, and unction. And do openly protest,
"before God and man, that I am contented in all things
"to conform myself unto the same; as trew subjects of
"this realm have done, and do, without ony murmuring,
"grudging, or scruple thereyn.

404   "Secondly, I sai, as there is nothing done by man (as of
"man) that cannot be amended, so I say, that the service set
"forth in England in the time of King Edward VI. was
"not, in all points, so godly and Catholic, but that, in some
"things, it both ought and might have well been mended.
"And I would to God, that it, which is now used within this
"realm, were also faultless.   Then doutless it should be
"no occasion of horrible bloudshed, as it is.

"Thirdly, I say, thoughe I am nether by the law of
"God, nor yet by the law of this realme, under any penal-
"tie bound to ether place or tyme, to heare or learne any
"thinges, whatsoever it be; thoughe it be ther and then
"never so well done: yet, I say, that the holy word of God
"doth teache all men, not only when they are at libertie,
"but also beynge prysoners, yf they may convenyently do
"it, to repaire to all places, where they may do good to
"others; much more where they may do good to them-
"selves: and chiefly, if they so can, for the avoidynge of
"offences.   The which is all mens part to avoid, if thei
"can; wher they are most resiaunte, and continually dwell-
"ynge.

"Fourthly, I say, as God hath geven no churche, peo-
"ple, or congregation, hie or low, or any rulers thereof,
"leave, authorite, or power to do what seemeth them good
"in ther own eyes; but hath straitly commanded, and
"geven them in charge, upon the payne of utter destruc-
"tion, both in this world and in the world to come, to leave
"undone what as is commaunded; and further, to do, if
"nede so require, what as may be to the benefit, and edi-

" fying of them that are under ther charge: which to do
" it is the right God's service and his trewe honour. All
" which holy ordynaunces, usages, and ceremonyes, thinges
" used and done by them, I knowledge myself, and all other
" inferiour persons, upon the like payne of utter destruc-
" tion, to be bounde to observe and kepe: and in no wise
" them, or any of them, stubbornly to breake or refuse.

" Fifthly, I say, a preste or mynister, in whose lippes is
" sure knowledge, and in whose mowthe is the word of
" truethe, over his charge appointed hyme by the ruler,
" hath power by the word, as occasion shall serve, to bynd
" and to lose. And that this charge ought, for order sake,
" and for avoydynge of offences, to receave of hym what as
" he ought and may lawfully mynister unto them, without
" any stubborne refusal of the same.

" Sixthly, I say, that all men, of what degre, dignite,
" estate, or calling soever they be, for an infallible trueth,
" are to hold and beleve the holy Scriptures of God, geven
" to us by the Holy Ghost; which is his wisedome: and
" them to take as a sure rule to walk by to eternal life.
" And also, that no inferior person thorow wilful boldness
" may be so male-pert, as to reject, or hold as frivolous,
" any determinations or order made by the holy Churche,
" not repugnaunt unto the same. And also, that no maner
" man follow or believe, after his own pryvate will or con-
" science, contrarye to the determynation and order, and
" doctryne of the same. For the Holy Ghost counteth
" him as a *foole that is wise in his own conceit;* and saith,
" *that strypes are prepared for the fool's back.*

" Seventhly, I say, that all things do not chaunge of a pre-
" sise, absolute power, and mere necessite; but that all 405
" men, except such, after transgression, as a just reward for
" ther synnes, are geven over into a lewd mynd, according
" to the knowledge they have received of God, have power
" in mynde; in that they know to will, and not to will.

" Agayne, I say, for that I am ignorant of many things
" which are allowed within this realme of England; and
" especially now used about the christenynge of infants,

VOL. III. PART II.   E

" therefore in them I will use silence, till I be thereyn bet-
" ter instructed ; lest that, in allowyng or disallowyng what
" I know not, I make myself to appear a foole in myne own
" judgment. I have not so learned with myne own heart,
" to rejoyce myne enemyes. But this I say, as all the or-
" dynances of God are very good and very holy, so I say,
" that baptysme, when and wheresoever it is ministred as
" the Holy Ghost doth teach it, is very good and very
" holye, and cannot but be effectual.

" Ninthly, For that I find them only to be saynets, the
" which, through faith, are sanctified in the bloud of Jesus
" Christ, by the Holy Ghost, and none other ; and that as
" they are all members of one body, so have they nede of
" help one of another : therfore, I say, that prayer unto,
" with, and for saynets is good ; and do not thynk it con-
" trary to God's words, but agreeable to the same, and
" nedeful to be used, bicause our necessity requireth. And
" also, for that I find in other places of the holy servantes of
" God what cannot be broken ; as, by the example of La-
" zarus and Dyves, after this life, hell to be the ymmediate
" place of the wicked, and heaven to be the immediate place
" of the good : therefore I dare not but say, as the Holy
" Ghost doth teache, that the good are in heavyn, and the
" wicked in hell. This notwithstanding, this I say, if there
" be a people departed which are neither good nor bad,
" and so to be are allowed of God, whereof as yet I am
" ignorant, I protest then, I think them to abyde till they
" be allowed before God, either as good or bad, in such a
" place as is neither good nor bad : 'till otherwise to be,
" they are allowed of God. What it is called, (if ther
" be any such place,) whether it be *purgatory,* or not, I
" know not. And if be prayer for the dead be beneficial
" for any, then must be nedes profit these or none.

" Tenthly, I say, for that no private opynion, be it true
" or false, is the cause of any man's salvation or damnation,
" or any just cause, but only an occasion for men to be
" justified or condemned therby ; and though they therein
" dyed never so stoutly ; therefore I will no more condemne

" frier Barnes, Garet, Jearom, Rogers, Howper, Cardmaker,
" Latymer, Taylour, Bradford, Filpot, Ridley, Cranmer,
" and such like; the which of late have suffered, then I
" will justify Feverston, Abell, Powel, friar Forest, Moore,
" Fisher, the monks of the Charterhouse, and such like,
" which before their tyme also suffered.   And for that all
" men, whatsoever they be, are utterly forbid the deter-
" minate judgment of salvation or dampnation;. because it
" is the office of God only, which therein will do accord-
" ing to his own will or pleasure, otherwise than we know,
" or as we shall know : therefore I say, as it ought not to be
" used among men, so it ought not to be required of any
" man. Wherefore if any man therein will excede, I will ex- 406
" hort him, from henceforth in charity to excede therein.
" For this much of some of them I am able to say of mine
" own knowledge, if they in their tyme had byn gredy by
" death to have such allowed their enemies, doubtless some
" of them that now succede, had not bene alive to rejoyce
" as they do.   I would advise either quality ; or else, if it
" be possible, more charity ; for it was never more needful.

" Eleventhly, I say, as fasting, prayer, and all deeds of
" charity, are the ordynances of God, taught by the testi-
" mony of his holy word ; so, I say, they are not only law-
" ful to be frequented and used in tymes and places con-
" venyent ; but also ought of every man, according to that
" he hath, to be frequented and used as they are taught
" by the same.   And also I say, that for the infyrmyties
" sake, them which want as well knowledge as power to
" bridle and rule themselves, the rulers have full power and
" auctority to appoint both days and tymes of common
" fasting and prayer ; so that they do it to the edifying of
" their Church, and not to snare them withal.

" Twelfthly, I say, that the institution of our Saviour
" Jesus Christ is not an idol, nor abhomynation, but is a
" most blessed, comfortable, and holy ordynance, most
" thankfully to be frequented and used of all his Church
" and people ; and do evidently believe, that so often, when
" and where it is dewly mynistred as our Saviour Jesus

E 2

" Christ did it for an example, that then and there, by the
" mynysters, is trewly gyven the same body and bloud of
" our Saviour Jesus Christ that was crucified and shed for
" our synns, and none other.   And also I say, it is no
" idolatry nor superstition to recyve it, and to kepe the holy
" ordynance of the same, nor to adore nor worship.   The
" same Christ sitteth and reigneth eternal God and King
" for ever.   To whom be all honour, glory, might, rule,
" and power, for ever and ever, world without ende, Amen.

" Thirteenthly, I say, as the great and honourable au-
" thority and power, and authority of rulers is not doubted
" of, and what they may lawfully do to undoubted offend-
" ers is not unknown : therefore I will therein, with re-
" verence, use silence.   But that, I say, as no ruler, of what
" degree soever they be, may lawfully punish any for that
" which is not spoken nor done : so, say I, a bishop, for his
" office sake, much less may do it. If all rulers, in all cases,
" be forbidden the use of unlawful rigour, as I am sure
" they are, how can he excuse himself of fault, that use
" unlawful rigour to any man for the secrecy of his con-
" science ?

" *The proud have laid a snare for me, and spred a net*
" *abrode with cordes ; yea, and set trapps in my way. But*
" *myne eyes loke unto thee, O Lord, my God.   For in thee*
" *is my trust.   Oh! cast not out my soul.   Keep me from*
" *the snare which they have laid for me, and from the*
" *trapps of wicked doers. And let the ungodly fall into their*
" *own nets together, until I be gone by theym.*"

This man, we see, by these wary expressions, and smooth,
seemingly complying paragraphs, under the distinct, con-
tested articles, shewed, or rather hid what his true thoughts
of religion were. And hence we may observe another sort of
professors of the gospel, (if we may call them so,) who, under this cruel government, endeavoured to save their lives,
by thus artificially concealing and keeping their opinions to
themselves ; and by an outward conformity to the present
superstitions, errors, and corruptions. And there were a

great many timorous men and women in these persecuting
days, that were feign thus to temporize, and shift to save
their lives, and salve their consciences, as well as they
could..

But neither would this confession serve Bishop Boner's
turn : for he saw well enough through it, however obscurely
Gybson had drawn it up to deceive him, and save his own
conscience.   That he therefore should speak fully home to
the purpose, and acknowledge divers things that the Bishop
laid to his charge, he required him to give such answer to
thirteen articles, as whereby he should effectually accuse
himself.   So Gybson drew up another seeming confession
cunningly worded, which if the Bishop would be deceived
by, he might.   But he framed it so, that it might be understood, not as though he acknowledged what was contained
in the words, but that Boner would have him so to acknowledge.   And the whole writing he intimated to be false, by
affixing two verses out of the Psalms, one at the top of this
paper, and the other at the end of it.   And this is a copy
of it.

O ye sons of men, why will ye blaspheme mine honour ?
Why have ye such pleasure in vanity, and seek after lyes ?

ARTICLES

Given by the Bishop of London, to be confessed or denyed
by Richard Gybson, in his answer to be made thereunto,
yea or nay.

First, I have both thowght, beleved, and spoken, and
so do thynke, beleve, and speke, that the fayth, relygion,
and ecclesiastical service observed and used now in thys
realm of England, is good and laudable, and not agaynst
God's commandments or word ; especially concerning the
mass and the seven sacraments : being contented in all thyngs
to conform myself unto the same, as true subjects of these
realms have don, and do, without any murmuring, grudging,
or scruple therin.

Second, I have likewyse thought, beleved, and spoken,
that the English servyce, set furth here in thys realm of

England, in the time of King Edward the Sixth, was in many poynts ungodly, and not catholick ; and therfore not to be received, continued, or used here in thys realm.

III.   Thyrdly, I have lykewyse thought, spoken, and beleved, that I am bounden, being at lybertie, to come to my parysh 408 church, and to be present, and to hear matins, mas, and even song, with other divine service sung and sayd.

IV.   Fowrthly, I have lykewyse thowght, beleved, and spoken, that I am bownden, being at lybertie, to come to procession to my parysh church upon days and tymes appoynted ; and to go therin with others, syngyng or saying accustomed prayers ; and also to bear a taper or a candel upon Candel-mas day, and take ashes upon Ashwensday, bear palme upon Palmsunday, crepe the cross upon days and tymes accustomed, to receyve and kyss the pax at mas-tyme, to receyve holy bread and holy water ; and fynally, to accept and allow all the ordynances, ceremonyes, and usages of the Church, after the maner and fashion as they are now used in thys realm of England.

V.   Fyfthly, I have lykewyse thought, beleved, and spoken, that I am bownd to confess my sinns to a priest, and to re-ceyve absolution of them at his hands, being God's minister ; and also to receyve of the priest the sacrament of the altar, at tymes accustomed, after the form and maner as is now used in the Church of England.

VI.   Sixthly, I have lykewyse thought, beleved, and spoken, in matters of religion and fayth, and beleve I ought to give credyt to the determynation and common order of the Ca-tholic Church and see of Rome, and members thereof, and not to follow or beleve after my private will or conscyence, contrary to the sayd determynation and order.

VII.   Seventhly, I have lykewyse thought, beleved, and spoken, that all things do not chance of a precise absolute power and mere necessity, but that a man hath, by God's grace, a free choyse and wyll in hys doyngs.

VIII.   Eighthly, I have lykewyse thought, beleved, and spoken, that the fashionyng and maner of christenyng here used in this realm of England, is not against the word, but agreable

and conformable unto the same: and that one may be effectually baptized, and therby saved, before he come to the
age of discretion.

Ninthly, I have lykewyse thought, beleved, and spoken,   IX.
that prayer to saints, and prayer for the dead, is not contrary
to God's word, but agreable to the same, and profitable: and
that the souls departed have a mean place, commonly called
purgatory, and do not sleep 'till the day of dome.

Tenthly, I have likewyse thought, beleved, and spoken,   X.
that such as in the time of King Henry VIII. and in the
time of Queen Mary now, have bene condempned and
burned for heresie, were hereticks, unfaithful, and no good
Christen people; specially fryer Barnes, Garret, Jerome,
Frith, Rogers, Hoper, Cardmaker, Latymer, Tayler, Bradford, Philpot, Cranmer, Ridley, and such like. I have not
liked, allowed, or approved any of their opinions so condempned.

Eleventhly, I have likewise thought, believed, and spoken,   XI.
that fastyng and prayer now used in the Church of England, and the appoynting of days and tymes for fastyng,
and abstayning from flesh upon fastyng days, and specially
in the tyme of Lent, is good and laudable, and not against
God's word. And therefore persons ought not at all tymes
to have liberty to eat all kinds of meat.

Twelfthly, I have lykewyse thought, believed, and spoken, 409
that the sacrament of the altar is not an idol nor abhomyna-   XII.
tion, but that in it is really, &c. the very body and blood in
substance of our Saviour Christ; and that it is no idolatry
or superstition to receyve and kepe the sayd sacrament, and
also adore it, yea, and to lift it up at the levation and sa-
cryng time.

Thirteenthly, I have likewise thought, believed, and   XIII.
spoken, that a person offending or trespassing by words or
otherwise in matter of religion, belief, and faith, within any
bishop's diocess of this realm, and being called for the same
before the said bishop, within whose diocess he doth so
offend or trespass, though he were not there originally born,

CHAP.
LII.

Anno 1557.
is bound to make answer thereunto, yea, upon his oath, if he be by the said bishop or ordinary so required.

Psalm xii. O that the Lord would root out all deceitful lips, and the tongue that speaketh proud things. Which say, Our tongue should prevail: we are they that ought to speak: who is Lord over us?

Gybson
sends two
papers to
Boner.
A little before this, as it seems, (upon occasion of his denying to be confessed and absolved, in order to the receiving the sacrament at Easter 1557, a priest, against this time, being provided for the prisoners in the Poultry Counter, where Gybson lay,) Bishop Boner objected and administered nine articles to him. He also, soon after, in the month of April, bantered the Bishop by ministering nine (that is, just as many) articles to him; and sending him a second paper, consisting also of the same number of nine articles, describing what manner of man a good bishop ought to be. By which he might see how far short himself fell of that character.

The former paper he began, according to his custom, with suitable verses out of the Psalms, applicable enough to this proud prelate, *viz.*

EMANUEL.

Fox's Acts,
first edit.
Psalm xlix.

Psalm ii.
When a man is in honour, and hath no understanding, he is compared unto the brute beasts, and becometh like unto them. Wherefore, O ye judges of the earth, be ye learned, and ye rulers, serve the Lord with fear, and rejoyce before him with reverence. Embrace righteousness and judgment. Accept not the persons of the ungodly; lest the Lord be angry, and so ye perish from the right way.

Then follow the paper of articles, thus entitled:

Articles proposed by Richard Gybson, unto Edmund Boner, bishop of London: by him to be answered by yea *or* nay, *or else to say,* he cannot tell.

Gybson's
articles pro-
posed to
Boner. P.1839.
Of these articles I shall only shew the contents, because they are already in print in the Acts and Monuments.

I. Whether the Scriptures are available doctrine to make men learned unto salvation, without the help of any other doctrine?

II. What is authority, and from whence it comes, to 410 whom it pertaineth, and to what end it tendeth?

III. Whether the word of God, as it is written, doth sufficiently teach all men, of whatsoever calling, their lawful duty in their office? And, whether every man is bound upon pain of eternal damnation, to do as they are hereby taught and commanded?

IV. Whether any man, the Lord Jesus except, is or shall be Lord over faith? And by what authority any man may use lordship or power over any man for faith's sake?

V. By what lawful authority any man may be so bold as to change the ordinances of God, or any of them?

VI. By what evident token Antichrist, in his ministers, may be known; seeing it is written, *Satan shall change himself into an angel of light, and his ministers fashion themselves as though they were the ministers of God?*

VII. What the beast is that maketh war with the saints of God, and doth not only kill them, but will not suffer any to buy or sell, but such as worship the image? Also, what the gorgeous and glittering whore is, that sitteth upon the beast, with a cup of gold in her hand full of abomination; with whom the kings of the earth have committed fornication, and she herself drunken with the blood of the saints?

VIII. Whether a king over all those people that are born within his own dominions, is lawful, supreme, and governor here upon earth? And whether a king over all those people lawfully may, and ought not otherwise to do, nor suffer otherwise to be done, than in his own name and power to govern and rule without exception? And whether a king, without offence against God and his people, may give away, and not himself use that authority and power given him of God? And whether any subject, without offence to God and the king, may do ought to his minishing or derogation of the supreme prerogative royal?

CHAP.
LII.

Anno 1557.

IX. Whether the holy written law of God be given of God to all men, of whatsoever dignity, state, or calling, as well thereby to govern all their dominions, and their people therein inhabiting, as themselves? Or whether any law or laws, not being made within a dominion, whereas it or they be used, may be lawfully used, before they be by public and common consent of the same dominion or country allowed? These were bones for the Bishop to pick.

Gybson's
second pa-
per to
Boner.

The second paper sent by Gybson to Bishop Boner, and is extant only in Fox's first edition, began thus; with the name of God, and a verse out of the Psalms.

411   " EMANUEL.

Ps. xxxix.

" *Ascribe unto the Lord, O ye mighty, ascribe unto the*
" *Lord worship and strength. Give the Lord the honour of*
" *his name, and bow yourselves to the holy majesty of the*
" *Lord.*

" *What manner of man a bishop ought to be, and the duty*
" *of him in his office, as the holy Scriptures of God most*
" *truly do teach.*

What a
bishop
ought to
be.
1 Tim. iii. a.
Tit. i. b.

" In general, a bishop, as the steward of God, must be
" blameless, the husband of one wife, and one that ruleth
" well his own house, and that hath faithful children in
" subjection with all reverence; and one that is diligent,
" prudent, sober, discreet, righteous, godly, temperate, a
" keeper of hospitality, not stubborn, not angry, not given
" to overmuch wine, no fighter," &c.

2 Cor. i. e.
1 Pet. v. a.

" In particular: I. He may not be a lord over the faith-
" ful, of them that are committed unto his charge; neither
" may he use any lordship over them for the same; but
" must become as one of them, that through his humble-
" ness he may win the more to well-doing.

Rom. xv. d.

" II. Neither may he be so bold as to speak any other
" thing, to make any man obedient to the same, than he
" himself hath learned of Christ.

1 Cor. vii. f.

" III. Neither may he do or teach any thing to tangle
" or snare any man withal.

2 Cor. xiii. e.
2 Cor. iv. a.

" IV. He may not walk in craftiness, neither use the

" cloak of unhonesty, neither handle the word of God de-

" V. He may not reject the weak in faith, in disputing
" and troubling their conscience, but must bear their frailty; Rom. xiv. a.
" and, in the spirit of meekness, must be ready to help him Gal. vi. a.
" that is overtaken with any fault, &c.

" VI. He not only lawfully may, but also ought, by vir- 1 Cor. ix. e.
" tue of his office, to preach the word sincerely, to minister, 1 Tim. iii. b.
" so as no man may be able to reprove him, and to expel, 2 Cor. v. b.
" put out, or to excommunicate from among the remnants 2 Cor. x. c.
" of his charge, all open, wilful malefactors: and yet to 1 Cor. xiii. e.
" fare fair with all men, and not to be rigorous; because
" his office is given him to edify, and not to destroy.

" VII. And he not only lawfully may, but also ought, Acts vi. a.
" by the virtue of his office, of virtuous able men, well
" known, and of honest report within his charge, to appoint
" sufficient number to help him in discharge thereof.

" VIII. And he in no case by violence may compel John iv. e.
" any man to be of his church or fellowship, or to be par- Gal. i. c.
" taker of any thing that is done therein. 2 Tim. iv. c.

" IX. And for his due administration, as one worthy of 2 Thes. iii. e.
" double honour, he may not only receive of his charge 1 Tim. v. d.
" what is necessary, but also ought of them, as of duty, 412
" without requests, if need require, to be provided of the
" same."

And then he concludes, " If the Bishop of London be
" such a manner of man as these Scriptures do teach, and
" hath done, and daily doth his duty therein, as he is
" taught by the same, as of duty he ought to do; then
" doubtless, as he is a meet and worthy man for his office,
" so am I worthy of the punishment I have, yea, if it were
" more. But if it be otherwise, as wherein for the tender
" mercy of Christ Jesu, I most humbly require righteous
" judgment; then, as I have unworthily sustained long pu-
" nishment, so is he not only most unworthy of his office,
" but also hath most worthily deserved to be recompensed
" blood for blood, as equity requireth.

" *I will hearken what the Lord God will say. For he* Psal. lxxxiv.

" *shall speak peace unto his people, that they turn not them-*
" *selves unto foolishness.*

 " *This 6 of April,* 1557." " By me Richard Gybson."

Gibson's
last exami-
nations.

 This whole summer he continued in prison, and in November his business came on again: for the Bishop, teased
with him and his writings, sent for him, intending to make
a speedy end with him. He offered an oath to him, to
swear to such interrogatories as should be put to him:
which he would not take, saying stoutly, the Bishop was
not his ordinary, and had therefore nothing to do with
him. But Boner procured several persons, upon oath, to
give in their testimonies concerning him; such as belonged
to the Counter where Gibson lay. Some of which said,
they never knew otherwise than well by him both in word
and deed. But some of them said, that he had not, in two
years, been confessed to a priest, nor in that space had received the sacrament. Which when it was objected to him,
he freely acknowledged it to be true, and gave God thanks
that he had so done. He was sundry times brought into
examinations. Once John Bishop of Winton present, said,
" It was no pity to burn an heretic." To which Gibson
replied, " That it was not requisite nor lawful to burn men
" as heretics." The said Bishop told him, " He would not
" talk with him, because he was an heretic, and excommu-
" nicate." Gibson told him again undauntedly, " Yours
" and other Bishops' curses be blessings to me." At another examination, much conference happened betwixt him
and Dr. Darbishire, the Bishop of London's chancellor.
Another time he appeared at Justice Hall before the Bishop and divers justices, as though he were some criminal
in law. And last of all at the Consistory: where Bishop
Boner having read the sentence against him, admonished
him to remember himself, and save his soul. But Gibson
called this talk of the Bishop *babbling,* and desired to hear
no more of it. And then protested, that he was contrary,
and an enemy to them all in his mind and opinion, though
he had aforetime kept it secret for fear of the law. And

added, " Blessed am I, that am cursed at your hands. We CHAP.
LII.
" have nothing now for law, but *Thus will I.* For as the
" Bishop saith, so must it be." He valiantly underwent Anno 1557.
the cruel death of burning, in the month of November, Is burnt.
with two more in Smithfield, named Halingdale and Spar- 413
row.

By all the foregoing relations, we may note the boldness His cha-
and great abilities of this man. For as he was a personable, racter.
stout, and comely man of body, so he was of vigour and
activity of mind too.

This and many other excellent men did the Bishop of
London bring to their ends.

CHAP. LIII.

The persecution hot still. Ralph Allerton, martyr. Dr.
Weston, dean of Windsor, under displeasure.

FOR the heat of the persecution abated not at all (as was The per-
hoped) by the death of Bishop Gardiner, that implacable secution in-
creaseth;
bloody-minded man; but it rather increased, that bloody
butcher Boner being left behind him, and bloody counsels
generally overruling now at the Council-board. For this
year they were burnt together in one fire, in good round
numbers. As, six at Canterbury: after that, five at Smithfield: then seven at Maidstone: seven more at Canterbury:
then ten at Lewis: ten more at Colchester. But notwith- And so do
standing all this rage and madness exercised towards the the profes-
sors, espe-
professors, their numbers seemed not to lessen, but to in- cially in
crease the more. And at the latter end of this year, they Essex.
did more boldly than before exercise their religion, and
make an open profession of it: particularly in the parish of
Much Bently in Essex, where Boner was patron, one Thomas Ty, the priest and commissary, writ the Bishop word,
" that they were never so bold since the King and Queen's
" reign: that they did not only absent themselves from the
" Church, but did daily allure many others away from the
" same, which before did shew signs and tokens of obedi-

" ence. That they assembled upon the Lord's days in time
" of service, sometimes in one house, and sometimes in an-
" other, and there kept their schools of heresy, as he wrote.
" Nor did the officers care to do what was enjoined them
" for discovery. The jurats said, ' the commission was
" out, and that they were discharged of their oaths.' That
" the quest-men in the archdeacon's visitation alleged, that
" forasmuch as the two-and-twenty had been once presented
" and sent home, they had no more to do with them."
These two-and-twenty were sent up to Boner from Colchester side, upon the charge of heresy laid against them
by the commissioners; but, upon a slight submission, by
means, as is said, of Cardinal Pole, dismissed, and sent home
again: but herein the Council, now in a good mood, had
the chief hand. For one Boswel, secretary to Bishop Boner,
said, " The Council sent them not home without good con-
" sideration."

Ty wrote also, " That at Colchester (where but a little
" before ten had been burnt) the *rebels*, as he called them,
" were stout. That the parish priests were hemmed at in
" the open streets, and called *knaves ;* the sacrament blas-
414 " phemed and reviled at in every house and tavern ; prayer
" and fasting not regarded ; seditious talk and noise was
" rife both in town and country, in as ample and large
" manner, as though there had been no honourable lords
" and commissioners sent for the reformation thereof." This
information was writ December 18. This letter provoked
much, and set the bloodhounds upon a new scent and
search after good men and women ; and ended in the burning of nine more in one day in Colchester.

And which was to be remarked, the friends and relations
of these Essex men imprisoned, instead of exhorting them
to comply, subscribe, and recant, and so save their own
lives, and restore themselves to their liberty ; wives and
children did, on the contrary, earnestly persuade them to
hold out, and that even to death. A letter of this nature
I find written to one Ralph : whom I conclude to be Ralph
Allerton, that suffered martyrdom with three Essexians

more at Islington this year, and lived at Bentley aforesaid on Colchester side. He was a tailor by trade, as I con- jecture by Boner's often calling him *pricklouse*, according to his rude way of misnaming such as came before him: but having good learning, did use to read the English Tes- tament, and other good books, and to pray with the well- disposed professors, meeting together in houses and woods, and sometimes in churches too: which Allerton continued to do, till he was taken by the Lord Darcy in the year 1556, and brought up to the Council, who sent him to Bi- shop Boner; when out of fear he subscribed, and made a recantation at Paul's Cross; but was exceedingly afflicted in his mind in what he had done; and soon recovered, and went on in the same course he had done before, but with more zeal and constancy: insomuch that almost all the in- habitants of those parts became professors. He being taken again in the beginning of this year by the information of Ty, and some other sworn men, boldly stood to the con- fession of the truth. And being in prison, he writ his exa- minations, with some letters, with his own blood instead of ink; which are preserved in Fox. During this last impri- sonment, a spiritual brother named Foster, and a spiritual sister named Tyms, (the wife of the one and the husband of the other dying in the flames,) wrote him the letter afore- said, for his confirmation, and it had its effect; for he made a good confession and a resolute end. This letter, among other such like monuments, I have preserved in the Cata- N°. LXIX. logue.

Several other pious men in the said county of Essex, Several de- tected in Essex. that preached and exhorted, and travelled about for the benefit and edification of the professors of the gospel in those parts, whom Ty also discovered to the Bishop, were these; Mr. Laurence of Barnhall, John Barry, his servant, John Jeffrey, Robert Coles, and John Ledley. These two last named were great concealers and harbourers of good men; and resorted to the King's Bench, to the prisoners there, about matters of religion. And they went over sea to some of the Protestants in exile, to carry intelligence of the state of religion at home, and to propound certain questions concerning religion, and to know their advice and judgment. There were also these: William Punt, who wrote books concerning some pious confessors and martyrs in these days, their doings, sayings, and sufferings; and caused them to be printed abroad, and brought over hi-

415 ther; and among the rest, a book against the errors of Anabaptists: John Kemp, a great traveller into Kent for furthering religion: William Pulleyn, alias Smith; William a Scot; these two travelled over to the Duchess of Suffolk, having been her chaplains: Henry Hart, he was the principal of the *free-will* men; so they were termed by the predestinators. This man drew up thirteen articles to be observed among his company; and there came none into their brotherhood, except he were sworn.

Bensfield an informer.

Besides this Ty, the priest aforenamed, there was also, among others, one Denys Benfield, of this county, a busy informer against the gospellers. Of this man, I find this memorial, written by John Fox, on the backside of one of his letters: "Denys Benfield stricken black on one side, " and speechless." This for Essex.

Professors in London.

And in London, notwithstanding all the burning in Smithfield, during the three years last past, yet great were the numbers there that professed the gospel, increasing considerably, as it seemed, or at least shewing themselves more boldly towards the latter end of the Queen's reign. A long catalogue of their names, procured by Boner's spies, his chancellor Darbishire had gotten, and read them to one Lyving, a priest, and prisoner for the gospel; for this end and purpose, to make him acknowledge how many of them he knew, that he might accuse and bring others into a snare. In the said city they met frequently this year and the following in great numbers. And it was one of the articles put to Sympson, once a tailor, now deacon of a congregation, and a martyr, "That he and others had " been at assemblies and conventicles, where there were " considerable numbers of people gathered together to hear " the English service set forth in King Edward's reign,

" and to hear God's word, and to have the communion
" ministered."

But to turn to some other matters. Westminster church
being last year turned into a monastery, consisting of an
abbot and monks, when Dr. Weston, the dean, was required
to resign up the church for that use, and he to be removed
to the deanery of Windsor, he refused so to do: but being
hereby under the displeasure of the Cardinal and the Bishops, at last he did it unwillingly, moved thereunto by im-
portunate suit. He was a man, that though he maintained
the Church of Rome, yet he was no friend to monks and
religious men. About this time at Windsor he was taken
in adultery; for which the Cardinal deprived him of all his
spiritual preferments: but he appealed to Rome, as dealt
unjustly with, and would have fled out of the realm, but
was taken in the way, and cast into the Tower of London;
and there remained till Queen Elizabeth was proclaimed,
when he was delivered: but soon after fell sick, and died.
It was the general opinion, that if he had lived, he would,
out of his anger towards the bishops and clergy of Queen
Mary, have revealed a purpose of theirs, which was, to have
digged up the body of King Henry at Windsor, and burned
it for an heretic.

To speak the truth of him, he cannot be represented well
to posterity; he was a mercenary man. Being a man of
boldness, and of some learning, much use was made of him
in the beginning of the Queen's reign. He was appointed
prolocutor in the first convocation. He was the chief com-
missioner sent down to Oxford, when Cranmer, Ridley, and 416
Latymer were to be baited; and there he domineered, and
in the end cried *victory*. As soon as that job was done,
away he comes to London; and was at the execution of
Wyat; who, when he, upon the scaffold, had cleared the
Lady Elizabeth and the Lord Courtney from having any
hand in his business, (though before the Council, upon
hope of his pardon, he had charged them to have been
privy to it,) Weston stood up, and cried to the people, not
to believe him, and that he had confessed otherwise before

the Council. This officious man had been a month or two before upon the scaffold with the Duke of Suffolk, being appointed, as he pretended, by the Queen, to be ghostly father to him, though the Duke thrust him down once or twice as he was going up the stairs of the scaffold along with him: and when the Duke had prayed all men to forgive him, as he said the Queen had, Weston cried with a loud voice to the people, that her Majesty had forgiven him; whereupon several of the standers by said, " Such " forgiveness God send thee."

CHAP. LIV.

Apprehensions of Spain.   Stafford's rebellion.   Matters in the north.

Earl of Pembroke's commission.

THE Earl of Pembroke had like commission granted him now, as he had the last year; which was, to be lieutenant and captain general of the Queen's army beyond sea, for the defence of Calais.

The fears of the Spaniards.

The government by this time became very uneasy, not only in respect of the bloodshed for religion, and the rigorous inquisitions made every where, but for the domineering of the Spaniards, which was intolerable. The English were very much disregarded, and the Spaniards ruled all; the Queen, half Spanish by birth, and still more so by marriage, shewing them all favour; hating the English, and enriching the Spaniard, and sending over her treasures to Spaniards. King Philip also had required twelve of the strongest castles here in England; which were to be put into the hands of twelve thousand of the Spanish soldiers, to be sent over against the time of his coronation, as was found by certain letters taken with Spaniards at Diep. This raised a great apprehension in the nation, that he intended to get this realm to himself by a conquest, and to reduce it under a tyranny. That nation also had carried themselves here very disobligingly to the English, and would say, that they would rather dwell among Moors and Turks than with

Englishmen; who sometimes would not bear their insolencies and oppressions without resistance.

This, together with a hope of restoring himself to the dukedom of Buckingham, made Thomas Stafford, of that blood, in April arrive in England out of France with forces, and possess himself of Scarborough castle; giving out himself to be governor and protector of the realms; intending to depose Queen Mary, whom he called, *the unrightful and* **417** *unworthy Queen of England,* as forfeiting her crown by marriage with a stranger, and for favouring and maintaining Spaniards, and putting castles into their hands, to the destruction of the English nation. Stafford, with his party, (who were the remainders of those who made the insurrection the last year,) put forth his proclamation. But the King and Queen, being greatly surprised herewith, April 30, sent out a proclamation against him and the other traitors with him; and they were soon quelled by the Earl of Westmorland and others in those parts. Stafford and four more were taken in Scarborough castle, April 28, and brought up to the Tower: and twenty-seven more, that assisted in that exploit, were prisoners in York. May 28, Stafford was beheaded on Tower-hill; and the next day three of the accomplices were executed at Tyburn, *viz.* Stretchley, alias Strelly, alias Stowel, Proctor, and Bradford; that Bradford, I suppose, who wrote a large and notable letter, mentioned before, against the Spaniards. The proclamation against Stafford, together with Stafford's declaration, and the names of the prisoners, may be found in the Catalogue.

Those that were in Stafford's treason were, according to letters from the King and Queen to the Council in the north, indicted of their treasonable fact, and condemned there at York, at a session of oyer and terminer and gaol delivery, that began May the 17th. And the Council appointed their execution in such convenient and requisite places, as well along the sea-coast as otherwise, as the Lord President was commanded by those letters: a schedule whereof he sent to the Lords of the Council, shewing the

places where they had appointed execution to be done, and
the disposition of the twenty-seven persons to die the death
of traitors at those places, being all in Yorkshire; *viz.*

At York, John Wilborne, Clement Tylled, John Cawse-
wel, alias Creswel, and Robert Hunter.

At Scarborough, Tho. Spencer, John Adams, John Watson a Scot, John Lewis.

At Hull, John Brown, Owen Jones.

At Beverly, Hary Gardiner, John Thomas.

At Whitby, Thomas Warren or Warden, and John Don-
ning, Scot.

At Maldon, William Palmer, John Montfurth, Scot.

At Flamborow, Syley, Thomas Wilkinson.

At Byrlyngton, John Wallys.

At Audborow, Anthony Perrival.

At Hornesey, William Williamson.

At Paul in Holderness, Roger Thomas.

At Hassyl, Roger Reynolds.

At Hallyfax, Lawrence Alsop.

At Doncaster, Thomas Jordan.

At Howden, John Grey, Scot.

At Wakefield, Robert Hawgate, Scot.

All these executed for entering into Scarborow castle.

The chief of these traitors, who were Stafford, John
Proctor, alias Williamson, Stowel, Saunders, and Grissel, a
Frenchman, were sent up by the Lord President, according
to the King and Queen's commandment, together with their
418 several indictments, and the examinations also of such of
the traitors as seemed material for any of them that were
already sent up.

The Privy Council had sent the Council in the north
instructions, when they which they appointed to be arraigned there were tried, that they should diligently examine them, what foreign or English aids or succours were
to have assisted or joined with them. But none such they
would acknowledge or be known of, but said, "that if any
"such were, Stafford, and the rest carried up to London,
"each knew thereof." In fine, here was a round execu-

tion: for of thirty-five persons concerned in this plot, but
two obtained pardon, *viz.* Saunders and a Frenchman; all
the rest died the death of traitors.

Things now looked very gloomy upon England, and
especially in the north parts, where this plot was executed,
and where continual disturbances were, partly between
Scots and English, and partly between English and English: so that in all haste musters were commanded there to
be taken, and soldiers to be raised.

For (to come to particulars) there were terrible feuds
between family and family in the parts bordering upon
Scotland: insomuch that people went abroad in danger of
their lives, and were fain to go armed, and in considerable
parties together. Such feuds were between the Carrs, of
the Scotch race, and the Herons, and other English. And
when these parties met, they fought sometimes most des-
perately together. So it happened in the beginning of
April at Ford; where, upon an affray, Robert Barrow,
mayor of Barwick, and Giles Heron, treasurer of Barwick,
were cruelly slain. The mayor had such mortal wounds,
that he never spake more. The treasurer had fifteen bloody
wounds given him. Some of the offenders were in Scotland, at one Robert Carr's house, lord of Graydon; and
had with them the treasurer's head and his dagger: which
occasioned, that at the sessions in April at Morpeth, before
the adjournment of the same, came in presence Sir John
Forster, knt. George Heron of Chipches, and Nicolas Dar-
mington of Wharnely, esquires, with a band of men to the
number of two hundred and fifty, in forcible and warlike
array of armour and weapon, contrary to the provision and
order of sundry statutes and ancient laws of the realm
against such behaviour expressly provided and established.
In excuse whereof, the said gentlemen openly acknowledged their said apparel and armour was not to offend the
laws, and that the same notwithstanding, they durst not
otherwise come to the said sessions, for fear of bodily hurt
and danger of such enemies, as they alleged it was not unknown they had. This the justices of the peace certified

to the Lord Warden, Sir Robert Ellerker, high sheriff, and some others: signifying withal, that they had suspended the consideration of that matter till the time of the said sessions appointed at Newcastle; and had made proclamation, that all obedient subjects should forbear the like misbehaviour; and from thenceforth in that point observe the laws and statutes according to their duties. But the parties whom these gentlemen took to be their enemies, (as the Carrs,) or any for them, were not then seen nor heard of.

Their malice.
Another way these *feud-men* shewed their malice to one another, which, though not so mortal, yet vexatious enough; 419 when by interest with some of the Council in York, and by false surmises, they would procure them to be sent for up thither; a great journey from their dwellings, to put them to expense and trouble, and perhaps to do them or theirs mischief in their absence from home. This, the Lord Dacre, warden of the west marches, advised the Lord President of that Council of, in July the last year, and told him, how that there were divers in that county of Cumberland, that procured letters missive against their neighbours for displeasure and malice, rather than for any just cause; and prayed him, for the ease of poor men, that they might be discharged of the same. Wherein he also offered himself to see them ordered as to justice appertained.

Matters in ill terms between England and Scotland.
The Scots also and English stood but in doubtful state at this time to each other: and to make themselves look the more formidable to the English, they extolled much the French King's power and forces abroad in Picardy with himself, and with the Duke of Guise in Piemont; and his aiding the Pope in Naples. And that the Great Turk had mighty armies ready. All which the Scots spake for the French King's glory. But in truth, notwithstanding these boasts, the French King had received now a great discomfit in Italy, as it was written to the Lord Wharton out of Scotland; wherein the Duke of Nemours, a young man, but as towardly as was in all France, was slain, with four-and-twenty gentlemen and nobles of France, and 4000 horse and foot according to some, 5000 according to others, de-

stroyed. The Scotch Queen mourned, and made a dole.
The voice went, it was for the Cardinal of Bourbon lately
deceased, who was nigh akin to her. But it was thought,
that she rather mourned for the death of the noblemen, and
the great overthrow of the French part. The Duke of Ferrara was the lieutenant general of the French King's army
in Italy, and the Duke of Guise lieutenant in the other's absence. The Duke of Nemours was the chief captain of the
horsemen. Monsieur Dose, the French ambassador at the
Scotch Court, told Dr. Hussey, the English messenger there,
that this Duke was only wounded; that the Duke of Alva
waxed strong in the field; that the Duke of Guise arrived
in Rome in peace, and that he was there received of the
Pope with great gladness; that the Duke of Ferrara led
the army, and marched towards the enemy. And this was
the present state of the French, upon whom the Scots so
much leaned.

Dr. Laurence Hussey, by the Queen's command, was now Dr. Hussy
in Scotland; who rode from Edenburgh to Sterling, April at the Scotch
5, in the Lady Lenox's causes. The said Doctor, April 12, Court.
wrote to the Lord Wharton, (whose agent he was,) that the
Dowager complained much of the rebels; that there was no
redress made on the Lord Dacre's side. To which Hussey
was instructed what to say, from a memorial given him by
the said Lord Wharton. But of him she complained not at
all. And Sir Robert Carnegie carried with him all that was Carnegie at
passed between the commissioners, to declare to the Queen's the English.
Majesty, that of the Scots' part all justice had been done.
And they looked for war or peace, as the King and Queen
should order matters with him. The Scots now sent out Seven ships
seven ships upon some exploit, which came to Holy Island: sent out by
three whereof were reported to be scattered from the rest; the Scots.
but they were returned again for Scotland for new victuals. 420
And the French had lately sent considerable forces into
Scotland.

The King and Queen, in this mean time, were busy in The King
raising soldiers, to be ready to oppose Scotland. Sir George and Queen
Bows, son of Sir Robert Bows, was ordered in April to raise men in the north.

muster and prepare all his servants, tenants, and others
under his rule and office; and all others as should be willing
to go with him. Which, accordingly as he wrote the Lord
President word, he had mustered together, with his friends;
who all would be ready, at the said President's commandment, willingly to serve the King and Queen to the uttermost of their powers. He sent him also the book of the said
musters, that he might understand the number and sort of
his men, to dispose of them as he should think fit for the
advancement of the King and Queen's service. To the Lord
President, who was Lord Lieutenant of Darbyshire, letters
came in May, with order for an hundred men to be levied
and taken in that county, furnished with weapon and harness, to serve with captains, such as were gentlemen, inheritors, or heirs apparent, to have the conduct of the same:
and the same to be led towards the borders against Scotland.
And the same number of men was ordered to be raised in
Nottinghamshire.

A difference
between the
Lord Whar-
ton and the
gentlemen
of North-
umberland.
Great disturbances, continually almost, arose in the parts
of England near Scotland, being a kind of boisterous, head-
strong, unquiet people. The gentlemen of Northumberland,
and the Lord Wharton, the captain of Barwick, had now in
May a falling out about musters, as it seems, very un-
seasonably, considering the present apprehensions from the
neighbouring nation. The King and Queen therefore,
knowing of what bad consequence these quarrels among
Englishmen in the very confines might be, sent a commission to the Earl of Westmoreland and the Bishop of Durham, in time to make up this difference. Both which, for
the appeasing of these matters, and other disorders also, repaired to Newcastle. And the King and Queen desiring to
know what was done by their commissioners in this necessary work, sent to the Lord President to understand of their
doings, which caused him to send to them for their advertisements in this affair. And the King and Queen having
commanded him, in respect of his office as President, and in
that he had their commission of lieutenancy, to take a time
with his commodity, as his health and strength would serve,

to repair to the frontiers; (wherein those two lords were
appointed to attend for that purpose.) The Earl therefore
prayed them to signify unto him their opinion, what time
they should think most convenient for his repair thither,
that he might prepare himself in order thereafter, for the
further quiet, and to direct orders to be taken in those
matters.

It was soon after, that the diligent Earl seems to have The dili-
travelled from York to Newcastle; where he took order gence of
for the sending five hundred men to Berwick, and for the President.
appointing of an army of such able men, as had been or
might be mustered within his commission, according to the
King and Queen's letters lately addressed to him for that
purpose. This the said Earl signified by his letters dated 421
May 23. The Lords of the Council, on the 27th day, sent Well ac-
their letters to him, to let him know that the King and cepted by
Queen took his diligence used in these matters in acceptable and Queen.
part, and willed them to give him their most hearty thanks
for the same. And whereas the said Earl had let them The Coun-
know that there were but very few corslets to be gotten in cil's orders
those parts, the Council therefore signified to him, that it for corslets.
was their Majesties wish, that the greater number, if possible, might be furnished with that kind of armour; yet
seeing that could not so suddenly be brought to pass, they
would nevertheless that he should take such order, as at
the least wise so many being furnished with corslets as
might be, the rest might have some other kind of armour,
as they might best encounter with the Frenchmen that
were in Scotland, who were not furnished with corslets, as
their Majesties in a former letter gave his lordship to understand at better length. He had also required furniture Bows and
of bows and arrows to be sent thither. But this the Council arrows.
thought very strange; for beside the statute made for the
maintenance of shooting, which being put in execution must
have well enough served to meet with this lack, they saw
not why that part of the realm should have had more need
to be supplied of those things than their Majesties' subjects
in other places, who through the realm did of themselves

provide for their sufficient furniture of this sort of artillery, according to their duties. And so they doubted not but he would see that those under his rule should do in time as appertained; whereby they might be the better able to serve their Majesties, and defend themselves and their country, when need should require. And as touching the

Ordnance.

supply of such ordnance and munition as should be thought convenient to be sent thither, they wrote to him, that they had already considered the matter, and had taken such order with the same master of the ordnance, as the same should be supplied, and sent thither with as good speed as might

Victuals.

be. And whereas he mentioned the want of victuals in those parts, they doubted not but his Lordship could well enough consider, that the same was not fit to be supplied from them, especially seeing their Majesties were not certain whether they should have occasion to use their army that was to be put in readiness there, the same being chiefly prepared to encounter such foreign powers as might happen to invade the realm that way: in which case all good subjects were bound to do what they might for the defence of themselves and their country, to the uttermost of their power, both in providing themselves of victuals and furniture of other necessaries, according to their duty. And even so they mistrusted not, but he would cause their Majesties' subjects there to see to the supply of this want, when need should require, with as good foresight as might be, without trusting to other provision.

And money.

The Lord President put the Council also in mind of money for the furniture of the army, when need should require. To which they answered, their Majesties would cause such order to be taken, as the same should be provided and in a readiness when need was. He desired also that

422 letters might be written unto such persons as were named in a schedule sent unto them in his letter. To which the Council answered, their Majesties thought the same should not need. For that such as were within his lieutenancy, he might himself write unto, and command to be in a readiness, according to the order heretofore given him. And as for

the rest that were in other shires, the King and Queen in- tended to reserve their service to be employed otherwise, as occasion should require. Lastly, as to the appointing of the meaner officers to serve in the army, their Majesties referred the naming of them unto his own discretion; who being lieutenant, and having charge of the whole, might direct these and other like things as he should by his wisdom think most convenient. This was writ from Westminster, May 27, and signed by

Nico. Ebor. Canc. Anthony Mountague. Tho. Ely.
Arundel. Edward Hastings. Henry Jernegan.
Winchester. Pembroke. Jo. Bourne.

But notwithstanding these cares and preparations, and the daily expectations of the French and Scots, things were still but in a miserable state as to military matters in those parts: Berwick in great need of men: to which therefore five hundred men were appointed to be sent for defence of the same. But the town also had need of necessaries for furniture of five hundred men; and five hundred workmen also to be appointed to be there. There was a dearth of victuals: the old garrison not paid for their half year ended 14 February last, and for this other half year that would end August the 16th, except money delivered in prest by the late treasurer slain: which would appear upon declaration of his accounts. There was no treasurer known; nor when the soldiers should be paid. And the inhabitants of the town, victuallers, were not able to provide for the soldiers and workmen without ready money. And the victuallers and purveyors complained for want of a pay called *Gower's pay;* and thereby they grudged to take men to board upon credit. All which the Lord Wharton, captain of Berwick castle, wrote to the Earl of Shrewsbury, June the 3d.

Things at Berwick in a miserable state.

Now also the Earl of Darby had letters from the said Earl, authorizing him to muster and prepare the inhabitants of the county of Chester, to be ready to repair unto the said Earl, with his servants and tenants, and such force as he should be able to make, to serve their Majesties in such

The Earl of Darby to muster Cheshire.

Anno 1557.
Things look more towards war with Scotland.

The Earl of Westmerland to the Earl of Shrewsbury, Ex Epist. Com. Salop.

423

order and place, as the Earl of Shrewsbury for the time should appoint.

In the beginning of July, things in Scotland looked all towards war with England, (which had indeed very lately openly proclaimed war with France.) Notwithstanding, in the mean time commissioners on both sides had been pretending fairly to accommodate differences and irruptions upon each other: insomuch that July the 9th, the Earl of Westmerland being then at Carlile, one of the commissioners wrote to the Lord President in these words: " These may advertise your Lordship, that before this day " I was never so far past all hope for peace, and looked so " certainly for present war. For the demeanour of Scot- " land, as well in their preparing for war, as in the heinous " attentates and grievous injuries committed daily upon " the subjects of this realm, and especially upon the east " and middle marches, since our coming to Carlile, is so ap- " parently repugnant to the talk and communications of " the commissioners of the said realm, that I can no other " do, but verily believe that they mind no truth, but to " delay and trifle the time with us, until they be prepared " and ready, if they may, upon a sudden to work some dis- " pleasure unto this realm ; as by such intelligences as we " have received this day from the Lord Dacre, and also " by the Lord Wharton's letter, with two attentates com- " mitted by the Scots upon the sixth and seventh of this " month, ye may more at large understand. I have thought " meet to give your Lordship knowledge hereof, to the in- " tent ye may make more haste in sending the 600 horse- " men, which your Lordship is, by the King's and Queen's " Majesties' letters, appointed to send to the borders for the " better furniture of the same. For I would wish we were " nothing behind with them, but as ready to withstand " their malice, as I believe, for all their fair speech, they " are to attempt some enterprise against us."

Horse and archers appointed to be ready against a day.

Of which also the Court was so sensible, that letters came, not far from the beginning of July, to the Lord President from the King and Queen, and Council, to prepare 600

horsemen and 400 archers, to be in a readiness against the
first day of August; and also to put the whole force of the
north riding of Yorkshire in such perfect readiness, as the
same might encounter any mean force of the enemy that
should invade the frontiers with any army.

Yet so cunningly did the Scots commissioners even at this
time, and in the midst of those injurious acts, carry themselves, that the Earl of Westmerland, however persuaded
he was before of the Scots' hostile intentions, yet now, the
conference being at an end, about the middle of July, he
conceived quite other thoughts of them. For so he wrote in
a second letter to the Earl of Shrewsbury; " I trust we
" shall have no present need thereof, [that is, of an army to
" be put in readiness.] For in the end of our conference
" with the commissioners of Scotland, they seem very de-
" sirous of peace, and rather to covet the same than war.
" So that I believe we shall part very friendly upon Thurs-
" day next. For yesterday [that is, July 13th] we agreed
" upon this good point, that if their instructions and ours,
" which we look to have from both the princes, as their
" answers and pleasures to our resolutions, agree not; yet
" we shall depart in peace as we came hither; making pro-
" clamation through all the marches of both realms, for the
" continuation of the peace for two months; and then to
" meet again upon the east borders. And in the mean time
" the princes' pleasure to be known; and the wardens to be
" charged to take certain care of the great riders of either
" side, to remain with them, for the better stay and con-
" tinuance of the peace."

CHAP. LV.

424

*The Queen, in distress for money, makes use of a loan. She
raises an extraordinary guard. The Scots' assaults. The
English worst them.*

AMIDST these offensive and defensive wars with France
and Scotland, that the Queen had pulled upon her head,

besides the fears and conspiracies at home, she was pressed
with want of money; which forced her, towards the latter
end of July, to send her letters throughout the nation for a
loan, to enable her to put herself in a posture of defence,
and to resist and quell her enemies, whether her disobedient
subjects, or others. To Sir John Porte, in Derbyshire, she
sent command to borrow of eight gentlemen in that county
an 100*l.* apiece, to be repaid at the feast of All Saints
next ensuing, or one month after. And the said Sir John
to pay it into her comptroller, Sir Robert Rochester. These
eight gentlemen were, Sir George Vernam, Sir Peter Fretch-
vyle, Sir William Candysh, Thomas Babyngton, esq. Sir
Henry Sacheveril, Richard Blackwall, esq. Sir George
Pierpont, George Sowche, esq. To all whom she addressed
her privy seals.

To her said receiver for Derbyshire she wrote her letter
as followeth, whereby may appear the reasons that urged her
to this course:

" Mary the Queen.

" Trusty and wellbeloved, we greet you well:

The Queen
to Sir John
Porte, to
receive the
loan in
Derbyshire.
Epist. Co-
mit. Salop.
" And where we be presently occasioned, for the better
" defence of our realm, and meeting with such practices as
" have been and are daily attempted by certain our un-
" natural subjects, to defray greater sums of money than
" we can at this time of ourselves without our great hin-
" derance well furnish; like as we have for our relief herein
" appointed to take, by way of loan, the sum of an 100*l.* of
" each of the persons whose names be contained in a sche-
" dule here inclosed, and have for that purpose addressed
" our letters of privy seal unto them; so, for the readiness
" and good-will which we have always found in you to serve
" us, we have appointed you to receive the said money, and
" have willed the same persons to pay the same unto your
" hands, and to take your bill for the receipt thereof;
" which, together with our said letters of privy seal, shall
" be unto them a sufficient warrant for the repayment of

" the said sum unto them at such days as we have by our
" letters foresaid appointed.

" We therefore require you to use all the diligence you
" may in the receipt of the said monies; which when you
" shall have gathered together, we require you to cause to
" be safely conveyed to the hand of our trusty and right
" wellbeloved counsellor, Sir Robert Rochester, knt. comp-
" troller of our household; who shall not only give you
" allowance of the charges, which you shall have been at for 425
" the receipt thereof, but allow you a sufficient acquittance
" and discharge for the same. Given under our signet at
" our manor of Eltham, the last day of July, in the third
" and fourth year of our reign."

The foresaid gentlemen, by appointment, met with Sir **Some re-**
John Porte at Darby, except three, *viz.* Sir George Vernon, **fuse.**
Sir William Candysh, and George Zowch. Nor did they
come, when they were appointed a second meeting; nor
yet did they send: which was a certain sign they had no
mind to lend. Whereat Porte sent to the Earl of Shrewsbury for his advice.

Preparations for defence against Scotland are now more **Orders for**
and more hastening. The Lord Wharton, July 26, sent to **the raising**
the Bishop of Durham and the Earl of Westmerland, im- **ric of Dur-**
porting a command given to the Lord President; by virtue **ham.**
of which, the said Lord Wharton required to have the
power of the bishopric, with fifteen days' victuals, to be
placed upon the frontiers, until other powers should be
sent. And since this, the said Lord President sent to the
Bishop, to put the whole force of the bishopric in a full and
perfect readiness to repair to the borders for defence and safety thereof, as they should be commanded. Accordingly the
Bishop caused proclamation to be made, that all men should
be in a readiness for defence of the borders, whensoever they
should be called, either by burning of beacons, proclama-
tions, or any other ways, whensoever the enemy did invade
the realm with a power. And further, he consulted with the
chief of the shire, and shewed them both their lordships'

the enemies; which the Lord Wharton, the captain of Barwick, signified to the Lord President; and that the inhabitants might not venture to the bounds and confines; which
proved very incommodious to them, and would be to the
town, without some speedy remedy to repulse their force.
The Earl of Huntly came the 1st of August, at night, to
Langton, from the Dowager at Dunbar: she said she would
visit Aymoth again shortly.   The Scots daily made incur-
sions, and prepared so to do, to destroy the houses and corn ;
and thereby the fortresses, towers, and holds were in dan-
427 ger to be left destitute. And great damage they did, whereby the borders were much wasted: of which, notwithstanding, the Lord President was informed from time to time.
But effectual order was not taken from above; and the corn
that was ready to be gotten in, was in great danger to be
destroyed.

And in fine, by all intelligence the English could get,
the enemy was about some great enterprise, to be done
hastily by the light of the moon that then shone.   Wherefore, on the English side, the best preparations were made
that they could ; and Mr. Henry Percy, a brave gentleman,
brother to the Earl of Northumberland, repaired towards
the borders, and was at Alnwick castle the last of July, with
sundry gentlemen of Northumberland, and many other honest men, who repaired unto him : with whom he continually, for four or five days, travelled, to put all things into
a good posture for defence, in such sort as they took but
very little rest by day or night.   On the 5th of August, by
five in the morning, the Scots, with all their forces, invaded
England on the east marches. There were among them the
Lord James and the Lord Robert, two of the late Scotch
King's bastard sons, together with the Lord Hume and
many other of their nobility, and all the power they could
make ; minding to have taken the castle of Ford, and burnt
the ten towns of Glendale: but upon the opposition they
met with from the English, who bravely acquitted themselves, they gave way, and some of them were slain, and
among the rest Davison, one of their best borderers.   Mr.

Henry Percy took this opportunity to invade their country, where he burnt sixteen towns, and carried off 280 neat, and 1000 sheep, and some prisoners. The next day, viz. Aug. 6, came 600 bishopric men towards Barwick, to be placed according as the Lord Wharton, captain there, should appoint. But Sir Henry Percy's letter to the Earl of Shrewsbury, and that of the Earl of Northumberland, the Lord Wharton, Sir James Crofts, and Sir John Clere, to the same, both dated the day after the fight, will represent this occurrence more fully, which will be found in the Catalogue.

The Scots came down again upon the English confines, August 13, with better success: for the Lord Lieutenant of Scotland, with other persons of great quality, as the Earl Huntley, the Earl of Sotherland, the Lord James, the Lord John, the Lord Arskin, the Lord Somervile, Lord Fleming, Lord Hume, and Monsieur Dosy, the French ambassador, entered into England near to Barwick; where were arrived but the night before, the Earl of Northumberland and Sir Thomas Wharton, with certain of the horsemen and foot, appointed by the Privy Council to have been under the leading of the said Sir Thomas; and considering they were coming to Barwick, and the danger that the country was in to be spoiled, they sent forth Mr. Henry Percy, and other gentlemen, and certain of the horsemen, to let their enterprise so much as might be. But the enemy being very strong, took such advantage, as the English lost about an hundred horsemen, and took about twenty Scots. Such were the chances of war. The Lieutenant of Scotland continued, after this success, to lie upon the borders within six miles of Barwick, and the Frenchmen within four miles, with great powers. Of this the Earl of Northumberland, warden of the east and middle marches, Lord Wharton, captain of the town and castle of Barwick, Sir Tho. Wharton, and Sir James Croft, certified the Lord President by letter, shewing him how it might hence appear in what danger that town and country stood: which that he might be informed of, Sir James Croft was presently despatched

G 2

CHAP. LV.

Anno 1557.

N°. LXXIV. LXXV.

Another invasion by the Scots.

The danger of Barwick.

428

thence to him. And by him, together with the said Earl of Northumberland and the Lord Wharton, was the said Sir James, in this juncture, sent up to the Queen, for to be directed in several matters in this present emergence.

Croft sent
to Court for
directions.

And on the 20th of August the Queen gave a memorial or note of answer to those things that were propounded to her Council by instructions to him given by the said noblemen : which instructions were to this import ; what the Queen and Council directed should be done for the preventing this present intended invasion ; and if such invasion were made, what course should then be taken.

Also, what to do for securing the cattle and the corn from the invaders. Likewise, what to do with men raised in the neighbouring counties. Also, that in case of an army to be raised to go against the Scots, what was to be done for victuals. About the Northumberland men to be placed in garrison ; which they advised. About the officers' wages. How far the Lord Lieutenant's power should extend. Concerning the payment of the east and middle marches. Concerning the first, it was ordered that a strong garrison should be placed upon the borders, to prevent the invasion, if it could be : but in case of invasion, the said garrison to impeach their marching, and other attentates. For the second, that the people should send their cattle out of the way, and put their corn in places of safety. For the third, that the Earl of Darby and others should see their men ready to march upon call. For the fourth, that every parish should be induced to send victuals for their own men. Concerning the fifth, that order should be given, that those Northumberland men should be in the garrison on horseback, and to be in such places and numbers, and others to be discharged for these to be put in their rooms, according to the discretion of the Lord Lieutenant and Earl of Northumberland, and such like : which may be seen at large in the said memorial ; to which the Queen's name is set both at the top and bottom.

Nᵒ.LXXVI.

Letters to
the King to
break with
the Scots.

By letters of the latter end of July and beginning of August, the Council informed King Philip of the treachery of the Scots.

the Scots, that had brought a great army upon the English,
even while they were treating about peace ; and what preparations the English had made by sea as well as land
against them : praying the King, that seeing this was their
condition in respect of Scotland, he would enter hostility
with that kingdom, and deal with them and their ships as
enemies, whensoever they should come to Spain or the Low
Countries. To which the King, in a letter dated the beginning of August, gave this answer : " That he understood
" all things which the Scots had done, *sua naturali perfidia,*
" *by a perfidiousness natural to them,* while they were treat-
" ing of keeping peace and friendship, and how they had
" decreed open war against England. He had also seen, by
" the English letters sent to him, what provisions they had
" made upon the matter, *viz.* of sending nine of the Queen's
" ships coming home from Iseland upon the Scotch coast,
" and the rest with the navy on the west parts : which re- 429
" solution, as very prudent, and done with so mature coun-
" sel, was extraordinarily approved by him. That he from
" that day should repute the Scots enemies, for the same
" cause as the English did, and would have them handled
" as such. That he had commanded it to be writ into
" Spain, that from henceforth they should be damaged, and
" their ships and others belonging to them ; but because
" there were certain treaties, conventions, and pacts between
" the states of the Low Countries and the Scots, it was not
" yet decreed after what manner it should be done there :
" for those treaties were first to be examined, that a form
" might be found, to be observed in the declaration and
" denunciation of war against them. And that this was now
" in doing by his [the King's] commandment with the
" greatest diligence : and that an ambassador should be
" sent to the Scots for this very thing, who, in the King's
" name and the States', should despatch what was to be
" done." The King added, " that it was there held for
" certain, that this Scotch war with England was promulged
" against the will of all the governors and natural people of
" that realm ; and that therefore what the Scots should de-

" termine and answer to his ambassador, he would presently
" signify to them [the Queen's Council.] And that if they
" should not keep themselves in their duty, and within
" their own bounds, and forthwith desist from the war so
" unjustly waged against the English, all care should be
" taken, that on that side open war should be made upon
" them, and to do them all the damage that might be. And,
" in short, that nothing should be omitted by him which he
" should understand to be for the profit, conservation, and
" utility of this kingdom: concluding, *Cum res omnes illius*
" [*regni*,] (*et vestrum omnium fides et amor promeretur*,)
" *charas admodum habeamus. Dat. in civitate nostra Ca-*
" *meracensi,* vii. *mens. August.* MDLVII. Subscribed,
" PHILIPPUS."

The Queen
sets forth a
fleet.
   As the Queen had made the best preparations she could
on the sudden by land, so, in the beginning of this month of
August, she set forth a fleet against her Scotch enemies, to
annoy them.   On the 6th day, Sir John Clere, her vice-admiral, arrived at Barwick, where he and others concerned
consulted together about the marine affairs. The result was,
that the ships should make a show in the Frith, to give
terror to such pirates as lay there: and thence to set course
to Bahomines, and to waste the Iseland fleet.   And therewith they considered, that the same wind as should lead the
pirates out of the Frith, would serve also to lead the Queen's
ships to the coast of England.   But neither was the Queen
successful in this fleet.   Sir John Clere, the vice-admiral,
was in the ship called the New Bark.   There were seven of
the Queen's ships, beside the Mynion; three ships of the
town of Newcastle; and one Oswald Fenwick, of Newcastle,
brought a ship of his own adventure : in all twelve.   With
this navy, the Vice-Admiral entered an island called Kirkway, in Orkney, upon Wednesday, Aug. 11, and burnt part
of the town of Kirkway: and so he and his company went
430 safe back to their ships : and upon Thursday, the next morrow, landed again, and burnt the other part of the town, entered the church, and battered the castle with five or six

pieces of ordnance; but they could not prevail against it, and so returned to the ships safely. Upon Friday the 13th, they entered again where they were before, intending to have taken the Bishop's house. They had six pieces of ordnance on land with them for that purpose. But the Scots now being three thousand men, as they esteemed them, put the English to flight: where Sir John Clere was drowned, and divers captains and soldiers were slain and drowned, to the number of ninety-seven: four pieces of ordnance, called *sacres*, were lost. The ships and all others in them, being safe, sailed away southwards. Three captains were slain, namely, the captains of the New Bark, the Henry, and the Bull; the captain of the Solomon drowned; the captains of the Tiger, of the Willoughby, of the Greyhound, and the Gabriel, saved. These tidings were sent to the Court, August 22, by John Southern, captain of the Gabriel.

CHAP.
LV.

Anno 1557.
Unsuccessful.

CHAP. LVI.

The Scots pursue their designs of invasion. The preparation of the English. The Scots retreat without action. The English burn and plunder.

THE Scots still pursue their purpose of invasion; and in the very beginning of the month of September, their army, consisting of the greatest force they could make, was moving apace toward England. And order was given by proclamation and otherwise, that all the subjects dwelling by North Sowtray, should march on foot, unless he were a nobleman, knight, manner [*i. e.* owner] of good lands, or captain, who might ride, and none others; and all from Sowtray southwards, with their west borderers, to be their band of horsemen. They had three thousand harquebutters (as the espials sent word) made forth of the charges of the borough towns in Scotland. At this time they had a consultation at Edenburgh, where were present the Dowager, the Duke, the Earl of Huntley, and their nobility. It was there reasoned, that it would be a great matter for their

The Scots resolve upon an invasion.

whole realm, if the army of England should give them battle ; the experience whereof they had felt before. The Dowager answered, " that there was much spoken of an army to " rise in England, but upon her creditable intelligence she " would assure them all, that there was no army towards ; " and if there were, the same was of no great force, so as " they might do their purpose without danger of England." The same day this consultation was held, at night the duke said to some, that the Dowager and Monsieur Docel, the French ambassador, were fully determined to assail Barwick, and that he was never otherwise moved by the Dowager and Docel, but to assay that piece. The ordnance, provision, and victuals came forward, and the nobility of their 431 realm, and the power they might make, were in this army, and in their best order. Upon the sixth or seventh of September they intended to approach near Twede, and the next day to fall upon their purpose. The report was, the Earl of Huntley had the vaward, the Duke the battle, and the Earl of Cassels and their nobility of the west, the reward.

The Lord Lieutenant, Sept. 16, sent the Council word what advertisements he had received concerning the Scots' preparations, and other intelligence to that effect, as Sir James Croft had procured out of Scotland. But notwithstanding all this, the Council seemed loath to be at the charge of raising such forces as must necessarily be done to make a good resistance, because it was not yet certain the Scots were coming down. Therefore the Council thought (as they signified back again) they ought to have such good espials in that realm, as to know more certainty in this affair : and that before any great stir were made, the Lord President should have certain intelligence, both from the Earl of Northumberland, the Lord Wharton, and other officers on the frontiers. And their judgment was, that if he had good espials upon the Scotch actions, they could not so secretly assemble their powers together, but that he might have knowledge thereof time enough to meet with them. By such good espials, the Council added, it might be known what preparations they made, what their numbers, how

The Council advertised of it.

many days' victuals they carried with them, and from day to day what their doings were; and he might reinforce the borders, as their doings should give cause, and as to his wisdom it might stand best for the Queen's service. The Council also advised, that he needed not to make a full assembly of the army, unless the Scots should with their main strength go about to invade the realm: which could not be kept so secret, but it should come time enough to his knowledge to provide for them, either by the whole or such part of the army as he by his wisdom should think most necessary.

The Lord President also sent for money and bows: in both which he had in like manner a dilatory answer. But the Council's letter in this important emergence lies to be read in the Catalogue.

Crofts was an active, crafty man, who, with Sir Rafe Bulmer of Yorkshire, such another, about this very juncture got by some means or other into converse with two gentlemen of the adverse party, a Scot and a Frenchman: where using free and open conversation together, (and perhaps that accompanied with liberal drinking,) they learned divers material points relating to the Scots' present designed enterprise; which Crofts soon got the Lord Lieutenant acquainted with, and he the Queen and Council. She liked it well. And from the Council the said Lord Lieutenant was ordered to instruct them, that they should continue this acquaintance, and carry themselves very frank with those gentlemen, and to endeavour from them to bolt out more and more the Scots' intentions: and to make themselves the less suspected, should protest to them, that this communication is all of themselves, without any order or commission.

The Lord Lieutenant, to be nearer the Scots, was got as far north as to North Allerton. Thence, on September the 20th, he wrote to the Earl of Darby, lord lieutenant of the counties of Chester and Lancaster, to let him know, that according to such advertisements and knowledge as he had, the Scots intended to have an army of the power of Scotland in a readiness within two days of Michaelmas day, and

CHAP.
LVI.

Anno 1557

Number
LXXVII.

Crofts converses with a Frenchman and a Scot.

The Earl of Darby summoned with the force of Lancashire and Cheshire.

432

therewith to invade, if not resisted. Therefore he required the said Earl, with all the speed he could, to come forward with the whole force of Lancashire and Cheshire; and that he would be with the same force at Newcastle the 5th of October. The Earl of Darby, on the 22d of September, sent word to the said Lord Lieutenant, that he intended to set forward upon Thursday the last of September, and to come forward with the best speed he could; lying the first night at Blackborne, the second at Gisburn, and the third at Skipton, or near those places. Trusting his Lordship would have consideration to give order for payment of coat and conduct money, as had been accustomed in time past, remembering the simple and poor estate of the subject at that present; who otherwise were likely to be in great want.

News of the Scots army from the Lord Wharton.

From the Lord Wharton, the Lord Lieutenant was, September 23, informed again, that the Scotch army would be together near Edenburgh on Michaelmas day, and had sent to set forward three shires presently to their borders, saying, " that the army of this realm would be on the borders be- " fore theirs." He signified also in the same letter, that he had learned the Scots grudged against this war, occasioned by the French; that there were sundry noblemen in Scotland, who would have peace with this realm, as an espial informed

His advice. the said Lord Wharton, and said, " that if device were " made, they would treat thereon." Whereupon the said Lord made this judgment, that though this was told him upon intelligence, not from any authority or power to treat, yet he thought that such practice might have been used, and that with money, so as at least a dissension might have been sown among them; whereupon their force should have been less: for division among themselves had already letted great enterprises, which had been undertaken by the Dowager to have been done before this.

Instructions to the Lord Lieutenant concerning Scotland.

It being now known about September the 20th, or sooner, that the whole army of the Scots was to be ready by the 2d of October, the Queen's Council hastened to give careful instructions to the Earl of Shrewsbury for the receiving of them, for the providing ammunition, bows, money, and victuals, and for the annoying of the enemy, ransoming of prisoners, wearing the cross for distinction according to certain Scots articles, and such like. All which I had rather may be read from the Council's own letter, September 24, to the said Earl, who had the leading of the whole English army.

Francis Slingsby had the care of the castle of Wark in the confines, which was in great danger at this time: for it was but in an ill condition. And so the said Slingsby wrote to the Earl of Shrewsbury, that, according to his order, he had viewed the castle, and found it not so well furnished, nor in such force to defend the siege as he could wish it were. Notwithstanding, he would go about with all possible diligence to help and amend, where it should be most needful for the defence thereof. But he promised however, notwithstanding all wants, he would defend it so long as his life or his power and strength otherwise should continue. This letter of Slingsby's bore date September 29: on which day I find the Lord Wharton despatching away from Barwick ammunition to this castle, and a demi-culverin of brass to Norham; for which he had demanded carriage of the Bishop of Durham.

And it was now high time this preparation should be made: for, as the said Lord informed the Lord Lieutenant, the army of Scotland was gathering with such power, ordnance, and provision, as he had not heard of the like in his time.

The Earl of Darby was now setting forward with his men of both counties: and these were his captains, with the numbers of the men they led.

Marginal notes:

CHAP. LVI.

Anno 1557.
Number LXXVIII.

Wark castle in danger.

433

A mighty army preparing in Scotland.

Earl of Darby brings the men of Cheshire and Lancashire.

Captains in the county of Chester.

CAPTAINS.					MEN.
Sir John Savage	.	.	.	. .	200
Sir Will. Brereton	.	.	.	.	200
Sir John Warberton	.	.	.	.	150 } 300
Sir Edw. Warren	.	.	.	.	150 }
Sir Thomas Holcroft	.	.	.	.	100
Sir Thomas Venables	.	.	.	.	100

CAPTAINS.		MEN.
Sir Lan. Smith, with others adjoined . .		100
Sir Philip Egerton, with others with him .		100
Sir John Dawne		100
Sir Will. Davenport, with others ⎱ Robert Hyde, of Narbury, esq. ⎰		100
Sir Rol. Stanley, with others . . .		100
Sir Hugh Cholmley, with others . .		100
Sir Edw. Fitton		100
Sir John Lee, of Booth, and others . .		100
Rafe Dutton, esq. and others . . .		100
Richard Brooks	20 ⎱	100
The Wards' tenants	80 ⎰	
Rob. Tatton, esq. ⎱ John Lee and others ⎰		100
	Sum total	2000

Captains in the county of Lancaster.

CAPTAINS.	MEN.
Sir Rich. Molineux	200
Sir Tho. Gerard	200
Sir Tho. Talbot	200
Sir Rich. Houghton, because he is not able to go himself, doth furnish but . . .	100
Sir Thomas Hesbeth, and others with him .	100
Sir Thomas Langton ⎱ Sir William Norrisse ⎰	100
Sir William Ratcliff, or his son and heir, ⎱ who is an handsome gentleman ⎰ Sir Thomas Atherton joined with him ⎰	100
Francis Tonstal and others	100
Sir John Holcroft, or his son and heir ⎱ Richard Asheton, of Midd. and others ⎰	100
The rest appointed in Lancashire were of the Earl of Darby's retinue.	

434   But the Queen, dreading the excessive charges of these
Remanded. forces brought from Cheshire and Lancashire, forbad the

Earl of Darby to go forwards, and to stay his forces at
home ; minding, for the present, to resist the Scots doings
with a less force than the whole army: and that notwithstanding the Lord President's former letter to him addressed. But yet to remain in a perfect readiness to come forward hereafter, if occasion required, upon any sudden warning. This good husbandry in this eminent danger, and
countermanding his orders, certainly did not much please
the said Lord President.

Now came this particular account to him of the proceeding of the Queen of Scots, sent by some spy, *viz.* " That
" the Queen of Scots had her army in readiness, and did
" intend to lay siege to Wark. That she was coming to
" Hume castle, where her provisions, *viz.* forty ton of
" wine, &c. were come already. That the Duke of Cha-
" teller was lieutenant general of the whole army. That the
" Earl of Argyle and the Earl of Huntley, with the whole
" nobility of Scotland, came this journey. That the 2d of
" October they were to muster upon Fallayr moor, and that
" night they would set forwards on their journey to the
" borders. That the spiritual men and the burgesses of a
" certain place [Edenburgh I suppose] did find 5000 their
" charges. He related where and what quantity of ord-
" nance they had. That it was proclaimed in Edenburgh
" for forty days' victual. And that all the nobility of Scot-
" land were presently at that city, save only the Earl of
" Sunderland, who lay at that time in Jedburgh with no
" great company." Thus minded they were at present ; but
yet it was doubted with many whether they should agree to
come forwards in their journey, or not.

Thus, as there had been much talk of the Scots invasion
of England, so the intelligence of their entry into the said
kingdom, and of their setting forwards, which came so hot
in the beginning of October, somewhat slacked, partly
through diversity of opinions among themselves, and partly
through the foul weather and rising of the waters. But now
being slipped further into the month of October, that is, to
the eleventh day, it was certainly affirmed that the whole

nobility of Scotland was come to the frontiers, and were
waiting for the fall of the waters, minded that night to en-
camp about Hawden Ridge, near unto Wark; and so to
bring their ordnance over the Tweed. Hereupon the Lord
Warden had assembled the garrison nearer together; which,
with the power of the wardenry, had lain scattered abroad in
the villages from Morpeth forwards; doubting, lest lying
together, they should waste the country, and want victuals.

By the Lord
Talbot,
On the 11th day, the Earl of Shrewsbury's son, the Lord
Talbot, who lay at Alnwic, set forward to the Lord Warden
with such power as the Earl sent with him, and he sent
after him 600 foot more, as a further supply. And the Earl
of Westmerland, notwithstanding he had been sore diseased
with the gout for four or five days, with the rest of his
horsemen, to the number of 300, purposed to be at Alnwic
the next day, and so to repair to the Lord Warden.

And Sir
Leo. Dacre,
Also Sir Leonard Dacre, son of the Lord Dacre, came
from the west marches with a number of the best borderers there, unto the east marches, for the service of the King
and Queen, with 250 of the best men and horse of the west.
435 But when they lay hereabouts for some days, and expected
some wages, Sir Leonard being called upon by them, repaired unto the Earl of Northumberland, to know his pleasure herein; either that his men might receive wages; or to
be told what way might be taken with the creditors for
victuals and horse meat. But the said Earl surprised him,
when he told him, that the Lord President had taken order
that they should have no wages: which indeed was but
the effect of an order from above for sparing of money.
Hereupon Sir Leonard wrote to the Lord President, shewing him, " that this would be a perpetual disestimation of
" himself, who had led these men ; and assuring his Lord-
" ship, that there never was any that came from the west
" marches to the east as he did, neither Sir Henry Whar-
" ton, nor any other being charged with men, but they had
" allowed both coat money, conduct money, and wages.
" The men also declared with one voice, that they never
" came but they had wages, charges, and conduct money,

" nor would they now do what was never done before. This
" Knight therefore urged to the said Lord President, that
" he was his poor kinsman, and was willing to serve with
" his body, heart, and purse, and the rather under his Lord-
" ship, having the government and charge, than any other.
" And being but a young man and beginner in service,
" should be glad to do for the men that came with him as
" others had done heretofore ; and would be loath to lose his
" poor estimation that his countrymen had in him." Upon
this letter, and the consideration of the present circumstances,
the Lord President sent a portion of money to Sir Leonard
Dacre for his men.

CHAP.
LVI.

Anno 1557.

The Earl of Westmerland, Oct. 13, came with his men.
The bishopric men were not above four hundred, and there
were no horsemen : whereas in former time the Earl of
Shrewsbury had seen the bishopric serve at such a time with
a thousand men, that is, upon an invasion. But the said
Earl gave the reason, saying, " That it would be so no
" more, so long as the gentlemen and rich farmers were
" suffered to tarry at home, and a sort of poor creatures
" and men hired for money sent forth, who had nothing to
" help themselves withal." This made him charge the bishopric with untowardness to serve, as was then well seen.
But the Earl of Westmerland, by a letter from Haggerston,
October 16, made his complaint to the Lord President, that
when he came thither with his men, he found no kind of
provision, and not so much as bread and drink. These wants,
no question, did much disgust and discourage the soldiery,
and might have proved of bad consequence, had it come to
the push. The Lord President was at hand with a thousand men.

And the
Earl of
Westmer-
land, and
the bishop-
ric.

But at length all this mighty preparation in Scotland for
invading England and taking of Barwick blew over, as if
some special providence were concerned in it on the behalf of
this realm. For on the 17th of Oct. the Scotch noblemen
had consultation together, and finding the weather most
contagious, the time of the year for armies not good, their
men running away, dying, and in misery, resolved to send

The Scots
nobility
break up
from their
intended in-
vasion.

436

to the Dowager, that they would not continue together with that power, and that she should thereunto trust.   And the next day they determined to confer and devise to furnish their frontiers for this winter.   The messenger was sent accordingly from the nobles to her: and they the next day, according as they appointed, to provide for their frontiers; and the next night, that is Oct. 19, they minded to retire, and depart to their countries.   The Earl of Huntley was against their opinion; and thereupon they were sore offended with him, and said, that he should have no rule of their doings, and restrained his liberty for that day expressly.   For they said, they could do nothing at this time to the honour of their realm.   This, an intelligence in Scotland signified to the Lord Wharton, who also certified, that on the 17th of this month they brought over Tweed four pieces of ordnance; but in the passing over, two men and eight horses were drowned.   Of this retreat of the Scots the Lord President sent word to the Privy Council, with the particulars.   Which letter may be found in the Catalogue.

Number
LXXIX.

Whereat
the Queen
Dowager
takes on.

The same day that the nobles of the Scots appointed to disperse the army, the Duke, the Earls Huntley, Murton, and Argyle came to the Dowager and Docye, in Kelsowe. There the Dowager raged, and reprehended these nobles for their promise, which was to invade and annoy England. Their determination to depart, and the consideration wherefore, these lords also told her.   And thereupon arguments grew great between them; whereat she expressed much sorrow, and wept openly.   Docye was in great heaviness too, and with high words between them to this effect, they departed.   Docye wished himself in France.   The Duke, with the others, passed to Jedworth, and kept the chosen men on their borders.   The others in their number passed to their countries.   Yet it was said, that the Earl Huntley, standing with the Dowager's opinion for war against England, the others asked him plainly, whether he would be a Scots man, or a French man.   He, seeing therefore how they were bent, agreed to their opinion.   There was a talk also now arisen, that the Duke and the nobles minded to restrain the

Dowager of her authority, and Docel of his great meddling in Scotland. It was said moreover, that they intended to treat for peace with England by France; and that the Duke would give fair words to the borderers, until he might see what way could be made with England.

The English, soon after this retreat of the Scots, revenged themselves. For the Earl of Northumberland sent his brother Henry Percy, accompanied with Sir John Forster, Mr. Norton, and other gentlemen of the country, (who were very forward,) to enter into Scotland, with the gentlemen of the middle marches. In which journey they burnt the houses and corn of Lynton, and sixteen towns more, and won the tower of Lynton, and slew therein the laird's son, and had there a good spoil both of horse and goods, and after burnt it. Sir Andrew Car, and a great party of Tividale came up unto them, and skirmished: in which skirmish was slain one George Car of Hatton, a notable borderer and evildoer to this realm, and divers their best prickers, to the number of twelve, taken prisoners. With which doings, and a great booty of cattle, horse, sheep, and householdstuff, they returned home safe without loss, save one man hurt and taken.

But notwithstanding all these warnings and alarms from **437** Scotland, still the discipline of the English soldiery on the borders was strangely neglected; and the officers appointed by the King and Queen for Barwick, the chief bulwark against Scotland, were very negligent: of which the Lord Wharton, governor of the place, complained by a letter writ in November to the Lord President; wherein he certified him, that there were these ordinary officers of the town appointed by letters patents, a captain, a marshal, a chamberlain, a porter, a master of the ordnance. These, with the mayor for the year, were counsellors of the town. Every one of them had a yearly entertainment, and a certain number of men allowed in wages. The state of whom, at this present, was thus: Tho. Cary, the marshal, was a good true gentleman, and an old servant. The chamberlain, Sir Robert Elerker, had discontinued from his office and charge sithence the war began, and a long time before. The treasurer, Alan Bellingham, was also absent. John Selby was the porter: who, together with all the other officers, had neither of them their numbers in a readiness to serve, as they ought to have been.

I have been the longer and more particular in this part of history, because none of our historians mention any thing at all of the present state of affairs between Scotland and England, wherein the Queen and Council, and the north of England were now so much concerned.

CHAP. LVII.

The Queen makes war with France. The Cardinal's counsel to the Queen in this emergence. Calais lost. The Spaniard the occasion thereof. A Parliament.

HAVING thus seen the success of the Queen's war with her neighbouring kingdom of Scotland, where she was only on the defence, let us now consider her war with France, a more powerful dominion; where she made the assault, but to her cost.

The English break with France by King Philip's means. King Philip, who had been absent abroad in Flanders a great while, in March, the latter end of the year 1556, came into England for his own ends; and the Queen and her nobles conducted him through London with great magnificence. Being here, he dealt with the Queen and Council to break with the monarch of France, with whom he was fallen out, and to assist him with an army of English to go over and annoy that dominion; which most fatal counsel was taken, to the irreparable loss of England, Calais in this war being conquered: though it were one of the articles of this marriage, comprised in the conditions by act of Parliament, that the realm should not for his cause enter into war with France; as Sir Tho. Smith in a discourse writes. The English army made a brave shew, consisting of abundance of nobility and gentry, and headed by the Earl of Pembroke,

their general, and got themselves glory by a victory at St.
Quintins. The King stayed in England all the spring, to effect his purposes here with the Queen and her counsellors;
and leaving divers orders with them, in the summer he departed.   In this expedition of the English against the 438
French, among the rest of the gallant officers that were to
go, the Earl of Pembroke, the general, appointed the Lord
Gray, a brave captain, for one, late captain of Guisnes, Lord Gray.
who had there signalized himself against the French; but
the Privy Council did not seem to approve of his going;
and belike had some peculiar suspicions of him, of which
they wrote to King Philip: and he accordingly writ to
the Earl, to advise with himself whether it seemeth good
to him, that the said Lord Gray, for the cause which the
Council signified, should not rather tarry in the place where
he was.   But the Earl was not of that opinion, but that by
all means he must go with him to the King's army, as it was
appointed; and so it was done.   And so King Philip, by
letter, informed the Council.

The Queen was now full of thought and care to fulfil her The Queen
husband's mind, and to gratify him in this dangerous af- wants mo-
fair; though she needed money greatly to pay her debts; on this war.
and this war would ingulf her into greater need of it;
and a Parliament was therefore to be moved for a large tax,
which would not be very acceptable to them.   She being
minded therefore to lay matters before her Privy Council,
first consulted with Cardinal Pole, taking his advice, in
what method to put the business she was to propound before them that afternoon, and required him to give it her in
writing.

So the Cardinal, with his own hand, writ the Queen a The Car-
memorial, " That she should put her Council in mind of dinal's
" what the King had given in charge at his departure, to be the Queen
" executed by such lords as were to be employed against hereupon.
" France; and that, by having it reduced into articles, and
" put into writing, for their better taking notice of it.   That
" particularly, according as the King ordered, all the
" Queen's chief counsellors should be always present, and

" not be allowed to be absent; specially such weighty mat-
" ters being now in hand, to be prepared for the Parlia-
" ment, and the time so short before their sitting. That the
" Queen should know what her Council determined about
" the proroguing the Parliament till towards Candlemas, or
" the return of the King; or whether it were better not to
" prorogue it, considering the present extremity for money,
" both for setting out ships, as well for the Emperor's pas-
" sage to Spain as the King's return; and for payment of
" what was due to Calais and Ireland, and for the Queen's
" credit, who owed much money to the merchants. He ad-
" vised her also to call in her own debts; which was one
" of the points the King left in writing for the Council to
" consider of presently. It was his judgment therefore,
" that she should charge the Council that were concerned in
" this matter, to be very diligent in the prosecution thereof,
" and that every week they should let her know what money
" came in, and what order was taken for the rest; and that
" all who had received any commissions from her for any
" business, should not let a week pass without giving in ac-
" count to her of what they had done. Which he thought
" would help much to the speedy execution of all causes."

No.LXXX. But I refer the reader to the Catalogue for this paper.

439

Treachery
in the loss
of Calais.

But this compliment to King Philip, in taking his quarrel
with France, cost England dear, even the loss of that important town of Calais, as was said before, and the territories
thereunto belonging: which being all taken so easily and
so suddenly by the Duke of Guise, occasioned great jea-
lousies and suspicions among the people, that there was
some base treachery used in some of Queen Mary's courtiers,
that betrayed it to the French. And to conceal the great
men that had their hands in it, the blame was cunningly
conveyed upon some others of less note, that were innocent.
To justify this that I write, I find these notes following un-

Fox ii MSS. der John Fox's hand in one of his papers: " At the losing
" of Calais, the bailiff of S. Katharine's [to lay the blame
" upon him, an innocent person, as it seems] was sent down
" with letters by Sir Richard Southwel, [a great privy

"counsellor,] to Dover, the Council then sitting there, and
"all the fault laid upon him by privy letters from the said
"Southwel to the Council; which letters the said bailiff
"carried himself, [little knowing the contents of them.]

"Cardinal Pole was noted to be a doer therein, for the
"composing of the French King's mind towards the Pope.

"Thirlby also, when he heard of the loss of Calais, drank
"carouse to it, and called it a *fishertown*.

"Certain men were sent from Westminster to Calais, and
"the good soldiers dismissed."

Yet truth it is, the King of Spain, soon after the taking
of this town, (perhaps yet for some ends of his own,) made
an offer to England to assist them in the recovery of its honour, which he saw suffered much by the loss of it. But the
Queen's condition was so low, both in purse and courage,
that the thoughts of the charge, and despair of providing fit
officers, made her wholly to decline it, and patiently to sit
down under the loss. And so her Council signified in a
message back to the King, dated February 1, 1557; which
I shall exemplify from a Cotton MS. wherein may be seen
how sunk the hearts of the English nation now were.

"First, to say, That we be most bounden unto his Ma-
"jesty for his good affection towards this realm, and his
"gracious disposition and offer to put his force to the field
"this year, (being else otherwise determined,) for the reco-
"very of that honour and reputation which this realm hath
"lost by the loss of Calais.

"To say, That this offer of his Majesty we should not
"only have upon our knees accepted, but also in likewise
"have sued first for the same; and so undoubtedly we
"should have done, if other respects hereafter following
"(which we trust his Majesty will graciously understand)
"had not been, to our great regret, the let thereof.

"First, We do consider, that if we should send over an
"army, we cannot send under two [rather to be read *twenty*]
"thousand men: the levying and sending over whereof
"will ask a time; before which time (considering also the
"time the enemy hath had, being now almost a month, to

The King of Spain offers his aid for recovery of it.

Titus, B. 2.

The English decline it, and why.

" fortify and victual the place) it is thought the same will
" be in such strength, as we shall not be able alone to re-
" cover it.

" We do consider, how unapt and unwonted our people
440 " be to lie abroad, and especially in the cold ; and what in-
" convenience might follow also at their hands, (besides the
" loss of charges,) if their hope for the recovery of Calais
" should not come to pass.

" The charge of this army, if it should go over, would
" stand the realm in 170,000l. at the least, for five months ;
" which sum (having regard to other necessary charges for
" the defence of the realm both by land and by sea, which
" the people only have in their heads, with a wan hope of
" the recovery of Calais) neither, we doubt, will be granted
" of the people ; nor if it were, can be conveniently levied
" in time to serve the turn.

" Great garrisons continually, and an army for defence
" against the Scots and Frenchmen by land, must of ne-
" cessity be maintained.   The charge whereof will be one
" ways and another, go the next way we can, ere the year
" go about, 150,000l.

" The defence of the seacoast and isles, and the setting
" forth of an army by sea, will cost the realm in a year, all
" things accounted, above 200,000l. And yet all will be too
" little that way, if the Danes and the Stedes, [Swedes,]
" which we have much fear of, should be our enemies.

" The sum, amounting in the whole to 520,000l. beside
" provision of munition, which will be chargeable, and fur-
" niture of ordnance, whereof we have great lack by the
" loss of Calais and Guisnes, we see not how it can be le-
" vied in one year to serve us, unless the people should of
" new have strange impositions set upon them, which we
" think they cannot bear.

" The Queen's Majesty's own revenue is scarce able to
" maintain her estate ; the noblemen and gentlemen, for the
" most part, receiving no more rent than they were wont to
" receive, and paying thrice as much for every thing they
" provide, by reason of the baseness of the money, are not

" liable to do as they have done the times past. The
" merchants have had great losses of late, whereby the
" clothiers be never the richer. The farmers, graziers, and
" other people, how well willing soever they be taken to be,
" will not be aknown of their wealth, and by the miscon-
" tentment of this loss be grown stubborn, and liberal of
" talk.

" So that, considering our wants on either side; our lack
" of money at home; our want of credit, by reason of this
" loss abroad; the scarcity of captains and leaders of our
" men, which be but few; the unwillingness of our men to
" go abroad, and leave their things at home, without any cer-
" tain hope of recovery of their loss; the need we have to
" defend home, (looking, as we do, to be assailed both by
" land and by sea,) how desirous soever we be to recover Ca-
" lais, and well willing to serve his Majesty, (either for that
" purpose, or for any other thing wherein it shall please
" him to employ us;) we see not how we can possibly, at the
" least for this year, send over an army; nor until we may
" be assured of fewer enemies than we fear to have cause to
" doubt, and have time to bring such as be evil men among
" our people, and now be ready against their duties to
" make uproars and stirs among ourselves, to order and
" obedience.

" Wherefore, in most humble wise upon our knees, we
" shall beseech the King's Majesty to accept in gracious part 441
" this our answer, which we make much against our hearts,
" if we might otherwise choose. And as for our own persons,
" we shall bestow them, with all that ever we have, to the
" death, where and howsoever it shall please him; submit-
" ting ourselves to his Majesty's judgment in this matter,
" and to the execution and doing of that whatsoever, either
" his Majesty or any other man shall devise to be done
" better than we have said in this answer, and more for the
" honour and sureties of their Majesties, and commonwealth
" of this their realm."

But to see what was commonly talked of the above- The ill re-
mentioned expedition, wherein were employed many Lon- of this expedition.

The ill re-
sentment
of this ex-
pedition.

C H A P.
LVII.
_____
Anno 1557.
Printed at
Geneva,
an. 1558,
p. 207.

doners and many gospellers, take a passage of Christopher
Goodman's book, entitled, *How to obey, or disobey*, which
spake the sense of many English : " I will speak a word to
" them which be called gospellers, and yet have armed
" themselves against the gospel, drawing forth with them
" out of their country to maintain Philip's wars, and to
" please Jezebel, (who seeketh by that means to cut their
" throats craftily,) their poor and ignorant tenants, and
" other soldiers without knowledge, while their brethren
" be burned at home, and their country like to be wasted,
" spoiled, oppressed, possessed, and replenished with un-
" godly Spaniards.   Is this the love that ye bear to the
" word of God, O ye gospellers?   Have ye been so taught
" in the gospel, to be wilful murderers of yourselves and
" others abroad, rather than lawful defenders of God's peo-
" ple and your country at home?   This hath not the gos-
" pel taught you : but chiefly, in all your doings, to *seek*
" *the righteousness of God*, next, to *love your neighbours as*
" *yourselves*, and in no case to be murderers, as all you
" are, that either for pleasure of princes, or hope of pro-
" motion, or gain of wages, are become captains or soldiers
" in unlawful wars ; especially in this cause and dangerous

P. 211.

" time."   And a little after, speaking to London, " Thou
" canst not herein defend thyself, which since hast been
" ready, and yet art, to maintain wicked Jezebel in her ty-
" ranny at home, and in her ungodly and needless wars
" abroad, with thy goods and body at her commandment,
" being thereby made an aider, helper, and furtherer of all
" her ungodly oppressions and tyranny."

Kethe's
poetry up-
on it.

And Will. Kethe, a Scot, and exile at Geneva, endued
with a vein of poetry, shewed his good will to the Spaniard
and this expedition, with respect to the English assisting
them, in these stanzas :

For France spighteth Spain, which England doth treat ;
And England proud Spaniards with salt would fain eat.
Yet England proud Spain aids with men, ships, and boats,
That Spain (France subdued once) may cut all their throats.

A people perverse, repleat with disdain,
Through flattery, fain hide would their head and vile train;
Whose rage and hot lust, deceipt, craft, and pride,
Poor Naples, their bond-slave, with great grief hath try'd.

Lo! these be the birds which England must feed,
By planting of whom to root out their seed;
Their own lands and life by them first devoured,
Their maids then and wives most vilely defloured.

Is this not strong treason, yea, unnoble blouds,
To aid such destroyers both with lands and goods?
But when they thus pinch you, and ye put to flight,
To what fort then flee you, or where will you light?

For England thus sold for Spaniards to dwell,
Ye may not by right possess that ye sell,
They seeing your treason against your own state,
Will not with theirs trust you, which they know you hate.

To Scotland or France, if ye then should cry,
Your vile deeds now present, they may well reply.
And Dutchland abhors you. This then doth remain,
When Spaniards are placed, ye must to New Spain.

But oh! dreadful plague, and sign of God's wrath,
On such noble *gnatos*, strong foes to God's truth,
Whom fond fear hath framed to prop such a stay,
As country and people so seeks to betray.

This war, which was maintained, not only against France, but Scotland, ran the Queen into extraordinary charges; and the nation was in daily expectation of being invaded by one or both enemies: so that she was forced to require aid of her people, for maintaining an army to resist any invasion; and she obtained it of the Parliament, that began to sit Jan. 20, in this 4th and 5th of the King and Queen, and brake up March 7 following. The clergy gave her an entire subsidy of eight shillings in the pound, " now," as the act ran, " when the imminent necessity of the defence " of the realm required present aid and remedy." The Parliament gave her one subsidy, one 15th and one 10th. Then she also obtained an act for the turning all French-

A Parliament gives the Queen money.

CHAP. LVII.

Anno 1557.

Private acts.

men out of the nation, as such as privily informed her enemies of the counsel, state, and privacies of the realm: and not only so, but for the making void all letters patents for denizenship of any aliens or strangers born French, since the 32d of Henry VIII. as to her Highness should seem good; which was very hard. In this Parliament were these three private acts: I. For assuring the honour of Raleigh to the Queen. II. For the restitution of Sir Ambrose and Sir Robert Dudley. III. For the foundation of an hospital at Stoge-Podgies, in Berks. But now proceed we to ecclesiastical matters.

443

CHAP. LVIII.

A journal of memorable matters, happening in the months of February and some part of March.

February.

A grant to the friars of Greenwich.

Febr. 1. THE Queen, under her hand and seal, granted to the friars of Greenwich, towards their relief and succour of fuel, one acre of wood, in her wood called *the west wood* in the parish of Lewisham.

Sir Hary Capel buried.

Febr. 3, Sir Hary Capel, knt. was brought into little St. Bartholomew's beside St. Anthony's, [that is, near where the French church now stands in Threadneedle-street,] to be buried by his grandfather, Sir Will. Capel, knt. and lord mayor of London; which Sir Hary was son and heir to Sir Giles Capel, who was buried in Essex. At this funeral were three heralds of arms, a standard, a pennon of arms, &c. All the church hanged with black and arms; four great tapers, four gilt candlesticks, two great white branches; and twelve poor men had black gowns. And after, all repaired to his house to dinner. Dr. Bricket made the sermon at the mass.

Forgery.

One Langerich of Chesterton, for forging of divers writings and testimonials, was, February 4, by the Star-chamber adjudged to go about Westminster-hall with a paper on his head, with these words therein written, *For forging of*

false testimonials ; and after to be set on the pillory in the
palace at Westminster, and also at Cambridge, on a market
day, for more knowledge and publication thereof.

February 6, the Bishop of Westchester preached at Paul's
Cross.   This audience was made up of sixteen bishops,
the lord mayor and aldermen, and many of the judges.   And
there he declared, that on Wednesday next, all persons
were required to go on general procession, and to pray to
God to avert his judgments.

On the 9th, a commandment came, that all bishops, priests,
and clerks should go a procession about London, and the
lord mayor and aldermen, and all the crafts in London, in
their liveries, to pray unto God : and all the children of
all the schools, and of the hospitals, in order about London,
were called to this general procession.

On the 10th, the Lord Dacres of the north his son was
arraigned at the King's Bench at Westminster, for the death
of Mr. West, son and heir of Sir William West, knt.   The
which West was slain coming from Rothegam fair.   There
were upon him and his six men forty of Mr. Dacres' party,
all in harness, by whom he was shamefully murdered in
May 1556.   For this murder he took sanctuary in Westminster, and in a procession suffered himself to be whipt for
it.   Now a year and three quarters after, he was brought,
I know not how, to answer at the King's Bench bar, where
it is remarkable, certain men of the friends of Mr. West
deceased, offered battle with Mr. Dacres and his party, and
to fight at combat on a day set.

On the 11th, Anthony Sturton, esq. the keeper of Whitehall, and brother to the Lord Sturton, was buried at St.
Martin's in the Fields.   This man was receiver of all the
copes of cloth of gold, that were taken away out of all
churches in King Edward the Sixth's time, by the device of
the Duke of Northumberland, and certain of the then bishops.   And he delivered the said copes back again for the
same parishes' use to which they formerly belonged ; that
is, as many as could be known and owned ; if they had not

been disposed to other places in the realm. And this by the allowance of Queen Mary, when she came to the crown.

Anno 1557.
Mr. Py-
nock, a
brother of
Jesus,
buried.

On the 16th, Mr. Pynoke, fishmonger, and merchant of Moscovia, and a brother of Jesus, was buried with two good white branches, &c. attended with the company of the clerks, and many priests. Then came the mourners, and after, the brotherhood of Jesus, four and twenty of them, with black satin hoods, with I H S on them, and after, the company of the Fishmongers in their liveries. All being performed at church, the company retired to his house to drink. This brotherhood of Jesus seems to have been a guild or fraternity newly founded after the old popish custom; and perhaps called themselves the brotherhood of Jesus, in favour of the new order of Jesus, founded by Ignatius Loiola.

Sir George
Barnes dies.

The 18th of February, died Sir George Barnes, knt. haberdasher, late mayor of London, viz. at the time of the Queen's coronation.

Bishop of
Lincoln
preaches at
Paul's
Cross.

Feb. 20, Dr. Watson, bishop of Lincoln, preached at Paul's Cross. There were ten bishops present, besides the lord mayor and aldermen, judges, and men of the law; and a great audience.

Sir George
Barnes
buried.

On the 24th, Sir George Barnes aforesaid, chief merchant of the Moscovy company, was buried. There was borne the pennon of the Moscovy arms. The mayor and swordbearer had black gowns; and fourscore poor men were clad in black gowns. There was a standard and five pennons of arms, and coat armour, &c. a goodly hearse of wax. Dr. Chadsey made the sermon on the morrow; and after, a great dinner. Mr. Clarencieux and Mr. Lancaster were the heralds.

Lady Eliza-
beth comes
to town.

On the 25th the Lady Elizabeth, the Queen's sister, came riding from her house at Hatfield to London, attended with a great company of lords and nobles, and gentlemen, unto her place called Somerset-place, beyond Strond-bridge, to do her duty to the Queen. And on the 28th she repaired unto her Grace at Whitehall, with many lords and ladies.

On the 26th the Lady White died, wife to Sir Thomas White, late mayor of London, merchant tailor, and merchant of the Moscovy.

March the   day, the Queen's pensioners mustered in Hide-park, and all their men in green cloth and white. The Earl of Rutland took the muster of them.

March the 2d was the Lady White buried in Aldermary parish. There was a goodly hearse of wax, and eight dozen of pensils, &c. The chief mourner was the Lady Laxton, whom Mr. Roper led. After came the lord mayor and twenty aldermen following the corpse. Four banners of images, two great white branches; the morrow-mass, and a godly sermon; and all the crafts in their liveries. Poor men had gowns, and poor women. There were three masses sung; one of the Trinity, and one of our Lady, and the third of *requiem*. After, to the place to dinner; whither resorted the lord mayor, aldermen, and gentlemen. For there was as great a dinner as had been seen.

March the 4th, aforenoon, the Lady Elizabeth's Grace took her horse, and rode to her place at Shene, with many lords, knights, ladies, and gentlewomen, and a goodly company of horse.

The   day, never was so low an ebb: for men might stand in the midst of the Thames, and might have gone from the bridge to Billingsgate; for the tide kept not his course; the which was never seen afore that time.

The 6th day, being the second Sunday in Lent, my Lord Abbot of Westminster preached at Paul's Cross before the lord mayor and bishops.

The 7th, the Parliament was that day holden at Whitehall, and ended at seven a clock at night. Divers acts made.

The 10th, the Queen removed unto Greenwich, in Lent, in order to her keeping Easter there.

The 14th, the Lady Jennings, daughter to Sir John Cage, knt. late constable of the Tower, died: and on the 16th was buried in the Minories.

The 16th, the Lord Mayor and Aldermen assembled at

CHAP.
LVIII.

Anno 1557.
Lady White
dies.

March.
The pen-
sioners
mustered.

Funerals of
the Lady
White.

445

Lady Eli-
zabeth goes
to Shene.

An extra-
ordinary
ebb.

Lord Abbot
at Paul's
Cross.

The Par-
liament
ended.

The Queen
goes to
Greenwich.

Lady Jen-
nings dies.

An assem-
bly at

CHAP.
LVIII.

Anno 1557.
Guildhall
by the
Queen's
command.
The city
lend the
Queen
money.

The paschal
for the ab-
bey made.

Earl of Sus-
sex goes to
Ireland.
Four con-
demned to
the fire.

TheQueen's
Council go
to Guild-
hall.

446
Proclama-
tion.

Guildhall; for they had a commandment from the Queen, to procure of the city to lend her a round sum. There sat the Lord Chancellor, the Lord Treasurer, Lord Privy Seal, the Bishop of Ely, with others of the Council, as commissioners.

The 19th, the Mayor and Aldermen went unto Guildhall; and there all the crafts in London brought in their bills, what their companies would lend unto the Queen, to help her in her affairs toward the wars.

The 21st was made the paschal for the abbey of Westminster, which consisted of three hundred pound weight of wax. There were at the making, the master and warden of the waxchandlers. And after, a great dinner.

The same day the Earl of Sussex took his journey in post for Ireland.

The same day were brought before the Bishop of London and other learned men of the temporalty, four men, whose opinions were such, that they were judged and condemned to suffer death by fire. One whereof was a hosier, dwelling in Wood-street. Three of these four were burnt in the latter end of this month: one whereof was Cuthbert Simpson, the faithful deacon of the congregation, who endured infinite tortures, to make him confess and discover the names of the members of this congregation: which he would not.

The 22d, the Lord Mayor and Aldermen went unto Guildhall; whither the Queen's Council also came about the loan; as first, the Lord Chancellor, the Lord Treasurer, Lord Privy Seal, the Bishop of Ely, Sir John Baker, Secretary Petre, and many more. And after, went to the Lord Mayor's to dinner.

The 23d, a proclamation was set forth of certain acts made by the last Parliament, ended the 7th of March last.

Among other women burnt to death this year, upon pretence of heresy, that is, for adherence to the profession of the gospel, Alice Drivers was one; who, before this execution, underwent a very severe punishment, for comparing Queen Mary, in respect of her persecutions, to Jezebel, and

calling her Jezebel; who was adjudged by Sir Clement Higham, a judge in that reign, to have both her ears cut off:
and so they were.

CHAP. LIX.

Preparations against an invasion in the west. Instruc-
tions to the Lord Lieutenant of Devon and Cornwal.

THIS year went out in great fears of storms ensuing, and
with a prospect of dangers from abroad. For about the
middle of March were grounds to expect some sudden invasion from France on the coast of Cornwal or Devon, and
that some in those counties were ready to rise upon the
landing of any such insult: which occasioned the Queen
hastily to send down the Earl of Bedford, a good soldier,
and lord lieutenant of those western shires, to put them in
a readiness, to take order for the beacons, to muster the mi-
litia, to see to the horse and arms, to punish vagabonds and
spreaders of tales and rumours, and to see to the preserving
of peace and quietness, especially at the collecting of the
subsidy lately given by Parliament. But to give more light
to all this, I will set down at large the instructions given to
the said Lord Lieutenant at his departing.

The Earl of Bedford sent down into the west.

Instructions given by the King and Queen's Majesty to
their right trusty and right well-beloved cousin, the Earl
of Bedford, appointed their Highness's Lieutenant of the
counties of Dorset, Devon, and Cornwal, and their city
of Exeter, the xvi. *day of March, the* iv. *and* v. *years*
of their Majesties' reign.

His instruc-
tions. Ti-
tus, B. 2.

" Mary the Queen.

" *Imprimis*, The said lieutenant to have with him his
" commission, his instructions, and his letters. To depart
" forthwith to his charge with all diligence. To give order
" strait for the raising of beacons, and watching of the
" same, according to such orders as be appointed; and to
" give the charge of the beacons to men of understanding.
" To cause muster to be taken of all persons within his

" lieutenancy, of their weapons and of their armour; and
" to pick out and describe all the able horsemen and foot-
" men, their names and dwellingplaces. To call all the
" gentlemen of the shire together, and to take view of all
" their serving-men, and of all such horses and geldings as
" they have meet to set the serving-men upon; and to
" consider what number there is of them able to carry a
447 " demi-lance; and how many light horsemen; to appoint
" meet captains for the horsemen and for the footmen,
" such as he shall think most convenient, dividing the shire
" by hundreds, or such numbers as he shall think meet.
" To appoint to every captain the number he shall lead.
" To deliver him the names and dwellingplaces of his
" number, and to deliver him a precept or commandment
" for the numbers within that hundred, to obey him, and
" to all officers for his assistance, if any will disobey. To
" order every captain to take often musters and views of
" his band; seeing them furnished with weapons and ar-
" mour convenient, so as he may well know them, and have
" them always in a readiness. To appoint to what places
" and upon what warning every captain shall resort with
" his men for defence. To consider what dangerous places
" there be for the landing of the enemies upon the sea-
" coast, and to cause the inhabitants next unto the place,
" and, if they be not able, their neighbours next unto
" them, to help them to make of new, or repair, as the case
" shall require, for defence of the place, trenches and bul-
" warks of earth. To cause the inland-dwellers of the shire
" to furnish the numbers that go from their quarters for
" their defence at the seacoast, not only of sufficient money
" to pay for their victuals when they come there, but also
" to have consideration of their charges in coming back
" again, and of the time (which may be ten or twelve days)
" of their abode upon the seacoast: whereunto the said
" inland-men may be induced, seeing the other go forth to
" adventure their lives for their defence, and to the intent
" that they may remain the more quiet at home. The
" lieutenant, if he see the force of his enemies on land so

" great, as he shall not be able with the force of his charge CHAP.
" to withstand them, then to withdraw himself, with his LIX.
" forces, to places of advantage within his charge, breaking Anno 1557.
" the bridges behind him, cutting of trenches, throwing
" down of trees, and giving such other impediments to the
" enemy as may be devised, until a greater force may come
" unto him for his aid : giving immediately upon such land-
" ing, advertisement unto the Queen's Highness, or her
" Privy Council, or to other lieutenants next joining unto
" him, for his further aid. To cause diligent watch to be
" kept in all towns and boroughs within his lieutenancy,
" according to the order prescribed for the same. To have
" special regard for the punishment of vagabonds, spreaders
" of evil tales, and devisers or reporters of seditious ru-
" mours, by such pains as are ordained by the laws of the
" realm in that behalf. To see the King and Queen's
" Highness served of all able men indifferently ; that no
" man meet to serve be withdrawn from service by par-
" tiality, favour, or other like pretence, and unmeet men
" placed in lieu of them. To have a special care to keep
" the shire in good order and quietness, especially at the
" time of levying the subsidy. To see the statute, made
" for musters and furniture of armour in this last session of
" Parliament, truly and uprightly executed and kept of all
" such as they shall put in trust to muster or levy any
" number of men. And therefore to have a special care,
" as they tender their Highnesses service, and the main-
" taining of the subjects good will and duty towards them.

" Mary the Queen."

CHAP. LX.

448

A fleet equipped against France. Divers memorials of
matters and events in the months of August, September,
October, November, and December.

THERE was great talk in May 1558, and expectation of Anno 1558.
King Philip's coming over with speed in England, though The King expected.

the merchants, strangers in London, thought otherwise, and
that he could not yet conveniently be spared.   For indeed
the wars grew hot between him and the French.   However,
the Queen earnestly looked for him, and horses and his
wardrobe were gone as well to Dover as to Harwich.   The
Lord Admiral went also to Dover to prepare the fleet and
shipping.

Great pre-
parations
against
France..

For all things were putting in a readiness for him, and
preparation was made of a very great army of soldiers,
which were to serve him upon an expedition now resolved
against France.   And the Lord Treasurer, who was the
Marquis of Winchester, was made lieutenant general south
of Trent, and the Earls of Huntingdon and Rutland were
appointed to be head officers of the army.   At Portsmouth
there were then ready two hundred and forty sail ready
victualled.   However, the merchants and others now reported, that peace was ready to be concluded between King
Philip and the French King.   The first occasion thereof
was by means of the Duchess of Lorain.   This news was
writ from London by a servant of the Earl of Shrewsbury
to him ; who, being president of the north, was providing
forces in those parts.   The money was at this time extreme
scarce, and never so hard to come by at London ; and as
hard to be gotten at the Exchequer.   From both which
places the said Earl had expected money for the present
purpose.   But at length his receiver wrote him, that he
was in hope to receive his money at the Exchequer.

A design to
take Brest.

The present design was, by the help of the English fleet,
to which that of Spain was to join, to assault and take Brest
in Britain from the French.   But after the taking and spoil-
ing of another seaport in Britain, called Conquet, and some
other neighbouring towns, they departed, finding it not safe
to make any further attempt against Brest.   And soon after
were overtures made of peace between King Philip and
France : which nevertheless took not place, because the
French would not hear of restoring Calais.

Men raised
in the
north.

In July they were raising men in the north ; and 1500
men were appointed to be raised in the county of Darby,

by the Earl of Westmerland.   Which county, consisting of
eight hundreds or wapentakes, six of them, together with
the town of Darby, pertained unto the Earl of Shrewsbury,
and which were parcels of the rules, offices, and inheritance
of that nobleman.   These hundreds were, Scarsdale, High
Peak, Appletree, Wirksworth, Hartington Soyle, Melbourn
Home.   Therefore it lay in this Earl to assign the propor-
tion of men to be raised in these his hundreds.   And he
accordingly assigned 400 men only, having, it is probable,
raised for to serve under him good numbers before.   But 449
this caused some discontent in the Earl of Westmerland,
that so many as 1100, being the remaining number to
complete 1500 men, should be taken out of two hundreds, namely, Morlaston and Repton.   Which therefore
caused him to write a letter to the Earl concerning this
matter.

August the 3d, the Lady Rowlet, late wife to Sir Rafe
Rowlet, knt. was buried in St. Mary Staining, honourably.
And after mass, the company retreated to the place to dinner, which was plentifully furnished with venison, fresh sal-
mon, fresh sturgeon, and many other fine dishes.   This
seems to have been her anniversary; for she was buried in
December 1557.

The 12th day died Mr. Machyl, alderman of London,
merchant of Moscovy, and clothworker.   He was (saith my
MS.) a worshipful man, and a *Godys man* to the poor, and
to all men in the parish of St. Mary Magdalen in Milk-
street, where he lived and died, in a house wherein Alderman Hind died.   Had he lived, he had been mayor the
next year.   And on the 21st he was buried in the said
parish church, with five pennons of arms and coat armour,
and four dozen of torches, and four branch tapers double
store, with arms and pensils upon wax.   All the church,
the street, and the place [his house] hanged with black and
arms.   There attended the funeral the mayor and aldermen, and an hundred in black.   Eight dozen of escutcheons, and four dozen of pensils, and an hundred men in
mantle frieze gowns.   And on the morrow-mass three masses

sung; two of pricksong, and the third of *requiem ;* and a sermon made by a Grey friar. After the offices of the Church were performed, the lord mayor and aldermen, and all the mourners and ladies, went to dinner, which was very splendid, lacking no good meat, both flesh and fish, and an hundred March pains.

An Irish archbishop buried.

August 17, a Bishop of Ireland, [*viz.* Dowdal, archbishop of Ardmagh,] who died the 15th, was carried from the Gorge in Lumbard-street by water to be buried.

The Bishop's crosier buried.

On the 20th, Mr. Morton, one of the Gray Amisis of Paul's, and the Bishop of London's crosier, was conveyed from London to Fulham, to be buried.

Prior of St. Bartholomew's buried.

On the 22d, Dr. Peryn, master of the Black friars in Smithfield, (which was the first house of religion set up by Queen Mary in her time,) was buried at the altar-side afore St. Bartholomew. When King Henry VIII. rejected the Pope, and dissolved monkery, he became a voluntary exile, and after twenty years returned home; and under this Queen was made much use of to preach up the papal superstitions. He remained a stiff opposer of the reformed religion to the last. Four sermons of the eucharist, preached by him, he caused to be published, wherein he extolled the mass. Against whom, with respect to those sermons, Parkhurst made some verses; beginning,

Desipis, insulsas qui fers ad sydera missas, &c.

Dr. Cook, dean of the Arches, buried.

On the 23d, Dr. Cook, dean of the Arches, and judge of the Admiralty, a right temporizer, was buried in St. Gregory's beside Paul's. The church hanged with black and

450 arms, &c. There were present all the brethren of Jesus in satin hoods, and J H S upon them, with all the priests of St. Paul's. In January following was set up for him a coat armour, and a pennon of arms, and two banners of saints.

One buried in St. Bartholomew's.

On the 24th, a gentleman, unnamed, was carried from Grays-Inn in Grays-inn-lane, unto St. Andrew's parish in Holbourn; and there dirge sung. And after, carried through Bartholomew fair unto the Black friars there. And at the gate all the friars met him, and had dirge sung, and then buried him there. Such was the opinion of being buried within the walls of a monastery.

Ditto, Sir George Paulet, knt. brother to the Marquis of Winchester, was buried honourably. This gentleman married one Mrs. Lark, once a mistress to Cardinal Wolsey.

On the 29th was the Lord Windsor buried very splen- didly according to his quality.

Septemb. *initio*, Judge Stamford was buried at a town beyond Barnet. He was one of the Queen's sergeants at the famous trial of Sir Nic. Throgmorton anno 1554.

The 5th, the Queen had of late been very ill, and indis- posed in her health, but now she was better than she had been ten or twelve days before : which Sir William Cordel, one of the Privy Council, thought fit to signify in a letter dated September 5, from St. James's, to the Earl of Shrewsbury in the north.

The 6th day, Judge Morgan was buried in Northamp- tonshire honourably, with four banners of images.

The 14th, was buried Sir Andrew Jud, skinner, mer- chant of Moscovy, and late mayor of London, with ten dozen of escutcheons, an hearse of wax, and five principals, garnished with angels, many poor men in new gowns, and two heralds.

On the 20th, the Lady Southwel, wife to a privy coun- sellor of that name, was buried at Shoreditch.

Ditto, the Lady Cecilie Mansfield, deceasing at Clerken- well, was brought unto the Black friars in St. Bartholomew's, Smithfield, with banners of saints. The Lady Peters, wife to the Queen's secretary of state, was chief mourner ; and her servants bare the Lady's train, and bare torches also in black coats. She was buried afore the high altar, at the head of the old Prior Bolton. The church, choir, and rails, hanged with black and arms. The friars sung dirge after their song, and buried her after their fashion, without clerks or priests. And after, to the place to drink. And on the morrow were three masses said. And there was a godly sermon preached by the father of the

CHAP.
LX.
house, as ever was heard, (saith my MS.) teaching and admonishing to live well.

Anno 1558.
Lord Cobham dies.
On the 25th died the Lord Cobham, in Kent, knight of the Garter.

Lady Pecksal dies.
On the 26th died the Lady Pecksal, in the country, wife to Sir Richard Pecksal, knt. and daughter of the Lord Marquis of Winchester, lord treasurer.

October.
Mr. Wentworth dies.
October 23, Wentworth, esq. cofferer unto Queen Mary, died, and was buried at St. Margaret's, Westminster.

451
Cotton, a lawyer, buried,
Dr. Owen buried.
Ditto, Mr. Cotton, a great rich man of the law, was buried at St. Giles without Cripplegate.

On the 24th, Dr. Owen, physician to the Queen, was buried at St. Stephen's, Walbrook. He had also been physician to King Henry VIII. and no doubt to his son King Edward.

November.
A woman pillorized.
November 12, a woman was set on the pillory for saying the Queen was dead.

The Queen dies.
On the 17th, being Friday, in the morning, Queen Mary died. And though her reign were now expired, yet I will continue on my journal a little farther, till her interment.

Queen Elizabeth proclaimed.
The same day Queen Mary deceased, in the morning between eleven and twelve aforenoon, the Lady Elizabeth was proclaimed Queen by divers heralds of arms, and trumpets, many noblemen and knights present, as namely, the Duke of Norfolk, the Lord Treasurer, the Earl of Shrewsbury, the Earl of Bedford, the Lord Mayor and Aldermen, and many more. In the afternoon all the churches in London rung their bells: and at night were bonfires made, and tables set in the streets, and the people did eat and drink, and make merry.

Cardinal Pole dies.
On the 18th, the Lord Cardinal Pole died at Lambeth, between five and six in the morning. And there he lay till the Council set the time that he should be buried: and where, and how.

Te Deum sung.
The same day *Te Deum laudamus* was said and sung in every church in London.

November 20, Dr. Bill, Queen Elizabeth's chaplain, preached at Paul's Cross, and made a godly sermon.

Ditto, Gruffith, the bishop of Rochester, and parson of St. Magnus on London-bridge, died.

November 22, Robert Johnson, gentleman and officer to the Bishop of London, was buried honourably in Jesus chapel, (a chapel, I suppose, in St. Paul's or St. Faith's,) many mourners in black; and all the masters [or brothers] of Jesus in their black satin hoods. The morrow-mass, and a sermon. And after, a great dinner, and a dole of money.

On the 26th, Basset, esq. one of the privy-chamber to Queen Mary, was buried at the Black friars in Smithfield, with tapers, arms, heralds, &c.

On the 30th, the Bishop of Rochester was carried from his place in Southwark unto St. Magnus in London. He had an hearse of wax, and five dozen of pensils, and the choir hung with black and arms, two white branches, two dozen of torches, two heralds of arms. Sir William Petre chief mourner; many mourners; twelve poor men had black gowns, and twelve of his men bare torches. The Bishop of Winchester preached. After he was buried, they went to the place to dinner. He had a great banner of arms, four banners of saints, and eight dozen of escutcheons.

December the 7th, the Lady Cholmely, wife of Sir Roger Cholmely, knt. late lord chief baron, was buried in the parish of St. Martin's, Ludgate, with four banners of saints.

December 8, Dr. Weston, sometime dean of Westminster, was buried at the Savoy.

The 9th, Mr. Richmond, herald, was created Norroy by the Queen at Somerset Place. And Ricebank created Bluemantle.

The 9th, Dr. Gabriel Dune, priest, was buried honourably at St. Paul's.

On the 10th, the deceased Queen was brought out of her chapel, with all the heralds, many lords and ladies, gentlemen and gentlewomen, and all her officers and servants in black.

The same morning the corpse of the Lord Cardinal was removed from Lambeth, and carried toward Canterbury,

I 4

CHAP.
LX.

Anno 1558.
Bishop of
Rochester
dies.

Johnson, an
officer to the
Bishop of
London,
buried.

Basset buried.

Burial of
the Bishop
of Rochester.

December.
Lady
Cholmley
buried.

452
Dr. Weston
buried.

Heralds
made.

Dr. Dune
buried.

Queen Mary
brought out
of her chapel.

The Cardinal's body
removed towards Canterbury.

CHAP.
LX.

Anno 1558.

with a great company in black; drawn in a chariot with bannerols wrought with fine gold, and great banners of arms, and four banners of saints.

Mr. Verney
buried.

The 11th day, Mr. Verney, master of the jewel house, was buried within the Tower.

Sir George
Harper buried.

The 12th, Sir George Harper, knt. (one of those in Sir Thomas Wyat's business,) was buried at St. Martin's, Ludgate.

The Queen's
funeral.

On the 13th were the funerals of the late Queen magnificently celebrated at Westminster.

But now we turn back to see how matters stood with the Church, and in what state religion was, this last year of the Queen.

CHAP. LXI.

Cardinal Pole's commissions.   Advowsons settled upon the see.   Causeth some to be burnt.

Commission for
heretics.

IN the beginning of this year, Archbishop Pole (pretending to take some care of his diocese) issued out a commission, dated March the 28th, against the *heretics* there, (as the honest professors of the gospel were now called,) to Nicolas Harpsfield, Rob. Collins, Richard Fawcet, Hugh Turnbul, S. Th. PP. John Mills, Hugh Glazier, and John Warren, S. Th. BB. canons and prebendaries of Canterbury: these were commissioned to absolve, admit, and receive into the bosom of the Church those that confessed their errors, and retracted and abjured them; and to enjoin them penance. But the obstinate, and such as would not be brought to the unity of the Church, to reject, and cast them out of the communion of the Church, and to commit and deliver them to the secular power: yet adding this condition, *si facti atrocitas ita exposcerit; if the heinousness of the fact shall so require.* And to such sentences he required two of them, at least, to join and give their assent and consent. This commission opened a door to a great persecution in Kent this year.

The Archbishop gave another commission to Maurice, bishop of Rochester, dated May the 24th, to confer orders, as well in his diocese, as elsewhere in other dioceses of his province.

The Cardinal, as he was Archbishop of Canterbury, had a power of visiting All-Souls college, Oxon. And on July 20, signed a commission to Dr. Henry Cole, his vicar general, to visit the said college.

But the said Dr. Cole, whether by resignation, or otherwise under some cloud with the Cardinal, was this year divested of the spiritual offices conferred on him the last. For I find a commission, dated October 28, from the Cardinal, to Nic. Harpsfield, to be his official; and another of the same date to be dean of the Arches. And yet a third, two days after, authorizing him to visit All-Souls college abovesaid.

There were letters dated November 5, in the fifth and sixth year of the King and Queen, whereby were granted to Cardinal Pole and his successors, archbishops of Canterbury, the perpetual advowsons of divers vicarages, rectories, and churches, in the county of Kent, and within the diocese of Canterbury; viz. Hernehil, Folkeston, Reynham, Bredgar, Selling, Merden, Graveney, Sittingborn, Lydd, Tilmanston, Kennington, Maydston, Monnington, Godneston, Asse, Whitstable, Leed, and Salmiston, cum Dean. These letters patents were pursuant of an act of Parliament, as is mentioned in the said letters; which Parliament was held on the 21st of October, the 2d and 3d of the King and Queen: importing, "that whereas di- " vers rectories and benefices impropriate, glebe-lands, " tithes, oblations, pensions, portions, profits, and emolu- " ments ecclesiastical and spiritual, which from the twen- " tieth year of King Henry came into the hands of the " said King, and at his death into the hands of King Ed- " ward, and after into the Queen's hands and possession, " should be disposed, ordered, and applied, and converted " by the most reverend father, Cardinal Pole, then legate " a latere, and now archbishop of Canterbury, for these

" uses ; *ad inaugmentationem et incrementum victuum in-*
" *cumbent. prædict. aut aliarum curarum et beneficiorum*
" *indigent. Vel aliter in prædiatorum,* [*prædicatorum,*]
" *sustentationem, aut scholarium sustentationem :*" that is,
" for the augmentation and increase of living for the fore-
" said incumbencies, or other poor cures and benefices ; or
" else for the sustaining of poor preachers, or the mainte-
" nance of poor scholars within the kingdom, and being
" denizens of England, according as should seem best to
" the wisdom of the said Cardinal ; the patronages of which
" benefices, rectories, and vicarages were then in the Queen.
" And when she was given to understand that many of
" the rectories and vicarages were then void and destitute
" of curates ; and likewise that such a want was throughout
" all the dioceses of her kingdom, partly through the death
" of the incumbents, but chiefly because the rents and re-
" venues of the said livings were so small and strait, that
" they sufficed not for the sustaining of able and learned
" curates ; by the defect of which it was come to pass, that
" the people were not instructed in the sincere and Catholic
" doctrine and religion ; nor were the sacraments and sacra-
" mentals administered to them ; not without the anger and
" indignation of Almighty God, and the great danger and
" hazard of many Christians ; the burden and care of all
" which did especially and properly belong to the ordina-
" ries of such dioceses : to which if the distribution of the
" patronages of all and singular the benefices were com-
" mitted, they would be so much the more obliged to pro-
" vide and collate fit and able persons for those places : We
454 " therefore, as the letters proceed, desiring to be disbur-
" dened altogether of this care, and in consideration of the
" sum of 7000*l.* of lawful money of England, by the said
" most reverend Cardinal offered to us ; together with the
" consent of the rest of the prelates of this kingdom, of
" their mere and free will unasked, out of the rents, reve-
" nues, and profits of the said benefices, and delivered into
" our hands, for the sustentation and better supportation of
" our great burdens in defence of our kingdoms and sub-

" jects; have granted to the said Cardinal and his succes-
" sors, the archbishops, all the patronages, advowsons, do-
" nations, and free dispositions and rights of patronage of
" the churches aforesaid." The procuring this to the archbishopric must be recorded for one of the good deserts of
this Cardinal to his see.

This last year of the Cardinal's life he foully polluted
his hands in blood, which he seemed hitherto to be shy of
doing; and this as the effect of his late commission against
heretics. For he issued out an instrument, called a *signi-
ficavit*, dated from Lambeth, July the 7th, to the King and
Queen, against certain heretics in his diocese. These were,
John Cornford of Wrotham, Christopher Brown of Maid-
ston, John Hurst of Asheton, Katharine Knight of Thorn-
ham, and Alice Suoth, or Snoth, of Biddenden. Of whose
heresy his commissioners, Harpsfeld, Collins, and the rest,
had informed him. The Cardinal therefore, in the said instrument, prayed the King and Queen, that they might be
cast out of the fold, as diseased sheep, lest they might infect
others. *Cum igitur sancta mater Ecclesia non habeat quod
ulterius facere, et exequi debeat, in hac parte vestris regiis
Sublimitatibus, et brachio vestro seculari, dictos hæreticos et
relapsos, relinquimus, condigna animadversione plectendos.*
" When therefore," as the instrument proceeded, " holy mo-
" ther Church hath not any thing further that she ought
" to do in this behalf, we leave the said heretics and re-
" lapsed persons to your royal Highness, and your secular
" arm, to receive condign punishment." And a warrant, I
suppose, hereupon, being sent down for their execution,
they were all burnt alive at Canterbury, November 10,
being but seven days before the Queen's death and his, and
the last that were burnt in that reign.

We have seen what commissions went forth from the
Cardinal this year 1558, and what his commissions were for
the other two years past, as I carefully took them out of
the register. By which we may perceive, that the Cardinal
never did, in his own person, ordain, or consecrate, or visit,
but did all by others. Whether it were his exalted station,

or his constant employment about the Queen in matters of state, or his infirmities, that made him neglect the offices of his function, I leave to others to determine.

455

CHAP. LXII.

Proceedings with the heretics. Commissions for inquiry after such in Essex. A loan. The statute for burning heretics examined.

They begin to think of other courses to check religion.

WE are now in the last year of Queen Mary; and the persecution still held; which though sharper, yet was less dreaded: insomuch that the Papists, seeing how little all their endeavours had prevailed, began now to think of some other ways to suppress the religion. There was one Dale, a promoter, who told Mr. Living, a minister, and in bonds for religion: " You care not for burning; by God's blood, " (as he swore,) there must be some other means found for " you." Such was the courage of good people in those days. And so far were the persecutors from obtaining their ends, (*viz.* that by burning some, the terror thereof might reduce the rest to submit to the old superstitions,) that it had a quite contrary effect. They were encouraged and made more strong and resolute to persist in their principles, by the many examples of constancy they had so often before their eyes.

Songs made against the mass.

Some of these vented their resentments of the cruelty of this time, by making songs against the government, and against the barbarous usage exercised to the Queen's poor quiet subjects. There was one Cornet, a minstrel's boy, suffered for it. As at a wedding near Colchester, being bid to sing some song out of the Scripture, he sung a song called *News out of London;* which was against the mass and the Queen's proceedings. For which he was complained of, and committed to custody, and brought before the Earl of Oxford, and was whipped for his pains.

In the beginning of this year, in the month of April, by

virtue of a commission from Boner the bishop, and some
warrants also from the Council, Dr. Chedsey and Thomas
Mowrton, the Bishop's chaplains, and John Boswel, his secretary, went down to Colchester and Harwich, to examine
the heretics in those parts of Essex, and to condemn them
to be burnt. For though they had burnt so many, yet
many more remained here. Bonner gave them a letter to
the Lord Darcy, to countenance and further them in this
business. And the officers and under-sheriff were zealous
to serve them. Upon their first coming down, they examined six in one day, and condemned them the next.
And so were making quick work with many more. Some
whereof had been not long before spared and sent home by
means of Abbot Feckenham, who grew weary, as it seems,
of these butcheries. But by the providence of God, or
some secret friends at Court, while these bloody men were
very earnest at this their cruel business, the Council sent
for the chief of them up to Court immediately, *viz.* Chedsey, to confer with him upon certain matters. The letter
ran thus :

" After our hartie commendations, having certain mat-
" ters, wherein we would furder talk with you, we have
" thought good to will and require you in the King and
" Queen's Majesty's names, to make your indelayed repair
" unto us. At which your comyng, you shall furder under-
" stand the cause of your sending for. Whereof we require
" you not to fayle, as you tender their Majesties favour.
" From Grenewych, the 20th of April, 1558.
                    " Your loving frends,
          " Nic. Ebor. Cancel.   Thomas Wharton,
          " T. Cornwalleis,   H. Bedyngfeld,
          " T. Clynton,   Jo. Boxal."

This was a mighty surprise to the Bishop's commissioners ; for they were very loath to be taken off. " Be-
" cause," as they said, " there were so many obstinate he-
" retics, Anabaptists, and other unruly persons then in

" Essex, as never was heard of." So Chedsey wrote first to the Lord Chancellor, to excuse coming up; " because of " the great employment he was busie upon ; and that he " would repair up as soon as he had done the King and " Queen's affairs." And likewise to the Bishop to further his stay, writing to him in this manner:

" After my most humble commendations to your honour- " able good Lordship : This present Thursday, I, with the " residue sitting in commission at Colchester upon the he- " retics, received letters by a pursevant, directed to me " only, to appear indelayedly before the Council for certain " matters. We be now in the myddest of our examination " and articulation. And if we should give it off in the " midst, we should set the country in such a rore, that my " estimation, and the residue of the commissioners shall be " for ever lost. And principally the Queen's Majesty, with " her honourable Council, shall be less regarded, and your " honourable good Lordship utterly condemned, *quid cœ-* " *pit ædificare Dominatio vestra*, &c.

" Wold to God the honourable Council saw the face of " Essex as we do see. We have such obstinate heretics, " Anabaptists, and other unruly persons here, as never was " heard of. And now to be called from our doings, it wyl " be taken that we have no commission, but came of your " Lordship's commandment, without any other warrant " from the honourable Council.

" I have written to my Lord Chancellor's Grace, and " have made my lawful excuse, with promise to make my " repair indelayed, as soon as I have done my service in " the King and Queen's affairs. I beseech your Honour " to further this matter to God's glory, the majesty of the " Quene, the honour of the Council, the estimation of your " Lordship's dignity, our honesty, and the quietness of the " country, now drawing to some conformity. And thus I " commit your Honour to the tuition of Almighty God. " Written at Colchester, 21 *Aprilis*, 1558, by your perpe- " tual and daily orator,

" Wylliam Chedsey, priest."

This Dr. Chedsey was a very zealous man for the popish **CHAP.** religion; and in King Edward's days maintained a public **LXII.** dispute about the *presence* in the sacrament, with Dr. P. Anno 1558. Martyr. Under Queen Mary he was preferred to two good 457 canonries, *viz.* first, that of Windsor, afterwards, that of Chedsey preaches at Christ Church, Oxon. I have this note further to make Thame of him. At Thame in Oxfordshire, not long before he against the was put into the commission abovesaid, about 1556, or professors. 1557, as I conjecture, he made an earnest sermon against the gospellers, and therein willed his auditors to make their complaints against such as were suspected to profess God's word, or to keep any books contrary to the papal religion. "At this sermon was one Robert Runsse, alias " Child, present; who was an horrible Papist, and being " glad that he might have occasion to trouble the pro- " fessors, did marvellously rejoyce that day, and glorying " in the same, was suddenly stricken, being in the church A judgment " at evening prayer; and after that never spake, but died secutor. " miserable. This man's life was evil, and his religion Fox. MSS. " such, joined with presumptuous boldness, that there was " not such an impudent Papist in the whole country. He " was a singing man in the choire, and a great persecutor." This was part of a letter written in the year 1569, from Francis Hall of Thame, and minister there, as I suppose, to Mr. Field, living at London. Who conveyed it to Mr. Fox, as a matter proper for that ecclesiastical historian's cognizance.

But though Chedsey was called away from the exercise of his bloody office, yet the two other that remained behind followed their work. And concerning what they had already done in this commission, they wrote the Bishop this account, April 22.

" Yesterday, being Thursday, we finished the examina- What was " tion of three most obstinate and comberous heretics: for done by these in " one of them held us all the forenoon, and the other two commis- " all the afternoon. This morning, being Friday, we in- sion. " tended to finish the examination of the other three, and " at afternoon to pronounce sentence of them all, if we

" shall find cause. There is little hope in them. One of
" these to be examined is a woman, and of those that my
" Lord Abbot did deliver. The officers of this town be
" very diligent with us, and the undershereve. To-morrow,
" being St. George's day, we intend to ryde to Harwich.
" My Lord Darcy and my Lord of Oxford sit here dayly
" for the assessement of the countrey. We delyvered your
" Lordship's letters to the Lord Darcy on Wensday, and
" his Lordship gave unto us good swete words for his as-
" sistance. We shewed my Lord of Oxford, that for so
" much as we were sure of my Lord Darcy to have his
" presence, nere unto Colchester, and supposing we should
" not have seen his Lordship, therefore your Lordship dyd
" not wryte to his honourable Lordship. And thus hasting
" to mass, and so forth with our business, I wysh to your
" Honor *omnem felicitatem.*

" Your Lordship's most bowden bedesman
" and humble servant,
" Thomas Mowrton, priest.
" Your Lordship's daily orator and poor officer,
" John Boswel."

458   The assessment of the country, mentioned in this letter,
The people in the making of which the Earl of Oxford and the Lord
murmur at
a loan. Darcy are said to sit daily at Colchester, was a great loan
Coop. of money the Queen at this time borrowed of her subjects,
Chron.
to carry on a war with the French, which she had impru-
dently undertaken for the sake of her husband King Philip.
Of some she took ten, of others twenty, forty, or fifty
pounds, according as their abilities were judged. Which
caused a great grudging among the people. Because but
the year before she had borrowed from the City, and of
most rich men in all parts of the nation: sending abroad a
number of privy seals, by which she required a hundred
pounds apiece of all such as were counted able, whether
they were gentlemen or others. This was in 1557. Which
also caused grudging, because great payments had been
granted before by act of Parliament. This opened people's

·mouths against the Spaniards; thinking these payments to come especially upon their account, and for the charges of their wars.

In all these bloody doings beforesaid, it is to be remarked, that they bare out themselves by the pretended laws of the land. And so did Cope and Parsons, and other Papists, throw in Mr. Fox's dish, when he charged them with their cruel putting to death such numbers of poor people, only because they differed from them in some points of religion. They commonly proceeded upon two acts of Parliament; one was from *anno quinto Richard. II.* which was occasioned by certain preachers, who went about the towns and countries to draw away people to their sermons. Such preachers were to be imprisoned at the certificates of the prelates. But here is no mention made of burning, but only of arrests to be made of them. The other statute was in the next reign, *viz. anno 2 Hen. IV.* By virtue of which, the secular power had authority to bring such heretics to the stake, and burn them, whom the bishops delivered to them. Now both these, in truth and reality, were of no force at all as laws of the land, as appeared to the industrious Mr. Fox, who searched the rolls.

For he found the former act to be revoked the year after it was made, *viz.* anno 6, upon the words of the Commons, which were these: "Forasmuch as the same statute was "never assented, ne granted by the Commons: but that "which therein was done, was done without their assent, "and now ought to be undone. For that it was never "their meaning to be justified, and to bind themselves and "their successors to the prelates, no more than their ances- "tors had done before them." And yet, notwithstanding this revocation, they inquired upon this statute in Queen Mary's days.

As for the latter act, *viz.* that of King Henry IV. it was never assented to by the Commons, and so could be no law of the land. For in the rolls the statute is thus entitled, *Petitio Cleri contra Hæreticos.* And assented to in

this form: *Quas quidem petitiones prælatorum et cleri su-
perius expressatas, Do. noster Rex de consensu magnatum,
et aliorum procerum regni sui in præsenti Parliamento ex-
istentium, concessit; et in omnibus et singulis juxta formam et effectum eorundem ordinavit, et statuit de cætero
firmiter observari,* &c. Where is no mention at all of the
Commons. The clergy being aware of this, in a printed
statute-book, and in the Latin and English provincial councils of Oxford, corrupted the rolls, and foisted in a clause
to make it a law of the land, *viz. Ac etiam Communitates dicti
regni.*

CHAP. LXIII.

*Books prohibited under severe penalties. Goodman's book.
Protestant congregations in London. Goldwel. New Bishops nominated. Horn, a martyr.*

A severe
proclama-
tion against
certain
books.

A SHORT but terrible proclamation was this June put
forth by the King and Queen: whereby the having of certain books, and not burning them, was attended with this
penalty, to be executed presently by martial law; and the
persons to be taken and reputed for rebels. Nor is it specified particularly what books these be by name, nor what
sort of books, any more than " books filled with heresy, se-
" dition, and treason, and whereby God was dishonoured,
" and encouragement given to disobey lawful princes:"
under which words, or some of them, any Protestant books
might be comprised. The proclamation being short, I will
insert it.

" By the King and Queen.

" Whereas divers books filled with heresy, sedition, and
" treason, have of late, and be daily brought into the realm
" out of foreign countries and places beyond the seas, and
" some also covertly printed within this realm, and cast
" abroad in sundry parts thereof; whereby not only God is
" dishonoured, but also encouragement is given to disobey

" lawful princes and governors ; the King and Queen's Ma-
" jesty, for redress hereof, do by this their present procla-
" mation declare and publish to all their subjects, that
" whosoever shall, after the proclaiming hereof, be found to
" have any of the said wicked and seditious books, or find-
" ing them, doth not forthwith burn the same, without
" shewing or reading the same to any other person, shall, in
" that case, be reputed and taken for a rebel, and shall,
" without delay, be executed for that offence, according to
" the order of martial law. Given at our manor of St.
" James, the 6th day of June."

Of which proclamation Alexander Noel, a learned and a Noel's re-
good man, living in these times abroad, afterward dean of mark thereon. Confu-
St. Paul's, made this remark : " This is the proclamation pro- tat. of Dor-
" cured by Papists against our books, the bringers in, sell- man. fol.
48. b.
" ers, buyers, readers, or keepers of them : assigning the
" penalty of cruel and sudden death by law martial, without
" examination, question, verdict, and judgment : not only 460
" unusual in this realm, but more hasty and cruel than is
" used for any murderers, rebels, or traitors."

There was one book indeed, that came out this year, Goodman's
which this proclamation might have a particular eye to, *viz.* book.
Christopher Goodman's book. It was entitled, *How supe-*
rior Powers ought to be obeyed of their Subjects, and
wherein they may lawfully, by God's law, be disobeyed
and resisted : wherein is declared the cause of all this pre-
sent misery in England, and the only way to remedy the
same. Printed at Geneva, by John Crispin, MDLVIII. The
preface is writ by Will. Whittingham, then also at Geneva.
Though a little book in *decimo sexto,* it is full of bitterness,
and encourageth to take up arms against Queen Mary, and
to dethrone her ; and that upon this reason, among others,
because it is not lawful for women to reign. As it had
Whittingham's preface at the beginning of it, so had it
William Kethe, another divine at Geneva, his approbation
in verse at the end ; which verses will shew the intent of
the book :

CHAP.
LXIII.

Anno 1558.
Kethe's
verses on it.

Whom fury long fostered by suff'rance and awe,
Have right rule subverted, and made will their law,
Whose pride how to temper, this truth will thee tell;
So as thou resist may'st, and yet not rebel.

Rebellion is ill, to resist is not so,
When right true resisting is done to that foe,
Who seeks, but by ruin, against right to reign,
Not passing what perish, so she spoil the gain.

a Queen
Jane.

A public weal wretched, and too far disgraced,
Where the right head a is off-cut, and a wrong instead placed;
A brute beast untamed, a misbegotten,
More meet to be ruled, than rule over men.

A marvellous madness, if we will behold,
What sighs shall assure men, to see themselves sold.
And yet when from slavery their friends would them free,
Do stick to their foes; so still slaves to be.

Such treating of the Queen as this was, did, no question,
irritate her much, and provoke her to issue out such angry
declarations of her mind, and resolutions of taking vengeance
of all such like book-writers or book-readers.

Bentham,
an exile,
becomes
minister to
the congre-
gation in
London.

But to proceed with our history. Many congregations of
gospellers continued in London throughout this reign, from
the beginning to the end of it, in spite of the hardships
thereof, and notwithstanding the taking off so many of their
members. There was one chief congregation above the rest,
the pastor whereof was as superintendant. These pastors
were, Mr. Scamler, afterwards bishop; Mr. Fowle; Rough,
a Scot, afterwards burnt; Aug. Bernher, Latymer's faithful
servant. The last year of the Queen, succeeded in this office Thomas Bentham, lately an exile in Germany, (afterwards bishop of Litchfield,) who, as it seems, was sent
461 thence, or went voluntarily, chiefly by the persuasion of Mr.
Lever, and became preacher to this congregation, administered the sacraments, and performed the whole office of a
minister; and, besides, governed the church, in appointing
and ordering the matters thereof, according as things oc-

curred. To him they betook themselves for resolution in cases of conscience; whereof there were three happened this year: one was about a young woman married in her non-age to a certain person, with whom she was altogether unwilling to live, but was forced to it: the second was about going to the papistical courts, and following their suits and causes there: the third was about paying tithes and duties to the popish priests. Which cases, though Bentham himself did give his resolution to, yet he thought good, for the better satisfaction of his people, to send beyond seas for the judgment of the eminentest learned exiles there, and for Peter Martyr's opinion also. For which purpose he wrote this letter to Mr. Lever, (a person of great fame among the exiles for his learning and piety,) then pastor of the English congregation at Arow in Switzerland.

CHAP. LXIII.

Anno 1558.

" The grace and favour of Almighty God be with you
" and your godly congregation, *Amen.*
" My duty binding me to remember my dear friends,
" and our great dangers moving me to desire their help, in-
" force me at this present, both to write unto you, and de-
" sire your most godly and effectuous prayers, dere brother
" and lovyng freynde, Mr. Levir. For now I stand in the
" gapp, whereas you have so earnestly talked with me.
" Now therefore help me with your prayers, and I shall
" think, that you stand present at my back, or on my right
" hand. Whiles I was in Germany, at liberty of body,
" havyng sufficient for it for the time, I was yet many
" tymes in great greyf of mynd, and terrible torments of
" hell; and now here beying every moment of an hour in
" danger of takyng, and fear of bodily death, I am in mynd,
" the Lord be praysed, most quiet and joyful, seyng the
" fervent zeal of so many, and such increase of our congre-
" gation in the myddest of thys cruel and violent persecution.
" What shold I say, but *A Domino factum est.* There were VII
" men burned in Smithfield, the 28th day of July, altoge-
" ther; a fearful and cruel proclamation beyng made, that
" under payne of present death, no man shold either ap-

Foxii MSS.

Bentham to Lever, concerning the present persecution.

" proche ny unto theym, touche theym, nather speak unto,
" nor comforthe theym : yet were they so mightily spoken
" unto, so comfortably taken by the hands, and so godly
" comforted, notwithstandyng that fearful proclamation, and
" the present threatnyngs of the sheriff and sergyants, that
" the adversaryes themselves were astoyned. And synce
" that tyme, the Byshop of London, either for fear or craft,
" carryed seven more, or six at the least, forthe of his cole-
" house to Fulham, the 12th day of this moneth, and con-
" demning theym there the 13th day at one of the clock at
" afternone, caused them to be carryed the same tyme to
" Braneford besyde Syon; where they were burned in post-
" haste the same night. This fact purchaseth hym more
" hatred than any that he hath done, of the common mul-
" titude.

462   " This I signify, that you, knowyng owr great daungers,
" may the rather move your godly company to pray more
" earnestly for us.

" It is constantly wrytten by letters to London, that
" two townes a little from Nottyngham, about the 4th
" or 5th day of this month, were wonderfully beten and
" shaken with thounder, and such storms, many were slayn,
" and mo were hurt, with great wonders : which I take
" to be a token of God's great displeasure for synne, who
" will make heaven and earth wytness agaynst wicked-
" ness. And yet men, for the most part, were never more
" careless, nor malyciously merry, than they are now. God
" amend theym.

" I would gladly have your counsel, and Mr. Martyr's,
" in these three questions, if you have leasure at any tyme
" to walk to Zuriche. First, Whether a yong woman mar-
" ryed at non-age against her will, and so kept by force, be
" a lawful wife, or not, unto hym with whom she ys com-
" pelled to remayne against her wyll. Secondly, Whether
" the professors of the gospel may prosecute theyr right
" and cause in any papistical court, or answer, beyng called
" thereunto ; or take administration of goods in such court.
" Thirdly, Whether the professors of the gospel, not com-

"municating with Papists, may yet as well pay their tithes
"and such dutyes to the Papists, as tribute, custome, and
"subsidy to evil rulers and wicked magistrates. I trust,
"that I have answered some of my frynds in these questions
"according to the truth; yet wold I have your judgment,
"both for greater confirmation and comforth unto theym,
"and for my further instruction also. If you can shortly
"send me word of these, you shall greatly comforth me,
"and help to confirme my fryends in the ryght ways. I
"pray you commend me to all your company by name
"most hertily in our Lord Jesus Christ, who bless and keep
"you, to the comforth of his congregation. Written at
"London, the 17th of July.

       "By yours, to his power,
"Salute all my friends at   "Thomas Bentham."
"Zurich by name, I pray.

  "*To his dear friend and godly brother, Mr. Levir,*
  "*these be dd. at Arowe.*"

At the burning of those seven in Smithfield, mentioned Bentham
in this letter, was Bentham himself present; and could well present at the burning
testify what he wrote, that little regard was had to the se-of some in
vere proclamation, that none should speak to them, or com-Smithfield.
fort them, or pray for them. For he himself, as soon as he
saw fire put to them, cried aloud to the people, "We know
"they are the people of God; and therefore we cannot
"choose but wish well to them, and say, God strengthen
"them:" and added, "God Almighty, for Christ's sake,
"strengthen them." And he was presently answered by
multitudes, "Amen, Amen," to the amazement of the officers.

In October, Sir Edward Carne, knt. and doctor of laws, Goldwel,
that had been long ambassador at Rome with the Pope, was bishop of St. Asaph,
now, upon his desire, called home; and the Queen was upon to be des-
despatching Thomas Goldwel, the bishop of St. Asaph, in patched to Rome.
his room; a person, as she wrote to the Pope in her letters 463
credential, well approved by him. For he had lived long
abroad for the sake of the Roman Catholic religion, and

had conversed much with Cardinal Pole there, and was employed by him in a message into England to the Queen. But he went not to Rome in this intended embassy, the Queen dying before he could be despatched. Yet the next year he fled away beyond sea, and left his bishopric. And was afterwards famous for nothing I know of, but for obtaining of the Pope, with much ado, an enlargement of the patent for pilgrimage, and offering to St. Winefrid's well in Flintshire.

In the month of October, divers sees being vacant, the Queen made a promotion of bishops: whereof this Goldwel, above mentioned, was to be translated to Oxon: her chaplain, Francis Mallet, D. D. upon the death of John late Bishop of Salisbury, to be made bishop of that see: and Thomas Wood, B. D. she appointed for St. Asaph. And there were accordingly three letters prepared from King Philip and Queen Mary to Pope Paul IV. to admit these three; which letters were all dated in the month of October.

In the letter for Mallet, she signified to the Pope, that she had first offered this bishopric to William Peto, of the Franciscan order: whom, she said, she would have preferred the rather to this place, because she heard he had been thereunto nominated by the apostolic see; but that when she sent for him, he excused his acceptance of this

dignity by reason of his age, and other causes alleged. In her letter for Wood, she told the Pope, that she chose him to this honour, for his constancy in the Catholic religion in the most difficult times, not suffering himself to be allured by rewards, nor terrified by punishments. But these letters, I guess, were never sent away, at least not delivered; the Queen's illness, and her death the next month, preventing.

About eight weeks before the end of this reign, suffered, for the profession of the truth, one Edward Horne, of Newent, in the diocese of Gloucester, or Worcester. He was burnt in a place called the Court Orchyard, near the churchyard; and his wife was condemned with him, but she recanted, and refused to suffer with him. He sung at his burning the 146th Psalm, until his lips were burnt away; and then they saw his tongue move, until he fell down in the fire. This I relate the rather, because it was omitted by Fox, in his Martyrology, as probably many others that suffered in those cruel times might be, for want of information. He makes mention indeed of one John Horne, and a woman, that suffered martyrdom for the testimony of their faith, at Wotton-under-Edge, in Gloucestershire. One John Deighton, a worthy minister, as it seems, somewhere in those parts, above seventy years after, had been so curious to inquire after the truth of this, and other relations of Mr. Fox, and could not be satisfied that any such persons had suffered there: but in such a space of time the memory of it might be worn out. But he concluded hence, that it was a mistake through the default of others, that made the certificate for Mr. Fox out of the registers of Gloucester or Worcester. Whereupon this gentleman, a new edition of Fox being then in hand, sent up this information: and out of that reverence that he bore to the memory of Mr. 464 Fox, whose person and place of dwelling he knew, and the honour and love he bare to his works, he wished that this small error, which was none of his, were amended. But whether that were a mistake or not, it is certain that one Edward Horne suffered at Newent; where this Deighton had been, and spake with one or two of the same parish, that did see him there burnt, and did testify that they knew the two persons that made the fire to burn him: they were two glovers, or fellmongers, whose names he had in his note-book. And his son was then alive in the same parish, called Christopher Horn, an honest poor man, being about seventy-five or seventy-six years of age, and born in Queen Mary's time, about a quarter of a year before his father suffered. His mother, that promised to suffer with her husband, but recanted after she was condemned, was afterwards married to one that lived at Teynton, within a mile or two of Newent.

CHAP. LXIV.

Treaty about Calais. The Queen's sickness and death, with Cardinal Pole's. Her character. Her funerals. Remarks of her reign. Meetings of Protestants in this reign; and their persecutions.

Anno 1558. TOWARDS the end of the Queen's reign, there was a
Treaty a- meeting near Dorleas, between the commissioners of France,
bout Calais. of Spain, and of England: and some overture of peace was
made, but broke off upon the article of the restitution of
Calais. And (to shew what further became of the business
of Calais) after Queen Mary's death, the King of Spain renewed the like treaty, wherein Queen Elizabeth concurred.
The commissioners for the said princes met at the castle of
Cambray. In the proceeding of this treaty, at the first, the
commissioners of Spain for form, and in shew only, pretended to stand firm upon the demand of Calais; but it
was discovered, that the King's meaning was, after some ce-
remonious and perfunctory insisting thereupon, to make a
separate peace with the French, excluding the Queen,
which he did. And so left her to make her peace, after her
Cott. Vol. realm had made his wars: as we are told in an answer to a
Jul. F. 6. libel against Queen Elizabeth, touching her proceedings
with Spain. So little beholden was this kingdom to that
match with Spain.

The Papists   As the Queen declined in her health, and grew worse and
contrive to worse, by a feverish distemper wherewith the kingdom was
put by Lady
Elizabeth. then grievously infected, insomuch that there was little
hope of her life, the Papists beat their heads to put by the
succession of the Queen's sister, the Lady Elizabeth. And
they chiefly thought of Cardinal Pole, and fancied much
his fitness to be promoted to the imperial crown of this
realm, being of the blood royal: and besides him, several
others they had in their minds, probably of royal blood
too, that might serve their ends, and keep up their religion.

465 As seemed to appear by this passage. When Queen Mary
was sick, one Date, a promoter, used these words to the wife

of one Living, a prisoner before mentioned ; " *You hope,*
" *and you hope; but your hope shall be aslope :* for though
" the Queen fail, she that you hope for shall never come at
" it: for there is my Lord Cardinal's Grace, and many
" more between her and it."

    In her sickness she carried herself very devoutly : and
taking this fatherly chastisement patiently, she surrendered
herself to God, and prepared herself for death after the
manner of the popish superstition, wherein she had been
bred ; for she devoutly called for and partook of the sacraments of the Church. After she had received her supposed
saviour, the wafer, the extreme unction was administered to
her; and she repeated the Psalms of the Office without book,
as the priest read them. When the strength of her body
was quite wasted, and the use of her tongue failed her, yet
in mass-time, when the sacrament was to be elevated, she
lifted up her eyes towards it: and at the pronouncing of the
benediction, she bowed her head, and soon after yielded up
her spirit.

    The sickly Queen held out to the month of November,
when, on the 17th day thereof, she ended her life, to the
great joy of the poor professors of the purer religion ; who
had been sufficiently harassed by some of her zealots, that
shed abundance of innocent blood, and set a stain upon the
Marian days which will never be wiped off.

    If we would therefore have some fair character and praise
of Queen Mary, we must not expect it from Protestants, to
whom she was very severe; but the Papists are not sparing
herein. He that made her funeral sermon, on the 13th of
December, (when her funeral obsequies were celebrated in
Westminster with great solemnity,) saith, " that the world
" was not worthy of her, and that she was too good to tarry
" any longer here. A virtuous and a gracious lady, an in-
" nocent and unspotted Queen. And he did verily think,
" without prejudice to God's judgment, that then she was
" in heaven, and there offered up a sacrifice for them. That
" she feared God as much as the poorest creature. That

" she married herself unto her realm; and, in token of faith
" and fidelity, put a diamond ring upon her finger, which
" was never put off after, during her life. That she was
" never unmindful of her care for the nation: that she used
" singular mercy towards offenders, and much pity and
" compassion towards the poor and oppressed: clemency
" among her nobles. That she restored more noble houses
" decayed, than ever did any single prince of the realm,
" [namely, of such as had been arraigned or executed, upon
" the quarrel of the Pope and the supremacy, in the reign
" of King Henry VIII.] That she found the realm poi-
" soned with heresy, and she purged it; restored to the
" churches the ancient ornaments that had been taken away
" and spoiled. And that she, who was a member of Christ's
" Catholic Church, refused to write herself *head* thereof:
" and was herself able, by learning, to render a cause why;
" no prince having for 1500 years usurped that title, [as
" had King Henry her father.] That she argued it from
" Scripture thus, that a woman is forbid to speak in the
" Church, but the head of the Church must preach in the
466 " Church; and he must offer sacrifice for the sins of the
" dead: but it was not read, she said, either in the Old or
" New Testament, that ever woman did sacrifice. That
" there was never prince on earth that had more either of
" learning or virtue. She was praised, lastly, for her well
" taking her sickness, and disposing herself against death;
" committing herself to God, and the realm to his provi-
" dence, [not to her sister."] All this, and the like, may be
read in the sermon preached at her funeral; which I have

Number
LXXXI.
The preach-
er of her fu-
neral ser-
mon con-
fined.

transcribed from a manuscript into the Catalogue.

The preacher was White, bishop of Winchester: against
many passages in whose sermon (wherein, as he did over
extol the deceased Queen, he too much depreciated her present Majesty) such offence was taken, that he was commanded to keep his house. And there he was confined till
January 19: when being called before the Lords of the
Council, after a good admonition given him, (I use the

words of the minutes of the Council-Book,) he was set at liberty, and discharged of the said commandment of keeping
his house.

She was buried with a pomp suitable to her princely quality, by special order of the Queen her sister, and her Council, to the Marquis of Winchester, lord treasurer: to whom,
within a day or two after her death, were sent from Hatfield, (where the Queen as yet was,) the names of such persons as should be mourners at the interment; and orders
withal were given him to take care of the funerals. In answer to which, he wrote to the Council what his judgment
was of these mourners, and feared that some of them would
not care to be present; and moreover requested a warrant
of 3000*l*. for defraying the charges. To which the Lords,
November 21, gave this return: That if he should need
commandment from the Queen to such of them as should
refuse, it should be procured. And for the 3000*l*. the Lords
would consider that matter at their coming to London:
which was not above two or three days after.

When the day was come, after this manner were her
funerals performed. Her corpse was brought from St.
James's, where she died, in a chariot, with a picture or
image resembling her person, adorned with crimson velvet,
her crown on her head, and her sceptre in her hand, and
many good rings on her fingers. And so up the high way
went the foremost standard, with the falcon and the hart.
Then came a great company of mourners. And after, another goodly standard of the lion and the falcon, followed
by King Philip her husband's servants, two and two together,
in black gowns; heralds riding to and fro, to see all go in order. After, came the third standard, with the white greyhound
and the falcon. Then came gentlemen in gowns, mourners.
Then came riding esquires, bearing banners of arms. Next
came the Lord Marquis of Winchester, on horseback, bearing
the banner of the arms of England embroidered with gold.
Then Mr. Chester, the herald, bearing the helm and the
crest and mantles. Then Mr. Norroy, bearing the target,
with the garter and the crown. Then Mr. Clarencieux,

bearing the sword. And after, Mr. Garter, bearing her coat armour: all on horseback. Banners were borne about her by lords and knights; with four heralds on horseback, bearing four white banners of saints wrought with fine gold, *viz.* Mr. Somerset, Mr. Lancaster, Mr. Windsor, and Mr. York. Then came the corpse with her picture lying over her, covered with cloth of gold, the cross silver. Then followed Mr. —— with the chief mourners. And then ladies riding all in black trailed to the ground. In the chariot wherein the Queen lay, rode the pages of honour with banners in their hands. Afore the corpse, her chapel, and after, all the monks, and after them the bishops in order. And all in this equipage passed by Charing-cross to Westminster-abbey; where, at the great door of the church, every body alighted off their horses. Then were gentlemen ready to take the Queen out of her chariot: and so earls and lords went before her towards the hearse, with her picture borne between men of worship. At the church door, met her four bishops and the abbot, mitred in copes, censing the body; and so she lay all night under the hearse with watch. *Item,* There were an hundred poor men in good black gowns, bearing long torches with hoods on their heads, and arms on them. And about her the guard bearing staff-torches in black coats. And all the way chandlers having torches to supply them that had their torches burnt out.

467

On the next day, *viz.* December 14, was the Queen's mass; and all the lords and ladies, knights and gentlemen, did offer. And there was a man of arms and horse offered, and her coat armour, helmet, sword, and target, and banner of arms, and three standards. All the heralds standing about her. The Bishop of Winchester made her funeral sermon. There was offered also cloth of gold and velvet, whole pieces, and other things. After the mass and all was done, her Grace was carried up to the chapel that King Henry VII. builded, with bishops mitred. And all the officers went to the grave. And after, they brake their staves, and cast them into the grave on her. In the mean time the people plucked down the cloth, every man a piece that

could catch it, round about the church, and the arms too.
The Queen being buried, the Archbishop of York came and
declared a collation, and as soon as he had made an end, all
the trumpets blew a blast. And then the chief mourners,
the lords and knights, the bishops and the abbot went into
the abbey to dinner, and all the officers of the Queen's Court.

The news of the Queen's death was brought to King Philip her husband, by the Lord Cobham, sent to him in embassy, November 23, by Queen Elizabeth, now newly come
to the crown. Which ambassador had instructions also to
desire of the said King the renewing of such treaties and
leagues, as had passed before between the two crowns of
Spain and England. The same commission Queen Elizabeth
repeated by other succeeding ambassadors, *viz.* Sir Tho.
Chaloner and Sir Thomas Chamberlain, successively ambassadors resident in the Low Countries. And though all
these had divers times made overtures thereof both unto the
King and certain principal persons about him, he still declined it by this specious pretence, that former treaties did
stand in as good force to all intents, as new ratifications
could make them. A strange answer at that time, but conformable to his proceedings afterwards.

Cardinal Pole died the same day that Queen Mary did ;
and not many hours after her. His last will may be seen
in Holinshed's History. Therein he desired his successor
would not sue his executors for dilapidations, seeing he
had bestowed more than a thousand pounds within these
few years in repairing and making such houses as belonged
to the see, since he came to it. The overseers of his will
were Nicolas Archbishop of York, lord chancellor ; Thomas
Bishop of Ely ; Ed. Lord Hastings, lord chamberlain ; Sir
John Boxal, the Queen's secretary ; Sir Edward Cordal,
master of the rolls ; Henry Cole, vicar general of the spi-
ritualties.

There seemed to have crept about a secret report among
Papists, abroad soon after, that both Queen Mary and Car-
dinal Pole came to their ends by poison. And Osorius, a
Portugal bishop, in a book of his writ against our country,

CHAP.
LXIV.

Anno 1558.

Answer
apologeti-
cal against
Osor. f. 28.

They died
of an infec-
tious fever.

(by way of address to Queen Elizabeth,) confidently avers that Queen Mary was destroyed by poison, and putteth it to Dr. Haddon, (who had answered his scurrilous letter to Queen Elizabeth,) whether he understood any thing of that conspiracy, wherein wicked men had practised the destruction of Queen Mary and Cardinal Pole. " But," said Haddon, a knowing man, " that this was so far from truth, " that none ever believed or so much as reported this but " himself: and that all the English nation, and all other " strangers that were then in England, would manifestly re- " prove and condemn this his malicious and shameless impu- " dency. And that in truth they both died of an infectious " fever that the nation then laboured under, and seized upon " many persons of quality and honour. For there ranged " at that time a certain outrageous burning fever, which " infected all the estates in the realm, and among the rest, " shortened the lives of the richest and most honourable per- " sonages. At what time, Queen Mary, in many things " most commendable, after a few months, died of the same " disease: in like manner, Cardinal Pole, an excellent " learned man, being sick of a quartan, departed this world " the same time. He added, that as to this report, or ra- " ther invention of Osorius, (who appealed to Haddon, " whether himself understood nothing of a conspiracy to " take away the Queen's life,) he protested that there was " never any such matter spoken, written, feigned, or sur- " mised, unless by some such as himself, which having else " nothing to snarl at, did bark and howl at the clouds, " moon, and stars, ——: and that they were flying vapours, " and drowsy dreams, imagined by Osorius, whereof nei- " ther he [Haddon] or any man else ever heard, or could " hear one word."

The Queen was learned, and well disposed to religion, had she not been so misguided by her pontifician clergy. She seemed to be devout, and addicted to prayer. I have seen a prayer used by her, when she was Lady Mary, against the assaults of vice. At the end of which prayer she wrote these words, " Good Francis," [meaning, I suppose, her chaplain, Dr. Francis Mallet,] "pray that I "may have grace to obtain the petitions contained in this _____ "prayer before written : your assured loving mistress during "my life, Marie." There is also a meditation touching adversity, made by her in the year 1549 : which, I believe, was occasioned by her sickness that year. At the end of which she hath these words, written to one whom she styled 469 _cousin_, and to whom she seemed to send it, "Good cousin "Capel, I pray you, as often as you be disposed to read this "former writing, to remember me, and to pray for me, your "loving friend, Marie." In the same book is another prayer proper to be read at the hour of death ; which also might belong to the said Queen's devotions. These three prayers being very devout, and for the sake of the royal person that used them, I have put into the Catalogue.

She left the nation in a poor mean condition, sunk in their spirits with persecution, and the sense of their shame in the loss of Calais ; London, her royal chamber, impoverished, poorer by much than it was at her accession to the crown. This is set out notably by the learned Sir Thomas Smith, in an oration by him penned upon this argument : "Whe- "ther it be best for the Queen [Elizabeth] to marry a no- "bleman within her own kingdom, or some foreign prince :" wherein he hath these words ; "What decay came that time "(_viz._ of Queen Mary's reign) to the substance of the "realm, and riches both public and private, it would be no "less pity than needless to tell you. For first, what debts "the realm was left in to be paid beyond seas, you heard it "declared by Mr. Secretary in the first Parliament of the "Queen's Majesty, [_viz._ Queen Elizabeth,] and how much "it did exceed the debts of King Edward VI. What was "owing also to her subjects within the realm. It was mar- "vellous to hear how the private substance was diminished : "part might be seen by the subsidy books. In the last Par- "liament of King Philip and Queen Mary, you heard a "burgess of London make declaration and prove, that the "city of London alone was worse in substance in those five

" years [of Queen Mary] by 800,000*l.* than it was at the
" death of the late King Edward."

The nation was quite dispirited, partly with the manner of government, partly with a raging sickness that
reigned towards the latter end of this Queen, and partly
with the bloody doings and executions of poor people. To
this purpose the same writer : " I was, I assure you, ashamed
" both of my country and countrymen. They went to mus-
" ter with kerchiefs on their heads [by reason of ther sick-
" ness] to the wars, [in France,] hanging down their looks ;
" they came from thence as men dismayed and forlorn.
" They went about their matters as men amazed, that knew
" not where to begin or end. And what marvel was it,
" when here was nothing but fuming, heading, hanging,
" quartering, and burning, taxing, levying, and pulling
" down of bulwarks at home, and beggaring and losing of
" strong holds abroad. A few private men in white rochets
" ruled all : who, with setting up of six foot roods, and re-
" building of rood-lofts, thought to make all cocksure."

And the reasons of all the evils of this Queen's reign
were, by the wisest men then, attributed chiefly to two
things ; *viz.* her marriage, and her great and manifold executions of her subjects. So doth the afore alleged Sir
Thomas Smith bring in one Agamus, making an oration for
the single life of princes ; who hath these words : " We do
" not read of many, who being sole inheritors and princesses
470 " of any country, which after took unto them husbands, who
" had success after. Even in our days, Queen Mary took
" King Philip to her husband, a noble prince, was discreet
" and fortunate ; and yet many think that she lost thereby
" the hearts of the most number of her subjects. And it is
" too manifest, that immediately upon it, in a very short
" space, an incredible number of her subjects were, by or-
" der of such laws and justice as was used in those days,
" most cruelly put to death. And God for his part, whe-
" ther offended that she living solely, and as me bethought
" a virgin, did suddenly choose to marry ; or rather that she,

" finding the light of the gospel abroad in her realm, did
" what she could to extinguish and put it out; did so pu-
" nish the realm with quartan agues, and other such long
" and new sicknesses, that in the two last years of her reign
" so many of her subjects were made away, what with the
" executions of the sword and fire, and what by sickness,
" that the third part of the men in England was consumed."

And it was little to the credit of this independent kingdom, but not a little to the prejudice of it, that all Queen
Mary's counsels were seen unto and influenced by Spaniards
that belonged to King Philip; and nothing done almost but
by their direction. And a prince abroad, and that had distinct interests of his own, overruled all the counsels at
home: which occasioned Queen Elizabeth, upon her first
access to the crown, to make this order, (as I find in a diary
of Sir. W. Cecil,) " That where in the time of the late
" Queen, the King of Spain then being husband to the said
" Queen, nothing was done on the part of England, but
" with the privity and directions of the said King's minis-
" ters: now the Queen's Majesty being and professing her-
" self a free Princess, to direct all her actions by her own
" ministers, and with the advice of her Council of England
" only; meaneth in this matter to proceed and direct, with-
" out a participation toward the Spaniard of any thing,
" otherwise than shall be for the nature of her matters ex-
" pedient."

The nation governed by Spa-niards.

*Cott. Libr.
Titus C. 10.*

But notwithstanding those merciless executions for religion, it is not to be passed over without remark, that there
was a congregation of godly men at London, in the very
mouth of danger, who met together for religious worship all
the Queen's reign, from the beginning to the very end of it.
Their ministers were these among others: Edmund Scamler,
afterward bishop of Peterborough; Tho. Foule; Augustin
Bernher, sometime Latimer's servant; Tho. Bentham, afterward bishop of Coventry and Litchfield; Tho. Rose, who
endured much in those times, but escaped; John Rough, a
Scotchman, that was taken and burnt. A deacon of this
congregation latewardly, who had a list of their names, was

Gospellers meet to-gether in London all Queen Mary's reign.

Their mi-nisters.

Cutbert Simpson, who was also taken and burnt; and who endured great tortures, because he would not produce his list, nor discover the names of the brethren. Upon any cases of difficulty or emergences, this congregation sent some of their members beyond sea, to some of the learned exiles there, for their resolution, counsel, and advice; and so they returned again to the flock. And some they had, whom they sent to the prisons, to visit, counsel, comfort, and relieve those that lay there for religion. Of these, the names **471** of two were Coles and Ledley, who were about the year 1557 detected, by one Ty, a priest, to bishop Boner, as were a great many more by false brethren.

Their meetings were at several places, as it was appointed by themselves; for they often changed their places for more privacy and security. Sometimes it was at Black Friars, at Sir Tho. Cardine's house, who was of the privy chamber to King Henry VIII. Again, sometimes the meeting was somewhere about Aldgate; sometimes in a clothworker's loft, near the great conduit in Cheapside. Once or twice in a ship at Billingsgate, belonging to a good man of Lee in Essex. Other times at a ship called Jesus Ship, lying between Ratcliff and Rotherith; there twice or thrice, till it came to be known. Other times in a cooper's house in Puddenlane. Sometimes in Thames-street; sometimes in Bow-churchyard; and sometimes in Islington, or in the fields thereabouts. These meetings were often in the night times. There would be in these assemblies forty, and sometimes an hundred, or more, met together; and toward the latter end of the Queen the number increased, though the malice of their enemies decreased not. At these meetings they had collections for Christ's prisoners, and would gather sometimes ten pounds at a night-meeting. But they could not be so private, but that now and then they were discovered and taken. To some of these secret assemblies resorted such as were spies, who were sent to serve as informers and witnesses. Such an one once came to take their names and spy their doings; but while he was among them, he cried them pardon, and was converted to become one of them.

And as in the south parts, so likewise in the north, there were divers that professed the gospel, and had their preachers and pastors. As George Marsh, who suffered burning at Chester. In Yorkshire was Mr. Best, who was after bishop of Carlisle; Mr. Brodbank, Mr. Reneses, Mr. Russel. And these privately went from place to place in Lancashire, and in those northern parts bordering, and preached the gospel to select companies, assembled by assignation, and sometimes gave the communion. One Jeffry Hurst, of Shakerly in Lancashire, but fled from thence, being known to be a professor of the gospel, and being sought for; and dwelt privately in Yorkshire and thereabouts: such was his love to his friends and country, that he would sometimes bring some of these ministers to Shakerly. In the bishopric of Durham was Bernard Gilpin, afterwards commonly called Father Gilpin, placed at the rectory of Essington, by Bishop Tunstal, his great uncle. This man, though he made a shift to comply with the Church at that time, yet he preached the word of God honestly and sincerely, and sharply taxed the vices that then reigned in it, and propounded the doctrine of salvation plainly and soundly; and the clergy's faults he touched to the quick. He believed not transubstantiation, and justification he explained after the manner of the reformers. So that had he not had the Bishop of Durham to his friend and relation, he might have undergone great danger. For some accused him to the Bishop as a man that deserved burning. But hereby the seeds of true religion were sown in those parts. And which tended more to the spreading of religion through those northern quarters, he was after removed to Hough- ton, a parish containing fourteen villages; where he persevered constantly in the duty of his ministry. And such was his pity of many parishes in Northumberland, through impropriations destitute of ministers, in the parts called Riddesdale and Tyndale, (among the inhabitants of which the word of God was never heard to be preached; and the most they had was an ignorant priest hired by the impropriator to read the mass,) that hither, out of zeal to God's glory, and compassion to the souls of the people, he resorted once a year to preach, teach, and instruct them; and so continued to do in the reign of Queen Elizabeth.

That five years reign consisted of abundance of violences, oppressions, injustices, and slaughters: insomuch that they who felt it, and outlived it, made hideous descriptions of it. Her they called *Jezebel, Athaliah,* and *unnatural woman.* " No, no woman," saith one of them, " but a monster, " and the Devil of hell, covered over with the shape of a " woman." The injustices and cruelties exercised by her authority, wrung from them expressions too unseemly to be given to a crowned head. They were the more offended with her, because it was, in a great measure, by the means of their party that she arrived to the crown. For they were the great instruments of setting her in her throne, and expected to have some better usage for their pains. And so all their love to her turned into hatred. And black are the representations that some of these men made of her government. As, " that they could not be suffered to enjoy their " right inheritances, but whatsoever they had was, either by " open force or crafty dealing, pulled from them. They were " more ungentle than common thieves, more empty of mercy " than common murderers. For they were not only con- " tented to have the goods of the people, but they would " have it delivered to them by the owners own hands, that " it might be said to the world, they gave it with the heart. " Nor were they herewith pleased, but would have their " lives, that they should not bewray them. And yet herewith " they were not satisfied, but they meant to root out the " whole progeny and nation of Englishmen, that none " should be left to revenge or cry out of their extremities, " and to bring our country into the Spanish dominion. One " brother killed another, children laid violent hands on " their parents, children were murdered in the sight of their " parents, and parents in the sight of their children. Nay " further, these unnatural English tormenters and tyrants " would be gods, and reign in the consciences and souls of " men. Every man, woman, and child must deny Christ

The Pro-
testants
speak plain-
ly of this
Queen.
Hales ora-
tion.

"in word, openly abhor Christ in deed, slander his gospel
"with word and deed, worship and honour false gods, as
"they would have them, and as themselves did, and so give
"body and soul to the Devil, or secretly fly, or after un-
"heard torments to be burnt openly. They compared this
"persecution to that of Pharaoh, Herod, Caligula, Nero,
"Domitian, &c. nay exceeding it."

Another that lived in and after these evil days wrote
thus: "For refusing that most unlawful and wicked oath
"of the Pope's supremacy, and not acknowledging of his
"usurped authority, a great number both of learned and
"unlearned, as well of the laity as of the clergy, of women
"as men, of young as old, have lost not only their livings
"and all their goods, but also as many of them as escaped
"not out of their country into miserable exile, were appre-
"hended, and cast into most vile prisons; being not set, but
"hanged, in stocks and irons, both feet, hands, and neck; and
"after long punishments and pining, most painful and piti-
"ful also to all, saving only pitiless Papists, have finally
"lost their lives, being most cruelly consumed by terrible
"flames of fire into ashes; if they might obtain so much
"mercy, as to escape that usual long, lingering and roasting
"in smoke, and smoky fire."

Very many they were that fell under the severities of this
reign for their religion only: but the exact number I perceive is not known, because of the variety I observe among
the historians, that pretend to set down how many: as, for
example, one historian thus:

"Anno 1555. Burnt, in sundry places and times, eighty;
"besides those that died in prison: of which some were cast
"into the fields unburied, and some buried in the courts and
"back-sides of the prisons where they died.

"Anno 1556. Burnt eighty-six: whereof many were wo-
"men and maidens.

"Anno 1557. Burnt sixty-seven: of which about twenty
"were women."

Anno 1558. The number not mentioned, only it is expressed to be a great many in divers places.

Marginal notes:
CHAP. LXIV.
Anno 1558.
Imprisonment, torture, burning, exercised. Noel's Reproof, p. 12. 473
The number bers that suffered under Queen Mary.
Cooper.
80.
86.
67.

CHAP.
LXIV.

Anno 1558.
Vol. ii. p.
364.

According to Bishop Burnet, in his History of the Reformation, the numbers consumed by fire under those years
stood thus:

Anno 1555, burnt 72
Anno 1556, — 94
Anno 1557, — 79
Anno 1558, — 39
In all 284

Wev. Mon.
p. 116.

Speed the historian recounts the numbers in this method,
at it was transcribed by Wever in his Monuments: " In the
" heat of whose flames were burnt to ashes five bishops,
" one and twenty divines, eight gentlemen, eighty-four arti-
" ficers, an hundred husbandmen, servants, and labourers,
" twenty-six wives, twenty widows, nine virgins, two boys,
" and two infants; one of them whipped to death by Boner,
" and the other springing out of the mother's womb from
" the stake, as she burned, thrown again into the fire.
" Sixty-four more were persecuted for their profession of
" faith: whereof seven were whipped, sixteen perished in
474 " prison, twelve buried in dunghills. Many lay in captivity
" condemned, but were released and saved by the auspi-
" cious entrance of peaceable Elizabeth:" and fled the land
in those days of distress, which by her, upon their return,
were honourably preferred. So that, according to this cal-
culation, the number of those that were burnt amounted to
277.

The reason
of the va-
riety of
historians
herein.

And no wonder need be made at this variety, considering
how the accounts of the numbers of the burned were gathered up by divers men, and the intelligences they received
thereof from their friends throughout all the parts of the
nation; which were more or less perfect, according to the
informations they could come by.

Those that
suffered un-
der Queen
Mary, and
those that
suffered un-
der Queen
Elizabeth,
compared.

But we may best depend upon the account given us by
the Lord Burghley, in his treatise, called *Execution of Justice in England*, writ in the year 1583: who there reckon-
eth the number together of those that died in that reign by
imprisonment, torments, famine, and fire, to be near 400.
And among that lord's MSS. I find a paper, making the

burned to amount to the number of 290: which, setting down the particulars, may deserve place in the Catalogue.

The Papists have studiously laboured to lessen the charge of blood that the Protestants lay to this unhappy Queen Mary, and think to stifle it by aggrandizing the sufferings of their own party under her sister Queen Elizabeth: hoping to make the world believe, that even those that were put to death for treason were martyrs for religion; crying out loud of the great numbers that have been executed under that Queen. To lay therefore this matter plainly open before every impartial man, that he may make a true comparison between those that were burnt and made away under Queen Mary, and those that died under Queen Elizabeth, I shall recite the words of the great noble author before mentioned, who had opportunities of being thoroughly acquainted with the matters of those times, and lived in the middle of them, and who was withal an observing and honest man. He writes thus:

" To make the matter seem more horrible or lamentable, " they [who had writ infamous libels against the Queen] " recite the particular names of all the persons, [that were " put to death,] which by their own catalogue exceed, not " for these twenty-five years' space, above the number of " threescore; forgetting, or rather with their stony and " senseless hearts not regarding, in what cruel sort, in the " time of Queen Mary, which little exceeded the space of " five years, the Queen's Majesty's reign being five times as " many, there were by imprisonment, torments, famine, and " fire, of men, women, maidens, and children, almost the " number of four hundred. And of that number, above " twenty that had been archbishops, bishops, and principal " prelates or officers in the Church lamentably destroyed; " and of women above threescore; and of children above " forty: and amongst the women some great with child, out " of whose bodies the child by fire was expelled alive, and " yet also cruelly burnt: examples beyond all heathen " cruelty. And most of the youth of them suffered cruel " death, both men, women, and children, (which is to be

" noted,) were such as had never by the sacrament of bap-
" tism, or by confirmation, professed, nor were ever taught,
" or instructed, or ever had heard of any other kind of reli-
" gion, but only of that which by their blood and death, in
" the fire, they did as true martyrs testify. A matter of
" another sort, to be lamented with simplicity of words, and
" not with puffed eloquence, than the execution in this time
" of a very few traitors: who also in their time, if they ex-
" ceeded thirty years of age, had in their baptism professed,
" and in their youth had learned the same religion, which
" they now so bitterly oppugned. And beside that, in their
" opinions they differ much from the martyrs of Queen
" Mary's time: for though they continued in the profession
" of the religion wherein they were christened, yet they
" never at their death denied their lawful Queen, nor main-
" tained any of her open and foreign enemies, nor procured
" any rebellion or civil war, nor did sow any sedition in se-
" cret corners, nor withdrew any subjects from their obe-
" dience, as these sworn servants of the Pope have conti-
" nually done."

A passage
of Archbi-
shop Bram-
hal con-
cerning the
cruelties
under
Queen
Mary.
Just. Vin-
dic. cap. 3.

To which I will add the vindication of our nation, which
a later worthy author made to the same clamour raised by
Papists against the severity used towards the Roman Catholics in this kingdom. " He might have considered,"
saith he, " that more Protestants suffered death in the short
" reign of Queen Mary, men, women, and children, than
" Roman Catholics in all the longer reigns of all our
" princes, since the Reformation, put together. The former
" by fire and fagot, a cruel lingering torment, *ut sentirent*
" *se mori, that they might feel themselves to die* by degrees;
" the other by the gibbet, with some opprobrious circum-
" stances, to render their sufferings more exemplary to others.
" The former merely and immediately for religion, be-
" cause they would not be Roman Catholics, without any
" the least pretext of the violation of any political law; the
" latter not merely and immediately for religion, because
" they were Roman Catholics; for many known Roman
" Catholics in England have lived and died in greater plen-

" ty, and power, and reputation, in every prince's reign
" since the Reformation, than an English Protestant could
" live among the Irish Roman Catholics since their insur-
" rection. If a subject was taken at mass itself in England,
" which was very rare, it was but a pecuniary mulct. No
" stranger was ever questioned about his religion. I may
" not here omit King James's affirmation, that ' no man in
" his reign, nor in the reign of his predecessor Queen Eli-
" zabeth, did suffer death for conscience sake, or religion.'
" But they suffered for the violation of civil laws, as either
" for not acknowledging the political supremacy of the King
" in ecclesiastical causes over ecclesiastical persons; or else
" for returning into this kingdom so qualified with forbidden
" orders, as the laws of the land do not allow; or, lastly,
" for attempting to seduce some of the King's subjects from
" the religion established in the land."

But to make some few reflections more upon the professors and sufferers in Queen Mary's reign: which are not
mine, but made by one who lived in the middle of those
evils, and narrowly escaped himself.   " The faithful Lord
" in all these turmoilings preserved his servants, giving unto
" a number of them such a princely spirit, that they were
" able to deride and laugh to scorn the threatenings of the
" tyrants, to despise the terribleness of prisons and tor-
" ments, and in the end most joyfully to overcome and con-
" quer death, to the praise of God, and their own endless
" comfort.   Unto other some the self-same most gracious
" God gave such a valiant spirit, that they were able, by
" his grace, to forsake the pleasures and commodities of this
" world, and being armed with patience, were content to
" travel into far and unknown countries with their families
" and households, having small worldly provision, or none
" at all, but trusting to his providence, who never faileth
" them that trust in him.   Besides this, the same God pre-
" served a great number even in the midst of their enemies,
" not only from bodily dangers, but also from being in-
" fected with that poisoned and blasphemous doctrine, that
" then in all pulpits, with shameless brags and ostentation,

CHAP.
LXIV.

Anno 1559.

The con-
stancy of
the profess-
ors.
Aug. Bern-
her Pref. to
Lat. Ser-
mons.

476

CHAP. LXIV.

Anne 1558.

"was set abroad. I will not speak now of that wonderful "work of God, who caused his word to be preached, and "his sacraments ministered even in the midst of the enemies, "in spite of the Devil and his ministers."

The evils of this reign.

In short, it was a sad and uncomfortable reign to this nation; and those that lived in it, and outlived it, were best able to describe it. One, a wise and observing man, thought to be Archbishop Parker, in his preface to a book writ by

Def. of Priests' Mar. Pref. fol. 8.

another, in *Defence of Priests' Marriage*, speaks of the miseries of this time, and calls them "the plagues that Al- "mighty God revenged the contempt of his holy institution "in the aforesaid reign, and that it was not like the notabi- "lity thereof would be forgotten to be transmitted to their "posterity in writing." And he proceedeth to enumerate

Rains, tempests, drought, famine, fevers. Coop. Chron.

the evils of this reign. "What immoderate rains and tem- "pests raged in one year! What intolerable heat and "droughts in another year! What penury and scarceness of "corn and victuals! What hunger and famine thereof fol- "lowed!" Add, what diseases and sicknesses every where prevailed! the like whereof had never been known before, both for the lasting and mortality of them: which being hot burning fevers, and other strange diseases, began in the great dearth 1556, and increased more and more the two following years. In the summer 1557, they raged horribly throughout the realm, and killed an exceeding great number of all sorts of men, but especially gentlemen, and men of great wealth. So many husbandmen and labourers also died, and were sick, that in harvest time, in divers places, men would have given one acre of corn to reap and carry in another. In some places corn stood and shed on the ground for lack of workmen. In the latter end of the year, quartan agues were so common among men, women, and young children also, that few houses escaped: and these agues were not only common, but to most persons very dangerous, especially such as had been sick of the burning fevers be- fore. In 1558, in the summer, about August, the same fevers raged again in such manner, as never plague or pesti- lence, I think, saith my author, killed a greater number. If the people of the realm had been divided into four parts, certainly three parts of those four should have been found sick. And hereby so great a scarcity of harvest-men, that those which remained took twelve pence for that which was 477 wont to be done for three pence. In some shires no gentleman almost escaped, but either himself, or his wife, or both, were dangerously sick, and very many died: so that divers places were left void of ancient justices and men of worship to govern the country. Many that kept twenty or thirty in their houses, had not three or four able to help the residue that were sick. In most poor men's houses, the master, dame, and servants, were all sick, in such sort, that one could not help another. The winter following also, the quartan agues continued in like manner, or more vehemently than they had done last year. At this time also died many priests, that a great number of parish churches, in divers places of the realm, were unserved, and no curates could be gotten for money. All which, and a great many miseries more now lying upon the nation, and the loss of Calais not the least, looked like the frowns of God upon the Queen and her government. And in the midst of these calamities she expired. And she that wrote herself by her marriage, Queen of so many kingdoms, Duchess of so many dukedoms, and Marchioness of so many marquisates, left less riches in her coffers, and wealth in the realm, at the time of her death, than any of her progenitors did.

This destruction of the ministers of the gospel, partly by burning and execution, and partly by exile and discouragement of the study of divinity, had this inconvenience, that in the next reign there was great want of clergy to supply the churches of the kingdom, and to perform divine service, according to the reformation of religion established. For the remedy whereof, many laymen, and such as had followed secular callings, were ordained ministers: namely, such as could read well, and were pious, and of sober conversation, to serve in some of the parish churches for the present necessity. This was thrown by Papists in the teeth of the reformers, in the beginning of Queen Elizabeth. Dorman,

Want of clergymen.

Anno 1558.
Artificers
made mi-
nisters.
Dorm. Re-
proof. one of these in these times, thus in foul terms describes it. And first, concerning Nowel, dean of Paul's, that had been master of Westminster school in King Edward's days, and fled abroad under the persecution, " that so soon upon his " returning home, of a mean schoolmaster, became so va- " liant a preacher : unless perhaps the same spirit that hath " of late divines in their shops, and disputing upon the ale- " bench for their degrees, (so many tinkers, cobblers, cow- " herds, broom-men, fiddlers, and such like,) have also made " him a preacher among the rest."

To which slander, Nowel gave this sober answer : (which will acquaint us with the true state of this matter, and suffi- ciently throw the reproach upon the priests of those days :) " None such reputed or counted divines among us, as you " lyingly slander us. Indeed, your most cruel murdering " of so many learned men hath forced us, of mere necessity, " to supply some small cures with honest artificers, exer-

The reason
thereof.
Noel's Con-
futat. " cised in the Scriptures ; not in place of divines, bachelors, " or doctors, but instead of popish Sir John Lack-Latins, " and of all honesty ; instead of Dr. Dicer, bachelor Bench- " whistler, master Card-player, the usual sciences of your 478 " popish priests : who continually disputed, *pro et contra*, " for their form upon their ale-bench ; where you should " not miss of them in all towns and villages : instead of " such chaplains of trust, more meet to be tinkers, cow- " herds, yea, bearwards and swineherds, than ministers in " Christ's Church. That some honest artificers, who, in- " stead of such popish books as dice and cards, have tra- " vailed in the Scriptures."

CHAP. LXV.

Creations under this Queen. Her privy counsellors. Li- cences of retainder. To whom granted.

Creations of
noblemen.
E MSS.
Rev. Patr.
Johan. D.
Epis. Elien. THOSE that were ennobled by this Queen, or restored to their ancient honours, were these :

Edward Courtney, son to Henry Courtney, marquis of

Exeter, was restored, and created Earl of Devonshire, at Richmond, September the 3d, in the first year of the Queen, and died at Padua in Italy, without issue, being the last of this noble and ancient family.

Thomas Percie, son of Sir Tho. Percie, knt. was restored, and advanced to the degree of a baron, April 30, the 3d and 4th of Philip and Mary, and the day following to the earldom of Northumberland. He was made general warden of the east and middle marches, 10 *Elizab.* After attainted, and suffered death at York for treason, in the twelfth of the said Queen.

Anthony Browne, created Viscount Mountague, 2 Sept. 1st and 2d of Philip and Mary, and made knight of the most noble order of the Garter. He was the son of Sir Anthony Browne, and of Lady Lucie his wife, daughter and one of the heirs of John Nevyl, marquis of Mountague.

William Howard, third son of Thomas Duke of Norfolk, was created Lord Howard of Effingham, March 11, 1 *Mar.* and March 20, Lord High Admiral of England, Ireland, and Wales, and knight of the most noble order of the Garter. Had issue by his first wife, a daughter, named Agnes; by his second, Charles and other sons.

Sir Edward North, knt. baron of Carteleigh, by summons to Parliament 1st *Mariæ.* He was father to Roger Lord North; and took his place in Parliament April 7.

Sir John Williams, knt. created Lord Williams of Thame, April 5, at St. James's: and upon the Queen's marriage was made Lord Chamberlain to King Philip. He had issue, two daughters and heirs: one married to Henry Lord Norris, and the other to Sir Richard Wenman, knt.

Sir John à Bruges, knt. was, April 8, 1 *Mariæ,* created Baron Chandois of Sudeley, and died the same year. Whose son was Edmond Lord Chandois, succeeding his father in this honour. In the first of the Queen, he was made lieutenant of the Tower.

Sir Edward Hastings, knt. third son to George Earl of Huntington, became Lord Hastings of Loughborough, by 479 summons to Parliament, the 4th and 5th Phil. and Mar. He was lord chamberlain to Queen Mary, and knt. of the noble order of the Garter: having been made in the first of the Queen a privy counsellor, master of her horse, and receiver of the honour of Leicester. Died without issue.

The
Queen's
Council.

The Queen's counsellors towards the latter end of her reign were these that follow: whereof those that have asterisks were laid aside the next reign, as I took them out of a journal of the Lord Burleigh's; the rest continued privy counsellors to Queen Elizabeth, viz.

* Reginald, Cardinal Pole.
* Nicolas, Archbp. of York, Lord Chancellor.
Powlet, Marquis of Winchester, Lord Treasurer.
Fitz Allen, Earl of Arundel.
Talbot, Earl of Shrewsbury.
* Henry, Earl of Bath.
Stanley, Earl of Darby.
Herbert, Earl of Pembroke.
Edward Lord Clinton, Lord Admiral.
Lord Howard of Effingham.
* Brown, Viscount Mountague.
* Thirlby, Bishop of Ely.
* William Lord Paget.
* ——Lord Wentworth.
* Richard Lord Ryche.

* Edward Lord Hastings of Loughborough.
* Sir Thomas Cornwalleys.
* Sir Francis Englefield.
* Sir Edward Waldgrave.
* Sir John Mordaunt.
Sir Thomas Cheyney.
Sir William Petre.
Sir John Mason.
Sir Richard Sackvil.
* Sir Thomas Wharton.
* Sir John Bourn.
Dr. Wotton, Dean of Canterbury.
* Dr. Boxal.
* Sir Henry Jernegam.
* Sir Henry Beddingfield.
* Sir Edmund Peckham.
* Sir Robert Peckham.
* Sir William Cordell.
* Sir Clement Higham.
* Sir Richard Southwel.

Licences to
retain.

It was a fault in this reign, that so many retainers were granted. For Queen Mary granted more by half in her short five years, than her sister and successor in thirteen. For in all that time there were but fifteen licences of retainer

granted: whereas Queen Mary had granted nine and
thirty. She was more liberal also in yielding the number of
retainers to each person; which sometimes amounted to two
hundred: whereas Queen Elizabeth never yielded above
an hundred to any person of the greatest quality, and that
rarely too. But Bishop Gardiner began that ill example,
who retained two hundred men: whereas under Queen
Elizabeth, the Duke of Norfolk retained but an hundred,
and Parker, archbishop of Canterbury, but forty. A retainer
was a servant, not menial, (that is, continually dwelling in
the house of his lord or master,) but only wearing his livery,
and attending sometimes upon special occasions upon him.
The livery was wont to consist of hats or hoods, badges
and other suits of one garment by the year. These licences
were given many times to lords and gentlemen on purpose
for maintenance of quarrels, and many murders were committed by the means thereof, and feuds kept up among the
nobility and gentry. The catalogue of the retainers in this
reign was as followeth :

CHAP.
LXVI.

Anno 1558.

Anno primo regni Mariæ.
Stephen Bishop of Win-
  chester 200
Sir William Petre, knt. 60
Henry Earl of Arundel 200
Nicolas Bp. of Worcester 10
William Lord Paget 100

*Annis 1st and 2d Phil. and
  Mary.*
William Earl of Pem-
  broke . . . 100
Sir George Herbert, knt. 40
Sir Henry Tirrel . 20

*Annis 2 and 3 Phil. and
  Mary.*
Sir Richard Southwel, kt. 40
Sir Robert Southwel,
  knt. 20

Sir Edward Hastings,   480
  knt. . . . . . 100 To whom
Sir Francis Englefield   granted:
                              and the
  knt. . . . . . 100 numbers of
                              retainers to
Sir Edward Gage, knt. 30 each.
John Wadham, esq. 10
Edward Lord Clynton 100
Sir Nic. Hare, knt. . 40
Sir Robert Brooke, knt. 10
Sir John Bourne, knt. 40
Roger Lygon . . . 16
Sir Henry Jerningham
  knt. 100
Anthony Visc. Moun-
  tague . . . 60
*Ann. 3 and 4 Phil. and
  Mary.*
James Basset . . 20

Nic. Abp. of York .	60
Sir William Cordel, knt.	12
Sir Tho. Wharton, knt.	30
Anthony Hungerford	20
Richard Forest . .	40
Sir Robert Rochester, knt.	60
Henry Earl of Westmerland . . .	100
Anthony Brown, sergeant at law. . .	20
Lady Jane Dormer .	10
Sir William Dormer, knt.	30

Ann. 4 and 5 Phil. and Mary.

Sir John Tregonwell, knt.	30
Tho. Earl of Northumberland	100
Thomas Babington and William his son .	30
John Arundel . .	40
Richard Manxel . .	50

Ann. 5 and 6 Phil. and Mary.

John Boxal, clerk .	10
Richard Wilbraham .	10

CHAP. XLVI.

The Lady Elizabeth succeeds to the crown. The exiles return. Good omens of her ensuing reign.

The exiles return.

To Queen Mary succeeded the excellent Princess Elizabeth, her sister; whom God raised up to rescue this land from the ruin impending over it. The exiles now returned apace from their several towns and cities, where they were retired from the late stormy wind and tempest at home. Those at Basil had the news of their speedy return told them the day before the Queen's death. It was strange, but true. For Elmer (bishop of London afterwards) was present when John Fox preached there: where, among other arguments which he used for the consolation of the poor English, he bade them be of good comfort; for the time drew near, that they should be restored to their own country; and said, that this he told them, *Dei monitu,* being *warned by God* so to do. He was reproved by the elder sort for thus preaching. But the issue of things excused him. And by comparing the times, it appears that he preached this sermon but the day before the Queen's death.

The news of it first came to Strasburgh : and some gentlemen there sent messengers to Zuric, to the English there,
coming thither with the tidings on the last day of November ; which was but twelve or thirteen days after the Queen's 481
death. The next day, being December 1st, P. Martyr
(then professor at Zuric) sent the news of it to Calvin,
whereby it became known to the English at Geneva, if they
had it not before. Great expectation now there was among
the chief professors of religion ; but yet not without some
fear : as appeared from this clause in Martyr's letter to
Calvin : " Perhaps now is the time for the walls of Jerusa-
" lem to be built again in that kingdom ; that the blood of
" so many martyrs so largely shed, may not be in vain."
And December 22d following, the same Peter Martyr sent a
letter to Queen Elizabeth, full of good exhortations ; stirring
her up to reform the Church : which, I suppose, he did by
the secret advice of some of the Protestant exiles at Zuric,
as well as by his own inclination.

The joys and benefits of this change of government from
one sister to another, of such different minds and religions,
I will declare in the eloquent words of one that had opportunity of knowing them.

Domi quid est, quod ad salutem vel solatium quispiam
excogitare possit, quo homines non prius frui quam sperare
inciperent? Qui domi profugerant, revocati, qui carceribus
astricti, liberati, qui bona amiserant, donati, qui dignitate
exuti, restituti. Sunt leges interim iniquæ abrogatæ, latæ
salubres. Pax mentibus, conscientiæ libertas, concordia
ordinibus, securitas bonis, redierat. That is, " What was
" there here at home, which any could think of, tending
" either to safety or comfort, but the people began to en-
" joy, even before they could hope for ? The exiles were
" called home ; the prisoners were set at liberty ; they that
" had lost their goods had them bestowed on them ; they
" that were deprived of their honours were restored. Un-
" just laws in the mean time were abrogated, and wholesome
" ones made. Peace was recovered to men's minds, liberty

" to their consciences, concord to the states, and security to
" good men."

The nation felt themselves quite in another condition.
Their hearts were filled with joy, and replenished with
vigorous hopes of blessed times a coming, and their mouths
with praise for their new Queen. Hancock, one of the exiled
clergy, hath these words: " Had not our godly, wise,
" learned, and merciful Queen Elizabeth stood in the gap
" of God's wrath, and been the instrument of God to restore
" the everlasting word of God unto us, we had been bond-
" slaves unto the proud, vicious Spaniard :" and then he
makes this prayer for her:

" O eternal, omnipotent, and most merciful God; who
" didst, by thy merciful providence, preserve our most
" gracious Queen Elizabeth, in the dangerous days of the
" reign of her Majesty's most unnatural sister, Queen Mary,
" to this end, that thou, a most merciful God, wouldst, by
" her Majesty, set forth thy glory, in restoring to us again
" the jewel and treasure of thy most sacred and holy word :
" we beseech thee, O Lord, make us thankful: preserve her
" Majesty, that, if it be thy blessed will, we may a long
" time enjoy this great treasure and jewel of thy most holy
" word: that her Grace may, by thy mighty power, so de-
482 " fend and protect this her realm, from the rule and govern-
" ment of strange nations, that we may never be spoiled
" again of the same. And that it may please thee, of thy
" merciful goodness, so to rule and govern us, that we her
" subjects, with thy grace, may be diligent hearers of thy
" word, and obedient followers of the same. So that for our
" unthankfulness we provoke not thy wrath (as in the days
" of good King Edward) to take from us so most godly,
" pitiful, and peaceable a Princess: but that she may a long
" time rule and govern both these her realms of England
" and Ireland; to the confusion of the Papists, her ene-
" mies, and to the great comfort of thy children, her loving
" subjects. Grant this for thy dear Son, Christ Jesus sake."
To which I will add another pious prayer, composed for

her and the Church, by another exile, (soon after Bishop of Durham,) upon her first coming to the crown, in the name of the people of England.

CHAP.
LXVI.

Anno 1559.

Another prayer for her. Bishop Pilkington's Exposit. upon Hagg.

" Most righteous Judge and merciful Father, which of
" love didst punish thy people, being negligent in building
" thy house; that by such sharp correction they might be
" stirred up to do their duty, and so have pleased thee:
" we acknowledge and confess before the world and thy
" divine Majesty, that we have no less offended thee in this
" behalf, than they have done; and that for all the sharp
" plagues which thou laidst upon us, we could not awake
" out of our dead sleep; and forgetting the earnest promo-
" tion of thy glory and true religion, rather consented to
" the persecution of thy true and faithful people: until
" now, that of thine infinite goodness, by giving us a
" gracious Queen, and restoring the light of thy word, thou
" hast letten us taste of the treasures of thy mercies: we
" fall down flat therefore before the throne of grace, de-
" siring pardon for this great negligence, and of all our
" former offences, and pray thee, that thou wilt not deal
" with us as we have deserved, but, as of thine own free
" will thou promisedst thy people, falling earnestly to thy
" work, and restoring thy temple, that from thenceforward
" thou wouldest bless all their works and fruits, overthrow
" their enemies, and save thy people. That thou wouldest
" make that house also more glorious than the first, by the
" preaching of thy gospel. So we desire thee, for Christ's
" sake, to be no less good and gracious Lord unto us, yet
" once again, going about to restore thy true religion, trod-
" den down and defaced by the cruel Papists. Send forth,
" O Lord, many such faithful preachers, as will set out thy
" glory unfeignedly. Open the hearts of thy people, that
" they may see how far more acceptable unto thee is the
" lively preaching of thy holy word, than all the glittering
" ceremonies of popery. Deliver us, we beseech thee, from
" all our enemies. Save and preserve our gracious Queen
" as thine own signet: endue her and her Council with such
" reverence and fear of thee, that all policy which is con-

M 3

CHAP.
LXVI.

Anno 1558.

483

" trary to thy word set apart, they may uprightly seek and
" maintain thy true glory, minister justice, punish sin, and
" defend the right. Confound, most mighty God, and bring
" to naught all the devices of such as go about to over-
" throw thy word and true worship. Open our eyes, that
" we may see how dearly thou hast loved us in Jesus
" Christ, thy Son our Lord. Hold us fast, O Lord of hosts,
" that we fall no more from thee. Grant us thankful and
" obedient hearts, that we may increase daily in the love,
" knowledge, and fear of thee. Increase our faith, and help
" our unbelief. That we, being provided for and relieved
" in all our needs by thy fatherly care and providence, as
" thou shalt think good, may live a godly life to thy praise,
" and good example of thy people; and after this life, may
" reign with thee for ever through Christ our Saviour. To
" whom with thee and the Holy Ghost, three Persons and
" one God, be praise and thanksgivings in all congregations
" for ever and ever. *Amen.*"

Good
omens in
Queen Eli-
sabeth.

And it was not without ground, that the nation conceived
such great hope of being happily governed under this lady,
both in regard of her mild and serene beginnings: whereas
the former Queen's first footsteps into her government, was
nothing but storm and ruffle, violation of laws, terrors and
threatenings, imprisonments and executions: and in regard
likewise of the excellency of her nature, her genuine modesty, learning, and piety. Of both these, take what is said
by one, afterward Bishop of London, but then living in the
Court, and so well knew her in her younger days, and at
her accession to the crown.

Her mild
entrance.
Harbour
for faithful
Subjects.
By J. Elmer.

" Mark her coming in, said he, and compare it with
" others. She comes in like a lamb, and not like a lion;
" like a mother, and not like a step-dame. She rusheth not
" in at the first chop, to violate and break former laws; to
" stir her people to change what they list, before order be
" taken by law. She hangeth no man, she beheadeth none,
" she burneth none, spoileth none."

Her modest
apparel.

And this was his character of her in her younger years.
" The King, said he, left her rich clothes and jewels; and

" that he knew it to be true, that in seven years after her
" father's death, she never in all that time looked upon that
" rich attire and precious jewels but once, and that against
" her will. And that there never came gold or stone upon
" her head, till her sister forced her to lay off her former
" soberness, and bear her company in her glittering gayness.
" And then she so ware it, as every man might see that her
" body carried that which her heart misliked. I am sure,
" said he, (and he that said it was about that time at Court,
" tutor to the Lady Jane Grey,) that her maidenly ap-
" parel which she used in King Edward's time, made the
" noblemen's daughters and wives to be ashamed to be
" dressed and painted like peacocks; being more moved
" with her most virtuous example, than with all that ever
" Paul or Peter wrote touching that matter. Yea, this
" I know, added he, that a great man's daughter, [the
" Duke of Suffolk's daughter Jane, he means,] receiving
" from Lady Mary, before she was Queen, goodly apparel
" of tinsel, cloth of gold and velvet, laid on with parch-
" ment lace of gold, when she saw it, said, What shall I
" do with it? Marry, said a gentlewoman, wear it. Nay,
" quoth she, that were a shame to follow my Lady Mary
" against God's word, and leave my Lady Elizabeth, which
" followeth God's word.

" And when all the ladies at the coming of the Scots
" Queen [in King Edward's reign] went with their hair
" frounced, curled, and double curled, she altered nothing,
" but kept her old maidenly shamefacedness.

484

" She never meddled with money, but against her will;
" but seemed to set so little by it, that she thought to touch
" it was to defile her pure hands, consecrated to turn over
" good books, to lift up unto God in prayer, and to deal
" alms to the poor.

She seldom
touched
money.

" She was virtuously and virgin-like brought up; honest,
" discreet, sober, and godly women about her; trained up
" in learning, and that not vulgar and common, but the
" purest and the best, which was most commended; as the
" tongues, arts, and God's word: wherein she so exceed-

Her learn-
ing.

" ingly profited, as I myself can witness, (saith my author,)
" that seven years past, [viz. in the year 1552,] she was
" not, in the best kinds of learning, inferior to those, that
" all their lifetime had been brought up in the Universities.

Her school-
master's ac-
count of
her.

" Her first schoolmaster [Ascham, with whom our author,
" viz. Mr. Elmer, was familiar] told him, that he learned
" every day more of her, than she of him. Thus expound-
" ing it; I teach her words, and she me things. I teach her
" the tongues to speak, and her modesty and maidenly life
" teacheth me works to do. I think, said he, she is the
" best inclined and disposed of any in all Europe.

Two rare
qualities in
her.

" An Italian, which taught her his tongue, (though that
" nation lightly praise not out of their own country,) said to
" Elmer, he found in her two qualities, which were seldom
" qualities in one woman: viz. a singular wit, and a mar-
" vellous meek stomach."

From which premises the foresaid writer made this conclusion: " We must needs conceive good hopes, yea, in a
" manner be assured, that as she hath passed so many of
" our kings, and all our queens, in these good studies and
" sciences, so she must needs exceed them in the rest of her
" life and government." And how happily true it so fell out
in her succeeding reign, all the world, especially her own
kingdom, knew.

A
CATALOGUE

OF

LETTERS, SPEECHES, PROCLAMATIONS, RECORDS,

AND

OTHER VALUABLE MSS. PAPERS AND MONUMENTS,

Relating to the History of this Reign, and to which reference
made in the foregoing Memorials.

CATALOGUE

OF

LETTERS, SPEECHES, PROCLAMATIONS,

&c. &c.

Number I.

Queen Mary's letter to Sir Edward Hastings, to aid her in her obtaining the crown.

Mary the Queen.

RIGHT trusty and right welbeloved cousin, we grete you MSS. G.
well: Advertising you, that to our great grief and heavi- Petyt, Ar-
ness of heart, we have received woful news and advertise- mig.
ment, that the King, our dearest brother, and late sovereign
Lord, is departed to God's mercy, upon Thursday last, at
night: by means whereof, the right of the crown of this
realm of England, with the governance thereof, and the
title of France, is justly come unto us by God's providence;
as appears by such provisions as have been made by act of
Parliament, and the testament and last wil of our late dearest father King Henry VIII. for our preferment in this
behalf: whereby you are now discharged of your duty of
allegiance to our said brother the King, and unburdened
and set at large, to observe, execute, or obey any commandment, heretofore or hereafter to be addrest unto you
by letter or otherwise, from or in the name, or by colour of
the authority of the same King, our late brother; and only
to us and our person are and owe to be true liegeman.

Wherefore, right trusty and right welbeloved, for the
special trust and affiance we have in you, and as you be a

nobleman, we require, command, and charge you, to have an heart and an eye, vigilant and fully bent to God's glory, our honour, and surety of our person, and the universal quietness of the whole realm; especially of those our counties of Middlesex and Bucks, where your habitation and mansion is: and that ye stir not in a forcible array, at the commandment, call, or bidding, by letters or otherwise, of any person or persons whatsoever, except for us your sovereign Lady: and except also, if any wilful, as God forbid, will dare and attempt otherwise violently and by force, that shall to you seem prejudicial unto us, our right and title aforesaid. For the prevention of which cause, and also to the intent you shall and may be ready to serve us at our command, hereafter to be addrest unto you, we will you shall, to the best of your power, fortify and prepare your self. And this our letter, signed with our hand, shall be your warrant and discharge in this behalf. Willing you further not to doubt, but that we shall in the ballance of equity, reason, and justice, consider your endeavour, and also employ our own person and study accordingly: and so prosecute you with such our good favour and grace, as shall avaunce God's glory, and the commonweal, to your comfort, with the help of God: who have us all in his blessed keeping. Yeoven at our manour of Kenningale, the ix of July, in the year of our Lord God 1553.

To our trusty and right welbeloved
Sir Edward Hastings.

4

Number II.

Queen Jane to certain gentlemen, to repair into Buckinghamshire, to quell the disturbances there.

To our trusty and welbeloved Sir John St. Lowe and Sir Anthony Kingstone, knts.

Jane the Queen.

MSS. D. G. Petyt, Armig. TRUSTY and welbeloved, we grete you well. Because we doubt not, but by this our most lawful possession of the crown, with the free consent of the nobility of our realm, and other the states of the same, is both plainly known and accepted of you, as our most loving subjects; therefore we do not reiterate the same: but now most earnestly wil and require, and by authority hereof warrant you to assemble, muster, and levy al the power ye can possible make, either of your servants, tenants, officers, or friends, as wel horsemen as footmen, (reserving to our right trusty and right welbeloved cousins, the Earls of Arundel and Pembroke, their tenants, servants, and officers,) and with the same to repair with al possible speed towards Buckinghamshire, for the repressing and subduing of certain tumults and rebellions moved there against us and our crown by certain seditious men. For the repressing whereof, we have given orders to divers others, our good subjects and gentlemen of such degree as you are, to repair in like manner to the same parts. So as we nothing doubt, but upon the access of such our loving subjects as be appointed for that purpose to the place where those seditious people yet remain, the same shall either lack hearts to abide in their malicious purpose, or else receive such punishment and execution as they deserve; seeking the destruction of their native country, and the subversion of al men in their degrees, by rebellion of the base multitude: whose rage being stirred, as of late years hath been seen, must needs be the confusion of the whole commonweal.

Wherefore our special trust is in your courage, wisdom, and fidelities in this matter, to advance yourselves both with power and speed to this enterprize, in such sort as by our nobility and Council shal be also prescribed unto you. And for sustentation of your charges in this behalf, our said Council, by our commandment, do forthwith give order to your satisfaction, as by our letters also shal appear unto you. And besides that, we do assure you of our special consideration of this your service to us, our crown, and especially to the preservation of this our realm and commonweal. Geven under our signet, at our Tower of London, the xviii of July, in the first year of our reign.

5   Number III.

The chief officers of Guisnes to Queen Mary, declaring
their proclaiming of her Queen.

IT may please your most excellent Majesty, that, where
it hath pleased Almighty God so to stir the hearts of all
your Grace's most loving subjects, as we do with most joyful chere accept, repute, and take your most vertuous Grace
to be now our rightful and natural Queen; and for the
better signification of our true hearts towards your Majesty, we have caused your Highness proclamation to be
published within this your Grace's castle, town, and marches
of Guisnes; and have solemnized the said proclamation
with bonfires, gunshots, and chiefly with such triumphant
shouts of us your joyful liege people, as the same may be,
to your Grace's great comfort, and the better tranquility of
all your Majesties realms and dominions: we therefore,
having charge of this your Majesty's house, piece, and fort,
considering the mutability and variety of this season, and
partly by uncertain bruits understand, that our captain and
governour under your Highness, the Rt. Honourable Lord
Gray of Wiltonne, should persevere and be in armes against
your Majesties person; and we having such experience,
good proof, and affiance in his Lordship's honour, faith,
fidelity, which he hath always born, and we trust doth bear
toward the crown of England, do neither believe the said
scandalous rumours; neither, according to our duties, wil
condempne him, until further knowledg from your Majesty.   And again, considering of what waighty moment
and respect this your Graces house and piece doth now rest
to be vigilantly defended and looked unto; and knowing
that we, with   sworn soldiers here, are able of
ourselves to preserve this house and your Grace's right,
title, and just interest, without the assistance of any others,
until your Graces plesure be otherwise signified: and where
Sir Anthony Aucher, high marshal of Calais, was appointed
hither for our better aid and assistance, altho' there be no
matter, as we can perceive, to mistrust his fidelity and alle-

giance; yet doubting the which, we think most requisite neither to admit him, nor any other person or persons, to bear rule or charge within your Highness piece, until your Grace may please to advertise the contrary. Notwithstanding we use here counsils and advices in all our proceedings, which shall tend to the better advancement of your Highness service : wherein hitherto he hath diligently and faithfully employed himself.

And upon the dispatching of this unto your Grace, it happened that Mr. Harry Duddely arrived here out of France, with four servants; whom we have stayed to be surely kept here, and his letters, which he had to be con-6 veyed, as may appear by a scedule here included, we have sent you here unperused by us unto your Highness by this trusty messenger. And as we do, for the good respect of your Majesties service, keep him in sure custody, until your Graces plesure be further signified ; so in all other orders, which it may please your Grace to signify unto us, we wil, like loyal, true, and loving subjects, receive them and obey them according to our bounden duties, and to the uttermost of our power. And in the mean season we will defend your Graces house, and answer it to your Majesties behoof, both with our bodies, substance, and lives. And thus we most heartily wish to your most excellent Majesty al things prosperous. From your Grace's castle of Guisnes, this 25 July.

> Your Majesties loving, faithful,
> and most loyal subjects,
> Sir Richard Wyndebank, deputy,
> William Sparrow, chief constable,
> Walter Vaugehan, chief porter,
> of your Majesties castle of Guisnes.

Number IV.

A copy of verses congratulatory, made by Dr. Walter Haddon, to Queen Mary, upon her access to the crown.

ANGLIA, sæpe tuis divina potentia rebus
Adfuit, et sævis te tempestatibus actam,
Impulit in portum salvam, terraque locavit.
Ista tamen postrema Dei clementia miris
Luminibus fulsit, radiisque illustribus arsit.
Ambitione volans, cæcaque cupidine regni,
Exacuit ferrum nimis immoderata potestas.
In tenebris miseri jacuerunt obruta regni
Sceptra, ruit vario discordia mista tumultu.
Ipse sibi dispar secum pugnare senatus,
Frendere nobilitas, incerto murmure ferri
Vulgus, et ancipites turbarum volvere fluctus.
Cum ratione furor pugnat, cum jure libido,
Vis trahit invitos, armis terretur honestas,
Officium pavor, et verum violentia frangit.
O! tenebras regni spissas, O! tempora dura!
Turbine quis tanto raptatos colliget artus,
Anglia? Quis laceris corpus componere membris,
Quis solitum poterit repræsentare decorem?
Tu, Deus, æterno qui dirigis omnia cursu,
Cujus inexhaustis manat clementia rivis;
Tu, Deus, e cœlo spectans, nostrisque misertus,
Aspera magnorum tollis tormenta malorum,
Classica civilis belli tu concita frangis,
Tu revocas lætam pacem, tu pectora sedas
Turbida, discordes animos tu fœdere jungis.
Fœmina virgo venit, descendens stemmate regum,
Fœmina virgo venit, Mariæ prænomine digna.
Salve flos regni, salve lectissima gemma,
Salve de cœlo lapsum venerabile sydus.
Optima sis nobis, et felicissima princeps:
Auxilium fractis fer mansuetissima rebus.
Fratris ut es regni, sic sis pietatis et hæres.
Justitiam serva, demissis parce, superbos

Contere, virtuti sit honos, doctrina colatur.
Fac tueare bonos, nec falsa calumnia quenquam
Opprimat, ipsa tuos et ames, et ameris ab illis.
Rex tibi frater erat, mors illum funere mersit,
Morte cades Regina soror : mortalia durant
Nulla diu, proprio se carpit tempore vita.
Hanc, supreme Deus, regno qui ponis avito,
Anglia cui fasces summittit læta supremas,
Imbue divino sanctissima pectora succo,
Semper ut ad cœlos sursum sua lumina tollat.
Vinciat ut pietas, communis, ut alliget ardor
Mutuus in Christo, studiis consentiat omnis
Nobilitas rectis, populus tractabilis artes
Suscipiat pacis, regnique statuta sequatur.
Aurea perpetuis omnes concordia vinctis
Nectat, ut ad Patrem communem supplice voce
Junctorum fratrum communia vota ferantur.

Number V.

8

*A proclamation set fourth by the Quenes Majestie, with the
aduise of her moost honourable Counsell, for the newe
seuerall monies and coines of fyne sterlynge syluer and
golde, and the valuation of euery of the same : newe set
furth by her Heighnes.*

THE Quenes most excellent Majestie, of her greate and
aboundaunte clemencie, callynge to her graciouse remembraunce what great and intollerable charges hath come and
chaunsed moost specially unto her Heighnes, and also to
her louynge subiectes, aswell by the reason of these base
monies of late made within her Maiesties realmes, as also
by greate quantities of the lyke base monies made and
counterfeyt in other realmes, and issued out within this
her Graces realme, and other her Heighnes dominions. For
the tender zeale her Grace beareth to her louinge subiectes,
in no wyse can longer suffer the same inconueniencie, but is
fully resolued and determined with all conueniente spede
to cause to be made and set forth certayne coynes, aswel of

golde as of syluer of the perfect fynes, accordinge to the rates hereafter ensewyng: which shall redounde muche to her Heighnes honor, and to the great wealth, commoditie, and profit of her louinge subiectes.

Wherefore her Majestie hath ordered and established to be made within her mintes these seuerall coynes, aswell of syluer in fynenes of the standerd sterlyng, as also of golde, as hereafter enseweth; that is to saye, the whole soueraigne of fyne golde, whiche shalbe currant within all her realmes and dominions for xxx*s*. of the lawful monies of England. One other pece of fyne gold, beyng half the soueraygne aforesayde, whiche shalbe called the royall of golde, shalbe currante for xv*s*. of the lawful monies aforesayd. One other pece of fyne golde, whiche shalbe called the aungell, currant for x*s*. of the lawfull monies aforesayd. One other pece of fyne golde, whiche shalbe called the half aungel, currant for v*s*. of the lawfull monies aforesayde.

And of coynes of syluer as here enseweth: that is to say, one pece of syluer monies, which shalbe called the grote, and shalbe currant for iiii*d*. of the lawfull monies of England. *Item*, One other pece, the half of the foresaye grote, whiche shalbe called the half grote, and shall be currant for ii*d*. of the lawful monies aforesayde. *Item*, One other pece, the half of the half grote, whiche shalbe called the penny, and shalbe currant for i*d*. of the lawfull monies aforesayde.

All whiche monies aforesayde, the Quenes Heighnes straytly chargeth and commaundeth all maner of persons 9 within hir realmes and dominions, (the realme of Ireland only excepted, forasmuche as her Heighnes coynes there hath a special standerd,) of what estate or degree soeuer they be, to receaue and paye the sayd seuerall peces of monies, aswell of golde as of sylver, at the seuerall rates before rehearsed, upon payne of her Heighnes displeasure, and to be further punished, as shal seme to her Grace most conuenient. And her Maiesties expresse commaundement is, that all suche base monies, whiche haue bene redused to the value of a lower rate, shal go currant in paiment in like maner and sort, as the same be currant at this daye, and as is declared in the proclamation last made in the tyme of the late most noble prince, Kynge Edward the vj. in that behalfe, untyl such tyme as her Heighnes, with the aduise of her Counsell, shall take further order touchinge the same. Geuen at our manor of Rychemonde, the xx of August, in the fyrst yeare of our most prosperous reygne.

God saue the Quene.

Londini in ædibus Johannis Cawodi typographi Reginæ excusum anno M.D.LIII.

Cum priuilegio ad imprimendum solum.

Number VI.

The Queen's proclamation for the remission of a part of a tax granted in King Edward's time.

By the Quene.

THE Quene our soveraygne Ladye, graciouslye considering the good wylles, forwardnes, and harty dispositions of her trewe louynge subiectes, always heretofore exhibited, to the ayde and succoure of the common weale, with their proper substance and goodes, when the servyce, the necessitie, and honour of the realme hath so required, as well in the tymes and several reygnes of the moost excellent prynces, our late soveraygne lordes, her deare father, and deare brother, Kynge Henry the Eyght, and Edwarde the Syxte; and speciallye synce the tyme of her vocation to the crowne, in the defence of her royal person, against the maliciouse force of the most arrande traytour Syr John Dudley, late duke of Northumberlande, and his complyces. Notwithstandyng it is well knowne to the multitude of her sayde good subiectes, howe by the euyll governemente of the realme in these late yeares, specially since the sayde duke hath borne rule, the treasure of the same is meruelouslye exhausted, and her Hyghnes nowe presently charged with payment of notable great sommes, beynge the debte of her sayde brother the Kynge, partly due to dyuers of her sayde servantes and subiectes, and partly to certayne marchaunt straungers and others; whiche, for her owne honour, and the honoure of the realme, her Highnes determineth, by the helpe of God, truly to discharge, content, and paye, in tymes conveniente and reasonable; yet hauynge both a speciall mynde to the weale of her sayde subjects, and accomptynge their louying harts and prosperitie as her owne weale, and the chiefest treasure that she desyreth, next the fauor and grace of God; and hauying a full affiaunce in her sayde subiectes, that yf the state, the cause, and honour of the realme shall so requyre, they wyll at all tymes hereafter exhibite their semblable service: notwithstandynge in the latter session of the laste Parliament, holden in the tyme of the sayde late Kynge Edwarde the Syxte, towardes the paymentes and discharges of the sayde notable debtes, there was graunted by acte of Parliament unto the sayde K. Edward two dismes, and two fyftenes, and one subsidie of four shyllynges of the pound, to be raysed and leuyed of the manours, landes, and tenements, and two shyllynges eighte pence of the goodes and catelles of her subiectes, whiche grauntes are nowe due unto her Hyghnes by the sayde acte, and wolde discharge one greate peece of the sayde debtes: her Maiestie, for the considerations aforerehearsed, of her mere grace and great clemency, for the releif and succour of her sayde good subiectes, hath freely for her, and her heyres and successours, pardoned and remytted, and by these presentes frely and fully pardoneth and remitteth unto her sayde subiectes, and their heyres and executours, the sayde subsidie of four shyllynges the pounde, and two shyllynges eyght pence the pounde, graunted in the latter session, and last parliament; trustynge her sayde good subiectes wyll haue louyng consideration thereof for theyr partes, whome she requyreth hartely to bende themselves wholly to serve God to his glory, with continual prayer unto the same for the honoure and avauncemente of her Grace, and the commonweale. Geven at oure manour of

Rychemonde, the fyrste day of September, in the fyrst year of our moost prosperous reygne.

God save the Quene.

Londini in ædibus Johannis Cawodi typographi Reginæ excusum anno MDLIII.

Number VII.   11

The knights of the Carpet, dubbed October the 2d, the day after the Queen's coronation, at the palace at Westminster, before her in her chamber of presence, under the cloth of estate; by the Earl of Arundel: who had of her Highness commission to execute the same.

THE Lord Garrat, (Gerrard.)

The Lord Borough.

The Lord Dudley.

Sir Thomas Stanley.

Sir Edmund Windsor.

Sir Henry Radcliff.

Sir Tho. Hastings.

Sir Will. Walgrave.

Sir John Browne.

Sir Rafe Chamberlain.

Sir John Teret, (Tirwhit.)

Sir John Hodelston.

Sir Rob. Peckham.

Sir Herry Ley.

Sir Christopher Alen~~Jrdox~~.

Sir Richard Freston.

Sir Will. Kelloway.

Sir Henry Gaston.

Sir John Tregonwel.

Sir Ambrose German.

Sir Leonard Chamberlain.

Sir Tho. Gerard.

Sir David Brook, lord chief baron.

Sir Rich. Morgan, lord chief justice.

Sir George Jefford.

Sir Tho. Pakenton.

Sir Tho. Lovel.

Sir John Spencer.

Sir John Fitzwilliams.

Sir Tho. Androuse.

Sir William Courtney.

Sir Will. Gresley.

Sir Tho. Cave.

Sir Edward Littleton.

Sir Philip Parreis.

Sir Tho. White.

Sir Tho. Metham.

Sir Rich. Lason, or Lawston.

Sir Tho. Dawney.

Sir Rob. Wyngfield.

Sir Tho. Knevet.

Sir Roger Wedowes.

Sir Francis Stoner.

Sir John Aly.

Sir Rich. Tutte.

Sir Edmund Green.

Sir Tho. Fynce, (Finch.)

Ex Offic. Arm. N° 7.

N 3

Sir Rob. Lame, (Lamb.)
Sir Rich. Stapleton.
Sir Will. Damsel, (Daunsel.)
Sir Joh. Chichester.
Sir Herry Crypes, (or Crisp.)
Sir Tho. Palmer.
Sir Henry Ashley.
Sir Rich. Stranguis.
12 Sir Geo. Matthew.
Sir John Cotton.
Sir John Pollard.
Sir John Walbelton, (Warburton.)
Sir John Fermer.
Sir Tho. Berenger.
Sir John Constable.
Sir Geo. Stanley.
Sir Rob. Stanley.
Sir Rauf Egerton.
Sir Rich. Molines, (Molineux.)
Sir Tho. Hesket.
Sir Tho. Wainam, (Wainman.)

Sir John Crofts.
Sir Edmund Molevery.
Sir Ric. Brags.
Sir James Fitz-James.
Sir Tho. Verney.
Sir James Williams.
Sir Will. Meringe.
Sir Edw. Pylson.
Sir Edw. Fytton.
Sir Will. Warren.
Sir Thomas White, lord mayor.
Sir Tho. Throgmorton.
Sir Edw. Grevyl.
Sir Herry Stafford.
Sir Will. Wygston.
Sir Herry Jones.
Sir John Bruse.
Sir Rob. Witney.
Sir Rich. Thudley.
Sir Tho. Baskerfield.
Sir Tho. Tyndal.
Sir Rich. Walwynn.

Number VIII.

Magistri Hugonis Westoni, decani Westmonasterii, oratio, coram patribus et clero in synodo congregatis habita.

CUM Demosthenes, totius Græciæ lumen, ante Philippum Macedoniæ regem verba facturus, obmutuerit, cum Theophrastus philosophorum doctissimus, et oratorum eloquentissimus, multum animo consternatus, inter dicendum sæpius conticuisse feratur, cum ipse denique Marcus T. Cicero, Latinæ facundiæ parens, et timorem quendam naturalem insitum habens, meticulose orationum principia solitus sit exordiri; mirum fortasse vobis videbitur, ornatissimi præsules, doctissimique viri, qua effræni audacia (ne dicam audaci temeritate) ego, qui neque usu multum, neque doctrina satis, et ingenio parum valeo, in hunc celeberrimum cœtum dicturus, prodire ausim, ubi ante oculos, quocunque inciderint, clarissima hujus regni lumina undique observantur. Sed neque vestræ excellentiæ (quam vehementer admiror) ignoratio, neque inanis de mea tenuitate (cujus sum mihi probe conscius) persuasio, sed difficile illud proloquendi munus ab isto venerandissimorum hominum cœtu mihi delegatum, huc me pertraxit adegitque. Mediocritatis meæ mihi probe conscius, facile intelligo quam longe sim impar gravissimis et maximis negotiis obeundis, quorum provinciam mihi benevolus horum venerandorum hominum consensus imposuit; eorum etiam amicum de me errorem satis agnosco, qui ex tam conferta doctissimorum hominum corona, ex tam venerando gravissimorum hominum cœtu, me nullius pæne eruditionis hominem, præterea impeditioris linguæ, totius hujus consessus, imo fere totius nostræ Ecclesiæ linguam et os præficerat. Non possum tamen quin de tanta et tam præsenti illorum in me benevolentia et gratias agam maximas, et vestræ authoritati sanctissimæ paream.

Eidem igitur vestræ benevolentiæ, quæ hanc mihi pro_ vinciam imposuit, confisus, breviter ab eo, quod in ipsa re mihi videtur esse præcipuum, orationis meæ exordium sumam. Convenistis, patres, consulturi de religione, id est, re omnium tum maxima tum sanctissima: convenistis visuri triste spectaculum, lugubrem matris vestræ Ecclesiæ vultum, convenistis, inquam, ut matrem nostram Ecclesiam Christi misere laceram ac quassatam resarciatis, hæreticorum telis jure oppugnatam, labefactatam, ac pæne solo æquatam, 13 erigatis, fidem pæne explosam reducatis, religionem excisam redintegretis. Cæterum quid vobis minus convenit, quam a me moneri, et ad sinceræ religionis instaurationem excitari, qui tanta animorum alacritate in hoc incumbitis, ut me præcedatis, ut me a tergo relinquatis hortantem, quantum et vos, patres, ab illustrissima nostra regina præcurrente, vos ipsos esse superatos vidistis. O! inauditam et admirandam Dei bonitatem! Nunquid enim unquam accidit admirabilius, in tanta omnium ærumnarum colluvie, in tanto afflictionum examine, in tanta Ecclesiæ ruina, in tanto fidei naufragio, religionis rebus fere conclamatis, virgini Ecclesiæ virginem Reginam, seu præsens aliquod numen a Deo Opt. Max. nobis dari, quasi cælitus demissum, cujus ductu et auspiciis, cuncta hæc tam misera, tam calamitosa et nefanda reprimuntur, dissipantur, abiguntur. Cujus encomiasten agere mecum non institui, partim quod temporis penuria (qua premor) haud sinit; partim vero, quoniam vereor ne laudibus (quas augere debeo) nonnihil angustiis orationis meæ, existimetur esse detractum. Quid enim multiplicem illius doctrinam, quæ in hominibus rara est, commemorabo? Quid illius animum plane masculum et infractissimum? An non vidistis constantissimam inter difficillima, in magnis erectam, diligentissimam in minimis? Quodnam obsecro felicius præsagium aut omen Ecclesiæ, ad nativum suæ puritatis splendorem instaurandæ præfigurari potuit, quam quod Reginæ nostræ, nescio quo fato, certe non data opera, eodem die regio diademate insigniri contigerit, qui ecclesiarum dedicationi solemnis esse solet? Et instaurandæ atque expurgandæ templi religioni tam enixe incumbit, quasi huic uni vel nata vel donata sit: huic tam sedulo se consecrat, ut piissimis omnibus imperatoribus aut æquari aut anteferri meritissime possit. Theodosius ille sanctissimus imperator nihil prius aut antiquius duxit ad retundendos hæreticorum impetus, quam ad antiquos Ecclesiæ doctores qui ante divisionem floruissent, confugere. Ita et nostra Regina in hisce suis purganda vineæ Domini quasi præludiis faciendum censet ac præcipit. Theodosius imperator intente orare solitus est, ut sibi cooperaret Deus ad veritatis electionem inter tot opinionum dissidia: et omnes sciunt nisi Reginam ignorantes, quam ardenter diurnis nocturnisque precibus Deum Opt. Max. solicitat, ut omnes, maxime tamen nos Angli, (quorum gubernacula suscepit,) Catholicæ fidei veritatem agnoscamus, agnitam excolamus amplexemurque.

Quid Constantinum illum, constantissimum religionis assertorem, dicam? Qui tanta pietate liberalitateque fuisse perhibetur, ut episcopis ex cunctis terrarum partibus Ni-

coram accitis, victum commeatumque præstiterit, tantaque
morum mansuetudine ac reverentia in Ecclesiæ præpositos,
ut non in throno aureo gemmisque ornato, sed minore sede
quam aliis posita in medio eorum, ad episcoporum pedes
consederit.   At quis tam cœcus, qui non clare perspiciat
nostram Reginam hiisce Dei donis perinde illustrari, ac cœlum suis stellis ; vosque patres, universumque clerum aut
pari aut majori reverentia prosequi ?   Quod si Jovinianus
laudibus celebrandus sit a posteris, quod ab Athanasio here-
ticorum propugnatore petierit, ut ei rescriberet perfectam 14
divinorum dogmatum disciplinam ; quanto magis æternam
nominis gloriam consequetur nostra Regina, quæ multos
Athanasios ex universis sui regni finibus coegit, coactos mo-
nèt, hortatur, imperat, ut cum dicendo, tum scribendo, Catholicam fidem miseris modis discerptam resarsirent, resar-
sitam tuerentur ac foverent ? Jovinianus ut imperii sui ter-
ras ingressus est, primum scripsit legem, ut Catholici episcopi extorres et exules de exilio redirent, et ecclesias iis
reddendas esse professus est, qui fidem inviolabiliter servas-
sent ; ita et sacratissima Regina vos celeberrimos Angliæ
proceres, vestris sedibus exturbatos ex teterrimis carceris
squaloribus eduxit, et ingenti cum populi applausu propriis
restituit ecclesiis.

Felicissima Anglia, quæ talem habet Reginam.   Beatis-
sima Anglia, quæ tales habet Episcopos.   Beatissimi et vos
præsides, quibus donatum est non solum in illum credere,
sed pro nomine ejus pati.   Audite, venerandi Episcopi,
sanctum Episcopum Chrysostomum, audite, incarcerati, in-
carceratum.   Magna dignitas (inquit Chrysostomus) et multa, regno et consulatu universisque major, pro Christo ligari.
Nam nihil ita splendidum, ut vinctum esse propter Christum.
Vinctum esse propter Christum illustrius est, quam sive
apostolum, sive doctorem, sive evangelistam esse.   Siquis
Christum diligit, hic utique prius habebat, (optione data,)
vincula ferre propter Christum quam cœlos inhabitare.   Ligari pro Christo illustrius est quam sedere ad dextram ipsius, honestius est quam sedere super duodecim thronos.
Quod siquis mihi vel universi cœli, vel hujus cathenæ co-
piam et optionem largitus esset, cathenam hanc ego plane

elegissem.   Deinde, si aut mihi cum angelis standum fuisset
sursum, aut cum Paulo vincto, carcerem utique praeoptas-
sem.   Ad haec, siquis me aut in numerum et ordinem collo-
casset caelestium potentiarum, earum etiam quae prope sunt
thronum Dei, aut talem ligatum fecisset, talis utique ligatus
esse voluissem.   Non ita beatum dico Paulum, quod in pa-
radisum raptus, atque quod in carcerem est conjectus, non
ita beatum aestimo, quod verba audivit ineffabilia, [quam]
quod vincula sustinuerit, non ob id adeo beatum praedico,
quod in tertium coelum raptus est, atque propter vincula.
Et in Scripturis me non tantum delectat miracula patrans,
quantum male affectus, flagellatus ac miserabiliter tractus.
Beati vos, ob carcerem, ob cathenas, ob injecta vincula :
beati, inquam, et ter beati, imo saepius.   Totum orbem vobis
conciliastis.   Etiam longe absentes, amicos vobis fecistis.
Ubique terrarum et marium canuntur vestra praeclara faci-
nora, fortitudo, constans sententia, animusque minime steri-
lis.   Nihil, non tribunal, quod aliis videtur grave, vos de-
terruit, non carnifex, non tormentorum coacervationes, non
minae, quae innumeras mortes nunciabant, non judex qui
ignem ab ore flabat, non adversarii qui frendebant dentibus,
et innumeris aliis insultandi modis gestiebant, non tantae ca-
lumniae, non impudentissimae accusationes, non mors ante
oculos quotidie proposita ; sed haec omnia vobis uberem potius et sufficientem consolationis materiam praestitere.

15   Et idcirco clari quidem vos et celebrant et praedicant :
vos omnes amici non solum, sed et inimici ipsi qui haec effe-
cerunt.   Tanta res est virtus, ut illam impugnantes admi-
rentur.   Tanta res est malitia, ut etiam qui eam operantur,
condemnent. Nondum decapitati estis cum Johanne Baptista,
sed longe acerbiora tulistis.   Non enim idem est, brevi temporis momento caput amittere, et longo tempore cum talibus
luctari doloribus, terroribus, minis, vinculis, abductioni-
bus, bonorum rapinis, carnificum manibus, sycophanta-
rum impudentissimis linguis, convitiis, salibus et dicacitati-
bus. Gaudete igitur, exultate, viriles estote, corroboramini,
cogitate quot vestro exemplo ad certamina armastis, quot
fluctuabundos confirmastis, quantos spiritus resuscitastis !
Nam afflictionibus vestris multum profuistis, non solum prae-

sentibus, sed et absentibus, nec iis qui viderunt, sed et iis qui audiunt. Angliæ Ecclesiam, quam vestris carceribus tam splendide illustrastis, quam vestris, inquam, carceribus Christo non tam servastis, quam comparastis, pergite reædificare, muros Hierusalem tam ab hæreticis dissipatos extruite, maceriarum ruinas implete, juncturas a schismaticis concussas et disruptas in unitatis Ecclesiæ compagine conjungite, stertant, obganniant, debacchentur hæretici, recto vos pede incedite in magnam Domini civitatem Hierusalem, domum Dei, unitatem inquam Ecclesiæ. Ubi altare unum, unum sacerdotium, unus Christus, extra hanc unitatem quisquis est, alienus est, profanus est, hostis est. A qua unitate desistere, a Christo exorbitari est, a qua unitate desciscere, errorum omnium seges est, a qua unitate desciscere, fundi nostri calamitas unica fuit.

Sit vobis patribus exemplo Dionysius Corinthiorum episcopus maxime celebris, cujus illud est dictum, oportuerit quidem etiam pati omnia pro eo, ne scinderetur Ecclesia Dei : et erat non inferior gloria sustinere martyrium, ne scindatur Ecclesia, quam est illa, ne idolis immoletur. Imo, secundum meam sententiam, majus puto hoc esse martyrium. Ibi namque unusquisque pro sua tantum anima, in hoc vero pro omni Ecclesia martyrium sustinet. Sit vobis exemplo magnus ille Cappadox Basilius, de quo ita scribit Nazianzenus, quod cum strenue Cæsaris præfectum alloqueretur, et acriter perstringeret, atque eo nomine a præfecto procax et superciliosus sit habitus notatusque, in hanc sententiam prorupit, " Fortasse antea in Episcopum non incidisti. Om- " nino enim pro religione certantes, hoc agimus modo, in " aliis modesti sumus, et omnibus hominibus humiliores ; " ita enim mandata jubent ; nec solum contra Cæsaris po- " tentiam, sed nec contra viles homines supercilia attollimus. " Ubi vero Dei periclitatur negotium, cunctis aliis con- " temptis, ad Deum solum respicimus." Vos igitur inimicorum hominum linguas, calumnias irrogatas, contumelias, probra, remoras nihil faciatis. Animos vestros non terrefaciant, quin despectui potius ac conspectui habeatis. Nam si ita se res habet (ut Cypriani verbis utar) quod iniquissimorum hominum timeatur audacia, ut quod mali jure et æquitate non possunt, temeritate atque desperatione perficiant, actum est de episcopatus vigore, et de Ecclesiæ gubernatione; actum est de sublimi et divina potestate. Nec Christiani ultra esse aut durare possumus, si ad hoc ventum est, ut perditorum 16 minas atque insidias pertimescamus. Nec nobis ignominia est, pati a fratribus quod passus est Christus, nec illis gloria est facere, quod fecit Judas.

Jam vero, ut ad finem properemus, unum a vobis (reverendi patres) hujus venerandi cœtus nomine, cujus me communi suffragio linguam et os præfecistis, non tam petere quam impetrare contendo obsecroque, nimirum ut pristina illa dignitas et authoritas cleri Angliæ jam quasi post liminio huic celeberrimo cœtui, doctissimorumque hominum conventui vindicentur, ac restituantur. Si enim verius sit, quam ut possit negari, et manifestius quam ut dissimulari debeat, quod in veteri lege Deus Opt. Max. Levitas et sacerdotes suæ legis ac controversiarum, quæ inde nascerentur, interpretes constituerit: si in Novo Testamento Christus omnia quæcunque Scribæ, et Pharisæi super cathedram Moysis sedentes dixerint, servare ac facere turbis præceperit: si non solum de apostolis, sed et de eorum successoribus dictum constiterit, *Qui vos audit, me audit; et qui vos spernit, me spernit:* si Spiritus Sanctus posuerit Episcopos, ut regerent Ecclesiam: si Paulus Apostolus Jesu Christi, hujus rei [causa] Titum in Creta reliquerit, ut quæ deessent corrigeret: si membra sic in suo corpore, quod est Ecclesia, digessit Christus, ut suum cuique locum, suum cuique munus attribuerit, alios apostolos, alios prophetas, alios doctores constituendo: si a majoribus denique nostris, et prudenter in initio institutum, et totius orbis consensu denique confirmatum fuerit, ut de religione non unice, potissimum tamen ad eos qui ministri Christi et dispensatores mysteriorum Dei a Paulo Apostolo dictitantur, pertractanda et definienda referretur; nunquam satis demirari possum, quo consilio id juris et potestatis nobis ademptum fuerit, quod omnibus majoribus semper fuerit concessum. Quorsum quæso ex ultimis totius regni oris evocantur decani, archidiaconi, theologi gravissimi, legum peritissimi, qui sensus habent in Scripturis exercitatos, quique in lege Domini meditati sunt omnibus diebus vitæ suæ, si illorum suffragia in sua (quod aiunt) arena nihil omnino ponderis habitura sit? Quid hic oleum et operam perdimus? Quid aliud quam larvæ habiti sumus? Sine nostro enim consilio, nedum consensu, facta, transacta sunt omnia. At quam pie et feliciter rerum exitus tandem docebit. Quid quod libro blasphemiis conspersissimo, erroribus refertissimo, qui nomine religionis religionem tollit, sacramenta diminuens universum orbem condemnat, quem *precatorium* nuncuparunt, universis obtrudendo, nunquam accesserit noster calculus. Qua de re quantopere nobis gratulandum esse arbitror, haud facile dixero.

Quæ accuratius evolventi in mentem mihi venit Chrysostomi querela, siquando vera, dubio procul nostra tempestate longe verissima. Quid tantum tandem peccavit Ecclesia Dei, quænam tanta res ipsius Ecclesiæ dominum excitavit induxitque, ut illa tanto cum ejus dedecore, tam ignominiosissimis, tam larvatis histrionibus, ganeonibus, fœdis episcopis regendam traderet. Adhibenda ergo (ut inquit Hilarius) omnis cura, ne hæretici sint peritiores in desperatione vitæ, quam nos in spe vitæ, ne plus solicitudinis ad falsa impendant, quam nos ad vera. Atque hoc nobis gravior incumbit cura, quod non apud homines solum, sed ipsum adeo tremendum Dei Opt. Max. tribunal; cujus cognitio-17 nem nihil latere, cujus justitiam nihil effugere potest; cum in rebus omnibus, tum vel maxime in religione peculiari Domini negotio, recte aut secus a nobis dictorum factorumque rationem constare oportet. Industriam porro meam tam maximam adhibiturum me polliceor, quam vos maximam in me benevolentiam exhibuistis. Adhibebo, inquam, quantum maximam possum, ut vestræ de me expectationi satisfaciam. Quod si per omnia non fuero consecutus, non tam vos mihi, qui quantum possum sum præstaturus imbecillitate, quam vobismetipsis amicissimum de me errorem vestrum condonabitis. Mihi deesse potero, vobis et huic venerabili consessui non sum defuturus unquam. Dixi.

Number IX.

Deploratio acerbæ necis heroidis præstantissimæ D. Janæ Grayæ, Henrici Ducis Suffolciæ filiæ: quæ securi percussa animo constantissimo mortem oppetiit. A D. Thoma Chaloner, milite, scripta.

JANA luit patriam profuso sanguine culpam,
  Vivere phœnicis digna puella dies.
Illa suis phœnix merito dicenda manebat,
  Ore placens Veneris, Palladis arte placens.
Culta fuit, formosa fuit: divina movebat
  Sæpe viros facies, sæpe loquela viros.
Vidisset faciem, poterat procus improbus uri:
  Audisset cultæ verba, modestus erat.
Ipsa sed ut facies erat insidiosa videnti,
  Lumina dejecto plena pudore tulit.
Ingenium (O Superi!) tenero sub corpore quantum
  Nacta fuit! nactum quam bene et excoluit!
Vix ea ter senos obiens exegerat annos,
  Docta, cathedrales quod stupuere sophi.
Et tamen ipsa humilis, mitis, sensusque modesti,
  Nil unquam elatum dicere visa fuit.
At quæ viva omnes mansueto pectore vicit,
  Elato gessit pectore se moriens.
Constantesque animos supremo tempore servans,
  Nescio Socraticis cesserit ante rogis.
Quod si me vatum quisquam de more loquutum
  · Arguat hæc fictis amplificare modis:
Juro tibi Veneris per et omnia sacra Minervæ,
  Perque Aganippæas, numina nostra, deas,
Quod nihil insinuo: non laudatoris agentem
  Quorsum opus ampullis tollere mirificis?
Novimus; et nostris hæc nuper vixerit oris;
  Objecta implacidæ blanda columba leæ.
Quam quia læserunt alia, quas debuit iras
  Vertere in autores, fudit in innocuam.

Judicet hæc justus Judex, qui pectora cernit.
　　Non quæ jura jubent, semper ut æqua licent.
Nec fuit, ut (si culpa fuit, quando inscia peccat)
　　Altera tam sævis surgeret ulta modis.
Juppiter æquanimis crudeles odit ab alto:
　　Hinc (puto) et ultrici fila minora dedit.
Languentique ægros longum sub corpore sensus:
　　Conscia quo stimulis cederet acta suis.
Puniit et lento primos Rhamnusia tabe
　　Autores, diri consilii osa nefas.
Hunc hydrops, alium confecit calculus: isti
　　Stilla gravis capitis, illi alia ingruerant.
Discite mortales, sortem reverenter habete:
　　Calcata ultorem sæpe habet illa Deum.
Tene ita non animos saltem potuisse propinquæ
　　Flectere? nec demum flectere fœmineos?
Non ignara mali, non hæc miserata jacentem est,
　　Quam pia dicta aliis, tam fera facta suis?
Non potuit quondam cultam tam culta movere?
　　Non raræ dotes, donaque magna Deûm?
Qualia vix uni tot contribuere puellæ?
　　Nec nisi perpaucis contribuere viris.
Mitto ego, quid fidibus scivit, numerisque sonoris:
　　Quid præstabat acu, pingeret aut calamo.
Quis putet? hæc Arabum Chaldaica verba loquelæ
　　Junxerat, Hebræum scite idioma tenens.
Nam Graio, sive Ausonio memorasse loquentem,
　　Parvum erit: has aliæ per loca culta sonant.
Gallus item et Thuscus sermo numerum auxerat Anglæ:
　　Si numeres linguas, bis quater una tulit.
Invideat Stridon te Pentaglotte ferendo
　　Sancte senex, vicit nostra puella tribus.
Quod si formoso veniens e corpore virtus
　　Gratior est, nihil est nobile stemma comes?
A proavis pater huic titulos dedit ordine longo,
　　Regales mater læva per astra dedit.
Hijs perijt, nec sponte tumens, nec sponte tyaris
　　Addita, sed procerum noxa peregit opus.

Hii se forte suis rationibus ut tueantur,
 Quid meruit pro tot sola puella luens?
Ignovit victrix aliis sine vulnere sceptrum
 Ablatum Janæ, quod Maria obtinuit.
Huic non ignovit, teneræ nec dura pepercit,
 Nec consanguineæ, (tam pia) nec gravidæ.
Janam ætas, genus et sexus, procerumque reatus,
 Quicquid erat, culpa solvere debuerant.
19 Nec tamen hæc Mariæ potuerunt omnia sensus
 Flectere: cervices quo minus illa daret
(Proh dolor!) albentes gladio generosa secandas,
 Intrepide indignam passa virago necem.
Qualis Achilleo mactata Polixena virgo,
 Dedecus immanis juge Neoptolemi, &c.
Turba dedit lacrymas spectatum effusa: decori
 Illa memor, moriens lumina sicca tulit.
Oraque tranquillo vultu suavissima pandens
 Verba dedit duras apta movere feras, &c.
Ah! Maria immitis, fluvioque pianda noveno;
 Par erat, hoc saltem sanguine pura fores.

Number X.

*Dr. Crome's declaration of some articles that he had con-
fessed before the bishops, anno* 1530.

MSS. Foxii.　THERE be some men that doo saye I have been abjuryd, and some saye that I am perjuryd, but the trewthe
ys, that I am nother abjuryd, nor yett perjuryd. Nor I
knowe nott what that I shold abjure; no, nor I wyll nott
abjure, nor yett revoke any thyng that I haue sayde in
tymes past: nor I haue no commawndment to saye or declare my mynde in anye thyng that hath ben contayned betwene me and diverse prelates: butt onlye that I have
been advertysed, cowncellyd by those that are my frendys
to declare them, the whych I myght not well saye naye.
Wherfore at thys tyme to certefye your myndys, somwhat

I shall touch of them, a lyttell of everye thyng, bycawse I haue troublyd you long. And at a more leasure, as tyme and opportunyte cawsyth me, I shall dilate and declare them more at large.

Fyrst of all, I wolde that you sholde know, how that I am moch bownde to praise the Kings Highnes, that he of his goodnes wolde take so moche payne (as ys knowyn well inowgh) to forbere hys meate and drynk, to here me and my matter declaryd. And the manner of his sayying unto me was thus; how "that he wolde se that I shold haue no "wrong, nor he wolde not mayntene me in any evyll," as God forbid he shold.

Some saye, that I shall go abowt to blame the people, and to pute them in the fawt, and saye, that they haue mystakyn me otherwyse than I haue spokyn; and thus to hyde my nowghtines. Also some saye, that I shall blame myne accusers, and putt grett fawlt in them. I goo not abowte to 20 blame the people that sholde call me evyll, no, nor yett I goo not abowte to blame nether my judgys nor my accusers; for so ytt myght bee, that they of a charytable mynde (for bycawse they herde thynges of me the whyche were nowght, and were not of trewthe) sent for me to knowe my mynde therin as I thynk; butt whether ytt were of a charytable mynde or noo, I am very well contentyd withall. And yff ytt were nott of a charytable mynde, I praye to God to forgyve them, as I wolde be forgyvyn my self. I doo nott putt fawte in no man. Yf I haue sayd any otherwyse then trewthe ys, (as to my knowledge I neuer dyd,) I am sory.

Now to my purpose, for bycawse I haue ben somwhat long with you here, now I shall declare unto you these answerys according as they were spokyn.

This is the answer of the parson of Saynt Antonyns parishe in London, made to certeyne questyons demaundyd of hym by dyverse prelates of the Churche, in the presence of our Lord Kyng Henry the VIIIth, in the yere of our Lord God, a thousand fyve hundryth and thyrty, and the elevynthe daye of Marche.

I. *I think that some sowlys, departyd from there bodyes, be punyshed and purgede in purgatorye.*

Forsothe what so ever you thinke, or haue thought, I wolde nott that you sholde be offendyd by me: for whatsoever I haue sayde in tymes past, the same I wyll now saye agayne, and the same prayour that I haue usyd in tymes past, the same I will now use agayne. For I haue prayed no other wysse then the trewth then, nor no other wyse then ys usyd at the Crosse and other placys. Of a trewthe I haue sayde, that in all the Scripture I can nott fynde this woorde *purgatorye*. But although I haue so sayde, yett I haue allwayys prayede for the sowlys in Christs faythe departyd, abydyng hys mercye. And my think that this manner of praying dooth not dysanull that place, whyche men callythe *purgatorye*, but rather standyth and agreythe well with thatt, though the name be nott rehersyd: insomuch as ytt confessyth a place abydyng. The whych place, as I thynk, ys a stoppe betwene the sowle departyd and the kingdom of God. The whyche lett ys more paynfull to the sowle then ys burnyng fyre. Some men doo saye, that after the dethe of the bodye, the sowle goythe other to hevyn or to hell: forsothe I am not of that opynyon. For I do thynk verelye, that God of hys goodness hathe ordynede a place for sowlys to be punysshede in, accordyng to hys pleasure and wyll. And as for the name of ytt, allthough I can nott fynde in the Scripture, (as the trewthe ys, ytt ys nott ther,) yett I wyll nott stryve therat: in so moch as there ys a place, giue ytt what name so euer you wyll; name ytt *purgatorye* or what you wyll call ytt, I am contentyd therwith. But my thynk theye hurte pur-21-gatorye sore, whych goo abowte to bryng in scriptures to prove purgatorye withall: whych doo make rather agaynst purgatorye then with ytt. To praye after thys maner, my thynk, ytt ys well. Now lett us goo forth.

II. *I thynke that holy martyrs, apostles, and confessours, now departyd from there bodyes, are to be honoryd, and to be callyde upon, and to be prayede.*

I thynk that holye martyrs and confessours (after they

be departyde oute of thys worlde) maye be callyd upon, yff
they be callyd upon as they sholde be ; that ys to saye, we
sholde praye to our Ladye after this maner, and saye, " O
" blessyd Virgyn and mother of God, praye for us, and be
" thou an intercessor for us." And so lykwyse to other
sayntts. And lett us saye to God, " Lord, haue mercye
" upon us, and graunte us our petycions, yff ytt be thy
" wyll." And thynk you nott that God wolde haue seyntts
prayed too, becawse he wyll gyve mercye, but beleve that
he wyll gyve mercye to all that repent and ask ytt of hym,
accordynge to hys promyse. And lett all the seyntts acknowledg, that they them selffe reseyve and take all goodnesse of God. Lett us nott thynk that we sholde take any
thyng of them ; for they have nothyng but that they reseyve of God. Wherfore let us put our full trust in God,
and trust sewrly to hys promesse that he wyll gyve us
mercye: and lett us call upon the saynts to be as interces-
sours for us, that we may obteyne his mercye: and let us
desyre God to gyve us soche gyftes of grace as those seynts
had. And thys ys a very good worshyppyng of sayntts.
For what can please the sayntt better, than to see God glo-
rifyed in your lyvyng. Some men there be, that thynk that
they please the sayntt well, when on the saynts daye they
wyll putt on goodlye aparell, and bankett and feaste ry-
ally, for the sayntts sake. O thou folyshe man, they haue
studyyd all there lyffe long to please God wyth abstynence
and humylyte, and wylt thou then worshype them wyth
pryde and glotonye? Therfore the moost sewryst waye
that Scripture doth teache to worshipe sayntts withall, ys
to lyve the lyffe that they lyvid, so nye as God wyll gyve
you grace. And to honor sayntts thys [way] ys very well,
after my opynyon. Now let us procede ferther.

III. *I thynk that sayntts in hevyn, as means, doo praye
for us.*

I thynk as I haue thought allwayes, and the last tyme
that I prechede here to my remembraunse, I sayde, that
there ys butt one Mediatour. And trewthe yt ys, there ys
but one Medyatour consernyng redempcyon, the whyche (as

o 2

Sayntt John sayth) is Jesu Christ : he yt ys that is a mean
for our synnys ; but yett I saye, that there be medyatours,
as one of us usyth to doo for another. And so I thynk that
seyntts maye preye for us to God, and be as meanys for us,
that he wolde graunte us hys mercye, and not that we
sholde reseyue any thyng of them ; for, as I sayde before,
they haue nothyng butt that they haue reseyvyd, and to
thynk them meanes after thys maner ys well in myne opynion.

22   IV. *I thynke that pilgrimagis and offeryngs may godlye
and meritoriouslye be doon, at the tombes and reliques of
sayntts.*

I thynke that pylgrimagis maye be well doon, I neuer
sayde otherwysse ; but I haue sayde oftyn, and now I wyll
saye ageyne, " Doo your dewtye, and then your devocion."
Fyrst, I saye, doo those thynges the whyche God hath
comaundyd to be doon ; the whyche are the dedys of
pytye : for those shalbe requyrede of thy hande agayne.
When thou comyst at the daye of judgement, he wyll not
saye unto thee, " Why wentst thow not to Wilsdon a pyl-
" grymage ?" but he wyl saye unto thee, *I was an hun-
grede, and thou gavyst me no meat : I was nakyd, and thou
gavyst me no clothys,* and soche lyke. They that wyll leue
the comawndements of God undon, and wyll followe and
doe voluntarye dedys, whyche were nether commawnded
by God, nor yett by the Churche, are greatlye to be blamyd,
and are worthy to be punyshed. But I saye thys, what so
euer you doo, whether you offer, whether you eate, drynk,
or slepe, se that yt be alwayes doon to the glorye of God.
And I thynk whatsoever you offer, consyderyng well wherefore you doo offer yt, I thynke yt maye well de doon after
my opynyon.

V. *I thynk that the Lent faste, and other fastyngs, commawndyd by the canons, and receyvyd by the customes of
Chrysten people, (except that nede otherwyse requyreth,)
are to be kept.*

I thynk that fastyng ys verye convenyente amongst Crysten people to be had ; and specyally for young people, the

whyche are in there boylyng bloode. And yff there were no abstynence, there wolde peradventure bryde moche more inconvenyence then dooth. Also dyverse men are of that opynyon, that they wyll saye, I haue a lycense of the Pope to eate fleashe: butt I saye, yff he doo offende hys brother in eating of fleshe, the Pope shall nott nor can nott excuse him. Ytt ys the propertye of many folks, that for bycawse they eate but one meale in the daye, therfore they wyll eate the more at dyner: and yet yff they eate no more that daye, they wyll saye that they fast a good fast. I thynk that yff fastyng were well doon, and in a dewe ordre, yt shold be boothe good and profitable, after my opynyon.

VI. *I thynke that ytt ys to be belyvyd upon necessyte of sowle helthe, that God by vertu of the sevyn sacraments of the Churche, gevythe grace to those that receyue them, or any of them, well after a dew maner.*

I thynke that God gevythe grace to them that reseyue the sacraments worthelye: that is to saye, he that with a pure and clene conscyence reseyvyth the sacrament of the aulter, (the whyche ys the very bodye of Cryst in forme of breade,) remembryng that hys body was brokyn and sett on the crosse for our synnys sake, and not that he soffryd any thyng for hym selfe, butt that he dyd ytt for the very loue that he had to the sowle of man. And to trust in hys 23 promesse, that he can and wyll fullfyll ytt accordynge to hys woords. And so lyke wysse to haue in remembraunse the blessyd sacrament of baptysm; remembryng that there we haue renowncyd and forsakyn the Devyll, with all hys pompys and prydes, and to folow Cryst with all humylyte and paciençe. And so lyke wyse of other sacramenttes. Butt, I saye, he that presumyth to reseyve the blessyd body of Cryst, (in forme of breade,) and ys nott in perfyte loue and charyte with hys neybour, he reseyvyth hym unworthelye, and resevythe hys owne dampnacyon; be cawse he makythe no dyfference of the Lordys bodye. And therfore se that ye regarde well the sacraments, and specially the blessyd sacrament of the aulter; trustyng sewrly in Cryst, that yff you reseyue them worthely, that you shall reseyue grace by them according to hys promisse. And, thus to reseyue them after a dew maner (as before re-hersyd) wyll com greate profyte by them, after my mynde.

VII. *I thynk ytt to be laudable and profytable, that wor-shipful imagys be sett in churchys, into remembraunse of Cryste and the saynts.*

I thynk that imagys maye well be woorshippyd, yff men doo not esteme them no better then they are ; but to use them as they be ordeynyde, (for laye mennys books,) and not to fantasye or thynk in them any influence or devyne power, wherwith they woork myracles. For I saye, that there ys no more devyne power in one image then ys in another. I saye, that there ys no image that can work my-racles. Yff there be any myracles doon, yt ys doon by God, and by no image. Some there be that knelythe before the image, and fantasythe or thynkythe in there mynde, that the image laffythe upon hym. Some saye, that they wyll bowe downe there hedys to them. Some saye, that he swetythe, and soche lyke sayyngs there ys among the com-mon people. And yff these people thought not that there were a devyne power in them, they wolde not thus thynke in [of] them. And yff they thynk that there ys power yn them, then they commyte idolatry. And therfore yt ys ne-cessarye to shewe you the use of them, that you maye the better knowe howe to ordre them. I woolde that you sholde take the imagys that standythe in the churche as thyngs that doo putt you in remembraunse of God and hys saynts. As when you se the roode, you then remembre how Cryst was doon on the crosse for your sakys, and how that hys handys and fete were peirced with nayles, and hys hert pierced with a spere, there ronnyng owt plentye of bloode and water ; by the whyche bloode our synnys are washyd away. And lykwysse when you see the image of our Ladye, haue in remembraunse the manyfolde gyftes of grace that were gevyn her ; remembre what chastyte, and humylyte, and soche other excellent gyftes, that she hade of her sonne Jesu Cryst ; and desyre God to endewe thee wythe part of soche excellent gyftes as she had. And praye to our Ladye that she wolde be an intercessor for thee, that thow myghtst obteyne them of hym. And thus to worshipe images ys very well, after my opynyon.

VIII. *I thynke that prayers of them that be alyve, doo profite them that be dede, beyng in purgatorye.* 24

I thynke sewrelye, that prayers dothe helpe them in purgatorye: for we are taught by the Scripture, one to praye for another. And yff we haue nede of prayers here lyvyng in thys worlde, moche more nede shall we haue in the other worlde, where we shall be lett from that celestyall syght. And forsomoche that the Cherche hathe ordeynyde that soulys sholde be prayyd for, I thynke ytt very good and commendable that soulys that be departyde, be prayyd for. For there ys nothyng more acceptable to God then prayour, yff ytt be well doon, and after a good fashyon. And for so moche as God hathe ordeynyd a place, where they rest from the visible syght of the joye, unto soche tyme as ytt shall please hys goodnes to delyver them thense, no dowte of ytt, that God of hys greate mercye, when he berythe our pyteous preyers made unto hym with sorrowfull herts, he of hys mercye wyll release them of that payne. And thys I thynk that prayer doothe profyte them that are departyd.

IX. *I thynke that men bothe by theyre fastyngs, and by other deadys of pytye, maye meryte.*

I thynke that men maye meryte by fastyngs, and by the deadys of pytye; doyng them well and after a dewe maner: that ys to saye, remembryng fyrst, howe that all that we other doo or can doo, ys not able to make God amendys for that he hathe doon for us; but neuerthelesse that that lyythe in us to doo for Crysts sake, we shall doo to the uttmost of our powre, and so farre as God wyl gyve us grace. Not that we wyll look to haue hevyn for our woorks sake, butt that we truste in the mercye of God to opteyne the kyngdom by hys promysys. Yff we then woork after thys maner, referryng all to hym, thynkyng when we haue doon all that we maye doo, how that we be yett butt unprofytable servanttes; and God of hys goodnes consyderyng thy good mynde towardys hym in thy woork ; he wyll rewarde thee, accordyng to hys promesse, doble that thow hast de-servyd by thy woorks, he wyll rewarde thee with a crowne of glorye, accordyng to hys grett mercye. And thus to faste and woorke ys very well, after my mynde.

X. *I thynk that they that be prohybyte of the byshops, as suspecte of the faythe, ought to cease from preachyng and teachyng, till they haue purgyd them byfore the supreme of soche suspicion.*

I thynk thys opynyon to be very good and necessarye ; for yff that there be some, (as I my selfe haue herde in thys cytye,) the whyche teachythe errors, and yt were so that they sholde nott be callyd to be examynyd of soche thynges, peradventure with a lyttyll sofferaunce they wolde bryng the people to the same blyndnes that they them selfe were in. And yff yt were so that they were accusyd wrong-fullye, yett ys yt good for hym to cease from preachyng and teachyng, untyll the tyme that he hathe cleryd hym selfe of that suspycion. Now let us foorthe.

XI. *I thynk that kyngs and governours are not bownde, upon necessyte of salvacyon, to delyver to the people the holy Scrypture in the mother tong, so long as the knowledge of the trewthe, necessary to salvacyon, may other wysse be knowyn to the people.*

I thynk that kyngs and governours are not bownde, upon necessyte of saluacyon, to delyuer to the people the holy Scrypture in there mother tonge, so long as they wyll so provyde, that the knowledge of the trewethe necessarye to saluacyon may otherwysse be knowyn to the people. In thys maner of sayyng I doo nott here dysannull, and saye, that the Scrypture ys not good for the people to haue in their mother tong ; for I haue allways thought ytt very good and profytable for the people to haue, so that they wolde use it well : and nott for to use ytt, as you be notyd that you haue usyd ytt. Some wyll haue ytt to cheke prests and other men withall, and nott to edefye themselfe ; some to sytt in the tavern babylyng of hytt, not regardyng that ytt ys the gospell, and glad tydyngs of hyt in there sowlys ;

and to desyre of God strength and grace to doo soche thynges as ys appointed hym to doo by the Scrypture; and to gyve hym grace to have perfayte fayth, to beleve soche promysys as God hath promysyd hym in hys Scryptures, that he may optayne them (yff he doo those thyngs that be commawndyd hym in the Scryptures) for hys promyse sake. Yet allthough that there be some that wolde use ytt well, and yff they had ytt, yett those men must be also contentyd to bere with there brethren, and to take paynes with them, untyll soche tyme as God shall appoynte, that both they that wolde use ytt well, and yff they had ytt, and the other, the whych haue ytt and use ytt nott well, shall reseyue ytt with joye, and gyve God grett thanks for ytt. And where as I saye, how that I thynk that theye are not bownde, upon necessyte of salvacyon, to lett the people haue the Scrypture in there mother tong, so long as they haue the trewthe of Crysts Scrypture, necessarye to salvacyon, taught and declaryd unto them, I thynk sewrly, that yff soche meanys be made, that the trewethe maye be knowyn (necessarye to salvacyon) by preachyng and teachyng, so long I thynk the people may forbere the Scripture the better; and so long as ytt ys so, I thynke that they maye withholde ytt from the people the better. And allthough that they so doo, yett the Scripture ys good for every man to haue, so that they use ytt well; yett I saye ytt maye be the better sparyd, yff men may haue soffycyent knowledg of the trewthe (necessarye to salvacyon) by preachyng and teachyng. And thus, as before rehersyd, I thynk, that kyngs and governours are nott bownde (of necessyte of salvacyon) to delyver to the people the Scripture in the mother tong, as beforesayde.

XII. *I thynk, that upon consyderacyon of the tyme, yt is* 26 *lawfull to kings and governours, upon some cawse to there judgment reasonable, to ordeyne, that the holy Scriptures be nott gevyn to the people, to be rede in the voulgare tonge.*

I thynk that, for tyme and cause reasonable, they may keep it away for a good entent and purpose, as now I thynk that ytt ys kept awaye, for by cawse they se so many of you abuse ytt. Yett the Scripture ys good of ytt selfe, and, as I sayd before, ytt ys very good for every man to haue to use ytt well. I praye God, that you be nott the cawse your selfe, that so good a thyng ys kept from you. For I trust, yff you be nott the lett of ytt your selfe, ye shall sewrly possesse ytt by the grace of God. Butt yff you sholde desyre ytt to ordre yt evyll, ytt were better for you a great deale that you had neuer sene ytt : for the more knowledge that ys gevyn to you, the more ys your payne, yff you doo nott ordre ytt well. Neverthelesse you may nott saye, how that for by cawse he that knowyth moche shall answere for moche, and therfore I wyll nother haue the woorde of God taught unto me, nor yett rede ytt my selfe; for by cawse I wyll excuse my self by ygnorancy : for he that knowyth butt lyttill hathe lyttyll to answere for. They that thus thynk deseyvyth themselfe ; for there shall no man excuse hym selfe by ygnorancye, nott so long as the trewethe of the woord of God myght haue been taught unto hym, yff he wolde dylygentlye haue reseyvyd ytt. So long as ytt ys so that you maye haue knowledg, and wyll nott, so long you can nott excuse your selfe by ygnorancye. And therfore they that haue knowledg, se that they use that knowledg (that God hathe gevyn them) to the pleasure of God and the profyte of your neyghbour. And thus I thynk, for a cawse and tyme reasonable, they maye ordeyne, that the Scripture shall nott be gevyn to the people, as before rehersyd.

XIII. *I thynke that consecracyons, halowyngs, and blessyngs, receyvyd in the Churche, by usage of Cristen men, are to be praysed.*

I thynke that blessyngs, and soche other thyngs doon in the Church, ys good, and worthy to be praysyd, though yt be nott of necessyte : for I thynk that no man wyll ageyne saye any ceremonye that ys in the Churche, the whych ys usyd and hathe ben usyd for a good purpose : for he that despisethe the lest ceremonye in the Church (the whych hathe ben usyd by the custome of good Crysten people) ys no Crysten man. No, nor I thynk that there ys no man so folyshe, that wolde dyspyse them, yff the trewthe of that thyng that the ceremonye dooth represent, were knowyn. For there is not the lest ceremonye in the Churche but ytt representythe some good thyng: as the *pax* that comythe from the preste (when he ys at masse) down into the bodye of the churche, and there they kysse ytt, as the preste dyd at the fyrst: the whyche thyng doothe sygnefye the loue that ys or sholde be betwene the preste and laye men; that ys to saye, the spiritualty and the tem- 27 poraltye. How be ytt, I thynk ytt be lyttill consydred of many of them that doo kysse the *pax*: and as yt ys by thys ceremonye, so yt ys with other lyke. And also as concernyng blessyngs and halowyngs, you knowe very well that there ys no blyssyng that ys ordeynyd by God but that ys good, and therfore yt ys worthy to be praysyd of all men; for of blyssyng comyth no maner of evyll but good, for to blysse ys as moche as to saye, as to wysh a man good; as thus, " The favor and grace of Allmyghty God lyght upon " you," and to saye, " God prospere you in all your busy- " nes," and soforthe. And so yt ys of halowyngs and soche lyke; for of them comyth no maner of evyll, but goodnesse: wherfore they are worthy to be praysyd of everye man as good thyngs. And I dowt nott, butt and yff yt were so, that euery man knew the very trew use of the blyssyngs, consecracyons, and soche other thyngs, yt wolde comfort and doo them moche more good to folow them then yt dothe now. I wolde that euery man knew the use of them. Now here folowythe another answere, and yt ys the last, and concludythe all.

XIV. *I thynk, and always haue thought, these opynyons to be trew, and they whych thynk the contrarye doo err, after my judgment.*

I thynk, and allway haue thought: These woords sownde nott, that I shold now thynk that thyng that I haue not thought before, or that I sholde saye that thyng that I haue not sayde before: for I haue sayde nothyng to my knowledge but that thyng that I wyll saye agayne. And therfore yff any man haue these answerys wryttyn, as there ys many of them wryttyn in dede, some men haue translatyd thys woord *sentio*, and saye, that *I knowledge*, and some saye, that *I confesse;* for those woords sownde that I sholde now confesse those thyngs that in tyme past I haue denyed; and that ys not true: for those thyngs that I haue sayde, I wyll saye agayne: and therfore I saye, how that I thynk now as I haue allwayes thought. And therfore yff there be any of you that doo desyre to haue the true copye of these answerys, resort hether to my paryshe preste, and there you shall haue them redy for you at all tymes. I shall desyre you at thys tyme to be contentyd wyth thys lyttyll declaracyon; and herafter, by the grase of God, as tyme and oportunyte doth cause me, I shall declare them unto you more at large. And now I commit you unto hym the whych allwaye preservyth hys servants.

---

28   Number XI.

A consolatory letter to a nobleman imprisoned for the profession of the gospel.

Foxii MSS. I HAVE hard, that your lordeshippe doth both desyre that men shuld write unto you, and that also yow doo take in good part, be it but simple, that ys writen. Wheruppon I dyd bolden my self, at thys tyme, to write unto yow; though I be unknowen, and also unmete hereunto. And for successe of my writing, I wyll committe that unto hym that ys able to fede without fode, and to comfort wher no hope of comfort ys; as out of myn unpleasant and unsaverie wordes, yow ar lyke to fynd no consolation at all. But yet ys Godds hande nor goodnes not shortened, but that hereby he may worke both your comfort and hys owne glorie, as semeth best to hys good wyll.

What greatt and continuall thanks ar all Godds children bounde to geve hym, for your Lordshipps incredible stoutnes in Chryst our master hys causse? Well, it ys to be consydered, that Godds woorde hath not altogether been taught and redde in vayne unto the nobles, all ar not gyrers and

mockers, all ar not covetuose and ambitiouse, all ar not
fleshlye and ryotuose. And wold God, that a fewe more
were of that ernest zeale and boldnes in Christ, whych yow
have declared your self to be: for then shuld not owr old
blyndnes thys hedlonge be tombled in upon us ageyne. The
masse, wyth all the dreggs of Antichrist therin, woold never
soo easelye nor willinglye have been receyved as yt ys. But
what shall we saye, that even as a fewe be sincere and harte,
so yet the major part by farre ar but holow harted and
cold. And such, bycausse they seke the light, but dyd not
walke therafter, and had no delyte therin, are justly be-
reyved of the same, and lyke to be thrown into palpable
darknes, wyth Pharao and the Egyptians, and that (as it Exod. vii.
doth appeyre) accordyng both to ther deserts and desyre.
For God can not alwaye souffre dissemblers to set forth hys
name, neither wyll he, that hys wyll shuld, of the unwyll-
yng, be sayed to be mayntened. And therfore, by takyng
awaye the libertie of hys worde, he myndeth now to trye
the true from the false, and shede out the gootes from the
shepe: whych is almost alredye come to pass. But it ys not
lyke to ende thus: for seynce that God dyd so plentifullie
send hys gospell and worde unto us, gevyng us therto hys
sacramentes so purely ministred; and yet the receyvors notwithstandyng, for the most part, lyke unto the people that
ys spoken of by the prophet Ezechiel: what should be Cap. xxxiii.
looked for, but that God indede wyll laye hys hevye hand
upon us; and that not perhaps so much corporallie, as by
takyng away from us the spirituall foode of our soules,
whych ys the ministerie of hys worde. The Lord be mercifull unto us: and yet I can not saye, to take hys plagues 29
utterlye from us, (for that I thynke were not good for us,)
but rather to geve us of hys grace and Spirite to bear his
angre, bycausse we have synned against him so soore. For Micheas vii.
if we shuld have still as we have hitherto had, we wold be
as we have hitherto been, yf we were not worse. Wheruppon that lesson, whych in pleintie and bryghtnes we wold
not lerne, it shall be tryed, how we wyll lerne it in scarcetie
and darkness: and bycausse we wold not serve God the

right and true waye, we shall prove how we can beare and away wyth the false, and suffre idolatre before our eyes.

But your Lordishippe must pardon me, for I have forgotten my self, that I am about to write to hym that is in prison; whych knoweth and fealeth metelye well hereof alredye. For sure I am, the punishments of God upon thys hys Church, wyth your owne synnes and infirmitees, besides other crosses and trialls, have somethyng broken your hart wyth ernest sorow and repentance: so that you have more nede of Goddes promyses yn the gospell to comfort yow, then (as I go about) to encrease your dolor and sorrowe, wyth puttyng yow in mynd of such evells and miseries. And yet even perchaunce even thys kynde ys unto yow Jerem. ix. pleasure, as it was unto Jeremye, when he desyred rivers full of teares, and a cotage in a corner, to bewayle the synnes and sorowes of hys people: and as he, in hys hoole booke of Lamentations, doth nothyng but lament and cry out for the desolation of hys people and citizens. In the whych, yff he had a delyte, doyng of it for the materiall citie and temple, that they was made desolate; how much more must teares and wepynge yssew from such, as now beholde the suddein ruine and destruction of our Church of England? Wherin who doth not see a most miserable change. For lyght, darkness; for truth, falsehed; for Godds worde, mans inventions; for spiritual worshyppyng, corporal idolatrye; for godlye lawes to maynteyne the truth, contempt therof; wyth more that I wyll leave to your owne meditacions and prayers.

And thys waye to bewayle the private and common miseries of our dayes, as yt hath with yt a present delectation; so also ys yt the onlye and sure waye to atteyne to the comfort whych the promysses of Christ yn the gospell do Matt. xi. bringe. Even as Christ doth tell us, when he sayeth, *Come unto me all you that labor, and are looden, and I wyll re-* Matt. v. *freshe yow;* and in an other place also, *Happie are thei which mourne, for thei shall fynde comfort.* Accordyng hereunto, the prophet and good Kyng Dauid affyrmeth Ps. cxxvi. lykewyse, that *such as sowe in teares, shall reape in joye.*

Wherof your Lordshippe, in thys grett shyne of Godds gos-pell, haue often both hard and redde, yea and by expe-rience practised it also; but yet never so swetelye (I dare well saye) as now, syns thys crosse hath been layde upon you. For now yow be in Godds propre scholehouse, wher as yow have not so many to trouble yow, as when yow went wandering in the wyde world, that ys so full of the Devills scales. Now yow haue tyme to talke unto God, in your often and most serious prayers; tyme also to geve eare unto hym, talkyng and speakyng unto yow out of hys worde. So that yow tast of that in dede now, of wych before yow 30 dyd but (as it were) here tell of. And that yow fynd veri-fyed upon your self, that the good scholer of the Lord, David, spekyth of hym self, in the long Psalme of hys owne experiences, sayeng, *It is good for me, O Lord, that I have* Ps. cxix. *been in trouble, that I myght lerne thyne ordinances:* as though he shuld have sayed; Before I came into affliction, I hadd so many lettes and hynderaunces, that I could not entende unto that wych thow (O Lord) dydst putt to me to lerne: but now, by these crosses, I am taught to avoyde suche impediments, and to withstande such affections, as drawe me from the markyng and kepyng of thye lawes and commandement.

And now therfore, I beseech yow, (my good Lord,) waye wyth your self, what a good master our heavenlye Father ys unto yow, that alone he doth make yow so good a scho-ler, that yow can find yn your hart, in comparison of hym and hys worde, to despyse all things els: as favor and fayre worde of men, honor both present and hereafter to folowe, riches and pleasure, lands and possessions, parents and frends, wyf and children, and what shall I speke of more, except it be lyf it self? Thus is the Lorde working in yow, to make yow to thynke with Moses, to be in the affliction Heb. xi. and danger that the children of God bee in, rather than to enjoye all the riches of the Egiptians. But such an one ys Godd, and so ys he mynded, to wynne yow with kyndnes for ever, to bynd yow unto hym in bonds of hys mercye, that never shall be unloosed agayne. Geve honor therfore unto hym alone, wych hath alredye begonne and wyll continue, and make perfytt hys power and myght in your imbecillitee and weaknes. That hys name may be knowen, and hys chyldren confyrmed the boldlyer to stycke unto hym. As I doo not doubt, but that alredye yt ys come to passe in some, and how manye moo shall it be wrought in, wych shall here and perceyve, that yow shall with patience and strength persevere to the ende. Be stronge therfore, and stablishe your conscience upon the Lords worde. For what so euer ys pretended and brought in ageynst yow, yet knowe, that to consent and receyve the masse cannot be but horrible, and grevouslye provoke the Lord unto angre. And to persuade yow herein, or rather to confirme yow in that wych alredye yow ar out of doubt of, I wyll not make much a doo. For doo but conferre thys masse of mans makyng wyth the supper of Christs institution, and see what sembleablenes ys betwene them; and yow shall perseyve them as lyke one to the other, both in substance and outward appearance, as an honest matrone ys lyke to the Devill, deckt in an hoores atteyryng. And yet have they noon other cloke or defense, save onlye to saye, that it is the Lords supper: but a man with half an eye maye judge thys matter easelye ynough. Howbeit, though we shuld graunt (wych Godd forbydd) the masse, wyth the appurtenances, to be tollerable, yet wych way can they bring it in to the congregation of idiotes and symple? Unto whome all that in ther masse ys spoken ys in a straunge language. Wheras St. Pauli commandeth noon to speke with tongues, onlesse he be interpreted. Wher as also *Amen* must be answered to the thanks gevyng, not as to a mans q in a playe, but by one that preyeth, wherunto he maketh hys answer. *Turn awaye your eyes*, therfor, from the vanitie of ther customes and conceiles, of ther tradicions and good ententes, of ther doctors and divines, of ther fathers and fansyes, of scholemen and sophysters: for thes ar for the doctors and byshoppes to beate ther braynes about. Yow and thei also, when thei have doon what they can, must be judged and quieted by Godds worde and Scripture, or els it ys but vio-

1 Cor. xiv. 31

Ps. cxix.

lence and tyrannie. And the scripture we have hereof ys playne to hym that meaneth and seketh playnnes, markyng the cheif ende whye the supper was ordeyned; to put us in mynd, and so to confirme us in the Lords death, and the lyvelye and present remembraunce of the same: wheras they goo about nought els but the contrarye; as ther Latin service, and takyng awaye of Godds worde, doth most manifestlye declare. Beware of them then; for ther ende ys but darkenes and blyndyng of the people, and to gett mens consciences to hange upon them. But such ys the sawce, that our synfull lyves undre the gospell hath sawced our self, and the hole Church of Christ here among us wyth all.

But now what remedie? Noon, but to humble our selfs under the mightie hands of the Lord. And in noo wyse wyth hart or wyth hande, wyth worde or wyth dede, privelye or openlye, to subscribe or consent to the defacyng of Christes kyngdome, the pullyng downe of hys worde, nor settyng up of that wych ys disagreyng therto. For we ar hys temple both bodye and soule, and must beleve wyth the hart, and confesse also wyth our mouth, yf we wyll be salved. As St. Paull doth teach. 1 Cor. vi.
Rom. x.

The Lord of all mercye, comfort, and strength, geve your good Lordishipp, wyth other in the same case, thys faith and boldnes to confesse Christ and hys glorye unto the ende. *Amen.*

Number XII.

Articles for the married clergy in the diocese of Litchfield and Coventry.

IN Dei nomine, Amen. Nos Richardus Walker, canonicus Foxii MSS. residens in ecclesia cath. Litch. reverendi in Christo patris et domini, Domini Richardi, permissione divina Coven. et Litch. episcopi, commissarius specialis in hac parte legitime deputatus, articulos infra scriptos, ac quamlibet partem et particulam eorum de vobis magistris, Hugoni Simonds, &c.

et cuilibet vestrum ex officio nostro mero objicimus, minis- tramus, et articulamur, conjunctim et divisim. Quibus et cuilibet parti et particulæ eorundem, verum, plenum, pla- num, et fidele, virtute juramenti vestri, et cujuslibet vestrum, volumus per vos et vestrum quemlibet dari responsum.

Imprimis, Vobis et cuilibet vestrum objicimus et articula- mur, quod vos fuistis et estis sacerdotes, sive presbyteri, atque in sacris ordinibus, et ipso etiam presbyteratus ordine constituti, eosdemque sacros et presbyteratus ordines, ad triginta, viginti, decem vel octo annos elapsos suscepistis; atque pro Presbyteris, et in sacris ordinibus constituti fuistis, et estis, communiter dicti, tenti, habiti, nominati, et reputati, palam, publice et notorie : sicque fuit et est ves- trum quilibet, et ponimus conjunctim et divisim et de quo- libet.

Item, Quod vos non solum in professione ordinis et regu- læ Sti. Benedicti, vel Sti. Augustini, aut Sti. Francisci, vel Sti. Dominici, sive Cistertien. vel Præmonstraten. seu Car- tusien. alteriusve ordinis sive regulæ cujuscunque religionis; verum etiam in susceptione dictorum sacrorum et presbyte- ratus ordinum juxta sanctorum patrum decreta, in ea parte pie et salubriter edita et stabilita ac promulgata, juxtaque et secundum sacros canones et constitutiones ac ordinationes, et laudabiles consuetudines ecclesiasticas, ab ipsa Ecclesia Catholica, et præsertim ab Ecclesia Latina et Occidentali, religiose, pie, et continue observatas, solenne votum castita- tis et continentiæ fecistis, et emisistis. Sicque fecit et emisit vestrum quilibet. Hocque fuit et est verum, publicum, no- torium, manifestum pariter et famosum. Et ponimus ut supra.

Itemque, Vos scitis, creditis, aut dici audivistis, quod ex sacris ecclesiasticis constitutionibus, quilibet profitens ali- quam regulam religionis, et quilibet etiam suscipiens sacrum ordinem aut sacros ordines, tam ex ipsa professione, quam ex ipsorum sacrorum ordinum susceptione, obligatur ad per- petuam continentiam : nec eidem licere ad seculum retro- cedere, et uxorem ducere, sive concubinam retinere. Et ponimus ut supra.

Itemque, Vos in hujusmodi sacris, et presbiteratus ordi- IV.
nibus constituti, missas et alia divina officia tam privatim
quam publice dixistis, et celebrastis, atque sacramenta et
sacramentalia aliis Christi fidelibus ministratis. Sicque dixit,
celebravit, et ministravit vestrum quilibet. Et ponimus ut
supra.

Itemque, Tu Magister Hugo, &c. præmissorum omnium V.
et singulorum satis sciolus, ipsis quoque non obstantibus,
sed præter et contra ea ; atque post ipsos sacros, et presbyteratus ordines per te susceptos, in magnum opprobrium et
grave dedecus ac scandalum ordinis clericalis, et propriæ
animæ tuæ salutis manifestum detrimentum, de facto, cum
de jure non potuisti neque debuisti quandam   in uxorem, imo verius concubinam, mensibus Martii, Aprilis,
Maii, Junii, Julii, Augusti, Septembris, Octobris, Novem-
bris, Decembris, Januarii, et Februarii, annis Domini millesimo, quingentesimo XLVI, XLVII, XLVIII, XLIX, L, LI, LII,
et LIII, eorundemve mensium et annorum quolibet uno sive
aliquo, temere et damnabiliter duxisti et accepisti ; atque
cum eadem publice cohabitasti, et cohabitas in præsenti :
eandemque sæpius carnaliter cognovisti ; ac in nephariis
fornicariisque amplexibus tenuisti, et tenes in præsenti ; 33
fornicationem, adulterium, et incestum ea ratione publice et
notorie committendo, ac votum castitatis et continentiæ hujusmodi per te solemniter, ut præmittitur, emissum et factum, notorie violando et transgrediendo. Hocque fuit et est
verum, publicum, notorium, manifestum, pariter et famosum. Et ponimus ut supra.

. Itemque, Vos præmissorum prætextu et occasione fuistis, VI.
et estis, dictorum sacrorum canonum, constitutionum, et or-
dinationum, atque consuetudinum transgressores manifesti,
ac dictorum votorum vestrorum solennium violatores ; eaque
ratione et prætextu ipso facto vestris officiis et dictis respective beneficiis vestris de jure privati, et ab eisdem, eorum-
que possessione et occupatione, auctoritate ordinaria amo-
vendi et destituendi. Sicque fuit et est vestrum quilibet.
Et ponimus ut supra.

Itemque, Præmissa omnia singula fuerant, et sunt vera, VII.

publica, notoria, pariter et famosa, atque de et super eisdem laborarunt et in præsenti laborant publica vox et fama.

Number XIII.

An appeal made to the Queen from a sentence definitive, pronounced by a commissary of the Bishop of Litchfield.

MSS. Foxii.

IN Dei nomine, Amen. Coram vobis publica et authentica persona, ac testibus fide dignis, hic præsentibus, ego Simon Pope, clericus, rector ecclesiæ paroch. de Warmington in com. Warwic. Coven. et Litch. dioc. dico, allego, et in hiis scriptis animo appellandi et querelandi propono;

Quod licet ego fuerim et sim vir bonæ famæ, opinionis illæsæ, vitæque et conversationis honestarum, atque pro tali et ut talis inter bonos et graves fuerim et sim communiter dictus, tentus, habitus, nominatus et reputatus, palam, publice, et notorie; venerabilis tamen vir Magister Richardus Walker, ecclesiæ cathedralis Litch. canonicus residens, pro commissario reverendi in Christo patris et dni. Dni. Richardi permissione divina Coven. et Litch. episcopi se gerens, in quodam prætenso negotio deprivationis et amotionis mei præfati Simonis Pope, tam ab officio et ministratione clericali, quam dicta ecclesia mea paroch. de Warmington, cum suis juribus et pertinentiis universis nulliter et inique, ex officio suo mero, ut prætendebatur, in omnibus et per omnia procedens, juris et judiciorum ordine non servato, sed neglecto, prætermisso, et penitus spreto, quandam prætensam sententiam definitivam, sive quoddam prætensum finale decretum, vim sententiæ definitivæ in se continens: per quam inter cætera me præfatum Simonem Pope, rectorem antedictum, non confessum, neque aliquo modo saltem sufficienti convictum, neque ad hoc vocatum nec citatum, sed longe ante tempus sive terminum per eum primitus assignatum et affixum, ab eisdem officio et ministratione clericali, et dicta ecclesia mea paroch. de Warmington, cum suis juribus et pertinentiis universis privand. et amovendum fore decrevit;

atque de facto, licet nulliter et inique, deprivavit et amovit, ad omnem juris effectum tulit et promulgavit in scriptis [licet] nullam et iniquam, nullumve seu iniquum. Atque ad alia graviora contra me procedere se velle publice comminatus est, et indies comminatur, in animæ suæ grave periculum, meique dicti Simonis Pope, rectoris prædicti præjudicium non modicum, et grave dampnum.

Unde ego dictus Simon Pope, rector prædictus, sentiens me tam ex prolatione dictæ prætensæ sententiæ definitivæ, sive prætensi finalis decreti antedicti, quam ex aliis gravaminibus, iniquitatibus, et injuriis dicti prætensi commissarii colligibilibus, indebite prægravari ab eisdem et eorum quolibet ad serenissimam in Christo Principem et Dnam. nostram Dnam. Mariam, Dei gratia Angliæ, Franciæ, et Hiberniæ Reginam, Fidei Defensorem, et in terris Ecclesiæ Anglicanæ et Hibernicæ supremum Caput; atque ad inclitam et almam curiam Parliamenti hujus regni Angliæ, seu alium judicem competentem quemcunque ad quem de jure, seu statutis hujus regni Angliæ michi licitum est, vel imposterum licebit, appellare, in hiis scriptis appello; apostolosque peto primo, secundo et tertio, instanter, instantius et instantissime, michi, edi, dari, tradi, fieri et liberari cum effectu: et protestor, quod non sunt decem dies elapsi, ex quo michi de productæ sententiæ definitivæ, seu prædicti prætensi finalis decreti, prolatione et aliis gravaminibus, iniquitatibus, et injuriis prædictis certitudinaliter constabat et constat. Et quod in præsenti nequeo habere judicis præsentiam, ut coram eo appellarem. Et protestor insuper de intimando hanc meam appellationem pro loco et tempore, congruis et opportunis omnibus et singulis, quibus jus exigit in hac parte, deque corrigendo et reformando eandem juxta jurisperitorum consilium prout moris est et stili.

Number XIV.

35

The Queen to the justices of Norfolk, to search for the broachers of vain prophecies and rumours.

To our trusty and welbeloved, the sheriff and justices of the peace of our county of Norfolk, and to every of them.

By the Quene.

Mary the Quene.

Cott. Libr.
Titus, B. 2.

TRUSTY and welbeloved, we grete you wel : And wheras we have heretofore signified our plesure, both by our proclamation generally, and by our letters to many of you particularly, for the good order and stay of that our county of Norfolk from rebellious tumults and uproars ; and to have especial regard to vagabonds, and to such as did spred any vain prophesies, seditious, false, or untrue rumours, and to punish them accordingly ; we have nevertheles to our no smal grief sundry intelligences of divers and sundry leud and seditious tales, forged and spred by certain malicious persons, touching the estate of our person, with many other vain and slanderous reports, tending to the moving of sedition and rebellion : whose faults passing unpunished seemeth either to be winked at, or at least little considered ; which is unto us very strange. We have therfore thought good eftsones to require and command you to be not only more circumspect in the good ordering of that our county, according to our trust conceived of you, but also to use al the best means and ways ye can in the diligent examining and searching out from man to man thauctours and publishers of these vain prophesies and untrue bruits, (the very foundation of al rebellion,) and the same being found, to punish them, as the quality of their offence shal appear unto you to deserve : wherby the malicious sort may be more feared to attempt the like, and our good loving subjects live in more quiet.

And for our better service in this behalf, we think good that you divide your selves into several parts of our county ; so that every of you have some part in charge : wherby ye may the better bulte out the malicious ; and yet nevertheless to meet often for the better conferring herein. And that you signify your doings and the state of that shire by your general letters once every month at least to our Privy Council. And like as we shal consider such of you to your advancement, whose diligence shal set forward our service in this part, so shal we have good cause to note great negligence and fault in them that shal omit their duties in this behalf. Yeven under our signet at our manor of St. James the xxiii. of May, the first year of our reign.

Number XV.   36

A proclamation, that all courtesy should be used to King Philip and his train, coming into England to marry the Queen.

By the Quene.

WHERE the Quenes most excellent Majestie hath lately concluded a marriage, to the honour of the mightie God, and the weale and benefite of her Graces realmes and subjectes, with the moste hygh and mightye Prince, the Prince of Spayne; her Highnes, consideryng the lightnes and evill disposition of diverse lewde and sediciouse personnes, who, seking alwayes nouelties, and beinge seldome contented with their presente state, might peraduenture at this time, by their naughtie and disordred behaviour, attempte to stirre discorde, and gyue occasion to breake the good and frendly agreament that ought to be nourished and continued betwene the subjectes of thys realme, and suche as shall come in wyth the sayde most noble Prince; hath thought good to signifie unto all her faythfull and louynge subjectes, that lyke as allready order is taken, on the behalfe of the sayde moste noble Prince, that all such, eyther of his owne or any other nation, as shall attende upon hymselfe, or any of hys trayne, at theyr commyng hither, shall in their behaviour use themselfes honestly, frendely, and quietly towardes her Highnes subjectes, of all sortes and degrees, without givynge anye maner of juste occasion of trouble or discontentation to

P 4

any person for their partes; even so doth her Hyghnes streyghtly charge and commaunde al and singuler her lovynge subjects, of what estate, degree, or condition soever they be, that they and every of them do semblablye, for their partes, use all suche straungers, as shall repayre hither wyth or to the sayde most noble Prince, or any of hys trayne, with curtoyse, frendely, and gentle enterteynement, wythoute ministryng towardes them any maner of cause of stryfe or contention, either by outwarde dedes, tauntyng wordes, unsemely countenance, or by any other wayes or meanes, whereby lacke of frendeshyppe or good wyll might be conceaved.

And further streyghtly chargeth and commaundeth all and singuler noblemen and gentlemen, wythin this her Graces sayde realme, that they and everye of them do, eche one for hys part, take suche ordre wyth their servaunts and others, attendyng upon them, and do give unto them suche streyght warnyng and charge, as neyther by themselfes, nor by anye other meanes, they do presume to attempt, either directly or indirectly, to break this her Highnes order and commaundement, or any wayes to trouble, 37 disquiet, or give occasion of quarel to anye of the sayde most noble Princes trayne: upon payne, that whosoever shall by worde or dede neglecte thys her Graces pleasure, or do contrary to the same, shall not only incurre her Majesties high displeasure and indignation, but allso be committed to prison without bayle or maynprize; to abyde there suche further punyshment, eyther by fyne or otherwise, as shall be thought agreeable to the qualitie of his or their offences, and maye serve for an example to other lyke disordred persons.

God save the Quene.
Anno M.D.LIIII.

Number XVI.

Articles of inquiry for Boner bishop of London's visitation of his diocese in the year 1554.

ARTICLES to be enquyred of in the general visitation of Edmund Bishop of London, exercised by him in the year of our Lord 1554, in the city and dioces of London; and set forth by the same for his own discharge towards God and the world, to the honour of God and his Catholick Church, and to the commoditie and profyt of al those that either are good, (which he wolde were al,) or delighteth in goodnes, (which he wisheth to be many,) without any particular grudge or displeasure to any one, good or bad, within this realm. Which articles he desireth al men of their charitie, especially those that are of his diocese, to take with as good an intent and mynd as he the said Bishop wisheth and desireth, which is to the best. And the said Bishop withal desireth al people to understand, that whatsoever opinion, good or bad, hath been received of him, or whatsoever usage or custome hath been heretofore, his only intent and purpose is to do his duty charitably, and with that love, favour, and respect, both towards God and every Christen person, which any Bushop shuld shew to his flock in any wise.

The first articles are concerning the clargy, because they shuld of duety geve good example, and that their fault is more indeed, and more worthy punishment, than the faults of the laity.

The first article.

First, Whether the clargy, to geve example to the laity, have in their lyving, in their teachyng, and in their doyng, so behaved themselves, that they (in the judgment of indifferent persons) have declared themselves to search principally the honor of God and hys Church, the health of the souls of such as are commyted to their cure and charge, the quietnes of their paryshyoners, and the wealth and honor of the King and Quene of this realm.

Item, Whether the person, vicar, or any other ministring 38

II.

as priest within the parysh, have been or is married, or taken for maried, not yet separated from his concubine or woman, taken for wife. Or, whether the same woman be dead, or yet livyng: and being living, whether the one resorteth to the other openly, secretly, or slanderously, maintaining, supporting, or finding the same in any wise, to the offence of the people.

III.   *Item*, Whether there be any person, of what estate, condition, or degree he be, that doth in open talk, or privily, defend, maintain, or uphold the mariage of priests, encouraging or bolding any person to the defence therof.

IV.   *Item*, Whether ye have the person or vicar resident continually with you upon his benefice, doeing his duety in the serving of the cure; and whether, beyng able, he do keep hospitalitie upon the same, feeding his flock with his good lyving, with hys teachyng, and his relievyng of theym to hys power.

V.   *Item*, Whether the person or vicar, being absent, have a sufficient dispensation and licence therin: and whether in his absence he do appoynt an honest, able, and sufficient learned curate, to supply his room and absence, to serve his cure.

VI.   *Item*, Whether your person or vicar, by hymself, or his good and sufficient deputy for him, do relieve his poor parishoners, repair and maintain his house or mansion, and things therunto appertaining, and otherwyse do his duety, as by the order of the law, and custome of this realme, he ought to do.

VII.   *Item*, Whether the sayd curate, appoynted in the absence of your person or vicar, do in al poynts the best he can to minister the sacraments and sacramentals, and other his duety in serving the same cure; specially in celebrating divine service at convenient hours, chefely upon Sundays, and holydays, and procession days; and ministring the said sacraments and sacramentals, as of duety and reason he ought, moving and exhorting earnestly his parishioners to come unto it, and devoutly to hear the same: and whether he hymself do reverentlye celebrate, practise, minister, and use the same, as appertayneth.

Item, Whether he the sayd curate, person, or vicar, have bene or is of suspect doctrin, erroneous opinyon, misbelefe, or evyl judgment; or do set forth, preach, favour, ayd, or mayntaine the same, contrary to the Catholick faith, or order of this realm.   VIII.

Item, Whether they, or any of them, doth haunt or resort to alehouses or taverns, otherwyse than for hys or their honest necessity or reliefe; or repayre to any dysing houses, common bowling allies, suspect houses or places; or do haunt and use common games or playes, or behave themselves otherwyse unpriestly and unsemely.   IX.

Item, Whether they, or any of them, be familiar, or kepe company, and be conversaunt with any suspect person of evyl conversation and lyving, or erroneous opinyon or doctrin; or be noted to ayd, favour, and assyste the same in any wyse, contrary to the good order of this realm, and the usage of the Catholick Church.   X.   39

Item, Whether there be dwelling within any your parishes any priest, foreigner, stranger, or other, who not presented unto the Bushop of this dioces, or his officers, examined and admitted by some one of them, doth take upon him to serve any cure, or to minister any sacraments or sacramentals within the said parish.   XI.

Item, Whether there be dwelling within any your parishes, or repairing thither, any priest, or other naming hymself minister, which doth not come diligently to the church, to hear divine service or sermons there, but absentyth hymself, or discourageth other by his example or words to come unto the same, expressing their name and surname, with sufficient knowledge of them.   XII.

Item, Whether there be any maried priests, or namyng themselves mynisters, that do kepe any assemblies or conventicles with such like, as they are in office or sect, to set forth any doctrin or usage not allowed by the laws and laudable customs of this realm: or whether there be any resort of any of them to any place for any privy lectures, sermons, plays, games, or other devices, not expresly in this realm by laws allowable.   XIII.

XIV.   *Item*, Whether there be any of them which is a common brawler, scoulder, a sower of discord among his parishioners, a hawker, a hunter, or spending his tyme ydelly and unthriftily; or being a fornicator, an advouterer, a drunkard, a common swearer, or blasphemer of God or his saints, or an unruly or evyl disposed person; or that hath come to his benefice or promotion by symonie, unlawful sute, or ungodly means in any wyse.

XV.   *Item*, Whether they, and everich of them, to the best of their powers at al tymes, have exhorted and stirred the people to quietnes and concord, and to the obedience of the Kyng and Quenes Majesties and their officers; rebuking al sedition and tumult, with al unlawful assemblies; moving the people to charity and good order; and charging the fathers and mothers, masters and governors of youth, to keep good rule, and to instruct them in vertue and goodnes, to the honor of God and of this realme, and to have them occupied in some honest art and occupation, to get their living thereby.

XVI.   *Item*, Whether they, or any of them, do admyt any person to receyve the blessed sacrament of the altre, who are openlye known or suspected to be adversaries and speakers against the sacrament, or any other article of the Catholick faith; or to be a notorious evyl person in his conversation or doctrin, an open oppressor or evyl doer to his neybour, not being confessed, reconcyled, and having made satisfaction in that behalf.

XVII.   *Item*, Whether they, or any of them, have of their own authoritie admytted and lycenced any to preach in their cure, not being authorized or admytted therunto; or have denyed or refused such to preach as have been lawfully lycensed. And whether they or any of them, having authority to preach within their cures, doth use to preach, or at the least doth procure other lawful or sufficient persons to doo the same, according to the ordre of this realm.

40   *Item*, Whether they, or any of them, sens the Quenes
XVIII.   Majesties proclamation, hath or doth use to say or sing the divine service, minister the sacraments and sacramentals,

or other things, in English, contrary to the ordre of this realm.

Item, Whether they, or any of them, in their suffrages, collects, and prayers, doth use to pray for the King and Quenes Majeste, by the names of King Philip and Quene Mary, according to a letter of commandment therin lawfully gyuen now of late unto them by their ordinary. XIX.

Item, Whether they, and everych of them, have diligent- XX. ly moned and exhorted their parishners how and in what màner children shuld be baptized in tyme of necessity ; and they the said parishners reverently and devoutly to prepare themselves to receive and use the sacraments, especially of the sacrament of the aultre. And whether any person have refused or contempned to receyve the said sacrament of the aultare, or to be confessed, and receive at priests hands the benefit of absolution, according to the laudable custome of this realme.

Item, Whether they, and everich of them, hath diligently XXI. visited his and their parishners in the tyme of syckness and nede, and ministred sacraments and sacramentals to them accordingly. And whether they have exhorted and monyshed them to have due respect to their soul health : and also to set an ordre in their temporal lands and goods, declaring their debts perfectly, and what is owing unto them ; and they so to make their testaments and last wills, that, as much as may be, al trouble and busines may be excluded, their wives and children, with their friends, may be holpen and succoured, and themselves decently buried and prayed for, and to have an honest memory and commendations for their so doing.

Item, Whether they, and everich of them, have solem- XXII. nized matrimony betwene any his parishners, or any other persons, the banes not before asked iii several Sundays or holydays, or without certificate of the said banes from the curate of any other parish, if any of them be of another parish. And whether, touching the solemnization and use of this sacrament of matrimony, and also of al other the sacraments of the Church, they have kept and observed the

old and laudable custome of the Church, without any invocation [innovation] or alteration in any of the same.

XXIII.   *Item,* Whether they, or everich of them, upon the Sonday
at the service tyme, doth use to set fourth and to declare unto
the people al such holydays and fasting days, as of godlye
usage and custome hath heretofore laudably been accustomed to be kept and observed in the weke following and en_
sueing.   And whether they, and everych of them, doth observe and kepe themselves the said holy days and fasting
days.

XXIV.   *Item,* Whether the person or vicar doth repair and maintain his chauncel and mansion house in sufficient repara-
tion: and the same being in decay, whether he doth bestow
yearly the fift part of his benefit, til such time the same be
sufficiently repaired; doing also further his duty therin,
41 and otherwise, as by the law he is charged and bound in
that behalf, distributing and doing as he is bound by the
law.

XXV.   *Item,* Whether there be any person that doth serve any
cure, or minister any sacraments, not being priest; or if
any do take upon them to use the room and office of the
person, or vicar, or curate of any benefice or spiritual promotion, receyving the frutes thereof, not being admitted
therunto by the ordinary.

XXVI.   *Item,* Whether they, and everich of them, doth goo in
priestly apparel and habit, having their beards and crowns
shaven: or whether any of them doth goo in laymens ha-
bits and apparel, or otherwyse disguise themselves, that
they cannot easily be discovered or known from laymen.

XXVII.   *Item,* Whether they, or any of them, have many pro-
mocyons and benefices ecclesiastical, cures, secular services,
yearly pensions, annuyties, fermes, or other revenues, now
in tytle or possession: and what the names of them be, and
where they ly, geving al good instruction and perfect infor-
macyon therin.

XXVIII.   *Item,* Whether such as have churches or chappels appro-
priated, and mansions or houses therto appertayning, do
kepe their chauncels and houses in good and sufficyent re-

paracyons: and whether they do al things in distribucyons and almose, or otherwyse, as by law and good order they ought to do.

Item, Whether any such, as were ordered schismatically, **XXIX.** and contrary to the old order and custome of the Catholick Church, or being unlawfully and schismatically maried after the late innovation and maner, being not yet reconcyled nor admytted by the ordinary, have celebrated or sayd either mas or other divine service within any cure or place of this city or diocese.

Item, Whether any person, or vicar, or other having ec- **XXX.** clesiastical promocyon, do set out the same to ferm without consent, knowledge, and lycence of his ordinary; especially for an unreasonable number of years, or with such conditions, qualities, or maners, that the same is to the great prejudice of the Church, and the incumbent of the same, especially of him that shall succeed therin.

Item, Whether there be any person or vicar, curate or **XXXI.** priest, that occupyeth buying and selling as a merchaunt; or occupieth usury, or layeth out his money for filthy lucre sake and gain, to the slaunder of presthode.

Item, Whether they, or any of them, do wear swords, **XXXII.** daggars, or other weapon, in tymes or places not convenyent or semely.

Item, Whether any priest or ecclesiastical person have **XXXIII.** reiterated or renewed baptism which was lawfully don before; or invented or followed any new fashion or form, contrary to the order of the Catholick Church.

Item, Whether the person, vicar, or curate doo, accord- **XXXIV.** ing to the laws, every quarter in the year, upon one solempne day or mo, (that is to wyt, upon the Sonday or solempne feast, when the parishioners by the order of the Church do come together,) expound and declare by himself, or some other sufficyent person, unto the people, in the common or vulgar tongue, plainly, truly, and frutefully, the Articles of the Catholick Faith, the Ten Commaundements, **42** expressed in the old law, the two commaundements of the gospel or new law; that is, of earnest love to God and to our neighbour; the seven works of mercy, the seven deadly sins, with their off-spring, progeny, and yssue, the seven principal vertues, and the seven sacraments of the Church.

xxxv.   *Item,* Whether that every priest, having cure, do admonish the women that are with child, within his cure, to come to confession, and to receyve the sacrament, especially when their tyme draweth nigh; and to have water in readynes to christen the child, if necessity so require it.

xxxvi.   *Item,* Whether the stipendary priests do behave themselves discretly and honestly in al poynts towards their parson or vicar; geving an othe, and doing according to the law and ecclesiastical constitutions, ordinaunces, and laudable customs in that behalf.

xxxvii.   *Item,* Whether any parson, vicar, or other having any ecclesiastical promocyon, have made any alienation of any thing partayning to their church, benefice, or promocyon; what it is, and what warraunt they had so to do.

Number XVII.

The confession of the bishops and divines in prison for religion.

Fox's Acts.   FIRST, We confess and believe al the canonical books of the Old Testament, and al the books of the N. Testament, to be the very true word of God, and to be written by the inspiration of the H. Ghost; and therfor to be heard accordingly, as the judg in al controversies and matters of religion.

Secondly, We confes and believe the Catholick Church, which is the spouse of Christ, as a most obedient and loving wife, to embrace and follow the doctrin of these books in al matters of religion: and therfore is she to be heard accordingly. So that those which wil not hear this Church, thus following and obeying the word of her husband, we account as hereticks and schismaticks; according to this saying, *If he will not hear the Church, let him be unto thee as a heathen.*

Thirdly, We believe and confess al the articles of faith

and doctrin, set forth in the symbol of the Apostles, which we commonly cal the Creed; and in the symbols of the councels of Nice, kept in *an. Dom.* 324; of Constantinople, kept in *an. Dom.* 884; of Ephesus, kept in *an. Dom.* 432; of Chalcedonie, kept in *anno Dom.* 454; of Toletum, the first and the fourth. Also the symbols of Athanasius, Ireneus, Tertullian, and of Damasus, which was about the year of our Lord 376. We confes and believe, we say, the doctrin of these symbols generally and particularly; so that whosoever doth otherwise, we hold the same to erre from the truth.

Fourthly, We believe and confess concerning *justifica-* 43 *tion,* that, as it cometh only from God's mercy through Christ, so it is perceived and had of none, which be of years of discretion, otherwise than by faith only. Which faith is not an opinion, but a certain persuasion wrought by the H. Ghost in the mind and heart of man. Wherethrough as the mind is illumined, so the heart is suppled to submit it self to the wil of God unfeignedly, and so sheweth forth an inherent righteousnes: which is to be discerned in the article of justification from the righteousnes which God endueth us withal in justifying us, although inseparably they go together. And this we do not for curiosity or contention sake, but for conscience sake; that it might be quiet: which it can never be, if we confound, without distinction, forgivenes of sin and Christ's justice imputed to us, with regeneration and inherent righteousnes. By this we disallow the papistical doctrins of free wil, of works of supererogation, of merits, of the necessity of auricular confession, and satisfaction to Godward.

Fifthly, We confess and believe concerning the exterior service of God, that it ought to be according to the word of God. And therfore in the congregation al things publick ought to be done in such a tongue as may be most to edify; and not in Latin, where the people understand not the same.

Sixthly, We confesse and believe, that God only by Jesus Christ is to be prayed unto and called upon. And therfore we disallow invocation or prayer to saints departed this life.

Seventhly, We confess and believe, that as a man departeth this life, so shal he be judged in the last day generally, and in the mean season is entred either into the state of the blessed for ever, or damned for ever. And therfore is either past al help, or els needeth no help of any in this life. By reason wherof we affirm purgatory, masses of *scala cœli*, trentals, and such suffrages, as the popish Church doth obtrude as necessary, to be the doctrin of Antichrist.

Eighthly, We confess and believe the sacraments of Christ, which be baptism and the Lords supper, that they ought to be ministred according to the institution of Christ, concerning the substantial parts of them. And that they be no longer sacraments, than they be had in use, and used to the end for the which they were instituted.

And here we plainly confess, that the mutilation of the Lords supper, the subtraction of one kind from the lay people, is Antichristian. And so is the doctrin of transubstantiation of the sacramental bread and wine after the words of consecration, as they be called. *Item*, The adoration of the sacrament with honour due unto God, the reservation and confirmation of the same. *Item*, The mas to be a propitiatory sacrifice for the quick and dead, or a work that pleaseth God. Al these we confess and believe to be Antichrists doctrin; as is the inhibition of mariage as unlawful to any state.

And we doubt not by Gods grace, but we shal be able to prove al our confessions here to be most true by the verity of Gods word, and consent of the Catholick Church; which 44 followeth and hath followed the governance of Gods Spirit, and the judgment of his word. And this through the Lords help we wil do, either in disputation by *word*, before the Queens Highnes and her Council, either before the Parlament houses, (of whom we doubt not to be indifferently heard,) either with our *pens*, whensoever we shal be therto, by them that have authority, required and commanded.

In the mean season, as obedient subjects, we shal behave

our selves towards al that be in authority, and not cease to pray to God for them; that he would govern them al, generally and particularly, with the spirit of wisdom and grace. And so we heartily desire, and humbly pray al men to do; in no point consenting to any kind of rebellion or sedition against our sovereign Lady the Queens Highnes; (but where they cannot obey, but they must disobey God;) there to submit themselues with al patience and humility, to suffer as the wil and plesure of the higher powers shall adjudge.

Number XVIII.

A letter, or discourse, to the true professors of Christ's gospel, inhabiting in the parish of Alhallows, in Bread-street in London: written by Thomas Sampson, sometime their pastor.

THE grace and favour of God our heavenly Father, purchased unto us by the bloudy death of Christ our Saviour, be felt and encreased in al your consciences to your everlasting consolation. E Bibliotb. R. D. Johan. D. Ep. Eliens.

The violence of this age doth not suffer me, most loving brethren, to come as I would do unto you, and by talk and brotherly conferring to put you in mind of the gospel of Jesus Christ, which, among others far more worthy, even I by Gods grace preached unto you. I therefore have thought needful by these letters now to do the same; now I say, when, through the perverse frowardness of men, the true preaching of Christs gospel is banished, and mans doctrin is taught with lyes and fables. And tho some perchance wil think, that this longeth not to me, but to him that is your pastor, to do; yet, forasmuch as once I was your pastor, I cannot but testify, that some piece of pastoral cure doth yet rest in my heart towards you. The which indeed doth much persuade me, as the present necessity also seemeth no les to require, to make a long and a large treatise, by which ye might have an whole armour against al the assaults of false prophets. But when I consider how truly, and that

45 with much diligence, ye have been taught, and therewith thinking that ye are not forgetful hearers of the word, I think that among you it shal suffice, if I do but name those greatest evils, which now are poured forth out of pulpits among you, and therewith put you in mind of the truth, (contrary to these lyes,) which once you both heard and received, desiring you to abide in the same. This wil I do shortly, as I have little, and the same unapt time to do it: yet truly I trust to do it, as let Gods word therein try it: if first ye wil suffer me to tell you, that through these false prophets, the castle of your health, the salvation of your souls is assaulted: whom if we suffer to be with you, if you yield up your selves to the believing and following of their doctrin, then know ye, that as by blind leaders ye be lead, so you with them then being blinded, shal with them fal into the pit of perdition, which is prepared as wel for the falsely seduced, as for the false seducers.

Of these I could be content to speak the less, but that I se that while of too many, and that Londoners, these beasts be followed, ye have even drawn and pulled upon your heads those abominations, which, if but reason had ruled, should not have been admitted before that by laws they had been thrust upon you; that I speak not what true Christianity should have moved you to have don. Oh! London, London, is this the gospelling fruit, to be the first that without a law shouldst banish true preaching out of thee; to be the first that against laws shal admit that massing idolatry; to be the first that shal give the example of stumbling to al England? Which shouldst yet have been the first in constancy, in humble standing for the continuing of the truth in thee; in quiet and patient suffering for the truths sake even death, if by the rulers it had been offered thee. What ground are those which, not in persecution, but before persecution cometh, do go back? A ground thou art, reserved for the Lords woful curses, to whose judgment, London, I leave thee.

Seeing in London these evils are received, as it is now meet for vigilant pastors to watch over their flock, to chace

the wolves away, least at the Lords hand they do hear the
name of hirelings; so now is it high time for you, my loving brethren, and al of them that be the children of God,
to take heed whose voice ye do hear, to beware of the leaven
of papistical Pharisees, and to keep your selves undefiled
from al their abominations. The greatest of which now I
wil recite.

Among al their abominations, one of the principal is **The error**
their doctrine of *transubstantiation;* the very pride of pa- **of transub-**
pistry, and the horrible offence even of the Turks and hea- **stantiation.**
then: that a popish priest, by his huzzing and buzzing,
and mumbling up of the words of Christ, more like a con-
jurer than a Christian, should work that miraculous alteration and changing of the substance of bread and wine into
the substance of the body and bloud of Christ; which then
is to be taken as Christ himself, God and man; and to be
adored.   But you know, my dear brethren, that there is no
such miracle to be believed without the certain doctrine of
God's word to warrant the same; which the Papists can
never shew. And therfore their miracle is not to be be- 46
lieved. Christ, in instituting his supper, meant not to leave
there his body and bloud really and substantially, as the
Papists do teach. For Christ in the substance of his body
was then to be crucified: he was to dy; he was to rise
again; he was to ascend; and he was, and in the same yet
now is, to appear before the glorious God, our Bishop, Advocate, and Mediator; there to remain until the last day, as
the Scriptures do teach.

In the supper he instituted a commemoration of the
breaking of his body, and shedding of his bloud, to be don
and made of them that do eat that bread, and drink of
that cup, according to his institution: which he called his
body and bloud, for that it is to the receiver a seal and confirmation of Christs body broken, and Christs bloud shed
for them; that is, the profit and commodity thereof is
theirs, which they do partake by faith. And so these words,
This is my body, and, *This is my bloud,* is to be understood; and not as the transubstantiators literally enforce

them. For their understanding of them is both contrary to Christ's meaning, and also to the office of his body. Besides, that it is against the nature of his very body. And that the same phrase of speaking is thus to be understanded as I have said, the like phrases in like matters of the Scriptures doth sufficiently teach us. As where of circumcision the Lord doth say, *This is my covenant*, where it was but the seal of the covenant, as Paul calleth it. In the same sort it is said, *This is the passover; This cup is the new testament in my bloud; Christ is the rock;* and in like maner are these to be understanded. So that if the adversary wil give the H. Ghost leave to expound himself, then these words, *This is my body, This is my bloud*, are *figuratively* to be understood, as the like phrases are: and so serve they not at al for their monstrous transubstantiation.

The sacrifices of the mass.

Their second abhomination is their doctrin of the *mass*. In which to let many things pas, (as the strangeness of the tongue, the Jewish apparel, the fond nods, crosses, becks, and ducks,) three evils most notable, and to a Christian conscience intolerable, are there.

First, Their wicked sacrifice, which their mas-book testifieth to be *propitiatory*, to take away the sins of al those, be they dead or living, for whom they do say mass: yea profitable and available for wars, peace, weather, sicknes, for murrain of beasts, and whatsoever ye lust to [have] by their application. Oh! shameful blasphemy! As concerning the sacrifice propitiatory for sin, ye must hold the anchor of your faith, that this sacrifice (was) Christ himself once offered for al in his own bloudy death. He was the priest and the sacrifice, the offerer and the thing offered: and by his own bloudy offering, purified he, in the shedding of his bloud, al his from sin; by it purchased he eternal sanctification and salvation for them that shal be saved; and by it finished he for ever the ful propitiation for sins: for saying these words, *It is finished*, or consummate, he yielded up the ghost. Detestable therfore is the papistical sacrifice, injurious to the bloudy death of Christ. Christ instituted this supper to be a sacrament to us, and not that of it a priest

Matt. xxvii. 47

should make a propitiatory sacrifice for sin: in the eating and drinking of it, that we should declare the Lord's death, offering the sacrifice of thanks therfore. And therfore it is called of the Fathers, *a sacrifice of thanks.* That we eating and drinking according to his institution, should by faith apply unto our consciences the benefit of his death and passion; and not leaving any more sacrifice propitiatory for sin to any priest to offer, to whom and to what he listeth.

Christ ordained his supper neither for the dead, which have no use of eating and drinking with us in the congregation, nor yet for beasts, weather, nor war: for which Christ did not dye; but for his Church living upon this earth, that nedeth his word, and nedeth his sacraments, for confirming of their faith. Thus plainly ye se one mischievous misuse in this mass.

The second evil is, that the bread and cup which the Lord instituted to be received of the faithful with thanksgiving, in their mas they do abuse, and make of it an *idol:* holding it up, not only for the people to gaze upon, but to give unto it the honor which is due unto God alone: and so both make of it an idol, and of the people gros idolaters and transgressors of God's commandments. The filthiness of which idolatry I know yee do se so plain, that I need not with many words to impugn it: for a Christian conscience cannot but abhor it.

The third evil is, that in their mas that that is eaten and drunken is don and devoured of the priest al alone, with quartering and sopping, with licking and supping, with washing and wiping, and such pretty tricks of his own inventing. Christ in his institution appointeth this supper to be celebrate of the whole congregation. *Take ye and drink* Matt. xxvi. *ye al of this,* saith he. *This do ye in remembrance of me.* Mark xiv. And, *So oft as ye eat this bread, and drink of this cup, ye* Luke xxii. *shew the Lords death, til he cometh.* Christ and Paul speaketh not unto the priest alone, but to the whole congregation, to observe this ordinance of eating and drinking at the Lord's supper. Wherby ye may plainly se, how contrary this doing of our popish massers is in this also to the institution of Christ. And to be short in this, their whole mas is nought else but an horrible prophanation of the Lord's supper. Wherfore, as a most injurious blasphemy to the bloud of Christ, as a most gross idolatry, as a most wicked prophanation of Christ's institution, of al Christians is this mas to be eschued and abhorred.

Celebrating under one kind. Out of this mischievous idol the mass, form they unto the people a new found sacrament of their own inventing, delivering unto the people, as they say, through the miracle of their transubstantiation, a body. In which body, because also there is bloud, therfore they do not minister their consecrated cup accordingly, for fear of spilling: and yet they give drink to their houshold, to wash down the crumbs withal. Oh! thieves, where learn ye to minister such a sacrament? Where have ye your ground in the Scripture for this your unwholsom housel? Who can with a good con-
48 science receive such a new found popish sacrament at any Papists hand; seeing it is thereto of them used, to put Christ's true institution out of his true use? Whose appointed ordinance is, that the bread of thanksgiving and the cup of thanksgiving should be eaten and drunken of the congregation as before I said.

Other abuses of the sacrament.
The Papists defend their doctrine with menacing words, with imprisonment, with fire and fagot, with axe and halter.
Justification. This their new found sacrament they hang up in the *pix*, they carry abroad in processions to be adored, with many such mischiefs of their own inventings, which to reckon up al were an endles labour. I leave them therfore, ever listening when I may hear them defend these their abominations by the written word of God. But this as they never yet could do, so shal they never be able to do it. And therfore of al Christians are they with their evasions to be forsaken.

In the doctrin of *justification* they wander, enwrapt in labrinths inextricable. They erre in extenuating sin, both original and actual, in not understanding the law, the force of it I mean, nor the end of it: in making a justification partly of Christ's grace, partly of man's freewil, good motions, and good works. And herein they so enwrap themselves with their terms of the first grace, the second grace, grace precedent, grace concomitant, grace following, with merit of congruence, and merit of condignity, that they neither understand the true justification, neither can other men understand what they do mean by their justification. But their doctrin is to bring men into a continual doubting of salvation; and leadeth them clean from that free justification which we have in Jesus Christ.

But you, my brethren, have out of the Scripture received, and I trust by the practices of your own consciences have tasted, that by nature ye are the children of wrath of your selves; and of your selves that yee are but such a lump of sin, that in you dwelleth no good thing. For which the law justly condemneth you, as guilty of God's curse and wrath: and so driveth you to Christ, by whose grace ye be freely justified; by whose bloud-shedding only and alone the attonement is now made betwene God and you: which you believing are made the heirs of blessing, and of which your consciences by faith being assured by the work of Gods Spirit, ye be at peace with God. Because yee do feal even in your hearts, by lively persuasion of faith, that *God hath* Rom. iv. *loved you, and given himself for you:* for whose only sake *ye are justified and saved.* Which you thus feeling are led Eph. v. by the same Spirit that worketh this in you, to render unto God the sacrifice of your body, in living and doing those works which in his sight are acceptable; and that in a freedome and liberty of the Spirit. I mean no fleshly liberty, but that liberty of the Spirit by which we draw nigh unto the sight of God's grace, calling him *Abba, Father;* that liberty that subdueth the liberty of the flesh, and maketh it captive, and bound to serve the Spirit. In which you also walking, when you have don al that you can do, if ye could do al that is commanded you to do, yet seing al mans righteousnes is but as a defiled cloth, ye seek not thereby the perimplishment of your justification, which is already fully given you in Christ Jesus; ye look not to the merit of 49 your good works, but on your part knowing your own want and imperfection, yea and sin, even in the best ye do, ye say, *We are unprofitable servants;* commending al your Luke xvii. doings to the grace of God through Christ; that by him they may be made pure on God's part, considering that the good ye do is the work of his Spirit in you; which *worketh in al men both to wil and to do.* Ye do give unto him the glory, seing by his grace only ye are that good that ye are. Nevertheles, yet this also ye know, that the Lord who through Christ hath accepted you unto his grace, doth, of the same grace in Christ, accept these your works into his favour, as just, perfect, and good; which, tho they be the works of his Spirit in you, yet is he content to have them called and esteemed as yours; and, as yours, doth he of his own free grace reward them, both in this life and the life to come.

In this that I have thus spoken, ye se the force of sin, original and actual; the force and end of the law, the power of man's freewil, the true justification, mans regeneration, and the life, fruits, and perfection of God's regenerate child. By which ye may the more easily perceive, how far the Papists wander from the truth of justification. By which they draw men into a desperate doubting of salvation. Which whoso liketh, let them taste therof.

Works of superero- gation, &c. Counterfeit good works.

Here is occasion also given me, to warn you of al those means that they have taught to be *meritorious*, and to deserve grace: as, works of supererogation, works don of a good intent, fish-fasts, vows, pilgrimages, pardons, and such like popish trash: which tho' as yet perchance they dare not teach, yet have they taught, and will hereafter teach it. But against al such I account you sufficiently armed, if ye hold fast this, that our only merit available before God is the merit of Christ; which he freely giveth, and God, for his only sake, freely imputeth to al true believers: which is unto them ful, perfect, and sufficient merit, righteousnes, satisfaction, and salvation.

Interces- sion of saints. 1 Tim. ii.

John xv.

They teach also invocation of saints, to make them mediators, if not to God for us, yet unto Christ, to speak the better for us. The Scripture teacheth plain, that between God and man there is but one mediator, the man Jesus Christ: who therefore became man, that for man he alone should make intercession; as for mans redemption he alone did dy. Wherfore he also teacheth men to cal upon the

Father in his name, promising to such that they shal be heard.

Prayer abuse they, not only in a strange tongue, contrary to the doctrine of Paul, which will have al things don in the congregation to the edifying thereof; in superstitious numbring of a certain number of Psalms, or Pater-nosters, (of which, because the people shal be sure, they teach them the use of beads; contrary unto which Christ our Saviour taught, condemning it as a pharisaical superstition, when for their much clattering sake they think themselves to be heard.) But also they teach and defend praying for the dead to be charitable and propitiatory; whereas the Scripture teacheth, that they that dye in the Lord are in solace and blessednes. As then they need not our prayers, so our prayers can add nought unto their blessednes: and on the contrary part, they that dy wickedly have no remedy everlastingly. So that, on all parts, this kind of prayer is in vain, the other being in most blessed safty; and with these the time of health and grace being past. Their curious charity, therfore, and their peevish propitiatory prayer, hath no ground in the Scripture. But through this they have picked the purse of many a poor man. For on this unhappy ground built they chauntries, trentals, universaries, [anniversaries,] diriges, purgatory, pardons for souls departed, and a piece of their expiatory sacrifice, with many such proper devices.

Auricular confession they teach; in which they enforce a numbring of sins: which is nought else but the tyranny of their kingdom; and, as they use it, a killing of Christian consciences, and hath no ground of the Scriptures. In an anguish and doubt of conscience, it is both good, necessary, and comfortable for a man to counsil with some such learned elder in whose lips doth ly the law of truth. Again, if the true ecclesiastical disciplin were used, a piece of it ought to be, that the man restored should of his fault make an open confession before the congregation, to declare publickly his repentance. Yea, and a minister may upon just grounds examine any of whom he hath cure, of such a fault as he

(marginal notes:)
Prayer abused by the Papists. 1 Cor. xiv.
Matt. vi.
50
Prayer for the dead. Apoc. xiv.
Auricular confession.

seeth him worth to be reproved for. But this is so far from their ear-shrift, that a man most blind may easily judge thereof.

Popish innovations. But the rabble of their errors are too many now to recite; as, of the authority of the Church, of the not erring of the Church, of disciplin, of their five new invented sacraments, of vows, of choise of meats, of images, and such like. Against al which that ye may be armed, my dear brethren, I require you not only to cal to mind the doctrin of the truth received, but also that, for the trial of them, ye do abide in the word of the truth, Gods word, I mean. And because here they have also an error, I wil but recite it, and so make an end.

Traditions and councils, doctors, customs. Their error is, that God's written word is not a sufficient doctrin unto salvation. But, say they, the voice of the Church, traditions, and councils, are to be heard of necessity. As for traditions, there is no tradition of any matter of faith to be received other than is in the Scripture expressed. Likewise doctors and councils, with the consent and custome of the Church, are so far to be heard in matters of faith, as they do agree with the written Scripture. For it is the touchstone to try them al by: and that in such

Es. viii. sort, that if they say not according to this word, then, as

Ceremonies. there is no light in them, so are they not to be followed. As for traditions, customs, and for the order of the Church ceremonies received and used, which be no matters of faith, they may be admitted and altered at the discretion of them that have the rule of the Church under Christ, according to the necessity of the time and the disposition of the people. So that in them be nothing els but true edifying to unfeigned godlines. And such are of the people with humblenes to be received.

51
The holy Scripture is a sufficient doctrine for our salvation, without the popish unwritten verities. But for the ful trial of such; yea, and for the ful and perfect institution of al men in such things as concern salvation, God hath left unto his Church and people his written word. In which tho al things that God might have caused to be written be not written, yet in it so much is written, as sufficeth to teach us that Jesus Christ is the Son of God;

and also, that we believing might have life everlasting, as John doth witness. By which we learn, that the written John xx. word of God is a sufficient doctrin to instruct us in that faith which bringeth to life everlasting. It is that sufficient doctrin, that alone can make men learned unto salvation, by the faith which is in Christ Jesus. It alone sufficeth to make the man of God perfectly instructed to al that is good, as witnesseth Paul. Therfore unto the Scriptures doth Christ 2 Tim. iii. send the Pharisees; Abraham to Moses and the prophets: John v. Peter also to the same word of the prophets, as to the doc- Luke xvi. trin that sufficeth to instruct us to salvation. The know- 2 Pet. i. ledge of which word whosoever goeth about to take from the people, by putting it into a strange language, to the end, that the more safely our popish merchants may keep their mart of falshood and Popery, he robbeth the people of their means to salvation, he openeth a door for thieves and murtherers to devour the flock of Christ. And if at the world's hand he sustaineth not the judgment of a thief, yet at Gods hands he shal be sure to have the judgment of a soul-murtherer.

Thus briefly have I put you in mind, my dear brethren, of the principal errors of the adversaries, and of the truth contrary to them; not so copiously as the matter deserveth, but shortly, measuring the needs of your knowledg. For I have not to do now with the ignorant, but with you, of whom, by the time and kind of your teaching, I judg that ye be able, not only to judge of the truth, but to be brotherly instructors of others in the same.

And thus I have don first to exhort you constantly to abide in the truth received. Cal to your minds, that God, of his great mercy and goodnes, hath long been in planting, sowing, and watering of you, as it were to make you a garden of plesure unto himself. These seeds of life the Devil, by his doctors, wil now go about to pick out of your hearts. But if in this gospelling age you have been worthy hearers of the gospel; if with the word heard with your ears the Lords Spirit hath touched your hearts, to believe the word of truth preached, as he hath done to so many as have usfeignedly desired it : if ye be the sheep which have rightly heard the shepherd's voice ; then surely the strangers supplanting voice shal ye not hear ; but ye shal flee from such hirelings, as from thieves, robbers, and murtherers. Hereby verily shal ye be known what ground ye are, fruitful or unfruitful, constant or servers of the time. Good gospel-hearers be not such as will be tossed about with every wind. They be no such ground as wil be dried up with every blast of burning heat : but they abide in God's truth, searching and learning the same in the holy Scriptures ; and that with such faithful diligence and constant obedience, that if any angel from heaven shal preach another gospel, they hold him accursed. Yea, and tho there be many counterfeit Christians, that fal away from the Lord's truth, yet abide they with Christ, and say, *Thou hast the words of everlasting life.*

Consider, my dear brethren, that not to hear alone, but to keep Christ's words, maketh a man happy. And in keeping, the principal part is to persevere in the doctrin of truth. This maketh Christ's disciples, this maketh you free ; yea, this it is that maketh a man safe : for he that persevereth to the end shal be saved.

This also have I written to exhort you, to keep you undefiled from al popish leaven. If ye do fal from the gospel, and embrace Popery, ye fal from truth to lyes, from the word of light and life to darknes and death, from salvation to damnation, from God to the Devil. Ye are then they, into whom the evil spirit re-entreth with seaven worse than himself : ye are then the foolish builders, which suffer the unrecoverable ruine. And as then with the filth that is in Popery ye be defiled, so of the damnation which is due to such abomination ye shal be partakers.

But if ye think that ye can both embrace Popery and the Gospel, ye do deceive yourselves. For ye cannot both hold the tast of Christ's death, and also allow that mass which is the defacer of Christ's death. You cannot embrace the right use of the Lord's supper, and also use and partake the horrible prophanation of the same. Ye cannot by faith appre-

Margin notes:

John x.

The property of good gospellers.

Gal. i.

52

John vi.

Christ's death and the popish mass cannot agree together.

hend free justification, and yet seek by your righteousnes and merits to be saved. You cannot accept God's written word as the sufficient doctrin of salvation, and also take mens doctrins and traditions as necessary to the same; and so forth of the rest. Thus can ye not do both, they are so contrary. But if ye could do it, yet may ye not do it: for God wil none of your mangled service. For as there is no convenience between Christ and Belial, so men must not halt on both sides in God's service, but either say that God is God, or else that Baal is God. God never allowed the service of the Samaritans, which both served their idols and worshipped the living God. But if ye be turned to the Lord, then al strange gods must ye clean forsake. The Lord is God alone; alone therfore, according to his word, wil he be served. God is over man a jealous God; wherfore he wil have whole man wholly to be his alone, as our first commandment teacheth us. Again, if you think that in your hearts ye wil serve the Lord, but yet will be and may be present in person at their idolatry, for your hearts shal be in heaven; this is but a fleshly policy, which faileth as many as trust unto it. How can you, to whom Christ's death is clear, abide to se that whorish thief, that stealeth from Christ the glory of his death? How can ye, who have been, and are ready to receive with thankfulnes the Lord's supper according to Christ's institution, abide to se the horrible profanation thereof? And so forth of the rest.

But if your conscience were thus, that ye could thus do, yet know ye this, that it is against your Christian profession. For we are taught, that to believe with the heart, and to confes with the mouth, maketh a man safe. Both heartbelief and mouth-confession must go together. Which doth not so in you, when inwardly ye are gospellers, and outwardly dissemblers with Papists. *Ye are bought with a price*, saith S. Paul; *glorify now God in your body, and in your spirit, which are God's.* Seeing both body and spirit are God's, not only by creation, but also by redemption, even in the price of Christ's bloud, ye cannot with a dissembling pretence couple your bodies with Papists: for

Margin notes:
Serve God according to his word.
2 Cor. vi.
3 Reg. xviii.

Exod. xx.

Fleshly policy.

53

Rom. x.
Heart and mouth must go together.

1 Cor. vi.

then ye do not glorify God in your bodies.   We read not that a child of God used ever justly any such dissimulation.

Examples of constancy in God's word. Dan. vi. 14. Dan. iii. Daniel used none such ; and therfore was he soon accused of not adoring the King, Bel, and the Dragon.   The three Children, whether they came of compulsion, or came of their own mind where the idol was, dissembled not : for forthwith they were accused as transgressors of the king's commandment.   Eleazarus would not dissemble eating even of lawful flesh.   These men glorified God in body and spirit.   These men believed in heart, and confessed with the mouth.   And so must you do without any other musing, if ye wil do the office of Christians.

Of offence-giving. And this to do, not only the profession of Christianity enforceth, but Christian charity also.   Our doings must be without offence-giving : but by this dissembling a double stumbling block is given, which even in things indifferent is to be avoided.   For what tho a Christian may eat freely of meats offered unto idols ?   Yet if there be an idolator, whose conscience in his superstition should be confirmed therby, Rom. xiv. 1 Cor. vi. it were better never to eat flesh.   And what tho al things be clean to the clean, to be eaten on al days with thanksgiving ?   Yet better it is not to eat flesh, nor to drink wine, than to offend therby thy weaker brother.   If this be to be observed in things indifferent, how much more in things Note, the dissembling gospellers. which are absolutely evil ?   Must ye take heed, that neither ye give occasion of offence concerning the conscience of an idolater, nor yet of offending the weak, to draw them to the like evil with you ?   Both which ye do, when both a Papist and a weak brother seeth you, as mungrels mingling yourselves with the Papists in their idolatry.   As much might I 1 Cor. xiv. speak now, how al things that ye do in the congregation must be done to edifying.   But of this to have ful instruc- Calvin. tion, I refer you to the mind of Master Calvin, lately translated and printed in English.

Thus now I end, wishing you all wel in the Lord.   Abide in the truth.   Keep yourselves undefiled.   Offer yourselves humbly to suffer al violence of bloudy laws for truth's sake. Keep safe your consciences, tho the sword taketh your lives from you. Suffer and bear with al humblenes and quiet obedience. Humble yourselves in unfeigned repentance before the Lord in the horrible plague of Popery, that of his mercy he may be moved to end these days of 54 delusion. And let your prayers always ascend up unto the Lord, begging of him such things as ye need. In which I beseech you to pray also for me,

Your loving friend and orator,
Thomas Sampson.

Number XIX.

Status familiæ Cardinalis Poli, et sumptus necessarii, sicut describebantur, cum regnum ingressurus est.

Rmus et illmus pater præter omnes suos reditus et Papæ provisiones, non potest impendere singulis mensibus plus quam mille coronatos aureos Italicos. E Biblioth. C.C.C.C. Miscellan. B. p. 411.

Isti mille coronati consumi debent circa opsonia personarum 130 præscriptarum domi, præter extraneos, quos arbitror esse alios homines 30. Qui numerum 160 complent. Quibus quidem hominibus consultum esse debet de victu.

Præterea, prospectum esse debet quadraginta equitationibus equorum et mulorum, qui ordinarii paratissimi erunt S. R.

Pro victu ordinario predictorum hominum panis computatur singulis mensibus, coronati centum   C. 100

Pro vino et cervisia singulo mense   C. 150

Pro lignis magnis et parvis et carbonibus tum hyeme tum æstate   C. 100

Pro luminibus funalium, et aliarum candelarum sebacearum omni ratione habita, ut supra   C. 25

Pro communi carne cotidiana pondo 300. Bovina, et vervecina, et vitulina, singulis mensibus pondo 6000.   C. 150

Pro piscibus et ovis in diebus vigiliarum et dierum jejunii   C. 100

Pro caseo, fructibus, condimentis, et aliis cupediis   C. 25

Pro caponibus decem singulo die, in altilibus, cuniculis,

et aliis ripariis volucribus pro mensa suæ R. in ferculis quinque prædictorum viginta dierum   C. 100

Pro equitationibus quadraginta, decem millia pabuli singulo mense   C. 50

Pro palea, et stramine, et fæno   C. 190

Pro sellis, ephipiis, et aliis appendicibus   C. 20

Stipendia ordinaria veteris familiæ singulo mense   C. 75

Præterea, pro stipendiis, et cultu, et aliis vestibus familiæ novæ singulis mensibus   C. 25

55   Pro loturis pannorum, cyathis, lebetum et scoparum usu singulo mense   C. 15

Pro parvis eleemosynis, transitu fluminis, pharmacis, et aliis similibus rebus   C. 15

Animadvertendum est, quotannis impendi in vestimentis suæ R. solius quingentos aureos   C. 500

Præterea, impenduntur alii coronati quingenti circa cultum suæ ipsius familiæ, hoc est, cubiculariorum, sacellanorum, et satellitum   C. 500

Notandum est, in præsentia opus esse 2000 pro renovatione argentariæ, et supplemento sacelli, mensæ et promptuariæ   C. 2000

Præterea, pro aliis æramentis, et vasis ferreis, stanneis, et æneis totius domi   C. 300

Præterea, pro linteis et aliis mantilibus mensæ et cubiculi   C. 600

Number XX.

The substance of a book, entitled, Pro Instauratione Reip. Anglorum, proque Reditu reverendissimi et illustriss. D. Reginaldi Poli, &c. Oratio ad prudentiss. Senatum Angl. Autore Jodoco Harchio Montensi.

E Biblioth. Rev. D. D. Johan. E-pisc. Elien.   *ETSI P. C. mea in dicendo infantia, animique pauca efferre gestientis sterilitas,* &c. In this oration the speaker frames his speech to the Parliament after that maner, as tho' the whole state of the kingdom, in the laws and religion of it, were disjointed in the late government under

K. Henry VIII. and K. Edward VI. He speaks of the
tot passim latrocinia, et tam horrenda parricidia, so
many rapines in one place or other, such fearful parricides
and frequent seditions. And what did al these portend
and presage, but that the natures of men were degenerated
(he said not) into certain lawless brutes, but rather into
horrid monsters. That it could be nothing but the monster
of a man, so to delight itself in its own destruction, or seek
in such a kind of cruelty to turn its sword into its own
bowels. He represents the times of the two last kings so,
that man could not be safe from man; that mutual society
was dissolved; that children were miserable, by the cruel
and violent death of their parents, and husbands by the
public adulteries of their infamous wives, and that the commonwealth itself was almost drowned and overwhelmed in
the bloud of its citizens. And now can any one in words
comprehend what a frightful appearance of mischieves was 56
lately risen up among us, either from the contempt or alteration of religion?

Then he flatters the Parliament for their seasonable succor
afforded to the welny undon commonwealth and state of religion; wherby they had heaped up eternal praise, not only
to themselves, but to al England, happy in such a senate.

Then he procedes to lay down the way and means for
the restoring the commonwealth. That when we know
this decay of the state happening by the contempt of the
laws and religion, it is our duty to cal back the vigor of
the laws, and restore the majesty of religion and divine worship. As long as learned and pious men were contemned,
and lived in banishment, so long did the commonwealth
lay void of vertue and barren of true praises, like a tree
destitute of its juice and aliment. And that happened
chiefly from the time that the people, driven with he knew
not what furies, had forbidden the most godly and noble
Reginald Pole to come into his own country, and banished
him from the house of his fathers. This, he said, he could
easily prove, but that they, the senate, were his silent witnesses. For what else was the cause the resplendent glory

of this realm was turned into so much blind darknes, unles that we (a wonder by what error deluded!) brought a cloud ourselves over that very thing we had before illustrated.

Then he ran out against the late government, for destroying al the true nobility, wherin this nation was once famous beyond others: when ignoble persons and Gnatho's soaring above their vocation, crept into their places: who endeavoured to suppress, either by banishment or death, those whom they could not equal in glory; but that by the just judgment of God themselves were immerged in their own bloud: wherof one fresh in memory ended his life by the halter, and another lost his head. Al wisdom also, wherin England so far excelled, as tho' the muses had chosen their seat here, that also was departed. What remained of so great wit, of so true literature, when for so many years we were turned back to the foul puddle of ignorance; when we enquired not so much after what was true and honest, as what was profitable and pleasant; when we turned the more secret mysteries of holy discipline, and the serious knowledge of divine things, either into open blasphemy, or distorted them into old wives fables. Whether these things were true or no, he left to them to judge which sate in the theatre, where for twenty years the stir about religion was agitated, and consultations were had of the lives and banishments of the best prelats, and the destruction of the wisest men: from which time we were given up by God to a reprobate sense; that we once by a voluntary wickedness having put off justice and reason, afterwards should both say and believe faithfully things which could not once come into the minds even of such as were mad, and bereft of reason. And then by that fury wherewith we are acted, we hurried on to the destruction, not of the good only, but of ourselves. So that to foreign nations we were an unheard of example of tyranny and madnes. And lastly, which is worse, we came to that degeneracy of distraction, that we hunted for praise from impiety, and catched at commendation from al kind of wickednes.

But because they, the present Parlament, were not

guilty, he advised them to comfort themselves with the testimony of their innocency, and manfully, as hitherto they had done, to set about the restoration of those things which might retrieve the ancient glory to their country. And for that purpose he persuaded them by al means to call back those godly and learned men that were banished. Because of that sort there were but few at home; those especially who were illustrious both for Catholic religion and piety. Among whom, above the rest, Pole shone, most eminent both for the number of his vertues, and for the greatnes of them. By whose banishment, because ye lost in a maner al the graces of the realm, ye must endeavour, that by his return ye may recover them again: and as by his departure piety and nobility received the beginning of their ruine, so by his return they may obtain the encrease of their assertion unto their antient dignity.

Truly it is a most unworthy thing, that that gem of vertues should enlighten foreign nations; and by the want of him our native soil be obscured: or to suffer that man to be wanting to you, who grieves that you are wanting to him: not indeed, I know it wel enough, because banishment or a foreign region is troublesome to him, (for he lives at home, whosoever lives wel,) but because no man can (if he have not wholly put off his own nature) but embrace and entertain them with exceeding love, from whom they have received the beginnings of their life, (which knit the bonds of mutual benevolence among men,) and also the beginning of their education. And next also, because he wil not think himself to have lived, unless he shal have left the better part of himself to his country, which deservedly calls for it from him. And that is a thing, O ye senators, can never be done more fitly, than if he in these times help the tottering commonwealth with his counsil, wherewith he is excellently furnished; and according to his piety assist them that are in misery, and also afford himself an example of a safer way to those that err in the faith.

This is the design of that nobleman; this is the intention of his mind: which unless he thought he could obtain, first by the favour of God, and then by yours, he had never brought his mind to the least desire of coming home, whatever his provocation of riches and honours were; (wherewith perhaps he aboundeth more already than he desireth;) at least, of them he hath obtained so great a share, as is enough for the necessity of life, and for the dignity of his quality. But if any ambition of honour had tickled his mind, yet it had not become a man most famous for the constancy of his faith and for his birth, to seek power in his own country, which he had heretofore layd down for piety sake, unles he had taken it up again for the same cause. Because otherwise in his banishment he might obtain most ample honours, and live with greatest security of mind, most dear to the meanest plebeian, and most grateful to those of highest quality.

The holy man therfore desires to se you again, and is possest with a desire of his own country : not to burthen his old age, burthensome of itself, with new honours, or to compass riches, his soul being now desirous of flying away to heaven : but with what authority he may, to assist the Church in her present jeopardy, and to restrain and repress the wanton boldnes of the Devil in overthrowing religion, as wel by the maturity of his counsel, as by giving fit examples of piety. If therfore ye neglect so singular a pilot in such a tempest of affairs, what else wil ye give the world occasion to suspect concerning you, O ye senators, but that you yourselves are meditating of a shipwreck ? If therefore ye do not recal to your assistance a Camillus, so notable in managing affairs, all things being now in a maner laid wast, what wil the foreign Gauls reproach you with, but that you are conspiring together for the destruction of the city ? In a word, if you wil yet longer suffer to continue in banishment the second father of eloquence, next to Cicero, by what mouth, by what eloquence do ye hope to eject them out of this island, who, ingrateful citizens as they are, have conspired against the religion, which now ye endeavour to establish, and against the domestic tranquility of affairs, which ye are consulting about ? Lastly, who can oppress the seditious Gracchi, who, the Catilines raging against you in clandestine counsils? ··

Nothing indeed, ye senators, can at this day come more welcome to the ears of the Italians, than that ye should reject him whom they both intyrely love and esteem, and desire to retain with them. Nothing can be a greater plesure to the Germans, than for you to despise that breast, from whence they themselves so often have received the safest counsil for the composing and dispatching of their most weighty businesses; which they fear they may hereafter want, if he come back to you. What doth it signify to lay before you the fearful minds of the French; who, altho they have hitherto dreaded your strength, I know not what they contrive in their secret counsils for your destruction, if he shal not be recalled? The Scotch shal also wel relapse unto his accustomed perjury, and with a new desire of war, shal break off the league of friendship made with you, when he shal know you decline his presence; at whose absence that people, otherwise most valiant, tremble and shake. But whatsoever the enviers of your clemency, whatsoever the enemies of your glory, bark against you, not my opinion only concerning you is different, but the opinion of all good men; much otherwise is their judgment of your love toward this desolate state. Whereupon we undoubtedly hope you can never so rashly envy your country, your wives, your children, so many vertues in one man, and so many benefits. If this man of a most innocent life, had committed any thing that had deserved perpetual banishment, I should then in truth approve your counsel, not to recal him. But if he were a person that would not be brought 59 to consent to falshood, if he refused to cherish the impiety of some, if he from his heart lamented the cause of religion; if, lastly, even to the danger of his head, he resisted, as much as he could, those who afterwards hanged your parents, and defiled your bodies with the bloud of your sons, spoiled churches, and demolished to the ground the sepulchres of your auncestors; I do not say, what praises do you hold him worthy of, but what rewards? He went away, indeed, and avoided the insatiable plesure of exercising cruelty against the best of men; wisely presaging that in a short time fair weather would come, when the showers were fallen; and tranquility succede, when the furious storms were ceased, which arose, Neptune either not consenting, or permitting it for a time.

Wherefore he prudently chose rather to reserve himself for these times, in which he might do good by his counsil, and allure by his piety, than at that time draw death upon himself by a rash and unsuccessful attempt: which if it had happened, together with him al hope of nobility and honour of piety had perished; which by departing he conveyed safe with him to foreign countries; and in his returning he wil restore them to his country as so many presents.

If ye shal therfore, O ye patriots, call home this man, yé shal receive nobility and piety, together with learning; which hitherto are things wanting in this kingdom. Moreover, ye shal not hereby cal in a foreigner, who may introduce some barbarous and wild maner of living, but your own countryman, but an Englishman, fitted as wel to your customes, as maner of life; and who, according to the highly commendable custom of the English, shineth more in liberality than covetousnes, and allureth rather by humanity than severity. Again, neither, as ye know, shal ye receive an ignoble person, who shal labour to obtain the favour of the populacy by feigned pretences of bloud, and who being unmindful of his condition, for a dignity obtained shal grow proud; but such an one who as he is sprung from a noble family, and eminent for its neerness to the royal dignity, so also a sober affecter of a more splendid fortune, and a noble despiser of a more severe one. I omit his constancy, wherby he rather chose, as it is well known, to se the carcase of his parent slain with the sword, than to be drawn away from the confession of catholic truth. There is no need to speak either of his erudition, or most sweet fountain of eloquence; because many rivulets from thence, which like a golden floud flow over the whole world, abundantly testify the man to be of a most perspicacious wit, as

well as of the most eloquent tongue: which two are of
great moment to persuade a thing very necessary in this
age, *viz.* the taking away bad opinions concerning religion.

No, what need is there to rake up those more hidden
vertues of this pious person, wherin he is better known to
God than to men, more frequent in heaven than on earth,
and oftener among the poor than the rich. I pas over also 60
the shape of his body; the hansome composure of his members I am silent of, which would not deserve praise, unless
they had received a guest [his soul] most absolute in all
respects of integrity and goodnes.

Wonder not then, ye senators, that any should exhort
you to call for so illustrious an ornament of this realm. If
some rich city by the treachery or strength of enemies were
taken from you, with what endeavour, with what gifts
would you treat for the surrender of it? But why are you
not with the like care concerned for his return, by whom
this kingdom would be more famous and more abundant in
true riches, than the empty ostentation of a golden moun-
tain, or than the pride or greatness of any external thing
could make it? 'Tis necessary that that great POLE be
called home, that by his presence shal bring to you and his
country immortal glory. Not the people alone with profuse
tears, but even infants as yet in their cradles, I know not
how, shewing their desires, wish for his coming. The
wrinkled old men, while they se him again, have prayed for
death. Nay, which is like to a miracle, both the cattle and
heifers joyfully as it were presaging you somewhat of good
news, dance in the meddows, and the fields grow green in
an unwonted maner, for the cattles pasture, &c. [it being
now, I suppose, spring time.]

*And thus he strains every string, and plays the poet as
well as the orator, to induce the Parliament to be willing to
let an act pass to recall the Cardinal.*

Number XXI.

The supplication of the bishops and clergy of the province of Canterbury to the King and Queen; to obtain a dispensation from Cardinal Pole, the Pope's legate, concerning Church-lands.

NOS, episcopi et clerus Cantuariensis provinciæ in hac synodo more nostro solito, dum regni Parliamentum celebratur, congregati, cum omni debita humilitate et reverentia, exponimus Majestatibus vestris; quod licet ecclesiarum quibus in episcopos, decanos, archidiaconos, rectores et vicarios præfecti sumus, et animarum, quæ nobis et curæ nostræ subjectæ sunt, et earundem bonorum, jurisdictio-num, et jurium et sacrorum canonum dispositione, defensores et curatores constituti sumus; et propterea ipsorum bona, jurisdictiones et jura in pernicioso hujus regni præterito schismate deperdita et amissa, omni studio, et totis nostris viribus recuperare, et ad pristinum ecclesiarum jus revocare, juris remediis niti deberemus: nichilominus tamen habito prius per nos super hac re maturo consilio et deliberatione, ingenue fatemur, nos optime cognoscere, quam hæc bonorum ecclesiasticorum difficilis, et quasi impossibilis esset recuperatio, propter multiplices ac pæne inextricabiles super hiis habitos contractus et dispositiones: et quod si ea tentaretur, quies et tranquillitas regni facile perturbaretur, et unitas Ecclesiæ Catholicæ, quæ jam pietate et auctoritate Majestatum vestrarum hoc in regno introducta est, cum maxima difficultate suum progressum et finem sortiri posset. Ideo nos bonum et quietem publicam privatis commoditatibus, et salutem tot animarum pretioso Christi sanguine redemptarum terrenis bonis anteponentes, et non quæ nostra, sed quæ Jesu Christi sunt, quærentes, Majestates vestras enixe rogamus, iisque humiliter supplicamus, ut reverendissimo in Christo patri Domino Reginaldo Cardinali Polo ad ipsas et universum hoc Angliæ regnum, sanctissimi domini nostri Domini Julii Papæ Tertii, et apostolicæ sedis de latere legato, hæc nomine nostro insinuari, et apud eum intercedere dignentur, ut in hiis bonis ecclesiasticis, in parte vel in toto, arbitrio suo juxta facultates sibi ab eodem sanctissimo domino nostro Papa concessas, eorundem bonorum detentoribus, elargientes et relaxantes, publicum bonum privato, pacem et tranquillitatem dissidiis et perturbationibus, atque animarum salutem bonis terrenis præferre et anteponere velit. Nos enim in omnibus quæ ab ipso legato statuta et ordinata circa hæc bona fuerint, ex nunc prout extunc, et e contra, consensum nostrum præstamus : imo etiam, ut in præmissis se difficilem aut restrictum reddere non velit, Majestates vestræ nostro nomine eum hortari et rogare dignabuntur.

Insuper Majestatibus vestris supplicamus pro sua pietate efficere dignentur, ut ea quæ ad jurisdictionem nostram et libertatem ecclesiasticam pertinent, sine quibus debitum nostri pastoralis officii et curæ animarum nobis commissæ exercere non possumus, nobis superiorum temporum injuria ablata, restituantur, et ea nobis et Ecclesiæ perpetuo illæsa et salva permaneant ; et ut omnes leges, quæ hanc nostram jurisdictionem et libertatem ecclesiasticam tollunt, seu quovis modo impediunt, abrogentur, ad honorem Dei, et Majestatum vestrarum, et universi hujus regni spirituale et temporale commodum et salutem ; certam spem etiam habentes, Majestates vestras pro sua singulari in ipsum Deum pietate, proque multis et insignibus ab ipsius Dei bonitate acceptis beneficiis, necessitatibus et incommodis hujus sui regni Ecclesiarum, maxime curam animarum habentium, nunquam defuturas esse, sed prout opus fuerit, consulturas atque provisuras.

Number XXII.

62

Cardinal Pole, the Pope's legate, his dispensation to those that possessed Church-lands, and contracted unlawful marriages.

REGINALDUS, miseratione divina Sanctæ Mariæ in Cosmodin S. Romanæ Ecclesiæ diaconus, Cardinalis Polus nuncupatus, ad serenissimos Philippum et Mariam, Angliæ

Reges, Fidei Defensores, et universum Angliæ regnum, sanctissimi Domini nostri Papæ, et sedis apostolicæ de latere
legatus, eisdem serenissimis Philippo et Mariæ Regibus,
salutem in Domino sempiternam.

Cum supremum concilium istius regni, Parliamentum
nuncupatum, Majestatibus vestris per suos supplices libellos
exposuisset, quod perniciosissimo schismate in hoc regno
alias vigente, quod nunc Dei misericordia et Majestatum
vestrarum pietate extinctum est, aucthoritate ipsius Parliamenti nonnulli episcopatus divisi, et ex his aliquæ inferiores
ecclesiæ in cathedrales erectæ, et scholæ, atque hospitalia
fundata, necnon plurimæ dispensationes et beneficiorum
provisiones factæ fuerunt, ac multæ personæ, quibus persua-
sum fuerat, juris canonici dispositiones hoc in regno amplius
locum non habere, inter se in gradibus consanguinitatis vel
affinitatis de jure prohibitis, et aliis impedimentis canonicis
sibi obstantibus, matrimonia per verba de præsenti contraxe-
runt, et multi actus judiciarii et processus tam in primis,
quam ulterioribus instantiis super rebus spiritualibus et ecclesiasticis, coram judicibus tam ordinariis quam delegatis,
qui authoritate laicali procedebant, habiti et servati; ac
super eis etiam sententiæ latæ et promulgatæ fuerunt, et
bona ecclesiastica per diversas ejusdem regni personas occu-
pata et apprehensa fuerunt. Quæ quidem licet ex sacrorum
canonum institutis irriti declarari possunt, tamen si ad
alium statum, quam in quo nunc sunt, revocarentur, publica
pax et quies universi regni turbaretur, et maxima confusio
oriretur, præsertim si dictorum bonorum possessores moles-
tarentur: et propterea Majestatibus vestris humiliter supplicaverint, ut apud nos intercedere dignentur, ut præmis-
sarum rerum firmitati et stabilitati, et simul hujus regni
quieti et tranquillitati de benignitate apostolica providere
velimus.

Cumque episcopi quoque deinde, ac reliquum provinciæ
Cantuariensis clerus totum fere corpus ecclesiasticorum
regni repræsentans, ad quos hæc bonorum ecclesiasticorum
causa maxime pertinet, exposuerint, quod hæc bona ad jus
ecclesiarum revocari non possunt, quin pax universalis, et

quies hujus regni turbetur, et causa fidei atque unitatis Ecclesiæ, jam toto omnium consensu hoc in regno introducta, in maximum periculum adducatur : et propterea ipsi quoque supplicaverint, ut apud nos intercedere velint, ut in his bonis ecclesiasticis, possessoribus relaxandis restricti et difficiles esse nolumus; Majestates autem vestræ, ad quas 63 maxime spectat providere ut regnum ipsarum potestati, regimini, et curæ commissum, in pace et tranquillitate conservetur; his supplicationibus et postulatis cognitis et mature consideratis, judicaverint ea omnia, et maxime illa, quæ in bonorum ecclesiasticorum causa petuntur, pro causa fidei et pro pace publica, per nos debere sine ulla dilatione concedi; et quemadmodum rogatæ fuerunt, apud nos intercedere dignatæ fuerint; prout in supplicationibus, per idem supremum consilium, et episcopos ac clerum præfatum, Majestatibus vestris porrectis, atque in libello intercessionis per easdem Majestates vestras nobis simul cum aliis supplicationibus exhibito, latius apparet :

Idcirco nos, qui ad Majestates vestras, et hoc nobilissimum vestrum regnum a sanctissimo domino nostro Julio Papa Tertio, ipsius et sedis apostolicæ de latere legati missi sumus, ut regnum istud, quod jam diu ab Ecclesiæ Catholicæ unitate separatum fuerat, Deo et Ecclesiæ Christi, ejusque in terris vicario reconciliaremus : et ut ea omnia quæ ad pacem et tranquillitatem hujus regni pertinerent, omni studio procuraremus, postquam Dei benignitate, et Majestatum vestrarum pietate, per aucthoritatem ejusdem sanctissimi domini nostri Papæ, cujus vices hic sustinemus, reconciliatio jam facta est, ut paci et tranquillitati regni præfati consulamus, atque ut unitas Ecclesiæ, ex qua salus tot animarum pretioso Christi sanguine redemptarum dependet, hoc in regno jam introducta corroboretur, et salva permaneat, cum utriusque rei stabilitatem in eo maxime consistere, si horum ecclesiasticorum bonorum possessoribus molestia nulla inferatur, quo minus ea teneant, tot et tam gravia testimonia nobis fidem faciunt, et Majestatum vestrarum intercessio, quæ pro unitate Ecclesiæ, et sedis apostolicæ aucthoritate hoc in regno instauranda, tam studiose et tam pie

elaborarunt, eam quam par est aucthoritatem apud nos habeat, et ut universum hoc regnum sedis apostolicæ maternam
vere indulgentiam et charitatem erga se agnoscat, et reipsa
experiatur; quoscunque ad quos infra scripta pertinent, a
quibusvis excommunicationis, suspensionis, et interdicti, aliisque ecclesiasticis sententiis, censuris et pœnis, a jure vel ab
homine quavis occasione vel causa latis, siquibus quomodolibet innodati existunt, ad effectum præsentium duntaxat
consequendum harum serie absolventes, et absolutos fore
censentes, aucthoritate apostolica, per literas sanctissimi
dom. nostri, D. Julii Papæ Tertii nobis concessa, et qua fungimur in hac parte, tenore præsentium dispensamus: quod
omnes et singulæ cathedralium ecclesiarum erectiones, hos-
pitalium et scholarum fundationes tempore præteriti schismatis, licet de facto et nulliter attentatæ, in eo statu in quo
nunc sunt, perpetuo firmæ et stabiles permaneant, illisque
apostolicæ firmitatis robur adjicimus; ita ut non ea authoritate qua prius, sed ea quam nunc eis tribuimus factæ ab omnibus censeantur: et cum omnibus et singulis personis regni
prædicti, quæ in aliquo consanguinitatis vel affinitatis gradu,
etiam multiplici, vel cognitionis spiritualis, seu publicæ ho-
nestatis justitiæ impedimento de jure positivo introductis, et
64 in quibus sanctiss. Dominus noster Papa dispensare consue-
vit, matrimonia scienter vel ignoranter de facto contraxerint,
ut, aliquo impedimentorum præmissorum non obstante, in
eorum matrimoniis sic contractis, libere et licite remanere,
seu illa de novo contrahere possint, misericorditer in Domino
dispensamus, prolem susceptum, aut suscipiendam legitimam
decernentes; ita tamen ut qui scienter et malitiose contraxerint, a sententia excommunicationis, et ab incestus seu sa-
crilegii reatu, absolutionem a suo ordinario vel curato, quibus id faciendi facultatem concedimus, obtineant; ac omnes
ecclesiasticas, seculares, seu quorumvis ordinum regulares
personas, quæ aliquas impetrationes, dispensationes, con-
cessiones, gratias, et indulta, tam ordines, quam beneficia
ecclesiastica, seu alias spirituales materias, prætensa aucthoritate supremitatis Ecclesiæ Anglicanæ, licet nulliter et de
facto obtinuerint, et ad cor reversæ Ecclesiæ unitati resti-

tutæ fuerint, in suis ordinibus et beneficiis per nos ipsos, seu a nobis ad id deputatos, misericorditer recipiemus, prout jam multæ receptæ fuerunt; atque super his opportune in Domino dispensabimus: ac omnes processus in quibusvis instantiis, coram quibusvis judicibus, tam ordinariis quam delegatis, etiam laicis, super materiis spiritualibus habitos et formatos, et sententias super eis latas, licet nulliter et de facto, quoad nullitatem, ex defectu jurisdictionis præfato tantum insurgentem sanamus, illosque et illas aucthoritate apostolica confirmamus: ac quibusvis hujus regni personis, ad quarum manus bona ecclesiastica ex quocunque contractu seu titulo oneroso vel lucrativo, jam devenerint, illaque tenuerint, seu etiam teneant, omnes et quoscumque fructus ex eisdem bonis, licet indebite preceptos, in totum remittimus et relaxamus: volentes ac decernentes, quod istorum bonorum ecclesiasticorum, tam mobilium quam immobilium, possessores præfati non possint in præsenti, nec in posterum, seu per conciliorum generalium et provincialium dispositiones, seu decretales Romanorum pontificum epistolas, seu aliam quamcunque censuram ecclesiasticam in dictis bonis, seu eorundem possessione, molestari, inquietari, vel perturbari; nec eis aliquæ censuræ vel poenæ ecclesiasticæ propter hujusmodi detentionem, seu non restitutionem irrogari vel infligi; et si per quoscunque judices et auditores sublata eis, qua suis aliter judicandi et interpretandi facultate et aucthoritate judicare et definire debere, et quicquid secus attemptari contigerit, irritum et inane fore decernimus, non obstantibus præmissis defectibus, et quibusvis apostolicis, ac in provincialibus et synodalibus consiliis editis, specialibus vel generalibus constitutionibus et ordinationibus, cæterisque contrariis quibuscunque.

Admonemus tamen, cum divisio episcopatuum, et erectio cathedralium ecclesiarum sint de majoribus causis, quæ summo Pontifici sint reservatæ, recurrendum esse ad suam Sanctitatem, et ab ea suppliciter postulandum, ut hæc confirmare, seu de novo facere dignetur. Et licet omnes res mobiles ecclesiarum indistincte iis, qui eos tenent, relaxaverimus, eos tamen admonitos esse volumus, ut ante oculos ha-

bentes divini judicii severitatem contra Balthesarem regem Babylonis, qui vasa sacra, non a se sed a patre e templo ablata, in profanos usus convertit, ea propriis ecclesiis si ex-
65 tant, vel aliis restituant. Hortantes etiam et per viscera misericordiæ Jesu Christi obtestantes eos omnes, quos hæc res tangit, ut salutis suæ non omnino immemores, hoc saltem efficiant, ut ex bonis ecclesiasticis, maxime iis quæ ratione personatuum et vicariatuum populi ministrorum sustentatio fuerint specialiter destinata, seu aliis cathedralibus, et aliis, quæ nunc extant, inferioribus ecclesiis curam animarum laudabiliter exercere, et onera incumbentia congrue supportare. Datum Lambeth. prope Londinum Wintonien. diocesios, anno nativitatis Domini millesimo quingentesimo quinquagesimo quarto, nono cal. Januarii, pontif. sanctissimi, in Christo patris et domini nostri Julii divina providentia Papæ tertii, anno quinto.

Reginaldus Cardinalis Polus, legatus.

Number XXIII.

The Friars Minors of Ireland, their supplication to the Queen and Cardinal Pole, to be restored to their monasteries.

Serenissimæ ac invictissimæ nostræ Reginæ Mariæ, ac reverendissimo in Christo Patri ac Domino, Dno. Reginaldo, miseratione divina, Cardinali Polo, de latere legato.

EX parte gardiani monasterii novi de Kylchullyn Fratrum Minoris ordinis Francisci de Observantia in regno Hiberniæ, nuncii ac oratoris pro hiis quæ sequuntur negotiis humiliter supplicando, exponitur et insinuatur, quod quædam loca religiosa dicti ordinis in dicto regno Hiberniæ, finita eorum temporali firma, jam ad vestras revoluta sint manus, *viz.* monasterium novum de Kilchullyn, quod Rolandus Ustas tenebat[a] : monasterium de Ynystorty, quod

---

[a] Ex firma. Sed quum finita est firma in futura omnium Sanctorum festivitate, jam monasterium ad serenissimæ nostræ Reginæ revolvitur manus.
(tametsi idem Rolandus tempore vicis suæ patiebatur Fratres monasterium prædictum inhabitare) nova concessione et gratia ejusdem Reginæ prædictum postulatur, cum omnibus suis pertinentibus bonis, monasterium.

sine aliquo titulo tenet Richardus Butler; monasterium vero de Traim, (cujus fundatores erant felicis recordationis Henricus Octavus et Katharina, rex noster et regina,) emptum per Episcopum ipsum Mediem, jam a sua dignitate depositum, ac per eundem concessum sive donatum officiariis seu ministris juris ejusdem oppidi pro expeditione communium causarum in domum ædificandum: monasterium Montis Fernandi emptum est per Thomas Cusack. Qui nempe Thomas religiosorum fautor et benefactor, ut ipse asserit, promptus est ac paratus, (dummodo ad vestrum fuerit vo- 66 catus conspectum,) habita in Hibernia parva recompensatione, vel Reginæ benevolentia aliis in suis negotiis, pauperibus fratribus conferre ipsum monasterium.

Omnes quum prædicti pauperes fratres, hiis monasteriis olim tempore schismatis suppressis, inter montes nemoraque fame frigoreque innumeras penurias atque afflictiones sustineant; in tantum quod neque verbum Dei seminare, neque divinum exercere officium valeant.

Idcirco ex parte eorundem fratrum, oratoris seu nuncii humiliter ac obnixe supplicatur, quatenus vestris literis ad vestros officiarios et ministros, et præcipue ad deputatum et cancellarium vestrum in regno Hiberniæ directis, firmiter præcipiendo mandetis prædicta loca cum suis bonis necessariis et cæteris pertinentibus prædictis pauperibus fratribus sine quacunque contradictione integre concedi et dari.

Et quum capitanei et milites Anglici, et maxime qui novissime venerint ad Hiberniam, suis parcentes crumenis, in contemptum Dei et scandalum proximorum faciunt, monasteria a prædictis fratribus jam possessa et erecta, stabula; equos suos collocantes, et in locis consecratis, et quam maxime in monasterio de Cragfaryssy, alias De Petra Fargusii; igitur eadem supplicatione in hiis remedium postulatur: ut sic prædicti pauperes fratres quietique Deum laudare, et pro vestro felici statu, eundem perpetuo valeant exorare, et verbum Dei inter fideles seminare.

Number XXIV.

A breafe treatise; wherin is conteynede the trewth, that Mr. Justice Hales never hurt hymselfe, until such tyme as he condescended unto ther papistical religion, and wexed wery of the truth. But now ther is hope he wyll repent, and continue in the same as he did before. Yet be ther many that daylie labore hym to the contrarie.

Foxii MSS. SAINT Peter the apostle (good Christian reader) doth teach, that we that ar Christians, are Christians to this ende,

1 Peter ii. *to shew furth the vertews of him, that called us unto his unspeakable lyght:* meanynge, that we shuld alwayes be setters furth of as many things as we cold to his honour and prayse. And that ys a very kynde of ingratitude, and a certen degree

67 of injustice, not to propulse and defend any man from violence and oppression. And a greater ingratitude, and more injustice, not to propulse and defend the iust cause of God,

Matt. xxii.
Luke xi.
Mark iii. whan iniustly by violence it is slandred and oppressed. For in tymes past, the condition of the ungodlie was alwayes to speake slanderously and falsly by God's doings; insomuch as whan Christe wrought the salvation of the people, thay sayde, he wrought all things by the power of Belzebul, the chiefest of the devells. Saint John could fast, but he was counted to have a devel. Christ could eate and drinke, but he was counted a frende to synners and publicans: so that hatred unto the trewth dyd alwayse falsly reporte and

Ose ii. calumniate all godly mens doinges. Agayne, ther was never evyll that happened to any country or commonwealth, although yt wear the iust plague of God for the synne of the people of the countrye, but it was allwayes laide to the good peoples charge: as whan the Lord toke away corne, wyne, oyle, frutes, and other thinges necessarie from the Israelites;

Tertull. in Apolog. the wycked people said, that the worde of God, and his trew preachers were the causes therof. Yf the water in Egypt, called Nilus, dyd not accustomably flow over Egypt, the wycked Egyptians laid the faulte to such as professed Christ. Yf that flowed too much also, the faulte was imputed to the good Christians. So the Romains, if Tyber the flood waxed eyther to hygh in flowinge, or to low by drowth, none bare the blame but the pore Christians. So at this tyme, if any myschiefe happen, our ungodly Papistes put the faulte styll in the gostpell of Christ, or in the professoures of yt. Yea, and if a man shuld kyll hymselfe, ther is none burthened wyth the cause thereof, but Godes ghostpell and Godes people: which false reportes all good men from the begynnynge hath written and spoken against, as yt appeareth by the holy Scripture, and also by the olde aunciaunt doctoures and others.

Forasmuche therfore as upon the xiiith day of Aprill, anno 1554, the Busshope of Winchestre, lord chauncellor of England, and a very ennymie and persecutour of Godes most trew religion, and a murtherer of his electe and chosen people, said in the reproch of Godes most trew and catholique religion, set furth by the blessed Kynge of noble memorie Edward the VIth, that yt was a religion that brought men to dispayre, and murtheringe of themselfes, falsly accusinge the trewth of Godes word, that comforteth and most preserveth weake consciencies from heavines and desperation; and also most untrewlie reportynge the professoures therof to be most desperate and wicked personnes; wheras indead it is most false: for from the begynnyng of Christes Church, both the Apostles, and many thousandes of martyres have boldly and wyllinglie contempned the tyrannie of all persecutoures, and most patiently suffered most cruel deaths. And yf the ungodly man wear not cleane blynded, and geaven over (as I feare me he is) to a reprobate mynde, he myght iudge this rather to be trew: that such as he hymself hath most cruellie put to death, or ben the chiefest cause of ther deaths, as John Fryth, D. Barnes, Jherom, Garret, 68 A. Askew, Jos. Lascelles, and a great numbre mo, knowen for ther lernynge and vertues to have been holy men upon the earth, and now blessed saintes through Christ in heaven, dyd likewise professe the said trew doctrine, and suffred ther bodies to be brent for the same, without any desperation. And yet the wycked man syttinge chiefe judge in the Starrechamber, to discomfort and to dryve backe all men from their salvation, (which cometh by the trew worde of God,) named it the *doctrine of desperation*, and the professores thereof *desperate people*.

And the occasion of this ungodly and untrew talke was the doynge of one Judge Hales, Syr James Hales, knyght, that the same xiiith day of April, being a prisoner in ¡the Fleet, wounded hymselfe in diverse places of his bodie : and savinge the providence of God, (that stopped the Devel's malice, that yt came not to passe, and to so devylish an end, as he entended,) very like the man wold have kylled hymselfe. But God provided his owne servant to be soner at hand wyth hym, than his Mr. thought of, belike. But now, forsomuch as upon this mann's hurte, my Lord Chancellour hath not onely spoken uncharitably by the hurt man, (whose lernynge, equitie, and wysdom, all England honoureth,) but also upon this man's faulte, he maketh faultye Godes worde, and all the professours therof : therfore, to certifie the truth unto the worlde, how this man, Mr. Judge Hales, came to this ungodly mynde to destroy hymselfe, for that I do know the truth, I can do no lesse of duty than to open yt unto all the worlde : that men may beware how they wax werye of God in denyghinge hym in the tyme of trouble. And God I take to recorde I wyll wryte no more, than that I have perfytly lerned, and leysurely searched the truth and prisonne wher Judge Hales dyd this deed upon hymself. And besydes this, I wyll not wryte the truth of this matter, for any hatred I bear to my Lord Chauncellour, whose body and sowle I wysh to do aswell as myne owne bodye and sowle ; nor for any love that I bear in this respecte to any, that is of a contrarie religion to my Lord Chancelloure ; but onely for the love and zeal I beare unto Godes word, which is slandered by my Lord Chancellour, through this mannes ungodly fact, which he much repenteth at thys tyme, and I trust God wyll forgeave hym. The matter is this.

Mr. Hales, as all men know, is imprisoned for the testimonie of Jesus Christ, and persecuted because he wyll not conform hymselfe to the false and most untrew religion, set furth at this tyme by the bysshoppes. And although the papistical sort seame not to care whether Mr. Hales return to ther part or no; yet all men may see by ther craftie doinges, that very gladly thay wold have men recant, and conform themselfes to ther false feyth and doinges. And to compare this matter, and to bringe yt to passe, Mr. Hales was diverse tymes exhorted by one Mr. Forster, a gentylman of Hamsher, and also a prisoner in the Flete, that he shuld geave over his opinion, and conforme hymselfe to the proceedinges now adayes set furth. And as the same Forster hath reaported to others, that are prisoners wyth hym, Mr. 69 Hales, condescended unto his advise, and resolved hymself to leave his former truth, and to cleave unto the errour that was offered by this mannes persuasion unto hym, because therrour was wythout daunegeir, that he shuld depart unto, and the trewth full of perell, that he shuld departe from. Thus the good man, Mr. Hales, waxinge fainte and feable in the trewth, was encreased more and more with anguishe and anxietie of mynde, his conscience rebukinge hym of his timorousness and fear. But assone as yt was known that Mr. Hales was mynded to relent from the trewth, and to consent to falshod, the xijth of April in the mornynge, came the Byshope of Chychester into the Flete, wher he had longe taulke with Mr. Hales in the garden. The contentes whereof I cannot lerne: but as many of the prisoners have said openly in the Flete, the Bishope had made uppe all together, and cleane removed Mr. Hales from his fyrst feyth, and established hym in the latter opinions allowed now by the bishoppes. The same day at afternoune came ther to the Flete Judge Portman, a Somersetsher man, and had great talke and longe wyth Mr. Hales; after whose departure, supper tyme beinge at hand, Mr. Hales came into the parlare, and satte at the table very hevylie, eatynge lytle or nothinge, but full of cogitations, and heavie wyth pensifenes: and sone after supper gat hym to bedde, wheras he had no reste, but watch wyth heavines and sorrow tyll the next morrow towardes syx of the clocke; at what tyme he commanded his servant to fetch hym a cuppe of beare, who saw the butler, as he was comynge to the stare hede, and prayed hym to bringe up a cuppe of beare for his master to his chamber, and immediately he returned to his master, who in that short tyme (whiles his man was callinge at the stare hedde for a cuppe of bear) wrought to hymselfe this displeasure, in puttyng of hymselfe in daunger of hys life, and gave occasion to my Lord Chancelloure, and to the rest of the ungodlie generation, to slander and deface the trew word of God, and the professours thereof.

But now let all men iudge indifferentlie, how this man, Mr. Hales, came to this desperation of mynd, and than all men shall perceave yt came into hert, whan he had surrendered hymselfe to accomplish the commandment of man. For as long as he was constaunt in the trewth, he endured, and strknglie passed ever more cruel imprisonment. For he was fyrst imprisoned in the Kinges Bench, and very Christenlie endured yt. Than was he for all the tyme of Lent in the Cownter of Bredstreate, and stronglie endured yt. At lengeth he came to the Flete, and bare it almost for the space of thre weeks stronglie, tyll at lengeth by persuation he wexed wery of the trewth, and than denyinge Christ, that was made man of the substance of the blessed Virgine Marie, and creditynge a false Christ, that was and is made (after the papistical opinion) of bread ; was it any mervell, though the Devel entred into this man ? No, doubtlesse ; for his new made Christ is not hable to keape the Devel away. For he can not come out of the box, although he 70 should rotte ther, and be brenned, as it many tymes happeneth. Therfore it is no mervel, tho such as trust in that faulse Christ faul into desperation. For Judas, although he chose not a new made Christ, whan he betrayed the olde, yet the Devel entred into hym, and he hanged himself for betrayenge his old mayster. Yt is no marvel therefore to see men that forsake the truth of God to be vexed with evyll spretes, and many tymes to kyll themselfes. But this we may see most evidently by Mr. Hales, that untyll such tymes as he consented to forsake Godes truth, which of long tyme he had most godly professed, he never fell into this daunger, and into this peryll, to kyll hymselfe. So that the papisticall doctrine by this mannes example is a very worme, that byteth the conscience, and never leaveth tyll yt have kylled the man that forsaketh the truth, and turneth unto lyes.

Wherfor my Lord Chanceller myght rather of this horrible fault don by Mr. Hales, have lerned to have detested and abhorred his own false and popish religion, that assoon as any of Christes members faule from the truth into yt, thay eyther dispayre or kyll themselves most commonlie, as evidentlie yt was, as is proved by Mr. Hales: for whose salvation all Christians most earnestly pray unto God. Further, my Lord Chanceller myght lern by this mannes deed, what horrible and develish wayes be used towards Christes membres by hymselfe and others, that the like was never used amonge the Turkes, by villanie and compulsion to drive men, and compell men to such a religion as the word of God never knew of. In case it were trew, as it is most false, wham dyd ever the Byshope of Winchestre read in Godes worde, that any outward law made by man cold enforse feyth, which is thonly gift of God, and shuld be truly and charitably taught to all men by Godes worde. But all men may see, that like as ther doctrine they preach is none of Godes, so may they perceave, that thay have non other arguments to defende yt wythall, but the tyrannicall sweard and fyre. For fear wherof many dissemble wyth God in outwarde obedience to idolatrie, wyth so much stringe and anguish of conscience, as many, after that they had condescended for fear unto this wycked and condemned religion by Godes worde, the old doctoures, and the lawes of this realme, thay never be mery in spirite afterward: and many tymes, for very desperation of Godes mercy kyll themselfes. Yf the Byshoppe, and his generation, dyd not delyght in bludde, and passe for nothinge but for ther own kingdom of Antichrist, thay wold lerne by this mannes hurtynge of hymselfe, to beware how thay persuade men to do against ther consciences.

But let all men pray to God for strength, and that he

wyll of his mercy mitigate this bondage and servitude, more cruel than ever was the servitude in Egypt or Babylon. For than wear the chyldren of God in captivitie in straunge landes, and under straunge kinges; but we pore English men be in captivitie in our own lande, and under our owne country men, that make us committe more vile 71 idolatrie than ever dyd the Israelites in Egypt. From the which, the Lord Almyghtie in the bludde of Christ delyver us, and amend our persecutoures, if it be his wyll. Let all good men say, *Amen.*

Number XXV.

Ridley, bishop of London, to Sir John Cheke; that he would use his interest to prevent William Thomas, clerk of the Council, from getting a prebend in his church.

MASTER CHEKE, I wish you grace and peace. Sir, in God's cause, for God's sake, and in his name, I beseech you of help and furtherance towards God's word. I did talk with you of late, what case I was in concerning my chaplains. I have gotten the good wil, and grant to be with me, of three preachers, men of good learning, and, as I am persuaded, of excellent vertue, which are able both with life and learning to set forth God's word in London, and in the whole dioces of the same; where is most need of al parts in England. For from thence goeth example, as you know, into all the rest of the King's Majesty's whole realm. The mens names be these, Mr. Grindal, whom you know to be a man of vertue and learning: Mr. Bradford, a man by whom (as I am assuredly informed) God hath and doth work wonders, in setting forth of his word: the third is a preacher, the which for detecting and confuting of the Anabaptists and Papists, both by his preaching and by his writing, is enforced now to bear Christ's cros. The two first be scholars in the University; the third is as poor as either of the other twain.

Now there is fallen a prebend in Paul's, called *Cantrelles,* by the death of one Layton. This prebend is an honest man's living of xxxiiii*l.* and better, in the King's books. But alas! Sir, I am letted by the means, I fear me, of such as do not fear God. One Mr. William Thomas, one of the clarks of the Council, hath in times past set the Council upon me, to have me grant, that Layton might have alienated the said prebend unto him and his heirs for ever. God was mine aid and defender, that I did not consent unto his ungodly enterprize. Yet I was then so handled afore the Council, that I graunted, that whensoever it should fal, I should not give it, before I should make the King's Majesty privy to it, and of acknowledge, before the collation of it. Now Layton is departed, and the prebend is 72 fallen, and certain of the Council, no doubt by this ungodly man's means, have written unto me to stay the collation. And wheras he despaireth that ever I would assent, that a teacher's living should be bestowed on him, he hath procured letters unto me, subscribed with certain of the counsellors hands, that now the King's Majesty hath determined it unto the furniture of his Highnes stables.

Alas! Sir, this is a heavy hearing. When papistry was taught, there was nothing too little for the teachers. When the Bishop gave his benefices unto ideots, unlearned, ungodly, for kindred, for pleasure, for service, and other worldly respects, al was then wel allowed. Now where a poor living is to be given unto an excellent clark, a man known and tryed to have both discretion and also vertue, and such an one, as before God I do not know a man, yet unplaced and unprovided for, more meet to set forth God's word in all England; when a poor living, I say, which is founded for a preacher, is to be given unto such a man, that then an ungodly person shal procure in this sort letters to stop and let the same. Alas! Mr. Cheke, this seemeth unto me to be a right heavy hearing. Is this the fruit of the gospel? Speak, Mr. Cheke, speke for God's sake, in God's cause, unto whomsoever you think you may do good withal. And if you will not speak, then I beseech you let these my letters speak unto Mr. Gates, to Mr. Wrothe, to Mr. Cecil, whom all I do take for men that do fear God.

It was said here constantly, my Lord Chamberlain to have been departed. Sir, though the day be delayed, yet he hath no pardon of long life. And therefore I do beseech his good Lordship, and so many as shall read these letters, if they fear God, to help, that neither horse, neither yet dog, be suffered to devour the poor livings, appointed and founded by godly ordinance to the ministers of God's word. The causes of conscience, which do move me to speak and write thus, are not only those which I declared once in the case of this prebend before the King's Majesty's Council, which now I let pas; but also now the man, Mr. Grindal, unto whom I would give this prebend, doth move me very much. For he is a man known to be both of vertue, honesty, discretion, wisdom, and learning. And besides al this, I have a better opinion of the King's Majestyes Council, than, (although some of them have subscribed at this their clark's crafty and ungodly suit to such a letter,) than I say they wil let and not suffer, after request made unto them, the living appointed and founded for a preacher, to be bestowed upon so honest and wel learned a man.

Wherfore, for God's sake, I beseech you al, help, that with the favour of the Council, I may have knowledg of the King's Majesty's good pleasure, to give this preacher's lyving unto Mr. Grindal. Of late there have been letters directed from the King's Majesty and his honourable Council unto all the bishops, wherby we be charged and commanded, both in our own persons, and also to cause our 73 preachers and ministers, especially to cry out against the insatiable serpent of covetousnes; whereby is said to be such a greedines among the people, that each one goeth about to devour other, and to threaten them with God's grievous plagues, both now presently thrown upon them, and that shal be likewise in the world to come. Sir, what preachers shal I get to open and set forth such matters, and so as the King's Majesty and the Council do command them to be set forth, if either ungodly men or unreasonable beasts be suffered to pul away and devour the good and godly learned preachers livings? Thus I wish you in God ever wel to fare, and to help Christ's cause, as you would have help of him at your most need. From Fulham, this present the 23 July, 1551.

Yours in Christ,

Nicolas London.

Number XXVI.

Joannis Hoperi Angli, nuper episcopi Wigorniensis et Gloucestrensis, de vera ratione inveniendæ et fugiendæ falsæ doctrinæ, breve syntagma.

Desiderantur quædam in initio.

. . . . ignarus, vel idiota diligit. Sed dilectio nostra vera, est amor in vera fide erga omnia præcepta divina, quibus humiliter obedimus cum quadam lætitia et animi exultatione: ut tum ad Deum propter se, tum proximum meum propter Deum honore afficiamur. Et hanc dilectionem verbum Dei tantum docet: ut fidem, spem, charitatem, timorem, tolerantiam, ac cæteras virtutes omnes, quæ ab hoc Christiano necessario exiguntur. Qui ergo populum Dei ad carbonarios, vel ad quoscunque alios quibuscunque titulis et nomine inscriptos, et non ad verbum Dei relegant, impostores sunt, Deique et hominum hostes: de quibus etiam Deus gravissime per Hieremiam conqueritur, inquiens, *Duo* Hierem. v. *mala, inquit, fecit populus meus: me dereliquerunt fontem aquæ vivæ, et foderunt sibi cisternas, quæ aquas continere non valent.* Idem et apud vos facere, qui vestræ saluti præficiuntur, conantur. Primum defectionem a verbo Dei docent, a quo uno omnis petenda est veritas in religione Christi: et per quod omnes spiritus qui in ecclesiis docent, a populo probandi sunt, num sint ex Deo. Deinde certitudinem fidei nostræ ab *ignaro*, indocto, atque imperito carbonario petendam esse docent; quicquid sit fides plane ig- 74 norat. Quid hoc aliud est, quam juxta verbum Christi; *Cæcum cæco præficere, ut ambo in foveam cadant?* Certe Matt. xv.
Luc. vi. Christus longe alia tam a ministris Ecclesiæ, quam a populo exigit. Nimirum ut minister verbum Dei duntaxat doceat, et populus id solum audiat, discat, et observat: et omnino Deus vetat, ne qui sapientissimi et sanctissimi inter homines habentur, faciunt ea quæ recta videantur in oculis ipsorum: multo magis non est credendum nec faciendum in causa fidei, quod rectum videatur in oculis illiteratissimi et stupidissimi carbonarii.

Quare pro meo erga vos officio, munere, et amore, quo tenacius veritati verbi Dei adhæreatis; breve syntagma de falsa religione dignoscenda et fugienda, vestræ charitati dedicavi. Unde facile intelligetis, quam horribiliter et impie quæ hodie in ecclesiis Anglicanis fiunt, a veritate verbi Dei dissonent, et ex diametro pugnent. Quod vulgari ac nostro idiomate scripsissem, si typographum aliquem idoneum qui Anglice librum emitteret, invenissem. Sed ut pii omnes probe norunt, hodie in Anglia vel prela in imprimendis fabulis sudant, aut penitus silent. Præterea nolui vestra causa hoc opus nostra lingua edere, ne episcopi (Dei ac hominum implacabiles hostes) severius et acrius in vos (quos in Christo Jesu unice diligo) animadverterent. Quam atrociter enim et inhumaniter pii hodie ubique in hoc regno tractentur; illorum lachrymæ et gemitus (quos Deus tandem dubio procul clementer in Christo aspiciet) testantur. Præterea Latine scribere volui (quanquam Latinæ orationis pompam, fucum et calamistra assequi nec valeo nec affecto) ut quæ a me de rebus divinis inter vos olim dicta, et a vobis accepta, piis fratribus sparsim universum orbem incolentibus, palam facerem: ut fidem meam atque vestram agnoscerent, judicarent, et approbarent verbi Dei calculo et autoritate; et eandem apud Deum patrem nostrum cœlestem suis precibus adjuvarent, ut constanter et intrepide in eadem ad finem usque (invitis etiam inferorum portis) perseveremus. Piis et religiosis viris, ac sacrarum literarum amatoribus scribo, quibus Dei gloria et illius verbi veritas summopere est cordi; quamvis orationis fuco et pigmentis non illiniatur. Et quemadmodum perantiquus ille Lucilius poeta dicere solebat, se sua non Persio scribere, sed Siculis et Tarentinis; sic ego non solum quæcunque de vera religione

Cur vulgari idiomate non scripsit.

Lucilius poeta.

scribo, verum quæcunque etiam cogito aut loquor ; ea omnia piis tantum scripta, cogitata, aut dicta esse volo : quid livor virulentus carpat non moror : nec plus Papistarum flammas aut ferrum curo, quam leæna latrantis catuli vocem.   Corpus tantum occidere possunt : sed anima statim in Christo præsenti et sempiterno gaudio fruetur.   Tantum igitur dum hic vivitur Deum supplici animo precemur, ut ipsi cor ac mentem nostram dedicemus : cujus tutela et gratia omnia pericula evitabimus.   Interim hostes evangelii fortiter propter Christum contemnamus, omnesque in Christo comiter juvare studeamus.

Hæc assidue cum animis vestris cogitate, et meditatione ac studio legum divinarum vos ipsos oblectate : ut Deo et sanctæ suæ Ecclesiæ chari habeamini.   Cavete etiam ab iis, qui vobis fodiunt (ut inquit David) foveas : quæ non sunt secundum legem Dei.   Et non per quem, sed quid dicatur, animadvertite.   Nam quemadmodum inter bajulum et Al-75 cibiadem supremo loco natum, si veram nobilitatem spectemus, nulla est differentia, modo absit virtus : ita nec inter Nota. idiotam et summum Pontificem, sicut cathedram Petri oc-Galath. i. cupantem, si veram religionem spectemur, nulla est differentia, modo absit verbi Dei authoritas.

. Imo qui aliud evangelium quam Christi docet, anathemate (licet sanctissimus) est feriendus.   Quare cum sanctissimo vate Davide dicite, *In æternum, Domine, verbum tuum* Ps. cxix. *permanet in cœlo et in terra :* illud non potest mutari, non potest antiquari, non potest augeri, nec potest diminui. Nam quicquid Deus ipse constituit, ratum ac fixum esse oportet ; hoc indicat et testatur cœlorum et terræ perennitas.   Quicquid ergo reges, principes, episcopi, sacrificuli, vel is, qui impie seipsum pro summo capite Ecclesiæ Christi militantis in terris jactitat, in causa religionis dixerint ; vos ipsos ad scientiam legum divinarum recipite, et earum presidio adversus omnis impietatis insidias et imposturas communite.   In causa fidei nullam authoritatem principum aut episcoporum agnoscite citra verbum Dei.   Nam ipsa universalis Ecclesiæ autoritas nulla est, nisi quatenus a verbo Dei pendeat ; ementitam ac fictam Romani Pontificis autoritatem contemnite, et ex animis vestris omnino profligate. Deus enim omnes apostolos, quo ad autoritatem et dignitatem pares fecit, omnibus dixit, *Accipite Spiritum Sanctum, quorum remiseritis peccata sunt remissa, quorum retinueritis sunt retenta.* Omnes pares in docendo evangelio constituit; omnes pariter *lucem hujus mundi,* et *salem terræ* appellavit; et omnes testes æternæ salutis pares assignavit. Quamobrem ex verbo Dei nullam prerogativam, præ ceteris apostolis, Christus Petro concessit; quod si concessisset, tamen nec cathedræ suæ, nec suis successoribus eandem concedere, Petrus a Christo potestatem habuit. Et si illi et aliis totius Ecclesiæ curam Christus principaliter concessisset, nihil Romani Antichristi partes adjuvaret. Nam an Petrus unquam fuerit Romæ, adhuc sub judice lis est. Præterea an unquam Petrus supremam dignitatem et imperium Ecclesiæ suis successoribus commendaverit, Papa ostendere non valet. Et si etiam hæc omnia vera essent, quod Christus Petro, et Petrus suis successoribus, ut Papicolæ fingunt, contulissent; tamen Romanis pontificibus nihil patrocinaretur. Hi enim qui Petri doctrinam promovent, veri sunt Petri successores; et non qui illius sedem ac cathedram occupant. Et quod suam autoritatem conciliis et autoritatibus patrum asserere conatur, figmentum est. Nam cum in concilio Carthaginensi 3°. nomen et dignitatem universalis Episcopi patres obtulissent R. Pontifici, Pelagius Romanus Episcopus omnibus modis, eodem tempore, illud nomen a se rejecit. Et Gregorius Magnus quinque epistolis gravissime et maximo impetu orationis adversus Joan. Constantinopolitanum, quod tam insulsum nomen a Mauricio imperatore tentaverat, invehitur, illum vocans *predecessorem Antichristi.* Affirmat præterea Gregorius Magnus omnes qui in hoc scelesto vocabulo (generalis episcopi) conseniserint, fidem suam perdere. Et quod autoritatem suam ratam esse voluerit, quasi a regibus et principibus concessam: certo scimus reges et principes, et si vellent non posse aliquam suæ dignitatis partem cuiquam conferre, nec a suo officio et honore deponere. Nam quod Deus necessario alicui statui conjungit, nemo in alium statum trans-

Joan. xx.

Matt. v.

Luc. xiv.

An Petrus fuit Romæ lis est.

Gregorius, Ep. xxxix.

76

faire valet.   Reges autem sub se ministros, qui Ecclesiæ et Reges.
Reipub. munia ministrent, habere possunt, sed pares vel
superiores in Ecclesiæ vel Reipub. ministerio habere, regibus non licet.   Et si forte quispiam vel regis permissione,
vel aliqua temporis præscriptione, vel tyrannide, in ecclesiis
autoritatem sibi vindicat : nemo tamen illius autoritati ob-
temperare debet nec Episcopo, nec Papæ, quatenus sunt
Episcopi ; quandoquidem a Deo talem potestatem non habent : nec quia a regibus missi, propterea quod talem potestatem reges Episcopo papali facere non possunt.   Sed hanc
potestatem Papæ clare indicat Joan. originem suam habuisse Apoc. xvii.
nec a Deo nec ab homine, sed ex abysso : et in interitum
procul dubio brevi ibit.

Sed hanc violentiam et satanicam autoritatem Papæ, non
est præsentis instituti ulterius prosequi.   Tantum admonere
volui, quamvis contra omnia jura divina et humana (nunc
iterum propter nostra peccata) inter Anglos caput Ecclesiæ
obtinuerit : non plus hic habere jurisdictionis, quam infimus
Episcopus Angliæ habet Romæ.   Et tandem denuo Dominus interficiet illum spiritu oris sui, ut antehac fecit.   Nihil
tam perfectum tamque absolutum oculis nostris videmus inter ipsa opera Dei, cujus interitus videri non possit.   At
ipsa lex Dei nulla vi, nullave tyrannide, dolo aut vetustate
consumi aut obliterari potest, ut Christus testatur ; *Cœlum
et terra transibunt ; verba autem mea non transibunt.*   Illud igitur amplectamini, ac omni studio et diligentia colite.
In hoc omnes vires nervosque intendite, ut vita nostra sic
instituatur, et gubernetur a sancto Dei numine, ut nunquam
ab illius legis observatione aberret.   Tunc futurum erit, ut
omnia vobis prospere succedant, ac felicissime cadant, si legem Dei ante oculos habueritis.   Præterea, si ad verbi Dei
regulam, quæ hodie a Papistis in ecclesiis fiunt, exigantur,
tunc omnia impia et prophana esse, nullo negotio judicabitis.   Quapropter ego hoc breve syntagma scripsi, ut pii et
impii, veri et falsi cultus discrimen collatione quadam de-
monstrarem : quanta supplicia impiis cultoribus, quantaque
piis proemia sint constituta.   Deus apud Hieremiam judicio
contendit cum Israelitis, et cum illorum filiis acerrime dis-

ceptat. *Transite,* inquit, *ad insulas Cethim et videte, et in Cedar mittite, et considerate vehementer, et diligentissime videte, si factum est hujusmodi.* *Si mutavit gens deos suos, et certe ipsi non sunt dii: populus vero meus mutavit gloriam suam in idolum.* An non de nobis etiam idem justissime ac merito conqueri potest Deus? Quæ enim gens usquam in toto terrarum orbe tam impia, fraudulenta, immanis et truculenta est; quæ deos suos tantum ad præscriptum suæ legis non colit et veneratur? Nulla certe tam barbara natio reperitur sub sole. Nam si cultus Christianorum hodie in ecclesiis sub Papæ tyrannide, ad præscriptum verbi Dei conferatur; omnia ex diametro cum verbo Dei pugnare videbimus. Imo nec usus, nec lectio evangelii in missa incognita lingua publicis ac sacris conventibus ad regulam verbi quadrat. Nam evangelium etiam iis a quibus non intelligitur, nihil prodest. Christus igitur sæpe

Matt. xv. jubet: *Audite et intelligite.* Et pulchre docet Chrysosto-
Chrysost. mus in 1 Cor. xiv. " Qui ignota," inquit, "lingua loquitur,
" quam non intelligit, nec seipsum nec alium ædificat."

77 Quænam potest esse utilitas ex voce non intellecta? Nulla penitus. Ideo Deus ad vocem verbi sui non tantum hominum presentiam, auditum, geniculationem, corporis erectionem, capitis denudationem, manuum expansionem, vérum hoc exigit a singulis suis auditoribus, προσέχετε λαός μου τῷ

Ps. lxxviii. νόμῳ μου; quod sonat; *Intendite et adhibete mentem, popule mi,* vel *adverte animum ad legem meam.* Κλίνατε οὖς ὑμῶν εἰς τὰ ῥήματα τοῦ στόματός μου. i. *Ita aures vestras ad verba oris mei applicate et accommodate,* quasi nihil aliud cogitetis, aut audiatis, quam quod de ore meo egreditur. Hanc attentionem et intelligentiam efficacius adhuc multo exprimit Ebræa veritas. הַאֲזִינָה עַמִּי תּוֹרָתִי הַטּוּ אָזְנְכֶם לְאִמְרֵי־פִי:

Non solum istorum vocabulorum et thematum proprietas; verum etiam grammatica constructio indicat mentis attentionem, et aurium diligentissimam auscultationem lectioni verbi Dei adesse debere. Chalidæus explanator pulcherrime hæc verba explanat per duo verba, quasi Deus ad hunc modum fuisset loquutus, *Populae mi, conservate et consecrate mentem vestram ad vocem meam:* et aures vestras verbis oris mei relinquite, me concionantem solum audiant et observent. Hoc mandatum generale est ac universale, ut cum docti tum indocti non solum legem, verum etiam ænigmata et propositiones, nec non et singula verba oris Dei audiant, intelligant, discant, et observent, exigit. Et qui id fieri potest, cum quid legatur, agatur, aut dicatur in ecclesiis populus non intelligit? Quare ex studio et observatione legum divinarum, impia et falsa fugite, sanctaque et vera exosculamini; nisi a via veritatis aberrare volueritis, et tandem meritas ignorantiæ et ingratitudinis vestræ pœnas luere. Hæc pro meo erga vos amore ad vos scripsi: amanter igitur suscipite quæso.

E carcere, 1. *Decembris,* 1554.

Number XXVII.

Bishop Hoper's letter consolatory, to certain professors suffering imprisonment, being taken at a meeting together for religious worship.

John Hoper, to the Christian congregation.

THE grace, favour, consolation, and ayd of the Holy Foxii MSS. Ghost be with you now and for ever, *Amen.* Dearly beloved in the Lord, ever sythe I harde of your imprisonment, I have bene marvelously moved with great affections and passions, as wel of mirth and gladnes, as of heavines and sorrow. Of gladnes in this, that I perceave how ye be bent and geven to prayer and invocation of God's help in 78 theis dark and wicked procedings of men against God's glory: I have bene sory to perceave the malice and wickednes of men to be so cruel, devilish, and tyrannical, to persecute the people of God for serving [him,] for saying or hearing the holy Psalmes and the word of eternal life. Theis cruel doings do declare, that the Papist-church is more bloudy and tyrannical than ever was the sword of the heathnicks and gentils. Whan I harde of your taking, what you were doing, wherfore and by whom you were taken, I remembred how the Christians in the primitive

Church were used by the cruelty of unchristen'd heathens in the time of Trajan the Emperor. About LXXVII years after Christys ascension into heaven the Christians were persecuted very sore, as though they had bene traitors and movers of sedition. The gentile Emperor Trajane required to know the trew cause of the Christian mens troubles; a great learned man, named Plinius, wrot unto him and sayd, yt was because the Christians sang certain Psalmes before day to one called *Christ*, whom they worshipped as God. Whan Trajan the Emperor understood that yt was for nothing but for conscience and religion, he caused forthwith by his commandment every where, that no man shold be persecuted. Lo! a gentile wold not have such as were of a contrary religion punished for serving of God. But the Pope and his chaplains hath caused you to be cast into prison, being taken doing the work of God, and one of the excellentest works that is required of Christian men, that ys to wyt, whyle you were in perfect prayer; and not in such wicked and superstitious prayers as the Papists use, but in the same prayer that Christ taught you to pray; and in his name you gave God thanks for that you have received, and for such things as you want in hys name did you ask yt.

Oh! glad may you be, that ever you were born, to be apprehended and taken while you were so vertuously occupyed. Blessed be they that suffer for righteousness sake. If God had suffer'd them that take your bodies, to have taken your lyves also, then had you now bene following the Lamb in perpetual joys, away from the company and assemble of wicked men. But the Lord will not so suddenly you to depart, but reserveth you gloriously to speak and to maintain the truth to the world. Be not careful what you shal say: God wil go in and out with you, and wil be present in your hearts and in your mouths, to speak his wisdom, yea although it appear folishnes to the world. He that hath begun that work in you, wil surely strengthen you in the same. And pray you continually unto him, that you may fear him only that hath power to kil both body and soul, and to cast them into helfire. Be of good comfort; al the haires of the head are numbred, and there is not one of them shal perish, except your heavenly Father suffer it. Now you be even in the field, and placed in the forefront of Christ's battail; it is doutles a singular grace of God, and a special love of hym towards you, to geve you this foreward and preeminence, and a sign, that he trusteth you above many other of his people.

Wherfore, dear brethren and sisters, continually fight the fight of the Lord, your cause is most just and godle: ye stand for the trew Christ, who is after the flesh in heaven; and for his trew religion and honor, which is fully, amplie, sufficiently, and abondantly contained in the H. Testament, sealed with Christes own bloud. How much are you bound to God, that doth put you in trust in so holy and just a cause? Remember, dear bretherne and sisters, what lookers upon you have to se and behold you in this fight, God and al his holy angels, who be ready always to take you up, if you be slain in this fight. Consider also who you have standing at your backs, al the faithful brethern, who shal take courage, strength, and desire to follow such noble and valiant Christians as you be. Be not afraid therefore of your adversaries. For he that is in you is stronger than he that is in them. Shrink not, although it semeth to the flesh painful. Your pains shal not be now so grievous, as here-after your joy shal be comfortable. Read the viiith and ixth chapters to the Romans; to the Hebrews the xith and xiith; and upon your knees thank God that ever you were counted worthy to suffer any thing for his treuths sake. Read the second chapter of St. Luke's gospel, and there shal you se, how the shepherds that watched al night upon their shepe, as soon as they heard that Christ was born in Bethlehem, by and by they went to se him. They did not reason and dispute within themselves, who shold kepe the wolfe from the shepe in the meanwhile, but did forthwith as they were commaunded, and committed their shepe unto his keping, whose pleasure they obeyed. So let us now we are called, commit al things to him that calleth us. He wil take hede that al things shal be wel; he wil surely comfort the husband; he wil doutles help the wife; he wil guide the servants; he wil kepe the house; yea, rather than any thing shold be left undone, he wil wash the dishes and rock the cradle. Cast therefore your care upon God, for he doubtles careth for you.

Besides this, you may perceave by your imprisonment, that the adversaries wepons against you be nothing but flesh, bloud, and tyranny. For yf they were able, they would maintayn their wicked religion by the word of God; but for lack of that, they wil by violence compel such as they cannot by the holy Scripture overcome, to deny that known truth they have before professed. Good Christian brethern, let not their cruelty force you to do any thing against your conscience, but boldly withstand them, though it cost you the price of your life.

I pray you al, pray to God for me, and I wil do the same for you. And although we be asonder in the flesh, yet in Christ, I trust, for ever joyning in the Spirit together: and so shal meet together in the palace of heavenly joys after this life ys ended, which is short and miserable. God's holy Spirit be with you now and evermore. So be yt. Jan. 4, 1554.

---

80 ### Number XXVIII.

Sententia contra Johannem Hooper, lata a Stephano, Winton. Episcopo, 29 die Januarii, 1554.

Foxii MSS. IN Dei nomine, Amen. Nos Stephanus permissione divina Winton. episcopus, judicialiter et pro tribunali sedentes. In quodam heretice pravitatis negocio, contra te Johannem Hoper presbyterum, olim monachum domus sive monasterii de Cliva, ordinis Cistercien. coram nobis in judicio personaliter comparentem, et nobis super heretica pravitate, detectum, denunciatum, et delatum, ac in ea parte apud bonos et graves notorie et publice defamatum, rite et legitime procedentes, auditis, visis, et intellectis ac æstimatis, et matura deliberatione discussis et ponderatis dicti negocii meritis et circumstantiis, servatisque in omnibus et per omnia in eodem negocio de jure servandis, ac quomodolibet requisitis, Christi nomine invocato, ac ipsum solùm Deum pre oculis nostris habentes. Quia per acta inactitata, deducta, probata, confessata, et per te sepius coram nobis in eodem negocio recognita, asserta, et affirmata comperimus et invenimus, te tum per confessiones tuas varias, et per recognitiones tuas judiciales coram nobis judicialiter factas, errores, hereses, et falsas opiniones subscriptas, jure divino ac Catholicæ universalis et apostolicæ Ecclesiæ determinationi obviantes, contrarias et repugnantes, tenuisse, credidisse, affirmasse, publicasse, predicasse, et dogmatizasse.

·*Viz.* Quod licet, tam de jure divino quam humano, cuicunque religioso etiam expresse professo, et presbytero cuicunque post susceptam professionem, et post susceptum presbyteratus ordinem, ducere uxorem, et cum eadem tanquam cum uxore legitima cohabitare.

Item, Quod propter culpam fornicationis sive adulterii commissam persone legitime conjugate possunt ex verbo Dei ejusque auctoritate ac ministerio magistratuum ab invicem pro adulterio a vinculo matrimonii separari et divorciari. Sic quod licebit viro aliam accipere in uxorem, ut mulieri similiter alium accipere in maritum, pro eo quod mulier non est amplius uxor prioris viri, nec prior vir amplius maritus prioris uxoris.

Item, Quod in eucharistia sine sacramento altaris verum et naturale corpus Christi, et verus ac naturalis Christi sanguis sub speciebus panis et vini, vere non est. Et quod ibi est materialis panis et materiale vinum tantum, absque veritate et præsentia corporis et sanguinis Christi.

Quas quidem hereses, errores, et falsas opiniones, juri divino ac universalis Catholice Ecclesie determinationi obviantes, contrarias et repugnantes. Coram nobis tam in judicio quam extra, animo obstinato, pertinaci et indurato, arroganter, pertinaciter, scienter et obstinate asseruisti, tenuisti, affirmasti, dixisti, pariter ac defendisti, atque te sic credere, asserere, et dicere velle, paribus obstinacia, pertinacia, malicia, et cordis cecitate, etiam prudens et sciens affirmasti: idcirco nos Stephanus Winton. episcopus, ordinarius, et

81

diocesanus antedictus, de venerabilium confratrum nostrorum dominorum episcoporum hic presentium et nobis assi-
dentium consensu et assensu expressis, quam etiam de et
cum consilio et judicio jurisperitorum et sacrarum literarum
professorum, cum quibus communicavimus in hac parte;
te Johannem Hooper memoratum demeritis, culpis, obsti-
naciis et contumaciis, per improbas et sceleratas tuas obsti-
nacias et pertinacias multipliciter contractis, incursis, et ag-
gravatis, in detestabili, horrendo, et impio heretice pravitatis reatu, et execrabili dogmate comprehensum fuisse et
esse, atque hujusmodi scelerata et impia dogmata coram
nobis sepe dixisse, asseruisse, atque scienter, voluntarie, et
pertinaciter defendisse et manutenuisse, per varias tuas confessiones, assertiones, et recognitiones tuas judiciales sepe
coram nobis repetitas, ita asseruisse, affirmasse, et credidisse, declaramus et pronunciamus, teque in hac parte rite
et legitime confessum fuisse et esse decernimus. Ideoque te
Johannem Hooper antedictum hominem tuos errores, hereses, et impias ac damnatas opiniones refutare, retractare, re-
cantare, et abjurare, in forma Ecclesie approbata nolentem,
sed obstinate et pertinaciter dictis tuis sceleratis heresibus
et execratis opinionibus inherentem, et ad unitatem sacrosancte Ecclesie redire nolentem, premissorum occasione,
causa et pretextu, hereticum, obstinatum, et pertinacem fuisse et esse, cum animi dolore et cordis amaritudine, etiam
declaramus, pronunciamus, et decernimus. Teque tanquam
hereticum obstinatum et pertinacem, ex nunc judicio sive
curie seculari, ut membrum putridum a corpore sacrosancte
Ecclesie resecatum, ad omnem juris effectum exinde sequi
valentem, relinquendum et tradendum fore decernimus et
declaramus, atque de facto relinquimus et tradimus. Teque
Johannem Hooper hereticum pertinacem et obstinatum hujusmodi majoris excommunicationis sententia premissorum
occasione innodatum et involutum eaque ligatum fuisse et
esse, et propterea merito degradandum, et ab omni ordine
sacerdotali deponendum et exuendum fore debere, juxta
sacros canones in hac parte editos et ordinatos, sententialiter
et diffinitive declaramus per hanc nostram sententiam defini-

tivam, quam in et contra te dolenter ferimus et promulgamus in hiis scriptis.

Lecta, lata, et promulgata fuit hec sententia in ecclesia paroch. Ste Marie Overey, alias voc. Sancti Salvatoris in burgo de Southwark Winton. dioc. die Martis vicesimo nono die mensis Januarii, anno Domini, juxta computationem Ecclesiæ Anglicanæ, 1554, presentibus testibus de quibus in actis illius diei habetur specifica mentio.

Number XXIX.

John Bradford's meditation of God's providence and presence.

THIS ought to be unto us most certain, that nothing is Foxii MSS. come without thy providence, O Lord; that is, that nothing is don, good or bad, sweet or sower, but by thy knowledge; that is, by thy will, wisdome, and ordinance: for al these knowledg doth comprehend in it: as by thy word we are taught in many places, that even the loss of a sparrow is not without thy wil; nor any liberty or power upon a poor porket have al the devils in hel, but by thine own appointment and will. And we must always believe it most assuredly to be al just and good, howsoever it seem otherwise unto us. For thou art mervaillous (and not comprehensible) in thy ways, and holy in al thy works. But hereunto it is necessary for us to know no less certainly, that although al things be don by thy providence, yet the same thy providence to have many and divers means to work by: which being contemned, thy providence is contemned. As for an example, meat is a mean to serve thy providence for the preservation of health and life here. So that he that contemneth to eat, because thy providence is certain and unfallible, that same contemneth thy providence indeed. If it were so, that meat could not be had, then should we not ty thy providence unto this mean, but make free as thou art free; that is, that without meat thou must help to health and life. For it is not of any need that thou usest any mean to serve thy providence. Thy wisdom and power is infinite, and therfore should we hang on thy providence, even when al is clean contrary against us. But for our erudition and infirmities sake, it hath pleased thee to work by means, and deal with us here, to exercise us in obedience.

And because we cannot (so great is our corruption) sustain thy naked providence and presence, grant me therfore, dear Father, I humbly beseech thee, for Christ's sake, that as I something now know these things, so I may use this knowledge to my comfort and commoditie. That is, grant that in what state soever I be, I doubt not but the same to come to me by thy most just ordinance, yea, by thy merciful ordinance also. For as thou art just, so art thou merciful. Yea, thy mercy is above al thy works. And by this knowledge grant that I may humble my self to obey thee, and expect for thy help in time convenient, not only when I have means by which thou mayest work, and art so accustomed to do, but also when I have no means, but am destitute: yea, when al things and means are clean contrary against me; grant, I say, that I may still hang upon thee and thy providence; not doubting of a fatherly end in good time.

83 Again, lest I should contemn thy providence, or presuming on it by uncoupling those things which thou hast coupled together, preserve me from neglecting thine ordinance and lawful means in al my need, (if so be I may have them, and with good conscience use them,) although I know thy providence be not tyed to them further than it pleaseth thee; but grant that I may with diligence, reverence, and thankfulness use them; and thereto add my wisdome and industry in al things lawful for me, to serve therby thy providence, if so please thee. That I hang in no part on the means, or in my diligence, wisdom, or industry, but only on thy providence; which more and more perswade me to be altogether fatherly and good, how far soever it appear or seem, yea, is felt of me. By this I being preserved from negligence on my behalf, and dispairing or murmuring towards thee, shal become diligent through thy mean, and

alone grace: which give me and increase in me, to praise thy holy name for ever thro Christ our Lord and Saviour. *Amen.*

There is nothing that maketh more to the true godliness of life than this, the persuasion of thy presence, dear Father, and that nothing is hid from thee, but al to thee is open and naked, even the very thoughts, which one day thou wilt reveal and open, either to our praise or punishment in this life; as thou didst David's faults, which he did secretly, 2 Reg. xii. or in life to come, Matt. xxv. for nothing is so hid that shall not be revealed. Therefore doth the prophet say, *Wo to them that kepe secret their thoughts, to hide their counsil from the Lord, and do their works in darkness, saying, Who seeth us?*

Grant to me, therfore, that I may find mercy and pardon for al my sins, especially my hid and close sins. Enter not into judgment with me, I humbly beseech thee. Give me to believe truly in thy Christ, so that I never come into judgment for them; that with David I might so reveal them, and confess them unto thee, that thou wouldest cover them. And grant further, that I always think myself continually conversant before thee: so that if I do wel, I pas not of the publishing of it, as hypocrites do: if I do or think any evil, I may forthwith know that the same shal not always be hid from men. Grant that always I may have in mind that day, wherin the hid works of darknes shal be illumined, and the sentence of thy Son, *Nothing is so secret, that shall not be revealed.* So in trouble and wrong I shall find comfort, and otherwise be kept through thy grace from doing evil. Which do thou work, I humbly beseech thee for Christ's sake. *Amen. Soli Deo honor et gloria.* 1554.

Jhon Bradforthe.

Number XXX.

84

Bradford's prayer, that God would shorten the persecution, and restore the true religion.

AS David, seeing the angel with the sword ready drawn Foxii MSS.

to plague Jerusalem, cryed unto the Lord, and said, *It is I, Lord, that have sinned, and even I that have done wickedly ; thy hand be upon me, and not upon thy poor sheep :* wherethrough thou wast moved to mercy, and baddest thy angel put up his sword into the sheath, for thou haddest taken punishment enough : even so we, O most gracious God, seing thy fearful sword of vengeance ready drawn, and presently striking against this commonweal, and thy Church in the same, we, I say, are occasioned every one of us to cast off our eyes from the beholding, and narrowly espying of other mens faults, and do set our own only in sight, that with the same David thy servant, and with Jonas in the ship, we may cry, and say unto thee, that it is we, O Lord, that have sinned and procured thy grievous wrath upon us. And thus we presently gathered, do acknowledge ourselves guilty of most horrible ingratitude for our good King, for thy gospel and pure religion, and for the peace of the Church, and quietnes of the commonwealth ; besides our negligences, and many other grievous sins ; wherethrough we deserved not only these, but much more grievous plagues and punishments, if that thou didst not presently, as thou art wont, extend thy mercy upon us ; that thou in thine anger dost remember thy mercy, before we seek or sue for it. We take boldness, O gracious Lord, and, as thou hast commanded us to do in our trouble, we come and cal upon thee to be merciful unto us ; and of thy goodnes in Christ we most humbly pray thee to hold thy hand, and to cease thy wrath ; or at the least so mitigate it, that this realm may be quietly governed, and the same eftsones to be an harborough for thy Church and true religion : and which it may please thee to restore again to us, for thy great mercies sake ; and we shall praise thy name everlastingly, through Jesus Christ our only Saviour, Mediator, and Advocate. *Amen.*

Number XXXI.

85

Mr. John Bradford to Mr. Traves : begging his prayers,
and lamenting his own sinful condition.

GRACE and mercy from God the Father, through our Foxii MSS.
Lord Christ, govern our minds, *ne dominetur in nobis pec-*
catum. Amen.

Yesternight a litle tofore supper, I was desyred by a
neighbour, my mother's frend, ayenst this day to dyner:
unto whom, for that a refusal wold have bene imputed dis-
daynful statelyness, I unwillingly, (God to wytnes,) but not
unadvysedly, yet folyshly, graunted to the same: which
I advertise you, as myne excuse of not comyng this day.
And for myne absence yesterday, my vayne lokyng for you
to have come with your nerest neighbour, (the rather for
that I hard hym commyt to you the surveye of his will,)
hath with some repentance deceyved me, though to my hurt
and loss, yet to your profyt, which else, by my comyng
and troublyng you, shuld have bene contrary. If you
come not to morrow hither, send me word by this bringer,
and if there be no sermon, I wil come to you to have
your counsail in such thyngs as by letters I wil not now
write.

In the mean season, in your communication with God, I
pray you have me, of al synners, a most negligent, unthankful, and wretched, (Oh ! that from the bottom of my hert I
confessed the same unfaynedly,) in remembraunce : that at
length I might truly convert and retourne from thies greasy
flesh-pots of Egypt, to feed with his manna, patiently and
assuredly expecting his mercy, joyfully sighing for, and
bearyng the badge of his disciples and servants, the cross :
I mean to crucify this luciferous and glotonous hart, more
than most worthy of the rych Epulo, his inquenchable thirst,
and gnawing wormes of Herod. This paper, pen, and ink,
yea, the marble stone, weepeth, to se my slothful security,
and unthankful hardness, to so merciful and long-suffering
a Lord. I confess it, I confess it, though not tremblyngly,

humbly, or penytently; yet I confess it, oh! hypocritically I confess it.

Therefore pray, pray for me, *ut resipiscam, et ut Deum convertar, non contemnens iram ejus, et mortem filii sui Jesu Christi; sed ut Spiritu incedam, et Spiritu vivam:* evermore to bewayl my carnal security, and this *philautiam:* that I may be made a new creature through grace, made mete to receyve the new wyne of the gospel into a new vessel, purifyed by faith, wrought by the Spirit of consolation. Which may vouchsave to lead us in al truth and godly lyving; *ut in ipso cognoscamus Deum patrem, solum verum Deum, et quem misit Jesum Christum.* To which most blessed Trinity be all honor and glory for ever. *Amen.* From Manchestre in haste, this Thurysday in the morning.

86

Yours as his awne,
John Bradford.

To my veray loving friend,
John Traves in Blakeley.

Number XXXII.

Mr. Bradford to some person of quality unknown; excusing his not coming, being desired: and debasing himself.

Foxii MSS.

GRACE and virtue from God the Father, through our Lord Jesus Christ, govern our mynds, that synne have not the upper hand of virtue in our souls. *Amen.*

Wheras your mastershyp hath desyred me to have bene with you this present day, which was never in your company, I being also a refuse, an abject, a wyrling of this noughty and wretched world; yea, a worse than so, one of the most wretched sinners lyving: these thyngs consydered on the one syde, and your humane gentilnes on the other, seyng, I say, that I have dysobeyed your most gentyl request and desyre, I am wurthy, if ye should intreat with me accordyng to my deservyng, not alonely to go without, or want al sych ghostly edifying and profyt, which I myght have had of your mastershyp, but also to have you from now furth ever to be heyvy master to me. But al this notwithstonding, I wil comfort myself with your gentilnes, trusting ye wil not take me at the wurst. And thus comforting myself with your gentyl humanity, I humbly beseche your mastershyp, that ye wil be content thys next week, or the Ester weke, or any other tyme at your pleasure. And surely, if ye wyl appoynt no tyme, I wyl come afore I be called. I thank you for your boke.

Number XXXIII. 87

A letter of Father Traves, as it seems, to John Bradford; concerning a debt of his, and making restitution; which he was not yet able to do.

GRACE, mercy, and peace from God the Father, and Foxii MSS. our Lord Jesus Christ. Ye shal understond, that after the receipt of your letters, I declared to Mr. Latymer the sum that ye writ to me concerning your matter with your maister. When I came to that place, that you offered yourself to be a bondman, he misliked it, and said, Though by Goddis word appearith, that to make restitution we ought to sel ourselves; yet wold I not, sayed he, that he shuld go so far with his maister. I asked him, what counsil he wold gyve you; he said, Better counsil, or more, than I have gyven him, I cannot. Let him tary, and commytting the whole to God, work by leysure. More cowld I not get of hym: nor I durst not troble hym, for bycause he was studiously occupyed in preparing a sermon to be preached, if God wil, before the Kyng this next Sonday. He knowith not certaynly whether he shal thereto be called, but as yet judgith. What his counsel is, ye have herd.

Ye procede and ask my counsel. Alas! you know that I am but a very block, yea, more dumb than a dumb idol; as lytel help in me as in the block of Walsingham. Ernestly I protest, that I know not what nor how to counsil you : but pray, pray, and commyt yourself wholly to God. Wish an encreas of that desire that ye have to make restitution. And whether that God wil so enrich you, that ye shal be able to pay it, or that he wil move your maister, so that he wil and shal pay it, commit it to God with ernest desire and faithful prayer, that at length, yet when his mercyful ey shal se most meet, he wil unburden you of your check ; and look for his help in peace. I mean no such beastly security as is in me ; but with pacyent suffering, without wrythyng, wrastyng, or doubtyng of his promis, without desperate voices, thoughts, gronyngs, or woes. For the Lord knowith whan and how to delyver them that trust in him, for their best avayle ; yea, mawgre the berdis of al hard harts, God wil at length, man, delyver thee. In the mean tyme, be neyther stock nor stone, but labour for your part towardis the ending of it, as opportunyty shal serve ; whether in moving him agayn, (as I-would surely wish to do,) or labouring to gather of your own for the payment therof. Do it freely, but do all in the name of the Lord, in al thyngs gyving thanks to God the Father, thorow Jesus Christ. And the most mighty God move the hart of your maister to enrich you to your unburdenyng, even whan his wil shal be.

88 Despair not, thowgh al in hast it be not repayed, as thowgh ye were a man forlore, for that the payment is not made ; but rather gyve thanks to God even hartily, for that he hath opened the fault unto you, and hath gyven you a conscience in it. For he might have gyven you up into a lewd mynd, which shuld, nothyng regardyng it, have cryed Peace, peace, untyl sudden destruction had cummen. But God of his mercy hath opened it to you; not that ye shuld delight in it, (as, Oh ! God forgyve me, that I do in commemoration of my iniquity much more delight, than sorrow,) but that it shuld be a schole, a cross, a vexation, and perturbation of mynd unto you. *Ita tamen*, that ye must be void from that desperate solicitude, and with this, that God hath gyven you an ernest desire to

recompence; which is a great comfort, a signifying, that
thowgh ye be a wretch and a synner, yet God is with you
and in you. Who can then harm you?

But how shal I do, if I dy, say you, this being unpayd?
I say, God hath gyven you a desyre to pay it, but not a
power. Is God so cruel, trow ye, that he wil exact of you
to do that that is impossible for you to do? Are ye able to
pay it? Then pay it. Are ye not able? Have a con-
tynual desire, which is to be begged of God, to pay, and, in
the name of God, work so long as ye lyve, as God shal lead
you towards the payment of it. And yf ye dy before the
satisfaction, yet I thynk ye shal go without peryl. For I
beleve the synn is forgyven alredy, for Christis sake.

There remayneth then by the doctor's mynd but restitution : and I beleve that you have *animum restituendi*, and
ernestly labourith and followith, upon Goddis preparation,
toward the restitution ; the same hath made a good restitution, if ye dy before a ful restitution.

But indede that substance that ye have at that tyme gathered together, must go fully towards it. But what talk
ye of death? God is able to make you to make restitution,
even tomorrow. Pray contynually for his help, and ease to
unburden that way, which he knowith to be best for you.
And I dare say, that for Jesus sake, he wil both hear and
help you. But pray not, appointing God ony tyme: *sed
expecta Dominum, donec misereatur tui*, with ful submission, even in a pacient, faithful mynd to his wil. O! how
arrogantly take I upon me to babble. But as I scribble,
so do I but partly: follow not me, Bradford, follow not
me: for I am a very impenitent beast. I tell you of restitution? Oh! Lord spare me; gyve me not up altogether to a lewd impenitent hart, in which I procure heaps of
wrath. Lord, help, for Christis sake, help me. Al that I
do, I do it in syn and vainglory. Yet shal not the Devil
let me to wryte. For out of the wyld figtree some profit
may cum. But no thank to the tree, but the Creator.

Now foolishly further wil I go. I wold not offer myself
into bondage to that erthly maister. Ye know not what

bondage meanith.   Be it that I speak but carnally, I speak
89 as I am.   I wold not but thynk assuredly, that as God
hath gyven me that grace to knowledg my debt, being free,
that the same Lord of his mercy wil, and is able at ease to
work in my freedom the discharge of my debt.

[Something is wanting.]

Number XXXIV.

The protestation of Mr. Hughe Latymer, rendred in writ-
inge to Dr. Weston, and other of the Quenes commis-
sioners with hym, in an assembly at Oxforde, concernyng
certeyne questions to hym proponed ; faithfully translated
out of Latyn into Englisshe ; holden the xxth of Aprill,
anno Dom. 1554.

Foxii MSS.
The conclu-
sions wher-
unto I
muste an-
swer are
thiese.

THE first, That in the sacrament of the altar, by the
vertue of Goddes worde pronounced by the prest,
there is really and naturally the very body of Christ
present, as it was conceyved of the Virgyn Mary, under
the kyndes of bred and wyne. And in like manner
his blood in the cupp.

2. The second is, That after the consecration, there remayneth no substance of bread and wyne, nor none
other substance but the substance of God and man.

3. The threde is, That in the masse there is the lively
sacrifice of the Churche, which is propitiatory, aswell
for the quick as the deade.

To these I
answer.

Concernynge the first conclusion, me thinketh it is set
furthe with certeyne newe termes lately founde, that be ob-
scure, and do not sounde according to the Scripture.   Neverthelesse, however I understand it, thus do I aunswer,
allthoughe not without perell of my life.   I say, that there
is none other presence of Christ required, than a spiritual
presence: and this presence is sufficient for a Christen man;
as a presence by the which we both abide in Christ, and
90 Christ in us, to the obteignynge of eternal life, if we perse-

vere in his true gospel. And this same presence may be called a *real* presence, because to the faithefull belever ther is the real or spiritual body of Christ: which thinge I here reherse, leste some sicophant or scorner should suppose me, with the Anabaptist, to make nothing els of the sacrament, but a bare and naked sign. As for that which is fayned of many, I for my parte take it but for a *papistical* invention. And therfore I thynke it utterly to be rejected from amonge Goddes children, that seke their Saviour in faithe, and to be taught among the fleshely Papistes, that wilbe ageyn under the yoke of Antichrist.

2. Concernynge the seconde conclusion, I dare be bolde to say, that it hath no stay nor grounde of Goddes holy woorde, but is a thinge invented and found out by man, and therfore to be reputed and had as false, and I had almoste saide, as the mother and nourse of all other errors. It were good for my masters and lords, the *transsubstantiators*, to take better hede to their doctryne, leste they conspire with the Nestorians. For the Nestorians deny that Christe had a true natural body. And I cannot see how the Papistes can avoyde it: for they wolde conteyne the natural body which Christe had, (synne excepted,) ageynst all truthe, into a wafer cake.

3. The thirde conclusion, as I understande it, semethe subtilly to sowe sedition ageynst the offering which Christe hymself offered for us, in his own person, and for all, and never ageyne to be don; according to the Scriptures written in Goddes boke. In which boke reade the pithy place of Heb. St. Paule to the Hebrues, the 9. & 10. where he saithe, that Christe his owne self hath made a perfect sacrifice for our synnes, and never ageyne to be done; and then ascended into heaven, and there sittethe a mercifull intercessor between Goddes justice and our synnes; and there shall tary till these lienge transubstantiators, and all other his foes, be made his footstole: and this offering did he frely of hymself, as it is written in the 10th of John, and neded not John that any man shulde do it for him. I will speak nothing of the wonderful presumptions of man, that dare attempte this.

thinge, without any manyfest calling : specially that which entrudeth to the overthrowing and frutelesse making (if not wholly, yet partlye) of the crosse of Christe. And therfore worthely a man may say to my lordes and masters officers, *By what aucthoritie do you this? And who gave you this aucthoritie?* When and where? A man cannot, **John iv.** saith St. John, take anything, except it be geven hym from above ; moche lesse then may any man presume to usurpe **Ebr. v.** any honour before he be called therunto.

1 John ii.   Ageyne: *If any man sinne,* (saithe St. John,) *we have,* saith he, not a masser, nor an offerer upon earthe, which can sacrifice for us at masse : but *we have,* saithe he, *an advocate with God the Father, Jesus Christe the righteous* **Hebr. vii. d.** *one ;* which once offered hymself for us long agoe. Of **91** which offering, the efficacie and effecte is perdurable for ever. So that it is nedelesse to have such offerers : but if they had a nayle dryven throughe one of their eares, every tyme they offer, as Christe had iiij dryven thorough his handes and feet, they would soon leave offering. Yeit, if their offering did not bringe gaynes withal, it shulde not be so often done. For they say, *No peny no pr. nr.* What **1 Cor. ix.** meaneth S. Paule, when he saith, *They that preache the gospell, shall live of the gospell?* Wheras he shuld rather have said, The Lorde hathe ordeyned, that they that sacrifice at masse, shuld live of the sacrificynge. But allthoughe the Holy Ghost appoynted them no lyving for their masse-sayenge in Goddes boke, yet have they appoynted themselves a living in Antichristes decrees. For I am sure, if God wolde have had a newe kynde of sacrificynge preste at masse, then he, or some of his Apostles, wolde have made some mention therof in their master Christ's will. But belike the secretaryes were not the massers frends, or elles they sawe it was a charge without profitt, it must nedes elles have ben remembered and provided for. As ther was a living provided for the sacrificyng priestes before Christes coming, in the Jewes times. For now they have nothing to allege for themselves, that is to say, for their sacrifysinge, nor for their lyving, as those that preche the gospell have.

For Christe hymself, after he had suffered, and made a perfect sacrifice for our synnes, and also when he rose ageyne to justifie us, commanded his disciples to go preche all the world over, sayeng, *Whosoever beleveths, and is baptixed,* Matt. xxviii. *shalbe saved.* But he spake never a worde of sacrificynge, or sayenge of masse; nor promised the herers any rewarde, but amonge the idolaters, with the Devell and his angelles, except spedy repentance with teares.

Therfor, sacrificynge prestes shulde nowe cease for ever: for nowe all men ought to offer their owne bodyes a quicke sacrifice, holy and acceptable before God. The supper of Rom. xii. the Lorde was instituted to provoke us to thankesgeving, and to sturre us upp by preshynge of the gospell, to remem-Apoc. i. ber his deathe till he cometh ageyne, according to his commaundyment. For Christe bad Peter fede the flocke, and not sacrifice for the flocke. I can never wonder ynoughe, that Peter, and all the apostles, wolde forget thus necligently the office of sacrificynge, if they had thought it necessary, seinge that at these dayes it is had in suche price and estymation. To fede the flocke is almost nothing with many; for if you ceasse of fedinge, you shalbe taken for a good catholike; but if you ceasse from sacrificyng and massing, you wilbe taken, I trowe, for an heretique, and come to suche place as I and many of my bretheren be in, shortly.

Thus, lo! I have written an answer to your conclusions, even as I will answer before the majestie of our Lorde and Saviour Jesus Christe, by whose only sacrifice I hope to possesse heaven. Therfor I beseche your good mastershippes to take it in good parte. As I have done it with gret paynes, having no man to helpe me, as I never was before denyed to have. O Sir, ye may chaunce to come to this age and weaknes that I am of, and then you wolde be 92 lothe to be used as I am at your handes; that no man may come to me, to help me for any nede, no not so moche as to mende my hosen or my cote. And you know that he that hathe but one payre of hosen, had nede sometyme to have them mended. I have spoken in my tyme before ij kynges, more than one, two, or three howers to either, without interruption : but nowe when I shuld have spoken the truthe out of Goddes boke, (for that I ever toke for my warrante,) I coulde (by your leave) not be suffered to declare my faithe before you, (for the which, God willing, I entende to geve my life,) not by the space of a quarter of an hower, without snakkes, reiagges, revilinges, chekkes, rebukes, and tauntes, such as I never herd the like in such an audience all my life longe. Sure it cannot be, but I have made some haynous offence : forsothe I thinke it be this ; I have spoken ageynst the masse, and did aske, if their god of the aulter had any marybones. For I said I had redd the Testament over vij tymes synce I was in the prison, with gret deliberation, and yet I coulde never fynde, as I said before, in the sacrament of the body and blood of Christe, (which the Papistes call the sacrament of the aulter,) neither flesshe, bloode, nor bones, nor this worde *transubstantiation.* And because, peradventure, my masters (that can so soon make Christes body of bread, which was not *made* but *conceyved* by the Holy Ghost in the Virgyn's wombe, as Goddes invaluable worde dothe testifie, and also all the auncient fathers) myght say, that I doted for age, and my wittes were gone, so that my wordes were not to be credited. Yet beholde ! the providence of God, which will have his truthe knowen, (yea, if all men heilde their tongues, the stones shuld speake,) did bring this to passe, that where these famous men, *viz.* Mr. Cranmere, archebysshopp of Canterbury ; Mr. Ridley, bisshopp of London ; that holy man Mr. Bradforde ; and I, olde Hugh Latymer, were imprisoned in the Tower of London, for Christes gospel preaching, and for bicause we wolde not go a massyng, every one in close prison from other, the same Tower beinge so full of other prisoners, that we fower were thrust into one chamber, as men not to be accounted of, (but God be thanked, to our great joy and compforte,) there did we together reade over the Newe Testament with gret deliberation and paynefull study : and I assure you, as I will answer before the trybunall throne of Goddes majestie, we coulde fynde, in the Testament of

Christes body and blood, non other presence but a spirituall presence, nor that the masse was any sacrifice for synnes: but in that heavenly boke it appered, that the sacrifice, which Christe Jesus our Redeemer did upon the crosse, was perfect, holy, and good; that God the heyenly Father did require non other, nor that never ageyne to be done, but was pacified with that only omnisufficient and most paynefull sacrifice of that swete slayne lambe Christe our Lord, for our synnes.

Wherfor stande from the aulter you sacrileginge (I shulde have said you *sacrificinge*) preistes; for you have no aucthoritie in Goddus boke to offer up our Redemer, neither will he any more come in the hands of sacrificing prests, for 93 the good chere you made hym when he was amonge youre sworne generation. And I say, you lay people, as you are called, come awey from forged sacrifices, which the Papists do fayne only, to be lords over you, and to get money; leaste your bodies, which are or shuld be Christes temples, be false witnes-berers ageynst the blood of our redemption. For the Holigost had promysed to St. John in the xviijth Apoc. xviii. of the Revelation, that if you come from them, you get none of their plagues; but if you tarry with them, you have sponne a fayre threde; for you shall drynke of the same cupp of Godds wrathe that they shall. And ther by your playenge at main chaunce, you bring all the ryghteous blood, that wicked Cayne hath shedd, even upon your own hedds. Chewse you nowe whether you will ride to the Devell with idolaters, or go to heaven with Christe and his members, by bering the crosse.

Nowe I am sure this speche hathe offended my lords and masters; and I have marvell at it, for I aske none other question, in requiring to knowe if their *bread-god* had flesshe, marrow, and bones, or not, as our dere Redemer had, and as they affirme and set furthe with fire and faggott, good doctors, I warrant you, that their white idoll, I shulde haue said their *alter god*, hathe. Therfor, me thynketh, they are angry with me without a cause. But one thing this troble hathe brought me unto; that is, to be acqueynted with Mr. Doctor Weston, whome I never sawe before: and I had not thought he had ben so gret a clerke. For in all Kynge Edward's time he was a curat besides Bishopps-gate, and held hym well content to fede his parissioners with the doctryne that he nowe calleth *heresie*, and is sent from the Quene to judge us for the same. But I pray God sende hym a more mercifull judgement at the hande of Christe, then we receyve of hym. And I wolde ever have hym, and all those that be in Romes, to remember, that he that dwelleth on highe lokythe on the things upon earthe; and

1 Cor.i. also that ther is no counsell ageynst the Lorde, as St. Paule saithe; and that the world has and ever hathe ben a totering worlde: and yet ageyne, that though we must obey the prynces, yet are we lymyted, howe farre; that ys, so longe as they do not commaunde things ageynst the manifest truthe. But nowe they do; therfor we must say with

Acts v. Peter and John, *We must obey God before man.* I meane none other resistaunce, but to offer our lives to the deathe, rather than to comytt any evell ageynst the majestie of God, and his most holy and true worde. But this I say unto you, if the Quene have any pernicious enemy within her realme, those they be that do cause her to maynteyn idolatry, and to wete her sword of justice in the blood of her people, that are set to defende the gospell: for this hathe ben alweys the distructions both of kyngs, quenes, and whole comon welthes: as I am afrayed it will make this comon wealthe of Englonde to quake shortly, if spedy repentaunce be not had among the inhabitaunts therof. But you cannot say but that you have had warnynge, and therfore take hede betymes, and be warned by a number of other countries, that have forsaken

94 Godds knowen truthe, and followed the lyes of men. If not, other lands shalbe warned by you. You that be here sent to judge our faith be not lerned *in dede,* I meane not a *right;* because you know not Christe and his pure worde. For it is nothing but playne ignoraunce to know many things without Christe and his gospell. Saynt Paule saithe,

1 Cor. i. that he did knowe *nothinge but Jesu Christe crucified.* Many men bable moche of Christe, whiche yet knowe not Christe,

but pretending Christe, do craftely cover and darken his glory. And indede these are meteste men to dishonor a man, that seme to be his frende. Departe from suche men, saithe the Apostell to Timothe. It is not out of the wey to remember what St. Augustyne saith ageinst the epistell of Petikanus: "Whosoever," saith he, "techethe any thing necessary to be beleved, which is not conteyned in the Olde and Newe Testament, the same is accursed." O! beware of that cursse, you that so stoutly set furthe mennes doctrynes, yea, wicked blasphemy ageynste the truthe. I am moche deceyved, if Basilius have not suche like words: "Whatsoever," saith he, "is besides the holy Scripture, if the same be taught as necessary to be beleved, the same is synne." Oh! therfor take good hede of thys synne. Ther be some that speke false things, more profitable to the purse, and more like the truthe then the truthe it self. Therfor St. Paule geveth a watche worde, *Let no man deceyve you*, saith he, *with probabilitie and persuasions of words.* O good Lorde! what a dampnable act have you don? You have chaunged the most holy communion into a wicked and horrible sacrifice of idolatry; and you deny to the lay people the cupp, which is directly ageynst Goddes institution, which saith, *Drink ye all of this.* And where you shuld preache the benefite of Christes deathe to the people, you speake to the wall in a forreyn tongue. God open the dore of your herte, that you may once have a more care to enlarge the kingdome of God than your owne, if it be his will.

Thus have I answered your conclusions, as I will stande unto with Goddes helpe to the fier. And after this I am able to declare to the majestie of God, by his invaluable worde, that I dye for the truthe; for I assure you, if I could graunt to the Quenes procedings, and endure by the worde of God, I wolde rather live then dye; but seynge they be directly ageynst Godds worde, I will obey God more than man, and so embrace the stake.

By H. L.

Libro iij. c. 6. contra Cras. Petilian.

Number XXXV.

Old father Latimer to one in prison for the profession of
the gospel; giving his judgment, whether it be lawful to
buy off the cross.

Foxii MSS. THE eternal consolation of the Spirit of God comfort and
stablish your faithful heart in this your glorious cross of
the gospel, until the day of reward in our Lord Jesu Christ.
Amen.

Blessed be God, dear brother after our common faith,
that hath given you hitherto a will with patience to suffer
for his gospel sake. I trust that he, which hath begun this
good work in you, shal perform the same to the end. But I
understand by your letters, that he which tempteth and
envieth you this glory, ceaseth not to lay stumbling blocks
before you, to bereave you of that crown of immortality,
which now is ready to be put on your head: persuading
you that you may for money be redeemed out of a glorious
captivity into a servile liberty; which you by your godly
Luke ix. wisdom and spirit do perceive wel enough, and that he
which hath put his hand to the plow and looketh back, is
not meet for the kingdom of God: and that none, which
is a good soldier to Christ, entangleth himself with worldly
Matt. viii. markets.   Christ saith, that *foxes have their holes, and*
birds of the air have their nests, but the Son of man hath
not where to hide his head. The wise men of the world can
find shifts to avoyd the cros; and the unstable in faith can
set themselves to rest with the world: but the simple servant of Christ doth look for no other but oppression in the
world.   And then is it their most glory, when they be under the cross of their master Christ: which he did bear,
not only for our redemption, but also for an example to us,
that we should follow his steps in suffering, that we might be
partakers of his glorious resurrection.

I do therefore allow highly your judgment in this behalf,
who think it not lawful for money to redeem yourself out of
the cros: unles you would go about to exchange glory for

shame, and to sell your inheritance for a mess of pottage, as Gen. xxv. Esau did, who afterwards found it no more: and to think the good gifts of God to be procured with mony, as Simon Magus, or els to sel Christ for xxx pence, as Judas did. Acts viii. Good aucthority you may have out of the Scriptures, to confirm your judgment against al gainsayers.

The first is, that our Saviour Christ saith, *There is none worthy of him, except he dayly take up his cros, and follow him.* If we must dayly take up our cros, how may 96 we then shift that cros, which Christ hath put upon us, by our own procurement, and give mony to be discharged of that we are called unto? If that in taking up the cros we must also follow Christ, then we may not cast the same off, until we have carried it with him unto death.

S. Paul to the Philippians saith, that *it is not only* Phil. i. *given to us to believe, but also to suffer for his name.* If it be the gift of God to suffer for Christ's sake; if it be the gift of God, with what conscience may a man sel the gift of God, and give mony to be rid thereof? God giveth this grace but to a few, as we see at this day. Therfore we ought to shew ourselves both faithful and thankful for the same.

Moreover S. Paul saith, that *every man must abide in* 1 Cor. vii. *that vocation, as he is called.* But we are called to suffer.

S. Peter doth manifestly declare, saying, *If when you do* 1 Pet. ii. *wel, and yet be evil handled, ye do abide it, this is a grace of God.* For ye are called to this; because Christ was afflicted, leaving us an example, that we should follow his steps.

Since then this is our calling, how may we, without the displeasure of God, go about to redeem us with mony out of the same? S. Paul affirmeth the same to the Romans, saying, *For we are al day long delivered unto death, and* Rom. viii. *accounted as sheep appointed to the slaughter.* Also he saith in the same chapter, that *we are predestinate to be like and conformable to the image of his Son;* that as they persecuted him, so shall they persecute us; and as they slew him, so shal they slay us.

John xvi.

And Christ saith in S. John, that *they shal excommunicate you and kil you, and think to do God worship thereby. And this they shal do unto you: and this have I spoken unto you, that when the time cometh, you should not be offended in me.*

I cannot se how we might go about to deliver ourselves from the death we are called unto, for mony. S. Peter sheweth what we must do that be under the cross, saying,

1 Pet. iv.

Let them that suffer according to the will of God, commit their souls to him, as unto a faithful Creator. And, *Let him not be ashamed that suffereth as a Christian man, but rather glorify God in this condition.* S. Paul also to the

Heb. xii.

Hebrews sheweth, that we may not faint under the cros, neither by any means flie aside, saying, *Let us lay away al that presseth down, and the sin that hangeth so fast on, and let us run with patience unto the battail that is set before us: looking unto Jesus, the aucthor and finisher of our faith; which, for the joy set before him, abode the cros, and despised the shame, and is set down on the right hand of the throne of God. Consider therfore that he endured such speaking against him of sinners, lest we should be weary and faint in our mind. For we have not yet resisted unto bloudsheding, striving against sin: and have forgotten the consolation, which speaketh unto us as unto children, My son, despise not the chastening of the Lord, neither faint when thou art rebuked of him. For whom the Lord loveth, him he chasteneth, yea, he scourgeth every son whom he receiveth. If we endure chastening, God offereth himself unto us, as unto sons.* And blessed be they that continue unto the end.

97   In the Apocalypse, the Church of God is commanded not

Apoc. ii.

to fear those things which she shal suffer. *For behold! the Devil shal cast some of you into prison, that ye may be tempted, and ye shal have ten days affliction. Be faithful unto the death, and I will give thee the crown of life. He that hath ears to hear, let him hear what the Spirit speaketh to the congregations. He that hath overcome, shal not be hurt by the second death.*

Be these undoubted Scriptures? We may be sufficiently taught, that here is no means for us to fly, that are caught under the cros, to any such worldly means as the flesh can devise. Again, we were created to set forth God's glory al the days of our life; which we, as unthankful sinners, have forgotten to do, as we ought, al our days hitherto. And now God, by affliction, doth offer us good occasion to perform, one day of our life, our duty. And shal we go about to chop away this good occasion, which God offereth us for our honour and eternal rest? And in so doing we shal declare, that we have no zele to God's glory; neither to the truth, which is so shamefully oppressed; neither to our weak brethren and sisters, who have need of strong witnesses to confirm them. Therfore we should now be glad with St. Paul in our afflictions for our weak brethrens sake, and *go about to supply that which wanteth of the afflictions of* Col. i. *Christ in our flesh, in his body, which is the Church.* Not that the afflictions of Christ were not sufficient for our salvation; but that we which be professors of Christ must be contented to be afflicted, and to drink of the cup of his passion, which he hath drank: and so shal we be assured to sit at his right hand, or at his left, in the kingdom of his Father.

Christ saith, in John, *Except ye eat the flesh of the Son* John vi. *of man, and drink his bloud, ye shal have no life in you.* Which, in the interpretation of most auncient and godly doctors, is, to be partakers, both in faith and deed, of the passion of Christ. The which if we refuse, what do we but, as the Capernaites did, go from everlasting life? And here we are with Christ, who hath the words of eternal life. Whither shal we go, or what may we give, to be separated from him?

But perchance the worldly wise man, or carnal gospeller, wil confes, and object this to be true, and that he intendeth not to deny the truth, although he buy himself out of the yoke of the cros; minding hereafter, if he be driven therto, to dy therin. But to him I answer, with Solomon, *Defer not to do wel to to-morrow, but do it out of hand, if thou have liberty.* So I say, that little we know, whether God wil give us such grace as he doth now offer us, at another time, to suffer for his sake: and it is not in us to choose it when we wil. Therfore let us offer the counsil of St. Paul ;

Eph. v. *serve the time,* which we are in, of affliction, and be glad to be afflicted with the people of God, which is the recognizance of the children of God ; and rather *to redeem the time* with our death for the testimony of the truth, to the which we are born, than to purchase a miserable life for the concupiscence of the world, and to the great danger of falling

98 from God. For as long as we are in the body, we are strangers to God, and far from our native country, which is in heaven, where our everlasting day is. We are now more near to God than ever we were, yea, we are at the gates of heaven ; and we are a joyful spectacle become, in this our captivity, to God, to the angels, and to all his saints, who look that we should end our course with glory.

Matt. xiii. We have found the precious stone of the gospel ; for the which we ought to sel al that we have in the world. And shal we exchange, or lay to gage the precious treasure, which we have in our hands, for a few days to lament in the world, contrary to our vocation? God forbid it. But let us, as Christ willeth us in S. Luke, *look up, and lift up our heads, for our redemption is at hand.*

A man that hath long travailed, and hath his journey's end before him, what madnes were it for him to set farther compas about, and put himself in more trouble and labour than needeth. If we live by hope, let us desire the end and

2 Tim. ii. fruition of our hope. *No man is crowned, but he that law-*

1 Cor. ix. *fully striveth : none obtaineth the goal, but he that runneth out.* Run, therfore, so as ye may be sure to obtain. You have run hitherto right wel, good Christen brethren. God be praised therfore. But now what letteth you but a persuasion, that is *not sprung of him that calleth you,* as it is

Gal. v. written.

Example hereof, we have first our Saviour Jesus Christ ; who being advised by Peter to provide better for himself, than to go to Jerusalem to be crucified, received the reproch, *Go behind me, Satan; thou knowest not the things of God. Shal I not drink of the cup which my Father giveth me?* If Christ would not, at his friend's counsil, provide to shun the cros, no more ought we, whose disciples we are, being called therto at our friends flattering motions. *For the disciple is not greater than his master. For if they have persecuted me,* saith he, *they wil persecute you.* S. Paul being in prison for the gospel, was ofttimes brought before Felix the judge, who looked for some piece of money for his deliverance: but I cannot read that Paul went about at al to offer him any. John and Peter being prisoned for the testimony of the word, did with al boldnes confes the same; and sought no other means of redemption than by faithful confession. Paul and Sylas being of God miraculously delivered from their chains and bands of death, having al the doors open of their prison to depart if they would; yet departed they not out of prison, but abode stil the good pleasure of God, and his lawful deliverance. God in time past was angry with his people of Israel, for sending into Egypt for help in their necessity; saying, by the prophet Esay, *Wo be unto you, runagate children, who go about to take advice, and not of me, and begin a work, and not of my Spirit. Cursed is he,* by the Prophet Jeremy, *that maketh flesh to be his strength.* Moses chose rather to be afflicted with the people of God, than to be counted the son of King Pharaoh's daughter. The martyrs in the old time were wracked, as S. Paul testifieth, and would not be delivered, that they might have a better resurrection.

Let us follow them, and leave the Popes market; who buyeth and selleth the bodies and souls of men to Baalam and his false prophets; who love the reward of iniquity.

If any man perceive his faith [not] to abide the fire, let such an one with weeping buy his liberty, until he hath obtained more strength; lest the gospel by him sustain an offence of some shameful recantation. Let the dead bury the dead. Let us that be of the lively faith follow the Lamb wheresoever he goeth, and say to them that be thus curious and wise, Dispute us in this matter with S. Paul, *Stretch*

John xv.

Acts xxiv.

Es. iii.

99

forth the hands that were let down, and the weak knees, and
se that you have streit steps to your feet, lest any halting
turn you out of the way.   Yea, rather, let it be healed.

Embrace Christs cros, and Christ shal embrace you. The
peace of God be with you for ever, and with al them that
live in captivity with you in Christ. *Amen.*

Written by Mr. Latymer, being in captivity.

Number XXXVI.

An epistle sent by Mr. Latimer to all the unfayned lovers
of Godds trewthe, owts of a prison in Oxenford, called
Bocardo; where the said Latimer was emprisonned for
the testimony of Criste, the 15th of May, 1555.

Foxii MSS.   THE same peace that our Saviour Criste left with his
people, which is not withowt warr with the world, Almightye God make plentifull in your herts now and ever,
Amen. Bretherne, the time is come whan the Lords grounde
Luc. viii.   willbe knowen: I meane, it will now appeare, who hath re-
cevid Gods word in their herts in dede, to the taking of
good roote therein.   For suche will not shrinke for a little
heate or sun-burning wether; but stowtlye stand and grow,
even mawgre the malice of all burning showers and tempests.   For he that hath played the wise buildre, and layed
his foundation on a rock, will not be afrayed that every
drisling raine or myste shall burte his buildings, but will
stand, althoughe a great tempest do come, and dropps of
raine as bigg as fyrye fagotts.   But they that have buylded
upon a sande wilbe affraied, thoughe they se but a clowde
aryse alitle black, and no raine nor winde dothe once touche
100 them; no, not so moche as to lie one week in prison, to
truste God with their lyves, which gave them.   For they
Rom. xiv.   have forgot what S. Pawle sayth, *If we dye we ar the Lords,*
and yf we lyve we ar the Lords: so that whether we lyve or
dye, we ar the Lords. Yet we will not put him in trust with
his owne.

And forasmoche, my dearly beloved bretherne and sisters

in the Lorde, as I am persuaded of you, that you be in the number of the wise buildres, which have made their foundation sure by faythe, uppon the unfallible woord of Godes trewth; and wille nowe bring forthe fruyttes to Godds glory after your vocation, as occasion shall be offerid; althoughe the sun burn never so hot, nor the wether be never so fowle: wherfore I cannot but signefye unto every of you, to go forwards accordingly after your Mr. Criste; not stycking at the fowle waye and stormy wether, whiche you ar come unto, or ar lyke to come. Of this being most certyne, that the ende of your sorrow shalbe pleasant and joyfull, in such a perpetual rest and blyssfulnes as cannot but swallowe upp the stormes whyche bothe you and they now feale, and ar lyke to feele, at the hands of those sacrefycing prelats. But set often byfore your eyes St. Pawles counsell to the Co- 2 Cor. iv. rinthians, and remember it as a restorative to refresh you withal, lest you faint in the way, wheare he saythe, *Thoughe our outward man peryshe, yet is our inward man renewed day by day; for our exceading tribulation (which is momentary and light) he hath prepared for us an exceding weight of glorye. Whilest we loke not on things that ar seen, but on things that ar not seene. For things that ar sene are temporal, but the things that ar not seene are eternall.* And ageyne he saythe, *Yf this bodye were destroyed, we shall have another*, whych shall not be subject to corruption nor to persecution. Besydes this, set byfore you also, though the wether be stormie and fowle, yet strive to go apace, for you go not alone, many other of your bretherne and systers passe by the same pathe, as S. Petre saithe and tellythe us, 1 Pet. iv. that company myght cawse you to be the more couragious and chearfull; but yf you had no company at all to go presently with you, stick not to go still forward. I pray you tell me, if any from the beginning, yea, the best of Gods frendes, have found any fayrer waye or wether to the place whyther we ar going, I meane to heaven, than we now fynde and ar like to finde. Except ye will with the worldlings, which have their parte and portion in this life, tarry still by the waye till the stormes be overpaste, and then either night will approche, that he cannot travaile, or ells the doores will be shut upp, that he cannot go in, and so without he shall have wonderful evil lodging; I mean in a bed of fire and brimston, where the woorme dyeth not, and the fyer goeth not owt.

Rede from the first of Genesis to the Appocalypse, begynne at Abell, and so to Noye, Abraham, Isack, Jacobb, the patriarchs; Moyses, David, and the saintts, in the Old Testament, and tell me whither any of them find any fairer ways than we now fynde. Yf the Old will not serve, I pray you come to the New, and begynne with Mary and Josephe, 101 and come from thence to Zacarye, Elyzabethe, John the Baptyste, Stevyn, James, Peter, and Powle, and every one of the appostells and evangelists; and se whyther any of them all founde any other way unto the citye whereunto we travayle, then by manny tribulations. Besydes this, yf you shuld caule to remembraunce the primitive Churche, Lord God, we shuld se many that have given cherfully their bodies to most grevous torments, rather than they would be stopped in their jorney. There was no day scarce in the yere, but I dare say a thousand was the fewest that with joye left their homes and lyves here; but in the citie that they went unto, they founde another manner of dwellings then manny mynds be able to conceyve. But if none of these were, if ye had no company now to go with you, yet have you me, your poorest brother and bondman in the Lord, with many other, I trust in God. But yf ye had none of the fathers, patriarks, good kings, prophets, apostles, evangelists, martyrs, holy saints, and children of God, whych in their jorney to heaven found that you are like to fynd, (yf you go on forwards, as I trust you will,) yet you have your generall captayne and master, Christe Jesus, the deare derling, and only begotten and beloved Sonne of God, in whome was all the Fathers joye and delectation; ye have him to go byfore you; no fayrer was his waye then ours, but moche worse and fowler towards his citie of the heavenly Jherusalem. Let us remember what manner of waye Criste founde, begynne at his birthe, and go forthe.

John xii.
Matt. xv.

Acts xiv.

Ebr. xiii.

untill ye come at his buryal, and you shall finde that every
step of his jorney was a thousand times worse than yours is.
For he had layd uppon him at one time, the Deavill, death,
and synne; and with one sacrifyce, never againe to be done,
he overcame them all.

Wherfore, my dere beloved, be not so daintie, to look to Ebr. ix. 10.
have at the Lords hands, your dere Father, that which the
patriarks, prophets, appostells and evangelists, martyrs and
saynts, yea, and his owne Sonne Jesus Criste, did not finde.

Hitherto we have found fayre wether and fayre waye
too, I trowe; but bycause we have loytered by the way,
and not made the spede that we should have done, our loving Father and heavenly Lord hath overcast the wether,
and hath stirred upp stormes and tempests, that we mought
the more spedily ronne out the race byfore nyght come,
and byfore the dores be barred upp.   Now the Devill, and
his ostelers and tapsters, stand in every inn-doore, in citie
and countrey of this world, crieng unto us, Come in and
lodge here, for here is Criste, and there is Criste; therfore Matt. xxiv.
tarry with us till the storme be overpast: not that they
would not have us wet to the skinne, but that the time
myght be overpast to our utter destruction.   Therfore beware of his inticements, and cast not your eyes uppon things
that be present, how this man dothe or that man dothe,
(for you may not follow a multitude to do evill,) but cast
your eyes on the wager or merk that you ronne at, or else
you will lose the game. Ye knowe, he that runnythe at the
merk, doth not loke on other that stands by, or of them
that offer to go this waye or that waye, but lokyth altogether on the glove or merk, and on them that ronne with
him, that those that ar behynde overtake him not, and that
he may overtake them that ar byfore.   Even so shuld we 102
do, and leve lokinge at those that will not ronne the waye or
race to heavens blysse by suffering persecution.   And we
shold cast our eyes on thend of the race, and on them that
go byfore us, that we may overtake them, and that we may
provoke others to come the faster after us.   He that shooteth, wil not cast his eyes in his shooting on them that stand

or, ride by the way, I trow not; but rather on the mark that he shooteth at, or els he were like to win the wrong way. Evin so, my dere beloved, let our eyes be set on the merk

Ebr. xii. 2. that we shote at, evyn Jesus Criste, *who, for the joye that was set byfore him, abode the crosse, and despised the shame;* therfore he now sittethe on the right hand of God, all power and rewle subdewed unto him. Let us therfore followe him; for thus dyd he, that we shuld not be feint

2 Tim. ii. herted; for we may be most sewer, that *yf we suffre with him, we shall allso reigne with him. But yf we denye him,*

Mark viii. *he will sewrly denye us.* For *he that is ashamed of me,* sayth Criste, *and of my gospell, byfore thys faythlesse generacyon, I wilbe ashamed of him byfore my Father and his angells in heavens.* Oh! how hevy a sentence is this to all those that know the masse to be an abhomynable idoll, full of idolatrie, blasphemy, sacrilege against God, and the deare sacrifyce of his Criste; as undoubtedly it is: and that you have well seene, bothe by disputing of noble clerks, and allso by willing sheding of their blodes against that heynous sacrelyge. And yet for feare or favoure of men, for the losse of lyfe and goods, (whyche is none of theyrs, but lent theime of God; as David saythe, *It is the Lord that maketh*

Rom. xiv. *ryche and poore;* and as Paule saythe, *Yf we lyve we ar the Lords, and yf we die we ar the Lords:* therfore let us gyve him his owne.) Yea, some for advauntage and gaine, will honour with their prescence this pernycious blasphemye againste the deathe of our Redemer; and so dissemble both with God and man, as there owne harts and consciences do accuse theime. Oh! vayne men, do you not remember that God is greater than your conscience? Yt had bene good that suche men had never knowen the trewthe, nor that the ghospell had never bene taught amongs theime, that thus wittingly and for feare of men (who ar but duste, and their breathe is in their nostrells) do dissemble, or rather in dede utterlye denye Criste and his sacrefice, the price of their redemption; and so bring on theime the

Luke xi. bloode of us, and all other that have sincerly taught the ghospell, with the adorning and honouring of that false idol with their bodies, being the temples of God. The end of suche men is like to be woorse then the begynnyngs. Suche men had nede to take hede of their desemblings and clokings; for it will once be espied: I meane, when our Criste shall come in his glorye, which I truste wilbe shortely. But if he tarries, the time of all fleshe is but shorte, and fadythe away like a flower. I woold wishe soche men to reade the terrible place of St. Paule to the Hebrews, in the vith chapter, where he saythe, *Yt cannot be, that they whyche were* Ebr. vi. *once lighted, and have tasted of the heavenly gyfte, and were bycome partakers of the Holy Ghoste, and have tasted of the good word of God, and the power of the world to come; yf they faule awaye, and, as concerning themselves,* 103 *crucefye the Sonne of God afreshe, making a mock of him.* And rede the xth chapter, lest ye fawle into the daunger of theim.

And let men beware that they play not *wylye begile themselves,* as I feare me they do that go to masse. And bycausse they worshipp not, nor knele not downe, as other do, but syt still in their pewes, therfore they thinke rather to do good to other than hurte. But, alas! yff suche men woold looke on their own consciences, there they shall see yf they be very dissymulers, and seking to deceave other, they deceave them selves. For by this meanes the magistrates thinke them to be of their sorte. They think that at the elevation-time all mens eys ar sett on theime, to marke how they do; they think that other hering of suche mennes going to masse, do se or enquyre of their behaviour ther, and thus they play *wyly, beguylyng them selves.* But yf there were in these men eyther love to God or to their bretherne, then wold they, for one or for bothe, take Gods parte, admonyshing the people of their idolatrye. But they Matt. x. feare men more than God, that hathe aucthoritye to caste bothe body and sowle into hell fyer. They halte on both Matt. vi. sydes, they serve twoo masters. God have mercye on suche men, and anoynte their eyes with salve, that they may se, that they which take not parte with God ar againste him; and they that gather not with Criste scatter abrode. The Luke xi.

counsell given to the Churche of Laodicea is good councell for soche men. But now, derly beloved, to come againe, *Be not ashamed of the ghospell of God: for it is the power of God unto salvation to them that beleve it.* Be therfore partakers of the afflictions of Criste, as God shall make you able to beare: and thinke that no small grace of God, to suffre persecution for Godds trewths sake, *for the spirite of glory and the spirite of God doth reste uppon you. Therfore yf any man suffre, as a Christen man, let him not be ashamed, but glorifye God on that byhalf: for whosoever,* sayth Criste, *shall lose his life for my sake, and for the ghospell, the same shall save yt.* Yea, happie ar you, yf that come so to passe, as ye shall finde one daye, *when the fyer shall trye every mans woorke, what it is.* And as the fyer hurtyth not the gold, but makyth yt finer; so shall ye be more pure in suffring with Criste. The flayle, or the winde, hurtithe not the wheat, but clensyth yt from the chaffe. And ye, dearly beloved, ar Gods wheat; feare not the fanning wind, feare not the mylstone, for all theis things make you the meter for Gods tothe. Sope, though yt be black, soyleth not the clothe, but maketh yt cleane; so dothe the blacke crosse of Criste help us to more whytnes, yf God stryke with the batteldore. Bycawse you be Gods shepe, prepare your selves to the slaughter, allways knowing, that in the sight of God our deaths is precious. The sowles under the aulter looke for us to fulfill their nomber, happie ar we, yf God have so appointed yt.

Dearly beloved, caste your selves wholly uppon the Lord, wyth whome all the haires of your head be nombred; so that not one of them shall peryshe without his knowlege. *It is appointed unto all men that they shall once dye.* Therfore, wyll we nyll we, we must drinke of the Lords cupp, which he hath appointed for us. Drinke willingly therfore, and at the first, whylest it is full, lest peradventure if we linger, we shall drinke at the last of the dreggs with the ungodlye, yf we at the begynning drink not with the childrene: for with them his judgment begynnethe. And when he hathe wrought his will uppon mount Syon, then

Marginal references:
Rom. i.
1 Pet. iv.
Mark viii.
1 Cor. iii.
John x.
Ps. cxiv.
Apoc. vi.
Matt. x.
Heb. ix.
104
1 Pet. iv.

will he visyt the nations rounde abowt. Submit your selves therfore under the mighty hand of God. No man shall once touche you without his knowledge; and when they touche you, yt is for your profyt: God will woork therby to make you lyke unto Criste here or elsewhere. That ye may be therfore like unto him, acknowledg your unthankfulness and synne, and blesse God which correcteth us in the world, bycawse he wold not have us condemnyd with the world. Otherwise might he correct us, then to make us suffre for righteousnes sake: but this he dothe, bycawse he lovith us. Call uppon God throughe Criste for the joye and gladnes of his salvation. Beleve that he is our merci-Heb. xii. ful Father, and will here us and help us; as the Psalmyst saythe, *I am with him in troble, and will deliver him.* Know, that the Lord hath appointed bounds, over the whiche the Divell and all the world shall not passe. Yff all things seme to be agaynst you, yet say with Job, *Though he kill me, yet will I hope in him.*

Reade the xth Psalme; and pray for me your poor brother and fellow sufferer for Gods sake; his name therfore be praised. And let us praye to God, that he of his mercye will vowchesafe to make both you and me mete to suffre with good consciences, for his names sake. Dye once we must, how and whear, we know not. Happie ar they whome God gyvyth to paye natures debt (I mean to die) for his sake. Here is not our home; let us therfore accordingly consydre things, having allwayes before our eys that heavenly Jherusalem, and the way thytherto is persecution. And let us consydre all the deare frends of God, how they Heb. xiii. have gonne after the example of our Saviour Jesus Criste, whose fotesteppes let us allso followe, even to the gallows, (yf Godds will be so,) not doubting, but as he rose again the thirde day, even so shall we do at the time appointed 1 Thess. iv. of God, that is, when the trompe shal blowe, and the angel shall showte, and the Sonne of man shall appere in the clowds, with innumerable saints and angels, in his majestie and great glorie; and the dead shall arise, and we shal be cawght upp into the clouds, to mete the Lord, and to be

x 3

always with him. Comforte yourselves with theis words, and praye for me for the Lordes sake, and God be mercyful unto us all. So be yt.

Hugh L.

---

105 Number XXXVII.

John Fox to Peter Martyr, concerning the troubles among the English at Frankford.

Foxii MSS. SALUTEM in Christo, vir doctissime.————Ulterius forsan progressus essem, sed in adventu totum fere semestre ecclesiasten egi. Quanquam nec ea res tantopere me remorata est, quantum infelix illa θεολογομαχία καὶ διχοστασία, nuper hic enata: quæ totam fere hyemem nobis sterilem ac infrugiferam reddidit. Ego etsi in eo negotio me scepticum fere gesserim, non potui tamen in totum spectator esse otiosus. Nec mirum, quum et adolescentes impuberes, imo et pueri septennes aliquot se adjunxerunt partium studiis. Neque adeo in illis id miror, quos ætatis fervor utcunque excusare poterat; in senibus magis canis ac theologis illud miror, quorum authoritas quum potissimum intercedere debebat ad concordiam, hi omnium maxime faces incendio subministrant. Perlongam hic texerem Iliada, si tabulam per singulos actus diducerem, si odia, convitia, sycophantias, ac maledicentissimæ linguæ virulentias, suspiciones, captiones, commemorarem. Sed mihi nec otium, nec animus est camarinam, jam utcunque subsidentem, exagitare: utinam potius cicatricem queam vulneri inducere. Hoc unum dicam, quod in re ipsa compertum haberem, nunquam essem crediturus tantum amari stomachi latere in his, quos assidua sacrorum librorum tractatio ad omnem clementiam mansuefacere debuerat.

Quod in me situm est, ubique suasor ero concordiæ. Nec desunt etiam rationes, quibus id efficiam, si mihi auscultari posset; idque facilius, primum, si nullos aculeos reliquissent fugientes istorum quidam, ac paulo moderatius egissent in concionibus. Deinde, si nunc pacificatis affectibus, ad id saltem redirent, ut privatim inter se literis, aut collo-

quiis mutuis, amice ac leniter rem agerent, potius quam ma-
ledicis linguis; ii potissimum quorum animi offenduntur.
Ita fiet, ut incendium hoc, sublata paulatim materia, vel
sua sponte subsidat tandem. Nunc vero dum meris viribus
funiculus utrinque tenditur, et quisque experitur quam fortiter possit alterum contemnere, quid aliud isti quam faces
majori præbent incendio. Postremum vero remedium fuerit, si aliis legibus nequeamus φρατριάζειν saltem ut delectis-
simorum quorundam judicio res dedatur, qui æqua moderatione utrinque intercedant, atque liturgiam præscribant aliquam, cui utraque pars sit assensura. Quanquam multo
mallem nostra συνκαταστάσει pacem inter nos coalescere,
quam aliena diremptione. Extrema autem anchora in
Christo ipso sita est, qui pro misericordia sua dignetur animos nostros flectere ad ea quæ pacis sunt, et veræ tranquil-
litatis.

Sed nimis ego abundans otio, qui negotia tua gravissima 106
obturbem tam prolixis næniis. Rem oppido gratum feceris,
si apud Dominum Sleidanum cubiculum aut receptum aliquem mihi impetres, ad mensem unum aut alterum, donec
negotia mea literaria in ea urbe expediero. Domino Ætono
multam opto salutem cum cæteris commilitonibus, inter
quos D. Nowellum, et Fauknerum tuum salutari cupio.
Singulari tuæ præstantiæ cum universa familia omnia læta
exopto, in Christo, frater ac pater suspiciende.

<hr />

Number XXXVIII.

*John Fox to Peter Martyr; urging him to accept the invi-
tation of the English at Frankford, to read divinity to
them.*

SUSPICIENDE Domine, salutem et gratiam in Chris- Foxii MSS.
to. Elmeri nomine, et subscriptione nostra, ad te veniunt
literæ, in quibus graves et necessariæ causæ ad persuaden-
dum continentur. Cæterum ne omnino occultis tuis cogitationibus satisfaciant, vereor. Scio enim quam difficilis sit
τρόπος ἢ μετάθεσις locique mutatio, præsertim in ea urbe, ubi

et diu assueveris, et plausibiliter victitas.   Quin nec scio an occultiora adhuc avocamenta in hac re subsunt, abs te perspecta, quæ nos non advertimus.   Verum quæcunque incerta sunt Deo permittentes, interim ut simpliciter tecum agamus, καὶ κατηγορικῶς, primum, cogitet modo eximia prudentia tua, sic te productum esse, ut multo maximas utilitates vitæ et reip. Christianæ pro singulari excellentia tua afferre queas; nec minus certe parem virtutibus industriam in te defuturam arbitror.   Jam etsi nullus locus te vendicare poterit, attamen si indigentiam spectet excellentia tua, nulla certe Germaniæ pars impensius eget opera tua : si voluntatem ac vota hominum, nulla impotentius desiderat, quam Anglia nostra Francfordiana.   Cui genti quoniam te peculiariter esse apostolum suspicamur, (suspicamur enim omnes) idcirco audacius in literis solicitare atque ambire ausi sumus.

Quod si vero ita res pateretur, ut per conjuges nostras, et conscientiam, aliquo pacto abesse ab Ecclesia liceret, facile isthuc momento traheremur. Nunc quum nobis non perinde licet Ecclesiam deserere, ut cæteris ad vos accedere : deinde quum in te uno situm sit, ut Anglos omnes ubicunque dispersos intra unas caules eademque septa compellere; magnopere obtestamur, ne quibusdam e nostris ita gratificeris, 107 ut reliqua Anglorum multitudo inopia tui destituatur.   Ut hic de Argentinensium studiis ac favoribus nihil dicam, ut quotidianos temporum ac vitæ humanæ casus præteream, certe si senectam hanc, etsi satis adhuc florentem, ac vividam, consideres, quid tam consultius, quam ut illic quod superest ætatis exigas, ubi quam plurimis esse queas utilis.

Postremo, vel illud reputa ad fovendam interim senectam tuam, quam non mediocri solatio fuerit, postquam tot tam diversis locis dispalantes Anglos, tua unius causa coire in unum coetum te amplecti, ex te, imo ex Christo potius per te pendere, tuis consiliis regi, te in illo observare, videas.

De salario, de propensione magistratus, quid cum illis, quid inter mercatores nostros conventum sit, fidelis hic Tychicus noster, frater in Dno. charissimus, abunde significabit : qui communem hanc causam multo felicius dicendo, quam ego scribendo, perorare poterit. Attamen hæc apud te seorsim pro audacia mea commentare libuit.

In versione libri Dni. Cantuariensis maturabimus, quantum Dominus dederit. Audio Crawlæum quendam esse, qui priores libros illius habeat ex versione D. Chyclæi[a], quos, si per Whittinghamum nostrum ad te mittendum cures, gratum feceris. Dns. Jesus te quam diutissime incolumem Ecclesiæ suæ servet, ac tueatur in omnibus. Francfordiæ, 12 Octob.

[a] Forte Chokæi.

Tuus Jo. Foxus.

Incomparabili ac summo viro
Dno. Doctori Petro Martyri.

Number XXXIX.

John Bale from Basil, to Mr. Ashley in Frankford: wherein is declared the troubles and controversies among the English exiles at Basil.

MY special friend, Master Ashley, after my accustomed salutations in the Lord: This shalbe to assure you I have received your gentle letters, and am very joyful for that you are willing now to resort unto us. And whereas you desire before your coming to know the state of our Church; to be plain in few words, it is troublous at this present. I find the admonishment of S. Paul to Timothy, and of S. Peter to the dispersed brethren, most true, and in full force in this miserable age. They said, that *in the latter times should come mockers, liars, blasphemers, and fierce dispisers.* We have them, we have them, Master Ashley; we have them even from among ourselves: yea, they be at this present our elders, and their factious affinity.

MSS. D. G. Petyt, Armig.

108

When we require to have *common prayers*, according to our English order, they tel us, that the magistrate wil in no case suffer it: which is a most manifest ly. They mock the rehearsal of God's commandments, and of the epistles and gospels in our Communion, and say, they are misplaced; they blaspheme our Communion, calling it *a popish mas*, and say, that it hath a popish face, with other fierce dispisings and cursed speakings. These mocks, and these blasphemies, with such like, they take for invincible theology. With these they build, with these they boast, with these they triumph, in erecting their church of the *purity.*

But wheras they report our Communion to have a *popish face,* I desire you to mark that which followeth here, and to judge their impudency. The face of a popish mas is the shew of the whole action, with the instruments and ceremonies thereunto appertaining. To that face chiefly belongeth a monstrous brothel, or ape of Antichrist, with shaven crowns, side-gowns, oyl in thumbs, tippet, portas, and masbook. Our Communion hath none such. To the face appertaineth an autre: which we have not. To that face belongeth a superaltare, a chalice, a cover, a cake, a corporas, cruats, candlesticks, censers, and lights: which we have none. To that face belongeth vestments, crisable, amyss, albe, girdle, stole, altar-cloth, torch, and towel; beside the holy suffrages for Pope, for pestilence, and for old meseled swine: which our Communion hath not. What then may be thought of our unnatural and bastardly brethren, that so falsely report it, so maliciously mock, so unlearnedly ly upon, so seditiously slander it, so wickedly blaspheme it, and so villainously contemn it.

Our Communion, on the other side, beginneth with prayer unto God in the mother tongue: so doth not the mas. It sheweth us the commandments of God; it teacheth us the necessary articles of our Christian faith: so doth not the mas. It bringeth both the law and the gospel, to shew us both damnation and redemption: so doth not the mas. It moveth us to acknowledg our sins; it stirreth us up to repentance for them; it exhorteth us to mortification of our sinful flesh: so doth not the mas. It preacheth the Lord's death til he come; it calleth for a worthy preparation for so heavenly a supper; it promiseth ful remission of our sins through Christ's gainful sufferings: so doth not the popish mas. It giveth high thanks to God for our redemption; it praiseth the eternal Majesty for the same, and wisheth the true receivers to depart from thence in his most holy peace and perpetual blessing, and continue always; so doth not the abominable mas: *ergo*, our holy Communion hath not the face of a popish mas, as our new Catharites have most wickedly, maliciously, mockingly, falsely, frantickly, unlearnedly, loudly, seditiously, blasphemously, and beastly reported and written to their affinity or proselytes: raging and railing, more like Athenians than Christians; yea, more like devils than men. And they boast of 109 the glory of God, of sincerity, of the world, and of the highest *purity* in religion.

But the truth of it is, they seek to set up in their idleness (as they are all idle, saving in this point) a seditious faction, in contempt of the English order, for their own Pharisaical advancement, planting the foresaid lyes, mocking, and blasphemies, as the first principles of their building.

This write I unto you, that they should not in this behalf pervert you, as they have done other men. I would not in the mean time, that this should discourage you from coming towards us, but that you might come the sooner, with other good men, to help to repress their malicious and idle enterprizes. Thus, though we be not in England among the wicked Papists now, yet are we molested of idle brethren, as wickedly occupied as they, though in another kind. The times are perillous. Thus farewel in the Lord, and commend us to al our good brethren.

Number XL.

A prayer used in the time of persecution.

O MOST omnipotent, magnificent, and glorious God and Father of al consolation, we here assembled do not presume to present and prostrate ourselves before thy mercy seat, in respect of our owne worthines and righteousnes, which is altogether polluted and defiled, but in the merits, righteousnes, and worthines of thine onely Sonne Jesus Christ, whom thou haste given unto us a most pure and precious garment, to cover our pollution and filthines withal;

to the end we might appear holy and justified in thy sight through him. Wherfore, in the obedience of thy commandment, and in the confidence of thy promises, conceived in thy holy word, that thou shalt accept and grant our prayers presented unto thee in favour of thy onely Sonne our Saviour Jesus Christ, either for ourselves, or for the necessity of thy saints and congregation; we here congregated together, doe with one mouth and minde most humbly beseech thee, not onely to pardon and forgive us all our sins, negligences, ignorances, and iniquities, which we from time to time incessantly do commit against thy divine Majestie, in word, deede, and thought, (such is the infirmity of our corrupted nature,) but also, that it would please thee, O benigne Father, to be favourable and merciful unto thy poore afflicted Church and congregation, dispersed throughout the 110 whole world; which, in these dayes of iniquity, are oppressed, injured, dispersed, persecuted, and afflicted, for the testimonie of thy word, and for the obedience of thy lawes. And namely, (O Lord and Father,) we humbly beseech thee to extend thy mercie and favourable countinance upon all that are imprisoned or condemned for the cause of the gospell, whome thou hast chosen forth and made worthy to glorifie thy name; that either it may please thee to give them such constancy, as thou hast given to thy saints and martyrs in time past, willingly to shed their blood for the testimony of thy word; or else mightily deliver them from the tyrannie of their enemies, as thou deliveredst the condemned Daniel from the lyons, and the persecuted Peter out of prison, to the exaltation of thy glory, and the rejoicing of the Church.

Furthermore, (most beneficial Father,) we humbly beseech thee to stretch forth thy mighty arm, into the protection and defence of all those that are exiled for the testimony of thy verity: and that because they wold not bend their backs and incline their necks under the yoke of Antichrist, and be polluted with the execrable idolatries, and blasphemous superstitions of the ungodly: that it would please thee, not only to feed them in strange countries, but also to prepare a resting place for them, (as thou hast done from time to time, for thine elect in all ages,) whereas they may unite themselves together in the sincere ministration of thy holy word and sacraments, to their singular edification; and in due time restore them home again into their land, to celebrate thy praises, promote thy gospel, and edifie thy desolate congregation.

. Consequently (O Lord) thou that hast said, that thou wilt not break the bruised reed nor quench the smoaking fire; be merciful, we beseech thee, unto all those that through fear and weaknesse have denied thee, by dissimulation and hypocrisie.

. That it may please thee to strengthen their weakness, (thou art the strength of them that stand,) and lift up their feeble hands, that their little smoak may encrease into a great flame, and their bruised reed into a mighty oake, able to abide the blustring blasts and stormy tempests of adversity: to the end, that the ungodly do no longer triumph over their faith, which (as they think) they have utterly quenched and subdued. Stir up thy strength in them, (O Lord,) and behold them with that merciful eye wherewith thou beheldest Peter, that they rising by repentance, may become the constant confessors of thy word, and the sanctified members of thy Church. To the end, that whenas by thy providence thou purposest to lay thy crosse upon them, they do no more seek unlawful means to avoid the same, but most willingly to be contented with patience to take it up and follow thee, in what sort soever it shall please thee to lay the same upon their shoulders, either by death, imprisonment, or exile. And that it will please thee not to tempt them above their powers, but give them grace utterly to despair of their owne strength, and wholly to depend upon thy mercy.

On the other side, (O Lord God,) thou righteous Judge, 111 let not the ungodly (the enemies of thy truth) continually triumph over us. Let not thine heritage become a reproach and common laughing-stock unto the impudent and wicked Papists: who, by all possible means, seek the utter destruction of thy little flock, in shedding the blood of thy saints, for the testimonie of thy word, seeking, by most devilish and damnable practices, to subvert thy truth. Confound them (O God) and all their wicked counsels, and in the pit they have digged for others, let them be taken; that it may be universally known, that there is no counsel nor force that can prevail against the Lord our God. Break (O Lord) the horns of those bloody bulls of Basan. Pull down those high mountains that elevate themselves against thee.

And root up the rotten race of the ungodly; to the end, that they being consumed in the fire of thine indignation, thine exiled Church may, in their own land, find place of habitation.

O Lord, deliver our land, which thou hast given us for a portion to possess in this life, from the invasion and subduing of strangers. Truth it is, we cannot deny but that our sins have justly deserved great plagues to come upon us; even that we should be given over into the hands and subjections of proud and beastly nations, that neither know thee nor fear thee, and to serve them in a bodily captivity, that have refused to serve thee in a spiritual liberty: yet, Lord, forasmuch as we are assuredly persuaded by thy holy word, that thine anger doth not last for ever towards those that earnestly repent, but instead of vengeance dost shew mercy; we most penitently beseech thee to remove this thy great indignation bent towards us, and give not over our land, our cities, towns, and castles, our goods, possessions, and riches, our wives, children, and our lives, into the subjection of strangers. But rather, O Lord, keep them from us and our country. Subvert their counsils, dissipate their devices, and deliver us from their tyranny, as thou deliveredst Samaria from that cruel Benhadad, Jerusalem from that blasphemous Senacherib, and Bethulia from that proud Holofernes.

Keep and preserve, O Lord, our prince and rulers, our magistrates and governors, as do and wil advance thy glory.

Erect up thy gospel, suppres idolatry, banish all pa-

pistry, and execute justice and equity. Water throughly,
O Lord, thy vine of England with the moisture of thy holy
word, lest it utterly perish, and wither away. Build up
again the decayed walls of thy ruinated Jerusalem, thy congregation in this land : lest the ungodly do attribute our
confusion, not unto our sins, as the truth is, but unto our
profession in religion.

Remember, O Lord, that we are a parcel of thy portion,
thy flock, the inheritors of thy kingdom, the sheep of thy
pasture, and the members of thy Son our Saviour Jesus
Christ. Deal with us, therefore, according to the multitude
of thy mercies ; that all nations, kindreds, and tongues, may
celebrate thy praises, in the enlarging of thy restored 11 2
Church to perfection again. For it is thy work, O Lord,
and not man's ; and from thee do we with patience attend
the same, and not from the fleshly arm of man. And therefore to thee only is due al dominion, power, and thanksgiving, now in our days, and evermore. *Amen.*

Number XLI.

*Another private prayer, for the use of the persecuted under
Queen Mary.*

O ETERNAL God, the dear Father of Christ Jesu, our Foxii MSS.
only Saviour, I beseech thee to look down with thy fatherly
eye of pity and mercy upon me, most unworthy, thorough
my manifold sins and wickedness, the which I have committed ayenst thy divine Majesty ; and upon every one of
my Christen brethern and sistern, the which are persecuted,
or appointed to dy for the testimony of thy most pure
gospel : desiring thee, of thy tender mercy, for the merits of
our good Christ, to send thy holy Spirit among us, to aid
and comfort us withal : that thorough the strength of the
same, we may so stedfastly cleave to thy word, that we may
never deny thee before men, for fear of any thing that they
can do unto us.

Also, good Lord, I beseech thee to be merciful to our
weak brethren and sistern, the which as yet dare not openly

confess thy holy name, for fear of this sharp storm of persecution. Good Lord, I beseech thee to send them grace and strength.

Also, good Lord, I beseech thee to be merciful to the poor wives and children of al those our godly brethren, the which have been put to death for thy names sake, or are imprisoned here or elsewhere for thy gospel: and also the poor wives and children of every one of us, that at this tyme be exiled for the same holy cause.

Be merciful also, good Lord, according to thy promise, unto al those, the which any maner of wayes do aid and comfort us in this time of our imprisonment and persecution. And as they comfort our vile earthly bodies, which be but earth and ashes, even so we beseech thee, most merciful Father, to comfort them both in souls and bodies, both in this world, and in the world to come, with everlasting life.

Also, I beseech thee to pardon our enemies, persecutors, and slaunderers. And if it be thy good wil, I pray thee that thou wilt turn their hearts.

113   Also, I beseech thee to be merciful to all those that have a troubled conscience for this plague, the which is now come again among us for our unthankfulness sake, whose hearts, Lord, thou knowest: and send both them and us thy grace, most earnestly to repent us of our sin and wickednes, the which we have committed against thy divine Majesty, and thereby drawn thy grievous wrath ayenst us. And I beseech thee, give us grace to be most contrite for the same: and that we may henceforth live in newnes of life, according to thy blessed commandments. And also, that we may have a faithful trust and belief, to have free remission and forgivenes of all our sins, only for the death and passion of thy dear Son Jesu Christ, our Lord and Saviour; who, with the eternal Father, and the Holy Ghost, three Persons and one God, be all honor and glory, praise and dominion, world without end. *Amen.*

> Written by me Thomas Spurge, in Newgate, condempned to dy for Christ's verity: and so is Richard Spurge, George Ambrose, John Cavel, William Tyms, and Robert Drake.

Number XLII.

*A pious letter against complying with idolatrous worship
in Queen Mary's days, written by a freewill-man.*

RYGHT derely beloved in our Saviour Jesu Christ, and _{Foxii} MSS. especial good frind, I do hertely recommend me unto you, and to my especiall good frind John Smyth the porter, and also to his wife, and also to my mother and yours, and to all my good fellowes, and to my brother Thomas Dodmer, yf he be in London, wishing grace, mercye, and increase of knowlege, in our Saviour Jesu Christ; beseching him always that ye myght be fulfylled with the knowlege of his will, in all wisdom and spiritual understanding; that ye myght walke woorthye of the Lord, to plese him in all things, and to be fruteful in all good workes, and to growe in the knowlege of God. Walke as the children of lyght, for the frute of the Spyret is in all manner of goodnes, and rightwisnes, and trewth; and prove what is plesing unto the Lord, and have no fellowship with the unfruteful work-ers of darkenes, but rather rebuke them. Bere not a straun-_{2 Cor. vi.} ger's yoke with the unbelevers. For what fellowship hath rightwisnes with unrightwisnes, what company hath lyght with darknes, how agreeth Christe with Belyall, or dronken-114 shippe; or what part hath the belevers with the infydell; how accordeth the temple of God with images or idolatrie? Ye are the temple of the lyving God: as God sayeth, I will dwell in them, and will be theyr God, and they shalbe my people: wherfore, come owte from among them, and separate yourselves, seyth the Lord: and touch none un-cleane thing: so will I receyve you, and be your Father, and ye shalbe my sonnes and dowghters, seyth the All-myghtye Lorde: this I say therfore, and exorte you in the name of the Lorde, that ye walke no more as the other heathen walke, in the vanitie of the mynd, blynded in the_{Eph. iv.} understanding, being straungers from the lyfe which is in God, throw the ignorancye that is in them, because of the blyndnes of theyre hartes; which being past repentaunce, have geven themselves over unto wantonnes, to worke all maner of unclennes with gredynes. Take hede, therefore, howe ye walke, cyrcumspectly, not as the unwise, but as the wise: and use well the tyme, for it is a myserable tyme, yea, and such a tyme, that yf yt were possible, the very chosen and elect shold be browght into errours. Therfore watch and serch diligently the Scriptures, and walke while ye have the lyght of God's worde, that the darknes fall not Matt. xxiv. upon you. Be sure of this, that yf the good man of the howse knew what hower the thefe would come, he would surely watch, and not suffer his howse to be broken up. Therfore be ye redy also, for in the hower that ye thinke not of, shall the Sonne of man come. Therfore, let us take his yoke upon us, and lerne of hym for to be meke and lowly of harte, and we shall find rest for our sowles. For his yoke is easye, and his burden is lyght.

And say no more, We be not able to kepe his commaundments, as many hath sayd, and doth say. But Christe sayeth, He that loveth me, kepeth my commaundments: and Christe came not to breake the lawe, but to fulfyl yt: and wyll we say, we are not able to kepe yt? Wold we not thinke, yf ye had a servant, and shold commaunde him to do our busines which were reasonable, and he shold make us answere before he went abowght yt, and say, he is not able to do yt, or yt lyeth not in his power to do yt, wold we not thinke that he were an evill servant, and a slowthfull? yea, and I thinke he were worthye to be tourned owte of service. Even so in like maner, God commaundeth us to love him with all ower herte, with all ower sowle, with all ower mynd, and with all ower strength. Here is nothing required of us, but that that is resonable, and that lyeth in ower power: for yf he had sayd, Thou shalt love me more than with all thy hert, sowle, and mynd, and above thy strength, then had yt bin no mervayle thowghe we had sayed, yt lyeth not in ower power, nor we be not able to kepe the commaundments. But God is not so unresonable, althowgh we have counted hym to be unresonable: for he knoweth what we are able to do, and doth nother not commaunde more than we are able to fulfylle, althowgh we be slowthful in fulfilling yt. Christe sayeth, Who soever brek- Matt. v. eth one of these lest commaundments, and tech men so, he 115 shalbe called the leste in the kingdom of heven. And Sainte James sayeth, Who soever shall kepe the whole lawe, Jacob. ii. and yet fayle in one poynte, he is gylty in all: for he that sayde, Thow shalt not commit adultery, sayde also, Thow shalt not kill: thowgh thow dust no adulterye, yet yf thow kill, that is to say, *yf thow be angrye*, or speake evill of thy neyghborh, thow arte a transgressour of the lawe. So speake ye, and so do, as they that shalbe judged by the law of libertye, &c. Now seing that we shalbe judged by the law, let us be willing servants, and say no more, We be not able to kepe the lawe; but let us saye with David the pro-phet, I will ronne the way of thy commaundments, when Psal. cxix. thow hast comforted my hart. God will have a free wylling harte, and not an unwilling harte come unto him: as Christ sayeth, Come unto me all ye that labour, and are laden, Matt. xi. and I will refresh you: take my yoke upon you, and lerne of me, for I am meke and lowly of hart, and ye shall find rest in your sowles.

Marke well, he biddeth us to *come to* him, yea, and take his yoke, and ye shall find rest. Yea, and moreover he biddeth us ask, and yt shalbe geven us: knocke, and yt shalbe opened unto us: and yet we will say, we have no *freewill*; we can do nothing of ourselves. Trewth it is, yf God had lefte us uncreated, and had geven us nether under-stonding nor reason, then myght we say, that we cold do nothing of ourselves: but God hath made us better than unreasonable beastes, and yet they have power to use them-selves according to theyre nature, and yet they are creatures without reason: are we not better than they? No, I thinke we are much worse, except we use reason reasonably, and according to the lawe of God, better than we do. God hath geven unto man a more principal gyfte than he hath don to the unreasonable creature, which doth all things by nature, as the sonne, the mone, and unreasonable bestes, which do all things to theyre nature: but man to do all things owt of his freewill. And therfore for man is the day of judgment sette, and not for the unreasonable creatures.

Eccl. xv. Thus Syrac sayeth, God made man from the beginnyng, and left him in the hand of his cownsell; he gave him his commaundments and precepts; yf thow wilt observe the commaundments, and kepe acceptably faythfullnes for ever,

Deut. xxx. they shall preserve thee. He hath set fyer and water before thee, reach owt thy hand unto which thow wilt: before man is lyfe and death, good and evell: loke what he leketh shalbe

Sapiens i. geven hym. O seke not your owne death in the errour of lyfe; destroy not your-selves throw the works of your owne hands: for God hath not made death, nether hath he plesure in the destruction of the lyving, but rather they shold lyve. Sey not thow, yt is the Lord's fawte that I am gon bye, for thow shalt not do the thing that God hatyth: sey not thow, he hath cawsed me to go wrong; for he hath no nede of the ungodly: for it was not God's will that man

4 Esdr. viii. shold come to nowght; but they which be created hath defyled the name of him that made them; and are unthankful

116 unto him, which prepared lyfe for them; and therefore is

Sapiens ii. my judgment now at hand. God created man to be undestroyed; but man, throw his wickednes, slayeth his owne

Sapiens xvi. sowle. O! turne ye, turne ye from your ungodly weyes: O!
Ezek. xxxiii. wherefore will ye dye? For they will not turne, and why?

Ps. liv. They fere not the Lord: they say, they know God; but with theyre dedes they deny him. For so mich they are abo-

Tit. i. minable, and disobedyent, and unmete to all good works.

These words are playne enowgh, except we will not hear them nor reade theym. But the multitude of ungodly childerne is unprofitable, and the things that are planted with whordom shall not take no depe rote, nor eny fast

Sapiens iv. foundation. Thowgh they be grene in the braunches for a tyme, yet shall they be shaken with the wynd; for they stand not fast: and through the vehemence of the wynd they shalbe roted owt: for like as the fyeld is, so is the sede also; and as the flowers are, so are the colours also; and soch as the workman is, so is the work also.

Wherfore, derely beloved, let us loke ernestly to the commaundments of the Lord; and let us fyrst go abowght

to kepe them, before we say that we be not able to kepe them. Let us not play the slowthful servants, but let us be willing, and go about to do them; and then, no dowght, God shall assiste us, and strengthen us, that we shall bring them to conclusion: and alwaye, derely beloved, have the fere of the Lorde before your eyes; for whoso feareth the Lorde, walketh in the right path; and regard not him that abhorreth the weyes of the Lorde; and at the last, God shall reward every man according to his dedes: namely, prayse, and honour, and uncorruption unto all them that, with patience in doing good, seke everlasting lyfe: where we shall rayne with the Father, and with the Sonne, and with the Holy Ghoste, in a world without end. *Amen.*

Number XLIII.

A letter to the congregation of freewillers, by one that had been of that persuasion, but come off, and now a prisoner for religion.

IN our Lord I most hartily salute you, and so do al my brethren: and after my loving salutation, and bounden duty considered, this shalbe to let you all understand, that if my learning or knowledg were answerable to my good will, you should surely find me, through God's grace, ready 117 therwith at all times to do you the good, that God through his Spirit hath endowed me withal; to the end that God may be glorified both by you and by me. For truly, my dearly beloved in the Lord, so oft as I behold the misery and calamity of this realm of England, it so much lamenteth my soul, that I cannot express it by tongue nor pen. And I protest before God and his elect angels, that it is the sins of us all that have professed the gospel here in England of late. But I doubt not but that it shalbe to our salvation, notwithstanding our fall. And one cause was, because we were not sound in the *predestination* of God; but we were rather enemies unto it. God forgive us: as I doubt not but that he hath already, to the end that we should set forth

Foxii MSS.

Ps. xxxvii.

Y 3

his honor and glory. And another cause is, that we have professed the gospel with our tongues, and denied it with our deeds, as I, for my part, can conceive no less.

What high lauds, thanks, and praise, am I bound to give always to God, who hath certified my conscience by his Spirit, that he will not impute my sins unto me, for his Son Jesus Christ's sake; in whom he hath chosen his elect before the foundations of the world were laid; and preserveth us al, so that there shall never any of us finally perish or be damned. For Christ our Saviour loveth us unto the end, according to his own word. And again he saith, *Al that the Father hath given me, shal come unto me.* And in the Acts of the Apostles it is written, that *so many believed, as were ordained to eternal life.* So that our election in Christ is the original and fountain of all grace, and through it we obtain the fruition of the glory of God; as we learn by the apostle S. Paul's words: doth he not say, I pray you, that *Israel could not attain that which he sought, but the election hath obtained it: the remnant are blinded.* According as it is written, *God hath given them the spirit of unquietness: eyes that they should not se, and ears that they should not hear, even unto this day,* &c. This is the infallible truth, the which you cannot deny, except you deny the truth.

I, for my part, repent that ever I was so bitter unto them that were the teachers of this undoubted truth. Verily, I am not able to express the sorrows that I have in my heart, most especially in that I went about by all means to persuade other, wherby they might be one with me in that error of *freewil;* albeit that God in his good time wil revele his truth unto you, as it pleased him to open it unto me, his name everlastingly be praised for it. I do not mourn nor sorrow, in that God hath given me the ful feeling of his aboundant bottomles mercy, with his truth in the same: but with joy unspeakable I rejoyce, giving thanks to God night and day, in that it hath pleased him to vouch me worthy his fatherly correction at this present, shewing me what I am by nature; that is to say, ful of impiety and all evil. Therfore the great grief which I daily feel is, because

Marginal references:
Rom. viii.
Ps. xxxii.
Rom. iii.
Eph. i.
John xiii.
John vi.
Acts xiii.
Rom. xi.
Es. vi.
Mark iv.

that I see the horribleness, and the great dishonour, that
the filthy freewil of man doth render unto God; therefore
I sigh and am grieved, because I spake evil of that good I 118
knew not. Yet I have obtained mercy, because I did it
ignorantly.

Wherfore, beloved, I am provoked by the Holy Ghost,
to visit you with my letter, hoping and believing that God
will give it good succes; because it is the undoubted truth,
wherby God's glory may be the more set forth. For I have
a good opinion of you, my dear brethren, trusting in God
that he will revele unto you the knowledg of himself.   For Eph. i.
I believe verily you be the vessels of God's mercy : therfore 1 Cor. ii.
I am assured that you shal lack no necessary article of your
salvation.   For I have good cause so to judg of you, not Rom. ix.
only because God hath opened his truth to me alone, but I
also se how mercifully he hath dealt with many of our
brethren, whom you do know wel enough, as wel as though
I did recite them by name. God forbid that I should doubt
you, seing that it hath pleased God to revele himself in these
days, to them that heretofore were deceived with that error
of the Pelagians; yea, and suffered imprisonment in the defence of that which now they detest and abhor.   God be
thanked for them.   This is the Lord's doing, and it is mar-
vailous in our eyes.

O! dear brethren, insomuch that it hath pleased God to
vouch you worthy of so great dignity, to suffer against the
wicked Papists; and as that is a truth which you stond in
against these bloudthirsty enemies of God; and like as you
have the truth as concerning the Papists sacrament, in dis-
pising and hating that I do, as it is wel worthy; so likewise
is freewil a most untruth, undoubtedly.

Dear brethren, I do not write this unto you, to the end 1 Cor. xi.
that you should contend among yourselves, nor yet that I Rom. xv.
would strive with you; for the congregation of God hath no
such custom; but of mere love, I am glad to open the Matt. xxv.
talent unto you that God hath given me.   For I think that
God wil receive me home unto himself shortly.   Therfore I
am moved to signify unto you in what state I stond, con-

cerning the controversy between the opinions of the truth of
God's predestination and election in Christ. I do not hold
predestination to the end to maintain evil; as there be some
hath ful ungodly affirmed that we do. God forgive them, if
it be his wil. Wo were it to us, if we should delight in that
which God abhorreth and hateth, and the which was the
cause of Christ's death. For we are sure, that none which
have the ful feeling of their election in Christ, can love or
allow these things which God hateth. Wherfore I would
wish that men should not allow the fruit of faith to be the
cause of faith. But faith bringeth forth good works, and not
good works faith. For then of necessity we must attribute
our salvation unto our good works : which is great blasphemy against God and Christ so to do. But I thank God
I do allow good works in their place. For I was created in
Christ Jesu unto good works. Wherfore I am bound to
allow them according to the Scriptures, and not to the end
to merit by them any thing at al. For then I were utterly
deceived. For Esay saith, *Al our righteousness is as a
filthy cloth,* stained with the flowers of a woman, and are
not as the law of God requireth them. Wherfore I acknowledg that al salvation, justification, redemption, and
remission of sins, cometh to us wholly and solely by the
mere mercy and free grace of God in Jesus Christ, and not
for any of our own works, merits, or deservings. For our
Saviour Christ saith, *Make the tree good, and the fruit
good, or else make the tree evil, and the fruit evil* also ; for
the tree is known by his fruits, &c.

My dearly beloved brethren, herein was I deceived, with
many mo besides me, because we could not discern the
truth in good works. And if you, dear brethren, did once
se in what respect they ought to be don, you should soon
agree with us in the truth. For I myself could not understand S. Paul and S. James, to make them agree together,
til our good preachers, which were my prison fellows, did
open them unto me. I praise God for them most humbly ;
and yet I cannot be so thankful for them as I ought to be.

First, Paul saith, *Faith only justifieth, and not the deeds*

Eph. i.
Matt. xiv.

Eph. ii.

119

Matt. vii.

Rom. iii.
Gal. ii.

of the law. And S. James saith, *Faith without deeds is dead.* Here are contraries to the carnal man. When I saw these two Scriptures plainly opened, I could not stond against the truth therin. And thus were they opened unto me, that faith doth only justify before God, and the good deeds that S. James speaketh of, justify before the world. Thus must you understand these Scriptures; or els you shal make them repugnant in themselves; which were a great absurdity to grant. Wherfore, when you se the truth in this matter, it may so chance with you, as it did with me. For I consider the loss of mine own friends, and their displeasure: and while I walked in the house of God, musing of this matter, it pleased God to move me with his Spirit, that although I lost the love of my friends, yet I should win him, in whom I do delight. For I considered the saying of the Apostle, wheras he saith, *If I should go about to* Gal. i. *please men, I were not the servant of God.* Albeit I was much addicted to the contrary part, yet at the length, while I was thus musing, the fire kindled; so that I was compelled, even as it were by violence, to speak with my tongue; which hath turned since to my great joy and comfort: I praise God therfore most humbly. And although I thought I should lose many friends; yet it hath pleased God to raise up many friends to me for one. And I thank God, that they, whom I thought would have been mine enemies, are become my friends in the truth: as in sample, by our brethren Ledley and Cole, and such like. If it had lyen in their own wills, they would have been enemies to that excellent truth which they do now allow. Praised be God for them: *for it is he that worketh both the wil and the* Phil. ii. *deed, even of good wil.* For if he had not been merciful unto them and to me, and prevented our wills, we had been still wallowing in the mire. And the prophet Jeremy saith, *Turn thou me, and I shall be turned: heal thou me, and I* Jer. xvii. *shall be healed.* And David saith, *The Lord hath prepared* Ps. x. *the hearts of the poor, and his ear hearkeneth unto them.* So that it is the Lord that doth al that good is. Again, 120 David saith, *Ascribe al honor and glory to God;* who alone Ps. xxix.

John vi. is worthy. For *no man cometh unto me*, saith Christ, *except the Father, which hath sent me, draw him.* And again he saith, *Al that the Father hath given me shal come unto me*, as is before said, *and he that cometh unto me, I cast not away.* For *I came down from heaven, not to do my own wil, but the wil of him that sent me :* speaking these words in that he was man, that he desired to do the wil of the Father ; and in that Christ is God, he did his own wil. For John xvii. he said unto the Father, *Glorify me with that glory which I have with thee, or ever the world was :* speaking now of his omnipotency and deity. Yet notwithstanding that he is very God, he did pray that the wil of his Father should be don in his manhood ; seing Christ, being perfect God and perfect man, gave al the honor and glory to God his Father : which doth condemn many of our Scribes and Pharisees, which say, they can do good, if they wil, Christ being the auctor and finisher of al truth, and every truth itself, which truth cannot ly, because he is God : yet, notwithstonding that his mighty power and divinity, he cryed, saying, *Father, thy wil be don.* Much more ought we to cast down ourselves, which be but partakers of his godly 2 Pet. i. nature. Wherefore I may say with Christ, that al shal John vi. come to him, which the Father did give him.

Col. i. Therfore I believe, that we shal every one be preserved and kept in him, and for him, according to his own word. And who, that wil not allow his word, doth not allow him. Therfore I dare boldly say, with our everlasting Saviour Jesus Christ, that al the elect shal be preserved and kept for ever and ever. So that none of them shalbe damned at ony time. They that say, that ony of them may be lost for ever, do as much as in them lyeth, to make Christ unable to preserve and keep them : so that at one time or other, they may perish and fal away, as some affirm, denying the John xiii. power of Christ in so saying. For he saith, *he loveth his unto the end.* Which love remaineth, and shall never be extinguished or put out, but it remaineth for ever without end ; and is not as the love of man, which is sometime angry and Col. i. sometime pleased. For God at no time is so displeased with any of his elect, to the end, that he wil deprive them of the purchased possession which he hath layd up in store for them in Christ before, and were elect according to the fore-knowledg of God the Father, through sanctifying of the Spirit unto obedience and sprinkling of the bloud of Jesus Christ: which Lamb was killed from the beginning, according to God's divine wil and providence. And to conclude, S. Peter maketh it plain and evident to the spiritual ey, whereas he saith, *Forasmuch as you know how that you were not redeemed with corruptible things, as silver and gold, from the vain conversation which ye received by the traditions of the fathers; but with the precious bloud of Jesus Christ, as of a lamb undefiled and without spot: which was ordained beforehand, ever before the world was made,* &c. I am sure you cannot deny but that Christ was ordained, concerning his humanity, and not concerning the Godhead. And therefore it must needs follow, that Christ was ordained to dy in the flesh: and all was for our sins. Or els I am sure, that he had not taken our nature upon him, but to redeem us from our sins.

. But it may fortune that some wil say captiously, (as I have been answered before this time,) If it be so, that Christ was ordained in the flesh, then God did induce necessity to Adam's fal: to them I answer, God did not induce any necessity to Adam's fal; but Christ was ordained in this respect, that the Father seing the fal of Adam, for that purpose only he ordained Christ, to the end that he would preserve a remnant of the posterity of Adam; even as it pleased his godly wisdom.

What, (wil some say,) a *remnant,* and not al? S. Paul saith, *Like as al dyed in Adam, even so al be made alive by Christ.* And S. John saith, *Not for our sins only, but for the sins of the whole world.* Ah! wil these freewil-men say, Where be your *remnant* now become? To whom I answer by the Scriptures, Wheras Christ shal say in the last day, *Depart from me, you cursed, I know you not:* I pray you tel me, did not God know them, as concerning their creation, and also their wickednes? Yes, verily, but he knew

Marginal references: 1 Pet. i.   Eph. i.   Rev. xiii.   1 Pet. i.   121   Gal. iv.   Rom. ix.   Rom. xi.   1 Cor. xv.   1 John ii.   Matt. xxv.

them not for his elect children. And in this respect he knew them not: but otherwise he knew them, as I have written So in like case, if that the *all*, that S. Paul speaketh of, be truly understanded, it shal come to pas according to his saying. For even, saith he, *as al fel in Adam, so shal al be made alive by Christ.* It is meant by them whom it pleased God to ordain to life eternal. For God, by his fore-know-ledge, did se to what end the vessels of wrath would come, before he made them; to the end that he would shew his justice upon them, and his mercy on al them that were made alive again by Christ. For the true Church of Christ doth understand these *all*, and al other such like Scriptures, to include al the elect children of God. None otherwise, I am sure, that these *all* can be understanded, except we should make the Scripture repugnant to itself; which were too much ignorance, and too great an absurdity to graunt.

Therfore let us pray to God, that he wil, for his glorious name's sake, defend us from al errors, according as he hath decreed before al things, to the profit of al his chosen chil-
Eph. i. dren, which he hath predestinate in Christ, and for him. So likewise let us pray, that God of his free mercy wil give us the ful sealing of his abundant grace, according to his ac-customed goodnes; as undoubtedly he doth to every one of his in due time. Yet, notwithstonding, we are bound always
Matt. xxvi. to watch and pray, lest we fal into temptation. Christ taught his disciples the same doctrin, although they were his very elect: yet did he give them this commandment, to the end that he might certify them to be his; albeit they were cer-tain with him already. Therfore I say, whosoever they be that do find unlust and tediousnes to do good, may opinion with themselves, that they be none of God's children.

Wherfore I affirm, that al they be blasphemers to God, that do slaunder the truth in predestination; that say, If I be once in, I cannot be out, do what evil I will or can do.
122 All such do declare themselves to be reprobates, and the children of God's ire and wrath, rather than any of his. For whosoever delighteth in those things which God hateth and abhorreth, doth declare himself to be none of God's:

but if he be any of his, he will give him repentance for to ₂ Tim. ii.
know the truth by his Spirit. *For the Spirit maketh inter-* Rom. viii.
cession for the saints, according to the pleasure of God.
For we know that all things work for the best unto them
that love God, which are called of purpose. For those which
he knew before, he also ordained before, that they should be
like fashioned unto the shape of his Son.

And seing God hath made al his elect like to the shape
of Jesus Christ, how is it possible that ony of them can fal
away? For whosoever he be that doth so hold, is against
God and Christ; and may as wel say, that our only Lord
and Saviour Jesus Christ may perish, as any of them. For
Christ said unto the Father, *Father, thou hast loved them* John xvii.
as thou hast loved me. Although Christ spake these words
to the comfort of his disciples at the present, so likewise is
it to the comfort of all us his chosen. And those words did
include al them that God *called of purpose,* and those also
which he *knew before,* according to the text: for I am sure
that there is none can deny, but that God knew the estate
of al people. But those that S. Paul speaketh of, that *God*
knew before, he meant it by al his elect; and immediately
he addeth, saying, *Which he appointed before, them also he* Rom. viii.
called; and which he called, them also he justified; and
which he justified, them also he glorified. What shal we
then say to these things; if God be on our side, who can be
against us? That is to say, If God have appointed to glorify us, and to save us, who can then deny [deprive] him of
any of us, or take us out of his hands? *My shepe,* saith John x.
Christ, *hear my voice, and I know them, and they follow*
me: and I give unto them eternal life; and they shal never
perish. Oh! most worthy Scriptures, which ought to compel us to have a faithful remembrance, and to note the tenor
thereof; which is, the sheep of Christ shal never perish.
Mark, I pray you, Christ's words, which he spake with zea-
lousnes and power, towards his sheep, only to the end to
comfort them in all afflictions. He made them this faithful
promise, to the intent that they should not quaile for any
tyranny that should be done unto them, saying, *They shal*

never perish; for my Father, saith Christ, *which gave them me, is greater than al, and no man shalbe able to take them out of my Father's hands.*

Doth Christ mean part of his elect, or al, think you? I do hold and affirm, and also faithfully believe, that he meant al his elect, and not part, as some do ful ungodly affirm. For I confes and believe assuredly, that there shal never any of them perish: for I have good authority so to say; because Christ is mine author, and saith, *If it were possible, the very elect should be deceived.* *Ergo,* it is not possible that they can be so deceived, that they shal ever finally perish, or be damned. Wherfore, whosoever doth affirm that there may be any lost, doth affirm that Christ hath a torn body. But my hope is, that I shal hear better of you al, 123 and have heard already that which doth rejoyce me very much. For my brother Robert Cole did give you a good report to me and to my prison-fellows, and said, that you would —————.

[Somewhat is wanting.]

Number XLIV.

A tract, shewing how all sorts of people of England have just cause of displeasure against the bishops and priests of the same, for involving them in perjury. *Written anno 1555.*

Foxii MSS. GOD Almighty, Father of our Lord Jesus Christ, which, of his only pity and mercy, hath bought us out of al the thraldome and captivity of Sathan, not with pure and most fined gold, nor yet with al other precious things in the world, but by the most excellent love-price of his unspeakable love and wisdom, hath he given to death, out of his own bosome, his own Son Jesus Christ; whose stripes and death hath healed our sores, and purchased for us the kingdom of everlasting joy and felicity: the same God, with his dear Son, and his sanctifying Holy Ghost, be with you evermore. *Amen.*

I cannot but be right joyful, in these most miserable days, to se that God doth so mercifully and lovingly keep his little flock, even in the mouths of the wolves, both stedfast in faith, constant and patient, and rather desiring to dy in the truth, than with a dissembling heart to get out of the snare, and time of opprobry, and shameful reproch, as almost al England doth at this present day; [which they could never dare to do,] if they warily and with God's wisdom did ponder their state, and the condition that they are in.

For what land or people doth not know, that the whole popish clergy of this realm have not only lived perjured, as they themselves confes, and compelled al the people, many against their conscience, to confes the same these twenty years last past, and above; but also have compelled al them that in these years have been admitted priests, to perjure themselves in like maner: yea, and in every law-day, the keepers of the same were sworn to cal for al the young men 124 of their hundred, even as they came to the years of their age, appointed to swear the same oath, never to receive the Bishop of Rome, nor no other potentate or power in earth, to be head of the people of England, under God, but only the King's Majesty, and his successors for ever. Now, if this oath be unlawful, as the clergy now saies, then may al the nobles of the realm of that opinion have great cause of displeasure justly against al the devilish bishops that so led them and knew it. Yea, and if they look rightly to the bearing of the sword of God's vengeance, they wil with repentant hearts strike with the same, and not leave one of the dissemblers alive. The magistrates and gentlemen may have like cause against them, and al the company of that mark, which both was cause of their perjury, and the perjury that they have caused al the rest of the subjects and common people of this whole realm to commit. The merchants of London, yea, the merchants of al London and England, also may think a great deal of their honesty and credence perished, to be known of their creditors to be perjured. Al the whole people have cause justly to bear wrath towards the wickednes of that clergy, not only for their own perjury, but also for theirs. The souls that are dead in this perjury, without repentance, now in hel, shal curse them al.

Oh! what an heinous work is this in the sight of God, if the Papists say truth! The deeds of this Romish clergy makes me to think, (welnigh,) that they think there is no God but the Pope, they have so slenderly looked upon their duties, seing that they have heard it read, *Cursed are al they that do the Lord's busines wretchlesly. Cursed are al they that are perjured, and depart from the law of the Lord their God. Cursed are al they that lead the blind out of the way.*

But to heal this their wickednes, their sacrament of penance, and the proper pardon, doth them great service. For they have aucthority to minister that sacrament to the people, and to themselves also: and God then must needs forgive them al. But if any take not their penance, they must be damned, as some of the clergy saith. And this I know, that the most part of the priests so handle themselves, that with one part of the people they falsely dissemble. For if one come, whose conscience is not satisfied with this way, and tel the priest his conscience, he wil say, " You say the " truth; my conscience is as yours is; but we must bear " for a time: yea, and wil say, that he himself looks for an- " other change." And to the other that are addict to the other side, they say to them, " Yea, we have been deceived; " but thanks be to God, that ye kept your conscience al " this while against it. For even so was mine, but that I " durst do no other, but trusted that this time would come, " as it is now, thanks be to God." Oh! what damnable beasts are these! Truly, friends, I know in this town, where two priests ministred either of them two ways to the people: which thing I take to be a witnes of their double hearts. 125 And I think, if it were searched, it might be approved in mo places than two. For I know the people that have reported their priests, as I have before said, and could, if I were at liberty, bring you, if ye would, to the hearing of both parties. Alas! how should the people of God go the right way, when their guides are thus mutable, and never constant?

Another thing much do I mervail at, that never one priest, that now be so stout, did venture his life for the souls of his people in all these twenty years and upwards, nor enjoyned them any penance, for their perjury against the Bishop of Rome: but suffered them even to dy in the black curse and excommunication, that they wel knew was upon us, as they now say they did.

But these things have I said of the mutable clergy, which is not Christ's clergy, but the Pope's, who sitteth in Christ's seat, even in the conscience of the people. But God, I believe, wil shortly, of his clemency and mercy, destroy his power. But, friends, for al my saying *shortly*, look not you for it with carnal eyes; nor seek after false prophets, that wil say, It wil change this year, or the next year; as the people did, when they were carried captive to Babylon, in the prophet Jeremie's time. For they got them a prophet called Hananiah, which said unto them, that their captivity should last but two years, and Jeremie said, *Amen, I pray God it may be so.* And the same false prophet came to Jeremie, which had made a chain of wood, and hanged it about his neck, declaring to the people therby, that for their sins they should be captives, and their King bound with chains at Babylon; and took the chain from his neck, and brake it, and said, " Thus saith the Lord, Even thus within these
" two years shal the yoke be broken off the neck of the
" King; and the people shal come to this place again to
" serve God. Then said Jeremie, The prophet is not known
" to be true, till that thing cometh to pass which he pro-
" phesieth. And immediately the word of the Lord came to
" Jeremie, and said, Bid the people at Babylon build them
" houses, plant them vinyards, and mary their sons and
" their daughters, and pray for the peace of the country
" wherin they dwel: for that shalbe their own peace. For
" their captivity shal last LXX years. And tel that false pro-
" phet Hananiah, that because he hath falsely prophesied,

" he shal dy this year. Which things came to pass." And our sins are greater than were theirs. But if God wil have a change, he can do it what way he wil. But our imaginations, I fear, hinder his work in the matter in your days.

But if it come so to pass, the clergy wil also, I think, as easily change, as these two times before they have don. That it may be done unto them as it was in Moyses time to the children of Israel, when they had sinned so against God, that God would have destroyed them, if Moyses had not stand in the gap, and turned away his wrath. But when Moyses came unto the people, he commaunded every man to girde his sword upon his thigh, and every man to kil his neighbour. Even so, if God se it good, may of good deserving be don to this mutable clergy of England; that other for honour, riches, or wealth, or for their lives, have 26 so wickedly don, to bring this whole land out of the true faith of Christ unto the faith of Rome; and to cause God's people to confess themselves perjured, for swearing to perform their true obedience unto their liege Lord and King, commanded of God. O! miserable England, defiled with bloud by the Pope's sword! O! wicked clergy, fighters with the same! your destruction is in your own hands. Ye have brought swift damnation upon yourselves and upon the people.

How few are they that can justly excuse themselves? For what difference now is there between these two sorts of people? The one have received the Pope's pardon, with penance for their perjury, and thinks that they were perjured, and have made amends, and are forgiven: and other knows, that they were not perjured, and yet have received the pardon, and don the penance. This latter sort, in my judgment, are more hated in the sight of God than the other; for, contrary to their own knowledge and their conscience, have they don in the sight of God: so that the saying of Christ may wel be said unto them, that he said unto Jerusalem, *How oft would I have gathered you together, as a hen gathereth her chickens under her wings, and ye would not!* And in another place Christ said to his disciples, *If any city receive you not, depart from them, and shake the dust off your feet: for it shal be easier for Sodom and Gomor in the day of judgment, than for that people.* Ye may not think here that Christ meaned, that there should any ease come to the Sodomites and Gomorrheans, but that their punishment should be les, in comparison of the just vengeance of God prepared for them that refuse and forsake the true preachers. Yea, then how much more for them that know the truth and forsake it?

Dear friends, I am sorry to write so sharply to you, but God's verity wil no otherwise. Look upon it betimes: for it hath, I wiss, in us no place.

Now, Lord, for thy mercies sake, help and defend the little sort, that knows they were not perjured, but lawfully sware the oath, that is a part of God's glory; and are contented rather to dy by the Pope's sword, than to slander thy truth. And help those forward that repent of their deed, and give them the strength of thy Ghost rightly to knowledg their fault. And to the other sort, that of ignorance doth that wickedness, give light and understanding, with grace to amend. But have no mercy, Lord, as David saith, *upon those that sin of malicious wickednes.*

Pray, good people; fear not to pray. Peradventure God wil turn his plague from us, that we have justly deserved. Make your hearts pure, or els your prayers are sin.

Number XLV. 127

John Bradforth to the Queen, and other great lords, concerning the Spaniards, and their designs against England.

To the Quene's Majestie, the Lords, and other of the realme of England.

THOUGHE yt be never so daungerous to me to sett Foxii MSS. this lyttell treatys abroad, yet the natural love that I beare to my natyve countrye, surpassing all daungers that maye

z 2

chaunce to my bodye and goods, so burneth in my brest, that yt wyll not suffer me to suppresse or kepe secret from you suche matters, as are pretended for the destruction, not only of the common estat of the realme, but of your Majestie, most myserably deceaved, and of your honnorable estates moste sottelye circumventyd, your lands and posterytie for ever. The thinges which I have put forth is not the device nor imagination of me, nor the saynge of anye other man, but a moste certayne experience of one John Bradforth, late servaunte to Sir Wyllyam Skypworth, and after for the space of ij years served with one of Kinge Philippes privye councell; as he had found yt not only by communication, but also by lettres, which he had read himselfe, of other mens, as in his lettres more at large he doth declare: the coppies of which lettres, written and subscribed with his owne hand and name, I have readye by me to shewe for my dyschardge: which thinge, bycause it contayneth the destruction of your Majesty, and of the estates and subversion of the whole realme, I could not thincke myselfe, not onlye noe good subjecte, but a double traytour, yf I shoulde kepe the same secrett, all the matter of the same belonging unto your Majestie; whom I praye God to preserve, for your owne savegard, and for the welthe of the realme. *Amen.*

To the right honorable Earles and Lordes of Arundell, Shrouesburye, Darbye, and Penbroke, ther trewe and faythfull sarvaunt John Bradforth wyshethe the increase of grace, and parfecte knowledge of Godes holey truth, the preservation of theire honourable estates and countrey.

Ther hath byne certayne bookes and letters touching matters of religion latlye imprinted in Ingleshe, under the cloke of a fervent health and love towards our countrie 128 agaynest Spanyards, by the advice of certayne Protestantes, thinking therby to ground in the hartes of the people ther new fangled fayth; wherin it doth appeare, that the autors of theise bookes knowe not perfectlye the nature of the same, but have rathar wrytten by report of other, than by perfect practyse: which bookes, bycause that fewe men dare use them openlye, least they shoulde, by your Lordshippes, and the Quene's most honnorable counseyll, for their doctrin, be weeded oute with the moste folyshe gatherers of the same, I thincke they have not comen before your Honours; so that though theis books had most trulye declared the nature of the Spaniards, and that at large, (as indeed they have not,) yet they coulde not parfectlye, bycause the doctrin that was put forth with them, made them seame too vyle to be brought before your syghtes. I have therfor, moste honnorable Lordes, pourposed not to meddell with anye matteres, or answering unto them; but somwhat to declare unto you, not that which I knowe by reportes, but that which I know perfectly by experience; I meane that subtyll   device agaynest you and all the realme; and the natural disposition of the Spaniards, whose vylenes doubtles I cannot showe and exprese with anye wordes, as the truth is; neverthelesse I shall declare the premedytate myschiffe, and pretenced treasons, not only agaynest your Lordshippes parsones, but also agaynest the whole realme; so farr as I have harde, seen, and proved, for the space of two or three yeares, in ther companey.

My frends put me to serve amonge them, that I myght learne langwage, and knowe the parfect truth, whether ther conditions were so vyle as the common voyce reported, or not. And I assure your Lordshippes, and all my frendes, that the vylest report that ever I hard Inglyshe men speake by the worste of them, ys nothing to the vylenes which remayneth in the best among them all. I saye, all the whole nation of the Spaniards, except the Kinges Majestie; he wyll saye, the noblemen be verye cyvel parsons. I have not sene so moche vertue among all the reste, as in the noble prince the Duke Medina Celi, a prince untainted, indued with great humilitie; who hath in my hearing to my master manye tymes lamented the myserable estate of our moste noble kingdome. There be many other noblemen, very wyse and politicke; which can, thorowe ther wysdome, reform and brydell theyr owne natures for a tyme, and applye their conditions to the maners of those men with whom they meddell gladlye by frendshippe: whose myschievous maners a man shall never knowe, untyll he come under ther subjection: but then shall he parfectlye parceyve and fele them: which thinge I praye God England never do: for in dissimulations untyll they have their purposes, and afterwards in oppression and tyrannye, when they can obtayne them, they do exceed all other nations upon the earthe. Besides an heape of ambitious fleshelye lustes, as pryde, ambytion, dysdayne, and all maner of lechery, in these of all other natyons they do excede. But to learne of their maners, and to declare to your Honours 129 suche thinges as I have hard with myne ears, and sene with myne eyes in their writing, which are pretended to your distruction, the loss of your lyves, lands, wyves, and children, and the ruin of the whole realme, the suppression of the comon welthe, and bondage of the countrie for ever. I take God to my wytnes, I wryte nothing for malyce of the Spanyards, nor to flatter Inglyshemen, but only to shewe their cursed wyckednes, that oure countrye being at lybertye, may be kept safe from their tiranny, and their Morish maners: as known to your Honours aforehand, ye may the more provide to kepe your estates, and the whole realme, out of their bondage.

Fyrst, where it is Godes commaundement, that one shall not wrongfullye covet an other's goodes; (whiche commaundement the Spanyards saye they will kepe.) Whatsoever, they saye, is done in Ingland, touching the crowne and governance of the realme, shall not come thorow their procurement, but of the counsell themselves. The Kinge knoweth perfectlye the stout and dyvellyshe hartes of the people of England, to worke treason and make insurrections; and therfor he wyll not desyer the crowne, except he maye fyrste have certayne of the stronge holdes, portes, and townes, (marke theis three wordes well,) for his refuge at all tymes, untyll his Majestye maye bringe in powre to withstand his enemyes. For he purposeth to make all our haven-townes mor stronger towardes the land, than they be towardes the sea; that a few souldiours maye kepe the realme in quietnes, and burne the counterye on everye syde three or foure tymes in one yeare, tyll they can be content to observe all the constitutions, ordenaunces, and lawes: for, saye they, yf we have the sea to vyttell us, we shall have powre to rule Ingland so longe, tyll they be abell to suffer yt no longer. What greate travayll wyll yt be, while the sea is our frend, to burne betwen Southampton and Dover? For, they saye, they wyll never make feilde; but let stronge walles prove their manlynes; they trust that the Quenes Highnes, to mayntayne the Kinge, wyll pull the realme so much as in her lyeth: and when our money is gonne, and gathered upp, the Kinge wyll inriche himselfe this tyme of peace, for a yeare or two; so that when we have but small store of money, they shalbe ready to worke myschife agaynest us. For they shall have money from all places, and mayntenaunce from manye countryes, and they truste to be ayded by the greatest parte of the realme. For the Quene, and all cathollycke men, wyll take their parte agaynest the hereticks. Ther be but fewe of the noblemen of the counsayll, but they wylbe contenteyd, either by gyftes of the Quenes Majestie, or ells for greate brybes, to graunt the Kinge a juste tytle; or ells to receave him in uppon th'one parte, that he maye overcome th'other.

Is not this to be lamented, that we Inglyshmen, for feare of chaunge of religion, whiche cometh by Godes ordenaunce, shall seke to plant suche a nation in our counterye, as do seke the utter distruction of the same? But this is moste detestable and abhomynable, that so noble and pru-130 dent governors as your Lordshipes, should, either for fayr words, love, fayr brybes, or anye kynde of covetousnes, seke the subversion of our countrey, the ruin of the realme, the utter decaye of the common welth, and the destruction of our owne bloud for ever. For yf ther myght anye of the noble bloud remayne alyve, and bare rewll, we shulde have some hope of restoring the realme and weall-publycke: but yf they delyver the crowne once oute of your handes,

(I doo not meane the crowne of golde onlye, but also the poure that gooeth with yt,) ye shall in shorte tyme have suche a fall, as ther shall not be left one of your lynage lyving, that shalbe able to defend his, or beare rule, as his predecessors have done. For this you must nedes graunt, that yt is necessarye for the King to worke the surest waye for his owne proffyt and preservation that can be devysed by his owne counsayll : and then I am sure ther is none of you, I thincke, that can bear rule in the comonwelth, or near the Kinges Majestie. For the worlde speaketh agaynst the detestable treasons of oure nobylytie ; and therfor Spanyards myght be counted men of small wysdomes, yf they could not forsee suche daungers. But they have provided for that well enough. I woulde to God that your Lordships knewe as muche as I have harde with myn ears, and sene with myn eyes, or ells woulde credyt my wordes. For then your most prudent wysdomes coulde provide to withstand their pretensed treason.

Ye woulde saye, what coulde this fellowe hear or see ? Howe coulde he knowe their counsayll ? I was chambarlayn to one of the privye counsayll, and with all dyligence gave myselfe to wryte and read Spanyshe : which thinge once obtayned, I kept secret from my master and fellow-servants, and served dyligently, bycause I myght be trusted in my master's closset or studye ; wher I myght read suche writing, as I sawe brought in dayly into the counsell chamber. Which thing I dyd as opportunytie served : yet I understood not their concluded counseylls, but the effecte of suche letters as I have sene, which wer sent from one counsellor to another. I sawe certayne letters sent from th'Emprour halfe a yeare befor the Kinge came oute of Ingland : wherin was contayned theise privities, " That the " Kinge shoulde make his excuse to the Quene, that he " woulde goo see his father in Flaundars, and that immedy- " atly he woulde retourne, seing the good simple Quene is " so jelous over my sonne, (I tearm yt as the letters dothe,) " we shall make her agree unto all our requestes before his " retourne, or ells kepe him here exercysed in our affayrs ;

" tyll [we may prevayl] with the Counsayll, who doubtles
" wylbe wone with fayre promyses and great gyftes, poly-
" tickly placed in tyme:" with manye other thinges, howe
this matter shoulde be handeled, and howe yt shoulde be
brought to passe; howe all partyes must be followed;
whome they maye trust, and what men shoulde retayn
them; who they myght make their frend with brybes, and
who they myght wyn with fayr words. That the Emprour
woulde apoynte the Kinges Counseyll for the same purpose, 131
such as he many years had provided to be just, prudent, and
wyse in their doings; so that the Kinge myght boldly put his
trust in them at the fyrst present, which his father in many
years, and by long experyence had proved, and pycked out
for trew and faythfull servaunts, amonge many dissemblyng
flatterers; with many suche prudent counsellers, touching
Flaundars, Fraunce, Napells, and Mylayne, Bohema, Hon-
gary, Turkey, and many other countryes, as betwixt Spayne
and the Mores; whereof I knowe they have so brought to
passe, and manye other they are lyke to obtayn, and all which
matters I passe, because they partayne not to our countrye,
I leave with silence.

   In other letters I have read the cause disputed, that the
Quene is bounde by the lawes of God to endue her husband
in all her goods and possessions, so far as in her lyeth : and
they thinke she wyll doo yt indeed, to the uttermoste of her
powre. No man can thinke evel of the Quene, thoughe she
be somwhat moved, when suche thinges are beaten into her
head contynually with gentyllwomen. But whether the
crowne belonge to the Quene or to the realme, the Spanyards knowe not, nor care not, thoughe the Quene to her
dampnation disheryt the right heyres apparant, or breake
her father's intayle, made by the whole consent of the realme,
which neyther she nor the realme can justlye alter. Nevertheles they can be contented to flatter with your Lordshippes, untyll he be proved and allowed ; and yf they once
receave comforte in that, to brybe you frelye, tyll the
same be delyvered, but afterwarde they must begyne to govern and bear rule : for which government, I woulde to

God ye'knew their counsaylles, or ells that ye would cre-
dytt me in that I have harde and sene.

I have sene other lettres touching my Lord Pagette, that
he shoulde be the Frenche Kinges feode man, and the Lorde
Tresorer the Kinges utter enemye. But in these are dyvers
other thinges contayned, as, the Lord Talbot is not their
frend, the Lord Clynton they love not, nor dare not trust
him. Therfor, thinke they, that yf theise and certayne
other lordes of the northe wer made awaye, they shoulde
obtayne their purpose the better. Your Honnors maye consyder, that this reporte of the Lorde Pagett is invented
trayterously to make him awaye with the reste; for theise
fowr, yf ever the Kinge bare rule, shall and are taken for his
enemyes. They wryte also, that ther be dyverse other men
in Ingland, whose stoutnes must be plucked lowe, and powr
abated. I declare nothinge to bringe these noblemen into
suspition, but to showe what wayes they invente to make
dissension amonge them, that they myght be called to make
agrement for their purpose, as appeareth by theyr lettres;
that yf the one parte of the nobylytie woulde withstand the
other, they shoulde be receaved upon one parte, thoughe
they cannot prevayl afore that tyme. But read further,
and you shall fynd they thinke your Lordships, the Lord Ad-
myrall, Oxforth, Arundell, Penbroke, and dyvers others, to
132 be their frends. Wherfor their purpose is, yf ever they
bare rule, to joyne with you in counsayll for a time, and
the state of the realme once knowne, immedyatlye to lett
you dye pleasauntlye, with hanging, racking, heading, and
whirling upon wheles, justlye according to your deserts.
Let me confesse the truthe; for doutles I never sawe anye
suche deathes named in their lettres, but onlye, *they shoulde
be used according to their lawe*, which all men know ys not
to burye anye offenders, but to use them as I have toulde
you. For their reason is this, they maye not trust them
longe in their counsaylles, nor kepe them in auctorytie,
which wyll be traytours to their natyve countrye. Undoubtedlye, saye they, that nation that wyll worke treason
agaynest their owne naturall kinge and countrey, they wyll

surelye, as soone as they begyn to smarte or be great, worke myschiefe agaynest us and our Kinge.

Well, these thinges must be provided for in tyme: but I assure ye most trulye, I wryte not of suspicion or rashe judgment, but those thinges which I have sene with myne owne eyes, and be most surelye pretended, and wyll undoubtedlye be wrought, yf you take not the better counsayll to withstand them: marke well, yf these be well gotten goods, that shall be the destruction of you and your country for ever. Thus have I found in their letters, and doubtles the Kinges counsayll have pretended mor wayghtie matters towards you, in devising howe theise matters maye be brought to passe. I speake nothinge but that I knowe parfectlye: you maye take my wordes as yt shall please your Honors. If you worke prudentlye, as you can, yf yt please you, I shall rejoyce at your preservations: yf you wyll wyllingly gyve yourselves over unto such bondage, who wyll lament your myserable myschieffes that shall fall upon you?

Hark ther wordes after wrytinges: they purpose, yf ever their wyll serve them, not to have one lyving that hath byn born these xx years; but either to dryve them into forren realmes, or ells to make them slaves lyke the Mores, or ells to destroy them at home. For we wer borne out of the fayth, and so, saye they, we shall dye; and specyallye all those, which by anye meanes maye lay any clame to the crowne. I call God to record, I have hard yt wyth myn eares, and sene the sayd parsons with myn eyes, that have sayd, yf ever the Kinge obtayne the crowne, he woulde make the Ladye Elizabeth safe for ever coming to inheryt the same, or anye of our cursed natyon. For they say, that yf they can fynd the meanes to kepe Ingland in subjection, they wolde do mor with the land, than with all the rest of his kingdomes. I speak not of anye fooles communycation, but of the wysest, and that no meane parsons. Yea, and they trust that ther shalbe meanes found, befor that tyme, to dispatche the Lady Elizabeth well enoughe, by the helpe of assured traytors, as they have allreadye in England plenty. And then they maye the more easier destroy the other, when she is rydd oute of the waye. I speake not

this as some men woulde take yt, to move dissension; for
that were the best way for the Spaniards to come to ther
prey. Suche a tyme they look for; and suche a tyme,
133 they saye, some nobleman hath promysed to provyde for
them. I know not their names; but let every man therfore be trew to the realm; and endevor themselves to lyve
and love one another charitablye and quyetlye; that ye go
all one waye, and so withstand all these thretened coun-
saylls.

God is my wytnes, that my harte wyll not suffer me for
verye shame to declare suche vyle reportes, as I have hard
them speake agaynst the Quene. And yet her Grace taketh
them for her faythfull frends; but this truthe maye I shewe
you convenyentlye, to edify all men to consider therfor their
most trew wordes. The Spanyards saye, that yf they obtayne not the crowne, they maye curse the tyme that ever
the Kinge was maryed to a wyfe so unmeet for him by natural course of yeares. But and yf that maye be brought
to passe that was ment in mariage-making, they shall kepe
olde ryche robes for highe festival dayes: therfore yf the
Quene wyll have anye favorable frendshyp of the Kinge,
let her kepe her as ryche, and as highe in auctorytie, as her
Grace is at this present, or ells her Grace shall well prove
and parceave, that Spanyards naturallye love younge and
freshe wares, and chaunge of old things. Besides this, howe
shamfull the Courte shalbe kept, more lyke an hosterye or
tavarn, than a nobleman's house, let them reporte, that
have byne at Bryssells, in the Kinges Courte, and in
th'Emproures Courte also; wherin is to be solde both
wyne and beare out of th'Emproures seller, as commonlye
as out of anye tavarne in the cyttye. Yea, and the best of
your lordships, that shall never be trusted to tarye at home,
but commaunded to tarye upon the Kinge in straunge countryes; wher leaving your plentouse provision, ye shall be
glad to lye in a vyttelling house, wher ye shall thinke ye
fare well, yf ye have halfe a leane rosted capon to dynner,
and as much to supper, with a good pynt of thyn wyne or
water; or ells halfe a loyn of lean mutton; a pygges pet-
tytoe, with halfe a dossen of grene salletts, as the best of

the Kinges Counsayll dothe lyve contynuallye: then wyll
ye saye, Wolde to God we had kept the crowne for the right
and lawful heirs, and byn true to our owne countrye, that
we and our successors myght have lyved mor honourably
and quyetlye than anye natyon of the wholl worlde. The
Spanyards saye, our nobylytie and counsayll hath neyther
learnyng, wytt, nor experyence. Therfor they doubt not,
though not speadely, yet in prosses of tyme, to have the
upper hand with learning, wisdom, and crafte, and experyence, and policye.

Alas! for pyttie! ye be yet in such good estate, God be
thanked, that ye maye, without losse of anye manes lyfe,
kepe the crowne and realme quyetlye: but yf you delyver
them up willinglye, wher ye ought rather wyllinglye to adventure lands, lyfe, and goods, with honour and all, for the
preservation of your countrey, ye shall not onlye lose lyf,
lands, goods, wyfe, and children, but also all honour, with
the most myghtie kingdoms on the earth, with the losse of
innumerable of your countryemens lyves, and with the pur-
chasing of yourselves perpetuall shame. For what nation 134
on the earth is able to suffer the pryde and crueltye of the
Spanyards? They can suffer no man to be fellowe with
them, much les to bear rule above themselves. Doubt not,
but they are the proudest men upon the earth. Yf they
maye once obtayne ther purpose, they wyll tread your heads
in the duste. You woulde be glad yf you myght dwell at
home, without bearing rule in anye matters of the commonwelthe: but they wyll not suffer you to lyve at home in
your countries: no, no, for whye, they knowe parfectlye,
that you wyll have the countries on your parte, to make insurrections to deceave them, and to dryve them oute. They
wyll provide for that matter, and put you to death lovinglye, before you make malyce in the countrye: so that they
maye gather up agayne ther great gyftes upon your treasures, and mayntayne ther gorgious garments with ther
false bryberye, and ther fine Spanyshe genets with the oppression of the pore people. Ye shall prove their lustie ly-
veryes to be bought with excedinge great excesse. Can
Inglyshemen pacyentlye abyde to paye for every chimney,

and every other place to make fyer in, as in ovens, fur-
nesses, and smythes forges, a Frenche crown a year? I
wyll not speake of their other crueltyes, and intollerable
vexations, and polling-pence, for all maner of grene corne,
bread, beafe, mutton, and capon, pygge, goose, and henn,
mallard, chicken, mylck, butter, egges, chese, appells, pares,
nuttes, bear, and wyne.

And paradventure some man wyll thinke, that they do
not use to oppresse the poore commoners; but I assure ye,
ther is no yeomen, farmar, nor husbandman, in theise parties,
that eate a capon in his house, yf his frends come to vysit
him, but yt must coste him a noble, yf the capon be not
worth xx*d*. and even so of all other poulterye, and all other
thinges. When ye are once trodden down under foot, every
knave shall come to your house, and take the best parte,
and leave the worste: you must let your servant serve him
in all pointes; you must cappe to him in all places wher
you see him, or ells you shalbe counted a rude rustical
knave; you must gyve place to speake at his pleasur, and
ye must holde your peace; you must gyve him the best
beddes, and take the worste pacyentlye for yourselfe. He
must have the best dyshe at your table, and syt in the
hyghest place. Breflye, you must prefer him in all thinges,
and in all maner of honour, because the worst of them is
seignior. The worste of them shalbe better estemed with
the King and his counsayll, than the best of our realme.
Yf he be appointed in your house, either by the Kinge or
his counsayll, or receaved in for his money, the house must
be at his commandment, and not at yours; and yet wyll
he departe without taking his leave at all, or paying for his
lodging. Yf anye man wyll saye, that theye paye for their
lodging in Ingland honestlye, I speake not now of that
which they have done in Ingland, but of that which I have
sene done here in theise countries, which undoubtedly they
wyll also use among us in Ingland, when they beare once
rule. And ther are some that payed not verye honestlye
135 for all thinges they had, when they wer amongest you; for
I myselfe knowe dyvers worshipfull men, that lodged Spanyards in their houses a year and a halfe together, and let

them have a dosen beddes, and most part of their fuel, and all other thinges; and yet, at their departing out of Ingland heither into Flaunders, they wolde make no recompence, neyther for manye thinges that were stoln at the same tyme; nor for manye things that wer broken and rent; nor for manye thinges, that wer so baudye with theyr pockeye plasteres and sores, that never man coulde lye in them afterwardes; nor yet woulde take their leave of their hoste; nor gyve onye dodkyn in the house to anye parson that had served them, and had byne at their commandement; nor paye for anye other thinges, as vyctualls receaved of the poore people, as of the bakers, bouchers, and bruars, and suche others. Yf they went away so stoutlye and so churlyshlye in those dayes, when they went about to countarfayte all goodnes and jentylnes, when they loked to obtayne the crowne and governaunce by their jentill behavor and good conditions, what wyll they do, think you, when they have the crowne indede.

I here saye ther are certayne bookes amongest you, which I never sawe, as, *The Lamentation of Napelles,* and, *The Mourning of Mylayne,* with dyvers others, which shew the tiranny which the Spanyards have and use in other places or countries: and in that poynte, I woulde counsayll you to consider those books well, and to take good hede that ye com not into the lyke bondage; for yf ye do, loke, as they have destroyed the nobylytie in other countryes, even so wyll they murder you pryvily one after another, so sone as they beare rule among you; and with the same bringe in excises upon cytie and vyllage.

But paradventure you thinke to provyde once for all suche myscheves: yf ye wyll heare a foolles counsayll, the best and surest provision that ye can make, is to kepe styll the crowne to the right succession in your handes, and gyve yt to no forren prynces: for when the King is crowned, who can or dare saye agaynst him, or withstand his doinges? Do not the lawes of the realme bynd all men to obey him, and seing they of his counsayll understand not our laws, thinke ye then that they wyll not chaunge them? Ye saye, the Quene hath the power in her handes, we must obey her. That is true, in all suche lawes as be alreadye made and passed by Parlement. But whether ye maye laufullye consent, [contrary] to the discretion of the whole realme and natyon of Ingleshemen, [to the giving away] of the crowne, and dysannull the auctoritye that was gyven by Parlement, I leave yt to your consciences. Yf the crowne wer the Quene's, in suche sorte as she myghte do with it what she woulde, bothe nowe and after her death, there myght appear some rightfull pretence in geving yt over to a straunger prince: but seing yt belongeth to the heirs of Ingland after her death, ye comytt deadly synne and dampnation, in unjustlye gevyng and taking awaye of the righte of others. Remember what a myserable estate and end 136 Achab had, for unjustlye desiringe of Nabothe's vynyard. I think you can never forgette the unjust enterpryse of the late Duke of Northumberland, and what myserable successe yt had. Be ye therfor wyse, and beware by other mens harmes; for ye maye perseave evidentlye, that God wyll take vengeance upon wrongfull dooers: otherwyse, the Quenes Majestie that now is, had not bene Quene of Ingland at this present.

But paradventure her Grace thinketh the Kinge wyll kepe her the mor companye, and love her the better, yf she gyve him the crowne; ye wyll crown him to make him lyve chaste, contrarye to his nature: for paradventure, after he wer crowned, he woulde be content with one woman, but in the mean space he muste have iij or iiij in one nyght, to prove which of them he lyketh best; not of ladyes and jentyllwomen, but of bakers doughters, and suche poore whores: wherupon they have a certayne saying, *The baker's doughter is better in her goune, than Quene Mary weythout the crowne.* Yt greveth my harte to heare suche reporte, suche unlyke similytudes. For they saye, olde wyves must be cheryshed for their young ryche gyftes. Olde wyves, saye they, for fayre wordes, wyll gyve all that they have: but howe be they used afterwardes? Yf the King do so lyttell esteme the Quene, when by her Highnes

he seketh to obtayne the crowne, after what sorte wyll he
use himselfe when he hath obtayned his purpose? Doth
the Quene thinke that he wyll remayne in Ingland, with
geving him the realme? The counsayll of Spayne purposeth to establyshe other matters, and to appoynt in Ingland a Vyce-roy, with a great armye of Spanyshe soul-
dyours, to kepe you in subjection, and let the Quene lyve
at her beades, lyke a good auncyent ladye. As for the
Kinge, he can better awaye with Antwerpe and other
places, wher he may go a mummyng and masking, yea,
even in the holy tyme of Lent, nyght after nyght. I wyll
tell you a trew tale, wherin the Spanyards do glorye: Ther
wer certayne marchants in Antwarpe, whiche had fayre
wyves, whome the Kinge coulde not have at his pleasure;
but hearing by chance that some of them wer with another
wyfe being in labour, the Kinge with certayne other went
thither in womanes apparrell: and the Kinge, as the Spanyards reporte for a great honour, held the childwyfes
backe, while she had brought forth the chylde, and was her
mydwyfe. But what was wrought afterwardes, let other
men judge: for doubtless I woulde not have wrytten this,
had not the good Bushoppe of Castyle byn checked in his
sermon: for he desyred the Kinge to kepe himselfe for his
owne wyfe, and wylled him to leave this lothsome lechery,
or woulde the Spanyards once be ashamed to boste of suche
shamfull deeds.

But yf I shoulde wryte all that I have harde them most
shamfullye reporte and boste, I know that many ladyes in
Ingland woulde be sore ashamed. I woulde to God the
honorable ladyes knew the vylenes that the Spanyards have
reported by them, and I thinke the good ladyes would not
love to kysse so pleasauntlye and so manye tymes with
straungers: they would rather cut ther owne throtes, or
kyll themselves as Lucretia dyd, than to use famylyarytie 137
with suche a vyle nation. Among other reportes, they saye,
they can have the best man's wyfe in Ingland for a small
porcyon of golde, or a juell: which reporte is spread so
farre, that the younge girles of Spayne (God is my judge

I lye not) do wryte to perryshe boyes, that ther princoxes be so famylyarlye receaved in (I wyll not wryte the worst) with the ladyes of Ingland, that they have no mynd of Spanyshe wenches. And of London they reporte, that for all their waches, ther hath byn mo moungrelles borne these ij years than right Inglyshemen. Oh abhomynable natyon! What woulde the vyllanes reporte, yf they myght have had suche lybertye as they most shamfully boste of? Yea, what wyll they do, yf they maye obtayne that which they loke for? I woulde to God ye knew how manye mens wyves and doughters in Flaunders lye at surgerye, and howe manye younge wenches, infected with stinking whordom of Spanyards, lye in the stretes uncurable of the poxe. I woulde wryte mor thinges that appartayne to their naughtie nature; how swynishlye they sytt at the table, and howe vylye they use themselves in their chambers: but bycause manye Inglyshemen knowe these thinges parfectlye, I wyll let yt passe, and make an end.

I have declared now to your Lordshippes some of the Spanyards policyes and purposes, which I have parfectlye sene and redd in their lettres with myn owne eyes, and parfectlye harde with myn eares, to be invented agaynst the Quenes Hyghnes, your honours, and the whole realme. I have also brefly shewed you some part of their naughtie condytions; as for their arrogant pryde, tyrannous policye, and beastly lecherye; which I have not learned by hearsaye, but by daylye experyence and conversation with them. Nowe judge you, whether yt be anye poynte of wysdome to put your honorable nobless under the heavye and grevouse yoke of suche a cruell and proud natyon, to be mocked, robbed, and dysheryted, tormented, and murdered, a thousand tymes: wherfor I beseche God to open your Lordships eyes, that you maye see; and to comfort and strengthen your hartes, that you maye do suche thinges as maye redound unto Godes immortal glorye, the saftie of your Highnes, landes, goodes, and honour, and of your wyves and children, and of your whole realme. *Amen*.

By your Lordships servaunt,
John Bradforde.

Number XLVI. 138

Adversaris principal against Farrar, bisshope of Saint Davides, vidz.

i. *Thomas Yonge, chaunter of the cathedrall churche of St. Davides.*

ii. *Rolande Merick, doctor of lawe, and canon resident of the same church.*

iii. *George Constantayne, to whome the Busshope gave the office of registership.*

ITEM, the Busshopes aunswer unto the first, second, third, fowerth, and xxxvjth articles, doth declare theffect of the contravarsie betwene him and his said adversaris. **I.** Foxii M

Item, The said George Constantyne being joyned in fryndship with his sonne in lawe Thomas Yonge aforesaide, and they both confederated with the saide Roland Merick, with divers other their adherentes, wer the original begynners of all this truble and contention betwene the said Bisshope and theym ; only throughe their awne wicked and most covetous behaivor, in spoyling the cathedral churche of plate, juells, and other ornaments, to a notable valor; converting it unto their awne usis, agaynst the Kinges right, and to thutter decaye of the same churche: also for omitting the Kinges Majesties injunctions, and commytting simony and bribrie, as is declared in th'exceptions agaynst the said Yong and Constantyne: and furdremore, for their abhomination in manifest bearing with most wicked and vile lyvers, as is declared in the Bishopes awnswer to the xijth article. For with their ill demerites, and willfull persisting therin, and their most stubburne disobeydyence agaynst the said Bisshope, (who first with gentlenesse sought their reformation, wherunto they in nowise woulde enclyne; and thinking then to fear theym with the lawe, as the father dothe fear the children with shaking the rod, to make theym obedient; throughe which attempt they became worse, and so) he at last put theym out of office. Sithens which tyme, they have bestowed all their wit and **II.**

cunnyng without ceasing, to invent mischieff agaynst the said Busshope, seking by all unjust meanes his utter undoing, and finally his death, as maye appeare by their proceadinges.

III.   *Item*, The saide Thomas Yonge, Roland Merick, and George Constantyne, to prevent the saide Busshope, who had (as they knowe right well) just and heynouse matter agaynst theym, did most maliciouslye conceyve, divise, and procure, aswell the pretensed matter of *premunire*, promoted by Roger Barloo, as also the false surmised articles promoted by Hughe Raulins, priest, and Thomas Lee, unto the Kinges highe Counsell: mynding therbye utterly to discredit and bring undre fote the said Busshope, to th'end that he shoulde not be able to prosecute any matter against theym, wherby their wicked doinges might be opened.

139

IV.   *Item*, They are the maynteyners and bearers of the chargis of Thomas Lee, brother in lawe to George Constantyne, uncle to the wiff of the saide Thomas Yonge, and promoter of the said articles by them divised, and came in for wittnisses unto their owne conceytes.

V.   *Item*, Furdremore they obtayned a commission into the countre, for better proff of the said articles. By virtue of which commission, and also by couller therof, they examined six score and vii wittnessis; and that very parcially and unlaufully, as apearith in the general exceptions herafter ensuing: which great nombre of witnesses did sound much in the counsells eares. Neverthelesse it is proveable, that th'one halff at the least of the said nombre are defamed persons, and manye of them have bene ponished for their demerites, by the said Busshope and his officers. And therfore were the redier to witnes against him; as adulterers, fornicators, baudes, drunkardes, brawlers, feyghters, theaves, runagates, and beggers. And the more part of the said witnessis are eyther kinsmen, familiar frindes, fermers of benefices, servantes, or by some other meanes adherentes unto the said advarsaris. And as for th'onest gentlemen, and other, which have deposed upon the said articles, they have said nothing that can hurt the said busshope, as it is thought by such as have sene the depositions.

Other capital enemies unto the said Bisshope of St. Davides, *vidz.*

Roger Barloo, brother to the Bishope of Bathe; Griffith Donne, gent. toun clerk of Carmarthen; Thomas John Thomas ap Harrye, gent. John Evans, clerk, the said Bisshopes chaplen.

Item, The said Roger Barloo is an utter enimie, and a VI. partie, and neverthelesse a witnesse agaynst the Bisshope; who woulde have had by lawe into his awne handes, as his due right, the parsonage of Browdie, and lordship of Ponchcastell, which the said Barlo holdith from him by a forged lease. And the said Roger Barlo, beinge very rich in monye, goodes, and landes, and also (knewe that the saide Bisshope had manifestly proved one lease, in thandes of Philipe Pyrrye, prest, upon parcel of the demaynes of the Bisshopes house at St. Davides, which lease was signed and sealed at Wels, by Bisshope Barlo, after he was transposed and clearly discharged out of the bisshoprick of St. David's) fearinge lest the Bisshop sholde prevaile agaynst his forged 140 lease to his shame, did of purpose (partly by the procurement of the forsaid principall adversaris) sue the said Bisshope in a pretensed matter of *premunire;* which yet dependith before the justice of assise in the shere of Carmarthen, to the great ympovrishment of the said Bisshope, bycause he shoulde not be able to wage the lawe agaynst him and other, for his awne right; as indede he is not, by reason of these and other great injuries done unto him; and therfore sustayneth intollerable wronges at divers handes.

Also the saide Roger Barloo holdith, by way of usury or VII. mortgage, a lordshype called Llandu, byside Brecknok, for one hundred pounde, which he lent unto his brother, now Bisshope of Bathe : which some, he saith, must be paide unto him in one whole some, by the Bisshope of St. David's that nowe is, or his successors. And untill such payment be made, the sayde -Roger Barlo and his assignes, to holde and enjoy the said lordshipe, with all and singular the rentes and profites therof, which is of yerely rent *communibus annis*, xx*l.* whereof the Bisshope hath not one peny, and yet payth tenth and subsidye for the same, with other lyke hindrances, by the saide Barlo, and other lyke unto him.

Griffith Donne, gent.

VIII.
Item, The saide Griffith Donne is an utter enemie unto the saide Bisshope, confederated with the principal adversaris aforesaide, and neverthelesse a witnesse agaynst him. For that the saide Griffith Donne, having to ferme th'archdeaconrie of St. David's, and was letted by the saide Bisshope from gathering of *procurations* bycause th'Archdeacon nor he dyd neither appoynt nor fynde anye sufficient officiall to visit the same according to the Kinges ecclesiastical lawes : by reason of which lett, the said Donne sustayned certayne damagis : supposing also, that the Bysshope did it for spite, and so conceyved an hatrede agaynst him, in which he doth still remayne. Sithens that tyme, one of the Bisshopes servaunts toke two of the said Griffith Donne's servaunts, destroyng a fewe conies, which the Bisshope did entend to have cherisshed for provision of his house ; and by reason of wordes that happened betwene the Bisshopes servaunt and theym, the saide Donne encreased his malice, and hath shewed the same divers waies.

Thomas John Thomas ap Harry.

IX.
Item, The said Thomas John Thomas ap Harry is the Bisshopes utter enemie, and neverthelesse a witnes agaynst him : for that wheras one Owen Guyne, gent. obtayned the Kinges presentation to the personage of Penbeyer, and solde it (as it was playnly saide) unto the forsaide Thomas John, &c. who did compounde with a certayne unlerned prest to take the name of Person, with half the frutes, and himself th'other half : which packing the said Bisshope was crediblie informed of, and for that cause utterly refused t'admitt th'unlerned prest. Notwithstandinge th'ernest requestes of 141 dyvers gentlemen, aswel his fryndes as other, who were not a little greved with his naye ; considering that it laie in

theym to do hym evell or good in the countre. Wheruppon
the forsaide principall adversaries, as their comen maner is,
assone as they perceave that any man hath matter of contention, or by any means can pike a quarell agaynst the saide
Bisshope, they ar redy by and by, with all their counsell,
ayde, and policie, to tease, eg, and sett on, and with all
their poure and diligence to fordre and mayntayne the
same; seking by all injust and subtile meanes the said
Bisshopes utter discredit and undoing, and finally his death,
as appeared in the sessions holden at Carmarthen in July
last past: when they, throughe helpe of the forsaide Thomas
John Thomas ap Harry, (who is a gentleman of estemation
in that countre, having many kynsmen and fryndes,) did
privilie pack a quest of ignorant persons of no reputation,
and indicted the said Bisshope uppon the wordes of Raulins
information concerning Marlin, as apeareth by a coppie of
th'indictment, to make the matter seme more heynouse. For
they woulde have made it either treason or felonie, notwithstanding that the same matter is depending before the
Kinges highe Counsell undetermined.

Item, In the toune of Carmarthen, at the sermon wherin   x.
the said Bisshope (by occasion) spake of Marlin, ther was
at least iii C. people, wherof ther ar but ix that hath witnessed anything agaynst the Bisshope concernyng that article. And of those ix, ther ar but two agreing with Raulins information, as maye appeare by the boke of depositions. Of which two, th'one is the veriest drunkerd in the
toune, and also a whoremonger; th'other is a simple carpenter, that can speak no Englishe, but Welshe; neverthelesse uppon that sklendre evidence, they indicted the saide
Bisshope, as is aforesaid.

John Evans, clerk, the saide Bisshopes chaplen.

Item, The said advarsaries have perswadid the said John   xi.
Evans, not onlye to forsake, but also to commence matter
in the Chauncerie, against the said Bishope; alledging that
the said Bisshope made him a promise of a personage to
ferme: which the said Bisshope did not, nor of ryght
coulde not doo. And it is to be thought by the said Evans

craftye proceedinges, that he sekith not so much the attayn-
ment of his sute, (having alredy a compitent lyving,) as he
doth to vex and molest the said Bishope; the rather to
bringe him under fote, for contentation of th'adversaries,
whose ayde, counsell, and encoragement, the said Evans
hathe to the same purpose. Albeit the said Evans was the
man whome the said Bishope estemed and trusted above
other, and made him privie to all his doinges; neverthelesse
he was a secrete enemie unto the said Bisshope, and confederated with his said advarsaries: the which nowe he sheweth
openlye, like one that afore-tyme fayned holines.

XII.   *Item*, The said advarsaries use another kinde of police,
vidz. they have entysed certayne gentlemen of that countre,
142 not the symplest, to desire such thinges at the Bisshopes
handes, as they knewe before he woulde not graunt. To
th'entent, that those gentlemen being denied their requestes,
shoulde rather hate him than love him, or at the least not
regarde nor esteme him.

XIII.   And last of all, they have repelled his visitation of the
chapter. Albeit the more part wer content to receve the
said Bisshopes visitation; yet they, in the name of the
whole chapter have appealed unto th'Arches, (by Doctor
Leyson's bearing,) only to put the said Bishope to truble
and expences; mynding alwaies his undoing: to which purpose they do spend the goodes of the Churche, which they
have (agaynst the lawe and the Kinges ryght) converted to
the mayntenance of their wicked enterprises and wronge
doinges, aswell agaynst divers other men, with whome they
ar at variance, as with the said Bisshope. And they have
noyzed and bruted abrode most shamefull sklaunders, as is
written in the conclusion of their information; and also have
said, that they woulde pull him doune out of his bisshoprick. And it semeth verilye, by their behaviour in the same
cathedral church, and the decaye therof, that they woulde
rather pull downe the church and all, than to be obedyent
unto the Kinges auctoritie, to the said Bisshope committed.
Yt wer too too longe, yea, it is doubt, whether one man
might comprehend to write all that maye be trulye verified

of their wicked lyves, and viperouse behaviour toward the said Bishope. Notwithstanding their stubberne disobedience, he was frindlye receaved in executing his office throughout the whole dioces.

Number XLVII.

143

Exceptions generall, leide and purposed on the behalf of Robert Bisshope of St. Davydes, agaynst all and singular the pretensed witnesses, producted on the behalf of Hughe Raulins, clerk, and Thomas Lee; uppon their untrue surmised articles, by theym exhibited to and before the Kinges most honourable Counsell; by the divise and procurement of Thomas Yong, clerk, and his father in lawe George Constantyne, and Roland Merik, clerk, agaynst the saide Bisshope.

FURST, The said Bisshope saith and allegethe, that by lawe ther ought no fayth or credence be geven or hadd unto the depositions and sayinges of the saide witnessis, or any part therof: bycause they are infamouse, false, perjured, and in some part of their depositions discording, partiall, conducted, subornate, instructed; and for favour of th'informers, and their boulsterers, have deposed of malice, more than th'articles wheruppon they wer producted dothe conteyne, and beside and without the compasse of the same articles. And in divers other partes of their depositions, they depose *unum et eundem præmeditatum sermonem :* as by their said depositions doth appeare. To the which the said Bisshope referrethe himself as much as it shalbe expedient for him, and none otherwise. And furdre, for other causes articularly and specially, as is declared in the boke of exceptions.

Exceptions agaynst th'unlawfull proceedinges of Hughe Raulins, clerk, and Thomas Lee, promoters of th'untrue articles, in executing their commission for proff of the same surmised articles.

Item, The said Thomas Lee, for himself and th'other promotor, did, contrary to justice, at th'execution of their

I.

Foxii M

II.

commission, examyne certeyne of the witnessis himself, in the house of his brother in lawe George Constantyne, and 144 he and Davide Walter, the Bisshopes enemie, and servaunt to George Constantyne, did write their depositions uppon th'articles at their awne pleasure; and also at the divise of the said George Constantyne, and his son in lawe Thomas Yonge and Rolande Merick, the Bisshopes mortal enemies, and the vere divisors and procurers of th'informations, and the bolsterors and bearors of the promoters in the sute there-of. These are the names of the witneses so examined, which are alredie knowne : David ap Richard of Bettus, a perjured and an adulterouse person, standing in two places of the boke, and so in the nombre for two wittnessis ; Jem. ap Ruddz of Kynnarth ; Griffith ap Howell Guyn of Kyn-narth ; Leowes David, clerk; David ap Harvie, clerke ; Sir Harrie Goughe, alias Morgan, &c.

III.   *Item*, One John Draper of Carmarthen, an adherent of the forsaid principal adversaris, and an enemie to the said Bisshope, did also, contrarie to the tenor of their comission, examyne certeyne witnessis ; and had to his clerk, one William Davides, servaunt in lyverey to the forsaid Gryffith Donne, the Bisshopes enemie : by which shamefull partialitie they have written more matter, mo wordes, other terms and sentences, than some of the witnessis have said and deposed, or could say or depose : namelye, Humphrey Toye the 5th deponent, Rice Goughe the 14th deponent, William ap Evan the 50th deponent, John Benguyn the 68th deponent, Richard Person, the 89th deponent, which are alredy knowen.

IV.   *Item*, The said Hughe Raulins was not present at the Bisshopes sermon, of which his information maketh mention, neyther yet at th'executing of the commission for proff therof. For the forsaid adversaris divised the same, and gave it unto the said Raulins to promote ; choseing him for the same purpose, knowing him to be a man willing, and setting his whole delyte to work mischieff, both with worde and dede. Who abuseth his tonge most wickedly, ever rayling uppon the said Bisshope, to every man that will hear him, with most unsemely wordes, without eyther respect or reverence of the Kinges Majesties aucthoritie to the said Bisshope committed. And the said Raulins hath iiij or v benefices above the value of two hundred markes a yere, and is resident uppon none of theym, but spendith his lyving, to the hindrance of other men; going about here and there, wandring to and fro, without eyther man or boye waytting on him, more lyke a light person than a man of his vocation, being a preacher: and indede he is taken for a lewed fellow of all that knowe his behaviour, in so much that when a certeyn man objected unto th'adversaris, that it was ill done to put so lewd a fellow as Raulins to promote their cause, they answered and reported his honestie in these wordes, " We knowe Raulins to be a very knave, and " so mete for no purpose, as he is to set forwarde such a " matter ;" of which report ther is sufficient witnes. And indede it is thought that he hath done muche ill with his spiteful tongue; for he speaketh as boldly in this cause to all the Counsell, as thoughe the matter were true, and muche 145 for the Kinges proffit.

Item, Th'other promotor, Thomas Lee, was a marchaunt, v. who hath solde all his ware, and spent the monye, and now, for want of other busines, is become a promotor of the forsayd articles, and hath his costes and chargis borne by the forsaid principall advarsaris, as it is alleged in th'exceptions, which shalbe proved, yf a commission might be warded to that purpose.

Number XLVIII.

JHS is God with us.

An apology of Jhon Philpot; written for spittyng on an Arian: with an invective against the Arians, the veri naturall children of Antichrist: with an admonition to all that be faithfull in Christ, to beware of them, and of other late sprung heresies, as of the most enemies of the gospell.

I AM amased, and do tremble both in body and sowle, Foxii M

to heare at this day certen men, or rather not men, but covered with man's shape, parsons of a bestly understandyng, who, after so many and manifold benefyts and graces of oure Lorde God and Saviour Jesus Christ, manifested to the whole world, and confirmed with so evident testimonis of the patriarches, prophets, and apostles, approved by wonderous signes and undoubted tokens, declared to be both God and man by the spirit of sanctification, the eternal Son of God with power, the very expres ymage of the substance of the Father, and reveled unto us in thes later tymes in the flesh, born of the sede of David. In the which he hath taught us all trewth, and marvelously. finished the mystery of owr salvation, and is ascended in body into heaven; from whens his divinitie abased hymself for owr glory, and sittith with equal power at the right hand of the Father in his everlasting kyngedom: notwithstandyng are not ashamed to robbe this eternal Son of God, and owr most marciful Saviour, of his infinite Majesty, and to pluck hym owt of the glorious throne of his unspeakable Deity. O impiety, of all others most detestable! O infidelity, more terrible than the palpable darknes of Egipt! O flaming fyerbronnes of hell, as I may use the wordes of the prophet Essay against such apostates. *Was it not ynough for you to be grevous unto men,* by so manifold hereses, divydyng yourselffes from Christ's trew Catholyk Church, [no like] therto hath ben harde by any heretical segregation, but [have offered such contempt] unto my God, the eternal Son of God? What harte may bare such blasphemy? What eye may quietly behold such an enemy of God? What membre of Christ may allowe yn any wyse such a membre of the Divel? What Christian may have felloship with such rank Antichrists? Who, havynge the zeale of the glory of God in his harte, cannot burst owt in teares and lamentations, to heare the immortal glory of the Son of God trod under the fete, by the vile sede of the serpent? whose head, by his eternal Godhead, he hath beaten downe; and therfor now lyeth byting at his hele, lurkyng in corners. But he shall be crushed in peces unto eternal wo, after he hath

Marginal notes:

Rom. i.

Heb. i.

The Arrians deny Christ to be the eternal Son of God, and of his substance.

146

Esa. vii.

Arians have many heresies.

Gen. iii.

spewed owt al his venym; for brighter is the glory of
owre God and Christ, than it may be darkned by all the
route of the prince of darknes: who dwellith yn the light
which is unapprochable, although thes ded doggs do take
upon them with their corrupt sight to perce and blemishe
the same, to their owne blynding forever. If the good ^{Esa. xxxvii.}
Kynge Esechias, after he had heard the blasphemis that
Rabsacie uttered against the lyvyng Lord, tore his royal
garments in pecis, in testimony of the great sorrow he
had conceved for the same; shall we be still at the blasphemous barkyngs against owre Lord, and show no token
of indignation for the zeale of his glory? If Paul and Bar- ^{Acts xiv.}
nabas perceving the people at Lystris to take the honour of
God, and attributyng the same to creatures, rent their garments, yn signification that we all shold declare by sum
owtward means the lyke sorrow, when he heare or see the
lyke blasphemies; how may we with patience abide to heare
the robbery of the majesty of owre Christ's equality with
God, who, as S. Paul witnesseth, *thought it no robbery* to ^{Philipp. ii.}
be equal with God? What faithful servant can be content to
heare his master blasphemed? And if perchance he show
any just anger therfore, all honest men do beare with his
doyng in that behalf: and cannot you, Christian bretherne ^{The cause}
and sisterne, beare with me, who, for the just zeale of the ^{why he did spyt.}
glory of my God and Christ, beyng blasphemed by an arro-
gant, ignorant, and obstinately blinded Arian, making
hymself equal with Christ, saying, that God was none otherwyse in Christ than God was in hym; makyng hym but a
creature, as he was hymself, [pretending] you to be without synne as well as Christ; did spyt on hym? Partly as a
declaration of that sorrow which I had to heare such a ^{We ought}
prowd blasphemer of our Saviour, as also to signify unto ^{not to be at peace with}
other there present, whom he went about to pervert, that he ^{such as be}
was a parson to be abhorred of all Christians, and not to be ^{not of the treuth.}
companied withal.

If this my fact seme to them that judge not all thyngs ¹⁴⁷
according to the Spirit of God, uncharitable, yet let them
know, that God, who is charity, allowith the same: for it is

written yn the gospell, that Christ came not to set us at
peace with men in the earth, but at division; and that is
for his cause and trewth. And whosoever will not abide
with Christ's Churche in the trewth, we ought not to show
the poyntes of charity unto any such, but to take hym as a
heathen and a publican. *If any man,* saith S. Jhon, *bringe
not unto you this doctryne which I have taught ye, sai not
God sped unto hym; for whoso saith God sped unto such a
one is partaker of his evill doyngs.* Consider you, therfor,
that have love and feloship with such, that the same damnation shall fall upon you therfor, as is due to wicked heretycks. God will have us to put a differens betwixt the
cleane and uncleane, and to tuche no uncleane parsons, but
to go owt from them; and what is more uncleane than infidelitie? Who is a greater infidel than the Arian; who
spoilith his Redemer of his honour, and makith hym but a
creature? What felloship is there betwixt light and darknes? and what concord can there be betwyne Christ and
Belial? Never was there more abhominable Belials than thes
Arians be. The ignorant Belials worship the creatures for
the Creator: but thes perverse Arrians do worship Christ
(who is the Creatour of al thyngs; by whom, as S. Paul
testifieth, both yn heaven and yn earth, al thyngs, visible
and invisible, were made: who is God blessed forever:
and, as S. Jhon witnesseth, very God, and life everlasting)
but as a creature lyke unto themselfs. What Christian
tongue may call hym to be a good man, that denieth Christ
to be the auctour and worker of all goodnes, as the Arrian
doeth? Wo be unto them, saith the prophet, that call evill
good, and good evill. Judge therfor uprightly, ye children
of men, and condemn not the just for the unrighteous sake;
neither by any means seme to allow either in word or dede,
the wicked, who say, there is no God: for they that honour
not the Sonne, honour not the Father: for Christ affirmith,
that all men must aswell honour the Sonne as the Father.
And he that hath not the Son, hath not the Father. And
if we beleve yn God, we must also beleve yn Christ: for
the Father and he be one: and none in the Spirit of God

Marginal notes (left column):

Luke xii.
Matt. xii.
Matt. xviii.
2 Jhon.
2 Cor. vi.
Coloss. i.
Rom. ix.
Jhon v.
The Arrians deny Christ to be the auctour of al goodnes.
Jhon v.
Jhon xiv.
Jhon x.
1 Cor. xii.

can divide Christ from the substance of God the Father, unles a natural son may be of another substance than his father, which nature doth abhorre. Who can abyde the eternal generation of the Son of God to be denied, synce it is written of hym, *His generation who shall be hable to de-* Esa. liii. *clare?* Is there any trew Christian harte that grudgith not at such faithles blasphemours? Can the eye, eare, tongue, or the other senses of the body, be content to heare their Creatour blasphemed, and not repyne? Should not the mouth declare the zele for his Maker, by spyttings on hym that depravith his divine Majesty, which was, is, and shalbe God forever? If God, as it is mentioned in the Apocalypse, Apoc. iii. will spew hypocrites owt of his mouth, such as be nether hot nor cold in his worde; why may not then a man of God spyt on hym that is worse than an hypocrite, enemy to the **148** Godhed manifested in the blessed Trinity, who will in no wyse be perswaded to the contrary? If Christ with a whippe Jhon ii. dryved owt of the temple such as were prophaners thereof, ought not the servant of God, by som lyk owtward significa- tion, to reprove the vilany of those as go abowt to take away the glory of hym that was the builder of the temple? If there were as much zele yn men of the trewth, as there is talkative knowlege, they wold never be offended with that which is don in the reproche and condemnation of froward ungodly men, whom nothyng can please but singularities and divisions from the Church of Christ, which ought to be Gal. iv. the mother and mistris of us, and lead us into all trew The trew knowlege of the word of God, and not yn . . by . . ig- ought to be norance taking the word of God, daily another gospel, and owre mo- another Christ, as every sect doth set furth, separating mistres. themselfs from Christ's spouse, which the same, that is the complishment of trewth, never knew. O insatiable curiosity! Eph. i. O arrogant self love, the original of all thes heresies! O pestilent canker of thyne own salvation! O Arrian, the right Esa. xiv. inheritour to Lucifer, that wold exalt his seat, and be lyke to the hyghest! Whose fall shalbe lyke, where the synne is equal.

If God did highly allow the minister of Ephesus, for that Apoc. ii.

he could yn no wyse abyde such as said, they were apostles, and were not yn dede, how may any lay uncharitablenes unto me, who, for the love of my swete Christ, do abhorre all fantasticall Arrians, yn such sort as all men ought to do, that love the Son of God unfaynedly. If Moises be commended by the Scripture for strikyng an Egyptian, that did injury to one of the people of God; how may he justly be blamed, which did but spyt at hym, that doeth such injury and sacrilege to the Son of God, as to pluck him from his eternal and proper Godhede? Was there ever creature so unkynd? Was there ever man so temerarious, as to stryve against the glory of his glorifier? Was there ever heretyk so bold and impudent as the Arrian is, that durst take from the Son of God that glory which he had with the Father from the begynning? If Christ be the begynning and ending of all things, as he testifieth of hymself to S. Jhon; how may he be but a creature lyke unto others? Who may dissemble such blasphemy, that hath any sparkle of the Spirit of God? Who may heare with patience the right ways of the Lord perverted by thes divelish holly Arians, and hold his peace? A lyvely faith is not dumb, but is alwais redy to resist the gainsaiers, as David saith, *I have beleved, and therefor I have spoken.* Speak then, you that have tongues to praise and confesse God against thes Arrians: exalt your voice lyke a trompet; that simple people may beware of their pharisaical vermyn, and be not deceived, as now many are unawares, of simplicitie: suffer them not to passe by you unpoynted at; yea, if they be so stowte, that they will not cease to speak against God owr Saviour, and Christ, as they are all new baptized enemies thereto, refrayne not to spyt at such inordinate swyne, as are not ashamed to tred under their feet the precious godhed of owr Saviour Jesus Christ. Owr God is a jealous God, and requireth us to be zelous in his cause. If we cannot abyde owr owne name to be evil spoken, without great indignation; shall we be quiet to heare the name of owr God defaced, and not declare any sign of wrathe against them? It is written, *Be angry, and sinne not:* a man then may show tokens of anger, in a cause

Acts viii.

Jhon xvii.
Apoc. i.

A lyvely
faith is not
dumb.
Psalm cxv.

The Arrians
do baptise
themselfs a-
gayn, as
enemies to
the gospel.
149

Exod. xx.

Psalm iv.

which he ought to defend, without breach of charitye. The prophet David saith, *Shall I not hate them, O Lord, that* ^Ps. cxxxviii. *hate thee, and upon thyne enemies shall I not be wrathfull: I will hate them with a perfect hatred: they are become mayne enemies.* Aaron, because he was not more zelous in God's cause, when he perceived the people bent to idolatry, he entred not into the land of promise. God loveth not ^Apoc. iii. lukewarme soldiours in the batil of faith, but such as be ^Matt. xi. earnest and violent shall inherit his kyngdome.

Therfor S. Paul bideth us to be *fervent in spirit.* And ^Rom. xii. you that are so cold in thes days of the conflict of the gospell, ^We must be earnest aswel against thes arche-hereticks, as others, whereof there ^in God's cause. be at thes days storen up by the Divel an infinite swarme, to the overthrow of the gospell, if it were possible; I exhort you not to judge that evill, which God highly commendeth; but rather pray, that God wil give you the lyke zele to withstand the enemies of the gospell, nether to have any maner of felowship with thes Anticrists, whom the Divel hath shyten out in thes days, to defyle the gospell: which go about to teach you any other doctryne than you have receved in Kynge Edward's days, in the which, praised be ^In Kynge Edward's days we had God, all the syncerity of the gospell was reveled, accord- ^the synce- rity of the gospel. ynge to the pure use of the primitive Churche, and as it is at this present of the trew Catholyck Churche, allowed through the worlde.

The Sprit of God, the Holy Ghost, the third Parson in ^The Arrians mock the Trinitie, whom thes wicked Arrians do chide and mock, ^Holy Ghost, and hath taught the Church according to Christ's promise all ^deny hym to be God. trewth; and shall we now receve another vayne sprit, whom the holy fathers never knew? Trye the sprits of men by God's word, and by the interpretation of the primitive Church, who had promise of Christ to receve, by the com- ^The inter- pretation of the primi- yng of the Holy Ghost, the trew understanding of all that ^tive Church is to be fol- he had spoken and taught. After the which, we have ben ^lowed. trewly taught to beleve three Persons in one Deitye, God the Father from whom, and God the Son by whom, and God the Holy Ghost in whom all thyngs visible and invisible do consist, and have their being and lyf. In the which bylief we were baptized, by the institution of Christ, in the name of the Father, the Son, and the Holy Ghost ; and shall we now begyn to stande in dowbt of this most firme faith, the which from the beginning hath ben confirmed, besides the undowbted testimonies of the Scriptures, with the precious blood of an infinite multitude of martyrs and confessours? It is no marvel though thes Arrians deny the Holy Ghost to be God, who refuse the testimony that he made of hymself in fiery tongues unto the primitive Church, and before that in the lykenes of a dove at the 150 baptisme of Christ. Thes must nedes deny the Sprit of trewthe, who be ledde by the sprit of errour, under the co-

The Holy Ghost is another Comforter besydes Christ. lour of godlines, denyinge their trew Sanctifier and Instructour, whom Christ evidently taught to be another Comforter besides hym ; and therfor, to the end he shold so be beleved, appeared visibly as Christ did : but as their corrupt faces bashe not to deny the eternal Son of God, so are they

The Arrians are paste shame. not ashamed to deny the Holy Ghost to be God; their forehed is lyke the forehed of a whore, hardned with counterfeted hypocrisye. Stiff-necked wretches they are, that wil not yelde to the trewth, though it be never so manifestly laid before their face; they have sworne to runne after their master, the Divel, without stay, and to draw with them as many as they can, in the which they are diligent. The Lorde confound them : the Lorde conserve his elect from their damnable poison : the Lord open all Christian eyes, to beware of them: the Lorde geve all his Church an uniforme zele and mynde to abhorr them, and to cast from them. You that be of the trewth, and have any zele of God in you, store it up, and bend it against thes enemies of owre livynge God, which is the Father, the Son, and the Holy Ghost; to whom be all honour, praise, and glory, for ever.

Canst thou be an angred with thy brother, being lawfully called to be a minister in Christ's Church, and to be a teacher in the same, for spettyng at an obstinate adversary of Christ, refusing to obey the trewth, and declare no maner of indignation against the Arrian, the thief that robbeth thy

God of his honour? Doth the injury of the Arrian more offend thee, than the defence of thy Redemer please thee? Art thou not ashamed rather to take part with an Arrian, than with a right Christian? Thou wouldest seme to have charity, by bearing with the wicked; and contrary to all charity thou backbitest thy brother, for doynge that which thou sholdest rather do, than to have any familiarity with them. If you dwell within the Church of Christ, what hast thou to do with them that be withowt, which go abowt no-thyng els but to build a new Babilon, and to destroy al the godly ordre of the gospel? I tell thee playn, that I am no-thyng ashamed of that fact, but give God thanks, that I bear evil for well doyng. If I should please men, I could Gal. i. not please God. I marvel that there should be so little zele in a trew Christian harte, that it can seme to take the part of an Arrian. We cannot serve Christ and Baal. How long 3 Reg. xviii. will men halt on both sydes? Let your haltyng be healed. Hebr. xii. If you be unfaynedly of the trewth, abide yn the trewth, and let all your will be toward the professours of the trewth, in the unity of Christ's Church; lest you might appear to be scatterers with heretycks, rather than gatherers toge-ther with Christ. Do ye not see what a rabble of new The Divel found scatterors there be, such a sort as never at ons have hath shaken owt his bag ben heard of yn one realme, the one contrary to the other: of hereses so that the Divel might seme to have powred owt all his against the gospel. poisons at ons against the gospell? And will you that glory of the trewth, go abowt by word, dede, or help, mayntayn any such in their hedy errours? He that toucheth pytche, 151 cannot chuse but defile his fingers therwith. *Be not decev-* 1 Cor. xiv. *ed,* saith S. Paul, *for wicked talk corrupteth good manners; therfor watch ye rightuously, and sinne not; for many there be that have not the knowlege off God. I spake it to your shame.* S. Paul willeth us to be circumspect in talk- Heretyks are to be yng or acquayntyng owre selfs with such hethen men as at avoided. this day be, to their incouragement and strengthening of their errour. The words of an heretyk, as he saith in an-other place, *eateth lyke a canker:* and therfor writyng unto 2 Tim. ii. Titus, he commawndeth all Christian parsons to *avoid an* Titus iii.

heretyk, after ons or twyce warning; knowyng that such a one is perverted, and sinneth, and is damned by his owne 2 Thess. iii. *judgement.* And to the Thessalonians he also saith, *We command you in the name of owre Lord Jesus Christ, that ye withdraw yourselfs from every brother that walketh inordinately, and not according to the institution which they have receved of us.* There can be no fellowship betwixt faith Luke xi. and infidelity. He that is not with Christ is his enemy, he that is an enemy to the unitie of and peace of Christ's Church. He may not be coupled with us : and Solomon Prov. xvi. rendreth a cause why, *A perverse man in his mouth doth carry perdition, and his lips hideth fyer.* Agayne, he saith, Prov. xvii. *An evil man obayeth the tongue of the unrightuous : but the just harketh not to lying lipps.* Also Ecclesiasticus Eccl. xxviii. warneth, saying, *Hedge thy ears with thornes, and do not heare a wicked tongue.*

This have I touched, to give you warning how to behave yourselfs with the Arrians, and other schismatyks and heretyks, whom al godly order and good learnyng displeaseth ; the which, if owre Christian bretherne and sisterne did well weigh and follow, there would not be so many stowte heretyks as there be : I dowbt that the heretyks be better provided for than the poore faithful afflicted Contention flock of Christ. If you hear that there is contention beamong twyne us and them that be in prison, marvel not therfor, those in prison. nether let your mynds be alienated from the trewth anything 1 Cor. xi. thyng therby ; for as it is written, *It is necessary that heresies should be, that the elect might be tried.* Christ and 1 Jhon ii. Antichrist can never agree. And as S. John saith, *Antichrist is come, and there are now many Antichrists ; they are gon owt from us, such were none of us; for if they had, they would have continued with us.* By this sayinge of S. The rule to Jhon, we may well trye and know all the rowte of Antetrye an heretyke by. christ's generation. Such they be as breke the unity of Christ's Church, nether abide in the same, nether submitte their judgment to be tried in the causes which they brable for, by the godly learned pastors therof ; but arrogantly deprave them, and take upon themselfs to be teachers, before they have learned; affirmyng they cannot tell what, and speakyng evill of that which they know not: prowde they are, and puffed up yn the imagination of their owne blynde senses, and judge themselfs best of all other, because they can make a pale face of hypocrisy to the world, and cast a glass of dissembling water before the eyes of the simple people, as thes Arrians do. But praised be God, his word is lyvely and mighty, and beateth them al downe, lyke an iron rod an earthen pot in peces: and yet they are so hard harted, and far from grace, that they wil not yeld to the manifest trewth, when they have nought justly to reply. Besydes cownterfeted words, there is no pythe in them. Ful of contention and backbytyng thes brawlyng heretycks are, under a pretence of fayned holines, whom owre Saviour Christ aptly compared to paynted sepulchres, which be nothyng els withyn but full of rotten bones: for whereas trew faith is not yn the unity of Christ's Church, there is nothyng but abhomination in the sight of God. For God, as the prophet saithe, maketh his people to dwell after one maner in one howse. But with all maner of sects can this perverse generation away withall, more than with the unity and communion of Christ's pure Catholyke Churche; to the which in no wise they will agree, albeit the same is the pillar and stablishment of trewth, as S. Paul witnesseth to Timothy. I never saw nether heard before of such a sight of gidy and fantasticall heds, who delight only in singularity; whom I do much pity, because they take so much paynes to go to the Dyvell. Arrogant syngularity and envious contention be redy pathes leadyng to the same, yn the which they walk manfully. Still they have the Scriptures in their mouths, and cry, *The Scripture, the Scripture;* but it cometh like a beggar's cloke owte of their mouths, ful of patches, and all owte of fashion: and when they be by the word rightly alleaged overthrowen, and they have not with reason what to reply, yet will they never be confounded, but either depart yn fury, or els stop their ears at the sayings of the wise charmers, lyke deaf serpents; or els fall to scoldyng, which is their surest divinity they fight withall.

The Arrians counterfet holines.

152

Matt. xxiii.

Ps. lxvii.
Heretyks can better away with sects than with the trew profession.
I Tim. iii.

The heretyks behaviour in argumentation.
Ps. lvii.

B b 3

And if perchance any of them be soberer than other, their answer is, I pray you let us alone, owre conscyens is satisfyed, you labour but yn vayn to go abowte to turn us. For in self-love, blindnes, and vayne hypocrisy thes heretyks continue, be they never so charitably or learnedly informed.

And where they have nothing to lay against their lovyng informers, then they ymagyne most spitefully and falsly (to declare whose children they are) blasphemies; spredyng the same abroad, both by themselfs and by their adherents, against the sincere professors of the gospel; that we make God the author of synne, and that we say, Let men do what they will, it is not material, yf they be predestinate: and that we mayntayn all carnal liberty, dice, cardes, dronkennes, and other inordinate thynges and games: and with thes I, among other, am most slaunderously charged and defamed by thes owtragious heretyks, to whom I have gon abowte to my power to do good, as God is my witnes: but I have receved the reward of a prophet at their hands, (although I am not worthy to be cownted under that glorious name,) which is shame, rebuke, slaunder, and slaying of my good fame. They are lyk Satan their grandsyer in this poynt, who was a lyar and a manquiller from the begynnyng. Thes presumptuous heretyks do daily declare their cold charitye, which procedeth owt of their cold faith; God forgive them, and inflame them with a better spirit. I protest before God and his angells, that I never ment, nether said, any of thes infames, wherof I am belyed of them, with many other good men. Only bycause I holde and affirme, being manifestly instructed by God's word, that the elect of God cannot finallye perish, therfore they have pyked owt of their owne malicious nailes the former part of thes blasphemies: and because at another tyme I did reprove them of their temerous and rash judgment, for condemnyng of men, usyng thynges indifferent, as shooting, bowling, hawkyng, with such lyke; provyng by the Scripture, that all men in a temperancy might use them in their dew tymes, and showing that honest pastyme was no synne, which thes contentious schismatyks do improve, wherupon they do ma-

Thes new heretyks are ful of blasphemous reports.

Jhon viii.

153

The heretyks condemn all

liciously descant, as is before mentioned. And whether I honest pastymes as synns.
have deserved to have thes reproches for tellyng them the
trewth, which they cannnot abyde, let al men judge that be
of an upright judgment. Might not thes hypocrites be Jacob. i.
ashamed of their bridleles, blasphemous tongues, if the Divell had not rubbed away all shame from their foreheds ?
S. James saith, that if any person, which would seme to be
a gospeller, refrayne not his tongue, his religion is yn
vayne. O! what a many of vayne caterpillers be there,
which corrupt the swete and wholsom flowers of the gospel,
to the shame therof, as much as it lyeth in them. It had
ben better for them never to have known the gospel, than
by their prowde freewill knowledge to go abowt to subvert
the same. I would they would be taught by the Church of
Christ, where they ought to be, and become syncere con- The heretyks clowt up the Scriptures without understandyng.
fessors, or els leve botchyng up of heresies, to their owne
damnation and decevyng of many, and fall to their owne
occupation, every man accordyng to his owne callyng, and
learne to eate (with the swett of their owne browes) their
bread, to helpe others as God's worde commaundeth them,
and not to lye in corners lyke humbledoryes, eatyng up the
honey of the bees, and do nothyng els but murmur and Heretyks be idle, and stick out against the trewth.
stynge at the verity, and at all faithful laborours yn the
Lordes vynyard. Thus, by the way, I thought it good to
admonish you of other heretyks besides the Arrians, who be
handmaidens unto them, and do daily make an entrance for
them to encrease who belong to one kyngdom of darknes,
although the one be not so high yn degree as the other.
Blynd guydes they are, and leaders of the blynd, and as Matt. xv.
many as follow them do fall into the dytche; for, as it is
said of Solomon, *there is a way that semeth to a man* Prov. xiv.
right, and yet the end thereof tendeth to destruction.
Direct therfor your steps with the Church of Christ in
the waies of the gospel, and in brotherly unity, and acompt
it as the synne of wichcraft, to make division from the same,
and God of his mercy either turn their hearts shortly, or els
confound them, that they be not a shameful slaunder to the

gospel, as alredy they have began to be, to the great grief
of all faithful hearts.

154　　　Now will I turne to the Arrian agayne, who transfigureth
2 Cor. xi. hymself into an angel of light, as Satan oftentymes doeth,
The Arrians that he might under the cloke of holines more mightily de-
counterfeit ceve the simple folk.　And verely he is a divil incarnate;
holines.
Apoc. iii. he hath a name that he lyveth, and indede is deade.　Judge
Jhon vii. them not by their owtwarde shew, wheryn they extolle
themselfs wonderfully, and dazel simple mens eys lyke
Matt. vii. larks.　For owr master Christ prophesied of such false hypocrites to come, gevyng us warning to beware of such as
pretend the simplicity of a shew owtwardly, and yet in-
wardely are ravening wolfes, devowring the sowles and
Acts xx. bodies of men unto perdition.　S. Paul, departing from
Ephesus, said, there shold ryse up men speaking pervers
things, that they might make scholars to runne after them.
S. Peter setteth me furth thes Arrians lyvely in their colours, and in manner pointeth at them with his finger:
2 Peter ii. *There hath ben,* saith he, *false prophets amonge the people,*
as there shall be among you false teachers, which privily
shall bringe yn pernitious sects, yea, deniars of the Lorde,
who hath bought them, procuryng to themselfs swyft de-
struction, and many will follow their poisons, by whom the
Arrians be *way of trewth shall be evil spoken.*　Who be such Judases
Judases to
Christ. unto Christ as thes Arrians, which cease not to betraye
hym of his eternal deity?　Who slaunder more the trewth
than they, denying Jesus to be the God of trewth?　Thes
be they of whom the good apostle Jude speaketh of, which
transpose the grace of owr God into the wanton imagination
of their own braynes, and deny God, who is the onely
Jude i. Lord God and owr Lorde Jesus Christ.　*My mynde ther-*
for, saith he, *is to put you in remembrance: for as much as*
ye ons know this; how that the Lorde, after that he had de-
livered the people owt of Egypt, destroyed them which be-
leved not: the angels also, which kept not their first estate,
but left their own habitation, he hath reserved yn everlast-
yng chaynes under darknes, unto the judgment of the great

day. Even so shall the Lord destroy thes unbeleving Arrians, whom he did once through baptisme deliver from the bondage of synne, bycause they have forsaken the deity of Christ their original justice, and compared hym unreverently and ungodly to themselfs, to whom eternal fyer belongeth, which is prepared for the Divell, and for thes Arrians, his chife angels. Worse they are than the divels, which, in the eighth chapter of S. Matthew, did acknowledg hym to be the eternal Son of God : and in the Acts of the Apostles, they confessed Paul and Barnabas, which were the servants and disciples of Christ, to be the servants of God most highest. The divels, yn S. James, do beleve and tremble at the majesty of Christ. The centurion, in the Gospel of S. Matthew, acknowleged hym verely to be the Son of God. But thes hell-hounds are offended at his eternal majesty, and wold have hym no better than themselfs, by creation. *Matt. viii. Acts xvi. Jacob. ii. Matt. xxviii.*

Is this the profession of Christ, O ye Antichrists? Doth your fayned hollines tend to this end, to dishonour hym that is most holliest, and one God, with the Father and the Holy Ghost, of all hollines? O you painted hypocrites, doth your counterfeited love and dissemblyng patience go abowt to abase the eternal love of God, his beloved Son, O ye haters of God? Put off your shameles vysards, O ye unbelevyng Arrians : put off your angelicall infidelitie, and walk as you be, O you decevers of the people. You say ye see, and yet be altogether blynded; for he that seith not Christ to be the everlastyng Son of God, seith no light ; for he is the veri light by whom all men be enlightned. Seke therfor of hym your eye salve, lest yn your blyndenes ye stumble shortly to eternal darknes. O what huge blyndnes are they yn, which say, thei have no synne yn them! Wheras S. Jhon playnely affirmith, that whosoever saith he hath no synne is a lyar : and David saith, that all men be lyars : the prophet Esai saith, that all our righteousnes is lyke the cloth of a menstruous woman. Shal we beleve lyars before the faithful servants of God? If they know not themselfs, is it any marvil though they know not God? He that is un- *155* *Jhon i. The Arians say thei have no synne. 1 Jhon i. Psal. cxv. Esa. lxiv. Luke xvi.*

faithful in a little will also be unfaithful yn much : he that
is not ashamed to belye hymself, it is no wonder though he
be bold to belye another, better than hymself. How may a
purblynded man behold the brightness of the son? Who is
so sore diseased as he, that beyng very syck beleveth that
he is whole? Who knoweth not owre flesh (as long as it is
in this life) to be a lump of synne? Yea, and who fealith
not the law of synne, which is yn owre members, still to
Rom. vii.   strive against the law of owre mynd? S. Paul, who was taken
2 Cor. xii.   up into the third heaven, and saw suche thynges as is not
lawful for man to speak of, whose godly life surmountith
the rable of thes Arians, and yet he durst not be so bold as
to compare in purity with Christ, nether to affirm that he
was withowt synne, but acknowleged synne to be in his
2 Cor. xii.   body, and desyred that it might be taken from hym ; to
whom it was not graunted, but that it shold remayne with
hym for his spiritual exercise, and by grace to overrun the
same ; that where synne abundith, there grace shuld super-
abund. Why do ye clense the owtwarde sydes of your
stynkyng vessels, O you impure glorifiers of yourselfs, and
see not the inward abhomination which is in you? Ye say
ye be swete before the Lord, and behold you stynk before
the face of the whole world, but specially before God and
all his sayntes : for how can God but abhorre al such as do
take away the swete savor of his divine nature from his Son,
and to attribute that excellency to themselfs which is not
yn them? Hath not God hymself witnessed of man's' im-
Gen. vi.   purity, saying, that *all the thoughts of man be only prone*
Psalm l.   *unto evill?* Is not this inclination to evil, which lurkith yn
owre flesh, synne, and the natural corruption, which we
sucked from owre first parents? Learne to know thyself
better, and then shall you judge more uprightly of the Son
of God. Clense thyne ynward filthines and synne, by an
humble and repentant confession of thyne owne unworthy-
nes and wickednes towards thy Redemer, and then thyne
outward shew of hollines might be somewhat worthy, which
now is duble divelishnes, for want of trew knowlege both
156 of thyself, and of faith to God. Know thyne owne poverty

and misery, and come to thy Saviour, which is riche with
God, and hable of hymself to enriche thee with all felicitye.
Thou art lyke them that be of the congregation of Laodicea,
mention'd in the Apocalips, whych sayest with them, that I Apoc. iii.
am rych, and enryched, and want nothyng, and knowest
not indeed that thou art wretched and miserable, both poor,
blynd, and bare. I cownsel ye therfor to the fyeri gold of
the deity of owre Christ, that thou mightest through trew
bylyf *wex rich*, and be clothed with his whyt garmentes,
that the shame of thy nakednes might not appeare : as it
doth now, to thy great confusion. If you see not this, thou
arte one of them whom Christ, for thyne infidelity towards Jhon xii.
hym, hath made blynd unto everlasting damnation.

Thes Arians wold not be cownted miserable ; and thei The Arians
cannot away with this godly praier, which the Church usith, would not
saying, *Lord have marcy upon us, miserable synners.* But miserable.
S. Paul was not ashamed to say, *miserable parson that I* Rom. vii.
am, who shall deliver me from this bodye subject to death?
He confesseth as well owre miserable as synful state in this
life ; and they that perceve the impurity of owre nature,
which it hath through the fall of Adam, and the want of Rom. iii. 5.
original justice, which we loste by hym, cannot but crye,
We are miserable, and say with David, *I am miserable and* Ps. xxxvii.
made croked, I went all day long sorrowfully: and pray
with the blynde man of the gospel, *Jesu the Son of David,*
have marcy upon us. What vayn religion is this of theirs?
What pharisaical leven do thei scater abrod, what lying
hypocrisy do they mayntayne?

But is this all? No, verely : it were too longe for me to The Arians
tuche their infinite errours they are infected withall. They deny the
deny the Old Testament to be of any authority; David's Old Testa-
Psalmes be not to be used as praiers and praises to God ; thePsalmes
and thei are almost as bold with the Newe ; for they fynd They find
fault with the Lord's praier, and affirme that they nede not the Pater-
to say for themselfs, let *thy kyngdom come,* for it is alredy noster.
come upon them. And what nede we pray (say they) for
that we have alredy? And we have no synne, wherfor then
shold we say, *forgive us owre trespases?* O impudency, of

all impudencies the greatest! O infidelitie, more than ever was among the brutish heathen! Was there ever any that went abowt to set God to schole before he hath taught us how to pray; and they say, we nede not so to pray. The godly men, saith S. Peter, which did write the Scriptures, *speak not of themselfs, but by the instinction of the Holy Ghost;* and thes frantyk Antichrists will both correct and teach the Holli Ghost to speak. Who, havyng any spytell in his body, may not thynk yt well to be bestowed upon such wicked blasphemers of God and his word? I wold my spytell might be of as great vertue against them, as the words of S. Paul were against Barjesus; whom resistyng the belef of Christ, he called the son of the Divel, and therwith struck hym blynd. Better it were for a man to lose his owtward sight, wherby corruptible thyngs be only seen, than to want the inward, wherby God is perceved. And more precious is the glory of my Christ in my sight, than all the men of the world. The blynd Pharises I know will be offended at this my saying, and thynke it is uncharitably spoken; but I passe not upon their offence, answering them with Christ, *Let them alone, they are blynd, and the leaders of the blynd. He that is ignorant, let hym be ignorant still; and he that is filthy, let hym be more filthy; but he that is holy, let hym become more holy:* and beware of thes pestiferous Arians leaven; who, besydes all this, deny the benefyt of repentance to any parson that synneth after baptisme, contrary to the manifest word of God, saying, that *in whatsoever howr a synner doth repent hym of his synnes, thei shall be forgyven hym.* Do ye thynk that thes beasts are to be borne withal? Say what yee wil, they

2 Peter i.

Acts xiii.

157

Matt. xv.
1 Cor. xiv.
Apoc. xxii.

Thei deny repentance after baptisme.

Esech. xviii.

[The rest is wanting.]

Number XLIX.

Philpot to a certain lady; encouraging her under the present evil times.

Foxii MSS.   THE sprite of joy and rejoycing be with you, and bee

you comforted, through his lovyng and comfortable leading
and governance, and make continually joyful your unfayned
harte, my dearest sister in the Lorde, agaynst all the fiery
temptations of the enemy in these oure dais, by Jesus Christ
owr Saviour. *Amen.* Praised and exalted be the name of
owre lyving God, for the trewth of his faithful promises,
which he maketh his people to fele in the tyme of extremitie,
when thei seme of the worlde to be forlorne and most miserable; such is the goodnes of the omnipotencye of owre
God, that he can and doth make to his elect sower sweet,
and misery felicitye. Wherfor it was not without cause that
the wise man in his proverbs writeth, *Whatsoever happen-*
ith to a just parson, it cannot make hym sorrowfull. All
thyngs work to good unto them which be good. Unrighteous we are, and wicked of owreselfs, yea, when we have
owre gayest pecocks fethers on: but through Christ, on
whom we beleve, we are just, and in his goodnes we are
good: and herby have daily experience of his marcy and
loving kyndnes towardes us yn owre afflictions and miseries,
contrary to man's judgment. Therfor let us alwais, as David did, put the Lord before us, and then shall we fynd as
he said, that *he is on my right hand, and I shall not be*
moved. Sure it is, as S. Paul said, *If God be with us, who*
shall be agaynst us: as who would say, that all that owre 158
enemies can do makith for owre glory, so long as we abide
yn God. What hurt had Sidrach, Mysach, and Abdinego
by the fyer, whyles the Lord walked with them? What
anoyance had Daniel by the fierce lyons in the dungeon,
the Lord beyng with hym? So mighty is owre Lord, and
hable, yea, and ready to comfort such as put their whole
trust in hym.

Therfor, myn owne hart, be of good chere in thes cruel
dais, for thes are to the yncrease of owre glory: they that
bringe us low do exalt us, and they that kill us do open
the gates of eternal life. You by the Sprit of God, wherwith your mynd is indewed, do see that I say, and I by
experience do feel it, praise be to God therfor. I cannot
but lament the blyndnes, or rather madnes of the world,

to see how they do abhorre the prison of the body, yn a most righteous cause, and litle or nothyng at all regarde the prison of infydelity, in the which their sowle is fetter'd most miserably, which is more horrible than all the prisons of the world. How much the sowle is more precious than the body, so much is the captivity and mysery of the sowle more to be lamented than of the body. God therfor be blessed, which hath gyven your tender parson to understand, that the libarty of the sowle surmountith all the treasures of the world; and that the sowle beyng free, nothyng can be hurtful to the body. Hold fast this liberty, for this is the freedom of the children of God, by the which we passe withowt fear, both through fyer and water: and where to the world those be terrible, to the elect thei are joyous, and full of glory. God spake to Moises in the mownt, in fyer, thunder, and stormes; and the voice was so terrible to the people, that thei trembled therat, and wished that God would not speak unto them yn such wyse: but Moises face, comyng owt of the same, was so bright, that the children of Israel could not behold his face. Even so shall owre faces be, yn the middest of owre fieri formes, that owr enemies shall hereafter never be hable to behold the brightnes of owr cowntenance. And although we be made as black as the pot's bottom, that hangeth over the fyer, yet sure I am, that we shall be made whyter than snow, and purer than silver or fine gold. If we have to joy in any thing yn this world, it is yn tribulations, by the which we are certefied to be the children of God, and inheritors of his everlastyng kyngedom. By this, saith S. Jhon, *we know the love of Christ toward us, that he gave his life for us.* And by this we know we love hym; that we are redy, at his callyng, to yeld owre life for the testimony of his trewth to owre brothers, that they might have occasion to learne by owre faithful example, to esteme more the thyngs of God than of the world.

O God, increase this trew faith yn you; for I see you hereby to be in possession of heaven. Continually through hope behold the thyngs that be not seen, but yet hyden for owre greater rewards; and then shall not this noble faith perish, but grow to perfection and fruition of God. What though this sack of dong which we carrye about us doth 159 pynch and repyne at this owre pure faith, shall it discomfort us? No, trewly, but make us more circumspect and vigilant, that we be not overthrowen in owre right wais, since we have so familiar an enemy

By faith we overcum; and he that overcumith shal be crowned. Therfore the assaults of the flesh and of the world, wherewith we are to be pressed as long as we lyve, ought to make us diligenter in spiritual thyngs, and to be more desyrous to be delivered owt of this body of corruption. Happy be we, that see the dawnger of owr conflict, wherby we are admonished to beware, and to runne to the strong hold of the name of the Lord owre defence, to the which, in all your temtations, I do most hartely commit your faithful harte for ever.

As concerning myne owne affares, synce I cam to the Bishop's colehowse, I have ben six tymes in examination, twice before the spitell bishopes, and ons of late before a great many of the Lords of the Counsel, before whom I have more frankly, I thank God, uttered my mynd than I did any tyme before. The matter laid against me was, the disputation in the Convocation-howse two years past, concerning their idol the masse; the which by all means thei wold have me recant; and I have answered, that if the clargy that now rule the rost, can prove yether their sacrament of the aultar to be a sacrament, or else themselfs to be of the trew Churche of Christ, that I would be as conformable to their doyngs as thei cowld desyer. I loke daily for my final judgment, which was promised me yer this; but I thynk now they will defer it until the end of the Parliament. God, in whose hands my lyfe is, hasten the tyme in his good pleasure, and make me worthy of that great glory. You are as present with me as I am with you. Christ gyve us a perfect fruition one of another in his kyngdome. Owre bretherne that be gon before us, do loke for us. Hasten, O Lord, owre redemtion, and suffer us not to be overcumed of evill. *Amen.* Owte of the Bishop's cole-house, wherof one Eleynye, dwellyng in Pater-noster Row, gailer of Lolar's Towar, and another named Fountayn, be kepers. The xiijth of November.

Your owne bowels in Jesus Christ,

Jhon Philpott.

To my right welbeloved and the very elect lady of God, which hath chosen the better part, this be delivered.

---

160   Number L.

A letter by an unknown person to Bishop Boner ; reproving him freely for his cruelty, and foretelling his downfall.

Wo be unto thee that destroyest, when thou wast not destroyed : thou brakest the league, when as none hath broken it with thee. For when thou shalt leave off destroying, thou thyself shalt be destroyed ; and when thou ceasest from breaking the league, shal they break it with thee. Esay xxxiii.

Foxii MSS.   OH ! thou bloudy Boner, and idolatrous bishop of London ; oh ! thou most cruel tyrant of Sodoma, and proud painted prelate of Gomorra, hear the word of the Lord, and harken unto the voice of his mouth. Be thou warned by the power of his hand, and hasten to escape the day of his fearful visitation. For his fierce wrath is already kindled against thee, and his heavy displeasure shal shortly take hold upon thee. For why, the great abundance of innocent bloud which thou hast so cruelly shed like water, both in the city of London, and in the country round about it, cryeth so sore for vengeance in the ears of the Lord God of hosts, that of his justice and most righteous judgments he can no longer forbear thee. The measure of thy sin and iniquity is filled up to the brim ; and thy wicked grapes of fiercenes and cruelty be now ful ripe. Therfor shal the angel of the Lord shortly come with his sharp sickle, and cut thee down, as a cluster of corruption and wickednes, and cast thee into the winefat of the fiercenes of God's wrath, or lake that burneth with fire and brimstone; there to be tormented for ever, as thou art most worthy, except thou repent, and turn to the Lord in time. And altho thou dost believe, and hast also in secret said, that there is no such place of punishment; yet I assure thee, even in the name and word of the Lord, that thou shalt shortly have perfect experience, and true tast and feeling of it, unles, I say, thou do speedily repent, and surcease from thy bloudy proceedings and butcherly slaughter of the Lord's poor simple sheep.

To reherse unto thee the fearful examples of cruel Cain, Nemroth, Pharao, Achab, and wicked Jezabel his wife, Pashur, Nabucadonasur, Hamon, Holifernes, Antiochus, Pilate, Herod, Annas, and Caiaphas, with thy predecessor desperate Judas, which hanged himself, I think it would little or nothing pierce thy stony heart, which is hardened 161 as Pharao's, because thou dost not only deny the holy Scriptures, but also that there is any God, or life after this. Therfore I will let them pass, and also the examples of cursed Nero, Domitianus, Trajanus, and divers other, whose steps thou dost so directly follow, that at the length thou shalt be sure to fall into the same pit of perpetual destruction that they are in, with them to be tormented together for ever; except, I say still, thou do truly repent, and turn to the Lord in time. But if the threatned vengeance of God, against whom thou dost strive, nor the fearful examples of them, whose footsteps thou dost follow in al points, will nothing quench the flaming heat of thy malicious mind, thy greedy thirst after innocent bloud, and thy unsatiable desire of destroying God's dear children; yet let the very shame and obloquy of the world, wherunto thou art deeply fallen, something abate thy ravenous raging, and asswage thy fierce tyrannous roaring against the people of God. For not only England, but also the most part of the whole world, speaketh shame of thy unmerciful doings. Every man almost can tel upon his fingers ends, how many of God's dear servants thou hast burned, and how many thou hast murdered and famished in prison, within these three quarters of this year. The whole sum surmounteth to a XL persons, or thereabouts. Every child can say, that can any whit speak, *Bloudy Boner is Bishop of London.* Thou art become the common slaughter slave to all thy fellow *bitesheeps*, (bishops I would say,) and so art thou called every where, and that of all sorts of men ; yea, even of the Papists themselves. There are thousands that bear thee a good fair face, and flatter thee for advantage, which speak shame of thee, as they may well enough, behind thy beastly back.

I am credibly informed, that divers of thy fellow bishops, and some of thine own chaplains, do heartily abhor thee, more than thy beastly proceedings, which be against al law, right, equity, and conscience.

Oh! bloudy Boner, and most filthy bastard born, as thy other brethren were, what hast thou to do to condemn any man, or keep them in thy cruel colehouse to famish them, which are not of thy dioces? Cannot thine own laws, which yet are too much cruel, bridle thy unsatiable desire of shedding the bloud of them, with whom, by no law or reason, thou hast any thing to do? Shal al the world say to thy shame, that bloudy Boner is the common cut-throat and bloud-shedder for all the bishops in England! Oh ravening wolf, art thou so hungry again so soon, that for haste to satisfy thy greedy desire, thy cubbs must be fain to bring the sheep forth of other mens folds? Oh! butcherly bloud-shedder, is there no mercy in thy cruel hands? Wast thou so handled, when thou hadst most justly deserved it? Hast thou found that at the hands of other, which so many at this day feel at thine? No, no, for then hadst thou come too short to the supping of so much bloud of them whom thou hast most cruelly slain. But trust unto it, thou cruel tyrant, thou hast not yet escaped the mighty and terrible 162 hand of God, no more than thy bloudy brother, wily Winchester, hath done, if thou do still despise his great mercy and long suffering, be thou well assured thou shalt not long escape his fearful judgment and violent fire, which shortly shal consume thee, and al other his adversaries, to the fore-warning and terrible example of al tyrants and cruel murderers, unto the world's end.

Repent, therfore, you priest's son, I say, repent in time, and surcease from thy most wicked procedings. Lay away thy tyrant-like tyranny, and be thou sure the Lord hath yet mercy enough in store for thee. Surely, his great patience and long suffering would fain draw thee, and all other, unto speedy repentance. But if thou have hardened thy cruel heart, as Pharao did his, so sinning against the Holy Ghost, be thou right well assured thy final destruction is hard at hand. Make as merry as thou wilt, thou shalt shortly know thy fare. Longer shalt thou not tary here, than thou hast wrought thy appointed feat. But then shalt thou also go to thy place, as the very man of God, good Fatter Latymer, said to that cursed Winchester; whose words he hath found true, as thou shalt do mine : for God wil get his name the glory over thee, or ever it be long; that our posterity, which is yet to come, may praise him for the same. Thou strivest against the stream, and dost wrestle with him in vain. Thou shalt not bring al thy pestilent purposes to pass, though thou wouldest brast thine heart about it. Hamon shal hang upon his own gallows, do the best thou canst. The little mustard wilbe the greatest tree in God's garden, though the godless Gardiner and thou have gon never so much about to root it up. Remember the saying of an old doctor, *The bloud of the martyrs*, saith he, *is the seed of the gospel.* When one is put to death, a thousand spring up in his stead. Zorobabel wilbe found no lyar, which said, that the truth should have the victory. Christ doth tell thee, and all the rest, that it shalbe too hard for you al to kick against the prick.

Therefore it were best for you all to follow the good counsil that Gamaliel gave your predecessors, which put Christ to death ; lest, while you be striving against God, you utterly perish in his anger ; for his wrath is already kindled hot against you. But if thou wilt needs still procede forth in thy wickedness, until thou fall into the pit of perdition, (the wrath and just judgment of God provoking thee therto,) yet for very shame of the world, if thou be not altogether a beast without shame, meddle with no mo than be of thine own diocess. Seek not to become the slave and common slaughter man to all thy bloudy brethren, and very children of Satan, whom Christ calleth rightly a murderer from the beginning. I say not this, for that I think thou canst shorten any of God's elect childrens lives before the time that God hath appointed by his divine will and pleasure, but because I would fain se some equity appear in their doings, which hitherto have shewed themselves most detestable and devilish, as the most simple in the world may easily discern. And I also thought it good, yea, and my

163 very bounden duty, to give you warning in God's behalf, that thou mayest be more excuseless at the great day, when I and many other are to be called in heavy witnes against thee. And take these my doings as thou list, yet shall my conscience hereby be freed before God, and thine the further burthened ; and also thy shameless doings the further known to al, and spoken of to thyne infamy and reproch.

Before God I speak it, if thou do cause that eminent servant of God, good Master Philpot, to be put to death, now thou hast [unrighteously condemned] him, I wil cause as many copies of this as I can to be cast abroad into every part of this realm ; so that thy swoln cheeks shal even tingle at the hearing of it. I know thou, or some other for thee, wil practice thine accustomed craft of conjuring, sorcery, or witchcraft, to come to the knowledg of me. But I set not a pin by al thy familiar spirits ; no, though thou have a principal devil, even Beelzebub himself. For you can do no more to me than God wil give you leave, for the setting forth of his glory and my commodity. Therfore his wil be don, for it is onley good. God graunt mine always to be obedient and subject to the same. *Amen.*

>It is not for fear I write not my name,
>Sith God can preserve me forth of thy hands ;
>Yet for to tempt him I were to blame,
>And needless to bring myself into bands.

My time is not come, therfore I wil tary,
Stil trusting in God I shal not miscarry.

Number LI.

164

Cardinal Pole, archbishop of Canterbury, his metropolitical
visitation of the diocese of Lincoln; with the articles of
visitation.

Comperta et detecta in visitatione reveren^{mi} Domini Car-
dinalis per reveren. Patrem Johannem Lincolniens. E-
pum. in dioc' sua Lincoln. a festo Pasch' anno Domini
millesimo quingen^{mo} quinquagesimo sexto; et deinceps
exercita; sequuntur.

THOM'S WALLER de Alwincle in dioc' Petriburgensi Foxii MSS.
detectus, q^d daret operam magicis artibus. Et q^d consulu- Ars magica.
isset quendam Willmu' Atkinson de Yardwel in com. Lin-
coln. et Johem. Tossell de Baltissham in com. Cantabr' homines preficos, et fatiloquos, confessus est. Et ulterius ex-
aiat' quid illi dixissent, respondit, alterum predixisse, imminere dco' Thome Waller suspendium in proximis comitiis
apud Northampton. Alterum predixisse, q^d evaderet suspendium; sed vix, et cum magna difficultate. Pendente hac
causa coram nobis, dicus. Thoms' Waller in proximis comitiis fuit convictus de sacrilegio; et pependisset apud Northampton (ut dicitur) ni aufugisset.

Ormundus Hill de Thorneton presbr' conjugat' in dioc' Presbyter
Lincoln. unde prius effugerat, comprehensus, ab uxore illi- conjugat.
cita separatus fuit; salutari penitentia utrique injuncta.

Dns. Thoms' Nix de Caisho in com. Bedf. presbr. quon- Presbr. con-
dam uxorat' et ante biennium per nos divorciatus, convictus jugatus.
fuit post divortium predcm. consuetudinem stupri cum uxore
sua pretensa h'uisse. Quod et confessus est, et penitentiam
sibi injunctam tam apud Caisho, quam apud Bedf. in maxima hominum frequencia peregit. Post penitentiam peractam, humiliter petiit· se admitti ad ministrandum, et fuit
admissus.

c c 3

Fuga. ex-co'icata. Domina Anna Graie, uxor Henrici Graie, militis, negle-ctis censuris ecclesiasticis, stetit per integrum jam annum exco'icata. Unde ad Dnos. Regem et Reginam pro brevi de exco'icata capienda scribendum decrevimus.

165. **Fuga.** Anthonius Meeres in com. Lincoln. armiger, citatus ut compareret coram nobis; eo quod eucharistiam in fest. Pasche non recepisset, fugit ad partes transmarinas. Ut dicitur, stat exco'icat.

Fuga. Grauntham vidua in principio visitac'onis 'nre simili de causa fugit ad Ducissam Suff. in part. transmarinis, ut dicitur.

Fasciculus. Thoms' Armestronge de Corbie in com. Lincoln. armiger, et Elizab. ejus uxor de heresi contra sacramentum altaris, et auricularem confessionem et auctoritat. sedis ap'lice convicti, se humiliter submiserunt, et publice recantaverunt: et feria tertia ebdomade Penthecostes in maxima hominum frequentia in processionibus in eccl'ia catho' Lincoln. fasciculos portaverunt: ac deinde dominica sequenti apud Grauntham fasciculos etiam portaverunt, habita utrobique concione ad populum.

Combustus. Thomas More in eccl'ia parochi Divi Martini Leicestrie, ac post etiam in eccl'ia Dive Margarite xxi die Aprilis 1556. coram nobis comparuit, et multas hereses defendit: dicens inter cetera, *This is my faith, that in the sacrament of the aultar is not the body of Christ, no more than if I myself shuld geve one a pece of bread, and saie, Take, eate, this is my body; meaning my own body within my dublet.* Unde sententia contra ipm' lata. Scriptum est ad Dominos Regem et Reginam: et per breve *De heretico comburendo,* apud Leicester predict. mense Junii fuit combustus.

Rasura pueri in ludibrium. Maior ville Bedford scripsit nobis, quendam in ludibrium ordinis sacerdotalis rasisse verticem pueri infra bimatum; exquirens nram' sententiam. Cui rescripsimus; et super eo pars rea peregit publicam peniten' in mercato de Bedford.

Simonia. Robertus Wakeley r'cor de Stoughton Parva, in com. Hunt. propter simoniam coactus bn'ficium suum dimittere.

Curato penitentia injuncta. Thomas Hulcocke, curat. ecl'ie Omnium S'ctor' in Huntingt. quia ministravit eucharistiam Simoni White, Georgio

Hasseley, et aliis, sine confessione auriculari, sed cum confessione generali in Anglica lingua, sicut fieri solebat tempore schismatis; primum in gaolam est per nos injectus. Deinde etiam, publica penitent. est illi injuncta: quam peregit. Et injunctum est eidem, ne amplius ministraret in diocesi Lincoln. Et super eo recessit.

Conquestum est nobis, qd Dns' Oswaldus Butler, nuper rector de Wodhall in com. Bedford. adhuc tenet mulierem suam in amplexibus adulterinis: quem citandum fore decrevimus. Compertum est etiam, q^d nunquam fuit presbr' ordinatus. Tamen omnia sacramenta tempore schismatis ministrasset. Pro quo submisit se; et injuncta est ei penitent' publica. Quam peregit in eccl'iis de Wodhall, et Sce' Marie in Bedford. *Oswal. Butler, rector de Wodhall.*

Anna Drewrie parochie de Noviell vivit in amplexibus adulterinis cum Dno. Johanne Gascoine, milite. Super quo citamus utrumque. D'cus Johannes comparuit, et submisit se. Cui injunctum est, ne dc'am Annam in suum consortium amplius admitteret; sed suam uxorem 'ltimam ad se reciperet. Quod promisit se facturum. Sed promisso non stetit. **166** *Anna Drewrie, adulterium.*

Eadem Anna non comparuit. Quare stat exco'icata. Quare decrevimus scribendum regie majestati pro brevi *De exco'icato capiendo.* *Exco'icata.*

Notati sunt Edmundus More et Maria Lee de Medmenam, q^d viverent in amplexibus adulterinis. Dict' Maria citata venit: de crimine objecto competenti numero manifeste purgavit. Ut in actis apud Missendem Magnam xxiiii^to Aprilis apparet. *Edmund. More et Maria Lee.*

Thomas Troughton citatus venit coram nobis et commissionariis regiis, sexto Julii, anno Dni. 1556to. Et convictus fuit maliciose protulisse hec verba Anglicana, *The belles of the church be the Devill's trumpettes.* Ac etiam ista verba, *The ivel Churche did ever persecute the goode Churche, as they do now:* precedenti sermone de hereticis cumbustis apud London. Super quo obligatus ad recantationem publicam per scriptum, *de recognitione.* *Thom. Troughton. Church bells. Blonham.*

Anthonius Redshawe de Leiton, et Thomas Bell de Mollesworthe in com. Hunt. citatis viis et modis, non com- *Presbyteri conjugati.*

paruerunt. Ideo stant exco'icati. Unde scribendum decrevimus pro brevi, *De exco'icat. capiendo.*

Carnes comederunt in Quadragesima. Henricus Burnebie, Johannes Marcie, Thomas Selbie, Xpo'ferus Kendal, Will'mus Maxey, Alicia Selbie, et Thomas Felde, de Aconberce Weston, convicti et confessi, q^d in Quadragesima absque dispensatione carnes comedissent, in carcerem sunt conjecti. Ac postea peregerunt penitent. sibi injunctam, viz. fasciculos portando in villa de Huntington. die sab'ti post Dominicam in albis, ac crastino ejusdem sab'ti in eccl'ia paroch. de Aconbery Westonne.

Palme Sunday.
Ceremony mocked. Vigesimo septimo die mens. Aprilis anno predco. Laurentius Burnebie de Brampton detectus et convictus q^d Dominica in Ramis Palmarum, cum vicarius aperiret valvas ecclie' baculo crucis, dicus' Laurentius per modum ludibrii dixit, *What a sport have we towards. Will our vicar ronne at the quintine with God Almightie?* Super qo. submisit se: et injuncta est ei publica penitentia: quam peregit, prout in actis.

Non residet rector. Eodem die Nicholaus Abbot, rector de Branfelde, officio notatur. Quòd non residet in rectoriâ suâ. Et citatus non comparuit. Quare Dns. decrevit eundem citandum in eccl'iâ suâ. Et vocandum ad residentiam sub penâ deprivationis.

167
Proles vicarii de Spaldwike. XVIII Aprilis anno Dni. antedict. injunctum est vicario de Spaldwike, ut prolem ex adulterino conjugio, tempore schismatis susceptam, in scandalum aliorum, amplius in brachiis suis non circumferret. Ac data est illi insuper quædam recantatio, quam publice in eccl'ia sua ex Spaldwike legit.

Dilapidatio Cancelli. Fructus eccl'ie de Spaldwike, parcelle prebende de Stowe sequestrat. fuerunt propter dilapidationem, et notabilem ruinam cancelli ibm. Ac reparatione sufficienti facta, eadem sequestratio relaxata est ult. Julii.

Fuga propter religionem. Rich'us Simpson, Ric'us Whittel, et Henricus Barrey de villa Sce. Ivonis notati sunt, q^d aufugerunt propter religionem. Se humiliter submiserunt; et hereses quas prius defenderant, recantabant. Unde a sententia exco'icationis absoluti, in gaolam primum intrusi, publicam peniten. fasciculos gerentes, peregerunt.

Vicarius de Stewkeley Mag.   detectus, q^d sacramentum eucharistie inconfessis ministrasset in festo Pasche ult. et confessionem auricularem petentibus negasset; convictus in gaolam est detrusus: ac recantationem publice coram parochianis suis pronuntiavit, prout plenius apparet in actis.   *Eucharistia data inconfessis.*

Rob'tus Cupies, sacerdos de Eiton, detectus, q^d h'ens pensionem quinque librarum, in otio vivit, nulli cure deserviens. Cui Dns. injunxit, q^d preparet se ad deserviend. alicui cure, cum ad hoc vocatus fuerit.   *Sacerdos in otio.*

Faucet, sacerdos ac pedagogus apud Sc'um Neotam, notatur, q^d tenet quandam Elizabetham Williams, quam tempore schismatis duxerat: antequam citatus fugit. Gitata tamen Elizabeth comparuit. Cui a Dno. est injunctum, ne de cetero admittat dcum' Faucet in suum consortium, quousque divortium aucte' eccl'ie sit inter eos factum.   *Sacerdos tenet uxorem. Fugit.*

Injunctum est parochianis Sce' Neotis, q^d citra ultimum diem hujus mensis reedificent omnia altaria, quæ ante schisma fuerunt in eadem eccl'ia; impositione sive taxa in parochianos ibm. facta. Iisdem etiam injunctum est, q^d citra finem Pasche prox. reedificent crucifixorium cum imaginibus ad hoc necessariis inposterum facta, ut prius.   *Reedificanda altaria.*

Injunctum est parochianis de Brampton, q^d reedificent crucifixorium, et quatuor cruces lapideas infra eandem parochiam, citra festum Natalis Dni. prox' sumptibus communibus.   *Reedificare crucifixorium.*

Injunctum est parochianis de Wrabie, q^d vestiarium plumbo coopertum per ipsos prius detractum, reedificent, citra finem Sci. Michaelis archangeli prox.   *Vestiarium reedificandum.*

Ambrosius Sutton de Burton in com. Lincoln. armiger, detectus est, q^d tempore Quadragesime carnes comedisset. Vocatus comparuit, et allegabat bullam dispensationis a Dno. Papa sibi concessam, quam produxit, cujus tenor continet, q^d durante infirmitate tantum, cum consilio utriusque medici citra scandalum, exceptis feriis, quarto, sexto et sabbato, comedere liceret. Compertum tamen est, q^d inconsultis medicis, omnibus diebus, indiscriminatim, cum nulla   168 *Bulla carnes vesci.*

laboraret infirmitate, in grave aliorum scandalum, comede-
ret. Super quo, se submisit. Cui Dns. peniten. injunxit.

Sequestra-tio pro re-paratione. Edmundus Pike, firmarius de Wilden, obligatus est pro reparatione omnium edificiorum rectorie ibm. infra bien-nium faciend. Quam reparationem d'cus Pike magna ex parte fecit ante mensem Junii. Quo tempore eccl'ia vacavit per mortem ultimi incumben. ibm. Unde Dns. posuit fructus ejusdem eccl'ie sub sequestratione pro reliqua reparatione faciend. dco' Pike interim manente obligato.

Houghton rect. appro-priator. Gardiani presentant cancellum esse in maxima ruina, culpa approprietarii: ac rectoriam predictam nuper perve-nisse ad dispositionem reverend^{mi} Dni. Cardinalis. Unde Dns. Epus' detulit detectum ad prefatum reverendissimum Dn'um.

Todington chancel. Gardiani presentant cancellum defectum pati in vitreis fenestris, atque rectoriam esse in magna ruina; ac quadra-gesimam partem fructuum non esse distributam. xx^{mo} Junii comparuit Thom's Coke, firmarius ac procurator rectorie ibm. ac promisit reparationem cancell. citra festum Sti. Johannis Bapte', ac rectorie ante festum Mich'is: et promisit distributionem xlme [quadragessime] partis ad sta-tim. Unde Dns. assignavit ad certificand. super premissis prox. curia apud Bedford post festum Mich'is.

Octo vaccæ de bonis eccl'ie. Magir' Will'mus Smithe de Chalgrave detectus est, q^d h'uit de bonis eccl'ie de Totern-hoo octo vaccas. Secundo die Junii anno Dni' 1556to comparuit Will'mus Smithe, et allegavit predictas vaccas esse Dni Regis, ex concessione statuti Parliamenti, ac se esse generalem supervisorem ac custodem humoi' bonorum pro parte Dni. Regis. Unde Dns. decrevit supersedend. in causa.

Dunstable. Ibi nec rec-tor, nec vicarius. Gardiani presentant, populosum esse oppidum: ac ibm. nec rectorem esse, nec vicarium perpetuum, qui divinis offi-ciis fungatur; sed conductitium tantum curatum, precio conductum. Qui predicatur, ut possit. Ac rectoriam jam esse in dispositione Dni. Cardinalis. Unde Dns. detulit de-tectum ad reverendiss^{um} Cardinalem.

Harlington. Rectoria Gardiani presentant, cancellum esse in maxima ruina, ac

rectoriam pertinere ad Dnum. Cardinalem. Unde Dns. de- ibm. in
tulit detectum ad predcm' reverendiss^{um} Cardinalem. ruina.

Item, Gardiani presentant horreum vicarie ibm. fere col- 169
lapsum esse. xxvi^{to} Junii anno predco' comparuit vica- Horreum
rius, et allegavit portionem vicarie sue esse perquam exi- lapsum.
guam; ac ruinam factam antequam ipse vicarius ibm. fuerit. Unde Dns. assignavit eidem, ut hoc anno expendat in
reparatione dci' horrei vicarie, xx$.

Cancellum eccl'ie detectum est indigere magna repara- Salford re-
tione: ac rectoriam esse Dni. Cardinalis. Unde Dns. detulit ctorii.
detectum ad rev^m Dnum. Cardinalem.

Thomas Lawton detectus est, q^d abfuit ab uxore sua viii. Cranfeld.
annos, ac q^d rediit cum duobus nothis. xxvi^{to} Junii, an- Lawton ab-
no Dni. 1556, comparuit curat. ibm. cum gardianis, et cer- uxore.
tificabant predict. Thomam inpresentiarum detineri in carcere Regis apud Bedford. Unde Dns. decrevit supersedend.
donec predict. Thoms' sui juris fuerit.

Cancellum eccl'ie, ac tota rectoria fere delapsa. xxvi^{to} Ampthill.
Junii anno predco' comparuit rector ibm. ac allegavit, se Rectoria
noviter institutum in eadem r'coria, ac non esse adhuc in delapsa.
reali possessione ejusdem; nec intendere se eandem possi-
dere: eo q^d decime maxime partis, ac maxime fructuos.
terre illius parochie, viz. earum terrarum, que parcis Dni.
Regis Henrici Octavi ibm. vicinis nuper incendebantur, a
rectore auferuntur: quemadmodum et ceteris rectoribus ac
vicariis ibm. vicinis. Ac allegavit ceteras decimas ibm. debit.
vix sufficere ad tenuem curati victum. Unde Dns. hoc detectum decrevit referend. ad reverend^{um} Dnum. Cardinalem.

Gardiani p'ntant vicariam ibm. vacuam fuisse tres annos; Litlington.
eo quod portio vicario assignata sit nimis tenuis. Et alle- Vicaria va-
gabant rectoriam esse Dni. Cardinalis. Unde Dns. retulit cua.
detectum ad reverendiss^{um} Dnum. ut supra.

Gardiani p'ntant, vicariam vacuam fuisse fere tres annos Fletwike.
propter tenuitatem dotationis vicarie. Ac allegabant r'co- Vicaria va-
riam perquisitam esse per quendam Magistrum Loude. cua.

Cancellum eccl'ie in ruina, culpa approprietarii. Ac gar- Potton.
diani putant rev^{mum} Cardinalem habere dispositionem re- Cancellum
ctorie ibm. in ruina.

Esworthe.
Cancellum. Cancellum eccl'ie est ruinosum. Est in dispositione Dni. Cardinalis. Unde Dns. retulit ad rev^{mum} Dnum. predict.

Dunton.
Vicaria va-
cua. Vicaria diu vacua permansit: quia tenuis dotatio ejusdem non sufficit curat. alendo. Rectoria pertinet ad rev^{mum} Dominum Cardinalem. Unde Dns. detectum ad eund. retulit.

Bedford
Pauli vi-
caria vacua. Gardiani p'ntant vicariam ibm. tres fere annos vacuam fuisse. Eo quod portio vicarii non sufficit curat. alendo. Unde Dns. detectum retulit ad rev^{mum} Dnum. Cardinalem. In cujus dispositione r'coria ibm. est.

170
Okely. Con-
fessio in
Quadrage-
sima. Milo Redshawe detectus est, q^d bis in Quadragesima non confitebatur vicario ibm. xxv^{to} Junii, comparuit dict. Redshawe, et confessus est, qd. semel in Quadragesima confitebatur. Unde Dns. injunxit sibi publicam peniten. et eum dimisit.

Wutton.
Cancellum. Gardiani p'ntant cancellum eccl'ie esse in ruina: ac rc'oriam esse reverend^{mi} Dni. Cardinalis. Unde Dns. retulit detectum ad reverenm^{um} Dnum. Cardinalem; eo q^d appropriata est clero.

Deane. Re-
ctoria im-
propriata. Presentant gardiani, q^d duos jam annos rc'oria ibm. habit. et impropriata est decano et capitulo Wigorniens: ac qd. interim nullus est ibm. dotatus l'time vicarius. Ac q^d sepenumero destituti sunt curato; cum interim ampla sit rc'oria, ac humoi' que anteactis temporibus laudabilem prebuit hospitalitatem.

Tilles-
worth. Vi-
caria vacua. Vicaria diu permansit vacua: quia nullus curatus eandem acceptare vult. Domina Longe perquisivit rc'oriam.

Roxton.
Magister et
socii coll.
Trin. Cant.
approprie-
tarii. Mag'ir ac socii collegii Sce' Trinitat' Cant. appropriatarii ibm. detecti sunt, qd. deberent comparare eccl'ie ibm. unam capam pro diebus festivis congruam. xx. Junii 1556, comparuit firmarius rc'orie, ac promisit se mertiaturum dict. appropriatariis, ut emendent detectum citra festum Mich'is. Unde Dns. decrevit supersedend. ad illum diem.

Risley.
Cancellum. Cancellum ibm. indiget reparatione. Rectoria est rev^{mi}. Dni. Cardinalis. Unde Dns. decrevit referend. causam ad predict. Dnum. Cardinalem.

Bednsm.
Vicaria va-
cua. Vicaria per quatuor annos vacua. Quia dotatio ejusdem non sufficit vicar. alend. Rc'oriam ibm. perquisivit quedam Anna Butler, nuper vidua.

Vicaria vacua permansit supra duos annos propter insuf- Willington.
ficient. dotationem ejusdem. Dns. Will'mus Peter perqui- Vicaria va-
sivit rectoriam.

Nullus rector, nec vicarius dotatus ibm. Decime perqui- Wooborne.
site sunt per Dum. Joh'em Russel, nuper defunctum. Nullus rector, nec

Gardiani p'ntant quandam domum hospitalem apud Bed- vicarius.
ford, vocat. Anglicè, *S. Leonard's Hospital*, occupatam fu- Bedford.
isse per multos annos jam tempore schismatis per Dnm. pitalis.
Joh'em Braie: ac jam eandem perquisitam esse per quendam Johannem Albainum de Bedford: ac valorem ejusdem *Index*
esse xvil. vis. viiid. annuatim consistend. in temporalibus.
Fundatio ejusdem in omnibus violata est, et fuit per plures
annos.

Presentant gardiani quandam fundationem hospitalis ibm. Tedington.
in omnibus esse et fuisse per plures annos violatam; ac Hospitalis
fructus ejusdem occupatos esse per laicos. Ac egregiam violata.
ibm. domum magistro et fratribus hospitalis constitutam, in 171
magnam prolapsam ruinam. Valor ejusdem domus hospitalis est viiil. annuatim iiis. iiiid.

Gardiani p'ntant cancellum reparatione indigere, culpa Derney.
approprietarii, et firmarii r'corie ibm. xviiiº die Junii, anno Cancellum.
Dni. 1556, apud Whitchurche comparuit Will'mus Tillx-
ley, armiger, firmarius r'corie ibm. et allegavit dcam' rectoriam concessam reverendmo. Dno. Cardinali: ac se non te-
neri ad reparationem. Unde Dns. retulit causam ad pred'cum
revmum. Dnm. Cardinalem.

Gardiani p'ntant Agnetem Comes innuptam gravidam Denham.
fuisse ex patre ignoto. viiiº die Junii anno pred'co apud Agnes in-
Whitchurche, facta fide de executione citationis, Dns. dict. vida.
Agnetem exco'icavit: ac eadem exco'icata permansit supra
xlta dies. Unde Dns. pro brevi, *De exco'icata capienda*,
scribendum decrevit.

Gardiani presentant cancellum ruinosum, culpa coll'ii de Dachet.
Windesor, approprietarii ibm. viii Junii, anno Dni. pre- Cancellum
dict. comparuit Will'mus Reade, firmar. r'corie ibm. ac ruinosum.
promisit reparationem ante finem Mich'is prox. sequen.
Unde Dns. injunxit ad certificandum apud Beconsfeld prox.
curia post fin. Mich'is coram commissar. Bucks.

Stoke Po-ges. Tho. Holl. non frequentat eccl'iam.

Thomas Hollowey detectus est per gardianos, q^d non frequentat eccl'iam parochialem temporibus divinorum. viii Julii anno predict. comparuit; ac confessus est detectum; ac submisit se correctioni. Quem correctum et emendatum Dns. Epus. dimisit a judicio.

Marloo Magn. Carnium venditor.

Johannes More, carnium venditor, detectus, q^d tempore divinorum diebus festivis h'et apertas fenestras officine sue. viii Junii, anno predict. comparuit, ac promisit emendationem detecti. Unde Dns. injuncta penitent. dimisit.

Sanderton. Rector non residet.

Rector Dns. Robtus' Frankishe detectus, q^d non residet. viii Junii, anno Dom. 1556to comparuit Mr. Morganus Jones, ac exhibito procuratorio l'torie concepto pro d'co rectore, allegavit illam esse Oxonie studiorum causa. Et obtulit se paratum ad id probandum. Unde Dns. Epus. injunxit, ut resideret ante festum Mich'is prox. Ac certificet prox. curia apud Ailebury post festum Mich'is.

Wendover. Meretrix.

Johanna Hales, detecta, q^d meretrix est. viii Junii, anno pred'co comparuit, et negavit crimen. Unde assignatum est eidem, q^d ad purgandum se quarta manu presentar. se xxiiii^to Julii apud Whitchurche. Quo die comparuit, et confessa est detectum. Submisit se correctioni Dni. Unde eandem peracta penitent. emendatam dimisit.

Non ibant in processione.

Hugo Roffe, Nich'us Hore, ac Nich'us Kepinge de eadem parochia, detecti, q^d quodam die d'nico, in processione cum 172 ceteris parochianis non ibant. Octavo Junii anno pred'co comparuerunt, et fassi sunt detectum. Unde eosdem post penitent. peractam Dns. dimisit.

Risbo-rough Principis. Margaret Mason.

Margareta Mason detecta est, q^d habuit partum ex illicito coitu. xviii Junii, confessa est se partum h'uisse per Nich'um Welche de Oxon. Cum quo etiam asseruit se matrimonium contraxisse. Unde Dns. injuncta peniten. predict. Margarete, decrevit scribendum ordinario Oxon. pro emendatione Nicholai Welche.

Weston Turvill. Cancellum ruinosum.

Cancellum detectum est ruinosum esse. viii Junii, anno Dom. pred'co rector ibm. per procuratorem suum lt'um confessus est detectum, ac promisit emendationem. Unde Dns. injunxit, ut emendaretur ante festum Mich'is prox. et certificaret apud Aylesbury prox. curia post, coram commissario Bucks.

Cancellum ruinosum, culpa decani et capit'li Roffen. appropertarii. viii Junii, anno pred'co comparuit Thomas Holman, firmarius rc'orie ibm. Qui promisit se renuntiaturum detectum Dno. Decano. Unde Dns. distulit causam ad finem Mich'is prox.

Codington. Cancellum ruinosum.

Will'mus Bawle detectus est, q^d non recepit sacramentum, nec confessus suo curato, hoc Paschate. Deinde per parochianos ac gardianos ibm. facta est fides, q^d idem Bawle mente captus est, ut plurimum. Unde Dns. decrevit supersedend. ad intervalla: quibus intelligi possit dict. famos. aliquid sane mentis recepisse.

Brill. Non recepit sacramentum.

Isabella Sharps, detecta, q^d innupta habuit partum, et pater ignoratur. Octavo Junii, anno Dom. 1556. comparuit dict. Isabella, ac confessa est se partum h'uisse per Johannem Westley de Hogshawe, pastorem ovium. Unde Dns. eandem peracta peniten. dimisit: ac Westley exco'icavit, non curand. comparere.

North Merston. Innupta habet partum.

Johannes Nutbrone detectus est, q^d non vult ire in processione diebus dni'cis. xi Junii, anno Dni. 1556. comparuit, et confessus est detectum: submisit se. Unde Dns. injuncta penitentia eundem dimisit.

Stowe. Ire in processione.

Will'mus Harte detectus est, q^d non recepit sacramentum infra suam parochiam hoc anno, nec confessus fuit. xiii^o Julii, anno Dni. pred'co comparuit d'cus Will'mus Harte, ac exco'icatus propter contumaciam suam, petiit absolutionem, &c. Et allegavit se recepisse sacramentum in eccl'ia de Brigstocke comitat. Barks. ac ibm. confessum fuisse: ac super allegatione humoi' fidem fecit. Unde Dns. eundem absolvit, &c. Restituit, &c. Ac preterea injunxit, q^d citra festum Mich'is afferat certificatorias l'ras a curato de Brigstocke.

Shenley. Non recepit sacramentum.

Will'mus Woodcocke detectus est, qd. commisit adulterium cum quadam Matilda   xiii^o Junii, anno pred'co gardiani certificabant pred'cum Will'mum et Matildam aufugisse. Unde Dns. decrevit supersedend. ad reddit. ipsorum.

Newport Pannel. Commisit adulterium.

Gardiani presentant vicariam ibm. vacuam esse ac fuisse tres annos; ac etiam ibm. plerumque divinis officiis desti-

173 Ejusdem vicaria vacua.

tutam esse diebus Dominicis ac festivis: ac neminem velle suscipere in se onus vicarie tam magne ibm. propter exilitatem portionis vicarii ibm. viz. x*l*. in pecunia numerata, cum rudi mansione. Ac presentabant rectoriam ibm. esse in dispositione rev^{mi} Dni. Cardinalis. Unde Dnus. retulit detectum ad dictum reveren^{mum} dc'um Cardinalem.

Bradwel. Cancellum. Cancellum ruinosum est, culpa approprietarii ibm. xvii° die Junii, anno Dni. 1556to comparuit Will'mus Wogan firmarius ibm. ac allegavit rc'oriam esse in dispositione rever^{mi} Dni. Cardinalis, ac se exoneratum esse per indenturam suam. Unde Dns. facta fide retulit causam ad dict. reverendiss. Dnum.

Olney. Cancellum. Gardiani presentant cancellum fere collapsum esse, ac vix centum marcas sufficere ad reparationem ejusdem: ac r'coriam esse Dni. Cardinalis. Unde Dns. decrevit detectum referend. ad reverend^{um} Dnum. Cardinalem.

Iving-hoo. Cancellum. Cancellum ibm. indiget reparatione, culpa approprietarii. R'coria pertinet ad rev^{um} Dom. Cardinalem. Unde. Dns. decrevit superseden. ac causam referend. d'co reveren^{mo} Domino.

Swanborne. Cancellum. Cancellum ruinosum, culpa approprietarii. Rc'oria pertinet ad rev^{um} Dom. Cardinalem. Unde Dns. decrevit causam referend. pred'co Dno. Cardinali.

Muresley. Cancellum. Cancellum indiget reparatione, culpa rectoris. Nono die Junii, anno Dni. 1556to comparuit curatus rectoris ibm. et promisit reparationem citra fin. S'ti Johannis Bapte'. Ac certificavit de reparatione, facta juxta mandatum Dni. Judicis.

Westbery. Bona eccl'ie. Johannes Morden parochianus detectus est, q^d habuit de bonis eccl'ie ibm. unum argenteum calicem: quem recusavit reddere eccl'ie. Tertio die mensis Julii, anno Dni. pred'co comparuit Johannes Morden, et confessus est, q^d vendidit calicem xxx*s*. Unde Dns. eidem injunxit, ut citra fin. Mich'is prox. solveret d'ce eccl'ie xxx*s*. Quos idem promisit; ac habet ad certificand. prox. curia post fin. Mich'is apud Bucks.

Ashbie Parva. Mansum r'corie. Mansum rc'orie et cancellus maximam ruinam patiuntur. Jam vacat per resignationem ultimi incumbent. ejusdem. Dns. Rex et Regina sunt patroni.

Cancell. ruinam patitur, culpa Magistri Rad'i Rowlet, ma-nentis juxta villam S'ti Albani: qui emit dict. capellam, (ut asseritur.) Wheston capella. Cancell.

Cancellus ibm. ruinam patitur, culpa Magistri Gressam, manentis apud civitat. London. qui emit dict. r'coriam. Ernisbie. Cancellum.

Vacat propter exilitatem. Comes Oxon. est patronus. Elmisthor.

Vacat. Magister Johannes Turvile, generosus, est pa-tronus. P. 174 Thurleston.

Valet per annum, viz. communibus annis in reddit. et emolumentis xxxi$l$. xxii$d$. ob. Inde solut. et distribut. in eleemosynis pro fundat. per ann. iiii$l$. et reddit. resolut. xiish. vd. ob. Sic remanet magistro ibm. xxvi$l$ ixsh. vd. Unde nihil distribuitur. Mansum et capella ruinam maximam patiuntur.. Magir' Broke, qui manet apud Turrim London. est magir' humoi' hospitalis: et tenetur habere unum sufficientem capellanum presentem ad ministrandum certo numero pauperum: et non sunt ibm. neque sacerdos neque pauperes; neque fuerunt per spatium trium annorum. Dux Suffolcie nuper fuit fundator: modo Dns. Rex et Regina sunt fundatores. Hospital S'ti Johannis de Lutterworthe.

Cancellus ruinam patitur, culpa Mri. Bolles, manentis apud Freston in com. Lincoln. qui emit dict. rc'oriam. Stonisbie. Cancellus.

Cancell. et mansum rc'orie maximam ruinam patiuntur, culpa rc'oris ibm. qui manet apud London. Mr. Everardus Asshelie est firmarius ibm. Dns. Rex et Regina sunt patroni. Coston. Cancel. et mansum.

Magir' Everardus Ashebie he't in manibus suis unam capam et vestimentum de le *crimson velvet*, ac aliam capam de la *green silk*. Quas eccl'ie restituere recusat. Commissa est causa commissario Leicestr. ut fiat justitia.

Fenestre vitree cancelli sunt ruinose. Dns. Cardinalis habet rc'oriam appropriatam. Barston. Fenestre.

Cancellus, cemeterium et rectoria indigent reparatione. Certificatur, q^d reparantur. Saxulbie. Cancell.

Muri cemiterii et capelle fuerunt in decasu, ac carent multis necessariis: nec altare reedificatum. Certificatur, q^d reparantur. Gaddesbie. Capella.

Will'mus Cockin et Will'mus Lacer, eo tempore quo Wymysworlde.

Bona sub-tracta. erant iconomi [oeconomi] subtraxerunt multa bona ab ' eadem eccl'ia. Sicut patet per billam parochianorum. Qui restituere recusant. Decretum est pro processu fiendo per commissarium Archidiac. Leicestr.

Will'mus Cockin antedictus officio detectus est de adulterio cum diversis mulieribus: specialiter cum quadam Alicia Crosse. De eadem citat. comparuit mulier, et submisit se peniten'. Et d'cus Will'mus non comparuit: in penam contumacie suspens' postmodum obtinuit inhibitionem a Dno. Decano de Arcubus in d'ca causa criminali. Qua occasione crimen manet impunit'.

Walton. Cancel. Cancellus et navis eccl'ie indigent reparatione, culpa r'coris et parochianorum. Habuerunt terminum ad reparand. **175** citra festum Penthecostes. Rector vero moram trahit apud Mancestr. in com. Warwici. Causa committitur commissario Leicestr.

Barkbe. Vacat.

Belgrave. Vacat: non habens rectorem neque vicarium. Dns. Epus' Litchfeldensis est patronus. Ad quem scripsimus.

Prestwolde. Vacat: non habent rc'orem neque vicarium. Dnus. Cardinalis est patronus.

Kirkbie Bellers. Vacat: non habens rc'orem neque vicarium. Dns. Cardinalis est patronus.

Lodington. Vacat: non habens rc'orem neque vicarium. Dns. Cardinalis est patronus.

Ulvestoune. Vacat: non habens rectorem neque vicarium. Dns. Cardinalis est patronus.

Billesden. Cancell. Cancellus ruinam patitur, culpa Mri' Thome Hasilwoode. Qui emit d'cam rc'oriam. Cemeterium indiget reparatione. Carent ornamentis. Hu'erunt terminum ad reparandum citra finem Penthecostes. Nondum certificatur. Ideo fiat processus per commissarium Leic. ad debitam correctionem.

Norton. Cancel. Cancellus ruinam patitur in fenestris vitreis, culpa Mri' Turpin. qui emit d'cam rc'oriam. Muri cemeterii indigent reparatione: ac violatur bestiis. Habuerunt termin' ad reparandum citra festum Penthecostes. Nondum certificat. Ideo decretum, ut fieret processus, ut prius.

Cancellus ruinam patitur. Appropriatur reverendissimo *Foxton et* *Thurnebie.*
Dno. Cardinali.

Rector non residens. Manet apud aliud beneficium in *Galbie non* *residens.*
com. Lincoln. Decer' vocand. per commissarium Leic.

Rector non residens. Fiat processus: ut prius. *Kibworthe.*
Vacat: ac diu vacavit propter exilitatem beneficii. Dns. *Non resi-*
dens.
Cardinalis est patronus. *Lubham.*

Mansum rc'orie patitur maximam ruinam. Fama publica *Medburne.*
est, q^d rc'or ibm. Dnus. Johannes Standish, qui trahit *Mansum.*
moram Leicestrie, est symoniace promotus. Dns. Le Scrope,
sive Dns. Le Conias, sunt patroni. Unde Dns. vocand. decrevit. Necdum comparuit. Ideo Dnus. decrevit ulteriorem
processum. Et causa commissa est commissario Leic.

Vacat, et diu vacavit: non he'ns rc'orem nec vicarium. *Bowden.*
Mra' Stirley he't rc'oriam in suos usus; perquisitam per vi-
rum suum, modo defunctum: sed non antea appropriatam.
Fiat melior inquisitio.

Mansum rc'rie maximam ruinam patitur. Fama publica 176
est, q^d rector est simoniace ea promotus, per conventionem *Higham.*
inter ipsum et Johannem Ridgeley, generos. D'cus Ridge- *Mansum.*
ley he't proficua beneficii. Dns. Rex et Regina sunt patroni.
Decernitur vocand. et committitur causa commissario.

Vacat: ac diu vacavit, ratione junctionis extra curiam *Bredon.*
Augmentationis. Causa est in audientia coram reven^{mo} Dno.
Cardinali.

Cancellus maximam ruinam patitur. Eccl'ia indiget repa- *Rotheley.*
ratione. Carent multis ornamentis et picturis. Habuerunt *Cancell.*
termin. ad reparandum citra fin. Penthecostes prox. Nondum certificatur.

Rector non residens. Trahit moram apud Cantabr. De- *Kegworthe.*
cernitur vocand. ad residentiam suam sub pena priva- *Non resi-*
dens.
tionis.

Will'mus Salisbury, et Ric'us Hodge de Shepston predict. *Shepston.*
queruntur parochianos a tempore coronationis Dne. Regine *Campana.*
maximam campanam eccl'ie de Shepston vendidisse pro ix*l.*
valentem xxxvii*l.* Dns. scripsit Archidiacono Leicestrie, pro
hac causa.

Thomas Aschelin notatur, q^d abfuit ab eccl'ia sua paro- *Yaxley.*
Absens.

chiali in die Parasceues. Sexto Maii comparuit, et submisit se. Ac penitentia est ei injuncta.

Glatton.
Ludibrium.

Henricus Clerke notatur, q^d ludibrio habuit sacrificium messe inter compotandum. Comparuit, et fassus est se cantasse particulas illas, *Et cum Sp'u tuo. Sursum corda. Habemus ad Dominum: dignum et justum est,* &c. Non tamen in derisione messe. Submisit se tamen correctioni Domini. Cui data est schedula recantationis. Quam legit prox. Dominica tempore misse, in eccl'ia sua parochiali.

Stangronde cum Sacell.
Offley
Sandon
Westome
Esenden

} Cancelli ruinosi. Sequestrantur fructus.

Shenley.
Calix.

Non habent calicem argenteum. Tectum eccl'ie ruinosum. Habent ad reparandum citra finem Sti' Johannis Bapte'.

Kimbaltoune. Crucifixorium.

Will'mus Smithe detraxit crucifixorium absque consensu paroch'. Et he'nt tantum parochum, cum sint amplius quam mille parochiani. Mra' Wilkinson habet appropriatam ecclesiam. Decretum est pro Smithe vocand.

177
Alcumbery.
Commisit fornicationem.

Georgius Kidd commisit fornicationem cum quadam muliere ibm. Sexto Maii comparuit d'cus Kidd, et fatetur se cognovisse quandam Elizabeth Powche. Et q^d contraxit cum eadem : sed noluit eam ducere, pro eo q^d quidam Everardus Burnebie etiam cognovit eam. Quem Dns. decrevit ad comparend. in prox. curia, ac etiam mulierem. Et monuit d'cum Kidd ad comparend. in prox. ad recipiend. penitentiam.

Bitham. In decasu.

Rectoria in decasu et cancellus. Ac nullum habent curatum. Fiat sequestratio.

Hatfeld Epi'. Sacramentum.

Agnes Mery notatur, q^d non recepit sacramentum Eucharistie hoc Paschali tempore. Peregit penitentiam.

Hertford Sti. Andree. Portare cereum.

Robertus Webbe renuit portare cereum die Purificationis Bte' Marie Virginis ult. Peregit penitentiam.

Welwin.

Agnes Thurste vidua h'uit prolem citra mortem mariti sui : et de patre ejusdem nescitur. Peregit penitentiam.

Bayford.

Eccl'ia in ruina. Habent reparare citra fin' Mich'is prox.

David Will'ms impregnavit quandam Aliciam Downer. *North Myms.*
Peregit penitentiam.

Cancellus in ruina. Ut fiat sequestratio. *Kennisworth.*

Domini Johannes Yngvey, et Thoms' Goldere, presby- *worth.* teri, habent accessum ad suas concubinas. Suspensi fuge- *Suspensi, fugerunt.* runt.

Robertus Rosse absentavit se ab eccl'ia sua parochiali die *Hemilhamstede. Dies* Purificationis Bte' Marie Virginis. xix die Maii apud Hitchin *Purifica-* comparuit dict. Rosse: et habet ad comparend. coram justi- *tionis.* ciar. habit. monitione. Peregit penitentiam.

Anthonius Bonninge citra t'pus schismaticale detinuit *Abbotsley.* candelam suam, et illam non obtulit modo solit. in die Puri- *Detinuit candelam.* ficationis Bte' Marie. Peregit penitentiam.

Rogerus Clerke suscitavit prolem de Johanna White. Per- *Barkehamstede.* egit penitentiam.

Quidam Alexander Allisonne detinet a vicario duas can- *Abbotesley.* delas vicar. debit. dicend. ista verba Anglicana, *That a* *Detinet candelas.* *wiser vicar than yee wil not require them.*

Quidam Rob'tus Newman recepit sacramentum absque *Paxton.* auriculari confessione. Peregit penitentiam. *Auricularis confessio.*

Russheden.   Fenny Staunton ⎱ Cancelli ruinosi. Dns' **178** Gaddesden.   Wimley Magna ⎰ Epus. sequestravit.

Rich'us Belgrave absentavit se diu ab uxore sua, et aliam *Berkehamstede. Peni-* duxit, et ipsa similiter alium. Quibus injuncta est penitentia *tentia.* more solito.

Quædam Agnes Seale h'uit prolem, et nescitur per quem. *Abbotesley.* Sexto Maii comparuit mulier, et fatebatur articulum, per *Habuit prolem il-* quendam Rob'tum Mydleton de Gramsden Parva, dum- *legit.* modo erat in servitio suo, &c. Et habet penitent. more so- lito.

Johannes Slowe notatur, q^d per duas noctes, et unum *Guncester.* diem erat in domo Thome Vintener cum quadam Ursula *Suspiciose.* ux' dict. Thomæ suspiciose. Peregit penitent.

Quidam Robertus Aleyne absentat se ab eccl'ia sua pa- *Somersham.* rochi. Et cum venerit, se non bene gerit. Peregit peni- *Absentat se.* tent.

Nich'us Philipp notatur, q^d laborat in sua facultate in die *Ramsey.* Pasche ult. Peregit peniten. Et di...... est populosa pa- *Laborat in die Pasche.*

rochia : nec h'et rectorem nec vicarium. Mr. Ric'us Crum-well habet eccl'iam appropriatam.

Stephinage. Lenocinium. Thoms' Enderbie et ejus ux' notant' q^d fovent lenocinium in domo sua, custodiend. suspectam mulierem : quam Ric'us Yarley de Weston impregnavit. Reformatur quoad virum. Vocetur mulier.

Aylton. Duas proles habuit. Elizabeth Cuthbert h'uit duas proles, et manet cum Thoma Welforde : ut vocetur ad respondend. certis artic'lis. xviii° Junii apud Hunt, injunctum est, q^d offerret cereum manibus sacerdotis, &c. Peregit peniten.

WardonVetus. Rectorem non habet. Populosa parochia rectorem non h'et, nec vicarium. Dna. Elizabetha est proprietaria.

179

Multon	Raisen Drax media.	
Freston		
Whaplode	Westerington	
Butterwyke	Ancaster	
Stirtonne	Bemyngton	
Pinchbecke	Honyngton	
Randebie	Burton	
Donington	Hekyngton	
Stainton	Hale	Rectorie sunt appropriate reveren^mo Dno. Cardinali. Et cancelli ac mansa rc'oriarum ruinam patiuntur. Quare Dns. decrevit referend. reveren^mo Dno. Cardinali antedict.
Frampton	Iwardbie	
Sibsey	Digbie	
Friskeney	Armeston	
Stepinge Mag.	Canwike	
Billesbie	Timberlande	
Billesbie mar'	Swinestede	
Kedington	Billingbrugh	
Southelkington	Sempringham	
Fotterbie	Threkingham	
Grimolbie	Swatonne	
Barrowe	Mortonne	
Barton	Barham	
Therneton	Tallington	
Ulcebie	Hacthorne	
Noneton	Alkebarough	
Warletbie	Winterton	
Esteraisen	Repham.	

Stickeforde	Rayson. Non	
Holbeche	pertinet ad	
Quadringe	Epum.	
Wigtoste	Tupholm me-	*Reparat.*
Brughen	dia.	Rectorie appropriate sunt
Winthorp	Scopwithe	Epo. Lincoln. Et can-
Hoggesthorp	Kirkebie Grene	celli ac mansa rectoria-
Alforde	Bichefelde. Re-	rum ruinam patiuntur.
Mumbie	paratur.	Ad reparationem qua-
Hotoste	Horblinge	rundam tenentur firma-
Cokerington	Morton	rii. Quibus datus est
mar'.	Aconbie	dies.
Cokerington	Northorpp	
Leonardi.	Gainsboroughe.	
Alvingham	Reparatur.	
Tetney		

Thedilthorpe omn' S'torum	Rectorie sunt appropriate heredib. Dni.
Langton	Caroli nuper Ducis Suffolcie. Et can-
Scothorne	celli ac mansa rectoriarum ruinam pa-
Hagnabie	tiuntur.

Toynton omn' S'torum.	**180**
Fulslowe	Rec'orie sunt appropriate Dne. Catharine
Elissham	Ducisse Suff. Et cancelli ac mansa rc'o-
Ingham	riarum ruinam patiuntur.
Frothingham	

Cancellus et r'coria ibm. egeat reparationem.   Et nuper Swineshed. appropriata fuit monast' de West'mer.

Cancell. et r'coria ibm. sunt in magn. ruina, negligentia Flitte. Dni. Gilberti Plumpton rectoris ibm.   Fact. processus.

R'coria ibm. eget reparatione : eo q^d nuper vastat. et dis- Lenertton. tract. fuit violentia ignis.

Cancell. et r'coria ibm. sunt admodum ruinos. culpa Dne. Sutton. Anne de Cleve, proprietarie ibm.

Cancell. et r'coria ibm. egent reparatione, negligen. De- Thorneton. cani et Capit'li Lichefeld, proprietar.

Stickney. Cancell. et r'coria ibm. sunt ruinos. culpa Dni. Simonis Lewes, r'coris ibm. nuper in ead. r'coria institut. Fit processus.

Skendelbie. Cancell. ibm. est in ruina, culpa Rob'ti Fawne, proprietar. ibm.

Grimesbie. Cancell. et r'coria ibm. sunt in magna ruina, culpa r'coris ibm. Fact. processus.

Dirington. Cancell. ibm. est in ruina, culpa tam Dne. Stanhope vidue, quam Johannis Thomson proprietar. ibm.

Lavington. Cancell. ibm. est in ruina culpa, Rob'ti Brodbank proprietar. ibm.

Saxbie. Cancell. et r'coria sunt in magna ruina, culpa Ri'ci Brokellesbie, generos. proprietarii ibm.

Cameringham. Cancell. ibm. est ruinos. Eo q^d non valet vicarius in choro celebrare, culpa Dni. Rob'ti Tirwhite senioris, militis, defuncti.

Ouston et Haxey. Cancell. et r'coria ibm. in manibus rever^{mi} p'ris Dni. Archie'pi Ebor. proprietar. earundem. Sunt valde ruinos.

Torkesey Maj. Torkesey Petri. Knethe. Cancelli ibm. sunt in magna ruina. Factus processus.

Dns. Thoms' Henneage, miles, jam defunctus, prophanavit cancellum eccl'ie ibm. in communia hospitia. Et Dns. Will'mus Willoughbie, miles, Dns. de Parham dict. cancell. sic prophanat. in pn'ti tenet. Et eccl'ia ibm. est ferme ad terram collapsa.

181

Conesbie. Auricularis confessio. Johannes Edenham communicavit, antequam auricularem confessionem subivit. xxii^o Maii anno Dni. 1556to coram dict. rev^{do} pre' comparuit d'cus Johann. Edenham, et fatebatur artic'lum. Cui jurat. d'ctus rev^{dus} pr' injunxit subire confessionem auricularem palam et publice apud suum altare die domi'co prox. coram parochianis per sacerdotem : et penitere in publico mercato apud Tatershal in prox. mercato ibm. presente, more penitentis, nudis pedibus, tibiis et capite, cum candela in manu sua.

Caborne. Duxit monialem. Will'mus Otbie in uxorem duxit quandam Janam Missenden nuper monialem. Sexto die Junii anno Dni. pred'cto coram prefato rev^{do} p're personaliter constitut. d'ci Will'mus et Jana fatebantur artic'lum. Et Dns. per sententiam definitivam ipsos, Will'mum et Janam tam a mensa, quam a thoro separavit, et divortiavit.

· Christoferus Sawer solut. in uxorem pretensam quandam Gains-
borough.
Monialis. Elizabeth Rider duxit. x° die Junii anno pred'co coram prefato rev^{do} p're personaliter constitut. d'ci Christoferus et Elizabeth, ac nullam causam poterant allegare, quare divortiari non debeant. Ac idem Dns. Ep'us per sententiam definitivam ipsos a conjugali consortio separavit, et divortiavit: cum monitione de abstinendo a mutuo consortio sub pena juris.

Andreas Lacie illegitime conjunxit se conjugali consortio Horke-
stowe.
Monialis. Margarete Jackelin, nuper moniale. Secundo die mens. Julii anno Dni. ante d'co coram d'co Dno. Epo' personaliter constitut. d'ci Andreas et Margareta nullam causam allegare poterint, quare divortiari non debeant. Unde idem Epus' per sententiam definitivam eosdem divortiavit, cum tali monitione ad abstinend.

Anthonius Strailes et Ric'us Langrake comederunt carnes Boston.
Comede-
runt carnes. quodam die Sab'ti. xxvii die Julii anno Dni. predict. comparuerunt d'ci Anthonius et Ric'us; et fatentur artic'lum, ac penitentie se humiliter submiserunt. Quibus juratis Dns. injunxit penitere in hunc modum. Q^d d'ci Anthonius et Ric'us in publico mercato apud Boston circumferant sup. humeris suis induti linthiamen, nudis pedibus et capite, unum quarterium agni, viz. *Le a lambs quarter.*

Will'mus Barde de eadem tenet quandam Emmam Kerke- Wintring-
ham.
Adulte-
rium. bie in amplexibus adulterinis. xii° die Junii anno pred'co apud Lincoln. comparuerunt personaliter dict. Will'mus et Emma: et exa'iat. fatentur artic'lum. Cui Dns. injunxit penitere in publico foro apud Lincoln. publice, more penitentis, viz. *That the said Emme shal ride thorough the city and market in a cart, and be ronge out with basons.* Et commisit eandem vicecom. civitatis Lincoln. ad vidend. executionem.

Johannes Miller als' Fawkener de eadem, carnaliter cog- 182
Kirkebie
Grene.
Carnaliter
cognovit. novit quandam Elizabeth Hardwan. xii° die Junii anno pred'co apud Lincoln. comparuerunt personaliter, tam dict. Joh'es quam dicta Elizabeth. Qui exa'inati artic'lum fatentur. Quibus d'cus rev^{dus} Dns. pr. injunxit penitere publice, more penitentis, in publico foro apud Lincoln. Donec et quousque penitent. suam peregerunt; prout sibi et eorum utrique erat injuncta per d'cum rev^{um} patrem.

D'cus Johannes Miller similiter cognovit quandam Jennettam Smithe. Qui similiter exa'inat. fatetur artic'lum. Cui d'cus rev^{dus} pr' injunxit penitere, ut supra cum suprano'inat. Elizabeth. Et similiter commisit eandem vicecom. civitatis Lincoln. ad vidend. executionem.

D'cus Miller als' Fawkener una cum prescriptis meretricibus commiss. maiori et vicecom. Lincoln. in biga circumferebantur. Et Miller nudatis scapulis alligatus bige, fuit flagellatus usque ad sanguinem.

Magister Will'mus Wiat, sacerdos olim conjugatus, notatus, quod ab illicito suo conjugio separatus, per biennium ab altaris ministerio se abstinuit, nec curavit officio restitui. Vocatus se submisit, ac restitui postulavit. Cui injuncta est concio in eccl'ia cathedrali Lincoln. et restitutus officio.

Magister Johannes Todd, presbyter conjugatus, ac ab illicito conjugio separatus ab altari se abstinuit, atque amplexibus indulsit, vocatus primum in gaolam est conjectus. Post, injuncta est concio in eccl'ia cathedr. Lincoln. et restitutus officio.

Dns. Oliverus St. John, miles, pretendit sibi indultum per Dnm. Papam comedere carnes in Quadragesima. Quo indulto utitur tam ipse, quam tota sua familia in scandalum aliorum. Requisitus ut proferret indultum hactenus non protulit. Ideo ————————

Magister   Williams' de Dentonne, detectus quod abstulisset plumbum cancelli de Ewarbie. Vocatus, allegavit commissionem sibi factam tempore Regis Edwardi Sexti. Ad quam proferendam coram commissariis regiis dat. est ei dies.

Christoferus Catlin de Harrolde in com. Bedford, detectus est, quod per duos annos jam elapsos non interfuit divinis officiis, neque recepit eucharistiam in sua parochia. Vocatus tam per apparitorem, quam per literas commissariorum d'norum Regis et Reginæ, fugit in aliam diocesim. Quare Dns. decrevit scribend. ad Dnm. London. Epum. et alios sibi adjunctos commissarios, pro ulteriori processu versus eundum.

Articuli de quibus inquisitum est in visitatione predict'. ¹183

1. Primum, de fide et unitate fidelium : sintne aliqui he-retici, aut schismatici in parochiis, qui defendunt pravas et hereticas opiniones, contra fidem Catholicam, aut Chri' sa-cramenta in eccl'ia contra auct'em sanctissimi Dni' nri' Pape, et obedien' ejusdem.

2. Item, An sint, qui sine licentia Dni. Pape, vel sui le-gati, aut epi' loci, palam in eccl'iis predicare presumunt ; quive etiam in angulis adinuatis hominibus prava dogmata instillant, librosve hereticos legant, habent, vendunt, appor-tant, scribunt, aut quoquo modo propalant.

3. Item, An sint in parochiis sacerdotes conjugati a suis nephariis conjugiis nondum separati ; quive separati suas admittant ; ad easve accessum habeant.

4. Item, An sint in parochiis alique persone religiose pro-fesse, que contra vota illicito mri'onio sese copularunt.

5. Item, An sint omnia altaria in eccl'iis re-edificata, ca-lices, libri, vestimenta, ac cetera ornamenta. Sitne cruci-fixorium, cum imaginibus crucifixi, Marie et Johannis, re-edificatum ; ac reposit. in locum imago patroni.

6. Item, An sint fideles iconomi in singulis parochiis : qui singulis annis fidelem computum administrationis reddunt parochianis. Sintne aliqua bona eccl'iarum tempore schis-matis per alios, quam per commissionarios regios ablata.

7. Item, An sint in parochiis adulteri, fornicarii, usurarii, simoniaci, fatidici, incantatores, ebriosi, criminatores, cere-moniarum ecclesiasticarum contemptores, aut vituperatores.

8. Item, An sint in parochiis, qui recusaverunt suis cura-tis confiteri in Quadragesima, aut sc'am eucharistiam sumere in Paschate.

9. Item, An sint violatores jejuniorum ab Eccl'ia indicto-rum, qui carnes comederunt in Quadragesima, aut sancto-rum vigiliis.

10. Item, Sintne eccl'ie aut cancelli, seu mansa rectoria-rum, sarta tecta.

11. Item, Sintne rectores residentes, hospitalitatem te-nentes, ac gregibus suis invigilantes.

184   12. Item, Sintne eccl'ie vacantes, ac sacerdotibus destituti. Sintne satis dotate ad sacerdotes alendos.

Injunctiones pro Decano et Capitulo Ecclesiæ Lincolniensis.

Johannes permissione divina Lincoln. epus', dilectis nobis in Christo, decano et capit'lo eccl'ie n're cathedral' Lincoln. Ac aliis ministris ibm. &c. Auctoritate qua fungimur, pendente adhuc visitatione prct' quam vice et nomine rev^{mi} Dni. Reginaldi Cardinalis Poli nuncupati inchoavimus; vobis mandamus, quatenus injunctiones subscriptas recipientes, easdem executioni mandetis ipsi, aliis etiam omnibus (quantum interest) intimandas; et debite executioni ab ipsis (quantum in vobis est) demandandas, in reg'ris insuper eccl'ie vre' transcribendas, in futuram rei memoriam, curetis. Dat. apud Bugden primo die Augusti anno Dni. millimo' quingen^{mo} quinquages^{mo} sexto. Et n're consecrationis anno tertio.

1. Ex parte choristarum ecce' nre' conquestum est, terr' tenementa et predia, que ad illos pertinent, fuisse et esse per nuper decanum et capit'lum, licet minus juste, ad illorum grave dampnum et prejudicium, ad firmam dimissa. Vobis igitur aucte' qua fungimur, injungimus, ne terr' ten'ta aut predia humoi' de cetero ad firmam dimittatis, seu etiam alienetis, dimissionemve aut alienationem ab illis fact' (inconsulto Epo') confirmetis; sub pena deprivationis omnium promotionum quas in dioc' nra' obtinueritis.

2. Domus sive mansa infra clausum ecce' nre' existen. et in quibus canonici aut ecclesiastice persone residere consueverunt, laicis ad firmam per vos nullo modo dimittantur.

3. Mandamus, ut ecce' nre' Lincoln. deinceps in omnibus secundum usum eccl'ie cathedral. Sarum, tam cantando, quam legendo, ac etiam ceteras ceremonias peragendo, citra finem Pasche prox. futur. deserviri faciatis.

4. Mandamus, ut omnes prebendarii dce' ecce' in habitu clericali deinceps, tam infra eccam' nram', quam extra, incedant; nec barbas nutriant, sub pena amissionis prebende.

5. Mandamus, ne prebendarii ad stallum in choro in propriis personis admissi tempore divinorum in eccl'ia, sine suis superpelliciis et amiciis obambulant, sub pena xij*d*. totiens quotiens in premissis deliquerent, in usum triginta pauperum scholasticorum convertendorum.

6. Vicarii coias' infra precinctum ecce' insimul, aut sepa- 185 ratim capiant: neque in civitatem aut suburbium convivandi causa in ecce' scandalum, post festum Sti' Mich'is prox. futur. ullo modo transeant.

7. Male consuetudinis est, ut homines uxorati altari adstant, et subdiaconi officium exerceant. Id quod posthac ne fiat, curabitis.

8. Optamus aliquem gravem virum infra ordines sacros constitutum, choristis in senescallum per vos prefici; prout antiquitus fieri solebat.

Number LII.

The Council to the Lord President of the north, against some players of interludes in those parts.

AFTER our right harty commendations to your good Lordsp. Wheras we have been lately informed, that certain leud persons, to the number of six or seven in a company, naming themselves to be servants unto Sir Frauncis Leke, and wearing his livery and badge on their sleeves, have wandered about those north parts, and represented certain plays and enterludes, containing very naughty and seditious matter touching the King and Queen's Majesties, and the state of the realm, and to the slaunder of Christ's true Catholic Church, contrary to al good order, and to the manifest contempt of Almighty God, and dangerous example of others; we have thought meet to pray your Lordsp. to give order forthwith to al the justices of the peace within your rule, that from henceforth they do in no wise suffer any playes, enterludes, songs, or any such like pastimes, wherby the people may any ways be stirred to disorder; to be used by any maner of persons, or under

Ex Epist. comit. Salop. in Offic. Armor. vol. p. 229.

any colour or pretence, within the limits of your charge. Praying you also, not only to write unto Sir Frauncis Leke, willing him to cause the said players, that name themselves his servants, to be sought for, and sent forthwith unto you, to be further examined, and ordered according to their deserts; but also to give him strait charge and commandment in their Majesties names, that he suffer not any of his servants hereafter to go about the countries, and use any plays, songs, or enterludes, as he will answer for the contrary. 186 And in case any persons shal attempt to set forth these sort of games or pastimes, at any time hereafter, contrary to this order, and do wander for that purpose abroad in the country, your Lordsp. shal do well to give the justices of peace in charge, to se them apprehended out of hand, and punished as vagabonds, by vertue of the statute made against loitering and idle persons. And thus we bid your good Lordsp. most hartily wel to fare. From S. James, the xxx of April, 1556.

Your good Lordsp's assured loving friends,
Nico. Ebor. Canc.   Wynchester.   Hen. Sussex.
Pembroke.   Arundel.   Tho. Wharton.
Will. Petre.   Tho. Ely.

John Bourn.
Jo. Mordaunt.

Number LIII.

Sir John Cheke's writing and subscription, for the doctrine of the carnal presence.

De veritate corporis et sanguinis Domini in Eucharistia.

MSS. penes me.
Hilar. li. 8.
De Trinit.

EOS nunc, qui inter Patrem et Filium voluntatis ingerunt unitatem, interrogo, utrumne per naturæ veritatem hodie Christus in nobis sit, an per concordiam voluntatis? Si enim vere Verbum caro factum est, et nos vere verbum carnem cibo dominico sumimus, quomodo non naturaliter manere in nobis existimandus est, qui et naturam carnis nostræ igni inseparabilis sibi homo natus assumpsit, et naturam carnis

suæ ad naturam æternitatis sub sacramento nobis communi-
candæ carnis admiscuit. Ita enim omnes unum sumus, quia
et in Christo Pater est, et Christus in nobis est.

Et paulo post.

De veritate carnis et sanguinis non relictus est ambigendi Idem.
locus. Nunc enim et ipsius Domini, professione et fide
nostra, vere caro est, et vere sanguis est: et hæc accepta et
hausta id efficiunt, ut et nos in Christo, et Christus in nobis sit. Anne hoc veritas non est? Contingat plane his verum non esse, qui Christum Jesum verum esse Deum ne-
gant, et cæt. quæ in eodem loco sequuntur.

Helias melotem quidem discipulo, filius autem Dei ascen- Chrysost.
dens suam nobis carnem dimisit. Sed Helias quidem exu- ad pplm.
Antioch.
tus Christus autem et nobis reliquit, et ipsam habens ascen- Ho. 2.
dit. Ne igitur decidamus, neque lamentemur, neque tem- 187
porum difficultatem timeamus. Qui enim sanguinem suum
pro omnibus effundere non recusavit, et carnem suam et
rursus ipsum sanguinem nobis communicavit, et nihil pro
salute nostra recusavit.

In omnibus itaque Deo pareamus, neque contradicamus, Hom. 68.
licet cogitationibus nostris adversari videatur, et oculis, ad pplm.
Antioch.
quod dicitur: sed sit et cogitationibus et visu dignior ipsius
sermo. Sic et in ministeriis agamus, nec solum præ oculis
posita respiciamus, sed ipsius verba contineamus. Ipsius
enim sermo infallibilis, sensus autem noster seduci facilis.
Ille nunquam decidit, hic autem ut plurimum, quoniam et
verbum dicit, *Hoc est corpus meum.* Et pareamus, et cre-
damus, et intellectualibus ipsum oculis intueamur.

Sanctum et vivificum incruentatumque in ecclesiis cele- Cyril. sup.
bramus sacrificium, non hominis alicujus nobis similis, et Canon. 12.
Concil.
communis. Corpus consimiliter et pretiosum sanguinem esse Ephes.
quod præponitur credentes, sed magis proprium vivificantes
verbi corpus et sanguinem accipimus. Communis enim caro
vivificare non potest. Et hoc ipse Servator testatur, dicens;
Caro non prodest quicquam, Spiritus est qui vivificat. Quoniam enim verbo facta est propria, ob eam causam intelligitur, et est vivifica; sicut Servator dicit, *Sicut me misit vi-*

vens Pater, et ego vivo propter Patrem, et qui manducat me etiam vivet ille propter me.

August. ex
Beda et
Ivone.
Quod videtis in altari, panis est et calix, quod etiam oculi renuntiant, quod autem fides postulat instruenda, panis est corpus, calix et sanguis. Et paulo post.

Quomodo, inquit, panis est corpus, vel quod habet calix, quomodo est sanguis? Ista, fratres, ideo dicuntur sacramenta, quia aliud videtur, aliud intelligitur.

Aug. Serm.
ad Neophi.
ex Ivone.
Hoc accipite in pane quod pependit in cruce; hoc accipite in calice, quod manavit de Christi latere.

Hæc est sanctorum patrum, Hilarii, Chrysostomi, Augustini, Cyrilli de veritate corporis et sanguinis Domini in eucharistia sententia: in qua me quoque esse profiteor, non modo quia propter authoritatem doctrinæ et vitæ sanctitatem digni sunt quos sequamur, sed etiam quia Catholicæ Christi Ecclesiæ eadem sit sententia. Itaque in hac causa, et in reliquis omnibus idem me profiteor dicere et sentire, quod sancta Christi et Catholica tenet Ecclesia.

Joannes Checus.

188 ### Number LIV.

Sir John Cheke to Cardinal Pole, when he sent him the abovesaid confession by the Dean of St. Paul's.

J H U S.

Ibid.
FINEM contentionum non disputatio sed submissio facit. Ego ex C. T. consilio et authoritate a varietate doctorum ad Ecclesiæ unitatem accedo. In quo et C. T. de consilio gratias ago, et de successu Deo. Precor autem C. T. ut hæc mea sententia, quam vir doctus et pius ecclesiæ Paulinæ decanus C. T. tradet, quemadmodum non est a me ad tempus ficta, sic sit C. T. accepta, et omnis reliquæ de me questionis finis. Magnam habeo de virtutibus tuis, de pietatis et clementis [clementiæ] laude, de doctrina humilitatis fiduciam. Vellem te mei, et pietatis et literarum etiam aliqua ex parte studiosi, nonnullam rationem habere. Reliquum spero vitæ meæ cursum talem futurum, ut gratia tua et favore non indignus videar.

Quæ necessariæ sunt meæ hoc tempore petitiones, eas D.
Decanus Celsitudini tuæ exponet. In quibus etiam atque
etiam supplex peto, ut me juves. Dominus C. T. servet.
Londini e Turre, 15 Julii 1556. C. T. addictissimus,

Joannes Checus.

Number LV.

*Sir John Cheke to Queen Mary ; intimating his compliance
in religion, and petitioning for his liberty.*

PLEASITH it your Majestie to understonde, that in mat- Ibid.
ters of religion I have declared my ful mynde unto your Majestie, by your virtuous and learned chaplin, Mr. Dean of
Paul's ; trusting, that as it is truly minded of me, so your
Highnes will agreeably receave it. I beseech your Majestie, 189
therfore, as I have been and am your faithful subject,
whom I do, as God's minister, faithfully honor and serve,
that your Highnes wil have that opinion present of me, that
my faithfulnes, I trust, and dewtie hereafter, shal shew unto
you. And I trust, among many obedient and quyot subjects, which God storeth your Highnes with, I shall be
found, tho' not in habilitie of other qualities, yet in wil and
redines, and obedience of your lawes, and other orders of religion, as glad to serve and obey as eny other : desiring your
Majestie most humbly to favour such poor suits for my
liberty, as Mr. Dean shal make to your Majestie in my behalf. Almighty God prosper and encrese your Majestie in
all honor and godlines. From your Majesties Tower of
London, the 15th of July 1556.

Your Majesties most humble and obedient subject,

John Cheke.

Number LVI.

The Queen to King Philip her husband, concerning doing
something in which her conscience was not satisfied.

Monseigneur,

JA'Y receu les lettres de V. H. par Francisco le xviii^e de ce present, tres humblement remercient ycelle pour elles, sespecialement que vous pleust escripre que V. H. print les myens en bon part, lesquelles j'assure a V. H. estoint escriptes avec bonne intencion, et veu que celle de V. H. estoint escriptes avec la mesme, je ne pourray icy dire aultre chose, sinon supplier tres humblement V. H. (veu que semble bon a ycelle que je examineroy ma conscience, pour entendre si seroyt conforme a la veryté ou non) de m'appoynter et nommer quelz persones il semblera a V. H. plus convenientes pour moy, de communicquer sur cest affaire, et je les ouyray de fort bon coeur sincerement quelconques seront. Neantmoyns en mes dernieres lettres a V. H. je fitz offerture a V. H. que je me conformeroy a ceste mariage touchant cest endroit ayant le consent de ce royaulme, et ainsy feray je, sans lequel consent je craints, que en la fin, ne V. H. ne ce royaulme seront bien servitz en cest endroit. Car unefois il souvient a V. H. par ma propre procuracion a V. H. je ouyoy les freres de V. H. mais doncques et Alphonses me proponoit questions si obscures, que mon simple entendement ne les pourroit comprehendre; comme pour exemple, il me demandoit, qui estoit roy au temps de Adam : et disoit comme jestoy obligée de faire ceste mariage par ung article de mon Credo. Mais il ne l'exposoit point les choses trop difficiles pour moy d'entendre, ainsy quil estoit impossible en si peu de temps de diriger ma conscience. Mais une chose je prometz a V. H. sur ma fidelité a ycelle, que quelconques hommes yl plaira a ycelle m'appoincter, ils ne me trouveront obstinate, ne sans rayson j'espoyr.

Mais veuque V. H. escript en ses dictes lettres, que si ung Parlament iroyt au contrarie V. H. en imputeroyt la coulpe en moy ; je supplie en toute humilité V. H. de differer cest affaire jusques a vostre retour ; et doncques V. H. sera juge sy je seray coulpable, ou non. Car aultrement je vivray en jalousie de V. H. laquelle sera pire a moy que morte. Car j'ay commencée desja d'en taster trop a mon grand regret ; et pour dire la verité en mon simple jugement subs la correction de V. H. veu que le ducque de Savoye sera asture en guerre, et aulcum nombre du conceil et de la nobilité de ce royaulme avec V. H. je ne pourray trouver par quel moyen la chose pourroit estre bonnement traictee, cependant, ne aussy en mon jugement (combienque ma conscience seroys si bien satisfie comme celle de V. H.) l'affaire ne viendra a la fin que V. H. le voudroyt avoyr, sans vostre presence.

Pourquoy, Monseigneur, en si humble sorte comme il est possible pour moy, estant vostre tresloyalle et tres obeissante femme a V. H. (ce que faire je me confesse justement obligee d'estree, et en mon opinion plus que toutes aultres femmes, ayant tel mary comme V. H. est, sans parler de la multitude de vos royalmes, car cela nest pas ma principal fundation) je supplie V. H. que nous deux cependant prions a Dieu, et mettons nostre firme confidence en luy, que nous viverons, et enconterons emsemble, et ce mesme Dieu, lequel a la conduicte des coeurs des roys en sa mayn, sans faulte jespoir, nos illuminera en telle sorte, que la fin tendra a sa glorie et vostre contentation. Suppliant V. H. cependant pardoner ma presumption de la bonte de Dieu en cest endroict. Car combien que je ne l'ay point merite, neant moyns je l'ay bien experimente oultra l'expectation quasi de tout le monde ; et j'ay le mesme espoir en luy que je souloy avoir.

191   Number LVII.

Oratio habita Pataviæ in sancto templo divi Antonii vige-
simo primo mensis Septembris, M.D.LVI. *In mortem*
illustriss. Angli Domini Edovardi Courtenai, Comitis
Devoniæ, per Thomam Wilsonum Anglum.

Foxii MSS.   FUNUS videtis, grave quidem, et triste spectaculum,
humum non hominem, cadaver non corpus, truncum non
spiritum, molem sine mente, vas sine liquore, annulum sine
gemma. Res dura, mutatio sinistra, casus lamentabilis. Juvenem videtis, non unum inter multos plebeium, sed unum
e multis, atque adeo ex omnibus singularem : non quem
pauci laudarent ; sed quem omnes admirarentur : non quem
vulgus tantum coleret ; sed quem principes mirabiliter sus-
picerent. Juvenem dico, natione nobilem, dignitate illustrem, ingenio excellentem, ornamentorum omnis generis
affluentia abundantissimum. Sed quem juvenem vobis com-
memoro? Juvenem Anglum, et eum quidem ex Anglis nobilissimum. Juvenem dico, Edouardum Courtenaium, Co-
mitem Devoniæ, spem patriæ, decus regni, ornamentum
Britanniæ. Dolens dico, qui modo in summam spem erige-
batur propagandæ, illustrandæque dignitatis suæ : is jam
depressus, humi jacet : ægritudine confectus, cophino, et
fasciis obvolutus. O cœlum, ô superos, ô lubricum, et in-
certum genus nostrum, ô spem fallacem, ô summam vitæ
inconstantiam. Quem tot principes qui de facie eum nunq;
cognoverunt, ob illustrem dignitatem et singulares animi
dotes observabant : quem exteri admirabantur, hunc jam
omnes hic presentes ad terram devolutum, vident, deflent,
lamentantur. Et ego quidem ex Anglis infimus, Anglorum
maximum, potentissimumque principem, morte (ah! nimis
matura) præventum, vobis commendo : ut is sepulchro ejus
habeatur honor, quem tam præstantis viri dignitas meretur.
Et ut altius intrent in memorias vestras tam illustris Angli
splendores, obverseturque ob oculos melius vestros viva ejus
imago ; dicam de eo, quemadmodum par est, et dicam vere.
Sed primo si expatiari vellem in regni laudes, frustra rem
vobis notam, et multo familiarem recensendo, aures credo

vestras plus æquo obtunderem. Quamobrem regni celebritate prætermissa, prosapiam ejus primo vobis evolvam, ut ex claritudine generis, nobilitatem juvenis colligeretis. Ex rerum gestarum scriptoribus domesticis, legimus Courtenaiorum familiam, post hominum memoriam illustrem fuisse, imaginibus claram et splendore Britannico multo excellentem. Jam inde enim ab initio (quantum quis memoria consequi possit) comites Devoniæ fuerunt ex hac eadem familia: quor' cum multa extarent in rempublicam merita, sæpissime affinitate regia digni habebantur. Et inter alios quidem, Dominus Gulielmus comes Devoniæ, avus hujus juvenis, Edovardi Regis, hujus nominis quarti, filiam Catherinam in matrimonium sumpsit, ex qua Dominum Henricum genuit, patrem hujus. Unde albæ rosæ insignibus utebatur is Henricus materno jure, Eboracensis familiæ illustrissimæ nota, cum Lancastrienses alterius factionis principes purpuream semper gestarent. Ex hac autem affinitate regia, Henrico septimo ejus nominis regi, qui alteram, et majorem natu Edovardi Regis Quarti filiam Elisabetam, uxorem duxit, frater consanguineus fuit. Longum esset in istius viri et avi hujus laudes intrare. Nam si virtutes et summa ejus in regnum merita recenserem, exitum credo non invenirem, et prius verba deessent ad expoliendum tantum principem, quam materia ad exornandum: sic ut labor non quærendæ laudis, sed statuendi modi susceptus videretur. Successit Gulielmo Henricus: patri filius, et pater hujus: sed, Deus bone, qualis? Vir sane omni laude superior, comes natus, marchio post Exonie suo merito creatus: vir non alicujus urbis, sed totius orbis; non hominum, sed humani generis; non unius nationis, sed universæ naturæ lumen, et ornamentum. Sed adversa tandem usus fortuna, dolendum sane, ab omni dejectus fuit honore, et vita privatus.

Patre mortuo, juvenis hic solus patri filius, puer admodum, et innocens, annum agens duodecimum, ob patris offensam duris custodiis annis plus minus quatuordecim coercebatur. Quo quidem toto tempore tanta animi æquabilitate et constantia naturam suam corroboravit, nunquam ut succumberet, aut ullo modo frangeretur.   Natura etiam ad literas natus, studiis se totum involvit, juvenis docilitate summa, minimo ut studio esset opus, diligentia tamen ejus-modi, quæ naturam posset etiam ex tarditate invitare : sic ut nec angustia loci, nec solitudo, nec amissio libertatis il-lum a literis avocarent.   Unde tam avide philosophiam arri-piebat, et tantas in ea progressiones faciebat, nemo ut illi ex principibus par esset.   Neque in hoc solum laudabili stu-dio se ipse exercuit, sed intima naturæ scrutatus mysteria, mathematicorum labyrintha intravit, studio exhausto, fructu summo et voluptate singulari.   Tanta etiam expingendarum effigierum cupiditate ardebat, ut facile et laudabiliter cujus-cumque imaginem in tabula exprimeret.   Testudinem vero sonorisque intervallis, et temperata varietate contrectavit, absolutam ut in illo diceres perfectionem.   Neque hac doc-trinæ, et ornamentorum contentus, accumulatione, adjunxit sibi etiam linguas, Hispanicam, Gallicam, et Italicam.   In quibus omnibus tam diligenter elaboravit et sic mentem ex-prompsit suam, ut cum quovis externo summa cum sua laude absque ullo interprete ad plenum argumentaretur et sermo-nem haberetur. Tandem vero aliquando cum Regina nostra Maria serenissima, summo Dei beneficio, et suo jure succes-sisset ad regnum, et tantas in hoc juvene tertio affinitatis gradu cognato, virtutes elucescere vidisset; illius miserta servitutem, et solitudinem ægre ferens, e custodiis illum primo quoque tempore evocavit, libertatem donavit, decus restauravit, et ad dignitatem summam evexit, sic ut pientis-sima Reginæ opera, Comes Devoniæ ab omnibus salutaretur, proavorum suorum antiquum stemma, et splendor illustrissi-mus.   Cum igitur hic juvenis Edouardus Courtenaius (Re-ginæ summa gratia et clementia) ergastulo sic solutus esset, et liber evolaret; tam se erga omnes facilem præbuit, et tantum suarum virtutum specimen edidit, ut omnes illum, summo non solum amore, sed etiam honore complecteren-tur.

Gravis erat sine superbia, comis sine levitate, in sermone prudens, in respondendo cautus, in disputando modestus, nec se ipse jactans, nec alios excludens, paucis plura dicens, rem potius, quam verba secutus, familiaritatem exercens cum multis, a paucis tamen intime cognitus. Et cum dignitate principibus par esset, tamen generosa quadam ingenuitate animi se cum infimis exæquabat, si quidem ullas aut virtutis aut ingenii notas in illorum orationibus inesse intellexisset. Tam autem ingenio ad res omnes gerendas promptus erat, et voluntate tam ardenti; ut ex iis omnibus nil illi abesset, quibus illustrem personam vel ornari deceret, vel institui conveniret. Et cum corpore tam esset spectabilis, quam animo excellens, compositio membrorum eleganti junctura partium et copulatione, egregia, et statura laudabili: ad militarem animum adjecit disciplinam; unde brevi tempore, tam scienter et militariter equo insidebat, et hasta ad palum tam strenue, et laudabiliter cursum incitabat, proavorum ut in illo cerneres præstantiam. At erit fortassis, qui me hæc auribus potius vestris dare affirmet, quam vera putet esse, et vel hæc in illo non fuisse, vel non tanta fuisse credat, quanta meis ego verbis illa facio; præsertim cum vix in uno tot simul aggregatas esse virtutes credendum sit, quæ in paucissimis singulæ inveniuntur. Sed testentur alii cum quibus intimam ille habuit consuetudinem, et me coarguant mendacii, si longius quam par sit, in ejus sim evectus commendatione.

Quapropter cum tam præstans is apud omnes esset, ut omnium oculos in se converteret; in tanta apud plures æstimatione fuit, ut illorum judicio, non tam regni subditus, quam regni Rex esse mereretur, et Reginæ maritus. Sed ille, qua fuit modestia, nihil de se magnum cogitans, indignissimum se, et perpetuum profitebatur Reginæ famulum, ab omni semper abhorrens ambitione. Unde cum postea regni Regem, et Reginæ maritum, potentissimum Philippum, Caroli Quinti imperatoris invictissimi filium, divina prudentia haberemus: et essent ex nostris, qui hunc juvenem seditiose et turbulente ad arma contra Regem Reginamque incitarent; ille memor officii, et fidei suæ, et beneficii nuper accepti, nunquam voluit ullius, aut persuasione, aut consilio ingratus erga eam videri, a qua tot et tam amplis affectus fuit dignitatibus: neque illam in pericu-

lum ullum adducere, per quam ipse fuit ab omni periculo
liberatus.   Ex quo liquet, quam divina in illo virtus fuit, et
quam animus vere generosus, qui ne regni quidem potiundi
spe ab officio nunquam deflecteretur.   At læsæ majestatis
accusatus fuit : at accusantur et innocentes. At coram principibus regni examinatus : at honorifice liberatus.   At vixit
in suspicione apud plures : at erat vita inculpata apud om-
194 nes.   At periculum erat ne offenderet : at certum erat quod
non offenderat : at timendum pejora : at sperandum meliora : at potuit semper : at noluit unquam : et hoc quidem
certe aperte testificabatur in universo vitæ suæ cursu, usque
ad ultimum mortis diem, qui tam caute se semper gessit,
nunquam ut cum iis consuetudinem haberet, quorum mores
fuerunt Reginæ vel invisi, aut vita quovis modo suspecta.
Equidem, ut id quod res est ingenue dicam, nihil tam illi
(improborum certe machinationibus) tanta inussit tormenta,
et tantas peperit calamitates, quam nasci ex familia nobili,
et ex stirpe regia.   Cum igitur aliquot haberet inimicos
(invidetur enim semper præstanti dignitati) et criminationi-
bus illorum aspergeretur, quibusque quælibet suspicio, etiam levissima, ingens scelus videtur ; tam egregie et viriliter
suam ipse tuebatur innocentiam, et tam præsenti animo
(adversis enim nunquam frangebatur) syncerum se, incul-
patumque ostendebat ; ut Regina omnium laudatissima, illum de integro in gratiam sumeret, et inter proceres regni
fidatissimos accenseret.   Unde postea, explorata ejus fide, et
virtute cognita, Regis Reginæque communi consensu, mittebatur Bruxelliam in Brabantia, curiam imperialem, ut
ipsi imperatori Carolo (quem honoris causa semper nomino)
officium suum faceret, et innocentiæ suæ apud illum etiam
testimonium exhiberet.   Quo cum venisset, et ibi aliquot
menses constitisset, superveniente postea Rege, in tanta fuit
apud patrem, filiumque authoritate et gratia ; nemo ut ex-
ternus majore apud eos loco esset.   Ille vero humanitatem
hanc meritis suis majorem conspiciens, et favorem multo
maximum, optimum se facturum putavit, si mentem suam
majoribus, et amplioribus excoleret virtutibus, ut melius
utrique et copiosius posthac inserviret, et illorum singulari

in se benignitati quoquomodo responderet. Intelligens autem Italiam bonarum artium esse mercaturam, et tanquam alteras Athenas ingeniis florentibus, exquisitisque judiciis abundare, hanc ab ipso Rege gratiam obtinuit, ut qui tam diu custodiis obsepiretur, libere tandem aliquando expatiendi facultatem haberet, præsertim cum Rex ipse certo sciret illum virtutis ac doctrinæ causa, tot loca tam diligenter perlustrare velle. Ut vero gratior apud plures Italiæ illustrissimos viros adventus esset, scripsit Rex optimus in ejus gratiam complures literas commendatitias, in quibus sic ejus virtutes extulit, ut quocunque gentium proficisceretur, perlibenter, semper et honorifice ab iis, ad quos literæ mittebantur, exciperetur. Id quod expertus est uberrime in iis locis, ad quæ perrexit, et in quibus diversabatur. Sed videte, jam jam progressurus, et alios præterea principes visurus, universamque quasi peregraturus Italiam, in medio itinere (pro dolor!) interceptus est, et in hac urbe Patavina annos natus circiter triginta, ex duplici febre tertiana mortuus, et prius sane mortuus, quam moriturum quisquam suspicaretur. Breves quidem hujus vitæ hic voluptates hausit, in ipso nimirum ætatis flore absorptus. Nam post annos vitæ duodecim, vix biennium in reliquo vitæ suæ cursu vixit securus, et ab omni liber molestia. Sed (ô profunditatem judiciorum Dei!) qui grave sæpius et multiplex hucusque periculum evasit, febrem evadere non potuit. Ex hoc igitur juvene illustrissimo nostram metiamur imbecillitatem, disjungamusque nos a corporibus, ut consuescamus mori, et vivamus hodie tanquam cras morituri, et sic quidem hæc vita (dum erimus in terris) erit illi cœlesti vitæ similis, et cum illuc ex hiis vinculis emissi feremur, minus tardabitur cursus animorum nostrorum, et sic moriemur ut vivamus semper. Nam qui vivit moriturus bene, morietur ut vivat melius. Juvenis iste qui sic virtutem colebat in vita, sic jam e vita discessit, ut certo certius perpetuo vivat, et pro terra, cœlum occupet; pro labore, quietem; pro incertis, certa; pro humanis, divina: nam mors quidem interitus non est, omnia tollens, atque delens: sed quædam quasi migratio, commutatioque vitæ, quæ in claris viris, et omnibus Christi præ-

195

cepta observantibus, dux in cœlum soleret esse. At ejulat mœrens D. Marchionessa Exoniæ, vidua provectiore ætate, et unico orbata filio, clamant famuli, vociferantur amici, et has voces semper ingeminant: *Mortuus est juvenis.* Respondeo, ut quos lugere scio, hos nunc consoler: mortis nullum certum definitur tempus. Nam natura quidem dedit usuram vitæ, tanquam pecuniæ, nulla præstituta die. Neque id intempestivum est, quod Deus fieri vult. At melius esset, si longius vixisset: at bene est, quod bene vixerit, et optime mortuus sit. Nec vero parum diu vixit, qui virtutis perfectæ perfecto functus est munere. Nam vita acta perficit, ut satis, superque vixisse videatur. Mortuus etiam est in summa Regis sui Reginæque gratia: fama secunda: summis bonorum studiis: probatus a Deo: æstimatus ab omnibus. At Anglia illum desiderat, et vivum requirit: at Anglia illo nunquam carebit. Nam si mens cujusque is sit quisque fama illius et recte factorum memoria per omnes obvolitabit oras, et omnium aures Angliæ laudibus opplebit: sic ut concidat omne cœlum potius, omnisque natura consistat; quam ut fœlix illius conteratur memoria, aut ex pectoribus hominum eruatur recordatio.

Vos igitur, honoratissimi legati, et omnes præterea cujusque gradus, quem audivistis tam in vita fuisse celebrem et illustrem, hujus jam defuncti memoriam pie inviolateque tenete, nomen propagate, et illi simul gratulemini in cœlis collocato. Nam si veram sequatur laus virtutem, si recte facta premium, ille nec debet nec potest felicitate summa privari, qui semper in virtute sola summum bonum collocabat, et ad cœlum cogitationes omnino suas intendebat. Neque vero cuiquam bono male quicquam evenire potest, nec vivo, nec mortuo; nec potest is a Deo in morte negligi, qui Deum in vita tam impense colebat. Nos igitur (qui adhuc jactamur in vita) si illius insistamus vestigiis, hoc est, solidam virtutis viam ingrediamur, ad illum perveniemus locum, ubi sedent angeli, sancti exultant, et Deus ipse in sua regnat majestate: et veniemus quidem filii ad patrem, creaturæ ad Creatorem, exules ad patriam, servi ad libertatem, peregrini ad sedes sanctas, et plane nostras. Ad quem quidem locum tunc gradiemur, cum Christus nostri misertus, nos vocabit. Quod ut cito, et quam primum fiat, æternus faxit Deus, et communis omnium noster unus et solus Pater.

DIXI.

Number LVIII. 196

John Moyar to John Boulton, concerning a book the latter had printed of his sufferings under Queen Mary.

JOHN Boultonne, after my hartie comendations unto Foxii MSS. you, &c. Wheras you caused to be put in print a serteyne storye of your great trouble, and my recanting, I thought good to answer to serteyne thinges conteyned therin, which are not true; leaste many thinges which are true, by the untruth therof myght be discredited.

First, Wheras you say, *you were taken uppone suspition for writinge of a letter, the writer therof longe tyme after unknown, and great searche made for the same;* I marvell you were not ashamed to cause so manyfest an untruthe to be writen; for the longe tyme after that it was unknown was not ij dayes after it was written. It was set uppe the Satterday before Mydlent Sonday within nyght, and on the morrowe taken downe; and the same Sonday I was taken, and you on the Munday mornynge; and by ix of the clocke on the Munday it was confessed by us bothe. Ther was no further search as I knowe; but one man was sent for, and asked serteyne questions, and so let goo; lykewise a mayde: and this was all: and all this was done on the same Sonday followinge.

Secondly, Wheras you say, *you were committed to warde for a week or a fortnyght into the lower prison, and then had uppe.* I marvell that you have forgotten that viij days, or therabout, after we were committed to prison, that the mayor caused us bothe to sitt in the stockes tenne dayes and x nyghts; but that the keeper's wiffe let us out sometymes to refreshe us; and uponne the Friday before Easter we were lette forthe by the mayor, and ij of the bretherne.

And on the next day following, being Saterday, in the
mornyng early, we were examyned, where the priest promysed us, that *we shuld receave eaven as Christ had lefte
it*.   And when we came on the Sonday to the church, we
found it contrary.   And when I refused to be partaker at
their idolatrous masse, they said I was madde, and was
sent to the stocks, and there cruelly handled tyll Monday
mornynge; and then you dissemblingly, as I may charitably
say, receaved at their masse before the whole parish, as the
rest did; and therfore then were set at lybertie in the
197 keper's house, and not before, nor for any other cause, as
the whole contrey dothe well knowe, although you forgate
to put it in the story amonge the rest.

Thirdly, Wheras you declare *your gret trouble after you
had bene before the Byshopp of Winchester;* I being then
delyvered, came many tymes unto you; where you were indede tyed with a longe chayne to a blocke, and wente at
the length of the chayne, and you called it my *Lord Chan-
celour's almes*.   But whereas you say, you lay in the stockes
handes and fete; that I deny to be true, and am habell to
bringe proofe for the same, if nede be.   It may be that you
might be put in the stockes in the keper's rage, and let out
againe; but I am sure that, being in yor right mynde, you
had never one finger or hand put in the stockes.   But all
this trouble that you speake of, was when you were luna-
tike, and not your owne man.   There were dyvers of your
frindes, being one my sealfe, which caused you to have your
handes made faste; for that you tare in peces yor clothes,
and sate in the colde froste naked in the prison: but for no
other cause was any man lett to come unto you, beinge in
that case ether to bring what they could to comfort you, or
els to watch withe you in the nyght season.   As touching
the *eating of yor owne excrements*, I am sure that you did
it not beinge in yor right mind: I was present with you
when you shewed yor sealfe first to be madde, and there
appeared in you then no lykelyhode of any suche wante.
The story also it sealfe doth geve occasion of grete doubt,
whether that be true or not: for that there is no serteyne

tyme spoken of, howe long you eat them, for some say one
tyme, and some another: I am sure no man sawe you do it,
and therfore know not but by yor owne mouthe. If you did
it, being in yor right mind, how chaunceth it that you
knowe not the sertenty of the tyme? It is not a thing, as I
thinke, so sone to be forgotten. I thinke also, that if you
had bene so used, you wolde have shewed yor griefe to
somebody, for that you were not wonte to hide yor trouble.
When you were out of your witte, I graunte you myght do
it as you did many other thinges, but not of nessessity, I am
sure.

As touchinge that *the keper and his servauntes kept yor
meate from you*, I wyll say nothinge therunto, because I
know not the truthe; there was no such thing used when
I was in prisonne: and besyde that, you myght have complained, for that there were that came unto you now and
then.

Laste of all, Wheras you *complayned upon yor hurt that
you had by the coller-maker*, I know it to be true: but
where you accuse hym of whordome, I may well doubte
that; because I understand, by comon report, that he had
a wicked woman to his wyffe, who was a whore, and sought
to poyson hym; and therfore, being divorsed, he married
with her that was with hym in the prison: and it was well
knowen, that for the little zeale that he had to the gospell 198
he was then prisoned; for they used not in those much
punishment for whoredome. And in that you *charge the keper
with cruelty, for that he gave hym lyberty, beinge madde,
to hurte you:* you know that he was not knowen to be
madde, tyll he presently did the hurt; and afterward was
more sharpely handled than ever you were, bothe in stock-
ing and whypping, as it may appear, for he continueth the
same untyll this day. And where you say, you *were kept
in the stockes whyle he hurt you*; I marvell that you shame
not to lye so openly: were you not abrode in the prison
with a paire of fetters on yor feete? Are you not ashamed
also to say, that *you were delyvered out of prison, being
madde?* Were you not come to yor sealfe before you came

out? I myght here speake of yor recantation at your comyng forthe; which, I think, myght have bene as well spoken of as myne. I leave to talk of my recantation, because I am contented to be judged by those that dwell there, and do know the whole matter. None of us both have any cause to rejoise, except we be overmoch desyrouse of vaine glory. And this is the truth of the story, the which I am able and wylbe redy to prove, as occasion shall serve; not that I desyre to have it regestred, but rather, as unworthy to be put there, I would it were put quite out.

Thus I end, desyring God to geve to you and me the sprite of humilite, that we may glory, not in our owne vanite, but in God's gret mercy bestowed plentifully upon us in Christ Jesu, who is praysed for ever. *Amen.* At Wotton, this 18 of March, anno Dni. 1564.

By me John Moyar.

To his frinde John Boulton,
geve this in London.

Number LIX.

Informations gathered at Reading, anno 1571, touching the storie of Julius Palmer, martyr.

Foxii MSS. BOLTON, of whom Thackam speaketh, was set at lybertie by Sir Fraunces Inglefield, without any suerties, as appeareth in the storye of Bolton. Also, Jhon Ryder, of Readinge, capper, and Wyll'm Dyblye, weaver, do beare witnes therunto. And of this, Bolton hymselfe, dwelling in Longe-lane, by Smythfield, in London, can tell more. He ys a sylke weaver.

That Mr. Palmer was fet from the Cardinal Hatt in the night tyme, contrary to Thackam's assertion; the goodwyffe
199 of the Cardynall Hatt, with her sonne in law, Harrye Singleton, and Stephen Netherclief, ostler of the howse then and yet, do beare witnesse. The tyme was, to theyr judgment, betwene x and xj of the clocke at night, or thereabowt. Also, Wyll'm Dyblye, weaver, being at the next

house the very same night, and the same tyme, even abowt
x of the clocke, saith, that he heard a great noyse at the
Cardinall Hatt; and comyng owt of the howse to learne
what the matter was, he mett some of his companyons comyng out of the Cardynall Hatt, who told hym that the offycers were come to fetch away Mr. Palmer.

And whether Palmer called for a close chambre or not,
yt ys confessed by them of the howse, that he was lodged
in the closyst chambre in the howse; to wyt, in the chambre
beyond the hall, and that there he was fetched owt. Also
Stephen Nethercliefe, the ostler, saith, that he called for a
close chambre.

The goodwyfe of the Cardynall Hatt saith, she was in a
marveilous feare when they dyd fetch hym; and therfore
belyke there were more than one seargeant. Nicholas Sawn-
derson of Readinge heard the woman speake thes woordes,
that she was marveylously afrayd; and she said the same to
Thomas Jhonson and others.

Item, The goodwyffe of the Cardinal Hat saith, that
Hampton, sometyme their scholemaster, came to her, and
asked for Palmer, requestinge that he might speak with
hym. Also he desired her to send for a quart of wyne, that
he might drinke with hym. And afterward she, comynge
in where they were, heard Palmer say, that *he would lyve
and dye in yt.* When she perceaved them whot in talke,
What, (quoth she,) do ye chide? For God's sake chide not
in my howse. No, hostys, (quoth they,) we do not chide,
but reason the matter. The very same night was Palmer
fet owt of the howse by the offycers, as the goodwyffe, and
her sonne, and her ostler, do all confesse.

Her sonne in law lykewyse said, that he heard hys mother oftentymes tell, that Hampton came to Mr. Palmer,
and talked wyth hym, the very same night that he was fett
owt of their howse by the officers. And this he rehearsed
agayne in the hearing of William Dyblye, Christopher Bernard, &c.

Wyllyam Dyblye, weaver, abovenamed, who often resorted to hym in pryson, saith, that Mr. Palmer imputed

the cawse of his trouble to no man so moche as to Thackam. And Stephen Netherclief, the ostler abovenamed, saith the same, that Thackam was his greatest enemy. He spake thes wordes to Thomas Jhonson of Reading.

Jhon Galant of Reading sayth, that Gateley confessed to hym, how that he watched Palmer, and brought hym first to examynatyon. And touching the intercepting of the letter, he sayth, that Gateley spake these wordes unto him; *We mett with the messinger, and receaved the letter of him, and cawsed another to be conveighed and delyvered to the messinger, written in Palmer's name, which Palmer knew not of.* He uttered this before William Dyblye, weaver, and Christopher Bernard, cutler. And he saith, that he wyll now affirme the same to Gateley's face, as he hath done 200 in tymes past. *Item*, Jhon Galant sayth, that Gateley set certayne of hys howsehold to watche Palmer at his hostys howse.

Christopher Bernard saith, that there was a studye in the schole-howse in Thackam's and Palmer's tyme. *Item*, Jhon Galant saith, that he heard one Richard Bewen reporte, that Gateley brake up that studie in his sight. Also, Richard Bewen confessed the same to Thomas Jhonson.

Item, Jhon Galant sayth, that he resortinge to Palmer in pryson, charged hym, that he was apprehended and punished for adulterye and prepensed murther. Unto whom Palmer answered, *Brother Galant, I am a greater synner than all the world knoweth; but for thes thinges wherwith I am now charged, I am as cleere as the child that was borne this night.*

Thomas Jhonson saith, he can bring forth dyvers persons that have seene Hampton play uppon the organs, and sing in the quyer, together with Thackam.

Wylliam Dyblye saith, that Palmer protested to him in pryson, that in the letter wherwith he was charged before the vysitours, hys hand was counterfeated, and that he was betrayed, and was not wytting nor waring of that letter.

Mr. Moyer's lettre agreeable to the same.

William Dyblye and Christopher Bernard do say, that

Downer was a dissembler and an hipocrite, praying God to save every man from soche frends. The lyke sayd John Galant *to* Mr. Sheper.

Harry Singleton sayd, that Gateley had bene with him to inquere whether Palmer was fett owt of that howse, and of other thinges, as, who was then constable, &c. He confessed this before William Dyblye, Christopher Bernard, Jhon Galant, &c. The said Harrye sayd, he answered hym, that he hymselfe, (to wyt,) Gateley, was then constable, and (as he remembred) one of them that dyd fetch hym.

Item, Whereas Thackam saith, that Palmer was taken leaping over a wall, Tho. Jhonson saith, that in that place there was never no wall.

Item, Wheras Thackam saith, that he payd Palmer all hys monye, there appeareth a letter of atturney of Palmer's owne hand to the contrarye.

Other notes.

Thackam speaketh of one Coxe in hys answer; and the story meaneth another, called William Coxe, the cook, which was Palmer's hoste.

Jhon Galant sayth, that Palmer's hoste was not at home when the letter was intercepted, and knew not of yt tyll he came home.

The mayd whom Thackam abused, and begatt with child, was one Stanshall's servant, a syllye impotent mayd, who, at the byrth of the child, protested that yt was Thackam's childe; and afterward, when God called her, she tooke yt also uppon her deathe.

Item, His swering for the child, and his false othes to 201 Jhon Galant, touching the boordes.

Thackam protested in the pulpytt, in the begynnynge of Queene Maries raigne, that he would seale hys doctryne with his blud, and stand to yt even unto death. Yet afterward he shranke backe, and sayd, that he would never be minister agayne.

William Dyblye wytnesseth, that Thackam brought into the church leaves of old popishe service, and that he, with others, dyd helpe to patche together the bookes, and to sing the fyrst Latin even songe in the church of S. Lawrence.

Item, Mr. Gresshop can report of hys doinges at Yorke, knowne to the old Ladye of Rutland.

Item, Jhon Galant sayth, that the Ladye Vane, talking with hym, called Thackam *dissemblynge hypocrite;* and told hym, how he deceaved poore people with that which she dyd skymme off, and would not geve to her dog.

Number LX.

The epistle of John Clement to the professors in Surrey. From the King's Bench.

Jesus. Emanuell.

Qui ex Deo est, verba Dei audit.

Unto the faithful, and suche as have yet any sparke of the true feare and love of God remaynynge in their hartes, dwellinge in the parishes of Nutfilde, Merstham, and Chaldon, or therabowtes, in the countie of Surrey, or els wheare soever this letter shall come: your poore brother, (in bondes for the testemony of Godes everlastinge truth,) John Clemente, wishethe the swete peace of God in Jhus' Christe, with the contynuall ayde, strengthe, and comfortes of his moste pure, holye, and mightie Spirite; that in all thinges you may onely seake his glorye, the comforte and commoditie of his poore afflicted Church, the encrease of your owne eternall joye and comforte in him. Amen.

Foxii MSS.   SEING (my dere neighbours and lovinge frindes) that the malice of this troublesome tyme is suche, that it will not suffer the true servaunts of God to lyve and enjoye the libertie of their consciences within this realme of Englande, 202 but forceth them to flye from their native countrye, or elles deprivethe their lyves in this worlde, excepte they will (as alas! too many doe) forsake theire deare Lorde and onelye Esai. xli.   Saviour Jhus Christe, by commyttinge of idolatrye and

abhominations agenste him; which thinge to doe is mooste
dangerous, and the very deathe of the sowle: and seinge
also that God, of his greate mercye and infynite goodnes,
hath chosen and placed me to defende his truthe, agenste
all those abhominations used and defended with lyes of the
Papistes, I have thought it good, and my bounden dewtie,
to write this rude and simple letter unto you; not onely to
take my leave and laste farewell of you in this mortal life,
(altogether replenishede with synne and miserye,) but also Job xiv.
of love to admonishe you, and, in the worde and name of
the Lorde, to warne you to consider well the tyme of your Luke xix.
visitation, leaste that come sodenly upon you that hathe
bene oftentymes (by the prophetes and trewe servauntes of
God) thretened unto you; and though perchaunce of some,
which seme wise in their owne conceptes, I shalbe lawghed
to scorne, and have many a drye mocke for my laboure, yet
I will not for that leave my dewtie in this pointe undone,
but will discharge my conscience towardes you, and then do
as you list: for sure I am, that you shall not have many
mo general warninges, before the Lorde performe his pour-
pose upon the shrinkinge people of this realme. Consider,
dere frendes in the Lord, and call to your remembraunce,
how often the Lorde hath both by the woordes and writinges Matt. xxiii.
of his faithfull preachers, called you from the Babylonical
filthines, the service of idolatrie, and abhominations, unto
earneste and spedye repentaunce: forgeate not howe thei
did threaten you, (as well with plagues that are come to
passe, as also withe more perill that is harde at hande,) if
you did forsake the Lorde for the love of any worldly
thinge. And do not you thinke, but as parte of their
wordes are proved true by theis daies experience, so shall
the reste be as verely performed, as God himselfe is God:
for they have moste constantlye confirmed their sayinges
with their deathe, and sealed the same with their blude.
What wolde you have more? I my selfe, when I was with
you, did, with my simple learnynge and knowledge, the
best I cowlde to call you from those thinges that will suerlye Col. iii.
bringe the wrathe of God upon you, excepte you repente in

tyme, and turne to the Lorde with your whole harte: but howe preachers warnings, and my poore admonissions, have ben or is regarded, God and you do knowe.

Well: I wolde yet have you repente in tyme, and turne to God, and geve him his dew honnor: and the greatest honnor that we can geve to God, is to confesse and answer trewlye and faithfullye to his holy worde, and in his trewthes cause: and that shoulde every man do, whatsoever the worlde, feares, displeasure, friendshipe, or other lettes shoulde say to the contrarye, upon paine (saithe Christe) Matt. x. that I will denye him before my Father, &c. Reade the xth Luke xiii. chapter of Mathewe, and iiijth of S. Peter's first Epistell, 203 and you shall se, that persecution for righteousnes sake is 1 Pet. iv. no strange or newe thinge to be marvelled at; for it hathe alwaies accompanied the preachinge and professinge of Godes worde, yea, even in the prophets and apostells; suche is the malyce of the wicked ennemye agenste the true servauntes of God; yea, sometime at Godes permission, he trieth them with fearefull threatenynges and harde persecu- Matt. x. tions: as it is saide by Christe, *Thei shal betraye you to the judges, and of them ye shal be beaten and judged to deathe.* On the other side he tempteth them with love of wife, kynrede, and worldely friendes; yea, with love of goodes, landes, and their owne lives. But he that is overcome by anye of theis means, hathe this judgemente; *he is not myte* Matt. xvi. [*meet*] *for me*, saith Christe; yea, he saithe moreover, *He that saveth his liffe*, meanynge by dissimulation in this matter, *shall lose it; and he that losethe his liffe for my sake and the gospelles, shall save it.* And againe, *What shall it proffit a man to wyn all the whole worlde, and lose his own sowle*, &c.

Dere frendes, flatter not yourselves in your wickednes, as to thinke that you may be presente at idolatrye, and be fawteles therof, for God abhorrethe dissimulation. I do reade in the word of God, that penytente synners, that confese and acknowlege their synnes, (in faithe through Jhus Christe,) have had remission therof; but I never reade of Esai. xv. any unpenitente synners, that called evill good, and idola-

trye reasonable servinge of God, that obteyned remission of
their synnes.   Further, I reade that a servaunte that know- Luke xii.
ethe his master's will, and doth it not, shal be beten withe
many stripes : but I never reade, that it was lawfull for a
man that had knowlege, to do evil, but he was worthie double dampnation ; once, because he did evill, which is lawful
for no man to do ; twise, because he did that evill that his
owne conscience and knowlege condempnethe to be evil.
And yet some men are not only contente to do evil them- Rom. i.
selves, but also they encourage others to do the like, whose
dampnation is not far off, excepte they repent ; for all they
that wolde make you beleve that you may for civill pollecye
without daunger towards God, be presente with your bodies, wheras you know an idol is honnoured for God, deceyve you and themselfes also ; for it is as filthie and as
haynous unto Christe that redeemed us, (both bodye and
sowle withe his precious bloode,) to see us beare him good
will and service in our hartes, (as we say we do,) and yet
owtewardlye withe our bodies to be presente before an idoll,
as it is to an honeste man to heare his wife saye that she
bearethe her husbande good will in her harte above all men,
and yet gevethe the use of her bodye aswell to another man
as to her husbande.   Reade the scripture and followe it,
and beware of flatteringe, carnall, fleshely, and worldely
mynded men. S. Paule saithe, that *Christe loved his churche,* Eph. v.
or congregation, *and gave himeselfe for it, to sanctefye it,*
and cleansed it in the fountayne of water, thorough the
worde, &c.   And after many wordes, he concludethe thus :
This misterye is greate, but I speake of Christe and his
Churche.   Well, I say no more ; but consider and weigh
the marriage betwene man and woman, with the marriage
betwene Christe and his Church, and judge with your owne 204
conscience whether the sowle and the body, redemed withe
Christes owne moste precious blude, be not asmoch bownden unto Christe, as the body and sowle of the woman or
wife is to her husbande : I dare saye theare is none amonge
you, but he will say, yes, and more bownde too, or elles
you know not your dewties : then tell me, whether the wife,

in gevinge her bodye to the use of another man, let her
prate and commende the knowlege, faithe, and love of the
harte to her husbande never so moche, whether she be not
an harlot in her doinge? I warrante you, bothe her husbande, and all them that knowe it, will say the same.
Suche is the partialytie, blyndnes, and wickednes of men,
that thinkethe that Christe, the husbande of the congregation and churche, hathe enowth, if a man geve him the
knowlege of his harte and mynde, and let his bodye serve
the use of whoredome and idolatrie never so moche. No,
no, (deare bretherne,) the ipocrites understande not the word
of God, neither the mariage betwene God and man: for as
the man and wife (at the time of mariage) dothe promise
faithe of the bodye, besides good will of the hart, eache to
other; so do we at our baptisme promise faith unto Christ,
aswell of bodye as of mynde: therfore our baptism declar-
eth, that we shoulde not lyve to synne, but unto God. And
Paule requirethe us to *appoint all our membres to the servyce
of God :* yea, he saithe, *Glorifie God in your bodyes, and in
your spirites, which are Godes.*

Rom. xii.
1 Cor. vi.

I praye you, bretherne, take hede and beware of all them
that counsaile you to the contrarye: for the time is not
longe, but ye shall all appeare before the Judge of all equity
and right, and ther shall no excuse prevaile ; but as ye be,
so shall you be judged. As for this wicked worlde, use
wisdome and discretion, as far as you may, (not offending
God,) to avoide all daungers ; and be ye assurede, if ye
knowe and understande the first commaundemente of God,
you shal be of good comforte, whatsoever shal happen unto
you. Saye, *he is God*, then can man do no more than God
hathe permitted him, and then you saie, he is your God.
Dowtles truste in him, for if ye do, he will not onlye take
hede of you, but also of the haires of your heades ; he will
not suffer you to be tempted above that you shalbe able to
beare. Beware you differ not from God in judgmente: he
saithe, *Blessede are thei that suffer persecution for righteousnes sake :* then do not ye judge them unhappie : yea,
he addethe, *for theirs is the kingedom of heaven.* Is not

Exod. xx.
Deut. v.
Matt. x.
Matt. x.
1 Cor. x.
Matt. v.

this a comfortable worde? Who owght not rather choose to
be blessed withe Christe in a littell tribulation, than to be
cursed with the Devill for a littell pleasure? And you have
bothe the blessinge and the curse set before you, therfore
choose the beste. Christe saithe, *The waye is narrow, and* Matt. vii.
the gate streight, that leadeth unto life: do not you saye, it
is brode and large, as those men do that be neither whote
nor colde, whome God will spewe owte of his mowthe. The Apoc. iii.
Scripture saithe, We muste enter into heaven by many trou- Acts xiv.
bles: do not you saye, we maye come thither with ease;
for if ye looke for it that way, you shall never come there. 205
Therfore, dere frendes, breake not Godes commaundementes
for mens traditions.

But I here saye, that some be of this opinion, that if the
Quene or superioure powers (by their authorities and laws)
deceave me, and make me do amise, they shall bare the
blame, and not I. But beware, my friendes, this sayinge
is not of the truth: for the Scripture saithe, that *every man* Gal. vi.
shall bare his owne burthen, and dye in his owne synnes. Matt. xv.
And in case a blinde superstitious superiour's authoritye
cause a sort of blinde subjectes for to erre and to do amis,
both of them shall perishe, and their blude be upon their
owne heades. Therfore take hede in time, or ever it be too
late, and remember that you have often tymes bene warned,
bothe by me, and other whiche coulde informe you by the
worde of God (if you wolde receave it) better than I. But
it greveth me to heare howe littell you do regarde it: I
wolde be lothe to be a witnes at the greate daye of judgemente agaynste any of you all.

Deare frindes and neighbours, I love you in the Lorde,
as I have no lesse cause, for the greate kyndenes I have
founde withe you: but speciallye with God, who hathe
commanded me so to do; and therfore, of love I am constrayned once more to call unto you, to come awaye from
that filthie whore of Babilon, and bye no more of her wares: Apoc. xviii.
medle not withe her merchaundice at this markete tyme of
Ester; for her synnes ar gonne up to heaven, and hath procured Godes plagues and vengeaunce shortlye to be powred

upon them all; wherof you shalbe suerlye partakers, if you do not repente of your backeslydinge and shrinkinge from the Lorde. Repente, I saye, repente, for the tender mercys of God, and have compassion upon your owne sowles before it be too late. Be not offended, dere frendes, that I write somwhat sharplye and earnestlye unto you; for trulye it is no tyme nowe to flatter withe you. Neither can I *Luke xix.* lawgh at your harmes, whiche I se to be at hand; though perchaunce it be hid from your eyes, as it was from them of Jerusalem, when Christe wepte at their mirthe and rejoicinge, because thei knewe not the time of their visitation. No more do you, as it semeth; but I wolde have you take hede, and knowe the tyme also of Godes first visitation amonge you: for I am sure the seconde is harde at hande: *Ps. cxxxiv.* do not you thinke to flye from his presence, for his heavy *Ose x.* hande will fynde you owte, thowgh you shoulde hide your *Apoc. vi.* *Matt. xxv.* selfes in hell, as the prophet saithe. Thinke not then that theis Romishe rockes (wherinto you dailye creape) can cover you from his fearfull face, when he shall begyne to call you to accomptes for the talente that he hath lente you: it is not then your feigned excuses of feare and frayltie of the fleshe, that shal excuse your follye, and fleeinge from him: no, no, you shalbe even specheles at that daye, when it shalbe seene you have defiled your marriage garmente withe superstitious filthines of the whore of Babylon; and howe you have withe her commyttede fornication in the spirit ageanste

206 your deare husbande Christe, whiche redemed you, *neither* *1 Peter i.* *with corruptible golde nor silver, but with his owne moste* *Eph. v.* *2 Peter ii.* *precious harte blude, and cleansed you in the fountayne of* *water through his worde, that you might be unto hymselfe* *a glorious spowse and congregation without spot or wrinkle* *in his sight.* O let not that be fulfilled in you whiche is *2 Peter ii.* spoken in the true proverbe, *The dog is turned unto his vomit ageane, and the sowe that was washed to her wallowing in the myre.* But repente in tyme, and take the earneste warnynge that God dothe send you, willinge you to turne to him before it be too late. Consider your dewtie towardes God in theis dangerous daies, wherin the Lorde is verely

mynded to trye the chaff from the good corne, and to pourge his floor with his fanne, or crosse of tribulation, that he may bringe the wheat into his barne, and burne the chaffe withe unquenchable fire: you are called unto a kingedome that muste be wonne withe sufferinge on every side, into the whiche you muste also entre (as S. Paule saithe) *thoroughe many tribulations and afflictions*, in the whiche you must travaile as strangers and pilgrims in this wretched worlde, whiche is not our natyve countrye, wherin we muste reste and inhabite for ever. Matt. xiv.
Heb. xiii.

Oh! then, learne to leave all thinges willingelye that you do here possesse, and lifte up your myndes alwaies to the heavenlye habitation, where you shall continually remayne. Set not your felicitye and pleasure in the pelfe of the worlde, whiche shall shortly perishe and come to naught: but set all your joye and pleasure in the lyvinge God, whiche in Christe, and for his sake, hath geven himselfe whollye to be your portion and inheritance for ever. And therfore ought you withe all gladnes to geve yourselfes whollye unto him both body and sowle: but that do you not, so longe as you go about to serve ij masters: which yet you cannot do, (as Christ affirmethe,) though ye wolde cloke, colour, and counterfet never so moche. Do you thinke it to be but a small thinge, for the Lorde himselfe, even the myghtie God, to geve himselfe whollye to be your owne good God, and moste deare lovinge Father? Do you thinke it but a light matter that he hathe geven unto you (even to the deathe of the crosse) his owne onlye deare Son Jhus Christe, in whom was and is all his whole pleasure and delight; yea, and that when you were his verye enemyes; by the whiche gifte he hath geven you all other thinges, ether in heaven or earth? Do you estime it but a trifle, that he hathe geven you the Holye Ghoste, by whose powre and mightye operation you are made the sonnes of God, and coheires, annexed with Christe, of all your father's goodes and possessions? Matt. vi.
Rom. v.
Rom. viii.

But paradventure you will aske me, who dothe not earnestlye regarde all theis aforesaide giftes? Verelye I saye, Luc. i.

that none of you all do regarde them that do not wholye geve over yourselves agean to serve him, yea, and that in suche holynes and righteousnes as is accepted before him: for if you did well consider the depth of his aboundaunte bottomles mercye in Jhus Christ, you woulde so love God 207 ageane, that you woulde bowldelye saye withe Sainte Pawle, *Who is he, or what is it, that shalbe able to separate us from the love of God in Jhus Christe our Lorde*, &c. Rom. viii. Read the whole chapter, and the xj and xij to the Hebrues, for your comforte.

But I know that some of you will say, Dothe none love God, and serve hime truly, but suche as lye in prison, and geve their lyfes for his sake? Then God helpe us, for fewe shalbe saved. Indede, dere frindes, even so our Saviour Christe dothe saye, that *many ar called, but fewe ar chosen:* and *streight is the gate, and the way narrowe, that ledeth unto life, and fewe do finde it.* And in another place Christe callethe his Churche a *littell flock*, and conservynge the firste parte of your question, Christe dothe make you a playne and directe answer also, sayinge, that *he that wilbe his disciple muste nedes take up his crosse and followe him.* And ageane, *he that lovethe father or mother, wife or children, goodes or landes, or yet his own life, more than me,* saith he, *he is not worthie of me.* And S. Paule affirmethe, that *all* withowte exception, *that will lyve godly in Christe Jhu, muste suffer persecution.* And in another place he saithe, *To you it is geven, not onely to beleve in Christe, but also to suffer for his sake.* Nowe tell me, I pray you, whether that theis textes of Scripture do not prove, that all suche as will not suffer withe Christe, do neither love him nor serve him, nor yet be any of his disciples. Say what you will, and thinke what you liste, yet shall you fynde this full true, that all suche as wilnot suffer with Christe here, shall not reigne with him elles where; neither is it mete they shoulde. Oh Lorde! that the crosse, that is to say, trouble and persecution, for righteousnes sake, whiche is come amongest us for the triall of our feith, shold seme a strange thinge unto us that professe the name and gospell

Marginalia:
Matt. xx.
Matt. vii.
Luke xii.
Matt. xvi.
Matt. x.

2 Tim. iii.

1 Peter iv.

of Christe! Wheras we shoulde be moste of all acquainted
with it, as with our unseparable companyon in this life:
looke upon all the apostelles, martyrs, and confessours, synce
the comynge of Christe, and tell me if any of them all did
not contynuallye carrye the crosse of Christe, and in a manner all (or the most parte) dye in the end for his sake: yea,
moste chefly of all, look upon Jhus Christe himselfe, the
verye deare and only Sonne of God, and tell me, if all his
life and deathe was not full of most paynfull crosses.   And
will you looke to be his disciples, and yet thinke scorne to
beare your crosses with him? Disdayn you to drinke of the
same cup that your Lorde and master hathe donne before
you? Will you loke to enter into the kingdome of God any
easier waye than all other have donne before you? I praye
you shewe me your privelege, and tell me where you have
this prerogative above the reste of your bretherne, yea,
above the Sonne of God himselfe? My deare frindes and
lovinge neighbours, be not deceaved with selfe love, and
your owne fleshlye imaginations; for at one worde, this
is true, even as God in heaven is true, that if you wilnot Apoc. viii.
flye from that filthy whore of Babylon, and all her abhominable idolatrie and superstition, you shall suerlye perishe
with her in the plagues that shall shortlye be poored upon
her.   And furthermore, if you will not here willinglye suffer 208
withe Christe, for the testimonye of his truthe, you shall
not reigne withe him in glorye at his gracious comynge,
unto the whiche I hope it be not longe: for this is the firme
decree and purpose of the unchangeable God, reveled in
his everlastinge worde, that *all thei that will lyve godlye in* 2 Tim. iii.
Christe Jhu must suffer persecution: and that *every one* Heb. xii.
of his electe sonnes muste be scourged: proved and tryed as
golde in the fornace.   And theis wordes of Christe shall
contynewe for ever, that *whosoever shalbe ashamed of him* Mark viii.
or of his wordes in this adulterous and synful generation,
of him shall the Sonne of man be ashamed, when he cometh
in the glorye of his Father: and *he that goeth abowte to*
save his life shall lose it, &c.

Therfore, deare hartes, looke to your selves in tyme, and laye awaye all vayne excuses; for verely God wilnot accept them at your handes for your discharge, but will require of you in this pointe all that he hath commanded you. Wherfore, if you fele your selves too weak to confesse his name before the tyrawntes, then, for your refuge, the Lorde hathe geven you leave to flee, and that is the uttermoste that you may do; whiche doinge is yet very commendable, and a good confessing of the truthe before the worlde. Beware of them that shoulde be your shepherdes and pastors, for they deceave you, and ar become very wolves; they knew the trewthe, and pronely wolde confesse it. But now see if they wex not worse and worse: and this is the juste judge-

Rom. i. mente of God, *because that when they knew God, they glorified him not as God, nether wer thei thankefull, and therfore hathe God geven them up to ther owne hartes lustes;* for it is a juste plague of God to them, that had the truthe

2 Thess. ii. offered them, and regarded it not, to send them stronge delusions to beleve lyes, that all they may be dampned which beleve not the truthe, &c. Dere frendes, followe not their example; for if you do, you shall have like rewarde withe them: and seing that God hathe called you by his worde,

Prov. i. if ye refuse to heare, the tyme will come that you shall call upon him, and he will not hear: therfore, deare frindes, obey his voice, and then feare not the tyrantes, for the Lorde wilnot suffer them to laye handes on you, untill he see it good for you; and thereon reste your faithe. Take no example of the worldly wise, rich, and highe mynded men, which are choked with the worlde. For on high mountaynes dothe not growe mooste plentie of grasse; neither ar high trees farthest from danger, but seldom sure, and alway shaken of every wynde that blowethe. Suche a de-

Matt. xiii. ceiptful thinge, saith owre Saviowre Christe, is selfe-love, honour, and riches, to them that ar affectioned therto, that

Gal. vi. it blyndeth them, and maketh them thinke themselves somwhate, when indede thei ar nothinge at all. For though, for owre honoure we esteme owre selves, and stand in owre

owne lighte, yet when we shall stande before the judgemente seate of God, ther shalbe no respect of persons; for 1 Tim. vi.
riches helpethe not in the daye of vengeance, neither can
we make the Lorde partial for money; but as ye have donne, 209
so shall ye be rewarded. But if ye will turne unto the
Lorde withe your whole harte, he will suerly turne to you,
forgeve your synnes, and never remembre them any more,
yea, he saithe, if you will harken unto him, *theare shalbe* Ps. lxxxi.
no strange God amonge you, neither shall you worshipe Ps. lxxxiv.
any other God, but the Lord owre God; whiche hath promised that no good thinge shalbe with-holden from them
that lyve a godly life, whiche thinge God graunte bothe
you and me, and all other his deare children, to do for his
gloryous name sake. *Amen.*

Thus I have bene bowlde, dere frendes, to trouble you
withe my rude and simple letter, the whiche I have written,
partlye in discharge of my conscience and bounden dewtie
towardes you, and partlye for the love and good will I beare
unto your sowle healthe, that I mighte therby stere, provoke, and allure you to go on still forwardes in Christes true
feithe, feare, and love, accordinge to your profession, and as
you once godly did begynne; that as in Christe we have
truely loved, here in this life, so we may withe him together
lyve eternally in that blessed life to come, wheare theare is 1 Cor. ii.
suche joyes as the eye hathe not sene, the eare hathe not
hearde, neither yet hathe entred into the harte of man, &c.
God he knoweth I love you, and in my hart wisshe you
good, making mention of you in my dalye prayers; and
glade wolde I be to have your companye in that moste joyfull place, which Christe hathe prepared for all those that
love him, and contynewe feithfullye unto th'end; which Matt. xxiv.
thinge God graunt you all grace and strength to do, for his
name sake. *Amen.* Fare well, deare frendes, and pray for
me, whilste I am yet in this life, as I neither will nor can
forgette you: and if this my poore sarvice shall be well accepted of you, and take good effecte in you, I have my
hartes desire therin, as knowethe the Lord owre God, to
whose moste merciful defence I hartelye commytte you all.

The Almightie God blesse you all, and send us a moste joyfull merye metinge in his gloryous kingdom. *Amen.* The grace of owre Lord Jhus Christe be withe you all. *Amen.*

Dns. mihi adjutor : et non timebo quid faciat mihi homo.

From the Kinges Benche the xxvth *day of March, anno Domini* 1556, *by youres unfeinedlye to my power, John Clemente, an unprofitable servaunte of the Lorde : but yet of his great mercye made prisonner for his sake, and for the testimony of his everlastinge truthe ; at all tymes abydinge his moste merciful will and pleasure. Praye, praye, praye, even withe youre whole harte. Praye unto hym that is able to helpe.* Amen.

Number LXI.

John Clement's confession of faith.

Jesus Emanuell.

A confession and protestation of the Christian faythe, written by me John Clement, anno Dni. 1556. 1° *Aprilis.*

Rom. x. *The beleve of the harte justifieth : to confesse with the mouthe makethe a man safe.*

John Clement unto the Christian reader.

FOR two causes, specyallye, (dearlye beloved in the Lorde,) I have thought it good presentlye to put furthe a shorte summe of my faythe, and a brieffe declaration of the substaunce of the same, grownded upon the sure rocke Christe, and the unfallible veritie of his moste holye worde. The first is, for that I se a wonderfull sorte of sectes swarminge every where, not onlye of Papistes, whiche violentlye impugne and persecute Christe in his membres moste tirannouslye ; but also of Arians, Anabaptistes, and all other kynde of heretiques, whiche (under a pretence of the gospell, and godlye lyvynge) goe aboute the countrye deceavyng manye a symple sowle, to whom the depthe of Sathan's subtiltie is not knowen, and bringeth into sundrye sectes and schysmes, causynge them to devyde and separate themselves from the true Churche of Christe, grownded upon

the fowndation of the prophetes and apostles, Jesus Christe
beynge the heade corner stone, and to breake out of this
mysticall bodye: this is one thinge, I saye, that hath caused
me to shewe thee my faithe, that thou (good reader) mayest
knowe, not onelye what I hold and beleve, but also what
the whole Churche of God, which is the true spouse of
Christe, ever hath and dothe holde, mayntayne, and defende; and also what thou, and every lyvelye membre of
Christes true Churche, ought faythfullye to beleve, fyrmely
to holde, and earnestlye by the Scriptures withe sobryetie to
mayntayne and defende, if they intende to be saved. The
second cause is, for that I woulde be readye (as the Scriptures requirethe) to geve a reckonynge of my faythe in the
face of all the whole worlde, and also to be readye, (as
Saynte Peter teachethe,) *with mekenes to geve an answere to
every one that shall aske me a question of my faythe and
hope*, that I have in Jesus Christe, and evydentlye to prove 211
and demonstrate it by the holye Scriptures, and by uniforme consente of the primitive Churche: from the whiche
in any wyse I dare not, nor will not in anye wyse dissent;
no more do thou, (deare reader,) if thou wilte not be deceaved. For I tell the truthe, Sathan, that subtyll serpent
hathe transformed hymselfe lyke unto an angell of lyght,
and so craftelye he conveyeth himselfe in these dangerous
dayes, that if it were possible, the verye electe shoulde be
deceaved: for those, that neither by feare nor by flatterye,
he can bringe to his bowe, to make them open idolators
and persecutors of the truthe, with the pestilent Papistes;
nor yet whoremongers, dronkardes, extortioners, brybers,
peelers, and poulers, with the wicked worlde; them dothe
he busylye goe aboute to bringe into a wonderfull estimation
of themselves thorough hypocrisie and vayne-glorye; makynge them beleve that they be farre better and holyer than
any other; and that they be more wyser, and have better
knowledge and understandinge in the pure sense and mean-
inge of the sacred Scriptures, than any other men, be they
never so godlye, vertuous, wittie, or well learned. And
when the Devill hathe gotten them into his lease of selfe-

love and singularitie, then headeth he them at his pleasure, and perverteth them as he lusteth; makynge some to denye Christe to be God; some denyinge him to be man; some denying the Holye Ghoste to be God; some denyinge originall synne; some denyinge the doctrine of Godes firm predestination, and free election of Almightie God in Jesus Christe, whiche is the very certayntie of our salvation; some denyinge the descension of Christe into hell; some denyinge the baptisme of infantes; some condempninge and denyinge all indifferente thinges at any tyme to be used of Christian menne; withe innumerable suche like, too longe to be recyted: and as he hathe caused them to denye all these thinges, whiche yet Godes worde dothe allowe; even so hathe he made them to affirme many madde foolishe fantasyes, whiche the worde of God dothe utterlye condempne; as freewill, mannes righteousnes, and justifyinge of workes, withe dyvers suche like, to the great dishonoure of God, to the obscuringe of his glorye, the darkeninge of his truthe, to the greate defacynge of Christes deathe, yea, to the utter destruction of many a symple soule, that cannot shyfte from these subtyll sleyghtes of Sathan, excepte the Lorde shewe his greate mercye upon them. This hath the subtyll serpent sought ever synce the beginninge; and muche of his pestilent purpose hathe he brought to passe in these present perilous dayes, permitted of God as a just plague to punyshe our unthankfulnes for his truthe, and true preachers of the same. The Lorde be mercyfull unto us, and pardon and forgeve us our synnes and offences, release our iniquities and myseryes, and geve us true repentaunce, and encrease our faythe. Good Lorde, defende thy flocke, and shorten these sorrowfull dayes for thy Sonne Jesus Christes sake. *Amen.* Farewell, (deare reader,) prayse God onelye for his truthe: and praye for me his poore unprofytable servante.

212 Put awaye contention, and reade with discretion:
Trye trulye by the touchstone: judge without affection.

O Lorde, encrease my faythe.

The confession of the true Christian faythe, and belefe

of me John Clement, the unprofitable servaunte of Jesus Christe, but yet, thoroughe his greate mercye and grace, made prisoner (with other moe in the Kynges Benche of the same faythe) for the testimonye of Godes everlasting truthe: whiche faythe and belefe I do entende (by the helpe and assistaunce of Almightie God) to confyrme with my deathe and seale with my bloude, when the tyme shall come that the Lorde my God hath appointed.

Firste, I confesse and undoubtedlye beleve, that there is **I.** one (and but one) lyvynge and true God, and he is ever-lastinge, without partes or passions, of infinite power, wise-dome, and goodnes, the maker and preserver of all thinges bothe visible and invisible; and in unitie of this Godhead there be three Persones, of one substance, power, and eternitie, the Father, the Sonne, and the Holy Ghoste.

Secondlye, I confesse and beleve, that the Sonne of God, **II.** the second Person in Trinitie, whiche is the Worde of the Father, did vouchesafe for our sakes to take mannes nature in the wombe of the blessed Virgine Marye, of her verye substaunce, and became trulye man in all poyntes, (synne onelye excepte,) so that two whole and perfecte natures, that is to saye, the Godhead and manhode, were joyned together into one persone, never to be divided; wherof is one Christe, very God and verye man; who trulye suffred, was crucified, dead, and buried, and rose againe, to reconcyle us to his Father, and to be a perfect sacrifice for all the synne of mankynde, bothe original and actuall: and therfore, he beynge perfecte God and perfecte man, is to be honoured and prayed unto of all men, as the Father is.

Thirdlye, I do undoubtedly beleve in God the Holy **III.** Ghoste, who is the lorde and gever of lyfe, and the sanctifier of all Godes elect. That he is God equal with the Father and the Sonne, and is to be worshiped and prayed unto of all men, as the Father and the Sonne is; to whom, with the Father and the Sonne, be all honour, glory, praise, thankes, power, rule, and dominion, for ever and ever. *Amen.*

Fourthelye, I do confesse and undoubtedlye beleve all the **IV.**

whole canonical Scriptures to be most true, and every sentence of the same; and that the holy Scriptures contaynethe all thinges necessarye to salvation: so that whatsoever is neither read therin, nor may be proved therby, (althoughe the same be sometyme receaved of the faithefull as godlye 213 and profitable for an order and comelynes,) yet no man ought to be constrayned to beleve it as an article of our faithe, or repute it requisite of necessitie to salvation; but whatsoever is directlye against it is abominable, and to be warelye avoyded of all men.

v.   Fyfthelye, I doe confesse and undoubtedlye beleve thoroughlye in all poynts the three Credes, Nycene Crede, Athanasius Crede, and that whiche commonlye is called the Apostles Crede. For they may be proved by moste certayne warrants of the holy Scriptures.

VI.   Syxthlye, I do confesse and faithfullye beleve, that there is one true, faithefull, Christian Catholike Churche; and but one in all the whole worlde; whiche Churche is buylte upon the foundations of the prophetes and apostles, that is to saye, upon the worde of God whiche they preached, Jesus Christe beynge the head corner-stone: who hathe purified and clensed this Churche in the fowntayne of water thoroughe the worde, and hathe made it a gloryous congregation unto himselfe, without spott or wrincle in his syght.

VII   Also, I do confesse and beleve Jesus Christe (and not the Bysshop of Rome) to be the onely head of this true Churche, who only is the gever of lyfe and salvation to every true membre of the same, whiche is the propryetie of a true head; and that in this Churche onelye is purelye preached, and sincerely taught the true worde of God, and his sacraments dulye ministred according to Christes institution, in all those thinges that of necessitie are requisite to the same; if they be not otherwise lett or hindered by persecutions. Whiche thinge often tymes chauncethe; for longe cannot this true Churche be without persecution, as the holye Scripture in divers places provethe, neither hathe it bene from the beginninge.

Also, I doe unfaynedlye confesse, and faithfullye beleve, VIII. that thoroughe the mere mercye of God in Jesus Christ, I am a true lyvelye member of this blessed Churche of Christe : and so I doe acknowledge, confesse, and beleve all those faithefull preachers, ministers, and other godlye persones to be, that of late have bene put to execution, within this realme of Englande, for the testimonye of God's ever last-inge truthe and veritie ; for whome the Lorde is to be praysed nowe and ever : and the same Lorde geve me, and all other his deare children, grace to follow their good doc-trine and good example of lyvynge.

Also, I doe believe and acknowledge this true Churche to IX. be Christes spouse, his mysticall bodye, the house of God, the grounde and pyllar of truthe, governed contynuallye by the Holye Ghoste : so that it can never whollye erre in any necessarye poynte of our salvation, but is able at all tymes (by the worde of God) to dissolve all doubtes. Therefore as God is my Father, so is this his churche and spouse my 214 mother : for she hathe, from tyme to tyme, nourisshed, fedde, and comforted me with the lyvelye worde of God and his blessed sacraments, and hathe brought me up in the true understandinge and knowledge of the same. Wherefore I do verelye purposse, by the grace and helpe of Almightie God, to contynue her true, faithfull, and obedyent childe for ever. For I beleve and knowe, that without this Churche is no salvation nor remission of synnes.

Also, because the Bysshop of Rome and his clargye do X. usurpe to themselves the auctoritie and tytle of this true Churche ; here I do openlye confesse, acknowledge, and beleve undoubtedlye, that the Bisshop of Rome and his clargye, with all their adherents, are the very synagogue of Sathan, and the malignaunte Churche of Antichriste, whiche dothe corrupte the pure worde of God, and abuse his blessed sacramentes, and hathe ever, from tyme to tyme, (as it doth nowe,) persecute the true Churche of Christe ; and I do verelye beleve, that all Jewes, Turkes, and other infydells, that beleve not in Christe, and all heretikes, be members of the same cursed synagogue ; and all they do make but one

bodye of Antechriste, the Devill beynge heade of that beaste-
lye bodye, who in his membres, from the begynnynge, hathe
impugned Christe in his true membres, and shall doe untill
the worldes ende; but yet more at some tyme than at some
other, as it shall please God to suffre him, for the tryall of
his electe.

XI.   And also, I do proteste and beleve, that the doctrine of
the papisticall Churche, concerning holy breade, holy water,
holy fyre, halowinge of asshes, palmes, candells, copes, vesti-
mentes, chalyces, and suche lyke; their makynge and guild-
inge of images, their serveynge and worsshipping of them;
their goynge on pilgrimage and procession, their purgatorye,
pardons, and prayinge for the deade, their masses, diriges,
and prayinge to sayntes, their forbiddinge of meates and
mariages, their doctrine of freewill, justifyinge of workes,
and, fynallye, their devillisshe doctrine of the sacrifice of the
masse and transubstanciation is mere idolatrie, superstition,
and most detestable blasphemye and abhomination in the
sight of God, and therefore to be abhorred of all Christian
men. And therefore I doe here confesse before God and
man, that I utterlye forsake, renownce, and dissent from all
Jewes and Turkes that are infidells, and from all Papistes;
from all Arians, Eutichians, Manichians, Sabellians, Pelagians, Donatistes, Anabaptistes, and all other heretikes and
sectaries, whiche be contrarye to the worde of God and his
true Churche. For, as I said before, the true Churche
(beynge Christes spouse) is obedient in all things unto the
voice of Christe her bridegrome, and will not declyne ther-
from to the right hande nor to the lefte: neither will she
adde to nor diminishe from the worde of her husbonde
215 Christe, to whome, with the Father and the Holye Goste,
be all honor, glorye, and prayse, for ever and ever. *Amen.*

XII.   And furthermore, I do confesse and undoubtedlye beleve, that I, and every lyvely member of this Catholike
Churche, is and shall be redemed, justified, and saved
oneley and solye by the free grace and mere mercye of
God in Jesus Christe, thoroughe his moste precyous deathe
and bloudsheaddinge, and in no parte, by (or for) any of

our owne good workes, merites, or deservings, that we can
do or deserve. Notwithstandinge I confesse, that all men
ought, and are bownde by the worde of God, to doe good
workes, and to knowe and kepe God's commandmentes, yet
not to deserve any parte of our salvations thereby; but to
shewe their obedience to God, and the frutes of faythe unto
the worlde; that the lyght of their good workes may so shyne
before men, that God our heavenlye Father may be glorified
thereby. But yet I doe confesse, that God dothe not forgeve us our synnes, or repute us juste for any of our owne
workes, merites, or righteousnes, whiche beynge compared
to the puritie whiche the lawe of God requirethe shoulde
all be fownde (as Esay saithe) lyke a fylthye clothe stayned
with menstrue; but for Jesus Christes sake onely, whose
moste precious deathe and bloude sheaddinge, I hartelye
acknowledge to be a full and perfecte sacrifice, and a sufficient ransome for the synnes of all the worlde; to obtayne
salvation therby. And this salvation, redemption, and justification, is apprehended, or receaved of us, by the onelye
faithe in Jesus Christe, in that sence and meanynge as is
declared in the homilye of Justification whiche was appoynted to be reade in the peculiar Churche of Englande
in good Kynge Edward's dayes the Syxte: whiche homilye,
with all the reaste, then set furthe by his auctoritie, I do
affirme and beleve to be a true, holesome, and godlye doctrine for all Christian men to beleve, observe, kepe, and
folowe.

Also, I do beleve and confesse, that the last boke whiche   XIII.
was geven to the Churche of Englande by the auctoritie of
good Kynge Edwarde the Syxte, and the whole Parliament,
contayninge the manor and fourme of common prayer, and
ministration of the blessed sacramentes in the Churche of
Englande, they ought to have bene receaved and alowed
with all readynes of mynde, and thankfullnes of harte: but
(alas) for our necligence and unthankfulnes, this great
plague of papistrie and schysmes is come agayne amonge
us: God (of his greate mercye) deliver us, and all Englande,
from it shortelye, for his gloryous names sake. *Amen.*

XIV.   Also, I do accepte, beleve, and alowe, for a verye truthe, all the godlye articles that were agreed upon in the convocation-house, and publisshed by the Kynges Majesties auctoritie, (I meane Kynge Edwarde the Syxte,) in the last yeare of his moste gracyous reigne.

216   Nowe I have declared my faithe, and beleve of and in the
XV.   holye and blessed Trinitie, of the worde of God contayned in the canonycall Scriptures, and of the blessed sponse of Jesus Christe his true Churche, with a fewe other thinges more; I will shewe you my faithe and beleve of the blessed sacramentes, whiche Christe hathe instituted and lefte with his true Churche; whiche Churche, and every membre therof, ought (as they may convenientlye) to use the same, aswell for their owne contynuall comforte, as also to the stirringe up of their owne hartes in thankfulnes towardes God for all his mercyfull benefites powred upon us thoroughe Jesus Christe our Lorde. And therfore I beleve and acknowledge that our Lorde Jesus Christe hathe knytt together a company of newe people with holye sacramentes, as but fewe in number, so moste excellent in signification, that is to saye, baptisme, and the Lordes supper: whiche sacramentes be not oneley badges and tokens of Christian mennes profession, as the Anabaptistes saye, but rather they be certayne and sure witnesses, and effectuall sygnes of grace and God's good will towardes us, by the whiche, the Lorde dothe worke invisiblye in us, and dothe not onelye quicken, but also strengthen and confyrme our faythe in him; whiche sacramentes were ordeyned of Christe, not to be gased upon, nor caryed aboute, nor to be worsshipped, as the Papistes do use their counterfecte sacrament, to the great disshonoure of Almightie God, and to the great daungier of many a symple soule: but for that we should rightelye use them to the ende that they were ordeyned for, as it is afore said. For in suche onelye as do worthelye receave the same, they have a holesome effecte and operation, (and yet not of the *worke wrought*, as papisticall schoolemen speake; whiche wordes, as it is strange and unknowen to the holye Scripture, so it engenderethe no godlye, but a very supersticious sence,)

but they that receave the sacramentes unworthelye, doe receave to themselves dampnation, as Saint Paull saythe.
Therfore let every man rightlye examine himself.

As concerninge the blessed sacrament of baptisme, I do XVI.
confesse and undoubtedlye beleve, that it is the pure ordinance of Almightie God; not onelye to be a signe of profession, or a marke of difference, wherby Christian men are
decerned or knowen from other that are not christened : but
it is also a sygne and seale of our newe birthe; wherby, as
by an instrument, they that receave baptism rightelye are
graffed into the Churche of Christe; and all the promises
of God's mercye concerninge the forgevenes of synnes, and
our adoption to be the sonnes of God, are visiblye sygned
and sealed to us; yea, faithe is confirmed, and grace encreased by vertue and prayer unto God. And therfore I
do here confesse and beleve, that the custome used in the
Churche of God to christen or baptise younge children, is
bothe good and godlye, and agreable to the worde of God; 217
and therfore to be commended, retayned, and used in
Christes Churche: and I do utterlye dissent from the Anabaptistes, whiche holde the contrarye; howbeit I do not
condempne the yonge children of Christian parents that dye
without baptisme, as the prowde presumynge Papistes doe;
but I doe rather beleve them to be saved by the great
mercye of God in Jesus Christe.

Also I do beleve, that if a childe be baptised in the name XVII
of the Father, and of the Sonne, and of the Holy Ghoste,
as Christe hath commanded us, that it is trulye and sufficientlye baptised, thoughe the minister be never so wicked
in life or in learning that dothe baptise it; for the effecte of
God's ordinance dothe not depende upon the worthynes of
the minister, but upon the truthe of God's promises. Therfore I do beleve that those children that have bene, bee, or
shalbe baptised of the papisticall ministers, be trulye baptised, be the minister never so great a Papiste: howe be it,
this I doe confesse and beleve, that no Christian man ought
to bringe or sende his childe to the papisticall Churche, or to
require baptisme of them, (they beynge Antichristes,) for

in so doynge, he dothe confesse them to be the true Churche of Christe: whiche is a grevous synne in the syght of God, and a great offence to his true congregation. Yet nevertheless the childe so brought, if it be baptised in the name of the Father, and of the Sonne, and of the Holy Ghoste, as is afore said, that then it is sufficientlye baptised: and as for the childe (beynge without understandinge) is not in the faulte, but the parentes or governours be in a great faulte for their so doynge. Therefore take hede and beware of them for God's sake, and bringe not your children to them. For you ought not to requyre Christes sacramentes at Antichristes Churche, but at Christes true Churche onely: and I do beleve that every true Christian man or woman maye lawfullye baptise in the tyme of necessitye, yea, thoughe it were his or their owne childe.

XVIII.   Also I doe confesse and beleve, that the blessed sacrament of the bodye and bloude of Christe, commonlye called the *communyon*, or supper of the Lorde, is the blessed and pure ordinance of our Lorde and Saviour Jesus Christe, instituted by him the nyght before his passion, not onely to be a bare and naked sygne of his bodye breakynge, and his bloud-sheadding, and of the love that Christians ought to have amonges themselves one to another; but muche rather to be a sure seale and a fyrme testimonye of our eternall redemption by Christes deathe and bloud-sheaddinge. In so muche, that to suche as with true faythe and feelynge of the mercye of God in his promises, do rightelye and worthelye receave the same accordinge to Christes institution, they doe spirituallye receave Christe, God and man, with the effecte and commoditie of all his mercyes, merites, pas-
218 sions, and suffringes for us, as effectuallye and advayleablye as they were our owne, as in dede they are freelye geven unto us by Christe; and also as a sure seale and fyrme testimonye to our conscyence, that all our synnes (be they never so manye, so greyous, and so greate) be clerelye pardoned, released, and forgeven, onelye for the mere mercye of God, thoroughe the deathe and bloude-sheaddinge of his deare Sonne Jesus Christe, and we made the children of God,

and heyres of his kyngdome, and incorporated membres of his misticall bodye, as it is full well to be seen and proved in the holye Scripture, and also full well declared in the late Bysshoppe of Canterburries bokes, and many other godlye workes set furthe in that most worthy Kynge Edwarde the Syxtes dayes; and as it was full trulye and syncerelye preached of these worthey preachers, Thomas Cranmer, late archebysshop of Canterburrye, Doctor Ridley, old Hughe Latymer, Master Houpper, Rodgers, Saunders, Bradforde, and dyvers other godlye preachers, who have sealed the same with their bloude; and as it is yet also godlye defended (by the Scriptures) of divers other that be yet lyvynge, and godly learned men in Christes Churche: whose determinations do fullye agree with the faythfull fathers of the primitive Church, but specyallye with the worde of God. And therefore I will not, nor dare not for my lyfe, dissent from them; but I doe undoubtedlye beleve and protest before Ged and man, that the doctrine of the Papistes, concerninge transubstantiation, reservation, and adoration, is devillishe, detestable, false, fayned, and hereticall, and bringethe with it many absurdities and inconveniences, to the utter distruction of all that beleve it. For Christe, as he is perfecte God, so is he perfecte man, of a reasonable soule, and humayne flesshe, subsistinge: and forasmuche as the truthe of mannes nature requirethe, that the bodye of one and the selfe same man cannot be at one tyme in dyvers places, but must nedes be in some one certayne place; therefore the bodye of Christe is not present at one tyme in many and dyvers places, (the Scripture not testyfying the same.) For the Scripture dothe testifie that Christe was taken up into heaven, and there shall continue unto the ende of the worlde. And agayne, he sayethe, *I went out from the Father, and came into the worlde; agayne, I leave the worlde, and goe into the Father.* At whiche sayinge, his discyples said to him, *Lo, nowe talkeste thou playnely;* with dyvers other suche like places in the Scripture. Therefore neither I nor any other Christian man ought to beleve, or openlye to confesse the reall and bodylye presence of Christes bodye and bloude to be in the sacramentall breade and wyne, or under the accidentes of the same, as the Papistes do saye at their pleasure, and would force us to beleve it. God shortelye put them to sylence, and diminisshe their tyrannous power. For this their transubstanciation, or chaungeynge of the substance of bread and wyne into the substance of Christes bodye and bloude cannot be proved by the holye Scriptures, but is cleane repugnante against it ; and so is the takynge awaye of the one halfe of the sacrament from the 219 lay-men against Christes worde, which said, *Drinke ye all hereof.* And it is a verye drifte of the Devill to deface the glorye of Christes deathe, by settinge up a newe sacrifice for synne, I meane that most pestilent, poysoned, papisticall masse, whiche the Antichristes do affirme to be a sacrifice satisfactorye and propiciatorye, to obtayne the remission of synnes for the quicke and the deade ; contrarye to all the holy Scriptures, especiallye againste the excellent epistle to the Hebrewes, wherein it is playnelye-proved that Christe offered himselfe upon the crosse once for all ; and with that one oblation he made a full satisfaction for the synnes of all that trulye repent and beleve in him. For *with that one offering* (saithe Sainte Paul) *hathe he made perfecte for ever them that are sanctified, and nowe is he set downe on the right hande of God, and from hence furthe tarriethe there untill his enemyes be made his footestoole :* and then, (that is to saye at the latter daye,) *to them that hartelye loke for him, shall he appeare againe, and receave them to glorye ;* whiche most desirous daye of thy comfortable commynge hasten (deare Lorde) for thy great mercye, truthe, and promise sake. *Amen.* Let all true, faithfull Christian hartes hereunto unfaynedlye saye, *Amen.*

XIX. Furthermore, seynge I do perceave that there is a wonderfull sorte of the Pelagians secte swarming every where, whiche doe mayntayne, teache, and defende, that all men (havinge faithe or not, beinge regenerate or not regenerate) have power, choyse, and freewill to chose life, and to kepe the commandementes of God in such wise as the lawe of God requirethe, I have thought it good to set furthe my mynde and beleve herein also : wherfore I doe confesse and beleve, that Adam by his fall lost, from himselfe and all his posteritie, all the freedome, choyce, and power of mannes will to doe good; so that all the will and imaginations of mannes harte is onelye to evill, and alltogether subjecte to synne and myserye, and bonde and captyve to all manner of wickednes, so that it cannot once thinke a good thought, muche lesse then doe any good deede, as of his owne worke, pleasaunte and acceptable in the syght of God ; untill suche tyme as the same be regenerate by the Holy Ghoste, and prevented by the grace of God. For as Saynte James saythe, *Every good and perfecte gyfte is from above, and cometh downe from the Father of lyght :* and Christe saithe, *Without me you can doe nothinge :* and Paule saythe, that *it is God whiche workethe in us bothe the will and the dede even of good will.* Therfore untill the spirite of regeneration be geven us of God, we can neither will, doe, speake, nor thinke any good thinge that is acceptable in his syght. Let us therfore alwayes praye unto God, that he will make in us a cleane harte, and renewe in us an upright spirite : that by the myghtye operation thereof, we maye doe, speake, and thinke all thinges to his glorye and commoditie of our bretherne, in respecte of his greate mercye, love, and kyndenes onelye ; for without this his good spirite, whiche dothe worke true faythe in us, all our doynges be verye synne and hypo- 220 crisie in the sight of God, howe gaye and gloryous soever the same appeare in the syght of men : but here I doe not denye, but that every reasonable man (duringe the generall influence of God) hathe in himselfe power and will in thynges humayne ; as to eate and drynke, to buylde and plante, to learne this scyence or that, to marye, &c. yea, to faste and praye, to doe almes-dedes, to heare or reade God's worde, and so of all other lyke operations. For men are not images nor deade postes. That men are free in thynges humayne, it doth appeare moste clearlye by the philosophers, and other heathen people whiche did and doe yett florisshe in morall vertues exceadinglye : but to doe any of these thinges in suche sorte as God's worde dothe require them to be done, and as is pleasante, acceptable, and alowed in his sight, is not in the power or lybertye of any man, not beynge regenerate by the Spirite of God ; because it is not in his power to have the supernaturall knowledge of God, seynge the same is so farre above his might : therfore when I saye, man hathe not free-will to doe good, I meane it of workes that are holye, spirituall, and divine, the whiche are pleasante and acceptable to God, as to have lyvely lyght, spirituall knowledge, and understandinge of God, to have in him fyrme faythe and hope, to love him, honor him, praise him, reverence him, and serve him with all his harte, soule, and mynde, to order all his lyfe to the glorye of God, to obey and committ himselfe whollye to his governance, with mortifyinge his flesshelye appetites, and denyinge himselfe the flesshe, and his own worldelye wysdome; to love his neyghboure as himselfe, yea, even his very enemyes for the love of God, with all his harte to praye for them, and to doe them all the good he can possiblye ; but to doe suche workes to the glorye of God is not in the power or lybertye of the naturall man, untill he be born anewe, as Christe said to Nicodemus : for (as Sainte Paule saithe) *the naturall man perceavethe not the thinges that be of God, neither can he perceave them*, for he is deade in Adam, and of nature the childe of wrathe : for as a man that is deade cannot raise up himselfe, or worke anythinge towardes his resurrection, or he that is not, worke towardes his creation ; even so the naturall man (whiche is deade in Adam as thoughe he were not) cannot worke anythinge towardes his regeneration; but as a bodye without the soule cannot move but downewardes, so the soule of man, without the Spirite of Christe, (whiche is his lyfe,) cannot lyfte up him selfe, but must of necessitie descende ever more downewardes, regardinge but his owne intereste. Therfore he cannot but synne, he cannot but remayne in distruste and in infidelitie, so displeasynge God in all thinges that he doth : he must be borne agayne, to doe the workes that be spirituall and holye, and by our selves we cannot be regenerate by any meanes, for it is oneley the worke of God. To whom let us praye with David, that he

will take awaye our stonye hartes, and create in us newe
hartes by the mightye operations of his holye Spirite, who
leade, guyde, and comforte us by the certayne feelynge of
his greate mercye towardes us in Jesus Christe, for his glori- 221
ous names sake. *Amen.*

Fynallye, for as muche as I do perceave that not onelye xx.
Papistes, but also dyvers other that be professours of Godes
worde, beynge moved of an earneste zeale, than of any true
knowledge of the Scriptures, doe, with wordes and wrytynges,
impugne the moste pure, heavenlye, swete, comfortable, and
true doctrine of Godes fyrme *predestination* and free *election* of us in Christe, accordinge to the purpose of his grace,
before the whole worlde began, whiche is the sure certayntye of our salvation in Jesus Christe; I will, with the helpe
of Almyghtye God, brieffelye declare a shorte somme of my
faythe in this article also: wherfore I do acknowledge, confesse, and undoubtedlye beleve, that God our eternal Father (whose power is incomprehensible, whose wisdome is
infinite, and his judgmentes unsearcheable) hath onelye of
his greate aboundant mercye, and free goodnes, and favoure
in Jesus Christe, ordeyned, predestinated, elected, and appoynted (before that the fowndation of the worlde was layed)
an innumerable multitude of Adam's posteritie to be saved
from their synnes thoroughe the merites of Christes deathe
and bloudsheaddinge onelye; and to be (thoroughe Christe)
his adopted sonnes and heres of his everlastinge kingdome,
in whom his great mercye shalbe magnified for ever: of
whiche moste happye number, my fyrme faithe and stedfast
beleve is, that I (althoughe unworthye) am one, onelye
thoroughe the mercye of God in Jesus Christe our Lorde
and Savyour: and I beleve, and am surely certified, by the
testimonye of Godes good Spirite, and the unfallyble truthe
of his most holye worde, that neither I, nor any of these his
chosen children, shall fynallye perisshe or be dampned, althoughe we all (if God shoulde entre into judgment with us
accordinge to our dedes) have justlye deserved it; but suche
is Godes greate mercye towardes us, (for our Lorde Jesus
Christes sake,) that our synnes shall never be imputed unto

us: we are all geven to Christe to kepe, who will lose none
of us, neither can anythinge plucke us furthe of his handes,
or separate us from him; he hathe maryed us unto him by
faythe, and made us his pure spouse without spott or wrincle in his sight, and will never be devorced from us: he
hathe taken from us all our synnes, myseries, and infirmities, and hathe put them upon himselfe, and hathe clothed
us with his righteousnes, and enriched us with his merites,
and mercyes, and moste lovinge benefites: and he hathe not
onelye done all this, and muche more for us, but also of his
greate mercye, love, and kyndenes, he dothe styll kepe the
same moste surelye safelye for us, and will doe so for ever;
for he lovethe us unto the ende. His Father hathe committed
us unto his safe custodye, and none can ever be able to
plucke us furthe of his hands: he is stronger than the Devill, deathe, synne, or hell, for he onelye hathe overcome
them all for our behove, and yelded unto us his glorious
222 victorie, so that they can never hurte us any more unto
deathe; (I meane the seconde deathe:) he hathe regestred
our names in the boke of lyfe, in suche sorte that the same
shall never be raced out. In consideration whereof, we have
good cause to rejoyce, to thanke God, and hartelye to love
him, and of love unfaynedlye to doe whatsoever he willeth
us to doe, for he loved us firste, &c. Fynallye, Christe testi-
fyethe himselfe, that *it is not possible that the electe shoulde
be deceaved.* Verelye then, can they not be dampned:
therfore I confesse and beleve with all my harte, soull, and
mynde, that not one of all Godes electe children shall fynallye peryshe or be dampned. For God, who is their Father, both can and will preserve, kepe, and defende them for
ever: for seynge he is God, he wantethe no power to do it;
and also seynge he is their moste deare lovynge Father, he
lackethe no good will towardes them, I am sure. Howe can
it be, but he will perfourme their salvation to the uttermoste,
sythe he wantethe neither power nor good will to do it.
And this moste heavenlye, true, and comfortable doctrine,
dothe not bringe with it a flesshelye, idell, carnall, and careles
lye, as some men unjustlye do reporte of it, whose eyes God

open, and pardon their ignorance and rasshe judgmentes;
but rather it dothe mayntayne and bringe with it all true
godlynes and Christian puritie of lyfe, with moste earneste
thankefullnes of harte in respecte of Godes greate mercye
and lovynge kyndenes onelye. For (as Sainte John sayethe)
*he that hathe this hope in him, purgethe himselfe, as he is
pure;* and he that hathe the certayne feelynge of this in his
harte, cannot contynue or delyghte in synne. Therfore is
this a moste true, godlye, necessarye, holesome, and comfortable doctrine to be receaved, embraced, learned, and
faithfullye beleved and folowed of all true Christian men.
Whose harte soever God movethe to be desyrous to knowe
further in the truthe of this matter, let him reade that godlye boke of Barnardyne Ochynes xxv sermons, or at the
leaste xiiii of them, (the laste xiiii,) which teachethe this
matter verye godlye, and at large; so that a godlye, meke,
and humble mynde, may therby be satisfied abundantley.
But be ware in any wyse of curiositie, that unsaciable beaste.
Reverence and worshippe the deepe secretes and judgmentes
of God, whiche are unsearcheable and past fyndynge out.
Reason not with God, why he dothe this or that, for he is
holye in all his workes and righteous in all wayes, and hathe
done all thynges with equitie and mercye, justice and judgment.

As for *reprobation,* I have nothinge to saye of it; for
Sainte Paul saythe, *What have we to doe with them that are
without?* God, for Christes sake, open our eyes, that we
may clerelye see his truthe, and geve us hartes mekelye to
yelde to the same. The Lorde encrease our faythe and
true feelynnge of our election, and sure certayntye of our salvation in Jesus Christe, to whom, with the Father and the
Holye Goste, for our election, vocation, justification, and
glorification, be all honor, glorye, praise, thankes, power,
rule, and dominion, for ever and ever. *Amen.*

The Conclusion.

Let it not offend thee, (deare reader,) that in the ex-
pressinge or declaration of my faythe, I doe so muche set
furthe the prayse and commendation of the true Churche,

and of the godlye learned preachers of the same; as thoughe
I shoulde seem to leane too muche to men, and to builde my
faythe upon the wisdome and learninge of men, and not
onelye upon the unfallible worde of God, wherin is contayned all veritie.   For doubtles I doe not depende upon
the judgement of any man, further than the same dothe
agree with the true touchestone, whiche is the holye Scriptures: wherin (I thanke my Lorde God) I have bene continuallye exercysed, even from my youthe up, as they that
have knowne my bringynge up, can tell: and some persecution I have suffred for the same.   And now it hath pleased
God to make me a prisoner for the testymonye therof: and
I thynke that shortelye I must geve my lyfe for it, and so
confyrme it with my bloude, whiche thinge I am well contented to doe: and I moste hartelye thanke my Lorde God
therfore, that is to saye, for this his specyall gifte of persecution for righteousnes sake.   And thoughe for my synnes
God myght justlye have condempned me to hell fyre for
ever, and also have caused me to suffre bothe shame and
persecution in this lyfe, for evyll doynge; yet hath he (of
his great mercye in Jesus Christe, accordinge to his owne
good will and purpose) dealte more mercyfullye with me;
as to geve me this grace and favor in his sight, that I shall
suffre persecution of the wicked, with his electe people, for
the testymonye of his truthe; yea, even with the prophets
and apostles, and with his deare Sonne Jesus Christe himselfe, to the ende I may reigne with him in glorye: for the
Scripture saithe, If we suffre with Christe, we shall reigne
with Christe; but if we denye him, he also will deny us:
and againe, All that will lyve godlye in Christe Jesu must
suffer persecutions.   Thus can I testifie, bothe by the worde
of God, and also by experyence, that the crosse of Christe is
an unseparable companion with the pure profession of the
gospell: and the truthe beyinge taken to harte, in youthe,
and planted therin diepelye with affliction for the same, it
will not be wasshed awaye with the stronge storme of troubles and persecutions, be the tempest never so greate.   I
have written nothinge but that whiche I am well able to

prove by the playne texte of the holye Scripture, whiche (as the prophete saythe) gevethe wisdome unto babes, and is a lanterne unto my feete, and a lyght unto my pathes; and I will not, nor dare not for my lyfe, steppe one foot further than I have that lanterne goynge before me: and so farre dare I boldelye goe, thoughe all the worlde would counsayle and command me to the contrarye. The worde of God is that measuringe lyne or rodde whiche was committed to Ezechiell and to John, to mete all thinges with: it is the true touchestone wherwith Sainte John willethe us 225 to trye the spirites; yea, the worde of God is the thynge that oughte to be judge of all our doynges: for by his worde that he hathe spoken, shall all thinges be judged in the laste daye. Verelye no man can geve the worde of Gode too hyghe praise, nor yet geve too muche credite unto it; for it is the everlastinge truthe, and the light of the worlde, and excellethe all mistes of ignorance and cloudes of erroure.

Notwithstandinge, as it is unto some the savor of lyfe unto lyfe; even so it is unto other some, the savor of death unto death: as Christe himselfe is unto some a rocke to ryse bye, and to other some, a stone to stumble at. I woulde wisshe all men to reade the holye Scripture with diligent prayer daye and night, yea, and to marke it well: and yet not to refuse the ordinarie meanes that God dothe sende to instructe them bye, (as some doe, whiche will allowe no mennes judgmentes but their owne; nor loke upon any mannes godlye expositions upon the same:) for God hath sett an order in his Churche, and doth geve his gyftes diverslye, to some more and to some lesse, as his godlye wisdome pleasethe, for the edification of his bodye, whiche is his congregation. Therfore he (whatsoever he be) that refusethe or despisethe this order, cannot but fall into dyvers errours and pernicious sectes, every man as his owne fantasye dothe leade him: for as David saith, *he that will understande the secretes of the Lord, must entre into his sanctuarye:* that is to saye, he muste be at unitie with Christes

Churche, whiche is grownded upon the word of God, and
governed contynuallye by his holye and mightie Spirite,
whiche judgethe and trulye discussethe all thinges. And
doubtles I dare affirme, that God hathe sent in our tyme
verye excellent preachers and ministers of his holy worde,
suche, as more excellent in lyfe, but specyallye in doctrine,
and more plentye of them hathe not bene seene nor hearde
in all this realme of Englande, who have syncerelye preached and testified his truthe unto the worlde, and have moste
constantlye confirmed and sealed the same with their bloude.
And albeit that I muste nedes confesse, that God hathe
used their wordes and writinges, as his good instrumentes
and meanes, to bringe me firste to the true knowledge and
understandinge of his everlastinge word : yet nowe I doe
not beleve it onelye because they have wrote and spoken it,
but because I know it my selfe to be moste true, though
they themselves, or an angell from heaven, woulde come and
saye the contrarye : as the people of Samaria saide to the
woman whiche firste brought them tydinges of Christe :
Nowe we (saide they) *beleve, not because thou haste tolde us,
but because we have hearde and sene him our selves.* Even
so (I thank my Lorde God moste hartelye) I have (by
faithe in him and in his holye worde) bothe sene and hearde
Jesus Christe to be my onelye and moste mercyfull Saviour
and Redemer : therfore I cannot but testifie that whiche
I have bothe sene and hearde.

225   Thus have I (deare reader) as brieffelye as I can, declared the whole some and substance of my faythe, grownded and established upon the sure and unmoveable rocke,
Christe, and the unfallible testimonye of his pure and holye
worde, as I am well able to prove before the face of all the
whole worlde : and I truste, by the grace, helpe, and
strengthe of Almightye God, to confirme it with my deathe,
and seale the same with my bloude. Strengthen and comforte me, good Lorde, with thy holye and mightye Spirite,
that I maye boldelye confesse my faythe in thee, and in thy
holye worde, before the face of all men ; and not to feare to

dye for the same, when the tyme is full come, whiche thou haste appoynted for that purpose. All faithfull hartes praye for me.   The blessinge of God be with you all. *Amen.*

Geve the glorye to God onelye :
For he alone is worthye.

By me, John Clement.

Dns. mihi adjutor: et non timebo quid faciat mihi homo.
Dns. virtutum nobiscum: susceptor noster Deus Jacob.
Dns. protector vitæ meæ.

Quod Johes. Clement.

Cleave faste unto Christe, and contynue in his worde, *quod*, i. e. *quoth*, Clement.

F I N I s.

Number LXII.

Cardinal Pole's absolution of three persons that were con-
demned as heretics, but revoked their heresies.

REGINALDUS miseratione divinâ Stæ. Mariæ in Cos- ^{Ex primâ} medin Stæ. Romanæ Ecclesiæ presbyter Cardinalis Polus, ^{editione} ^{Foxii Mar} archiepiscopus Cantuariensis, sanctissimi Dom. nostri Papæ ^{tyrol.} et sedis apostolicæ, ad serenissimos Philippum et Mariam, Angliæ Reges, et universum Angliæ regnum, de latere legatus ; dilectis nobis in Christo, Gulielmo Adams, Thomæ Freman, et Guilhelmo Stonarde, laicis Londinens. seu alterius diœcesis, salutem in Domino sempiternam.   Ex parte vestrâ nobis nuper oblata petitio continebat, quod licet vos in varias hæreses et errores, a puritate fidei Catholicæ ma- 226 nifestè deviantes lapsi, et super ipsis per ordinarium vestrum inquisiti, ac deinde convicti et confessi, per definitivam sententiam damnati, et potestati sæculari dignâ animadversione puniendi, derelicti fueritis ; nihilominus vos, posteà a nonnullis Catholicis piis, et doctis viris de veritate instructi, errores vestros cognovistis, eosque voce et scriptis damnâstis, ac de illis ab intimis doluistis, nobisque propterea humillimè supplicari fecistis, ut ab excommunicationis, aliisque sententiis, censuris, et pœnis per vos propterea incursis, et

hæresi crimine, vos et unumquenque vestrûm absolvere, et
Ecclesiæ Catholicæ unitati restituere de benignitate apostolicâ dignaremus : Nos igitur de verâ et sincerâ vestrâ pœni-
tentiâ per fide dignas personas plenè informati, et atten-
dentes quòd ad se redeuntibus gremium non claudit Ecclesia,
et nonnullis aliis justis et rationabilibus causis moti, authoritate apostolicâ, nobis in nostrâ legatione concessâ, et quo
fungimur in hâc parte, tenore præsentium vos et unum-
quemque vestrûm, quâvis hæreticæ pravitatis occasione a
jure vel ab homine etiam per sententiam definitivam, legiti-
mis desuper priùs formatis processibus, specialitèr et expressè latis, vel promulgatis, etsi per plures annos in eis in-
sordueritis, in utroque conscientiæ scil. et contentioso foro,
plenariè, ita ut super hujusmodi criminibus, peccatis, et
excessibus, etiam de quibus, ut præfertur, inquisiti, convicti
et condemnati estis ; nullo modo puniri, inquietari, vel molestari possitis, absolvimus, et liberamus, ac Ecclesiæ unitati
ac aliorum Christi fidelium consortio aggregamus, ac omnem
inhabilitatis et infamiæ maculam, ex præmissis circa vos
quomodolibet insurgentem, penitùs et omninò tollimus et
abolemus ; vosque in pristinum, et eum in quo ante præmissa quomodolibet eratis, statum restituimus, reponimus,
et redintegramus, præmissis ac regula de insordescentibus
editæ, ac quibusvis aliis constitutionibus, et ordinationibus
apostolicis, cæterisque contrariis, non obstantibus, quibuscunque.   Volumus autem, ut omnem eam pœnitentiam, et
alia pro præmissis, per nos seu alium, vel alios a nobis ad
hoc deligendos, vobis et cuilibet vestrum injungenda, quæ
vos subituros expressè professi estis, et promisistis cum effectu, adimplere, omninò teneamini.   Alioqui præsentes vobis nullatenùs suffragentur.   Datum in palatio regio apud
S. Jacobum prope Westmonasterium anno a Nativitate Domini millesimo, quingentesimo, quinquagesimo sexto, quinto
nonas Julii, pontificatûs sanctissimi in Christo Patris, ac Domini nostri, Domini Pauli divinâ providentiâ Papæ IV. an. 2.
Re. Cardinalis Polus Legatus.

M. Antonius Faita, secretarius.
D. Lampsonus.

Number LXIII. 227

The faith and godly agreement of such prisoners as, before
the Bishop of London at Fulham, the 14th day of June,
were condemned, and burnt together at Stratford le Bow
the 27th of the same month. Whose names hereunder
are subscribed.

WE al confesse, and constantlie beleve, that there is one Foxii MSS.
God, and but one true lyvynge and everlasting God, with- I.
out parts or passions; of infinite power, wisdome, and goodnes; the maker and preserver of al things, both visible and
invisible. And that in unitie of this Godhed there are three
Persons, of one equal substance, power, majestie, goodnes,
and eternitie, the Father, the Son, and the Holy Ghost, as
it is truly taught and beleved in the true Church of Christ,
grounded upon God's holie word, and ever shalbe. Of which
true Church we do acknowlege ourselves to be, and every
one of us doo also acknowlege our selves to be true and
livelie membres one of another.

And we confesse, and undoubtedlie beleve, that the se- II.
cond Person in Trinitie, which is the everlasting Son of
God the Father, did vouchsafe for our sakes to take our
humanity upon him, in the womb of the blessed Virgin
Marie, of her very substance, and became truly man in all
poyntes, synn onlie excepted. So that two whole and perfect
natures, that is to say, the Godhed and manhed, were joyned
together in one person, never to be divided, even in Christ
Jesus, which is verie God and verie man. Of whose kyngdom there shalbe no end.

And we hartilie confesse and beleve al and every article III.
of the Christen faith, conteyned and rehersed in the Symbol,
commonly called *the Apostles Crede*, and also the crede
called *Athanasius's Crede*.

Also we do confesse and beleve, and faithfullie acknow- IV.
lege, that al salvation, justification, redemption, and remission of sins, cometh wholly and solely by the mere mercy
and favor of God in Jesus Christ, purchased unto us through
his most precious death and blood sheddyng onlie, and in

no part or peece by or through any of our own merits, works, or deservyngs, how many or good soever they be. 228 Notwithstandyng, least any man should mistake us, that we do deny or destroy good works, we do acknowledge and confess, that al men are bound by God's word to do good works, and to know and keep the commaundements of Almightie God : yet not to deserve any peece of our salvation therbie, but to shew our obedience therbie unto God, and the frutes of faith unto the world ; that the light of our good works may so shine before men, that God our eternal Father may be glorified therby. And we utterly deny and defie the idle, barren, and dead faith, which holy Saint James speaketh of in his Epistle, which hath no good works following it. But yet stil we do affirme, that God doth not forgeve us our synns, or repute us just in his sight, for any of our own works : for the best of them, compared to the puritie which the law of God requireth, shal be found, as Esaie saith, like a filthie cloth stayned with menstrue ; but for Jesus Christ sake onlie, whose most precious death and blood sheddyng we hartilie acknowlege to be a ful and perfect sacrifice, and a sufficient ransom for the synns of al the whole world. So that al they which do trulie repent and beleve, shalbe saved. And that there is no decree of God to the contrarie, so that they do persever to the end.

V. Also we beleve, that the sacrament of baptism is not onlie a sign of profession, and mark of difference, wherebie Christen men are discerned from other, that are not christened, but it is also a sign and seal of our new birth ; wherebie, as by an instrument, they that receyve baptisme rightlie, are graffed into the Church : the promises of forgiveness of synns, and our adoption to be the sons of God, are visiblie signed and sealed : faith is confirmed, and grace encreased, by virtue of prayer unto God : and that the custom of the Church to christen yong children is to be commended, and in any wyse reteyned.

I. Also we beleve, that the supper of the Lord is not onlie a sign of the love that Christians ought to have amonges themselves one to another, but also a sacrament of our redemption by Christ's death : insomuch, as to them that rightlie, worthilie, and with faith receyve the same, the bread which they break is the communion of the body of Christ; likewise the cup of blessyng is the communion of the blood of Christ. Neither was it by Christ's ordinaunce commaunded to be kept, carried about, lifted up, nor worshipped.

Also we beleve, that as the godlie consideration of pre-   VII. destination and our election in Christ is full of sweet, pleasant, and unspeakable comforte to godlie persons, and such as feel in themselves the working of the Spirit of Christ, mortifying the works of the flesh and the earthlie membres, and drawing up the mynd to high and heavenlie things; aswel bycause it doth greatlie establish and confirme our faith of eternal salvation to be enjoyed through Christ, as bycause it doth ferventlie kyndle our love towards God: so for curious and carnal persons, lacking the Spirit of Christ, 229 to have continuallie before their eyes the sentence of God's predestination, is a most dangerous downfal; wherby the Devyl may thrust them either into desperation, or els into wretchlesnes of most unclene lyving.

Also we beleve, that the offering of Christ once for ever,   VIII. is the perfect redemption, the pacifying of God's wrath, and satisfaction for al the synns of the world, both original and actual. And that ther is none other satisfaction for synn but that alone. Wherfore, the sacrifice of the mass, in which is said that the priest doth offer Christ for the quick and the dead, to have remission of synne and payne, is most devilish and daungerous deceyt.

Edmund Hurst.	Henry Wye.
Rafe Jackson.	John Roathe.
Henry Adlington.	William Hollowel.
Lion a Coise.	Thomas Bowyer.
John Dorrifal.	Elizabeth Pepper.
Laurence Pernam.	Agnes George.
George Searle.	

[Al Essex men and women, except Lion a Coise, who was a Dutchman.]

Number LXIV.

Saunders' oration to the visitors of Oxford; sent from Cardinal Pole.

Foxii MSS. VEREOR, ne admirati sitis, ornatissimi legati, non modo quod tam præstantes viros laudare aliquando, sed quod vel coram prodire ausus sim, is qui nec unquam doctus fui, et ut maxime fuissem, in tanta doctissimorum hominum multitudine pro academia tam florente, has partes egisse primus non debebam. Neque vero quicquam reperiri potest, aut gradu hoc aut ingenio, magis ab instituto alienum, cum gradus pene infimi ordinis, ingenium nullius usus existat. At si animadverteretis, in communi civitatis negotio, non tam referre quis laboret, quam pro quibus laboretur, debereque suo quam minimum nomine actorem valere, ut summa rei ad solum referatur auctorem, profecto neminem in hac causa mihi fuisse præponendum facile statuetis. Nam ut Romæ scribarum munus servis mandabatur, non quod libero homine non esset dignum, sed quia cum jure civili nulla propria servi persona putaretur, eo facilius poterat, domini personam sustinens, ex stipulationibus ei quærere ; 230 sic, putate, quoniam mea persona, in tot illustrium dominorum cœtu, nulla aut certe quidem perexigua est, idcirco publicam ei consensionem potuisse imponi. Tantum enim abest, ut meum aliquid in hunc locum afferam. Vereor mehercule interdum, ne cum pro aliis dicere instituerim, minus commode dicendo ex causa aliena litem meam fecisse videar. Sed me recreat et reficit divina eorum comitas facilitasque apud quos dico. Qui si ea quæ minus recte facta arguentur emendanda, non tanquam   sed paterna quadam indulgentia hoc tempore adsunt. Quid tandem ab eis in eo genere sperabimus, quod in Poli amplissimi Cardinalis et ipsorum laudibus totum consumetur ?

Ac de Cardinale, cujus præcipue nomine hæc comitia nituntur, illud brevissime dicam, iis esse illum moribus, ea doctrina, et auctoritate, nihil ut putem in orbe terrarum castius, nihil in omni humanitatis genere perfectius, nihil in summo honoris fastigio augustius. Atque ut cætera taceam, quæ tamen summa sunt, quo genere ortus, quomodo educatus, quantas angustias iniquissimis temporibus quanta animi æquitate pertulerit, quemadmodum bona, fortunas, amicos necessarios, matrem, patriam postremo, Dei Opt. Max. causa, reliquerit, imo nihili putaret, ut etiam illa majora prætermittam, cum summum in terris magistratum [a] repudiavit oblatum, cum salutem ad eos ipsos, a quibus per scelus ejiciebatur, a Papæ sanctitate impetratam, ultro attulit : neque aliud quicquam commemorem hoc loco quam ea beneficia, quibus civitatem hanc affecit. Nomine illud vel maximum est, quod jam ante reverendum patrem de Soto ad academiam misit, qui tam vita, quam eruditione, adolescentibus præeundó, eorum et animos et studia confirmavit. Cui patri quantum omnes debeamus, qui vel in theologiam, vel in honestatem incumbimus, cogitari profecto non potest, nedum ex dignitate exponi. Accessit, nec multo quidem post eadem occasione omni amore dignus, pater Joannes de Villa Garcya; qui vir quanto flumine ingenii, quibus literis, qua comitate ? Nos habemus ex illo fonte rivulos ita patentes, ut quum nemo propter eorum dignitatem ad aquam aspirare audeat, omnes propter liberalitatem recedant expleti. Propius accedo. Idem illustriss. Cardinalis, cui parum fuit————

[a] Scil. pontificatum Romanum.

[*Quædam desunt.*]

turbam : quæ libentissime occurrit, quæ videre jamdiu expetebat, quæ nunc undique ex omnibus locis intuetur, Episcopo Gloucestrensi, Colo, Wryto, Ormaneto, doctoribus, magistro Morweno, ornatissimi Cardinalis illustribus legatis salutem dicere, adventum gratulari, utque diutissime apud se commoretur, etiam atque etiam flagitare. Deinde quod isti tacitis suis cogitationibus, ego autem aperte et palam dico, idem plateas, vicos, templa, scholas, si loqui possent testatum relinquere voluisse. Neque id magis ex consuetudine, quam quod vere ita sit, dico. Ea quippe fuit superiorum temporum calamitas, ii ad urbem legati, a quibus non modo studiosi omnes, atque in iis optimus quisquam maxime timeret, sed qui tectis, ædificiis, altaribus, ipsis adeo muris minarentur. Quo nunc metu liberata urbs, si omni-

231

bus lætitiis incessit, si gaudium ipsa suum non capit, si serio
triumphat, quid miramur? Miraremur potius, si ista non
faceret.   At videte, quantum intersit inter mentes hominum
et cogitationes.   Illis legatis, qui etiam ex eadem conjura-
tione fuerant, propter avaritiam nihil credebant; hiis, propter abstinentiam bona omnia, fundamentorum instituta,
collegiorum origines, status denique totius academiæ ita
commendabuntur, ut hæc non tam fidei suæ commissa,
quam permissa potestati recordentur.   Itaque illorum si
considerata consilia statim deleta sunt, vestra vero decreta
non hac tantum memoria, sed in omne reliquum tempus
rata firmaque erunt.   Si enim quæ pie, juste prudenterque
consulantur, illa æterna fore necesse sit: si debeat autem in
pontifice pietas, in jurisperitis justitia, in senioribus elucere
prudentia, profecto nihil neque injustum neque ineptum in
hac legatione statui potest: quam et Magister Morwenus,
senex gravissimus, et Colus, Wrytus, Ormanetus, juris-
consultissimi doctores, et Jacobus Glocestrensis, pontifex
optimus, moderabuntur et regent.   Quibus de causis cum
immortales immortali Deo gratias hæc academia egerit, cum
fausta omnia omnibus sui studiosis precata sit, quum eos,
qui in dicendo exciderint, errores condonari sibi ac remitti
petierit, tum in vestra, lectissimi legati, virtute, in ampliss.
Cardinalis authoritate, in illustriss. principum Philippi et
Mariæ tutela, in Pauli Quarti sanctiss. Papæ fide, in totius
Ecclesiæ consensu, amore, societate conquiescat.

Number LXV.

*King Philip and Queen Mary to Pope Paul IV. in behalf
of Cardinal Pole, and his legantine authority.*

Foxii MSS.   SANCTISSIMO patri, ac Domino nro', D. Paulo IIII°
divina providentia, pontifici max^{mo} Philippus et Maria Dei
gratia Rex et Regina, Angliæ, Hispaniarum, Franciæ, utriusque Siciliæ, Hierusalem, et Hiberniæ, Fidei Defensores,
&c. æternam salutem et humillimam nram' obedientiam.
Quum excellenti Dei bonitate, ad imperium paternum atque

avitum venissemus, nihil antiquius habuimus, quam ut religionis statum, hominum et temporum improbitate non solum collapsum, sed penitus deformatum, et sedis apost^{cae} reverentiam, ad pristinam dignitatem ac splendorem, quod in nobis erat, restitueremus. Qua in re, quos labores, quæ regni et status, atque adeo vitæ nræ' discrimina subivimus, nisi Sanct^{tem} V. multorum sermonib. atque adeo orbis Christiani voce, intelligere putaremus, esset nob' de eo, per has lras' plurib. exponendum. Illud certe magnæ nob. conso- 232 lationi fuit, quod in rebus nris. arduis et temporib. illis difficillimis, sedis apost^{cae} non solum gra' et favore, sed etiam auxilio usi sumus. Accepimus enim ab ea legatum, r^{m} prem' et consanguineum nrm' Reginaldum Polum Cardinalem, qui quum subditos nros' ad sedis apost^{cae} obedientiam reduxisset, magnam post illa tempora et vehementer utilem, in reb. Ecclæ' componendis et confirmandis semper operam collocavit, cujus ut legati authoritate, et ut viri sapientissimi consilio, magna ad pietatem est facta accessio, et major quotidie (nisi quid aliunde sit impedimenti) futura speratur. Itaque justis de causis, magno dolore affecti sumus, quum lris quibusdam et multorum sermonib. ad nos perlatum esset, legati authoritatem semper utilem, his vero temporibus etiam necessariam, qua, pietas in Deum, et in sedem apost^{cam} obedientia augetur, e regno nro', quod nondum satis confirmatum est, revocari, atque ita revocari, ut legationem sedi Cantuarien. innatam et penitus annexam, multor. retro summor. pontificum actis confirmatam, multor. qui ante nos fuerat Angliæ regum prærogativa usurpatam, V^{ra} S^{tas} non exciperet. Quod, quia aliorum, qui rem non satis intelligebant, consilio et impulsu, non V^{rae} S^{tis} judicio et sententia factum existimamus, si nos ad pietatem et religionem confirmandam, omnes nros' conatus, ita ut Christianos principes decet, semper contulimus, si erga sedem apost^{cam} ea, qua debemus, religione et observantia, et ante regnum susceptum, et in regno fuimus, si V^{am} S^{tem} omnibus pietatis et obedientiæ officiis prosequuti sumus; rogamus, ne nobis paternam pietatem, et regno nro' justa privilegia, ne populo nro', qui gregis vri' et Ecclesiæ Catholicæ

portio est non contemnenda, auxilia ad pietatem negare velit, ne eam nob. sine nro. merito, notam inurat, quæ a vᵃ
et sedis apostᶜᵃᵉ clementia, et nra' in eam pietate et obedientia, vehementer aliena est. Atque hanc postulationem,
quoniam religione et pietate nititur, et ad populi Christiani,
cujus vobis curam Deus commendavit, profectum et salutem
pertinet, vᵃᵐq; ad Sᵗᵉᵐ orbis Christiani parentem destinatur,
et audiendam libenter, et facile concedendam, non dubitamus. Deus vᵃᵐ Sᵗᵉᵐ diutissᵐᵉ conservet. Ex regia nra',
Westmonasterii, 21º Maii, ᴹºᴰºᴸºᵛᴵᴵº.

Vᵃᵉ Stis,
Humillimi et obedientissimi filii.

Sanctissimo Patri ac Domino nostro   R. Aschanus.
D. P. P. Paulo IIIIº. divina pro-
videntia Pont. Maxᵐº.

---

233   Number LXVI.

The Parliament of England to Pope Paul IV. in behalf of
Cardinal Pole; from whom he had taken the legatine
power, and cited him to Rome.

JHESUS.

Foxii MSS.   MAGNUM et incredibilem dolorem accepimus ex
Sanctitatis vræ. literis, quibus reverendiss. patrem Reginaldum Polum vræ. Sanctitatis ad principes nostros, An-
gliæque et Hiberniæ regna, legatum a nobis divelli, et vro.
mandato Romam revocari intelligimus. Cujus, ut legati,
authoritas, et ut viri sanctissimi et sapientissimi præsentia
tantum ad fidem ac pietatem apud nostros constituendam
momenti, adferre videtur; diu ut credere non potuerimus
illud consilium Sanctitati V. placere potuisse, ut legatum a
sede apostolica missum, a V. Sanctitate confirmatum, temporibus horum regnorum tam necessariis, revocandum putaret. Nam legatum a sede apostolica ad principes Christianos missum, dum ejus præsentia necessaria esset, sine
magno principis aut populi, ad quem mittebatur, peccato,
accepimus revocari non solere.

Reginæ autem optimæ et sanctissimæ erga sedem apostolicam religionem et observantiam, et orbis Christianus intellexit, et V. Sanctitas graviter et diserte verbis laudavit.

Atque ut de nobis ipsis aliquid dicamus, postquam ad Ecclesiæ unitatem aggregati sumus, quod vestris temporibus ut fieret Deus Opt. Max. concessit, non solum nullius nobis erga sedem apostolicam delicti conscii sumus, sed modis etiam omnibus laboravimus, ut obsequio et observantia priorem ignominiæ labem, cujus nos pœnitet, deleremus. Quæ quum apud nos diligenter cogitaremus, in eam tandem opinionem incidimus, ut Sanctitatem V. ignorare crederemus, qui rerum nostrarum, præsertim quod ad religionem et pietatem attinet, status esset. Atque eam ob causam officii nostri esse putavimus, ut eum Sanctitati V. per literas nostras declaremus; ne si id prætermissum a nobis esset, Deus Opt. Max. et V. Sanctitas posthac negligentiam nostram justis de causis accusare posset. Quod dum facimus Sanctitatem V. rogatam volumus per eum, qui communis est et summus omnium pastor, cujus in causa per has literas legatione apud Sanctitatem V. fungimur, ut ista non solum libenter legere et audire velit, sed etiam nos vera scribere existimet, et quum illa omnia mature et deliberate perpenderit, eam rerum nostrarum et religionis curam habeat, quæ 234 sede apostolica summa omnium in terra potestate, et sanctissimo Christi vicario, digna videri possit.

Itaque ut calamitates et vulnera nostra paululum perstringamus, ante reverendiss. Patris legati vestri ad nos adventum; etsi sanctissimæ Reginæ pietate, et bonorum virorum studio in restituenda religione nonnihil erat actum, tamen formam nos ecclesiæ, vix aliquam habebamus. Populares animis et sententiis divisi, vix quicquam sibi in religione commune esse judicabant; hæresis non clam et in cubiculo mussitabat, sed in foro et pene in castris exultabat: pontifices, qui eam coercere et castigare volebant, quod eorum auctoritas per annos ante complures labefactari et contemni erat solita, quantum debuerunt efficere non valebant. Plerique longo errore et depravata consuetudine seducti, sedi apostolicæ non solum obedientiam nullam deberi putabant, sed ab ejus vel mentione et appellatione abhorrebant. Ad hæc mala vel sananda, vel saltem minuenda deerat unus, cui et sedes apostolica authoritatem, et vitæ innocentia commendationem daret. Qui idcirco majore cum gravitate alios ab errore revocare posset, quod ipse ab eo per omnem ætatis cursum inimicus fuisset. Quo in genere etsi in sanctissimo illo collegio multi erant, tamen de quo nostri aliquid audire, et quem nosse possent, unus erat amplissimus Cardinalis Reginaldus Polus; quem præter egregias animi virtutes, etiam nobilitatis opinio, quæ popularium animos non nihil movere solet, nostris vehementer commendabat.

Qui suo adventu, sapientia, virtute, et in omnes ordines moderatione, multa quæ vitiosa erant emendavit, quæ difficilia temperavit, quæ bene antea cogitata et incepta confirmavit: postremo, ita omnia quæ ad Dei cultum et pietatem attinent, administravit, ut jam spes magna sit opus bene cœptum perfici et consummari possit, si eo præsente et legato aliquot adhuc annos frui possimus. Sed ut in corporibus accidere videmus, quæ diuturno morbo afflicta, ubi paululum cœperint recreari, si ante perfectam et penitus confirmatam valetudinem, medico destituantur, sæpe in deteriorem, quam in quo antea erant, statum devolvuntur; ita si hujus Ecclesiæ corpori per annos jam complures afflicto, et hæresi, velut morbo pestilenti, pene ad exitium redacto, a quo tandem Dei bonitate respirare et vires sumere incepit, legati vestri authoritas detrahatur, magna et gravia pericula, (quæ avertat Deus) imminere videntur. Videmus enim, et quasi jam ob oculos habemus, bonorum mœrorem et luctum, imbecillium in fide fluctuationem et casum, malorum lætitiam et exultationem: quæ ut nobis, perinde ac debent, magnam curam et sollicitudinem adferunt, ita V. Sanctitati, pro excellenti qua in Ecclesia fungitur authoritate, majorem, si fieri potest, adferre speramus.

Atque utinam, ut ærumnas et calamitates, quæ rebus publicis ex hæresi proveniunt, Sanctitas V. legendo animadvertit, ita nobis qui magno nostro et hujus regni malo eos sentiendo experti sumus, fidem habere vellet. Sunt autem hujusmodi, ut nemo nostrum sit, qui non mortem, quamvis acerbam, tamen præ illorum temporum calamitate, levem et optandam arbitretur. Quæ quoniam Dei in nos clementia, et sedis apostolicæ, quæ legatum misit, beneficio, jam de- 235 pulsa, et in melius mutata videmus, justis de causis Sanctitatem V. rogamus nequid de legatione, quæ sedi apostolicæ gloriosa, et huic Ecclesiæ salutaris est, innovetur. Illud enim vehementer mirum in literis Sanctitatis V. et inauditum videbatur, revocari non solum sanctissimam illam a latere legationem, sed etiam alteram, sedi Cantuariensi innatam, et cum ea ita conjunctam, ut disjungi non solum re et usu, sed nec opinione quidem et cogitatione possit. Quod perinde nobis esse videbatur, ac si Archiepiscopum Cantuariensem ab hujus ecclesiæ corpore divelli, et Romam Sanctitatis V. mandato revocari audiissemus.

Nemo enim post hominum memoriam ejus sedis Archiepiscopus, non idem legatus fuit : quod tot sæculorum usu confirmatum, summorum etiam pontificum decretis contestatum, et Divi Augustini Anglorum apostoli, ut existimare possumus, temporibus incœptum, ut a V. Sanctitate, quem post D. Gregorium in fide parentem habemus, commutetur, nec expectare nec timere possumus. Et quoniam ea causa non solum Archiepiscopi propria, sed totius nobilitatis atque adeo regum Angliæ, qui semper ea prærogativa usi sunt, communis est, etiam atque etiam Sanctitatem V. rogamus, nequid ejus potestatis, tanta cum juris et ordinum perturbatione, tanta episcoporum et cleri, tanta nobilitatis et principum ignominia, minuatur.

Non hoc Reginæ sanctissimæ pietas merita est, quæ toties fortunarum omnium ac vitæ discrimen ante susceptum regnum, et in regno, non nisi ob religionem et erga sedem apostolicam observantiam, adivit: non episcoporum collegium, non proceres selectissimi, non bonorum cœtus, qui sunt omnes singulari in sedem apostolicam pietate et obedientia meriti. Qui si uno ore loqui possent omnes, a sanctitate et supplices peterent, liceret illis aliquando ab hæresi et animorum divisione respirare ; liceret in suavissimo unitatis vinculo secum et cum aliis manere ; liceret legatum hujus conjunctionis sub V. Sanctitate authorem et ministrum apud se habere; liceret privilegiis, tam in sede Cantuariensi, quam cæteris regni partibus, quæ sanctissimi pontifices concesserunt, et quæ V. Sanctitas primum per legatum vestrum in nostra ad sedem apostolicam reconciliatione, deinde vestris ad serenissimam reginam diplomatibus per tres legatos vestros acceptis, sanctissime confirmavit.

Hoc nos pro ea, qua in sedem apostolicam observantia sumus, V. Sanctitati, nequid ignoraret, significanda putavimus, ut filii obsequentes patrem rogavimus.

---

236   Number LXVII.

The nobility of England to the Pope, upon the news of his intended revocation of Cardinal Pole.

Foxii MSS.   QUO majore in sedem apostolicam studio, religione et observantia sumus, et post reditum ad unitatem Ecclesiæ nostrum semper fuimus, eo magis admiramur Sanctitatem V. quod literis multorum et sermonibus ad nos perfertur, decrevisse, ut apostolicæ sedis legatus Romam a nobis revocetur; quem nos quoniam ab ea sede profectus est, libenter hoc in regno videmus, et cujus eam ob causam authoritate et consilio, non solum popularium, sed omnium ordinum animi ad pietatem, et sedis apostolicæ observantiam vehementer incitantur. Patrum nostrorum memoria solebant summi pontifices, quo melius unitati et paci consuleretur, et disciplina conservaretur, legatos suos ultro ad hoc regnum destinare, quos tunc reges et optimates aut remittebant, aut illis præsentibus minus libenter utebantur. Nos, quoniam sedi apostolicæ officium et obedientiam libenter præstamus, et religionem quæ Dei bonitate et legati apostolici authoritate restitui cœpit, penitus confirmari cupimus, legati præsentiam ultro exoptamus. Et quoniam is gemina legatione utitur, quorum una a latere Sanctitatis V. proficiscitur, alteram sedi Cantuariensi innatam et penitus annexam cum eo episcopatu accepit, utramque ut his temporibus necessariam, et Ecclesiæ nostræ salutarem, continuari vehementer cupimus: sed alteram etiam, ex æquo et jure a V. Sanctitate postulare nobis videmur.

Non enim oblivisci possumus, quum ad Ecclesiæ unitatem ante annos jam duos, rediissemus, omnia privilegia, prærogativas et beneficia, quæ ullis retro temporibus summi pontifices huic regno omnibusque ejus ordinibus concessissent, per Sanctitatem V. sanctissimis verbis restituta et confirmata fuisse. Inter quæ illud vel primum est, quod sedis Cantuariensis prærogativa reges Angliæ semper apud se legatum habent; hoc regno et ecclesiæ nostræ omnes post hominum memoriam summi pontifices concesserunt: hoc jure reges omnes nostri, qui multis non solum annis sed sæculis vixerint, usi sunt: hoc legibus nostris multis et antiquis constitutum est.

Ut jam siquis contra aliquid moliri aut id pati et perferre velit, gravissimis legum pœnis coerceatur. Itaque nos ut eam juris prærogativam tueamur, non solum voluntate nostra, sed etiam officio et necessitate adigimur. Omnes enim sacramenti religione astringimur, ut hujus regni dignitatem, justa privilegia, legum authoritatem et prærogativam, sanctissime conservemus et tueamur. A qua religione ut recedamus tanto nostro periculo, tanta nobilissimæ Reginæ et nostrum ignominia, idque V. Sanctitatis, quem pro parente habemus, voluntate et mandato, nec sedi apostolicæ gloriosum, nec nobis omnino ferendum videtur. Et quanquam principes nostros ita esse affectos non dubitamus, ut regni statum eum quem acceperunt conservandum et omni dignitatis prærogativa ornatum, posteris relinquendum, judicent; tamen siquid hac in causa concedere vellent, nos ne nostro officio deesse videremur, eos non contra admonere et hortari non possemus.

Atque ut hæc pro regni hujus, cui deesse non possumus, dignitate conservanda libere et juste scribimus; ita sedi apostolicæ et V. Sanctitati officium et observantiam omnem Christiana nobilitate dignam libenter offerimus, et nos sanctissime præstituros pollicemur; ut filii obsequentes a communi patre supplices petimus, horum temporum rationem habeat, legatum semper utilem, his vero temporibus etiam necessarium apud nos esse, et summa authoritate, quo magis prodesse possit, uti patiatur; ne nobis pietatem paternam, quam paulo ante amplissimis verbis promisit, sine nostro peccato, nec regno, sedis apostolicæ amantissimo, justa privilegia negare velit, quæ nobis pro nostra in patriam charitate, in principes fide et officio, in leges reverentia, juraque et majorum nostrorum existimatione, modis omnibus conservanda et defendenda sunt.

Number LXVIII.

Cardinal Pole's speech to the citizens of London, in behalf of religious houses.

[*The beginning is wanting.*]

Foxii MSS. less polytyke consell coulde never have byn geven, than utterlye to caste them [the monasteries] downe, and so to suppresse them: whereby, as I saye, was overtorned the welthe of the realme, and of the prynce also himselfe. And this nowe I have declarede unto you, exhortynge you bothe to penance, and to shewe the worthy fruyte of penance; to th'intent you maye knowe in your case what ys the worthye fruyte moste requyred of you. Notwythstandinge my meanynge ys not, that thys beynge a noble act, and gratefull to God, and profytable to the realme, that you sholde furthewyth take in hande the byldinge of these, whiche I 238 knowe you be not able to doo; and yf you were able, and had suche a gay mynde to restore the ruynes of the chyrches, yet there be other chyrches, that are nowe fyrste to be helpen, and these be your parryshe-chyrches: whiche albeyt they have not byn cast downe by coulore of authoryte, as the abbayes were, yet they have byn sufferede to fawle downe of themselves maynye, and yn lyke maner spoyled as the monasteryes were. And to thys I exhorte you furthewyth to sett your hande; the whyche you maye yn no wyse fayle to doo, excepte you wyll have your people wax brutyshe and wylde, and your commonwealthe wythout foundacion: and thys I saye to you nowe, that by lycence and dyspensatyon doo injoye, kepe, and possesse suche goodes and landes of the chyrche, as were founde yn your handes, that thys was doone of the chyrche your moother's tendernes unto you, consyderinge your imbecyllyte and wekenes, after so sore a sicknes that you had in a schysme, at the whiche tyme your appetyte served you to no mete, but to that fruyte that came from the lande of the chyrche, and by that you lyved. Whiche she was contente you sholde kepe styll, and made promesse yt sholde not be taken from you, and so yt was lefte yn your hande, as yt were an aple in a childes hande, gyven by the moother, whiche she perceyvinge him to feade too much of, and knowynge yt sholde doo him hurte, yf he himselfe sholde eate the hoole, wolde have him gyve her a lytyll pece thereof; whiche the boye refusynge, and where as he wolde crye out yf she wolde take yt from him, lettythe him aloone therwyth : but the father her husbande commynge yn, yf he shulde see howe the boye wyll not lett goo one morcell to the moother, that hathe gyven him the hoole, she askinge yt wyth so fayre meanes, he may, peradventure, take the aple out of the boy's hande, and yf he crye, beate him also, and caste the apple out of the wyndowe. This maye Chryste the husbande doo, yf you shewe suche unkyndnes to your moother, whiche ys his spouse. She askethe that she knowethe shulde hurte the chylde, and doo her great good, because yndede she ys yn a maner famyshed, and what unkyndnes were that to gyve her nothynge? Trowe you, her spouse can be content wyth such ungratfulnes? specyallye knowinge, that thowgh you deny yt her, yet she of herselfe wyll never constrayne you further. But this I truste you wyll doo, when you by his grace waxinge a lytyll stronger, your appetyte shalbe retourned to his naturale course. As I have harde that some have begonne veray well all readye, whereyn God strength them.

And this I am constrayned, for your welthe, to warne you of, exhortinge you to enlarge your hande more to the helpe of the poore, that are so deare to Chryste, that he saythe, What so ever is gyven to them yn his name, he taketh yt as gyven to hymselfe. And this ys suche a meane to come to the grace of God, that the prophete Esaie, spekynge of the specyall means to injoye the goodnes of God, and to come to the light of his knowledge, (as 239 ys penance and fastinge, whiche the Jues used veraye extremelye, and of prayer,) yet he sayde none of them sholde profyte wythout almesse-dede ; forbearinge firste to doe wronge to oother, or oppresse oother, and afterwarde to gyve to the poore, whiche ys the verye thinge that you ought the more to be putt in remembrance of yn this realme, the lesse yt ys used, yn comparryson of that I have seene in oother realmes and countreys where I have byn; beynge assured, for owght that I can heare, or knowe here of almes-dede, that in Italye in two cytes onelye, there is more almes gyven to monasteryes and poore folkes in one monthe, than yn this realme in a hole yeare: wherein I wolde wyshe you dyd stryve wyth them to overcome them, whiche doynge you shoulde overcome them in grace, and in all welthe and knowledge of God, whiche doe followe all of this doinge thes workes of mercye. As the prophete Esaie dothe playnlye declare after he had spoken to the Jues of this poynte, to doe deedes of mercye, then he sayethe, *Tunc lucebit in tenebris lux tua.* And the cause thereof ys, that the doctryne of the chyrche ys the doctryne of mercye and almes of God. Whyche mercye is receyved more wyth comforte: but of them that use mercye, and gyve almes to other, that ys the veraye waye to enjoye all the grace and benefyts of God graunted to the chyrche. And so nowe I have tolde you, howe this ys one fruyte of penance, that you be specyallye bounde to shewe above all other, havinge above all other offended, in takeing goodes from the chyrche, whiche ys as muche as to saye, to take frome the poore.

Another fruyte, joyntly with this, you muste shewe, whiche ys this: as you, above all other nations that I knowe, dyshonoured the mynysters of the chyrche and presthode ytselfe, so you shoulde nowe honour bothe the ordre instytuted of God, and the persons for the ordres sake, and him that they do represente; remembrynge ever what Chryst sayethe, *Qui vos spernit, me spernit*. And what sore venge-ance in the olde lawe God hathe taken of them that have rebelled from God's ordre touchinge prysthode, and howe to him that dothe not obeye the pryste, the lawe appoyntethe no lesse payne than deathe: and to avoyde the wrathe of God in this part, wherein you have gone further than any schismaticall natyon hathe done, that ever I redde of. And so muche the more you be bounde to shewe *dignos fructus penitentia*, for the dyshonours and injuryes done to suche persons. Wherein I wyll not requyre you to be at further charge at this begynninge, but that you will not denye them that whiche God hathe ordeynyd you shoulde gyve them, whiche ys that parte that God hathe reserved to him-selfe: and those be your tythes of all kyndes; the whiche when you denye the pryste, you denye to gyve God his parte. And that God taketh so grevouslye, as thowgh you dyd crucyfye or nayle him to the crosse. As he testyfyethe by the prophete Malachias, who in the person of God ac-cusethe the Jues, askynge them, *Si homo configit Deum suum*. Whiche he dothe impute to them: and they askinge God, *In quo te configimus*, he sayethe, *In decimis et primi-tiis*, because they made strange to paye them. Wherefore 240 you may see, howe God taketh this kynde of dyshonouringe his prystes, wythdrawinge from them that shoulde be theyr lyvinge, by the appoyntment of God.

Wherefore yf you will have the earthe to brynge plentye to you, wythdrawe not from God, that ys Lorde of heaven and earthe, his parte, whyche he hath gyven to the prystes, and so shewe *fructus dignos penitentia*, for your offences past: and above all, obeye theyr worde speakinge in God's name, whatsoever theyr lyves be: the whiche, yf they be not good, the greater accompt they have to gyve. And yf you woulde fynde fawte wyth your selves in that you re-prove the prystes lyvynge, and praye God therewithall to gyve you good prystes, surelye yf you were destitute of suche, God woulde sende you them that you praye for. But you yourselves make your prystes evyll many times,

makinge them oftyn tymes to condescende to your unlefull
desyres, and shewe your selfe nothynge contente when they
wyll not playe the good companyons wyth you, and reprove them when they doe not: whereby God many tymes,
for your scorges, gyveth you prystes of lyke manners to the
commun people, as Scrypture sayethe, *Sicut populus, sic et
sacerdos*. And to amende this, you shall find none other
waye, but as I sayde afore, whiche ys, that you shoulde beware yourselves not to be colpable in those thinges that you
charge the prystes wythall; and obey them in that you
thinke yn your owne conscyence they speke well, and praye
for them, yf they be not good, acknoweledgynge that you
deserve worsse, yf God woulde doe after your deserts.
Whiche to eschewe, you muste, wyth humble petytion, de-
maude of the mercye of God, that he wyll not chastyse you
by these meanes, as to gyve you prelates and prystes that
wyll conforme themselves to your desyres; whiche is the
sorest plage can come to man, but to gyve you those that
be *secundum cor ejus*. This yf you did, surely God woulde
here you: and then God wolde sende you those that shoulde
be moste to your comforte. And thus I have shewed you
the waye howe to bringe furthe *fructus dignos penitentia*,
in this parte wherein you have moste offended God, touchinge the injuryes ye have done to these mynysters of God,
whiche be the prystes, whome God hathe sett over you to
be honoured as you woulde your naturall fathers; whiche
yf ye dyd, ye shoulde be sure to have God for your Father,
to have his mercyfull and contynuall protectyon over you.
And this you cannot doe, yf you favour heretykes; who
beynge the veraye enemyes of God and man, yet specially
theyre enmytye extendethe ytselfe agaynst prystes, that are
onlye the staye and lett, that theyr pernycyouse attempts
doe take none effect. And therefore the heretyke hathe no
enymye, in maner, but the prystes, albeyt indede he ys enymye to all the welthe of men.

And here nowe ys another fruyte that you muste shewe
worthy of a repentante mynde, that whereas you have sore
offendyd God by gyvinge favour to heretykes: now tempre

your favour under suche maner, that yf you can converte
them by any wayes unto the unyte of the chyrche, then doo
yt; for yt ys a greate worke of mercye: but yf ye cannot, 241
and you suffre or favour them, there cannot be a greater
worke of crueltye ageynst the commonwelthe, than to nor-
ryshe or favour any suche.   For be you assuryd, there ys
no kynd of men so pernycyouse to the commonwelthe as
they be; there are no theves, no murtherers, no advouterers,
nor no kynde of treason to be compared to theyrs; who, as
yt were undermynynge the chefe foundacyon of all commonwelthe, whiche ys religion, makythe an entre to all
kynde of vyces yn the most haynouse maner, as we have
had no small experyence synce religion was chaunged. After
whiche tyme, what kynde of vyce ys there, but yt toke
place here, and had his favourers? Whiche shulde have
byn to the utter undoynge of the realme, yf oure retorne to
oure ancyent religion had byn differryd any longer. And to
this poynte the realme was browght, to see the foundatyon
of the commonwelthe undermyned and cast up: whiche was
a doynge, when prysthode, when the olde lawes of the
chyrche, and the sacrament, were cast awaye, and troden
under fote.   But to this you cam not sodenlye; for fyrste,
you toke nothinge from the chyrche, but the pre-emynence
and prerogatyve of the supreme hed, whiche you toke from
the highest pryste, and gave yt to the Kynge; all the sacraments standynge and remaynynge wyth streight lawes,
that they sholde not be violated, but reverentlye kept. But
what, trowe you, was the fruyte of this? You had the use
of the sacraments wyth you, but the grace and profyt of
them you had not, no more than the Philistines had of the
keping of the arche of God, wherein was the booke of the
lawe, wherein was *virga, manna,* and *virga Aaron;* whiche
all were put wythin the arche, and kept wyth great reverence wythin the arche: but what ensued of that, but
great plagues of God to all cyties where the arche cam;
they changynge from cytie to cytie, to eschewe every one,
for his part, the plague, whiche never ceased, untyll they
had rendryde the arche of God ageyn, to whome God had

ordeyned.   And in lyke maner, all the tyme the arche was
in the Kynge's hande, as yt was, he takynge that straunge
tytle upon him, to be Hedd of the Chyrche in his realme;
all that tyme, we may saye, he pretended to kepe that was
yn yt, those sacraments wyth reverence, (as I understonde
you dyd a good whyle,) yet you beinge out of the unyte of
the churche, cowlde receyve no more grace or profyt of
them then dyd the Philistiens of the arche, havinge the
same amonge them, they not beinge incorporate with the
people of God.   And so you, at last, as though you hadde
not byn of the numbre of the people of God, as you shewed
to be, kepinge the external forme of the sacraments; you
also caste them away, havinge afore caste awaye the lawe of
the churche and authoryte of prysthode, which were signy-
fyed by the table of the testament, and the rodde of Aaron,
whereby at last you cast awaye the celestyal foode, signy-
fyed by manna, whiche all were kept in the arche.   And
this you dyd with more despyte, and wyth more offence to
God, wyth your owne bretherne, than ever dyd the Phi-
242 listiens wyth the people of God, beynge theyr open enemyes,
and of dyvers religion: who dyd no dyshonoure to the arche
of God, nor removed owte any thinge of the place, they
founde wythyn the arche.

And this beynge a matter of great sorrowe and repentance, as cannot be greater, then shewe you the fruyte of your
repentance, by honorynge ageyn the lawe of the churche,
the ordre and authoryte of prysthode, and that blessed
manna.   Whiche be thinges now most necessaryly to be required of you, yf eyther you loke to enjoye suche graces
and benefyts graunted to them, that be cytezins of this celestial cytie, whiche ys the chyrche; or to avoyde the most
horryble vengeance that God thretened to them, whiche
whereas they are pryvilegyd with more grace, have lesse regarde and estimation thereof.   Such S. Paule lykenethe to
a grounde, that havinge receyved raine in dewe tyme, and
well laboured, yf yt bringe furth thornes and bryers, cannot
be but a nawghty grounde, touchede with maledictyon, to
be destroyed at last with fyer.   Albeyt, as S. Paule saythe

to them that he so wryteth unto, *Confido de vobis meliora:* and so wyll I saye unto you. I have surelye better hope, whatsoever I saye. But you see the greate peryll; and what peryll yt ys to receyve greate graces, and to neglect the same. The fawle of this people of Israel ys a perpetual testymonye, and shalbe to the worldes ende. Who were higher yn glorye than theye for a great space? Who were brought lower, to more shame and contempte? Moyses myght saye, *Quæ est gens tam inclyta, quæ habet leges, ceremonias, et Deo appropinquantes,* &c. Thys benefyte they had yn Moyses tyme, whereby they passyd all natyons; and yet all was nothinge, to that grace and benefyts they receyved afterwarde; whiche was, to have Chryste borne amonge them; to take his manhode of theyr stocke; to have him, which ys the lyfe of the lawe, whiche ys *ipsa justicia, ipsa sanctitas;* to preach amonge them, and never to departe out of theyr countrey, as longe as he dyd corporallye tarye yn earthe; shewinge them his example of lyfe, and his miracles doone afore theyr eyes. And who now be further from receyvinge the fruyte of this glorye? What natyon lyvethe yn more myserye and shame? And why? But for the cause whiche Chryste himselfe shewede. *Quia non cognoverunt tempus visitationis suæ.*

What a terryble example owght this to be to all them that have receyvede great benefits? As, I saye, we have contynually, from oure fyrste receyvinge the feythe, as at suche tyme as Chryste was fyrste planted in oure hartes here, and so contynuynge mayny hundrede yeares, bryngynge furth noble fruytes to the honoure of him that planted you; and at laste, by youre owne fawte, were cut off, and lyke to have byn wytherede, yf the high grace and power of him that fyrste planted you had not, as yt were, engraffed you yet once ageyne. What countrye hathe ever had the lyke grace? And nowe, therefore, take heade you be not lyke the grounde I spake of even now. Upon St. Paules wordes I truste, I saye, you be not: but this I saye to you specyallye, of the cytie of London, you beynge the fyrste that receyvede the fruyte of this grace yn the newe planta- **243**

cyon, this seede of benedictyon beynge cast fyrst upon you, and havinge more dyligent labour bestowede upon you, to make you a grounde to bringe furthe all fruyte of sanctitie and justice, wyth more frequent rayne of preachinge and teachinge than all the realme besyde; greater examples, and, as I maye saye, miracles, shewede amongst you than anye other. What then shall I saye, after all this done, that more bryars and more thornes hathe growen here amonge you, than yn all the realme beside? I cannot saye so, nor I wyll not, albeyt yt myght so seeme: for a greater multytude of
Brambles and briars cast into the fire a-mong them. thes brambles and bryars were caste in the fyre here amonge you, than yn any place besyde. But mayny of them be-ynge growne in other places, and brought yn and burned amonge you, maye gyve occasyon that you have the worse name wythout your deserte. But the thinge standeth not yn the name, bethinke you yourselfe howe yt standethe.

This I saye ageyne, none hath had better preachinge and teachinge, nor have seene greater examples wyth theyr eyes, and as maye be well called, as they be, miracles. As what a marvelouse example was that, when the realme was fawl-inge from the unytie of the churche, when the foundacyon began to move, that God shewede, to staye you? When he suffered one of your bodye, I meane a cytesyn of yours,
Sir Tho. More. who was Syr Thomas Moore, borne amonge you, and for his wytt, vertue, and lernynge, most estemyd of any tem-poral man wythyn the realme, and no lesse estemyd yn other realmes for the fame of his vertues, to be assauted of the envye of mankynde, bothe *a dextris et a sinistris;* onlye to make him leave the unytie of the churche, as greater tentatyon coulde not be come to a man: yet, to overcome all, shewinge suche constancye of feyth as he might be a *miracle,* marvelouse example, to staye all other. For this, fyrste, you may consyder, what tentatyon, trowe you, was that a cytysyn of yours, from a meane state so sodenlye to be exalted to the highest offyce of the realme, as to be Lorde Chancellor? What was yt, but a bayte layde to take him wyth? To make him agree to that hys successor dyd, to let himselfe be plucked from the stone of the foundacyon of

the churche, and to be a meane to plucke other from the same. Was yt any other as the effecte dyd shewe? And when the bayte coulde not deceyve him, nor make him wyllinglye to leave his holde of the sure stone layd yn the foundacyon, then what was to be done of the enemy to plucke him from thens but by force? And nowe consyder what bondes were put aboute him to make him leave his holde; suche bondes treulye that were as stronge as the love he bare to his wyfe, to his chylderne, and to his owne lyfe, cowlde make and bynde him wyth. The which he must nedes all breake, excepte he wolde leave his holde of the sure stone, and be pulled from the foundacyon; to the whiche, notwythstondynge he shewed himselfe to be so surely joynede and fastenyd, that all this force coulde nothinge prevayle to plucke hym from yt. What kynde of morter was this? Was yt anye suche that coulde be made by mans hande? Or by the power of nature, that shoulde make him stycke so faste, that no power of nature coulde once move him? This was the mortar that Chryste brought wyth him from heaven: that love, that charytie he bare to Chryste, to his churche, to the bodye of the commonwelthe of this realme. Was there any other thinge of that force, of that vertue, able to make him to overcome the natural love, than a love and charytie surpassyng nature? Was not this a greate myracle? An acte, and a greate example far above nature? Surelye a greater hathe not byn sene yn this realme, nor yn none other, many hundrede years. And that you may the better be assured that yt was a verye light above nature, and a love gyven from above, I shall shewe you howe far yn this matter his owne natural light dyd extende, whiche he shewede, reasonynge yn this matter of the unytie of the churche with a frynde of his, and a specyal benefactor of all catholyck and good persons, whome I wyll not leave unnamed, for worthy ys he of name, and I doubte not but his name ys yn the booke of lyfe: yt ys Antony Bonvyse, whome I think you all knowe, dwellinge from his youthe amonge you, beynge nowe a verye old man; who havynge entyre frendeshyppe wyth Mr. Moore, as frendes

244

Anthony Bonvise.

and wyse men be wont to do, communynge togyther of the
state of the commonwelthe of this realme, and of that was
lyke to come, for the dysturbance of the quyetnes thereof,
Mr. Moore began to shewe what feare he hadde of the
chaunge of religion yn this realme, whiche he tooke, as yt
ys, to be the grounde of the commonwelthe, and feared that
yt sholde begyn of the perverse and hereticall opinion that
he sawe some inclyned unto, touchinge the sacrament of the
aultar. Whereof, after they had spoken wyth great la-
mentatyon of that whiche was lyke to insue thereof, albeyt
the same semed not at that tyme so lykely to other. For
as muche as he that began to breke the unytie of the
churche, was verye styffe concernynge the use of the sacrament after the olde forme and honoure; but he was not so
muche movyd to feare this, for that he sawe the present
lykelyhode, but rather of an instincte that the feare of God
had put yn his mynde, when the unytie was not yet broken;
and when he that was bent to breake the unytie was most
erneste yn the defense of the sacrament, yet then began he
to feare that the faythe of the sacrament sholde decaye yn
the realme, not speakynge any worde of the feare of the
breche of the unytie, by reason of the schysme, and depart-
ynge from the obedyence to the see of Rome, whiche then
was most lyke to happen furthwyth, the Prynce beynge offendyd wyth the Pope; whiche feare made Mr. Bonvyse
aske him the more ernestlye of his opinion thereyn: to the
whiche questyon he sodenlye makyng answer, sayde as his
natural reason gave; and that was howe he tooke not that
for a matter of so great a moment and importance, but rather as inventyd of men for a polytical ordre, and for the
more quyetnes of the ecclesiasticall bodye, than by the verye
245 ordynance of Chryste. This was his sudden and fyrst answer; but he hadde no sooner sayde the worde, but as
though his conscyence had byn stroken for so sayinge, cor-
rectyng the same, wyth confessing that he had spoken wythout consyderatyon, sayde to Mr. Bonvyse, howe he should
not take that for an answer to his questyon, whiche he
wolde thinke better upon, for he had never studyed yt

afore : and therefore wylled him wythyn x or xij dayes to repayre to him ageyn, and then he would shewe him hys whole determynate opinion ȳn that matter. This was Mr. Bonvyse gladde to heare him saye, and fayled not at the tyme prefyxed to retorne to aske him his opynyon thereof. And at the fyrste sight of him, Mr. Moore brake out into a greate reproch of his owne selfe, for that he was so hastye to answer yn so greate a matter, touchinge the prymacye of the Pope, sayinge, Alas! Mr. Bonvyse, whither was I fawlinge, when I made you that answer of the prymacye of the chyrche? I assure you, that opinione alone was ynough to make me fawle from the rest, for that holdyth up all. And so then he began to shewe him what he had redde and studyed therein, whiche was so fixed in his harte, that for the defence of the same he wyllingelye afterwarde sufferyd deathe ; overcomynge all Satan's tentatyon by the light supernaturall, and by a supernaturall love that the mercye of God had gyven him for his salvatyon, and greatlye for yours, you takynge example of him.

Whereupon nowe yf you wyll looke, and of the bysshope that dyede wyth him for the same cause, whiche was the bysshope of Rochestre, Doctor Fysher, you shall see wyth Bishop all the greate provysyon of God that he made for this Fisher. realme, the greate tendre favour he used to this regyon, for the savegarde of the same yn trewe feythe and religion : gyvinge so muche grace to thes ij men of best fame in the realme, for theyr vertue and knowledge, to testyfye wyth theyr bludde the trewe doctrine of the churche. Whiche they dyd, when the rest of the whole body of the realme representede yn the Parliament, gathered of the *spiritual* parte and *temporal*, of the clergye and the laitye, had determyned the contrarye. To the whiche determynatyon, thes twayne nothinge agreynge, when it was put moste earnestlye unto them, either to agree, or abyde the payne of the newe lawe, whiche was deathe, they choosed rather that parte, and dyede, as the martyrs of God bothe, for testymonye to the trewthe of that article : and foreseynge howe this alone broken, the gate was set open to

Satan to breake all the reste, and brynge yn to the churche here, what pernycyouse opinions he lyste; as the successyon shewede he dyd. Whereof also he himselfe was not wythout feare, that was author of the breache of the unytie of the same; he, beynge warned what trouble yt myght brynge the realme unto, thought to provyde suffycyentlye for the same, even by the meanes that he brake the unytie, whiche was by the authorytie of the Parliament, that shoulde stablyshe the doctryne of the sacraments. Whereupon was

Act of Six Articles. made an acte of Parliament touchinge the vj articles. But the Parliament had not so greate force to establyshe them,

246 the unytie once taken awaye, as experyence shortelye after dyd declare in this, that the unytie was not so soon dissolvede, but that the faythe of the sacraments began to quayle yn so many hartes, though they durste not for a tyme utter yt : and of this were manye pryvey counsells made ageynst them yn his pryvye chambre that was most earnest, because he had dissolved the unytie, to maynteyne the sacraments, beynge, as I sayed, warned afore, that the same change woulde followe. Whiche tarryed no lenger to shewe ytselfe openly, but untyll he was deade, whose person onlye they feared ; and then they burste out yn suche manner wyth so many chaunges, tyll at laste openlye yn the Parliament the sacrament of sacraments was caste out. Whiche had byn the ende of religion yn this realme, yf God had not helped bothe at that tyme to restore yt, as the unytie was broken, and at this tyme also : workynge myracles at bothe tymes, as well yn the deathe of those that dyede, to lett the goynge downe of the authorytie of the churche, as for preservinge yn lyfe that woman that shoulde sett yt up ageyne ; gevynge you space yn the meane season to prove and taste the bytternes of the fruyte receyved by the swarvynge from the unytie of the churche. Whiche at the fyrste semed verey sweete, as dyd the apple to oure fyrste mother, eaten ageynste the commandement. And the lyke you have suffered.

But to th'yntent you shoulde not be utterly undone, as yt must nedys have followed, yf trewe religyon were taken

awaye, I have shewede what provysyon the goodnes of God
forthwyth begun to shewe you in the example of them, who
for theyr holynes, lernynge, and justyce, each one yn his
state, the one for the spiritualtye, and the other for the
temporaltye, were counted the chefeste yn the realme, by
the judgement of that prynce that put them to deathe, and
tempted them most to lyfe. Whom yf one woulde have
asked, afore the greate temptatyon came to him to leave
the obedyence of the churche, to whome of all men of the
Churche of Englande he coulde best have byn contented to
remytte his conscyence, yn matters of any doubte yn religion, for his lernynge, vertue, and judgement, he woulde
surelye have namede no man afore the same bysshope of
Rochestre, Doctor Fysher, that he put to deathe afterwarde. This I maye the bolder affyrme to be so, because,
when I myselfe came out of Italye from my studye, commynge to do my dewtye, and to see the Prynce, yt was al- The King's
moste the fyrste questyon he asked me, whether yn all the question to
Pole.
unyversities I had byn, and yn all the cyties and places
where lerned men and good men myght be best knowen,
I had found suche a lerned man as the same Bysshope of
Rochestre, byddynge me to saye playnlye as I thowght.
To whom I answered, consyderinge so manye partes together, although yn one parte one myght be found to be
comparede, and yn some qualytie to excede and passe him,
yet yn all together, by that I coulde judge, I remembrede
none that I myght preferre afore him; and yn truthe I had
not: so that a meeter man by man's judgement, to testyfie
the trewthe of this matter, yn this realme none coulde be
founde, for the estimation he was yn, not onelye wyth the 247
Prynce then, but wyth the rest of the realme. And besydes
this, bycause bothe states yn the Parlyament dyd fayle, as
well spiritual as temporal, havyng provyded such a guyde
to the spiritualtye as that Bysshope was, and such a one as
myght be an example for bothe the partyes to followe; yet
yf of his abundante goodnes he woulde have paynted one
for an example of the laytie to stay them, surelye a meeter
coulde not have byn founde than was Mr. Moore, for the

opynyon that all men had unyversallie, of his wytt, lernynge, and justyce; and what opynyon the Kyng had of
Mr. Moore, the gyvenge him the office of the high chan-
cellorshyppe dyd shew. So that yf God woulde send furthe
his messengers yn this doubte, or any doubte concernynge
religion or justyce to informe you the trewthe, more meeter
and more to be beleved coulde not have byn founde yn the
whole realme than those two, that for theyr hollynes and
justyce were moste famouse, and so taken of the Prynce
and of all men. And here nowe was the provysyon that
God made to staye the multytude, that they shoulde not so
deepely fawle, which was the example of thes ij great and
notable servants of God, that rather suffered theyr heddes
to be stryken off, than to consent that the realme shoulde
be cut off from the obedyence to the hedde, that Chryste
dyd appoynte yn earthe. The whiche men, so well knowen,
were sufficient to have persuaded all the rest. That the
obedyence was more precyouse than any lyfe, wyth all the
favoure and honoure, that any prynce coulde have gyven to
any man. Whiche they myght have hadde above all other,
yf they woulde have estemed any thinge yn this lyfe, above
the same obedyence to God and the churche. And those
were these ij alone that shewede this mynde of humble obedyence to the Churche of Rome. For God had selected and
chosen owte bothe prystes and religiouse men out of those
religiouse howses that were moste refourmede, suche as were
moste notable for theyr vertue and religion: as out of the
Charterhowses, owte of Syon, and the fryars Observantes,
and of St. Francys: *quorum nomina sunt in libro vitæ:*
Monks put that with theyr bludde testyfyede the same, havynge lyfe
to death. offered them, yf they woulde have swarved from the stone
set by Chrystes hande, yn the foundatyon of the churche,
to be the staye of the same; but they shewed by the high
grace that God had gyven them, that no so cruel deathe
coulde be offered them, but they had rather suffer yt, as
they dyd, than to have byn browght out of the bodye of
the churche. And why was all this, but for your staye?
but for your example? And to shewe you what you should

followe? And for this cause they were preserved; they were strengthned and augmented myraculously wyth grace above nature, and sent unto as guydes.

And now what shoulde lett you to followe them? What dyd lett you afore, yt ys too well knowen; whiche was, too muche love of the worlde, and feare to leave the worlde, and streyght and cruell lawe made ageynst the followers of those men. But nowe what shoulde lett you, that you do no faster followe them, when the favour of heaven and 248 of erthe agree together, when the prynces be so favorable, when the goodnes of the Kynge and Quene take yt for a specyal servyce done to them, worthy of all reward? Whose example they followe fyrste themselves. What shall I saye nowe, whome shall I *fyrst* accuse? Shall I saye, the youthe browght up yn a contrarye trade, be they that be most hardest to be brought to followe them, whiche never sawe them, nor hearde no good reporte of them? And this I thinke be one greate cause. And herein I have great compassyon of the youthe; but you that be olde, that have seene the way that thes other tooke afore you, and have gone the same, do you indede use all the diligence you can, to bringe the youthe to followe the same, that your fathers afore have followed? Do you thinke the youthe ys to be borne withall yn suche matters of religion, when they do so muche contrarye to the example of theyr fathers touchinge religion? Woulde any good father suffer yn his son, that he lovethe, any thinge contrarye to cyvyll ordre? And the more he lovethe hym, the lesse wyll he suffer any dysorder in the chylde, *contra bonos mores:* and muche lesse he shoulde suffer *contra fidem.* For yf he wyll wynke at suche dysorders, he shalbe sure to have suche a childe as wyll not suffer hym, but shalbe a scourge to him all the dayes of his lyfe. And the greater scourge, the lesse scourge the father useth with him fallinge yn dysobedyence to the churche, as I thinke manye fathers have proved wyth theyr chyldren these late years, synce this dysobedyence of the churche began. And so masters wyth theyr servants, more than was ever seen in this realme afore, to theyr great and utter dyscomforte : whiche wyll never cease, untyll the fathers and masters cease to suffer any alteratyon yn his sonne or servant touchinge religion, whereyn the good example of the father and master ys one of the best remedyes, and wythout that, there ys small hope of remedye.

But nowe seinge chefelye the prynces themselves, and after, wyth them the whole nobylytie, and the heddes of the clergye, begyn to shewe good example touchinge religion, what shoulde nowe lette the cytie to follow the same, everye man in his owne house? And so I truste they do. But *The citizens comfort the heretics.* whereof comyth this then, that when any heretyke shall go to executyon, he shall lacke no comfortynge of you, and encouragynge to dye in his perverse opynyon, gyven by those that come out of your howse: when he shalbe put yn pryson, he shall have more cheryshing; what signe this? But that the youthe that doeth this, hathe byn perverslye and perniciouslye brought up yn ill opinions, whiche for to chaunge, you will saye, yt muste require a greater tyme. But what tyme will you require to that? For as it is nowe, this maye not be suffered. And nowe iij yeares and mo be past, that you have byn brought into the churche, and this beinge a thinge not to be suffered one houre. Take hede, for Godes sake, what you do, and consyder what a thinge it is to be negligent in suche a point, whereupon dependethe your welthe, bothe of bodye and sowle; whiche, though it be 249 verye daungerouse, yet yt ys suche, whereof you maye yn one howre be delyvered, excepte you wyll take upon you to be wyser than your fathers, that ruled bothe spirytuallye and temporallye, when the realme was in moste welthe and prosperyte. What shall I saye here, that yt hurtethe muche *The youth.* to the youthe, and ys a great slaunder and obstacle to them, whiche aforetyme harde none other lerninge but that the heretykes, that be nowe condemnyd, doe teache, when they see the same confirmed by the constancye of those that wyllynglye offer themselfe to dethe for the defense of theyr opinion. This, men saye, ys a greate stoppe, and a great blocke yn theyr waye that have none other lernynge than theyrs, to let them to come to the ancyent doctryne, as I thynke yt be indede. Nowe therefore harken and marke well, for we cannot lett, *quin scandala veniant: oportet enim scandala esse: sed væ illi, per quem scandala veniant;* and wel be to them that labour to take them awaye. And nowe what maye be done to take awaye this stoppe? I shall shewe you, as far as God shall gyve me grace, that you may be partakers of the same benediction that God gyveth to them that delyvere any membre of the chyrche *a scandalo,* and specyallye the youthe. And this, because yt requyreth a great processe, I am wyllinge to shewe you the verye roote of this deceyte of Satan, and to dysclose his malycyouse crafte, and the waye he takyth to blynde you with the name of constancye yn his membres : whiche ys mere obstynacye, and a develyshe pertynacye : and to declare also howe one maye be dystinctlye known from the other. Because, I saye, that yt woulde requyre a greater processe than can be intreated at this present, specyallye nowe havinge so muche sayde in this matter, perteyninge to the feaste of this daye, for your happy retourne to the chyrche, and that yt shulde be too long to entre into so great a matter besyde.

Onely this I wyll saye, to remove some parte of this impediment by the waye, of the symple persons, that these heretykes pretendynge to dye constantlye for the faythe of the chyrche, and wythout feare of deathe, because by no meanes, neyther fayre nor fowle, they wyl be brought from theyr opynyon; this first I saye, yt ys not the constancy that is preysed in the chyrche to dye for our owne opinion ; and if the Byshope of Rochestre and Mr. Moore shoulde have dyed for theyr own opynyon, I woulde never have called them constant; nor yf they had dyede for suche an opinion touchinge the faythe that they had not founde themselves, but woulde have sayde yt had byn in the prymative chyrche renewed by them, or by any other, that were not harde of in oure fathers dayes : for yf theyr feythe shall be taken for trewe, yt must be suche as hathe byn contynuede from the begynnynge of the chyrche unto theyr fathers dayes, of whom they had receved yt. So that God

The heretics dying constantly

к к 2

sendynge them to be preachers of Christes faythe, might
saye to them, as he sayde to Moyses, sendinge him to deliver
the people of Israel from the servytude of Pharao; *Ego
sum Deus patris tui; Deus Abraham, Isaac, et Jacob*: joyn-
inge the feythe of his father wyth the feythe of Abraham,
250 Isaac, and Jacob; testyfyinge his father's feythe to be the
same that Abraham, Isaac, and Jacob had: or else he
woulde not have joynede them togyther. And as God sayde
to Moyses, when he sent him to delyver the people, *Ego
sum Deus Abraham, Isaac, et Jacob*: and that shoulde be
his name for ever; and that he woulde be for ever knowne
by that name.　So ys also every trewe faythfull man
knowne, not by the faythe he hathe founde of himselfe, or
taken of the fathers so fur off, not allegynge his next father,
but by the faythe of his next father, contynuynge the same
untyll he come to his fyrst father, as Chrystes stock was
contynued in the faythe of Abraham, evin untyl his moother
and Joseph, that was taken for his father.　And this pedegre
and famyle Pharao wolde have broken, gevinge commandement to the mydwyfes, that all men chylderne of the people
of Israel sholde have byn kylled, to make the generation of
faythfull Abraham to fayle: whiche the heretykes showe
hathe been extinct, when they saye nowe that these five
hondrede yeares the trewe faythe was never taught.　As
though Pharao had obteyned his purpose; as though Moyses and all the male chylderene had byn kylled of him.　And
they havinge kylled Moyses in theyr own hartes, when they
kylled the lawe of God, they breke the genealogye of the
faythe, that Chryst hathe made so stable, that soner heaven
and earthe shall fayle than this generatyon from father to
father, in confessinge the trewe faythe.　And this faythe
was yt for the whiche those great defenders of the catholyke
faythe, the Byshope and Mr. Moore, dyede, and all those
that for lyke cause suffered at that tyme.　And this was
veraye constancy, to dye for the faythe that they were
borne yn, and that they had receyved of their fathers,
whiche might yn theyr lyfe saye, *Deus patris nostri misit
nos ad vos.*　And of them when they dyede, and nowe also

True con-
stancy.

yt maye be sayde, that whiche was sayde of the patryarches, and all faythfull after them, *Appositi sunt ad patres*: whiche ys the greatest comfort that any faythfull man at his deathe can have, and that the heretykes have not; that cannot shewe theyr fathers faythe, but swarve from the same.

And as for theyr boldnes yn theyr deathe, that ys a small argument of grace to be yn them; Chryst himselfe shewing more heavynes and doloure at his dyenge houre, then dyd the theves that honge besyde him : whiche dyd blaspheme Chryste, settynge nowghte by him, speciallye one of them, shewinge no further feare ; and so doe these heretykes at theyr deathe lyke the blasphemer, whatsoever theyr wordes be in the honour of Chryste. But this nowe shall be suffycyent for your warnynge for this tyme.

And now I have shewede you what great and marvelouse causes you have to rejoyse this daye, for your happy retournynge to the chyrche. I have shewed you therewyth whereby you maye knowe the same suffycyentlye, to gyve infynyte prayses and thankes to God, for your retourne thereunto, declaringe the benefyts that you obteyne thereby, and the way to rejoyse therein, and to take the fruycyon of them. But, as they be in theyr excellencye, no toungue 251 can expresse, nor never wylbe knowen, but, as I have repeted often, by that waye that Chryste shewede to the apostle Andrewe, then commynge from the schole of penance, *Venite et videte :* that ys to saye, *Come after me, and ye shall se* where I dwell; whoso doythe the same at one tyme, shall bothe see and enjoye what he seethe.

And nowe wyth this I shall make an ende, shewynge you in that, howe you maye see and folowe Christe, no lesse at this present tyme, than yf he were corporallye walkynge afore you, as Andrewe sawe him : whiche is to folowe his commandements, and to folowe the commandements of the chyrche, his spouse, whiche moveth not a foote but where Chryste goyth afore her, havynge the Spyryte of Chryste for her perpetuall guyde and mover. And thys you shall doe, followynge hyr dyscypline as the wyse man doythe advertyse you, when he saythe, *Audi legem patris tuï, et dis-*

Joy for return to the church.

K k 3

ciplinam matris tuæ ne projicias.   Whiche a great whyle
hathe byn dyspysed, and specyallye the dyscipline of ceremonyes whiche hathe byn utterlye cast out; and the sooner
the more they were ancyent.   And bycause man cannot lyve
without ceremonyes, nor never was relygyon utterlye voyde
of them, they had rather in those dayes use none, than accept the olde, so muche they dyspysed the dyscypline of
theyr moother; delyting in theyr newe inventyons, wherein
yf they woulde spende theyr wytts all theyr lyfe-time, better
can they not fynde than hathe byn instituted allreadye of
theyr moother.   And of the observation of ceremonyes, be-
gynnythe the very educatyon of the chylderne of God; as
the olde lawe doythe shewe, that was full of ceremonyes,
whiche St. Paule callythe *pedagogiam in Christum.*   And
amonge all the pryvileges and graces that God gave the
people whiche he tooke to his owne governance; this is
reckonyd the fyrste grace, that they had suche ceremonyes
with theyr law, as no nation had.   And as God makythe
this the begynnynge of the good education of his childerne
wyth dewe ceremonyes, so the heretykes makythe this the
fyrste poynt of theyr schysme and heresyes, to destroye the
unyte of the chyrche by contempte or change of ceremonyes; whiche semyth at the begynnynge nothinge.   As
yt semyd nothinge here amongste you to take awaye holy
water, holy breade, candells, ashes, and palme; but what yt
came to, you sawe, and all felt yt: wherefore take you good
hedee, howe you breke these lytyll and smalle thinges, lest
you leese the fruyte of the greate and the lytell, and yourselfe withal.

   For there ys nothynge so lytyl commanded, or orderyd
by the chyrche, but breache or dysorderinge of the same
makyth a great offence.   What lesse thinge woulde there
be commanded, than to forbeare the eatynge of an aple?
But the eatynge of the same, agaynst God's ordre and commandment, was so great an offence, that the hoole worlde
smarted for yt, and all mankynde had byn utterly undone
thereby, had not the mercye of God gyven us another
meate to expell the poyson thereof: dysobedyence beyng a

very poyson to mannys sowle and body, as obedyence saveth 252
bothe.   Whiche begynnethe to shewe ytselfe, first, by the
observatyon and kepinge of ceremonyes, and there Chryst
began to declare his obedyence, whereby we were saved.
And whoso wyll be saved, there must he begyn his worke;
not that those doe gyve salvatyon, but that the contempt of
those bringeth damnatyon: not that those gyve us that
lyght, whereby we seeke for to see Chryste and his benefyts
in his chyrche, but the same doe rather blynde those eyes,
wherewith Eva sawe the aple to hyr damnatyon: whiche
were her eyes corporall, and the eyes of her naturall dys-
cours and understandyng.   And this ys counted a happy
blyndnes, whiche ys the veraye waye to light: but the
verey light the Spirite of God gyvethe, neyther the ceremonyes whiche the heretykes doe rejecte, nor yet Scrypture Reading the
whereunto they doe so cleve, as though the readynge there- Scriptures.
of were the onely waye to come to the knowledge of Chryste:
whiche, no fayle, bryngeth a greate knowledge, yf yt be
well understode.   But this I dare saye, whereunto Scrypture alsoe doth agree, that the observatyon of ceremonyes, Ceremonies
for obedyence sake, wyll gyve more light than all the read- give more
ynge of Scrypture can doe, yf the reader have never so light.
good a wytt to understand what he readythe, and thowgh
he putt as muche dyligence in readynge as he can, with the
contempte of ceremonyes: but the thinge that gyveth us
the veraye light, ys none of them both; but they are most
apte to receyve light, that are more obedyent to follow ceremonyes, than to reade: for those be *parvuli;* and suche
to whome the Scrypture gyveth light, as Scrypture itselfe
doth testyfye; where yt ys wryten, *Declaratio sermonum
tuorum intellectum dat parvulis: et testimonium Domini
fidele sapientiam præstans parvulis.*   Whiche *name* they
cannot justely beare, that refuse ceremonyes.
    But what gevythe the veraye light, and what sheweth
the veraye waye to come to the same, whiche all heretykes
pretende they seeke, and pretende they have more than
oother, because they saye they cleve more to Scrypture than
those that reprove them; I wyll nowe shewe you, as I have

byn tawght of the chyrche, as God tawght Esaias the prophete, howe he shoulde teache hys people that sowght light,
and woulde not have yt, because they went not by the trewe
waye to fynde yt : but God tawght Esaias the waye howe
to bringe them unto yt; first, byddynge him speke to the
people under this manner ; *Clama, ne cesses : quasi tuba,
exalta vocem tuam ; et annuncia populo meo scelera eorum.
Me etenim de die in diem querunt, et scire vias meas volunt.*
Here you heare the desyre whiche the people had, and the
same ys nowe in manye, and none pretende the same more
than suche as be heretykes.   The whiche onely desyre of
ytselfe beynge good, yet not takynge the right waye to the
accomplishing of the same, maketh many to falle into heresyes, thinkynge no better nor spedyer waye to be, for to
come to the knowledge of God and his law, than by read-
yinge of books, whereyn they be sore deceyved.   And yet
so yt be done yn his place, and wyth right order and cir-
253 cumstance, yt helpeth muche.   But the right and pryncy-
pal waye to come to the light of the knowledge of God, and
his wayes, as the prophete callethe them, yt ys not gotten
by readinge : and what that ys the prophete Esaias doyth
expresse, spekynge not a worde of readynge the lawe ; and
the fyrst lesson he gyvethe herein to all them that have this
desyre of light and knowledge, ys to take awaye the impe-
dyment of that light, whiche be oure synnes, whiche be
taken awaye by the sacrament of penance.   Whereof the
Jues, whiche had this desyre to come to knowledge and
light of God, were not all ignorant, as they shewede in
theyr fastinge, prayer, and afflictyons of theyr bodye, as
the prophete rehersethe of them, spakinge in theyr person,
and marvelinge why they, walkynge as they thowght in the
waye to come to light, found yt not, sayinge on this manner,
*Quare jejunamus et non aspexisti, humiliavimus animas
nostras et non aspexisti.*   In whiche wordes they shewe,
that neyther by fastynge nor prayer, they coulde atteyne
that light and comforte whiche theye desyeryd of God, and
yet there coulde be no redyer waye than that they had en-
trede in, yf they had walkyde thereyn as they sholde.   And

what was yt they lacked in this waye? They had lacke of that whiche the folyshe virgyns lacked, at suche tyme they went to mete the spouse. They wanted oyle in theyr lampes. They lacked the workes of mercye: whiche yf they had byn joynede wyth fastinge, prayer, and trewe repentance of theyr synnes, then followeth the wordes of the prophete, namynge the workes of mercye, that makyth all yn this waye to come to light, when he sayethe, *Frange esurienti panem tuum: ægros vagosque induc in domum tuam: cum videris nudum, operi eum, et carnem tuam ne despexeris. Tunc erumpet quasi mane lumen tuum, et sanitas tua citius orietur: et anteibit faciem tuam justicia tua, et gloria Domini colliget te: tunc invocabis et exaudiet te: clamabis et dicet, Ecce adsum: quia misericors sum Dominus Deus tuus.*

Here nowe you have harde the veraye waye to come to light, not by readynge Scryptures, whereof you speke so muche, that are breakers of the unyte of the chyrche: and the prophete spekythe nothinge, nor yet by any other waye that can be imagenyd, yf woorkes of mercye take: and the prophete shewethe the cause, why thes workes ought to be regarded moste: *Quia misericors sum Dominus Deus tuus.* Whiche ys as muche to saye, *Because God ys mercyfull*, he wyll not have his light seene, his benefyts of mercye receyvyd, but of them that use mercye. And that ys so, we shall knowe at the daye of judgment, where every man shall have that perteynethe other to mercye or to justyce, whiche ys other rewarde eternall, or payne everlastinge, and to be rejected from the face of God for ever, or enjoye his glorye. Then Chryste himselfe dothe saye, that when they shall come afore him that shall professe to knowe him, as they that saye, *Prophetavimus in nomine tuo;* and other that seme to have moste of his favours yn earthe, that can cast spiryts out of other in his name; yet he wyll not knowe any of them, yf they have not workes of mercye: the whiche whosoever bringe with them, they shall knowe him, and he wyll knowe them. And to thes he saythe, *Esurivi et non dedistis mihi manducare*, &c. *Venite et benedicti patris mei:*

The very way to light.

254

possidete vobis regnum a Patre meo, &c. and to all other he
saythe, *Ite maledicti in ignem æternum, paratum Diabolo
et angelis suis*, &c.   What horrible wordes be these to them

that be slacke in almes-dedes, in workes of mercye? What
a terrour shoulde this be unto us in this realme, and what a
terrour ought this to be to them, that not onlye themselves
do noe workes of mercye, but have taken awaye the fruyte
of the almes that was gyven by other? What shall I saye
here, shall I doe as God biddythe the prophete, *Clama, ne
cesses: exalta ut tuba vocem tuam: annuntia populo meo
scelera eorum.*   I sholde lacke no matter of cryinge and la-
mentynge, if I wolde crye the hole-daye; and soe my dewtye
were to doe, beynge noe lesse commandyd to crye than the
prophete; specyallye nowe, after you have receyved suche a
worde of mercye as this ys, whiche none other contreye
hathe had synce the chyrche began; and yet dyverse and
great contreys beynge fallen, but none reformede.   And
for theyr remayninge in schisme, great plages of God remayninge styll upon them: but you, by the great mercye
of God, be retourned to the unite of the chyrche, where
now, whatsoever you doe, accordynge to the ordre of the
chyrche, shalbe acceptable to God, and fruytfull to you,
but yet not wythout penance for that paste, nor wythout
doynge workes of mercye above other.   For the greater that
your offence to God hathe byn above oother, so shulde
youre workes of mercye more exceede oother.   But where
shall we see any of them bothe, whiche muste be joynede
bothe togyther? Where ys your fastynge, your prayer, your
corporall afflictyon, to come to joye spirituall? What! doe
you thinke to come to more light, to more knowledge of
God, lackynge all these, and beynge not so far onwarde in
the waye as the Jues were, whiche desyred the light and
comforte of God? They knewe they shoulde passe by penance, and so used all corporall penance.   You are not yet
aryved thereunto, and what! doe you thinke to come to
more light, to attayne more comforte and favour of God,
lackynge all these? I wyll say more yn the exaggeratyon
of these vyces that be contrarye to these workes of penance.

When was more excesse of meate and drynke than nowe?
More excesse of sumptuose apparel, bothe on your bodyes
and yn your houses; the chyrches remaynynge bare, robbed, and spoyled? When was lesse almesse gyven? What
shall I saye? Shall I not crye out withe the prophete,
and compare you to those that have not offendyd the lyke
unto you ageynste the chyrche; yet shewe more devotyon
to the chyrche, more prayer, more fastynge, and greater
workes of mercye yn one daye, than you doe yn the hoole
yeare?

I can speake of the contrey I cam from, whiche ys Italye, Italy.
where I knowe yn somme cyte to be above iii score monasteryes, as I am sure yn Venyce be; and yn Florence alone
above iiii score, and the most part founded by the voluntarye almes of the citesyns, one not knowynge of another's 255
almesse. If I woulde rehersse at Rome, at Bononye, at
Mylane, what a multitude of holly houses and hospitalls be
founded under this manner, yt were a wonder to heare,
and a great reproche to you yn this cyte, whereas there are The city's
not x places, neyther of hospytalls, nor monasteryes yn the reproach.
cyte, nor abowte the cyte; and yet for you they maye dye
for hunger: is not this a matter to crye out at, if I wolde
folowe as the matter wolde leade me? But the joye of the
feaste of this daye doth staye me at this tyme; and I shall
exhorte you at all tymes to be folowers of good workes, to
take from me all suche cause and occasyon of complaynt,
havinge afore your eyes the sayinge of St. Paule, *Qui parce
seminat, parce et metet: et qui seminat in benedictionibus
et benedictionibus metet.*

And what is the benedictyon of this stede of almesse, the
prophete Esaias shewethe in that same place that I have rehersed, whiche sayethe in this maner; *He that soweth workes
of mercye, shalbe made himselfe a garden of pleasure for
God to walke yn.* For these be his wordes, contynuynge his
matter of workes of mercye; *Cum effuderis esurienti animam
tuam: et animam afflictam repleveris,* &c. *Et eris tanquam
hortus irriguus, cujus non deficiet aqua:* and what a grace,
thinke you, is it by doynge workes of mercye to be brought

to that case, that the soule shalbe a place planted lyke to a garden? I saye, this is more than to be brought ageyne to the garden of pleasure, where Adam was fyrst put. yn, whiche is called *paradyse:* I saye, it is a higher benefyte for him to retorne to the churche, that was out of it, than Adam coulde have to retorne to the place of pleasure, whiche was paradyse; from whence, for eatynge of an aple, whiche God forbadde him, he was expulsed. But this ys not so well knowen: and why? Bycause we folowe not the waye to come to the joyfull knowledge thereof; and what that ys, I have nowe shewed you.

And shewinge one thinge besyde that Esaias also maketh mentyon of in the same place, as a veraye perfet meane to ***The means to quietness of mind.*** come to perfet quietnes and joye of mynde, I shall leave you, as yt were, in the high-waye to paradyse, and that ys this; that sekynge God, if you hope to fynde him, you sholde utterlye leave your owne wyll, whiche restethe speciallye in ii poynts: the one in the desyre of more knowledge than God hath lymyted unto us: whereyn our fyrste moother fyrste dyd disobeye. And the other poynt is touchinge carnall pleasure of the bodye; in whiche poynte, if we forsake oure owne wyll, and specyallye in the hollydaye, whiche shoulde be all dedycate to the wyll of God, then sayethe the prophete, Thowe shalt make a hollydaye to God. For as longe as thou folowest thyne owne wyll, thou makest God laboure, as it were in a workye-daye, to breke thy wyll. And thou folowynge the same art occupyede in more servyle laboure than when thou tyllest the grounde; therefore the prophet sayethe, *Si averteris a sabbato pedem tuum facere voluntatem tuam in die sancto tuo,* &c. *Vocaberis sabbatum delicatum.* And what shall folowe of this the 256 prophete shewethe, speakynge in the person of God, *Et extollam te super altitudinem terræ:* that is to saye, *I wyll extolle thee above paradyse terrestryall.* And what then? *Et cibabo te hereditate Jacob patris tui.* But nowe what rewarde ys this, to be fedde whyth the inherytance of Jacob? This we shall knowe, yf we marke well what ys the meate we have been fedde withall, folowinge your owne

myndes,   of oure moother Eve manye
yeares, whiche bringeth nothinge but deathe; and all that
wayte upon deathe, and goe before deathe, that ys sorrowes,
afflictyon, both corporall and spyrytuall. But this ys a newe
meate, that neyther to the eye, to the sensys, to any dys-
course of reason, shewethe any pleasure, as the apple dyd
to Eva; and passeth so fur yn pleasure, as the pleasure in
heaven passethe pleasure yn earthe. This ys *panis verus,
qui de celo descendit, et dat vitam mundo.* This meate ys Feast of the
gyven to every feaste in the sacryfyce of the masse; whiche sacrifice of
who receivyth with condigne faythe and reverence, this the mass.
maketh up the joye of the feaste greater than ever Adam
had yn paradyse in his most felycyte, whiche neyther sense
nor reason can abyde : and therefore thys meate ys gyven
us to represse the judgment of bothe, and to subdewe both
to the captyvyte of feythe, stayenge upon the worde of
God; as Esaias spekynge of the same meate, and so con-
cludynge, saythe, *Os Domini locutum est.*

And here nowe I make an ende, havinge shewede you,
not of myne owne hedde, but as I have byn taught of my
moother and yours in the house of God, bothe what the
churche ys, what pryvyleges and graces be graunted to
them that be of that bodye, and the waye howe to enjoye
them : whiche yf you doe marke well, receyvinge that knowledge by dewe feythe, and love, and charyte, and applye
your wyll to folowe the same; then shall you have cause to
retorne to your owne howses, syngynge yn your howses,
Lætatus sum in his quæ dicta sunt mihi. And that you
may so doe, this shalbe my prayer. And yf you, commynge
to your owne house, wyll praye every man for his owne
selfe, as this greate kynge and prophete dyd for hymselfe
in his prayer, when he sayede, *Unum petii a Domino, hoc
requiram, ut inhabitem in domo Domini omnibus diebus vitæ
meæ : ut videam voluntatem ejus, et visitem templum ejus :*
in that maner I have declarede, then surelye that benedictyon shall fawle upon you; that yn another place, speakynge of the same matter, the prophete wysheth yn his
prayer for Israel, sayinge, *Benedicat te Dominus ex Sion :*

ut videas bona Hierusalem omnibus diebus vitæ tuæ. And wyth this benedictyon I wyll leave you, whiche through the mercye of God Almyghty light and remayne upon you nowe and ever. *Amen.*

257

Number LXIX.

A letter to Ralph Allerton, imprisoned for the gospel; comforting him under the cross, and exhorting him to persevere.

Foxii MSS. GRACE and peace from God the Father, and from the Lord Jesus Christ, be with you, my dear brother Rafe. God strengthen you in his faith, fear, and love, and keep you in the same to the end. *Amen.*

My dearly beloved in the Lord, I have me most heartily commended. And this is the cause that I write unto you now, wishing to you as to myself: for as I am willing to take my cross and follow Christ, even so, good brother Rafe, go on still, and bear your cross, and follow Christ: and so you shalbe his disciple. There is nothing more requisite, necessary, and profitable for the confirmation of a Christian life, O dear brother, than the cros and persecution. But alas! there is nothing in these days more feared, shunned, and avoided; and that of those that would be counted Christians and earnest gospellers. But such is their imbecillity, weaknes, and foolishnes, much like to little children, who customably do desire the sweet meat, and fly from the bitter thing that may do them good.

Loving brother, truly the cros of Christ, which is persecution, if we will put childlesnes apart, wisely weigh the worthines therof, it is that sovereign tryed treacle, that quencheth the deadly digested poison of self-love, worldly pleasing, fleshly felicity, and carnal security. If we look well, it is the only profitable plough, whose property is not only to root up al briars, brambles, thistles, thornes, and weeds out of the earthly heart, and concupiscence of mortal men, but also to prepare and yield the same, apt to receive the seasonable seed of Christ's sowing in his gospel-preaching. It is that true touchstone, that tryeth gold from copper, the true from the counterfeit, and the tin from that which is brass. Finally, deare brother Rafe, the cros is that flourishing flayle and fan, that purgeth and delivereth the good corn of a Christian life from al chaff of corruption, wherwith before it was covered. O! profitable instrument; O! necessary towel; O! excellent exercise, that cannot be spared in a Christian life.

Wherfore, deare heart, these things well considered, with what alacrity of mind, with what desirous affection, with what earnest zeal, ought we to embrace this incomparable jewel, this sovereign medicine, this comfortable cup of the cros of tribulation? Wherin, without al doubt, the Lord hath prepared a draught for his saints to drink, although 258 somewhat tart and bitter unto the flesh; yet it is most comfortable and pleasant unto the soul. For it is written, *By many tribulations we must enter into the kingdom of heaven.* O! brother Rauf, if you desire, as I doubt not but you do, to be saved, and not to be condemned, to live, and not to dy, to have Christ confes thee, and not to deny thee before his Father and his angels, and to follow the Son of God into his kingdom, and not to be expulsed thence, give ear then unto this sentence, for therin he teacheth us the only way unto the same, saying, *He that wil follow me, let him take up his cros and follow me.* Wherby it is apparent, that we cannot follow Christ, but bearing a cros: not the cros that the Papists bear of gold and silver, which many now-a-days do follow, the more is to lament; but the cross of persecution, affliction, and mortification. For if Christ be the way, as he saith he is, unto his Father, and that beside him there is no other but by-ways, tending to perdition; then is it of necessity, if we will come unto eternal glory, that we do travail that way that he hath gon before us, in passing his footsteps.

Now, brother Rafe, I remember my sister Tyms, and I have a recompence to make to you for your good heart: take this in part of recompence; and for your bargain that you did give my sister and me, I wish you the same dishes of meat, that our Christ entred into the kingdom of his Father with; that is, his ignominy, reproof, shame, scandal, reviling, persecution, affliction, and such like. And though they be sowre to the flesh, yet they be sweet to the soul.

Good brother, take no grief, that I and my sister wish you such recompence, being they be such that Christ fed his disciples with. *If they*, saith he, *persecuted me, they shall also persecute you. If they have called the master of the house Beelzebub, how much more shall they call the household servants.* So our portion is in this life to weep and mourn, to taste the bread of adversity and the water of trouble; to be as sheep appointed to the slaughter. These be the dainty dishes that God hath prepared for his children to feed on in this world. Therfore I pray you feed of them gladly, while you be in this life, to the end, that in the world to come you may laugh and rejoyce, having all tears wiped away from your eyes, and fed with the celestial manna and water of life, in triumphing over your enemies. *For in this world,* as saith S. Paul, *we are judged and afflicted, because we should not be condemned* with the world.

And this, dear brother, I make an end of my simple and rude letter; and for lack of a love-token, I pray you take this as a love-token. And I pray you, pray for me, as I wil do for you; that is, that God may encrease your faith; that you, and all the elect of God may boldly stand in his battel, and fight the good fight of faith, against al the fiery darts of Sathan and Antichrist: wherby we may obtain the crown of glory. The which God graunt for his mercy sake. *Amen.*

59   I pray you take this letter as mine and my sister Tymms also. She hath her commended from the bottom of her heart; and prayeth you to pray for her. Pray, pray, pray, yea, continue in prayer. Ask in faith, and obtain your desire. Written the vij day of April, by your poor brother Foster, and

Your sister Tymms.

Number LXX.

A proclamation set forthe by the Kinge and Quenes Majesties, agaynst Thomas Stafforde, and other traytors, his adherentes.

WHEREAS Thomas Stafforde, and others, malicious and evill disposed subjects, his adherentes, havinge conspired to perpetrate divers heynous tresons agaynste the moste royall persones of their Majesties: and therupon feringe to receive juste punishemente for his and their dissartes, fledde into the partis beyonde the seas, and there remaininge for a tyme, have, persistinge in their sayde malice, divised and attented divers tymes to sturre seditions and rebellions within this realme, to the greate disturbance of the Quenes peace and tranquilitie thereof; by sendinge hither into the realme divers bokes, letters, and writinges, bothe printed and written, farced and filled full of untruthes and sedition, and moste faulse surmyses of thinges sayde to be done and divised by the Kinge oure soverene Lorde, and his servantes, which were never imagined or thought. And to shewe their utter malice with more effecte, the same Stafforde did latelye, with certayne of his sayde complices, unnaturall Englishe men, and some straungers, enter into this realme, and by stelthe tooke their Majesties castell of Scarborowe, in the countie of Yorke, and set oute a shamefull proclamation, wherein he trayterouslie namethe and affirmethe oure sayde soverene Ladie the Quene, to be unrightfull and moste unworthie Quene; and that the Kinges Majestie, our sayde soverayne Lorde, hathe induced and brought into this realme, the number of twelve thousande straungers and Spaniardes; and that into the sayde Spaniardes handes twelve the strongeste holdes of this realme be delivered. In which proclamation also the sayde traytor Stafforde did name and take himself to be protector and governor of this realme; by these moste faultie and unnatural means, myndinge to allure the good subjectes of their Majesties, to withdrawe their dewtie of allegiance from their sayde Majesties, and to adhere to him the sayde Stafforde, to their confusion. **260**

Foxii MSS.

Albeit the sayde Stafforde, and other traytors his complice be by the helpe of God, and diligence of the Erle of Wes merlande, and other noblemen and gentillmen, good sut jects of those partes, repressed, apprehended, and forth comynge, to receave juste punishement, accordinge to thei dissartes. And that it may be well thoughte, that no wis or honeste man thinkethe, or can justelie gather anye caus to thinke, that the Kinges Majestie myndethe anye othe thinge unto the Quenes Majestie and the realme, but only to be carefull and studious of all thinges tendinge to the benefit, sewrtye, honor, and defence of the same : and in this parte, moste lovinglie and daylie bestowethe the greate travell of his reyall persone, besydes the large expence of his goodes and treasure ; yet to the intente none of their lovinge subjectes shoulde by simplicite be seduced and de-ceved, throughe the develyshe devices of the forsayed, or anye other like traytors, ther Majesties, of their greate cle-mencie and tender zeale towardes ther sayde subjectes, have thoughte good to warne and admonishe them of the pre-myces : exhortinge and charginge them to give no eare or credit to the sayde faulse proclamation and brutes, set oute and sprede by the sayde traytors, or hereafter to be set oute by anye others : wherebye they shall the better avoyde the daungers which they maye otherwise incurre, by adheringe or resortinge unto the sayde traytors ; and that also ther sayde lovinge subjectes do use themselves quietlye, withoute stirre or resistinge, till theye be commaunded in the name of ther Majesties, by the leiutenauntes of the country where the sayde subjectes dwell or inhabit, or by the shrife, or suche justices as shall have auctorytie from their Highnesses in their behaulf, to rayse and levey them. And that the sayde subjectes, and evrye of them, shall indever themselves to apprehende and take, and before the same lieuetenante, shrive, or justice of the peace of the sayed county, bringe all and every suche persone or persones as theye suspecte or knowe to be of the companey of the sayde traytors, or to fa-vour and ayde them, and all suche other also as shall pro-cure the people unlawfullie to serve, or shall sediciouslie or maliciouslie spreade or tell any sedicious newes concerninge the doinge of the sayde traytors, or otherwise. Straightlie charginge and commaundinge all justices of peace, mayres, shrives, baylyfes, constables, and all other their Majesties officers and mynisters, to se this proclamation put in execution, as their Majesties speciallie truste them: and as the sayde officers and mynisters will answer to the contrarye at their uttermoste perilles. Geven at oure palice of Westminster the laste daye of Aprill, aᵒ 1557.

Number LXXI.

261

A proclamation sett forthe by Thomas Stafforde, from Scarborow castle; exciting the English to deliver themselves from the Spanyards.

TO all and every singular person and persons, of what estate or degree soever they be, that love the common wealthe, honoure, and libertie of this ower native countrye, and moste for the realme of England, the Lorde Thomas Stafforde, son to the Lorde Henry, rightfull Duke of Bockingham, sendythe greetinge. Knowe ye, most dearlye belovyd contrymen, that we travellinge in strange realmes, and forren nations, have perfectly proved owt manye detestable treasons, which Spanyardes shamfullye and wrongfullye have pretended, and at this present have indevered themselves to worke against ower noble realme of Englande; we therfore more tenderlye favouringe, as all trewe Englishmen owghte to do, the common commodity and weal publycke of this ower natyve contrye, than ower welthe, treasure, safegarde, health, or pleasure, have with all possible spede arived here in the castell of Scarborowe, levyng owr bande, wherwith we thoughte to have proved in other affayers, comynge after us, bycause we had perfect knowledge by certaine letters taken with Spanyardes at Depe, that this same castell of Scarborow, with xij other of the moste chefest and principall howldes in the realme, shalbe delyvered to xij thousand Spanyardes, before the Kinges coronation: for the

Foxii MSS.

ɪ. l 2

Spanyardes saye, it were but vaine for the Kinge to be
crowned, onlesse he maye have certaine of our strongest
castelles and holdes, to resorte to at all tymes, till he maye be
able to bringe in a greate armye to withstonde his enemyes,
that is, to overrun and destroye the wholle realme: for, so
long as Englyshemen have anye power, we truste they will
never submitte themselfes to vile Spanyardes.   Which treason we have disappointed; trustinge, and firmelye belev-
inge, by the mighte of the omnipotente, everlastinge God,
with the ayde and helpe of all trewe Englyshmen, to deliver
owr country from all presente peril, daunger, and bondage,
wherunto it is like to be broughte, by the moste develyshe
devize of Mary, unrightful and unworthye Quene of England, who, both by the will of hir father, Kinge Henrye the
viijth, and by the lawes of this noble realme of England,
hathe forfette the crowne, for marriage with a straunger.
And also hathe most justlye deserved to be deprived from
the crowne, because she being naturallye borne haulfe
262 Spanyshe and haulfe Englyshe, bearythe not herselfe in-
differentlye towardes bothe nations, but showinge herselfe a
whole Spanyarde, and no Englyshe woman, in lovinge
Spanyardes, and hatinge Inglyshemen, inrichinge Spanyardes and robbinge Inglyshemen; sending over to Spanyardes continuallye the treasure, gowlde, and silver of our
realme, to maintaine them for owr destruction, sufferinge
poore people of England to lyve in all carefull miserye,
manye of them dyinge for verye hunger: and not contented
with all thes myschyfes, she sekynge ernestlye by all possy-
ble meanes to place Spanyardes in our castelles and howldes,
contrarye to all statutes, customes, and ordinaunces within
this realme, that they maye burne and destroye the countrye
iij or iiij tymes yerelye, till Englyshemen can be contented
to obeye all their vyle customes, and moste detestable doinges, wherby the whole commonaltie of Inglande shalbe
broughte to perpetual captivitie, bondage, and moste servyle
slaverye, as evidentlye shalbe proved before all men, at owr
fyrste assemble.   ·
   We therfore, dearly beloved countrymen, preventinge

these miserable mischefes, have purposed here to remayne and tarrye, to receve all suche faythfull and trewe Inglyshemen, as willinglye will worke to preserve their owne lyves, landes, lyvynges, tresures, wyves, childerne, yea, and to speake bryflye, the crowne of the whole realme, from the possessyon of prowde, spytefull Spanyardes, whose Moryah maners and spytefull condytions no natyon in the worlde is able to suffer. And therfore we are fullye determyned to wythstande them in all their doinges for the defence of owr countrye, not myadinge to worke to owr own advancement touchinge the possessyon of the crowne, but onlye to restore our bloude and howse to the owlde pristinate estate, which all men knowe hathe bin most wrongfully suppressyd by the malyse of Cardynall Wolsey; and not for any offence that we commytted towardes the realme or the crowne; but have always endevered ourselves, as we pretende at this present, to withstablishe the crowne to the next righteful heyrs of the realme. So that yt maye remayne successyvely to the trewe Inglyshe bloude of owr owne naturall countrye, banyshinge and expellinge all straungers, marchauntes onlye excepted; and to restore againe all suche actes, lawes, lybertyes, and customes, as were establyshed in the tyme of that moste prudente prince, Kinge Henrye the viij. Wherby this whole realme of Englande shall not onlye be preserved from the tyrannie of forrayne princes, but also be delyvered from all suche powlinge paymentes, as the Quene dothe daylye geve to Spanyardes; and will geve contynuallye, till she have beggered and destroyed all the whole realme. We therfore are fullye determyned moste thankefullye to receve all persons, of everye state or degre, that willingelye will wythstande thes myserable myschefes; and as the Dukes of Buckingham, our forefathers and predecessors, have always byn defendores of the poor commonaltye againste the tyrannye of princys, so shoulde you have us at this juncture, moste dearlye beloved frendes, your protector, governor, and defendor, againste all your adversaries and enemyes; mynd- 263 inge earnestlye to dye rather presentlye and personallye before you in the felde, than to suffer you to be overrun so miserably with straungers, and made moste sorrowfull slaves, and carefull captyves to suche a naughtye natyon as Span-yardes, who affirme openlye, that they will rather lyve with Mores, Turkes, and Jues, than with Inglyshemen ; wherby all men maye perceyve plainelye, that ever lyke as they do use Turkes, Mores, and Jues, which be their captyves, so muche more worse will they use us, and if we do not man-fullye within shorte tyme withstande the pretendyd pur-poses.   We shall therfore most earnestlye and lovinglye desyer all maner of persons, of what estate or degree soever they be, that will gladlye withstande these miserable mis-chefes and workes, and to maintain the crown from all straungers, to the right heyrs of the realme, that they and everye of them, with all expedition, resorte to us, so well ap-pointed with horses, armoure, or otherwayes, as they possy-ble can appointe themselves, for the preservatyon of the crowne, and savegarde of the realme.

Number LXXII.

The names of the prisoners taken in Scarborowe castell, the
28th of Apryll, an. 1557.

Foxii MSS.

Thomas Stafford, gent. ⎫
Mr. Brissel, Frenchman. ⎪
Rychard Saunders, gent. ⎬ 5 prisoners in the Tower
Willyam Scowell, gent. ⎪   of London.
John Proctor, gent. ⎭

John Browne	John Momford, Scot.
Owen Jones	Thomas Spencher
Henrye Gardyner	William Wilke
John Watsone, Scot.	John Adames *Index* – 68
John Graye, Scot.	Willyam Palmer
Willyam Williamson	Laurence Alsop
Anthonye Parriuall	John Bradforde
Clement Tyled	Thomas Wilkinson
John Wilborne	Rogere Thomas
Rogere Raynoldes	Robert Hangate, Scot.

John Wallyce   Thomas Jurdyne
John Donnynge   John Creswell
Jaques Lartoys, Fren.   Thomas Warre.
John Thomas
    27 persons remanynge in prison in Yorke.

Number LXXIII.   264

*The Queen to Sir Edward Dimock; to attend her person
with his servants and tenants in arms.*

Mary the Quene.   By the Quene.

  TRUSTY and welbeloved, we grete you wel, and let you *Ex Epistol.* wit, that the wars being open between us and France, and *Comit. Sa-lop. in Offic* the King, our dearest lord and husband, past the seas in *Armor. re-* person to pursue the enemy; we have given order, as meet *posit.* is, our honour and surety so requiring, to have a convenient sort put in a perfect readines and preparation to attend upon our own person, as wel for the defence and surety therof, as to resist such attempts as may be by any foreign enemy, or otherwise, made against us and our realm: and knowing your fidelity and good wil to serve us, have appointed you to be one among others that shal attend upon us: therfore requiring and charging you, not only to put yourself in order accordingly, but also to cause your tenants, servants, and others, under your rules and offices, to be mustered: and of your said servants, tenants, and others, within your rules and offices, to furnish yourself with ten horsemen, and one hundred footmen, wel appointed: of the which, one fourth part to be harquebuttiers, or archers, one other fourth part pikes, and the rest bills: and with the same numbers of men, horse, and furniture, wel in order, to be ready to attend upon [us here] or elsewhere, by our appointment, upon one day's warning, at any time after the 25. day of August next coming: and in the meantime, until eight shalbe so called to serve us, remain in ful readines and order to serve under them that have charge in that county. And hereof fail not. Yeoven under our signet, at our manor of Richmond, the last of July, in the fourth and fifth years of our reigns.

L l 4

265 Number LXXIV.

Mr. Henry Percy to the Earl of Shrewsbury; concerning his success against the Scots, invading the east marches.

Ex Epistol.
Com. Sa-
lop. in Offic.
Armor.
reposit.

I PERCEIVE both your Lordsps. [*viz.* the Earls of Shrewsbury and Westmerland] to accept my repair to this country, [Northumberland,] in such good part, as I have cause to rejoice therof: and further, to be desirous to know the occurrents from time to time happening in these parts. It may please your good Lordsp. to understand, that upon my repair to Alnwic, the last of July past, sundry gentlemen of this country, with many other honest men of the same, repaired thither unto me: with whom I travailed til Wednesday at night last, in such sort, as we were suffered to take very little rest, either by night or day; but by the more part of nights and days on horseback attended the invasion of the enemy. And for the better resistance therof, placed myself and my company nigh to the frontiers; as at Eslingtone, and other places therabouts. And yesterday, being the 5. of this instant, about five of the clock in the morning, the L. James and L. Robert, the late Scotch King's bastard sons, the L. Hewne, and others of Scotland, with al the power they could make in three days assembly of men from Edenburgh hitherward, and with certain peeces of ordinance, did invade on the east march of this realm, minded, as I learned by credible intelligence, to have attempted to win the castle of Ford, and have brynt sundry towns therabouts, called the Ten Towns of Glendale. Which their purpose, upon my repair towards them with a good number of gentlemen and others of this country, they did quite alter and change. And after they had brynt a house or two in the town of Fenton, where was taken and wounded to death, as is supposed, one of their best borderers and guides, Riche Davyson, with great haste and more fear (as by plucking off and leaving a great number of white crosses; and the small spoil or prey of cattel by them seized, did appear) departed home into Scotland, before we could in order come to them: which considered, by the discrete advice of the gentlemen, (whose good conformity and forwardnes in service I cannot but of good cause much earnestly commend to your Lordsp. whom I shall much humbly beseech further to commend and advance the same, upon this my just report, as may tend to their more encouragement of service hereafter,) I did enterprize to invade the country of the Mars in Scotland: where were brynt sixteen towns, and won a booty or spoil of 880 neat, and 1000 266 sheep, besides many horses, and some prisoners.

This day one aid of 600 men of the bishopric is repaired towards Barwick: which being placed as my L. Wharton shall appoint, I doubt not but shalbe able, by God's grace, to withstand the enemy. And the same considered, upon conference therin had with my L. Wharton, I do, for sundry, my Lord, my brothers, and mine, much necessary busines, depart hence tomorrow towards Prudhow. And thus remaining, as I am therto most bound, your Lordsps. assured to command at all times; I beseech the eternal God to conserve your good Lordsp. with continuance and encrease of mich honorable estate. From Alnwic, the 6. of Aug. 1557.

Your Lordsps. most bounden to command,
Henry Percy.

Number LXXV.

The Lord Wharton, Sir James Croft, and Sir John Clere, to the Lords of the Queen's Privy Council; relating the success of the Scots' attempts upon England.

PLEASETH it your most honorable Lordsps. in our Ubi supra. due maner to be advertised, that the Scots, sithence our late letter, have continued in great power together upon their east borders. And we having intelligence, that they would invade these borders the 5th of this month, as they did; for resistance wherof, we gave warning to the whole power of these marches, to be ready to let their enterprize. The Scots entred between Wark and Chyviot, to Glendall, and Mr. Henry Percy had a power with him, Sir John Foster, and Mr. Grey, and divers other gentlemen, with their powers; and the garrison of Barwick, upon our appointment, joined them, and drew towards their strength, and offered themselves in such sort, as the Scots, who intended to have burnt sundry towns far within the marches, were glad to take the advantage of four or five little towns being left waste. And our men being not of power to encounter them, held them close from sparpling abroad to destroy the country. And upon their retyre, followed them with scowerage towards Tividale, til our men saw that with good ad-

267 vantage they might enter into the march: where they burnt ten or twelve such towns as were upon those borders, and have taken some cattel and sheep, and brought home with them, for their better relief. We sent to meet them 300 footmen out of this town; and so they returned to Barwick in safty.

This day we were advertised, that the power of the bpric. of Durham are coming at Alnwic, and towards this town and Alnwic: whom we intend for to place upon the borders, unto the coming of Sir Tho. Wharton, who we understand wilbe in Newcastle upon the 8. of this month. And his men being placed, we shal return home them of the bpric. unto we have further occasion, &c.

Number LXXVI.

Mary the Quene.

A memorial or note of answer to such things as were propounded to our Councel by Sir James Croft, kt. by instruction to him given by our right trusty and right welbeloved cousins, the Earl of Shrewsbury, our lieutenant in the north; the Earl of Northumberland, warden of our east and middle marches for anempst Scotland; our right trusty and welbeloved the L. Wharton, captain of our town and castle of Barwick, Aug. 20, 1557.

supra.   FIRST, for avoiding of excessive charges, it is thought that it be provided, that there may remain a good and strong garrison upon the borders, put in such order, as they may be defended, and annoy in all cases, except in cases of invasion of a great army : and to consider what number may be thought meet for that purpose ; and in what places the same may be placed. And in case any such invasion be made by an army, the said garison to be so directed, as they may by al ways and means impeach their marching, and other attemptates and doings : foreseing nevertheles, that the said garison-men may use their doings in such wise sort, as they retyre and save themselves, if necessity so require, until the coming of the army.

To give order to the common people for sending their 268 cattel out of the way, and putting their corn in places of safety, as near as may be, in cases of invasion.

To provide that the Earl of Darby, and al others, having charge to bring any numbers, may be in readines from time to time to march al, or such part of their numbers, as may for the time be thought meet to serve.

To give order by al ways and means, that in case of the going forward of a main army, that the inhabitants of every parish where men be levied, may be induced, to send victuals for their men. To which purpose, the travail of the noble-men and gentlemen, having charge of men in every country, shal much avail. And it is like that the people wel informed and advised, wil gladly do thus much ; considering it is for their own surety and defence ; and considering also, that in time past, the common-people of those and other parts of the realm have done the like.

And because it hath been thought by the L. Lieutenant, the Earl of Northumberland, and others, that some num-bers of the Northumberland men may be placed in garison, to serve on horseback ; her Majestie is pleased, that order shalbe given by them accordingly : and that there be placed of the said Northumberland men such numbers of them in places convenient as they think good ; discharging for them such others as may seem to their wisdoms meetest to be dis-charged, and best able to serve.

The rate of the officers wages shalbe sent after.

And notwithstanding the expres order and commandment that hath been given to the L. Lieutenant, yet her Highnes pleasure is, that touching the marching forwards with the whole army, and other things also concerning the good service of her Majesty, the said L. Lieutenant shal use and do, and cause to be done, as he shal think good by his discretion, and as the force of the enemy and other circumstances shal require.

Her Majesties plesure also is, that the said Sir James Croft shal, in his return, repair unto the said L. Lieutenant, and declare to him the premisses; and shal also, any former directions to the contrary notwithstanding, attend upon the said L. Lieutenant, so long as pleaseth the same : foreseeing, that if the said L. Lieutenant, shal by his discretion think meeter to send the same Sir James to the borders for the service, to be used there, either in Barwick, or with the L. Warden, that then the said Sir James shal haste himself thither accordingly.

And concerning the payments that are to be made for the ordinary and extraordinary garison of the east and middle marches, the said Earl of Northumberland shal give order, and make warrant to the treasurer, Allan Bellingham ; and for al payments concerning the castel and town of Barwick, both ordinary and extraordinary, the said L. Wharton shal give and make like order and warrant; her Highnes trusting the said lords wil every of them wel husband the premisses, as appertaineth.

Mary the Quene.

269

Number LXXVII.

The Privy Council to the Earl of Shrewsbury, lord president of the north; giving order upon the intelligence of the Scots intentions to invade.

E Liter. Comit. Salop. in Offic. Armor.

AFTER our right harty commendations to your good Lordship, We have seen your letter of the 16th of this month, touching such advertisements as ye have received from Sir James Crofts, kt. of the Scots preparations, and

such other intelligences to that effect, as he hath gotten out
of Scotland. And altho' we do commend the diligence of
master Crofts, and could wish your Lordships had procured
by that, or any other means, to have as espial upon the
Scots doings as ye might; yet, in a matter of such importance, we think it had been convenient that Mr. Crofts had
advertised his knowledg unto our very good Lord the Earl
of Northumberland; and that your Lordship also should,
in such a weighty cause, be thoroughly advertised of the
very certainty and truth thereof, both from the said Earl,
the L. Wharton, and the other officers also on the frontiers,
before any great stir were made for the same. And yet
considering, that if there be as good espial of the Scots
doing, as with diligence may be had, and hath been used
heretofore, they cannot so secretly assemble any power together, but that we may have knowledg thereof time
enough to meet with their malice. We think, that noting
wel their practices, and understanding what preparations
they make, what numbers they do from time to time gather
together, how many days victuals they do provide, with
such other like circumstances; the knowledg whereof (having
good espials among the Scots, that may from day to day se
and note their doings) ye may both easily come by; and
thereby also guess by your discretions what they can be able
to do; and re-enforcing there the frontiers, as their doings
shal give you cause, and as your Lordships by your wisdom
shal think may best stand with the Queen's Majesties service, and the surety of the borders.

Ye shal not need to make any ful assembly of the army,
unless they should go about with their main power to invade
the realm. Which in that case (if any good espial be had)
cannot be kept so secret, but that it shal come time enough
to your knowledg to provide for the meeting with their intent, either by the whole, or such part of the army as ye
shal by your wisdom think most necessary. For which purpose your Lordship shal do wel to have the said army in
such continual readines, as ye may upon any such occasion

be also upon the sudden to lead the same forwards, as the cause shal require.

270 As touchinge your request to have a further supply of money sent thither, like as the cause of the sending of the last treasure that went from hence was, to the end that in case of necessity the same might serve, and be employed about the setting forward of the army, if need should so require, until upon knowledg thereof from you some greater mas might be provided; so if there be any such occasion, and that the army shall be set forward indeed, the Queen's Majesty wil then take order for such forward supply of money as shalbe convenient. And in the mean time her Highnes hath good hope your Lordship wil se, that the tresure already sent be kept together, and in no wise spent, but about the purpose aforesaid.

As for the bows that ye say are wanting, and require, may be provided for, either from hence or from Hull; albeit, as we signified unto you by our late letters, the remain at Newcastle, together with such proportions as have been lately sent from hence, amount unto 4000 bows at the least: of the stowing whereof, and by what warrant, we pray your Lordship, according to our former request, to examine the surveighor of the ordinance there: yet for the better ease of the present necessity, your Lordship shall do well to cause some skilful bowyers, and other honest persons, to be sent from York, and some other places thereabouts, unto Hull, to view and survey the state therof; and as many of them as are or may be made serviceable, to cause to be put in such state and readines, as they may always be ready to serve at your Lordship's commandment, if that army should come forward, for the furniture of such of the said army as being archers shal want artillery for such purpose; or otherwise as ye shal of your wisdom think convenient. And, as shortly we may, we will cause such farther supply of that sort of artillery to be sent thither, as shal be convenient.

At the closing up of these our letters, we received yours

of the 18th of this month, together with such advertisements as ye have received from Sir James Crofts and Sir Rauf Boulmer, kts. which we have declared unto the Queen's Majesty: which taketh the same in good part. And because it shal serve to good purpose for the understanding of the Scots doing, to procure by this means to feel their inclination, it shal be wel done, that the said master Crofts and master Boulmer, when they shal meet with the Scot and Frenchman, be frank in their communication with them, and by that means bolt out as near as they can what they do intend: protesting always, nevertheless, that the same is of themselves without any order or commission from you or any other: and so we bid your Lordship right hartily wel to fare, from St. James's the xx. of Sept. 1557.

Your Lordships assured loving friends,
Nico. Ebor. Canc. Winchester. Tho. Elye.
Tho. Cheyne. Henry Jernegan. Jo. Bourne.
E. Waldgrave. W^m. Petre S.

Number LXXVIII. 271

Instructions from the Privy Council to the said Earl, in relation to the Scotch affairs.

AFTER our right harty commendations to your good Ubi supra. Lordship, we have received your letters of the 19th of this month, together with the copies as wel of our very good Lord the Earl of Northumberland's letters written unto you, as also of the French and Scots instructions touchinge the taking and ransoming of prisoners on either side. Upon the perusing whereof, and of such other letters as ye lately sent unto us touching the Scots doings, we have thought meet for answer unto the same to signify unto you as followeth:

First, the Queen's Majesty, considering the several advertisements that have been sent hither both from your Lordship, and from the L. Dacres and others, of the preparation that the espials se the Scots do make, to have the

whole force of that realm in a readines against the 2. of
October: thinketh good, and so requireth your Lordship,
that ye do not only write unto every of the wardens, and to
the L. Wharton also, to have continual espials in Scotland;
and to understand from day to day, and time to time, the
said Scots assemblies, what their numbers shalbe, what purpose or enterprize they mind to take in hand; against what
time; who shal have the charge, with such like: but also
that as ye shalbe enformed, and understand these things to
be true, so give order for defence of the borders, and to
have such numbers assembled in such places, where they
may both best defend themselves and the country, and cut
off the victuals, or otherwise annoy the enemy, as opportunity may serve. And therewithal, lest the enemy might
find relief of our own provisions, to forese that they find no
victuals, but that the cattel be brought further into the
realm, and al other victuals put in safety.

And because it appeareth that there is not now such
store of bows there as were convenient, if the army should
go forward, like as we signified unto you in our late letter,
that ye might take those that be at Hull, so is her Highnes
pleased that ye should do, and make as good shift with
them as ye can, until some further supply may be sent
from hence: which shalbe with as good speed as we can;
order being already taken with the master of the ordinance
for that purpose, as by his letters lately sent unto your
Lordship ye may at better length perceive.

272   As for money, it hath been already by our last letters
written unto you, that if the army do set forward, ye may
use that treasure that hath been already sent thither, about
the advancing of the said army. And upon knowledg from
your Lordship of the marching forward of the same, her
Majesty wil take order, that a further supply of money
shall be sent to you out of hand.

As touching such gentlemen as ye say are fallen sick,
and some dead, her Highnes seeth none other remedy for
the supply of their want upon this sudden, but that your
Lordship must in their sted appoint some other skilful per-

sons, as you shall by your discretion think most convenient, which her Highnes desireth you to do out of hand ; so as the army be in no wise unfurnished of convenient officers, when it shall set forth.

And because it is to be thought, that the Scots will not enterprize any invasion upon this realm with a main force, unless they be of some strength, her Majesty thinketh it convenient, that ye take with you from out of those hither parts 11000 men at the least: whereof as many to be horsemen as ye can by any means get. So as, together with the force of the borders, the army be of an 18000 or 16000 men at the least.

As for victuals, Abingdon, who is appointed to provide victuals for Barwick, is now remaining there, and wil provide for the victualing of all those that be upon the borders, which must be one great part of the army. And as for those that your Lordship shal bring with you, ye must cause the country to follow the army with victuals; and, as we think, if Abingdon have warning given him from your Lordship in time, he wil also help with some furniture for the army that shal come with you. For which purpose, I, the Lord Treasurer, wil in like manner write unto him.

And where your Lordship thinketh there wilbe lack of carriages, we doubt not but there are enough to be found in the country there, for the furniture of a greater number of men than shal go forth now, if your Lordship will use your authority, which in this case you must needs do.

We have also perused the Scots articles touching prisoners: and altho' we reckon the same to be of no great importance, and rather to be moved by the Scots for a brag, or for some practice, than for any good meaning: yet for some answer to the same, we think, touching the ransome of prisoners, that it is not convenient that any of the degree of a baron or upwards should be set at any certainty, but to remain at the Prince's pleasure. And for al under the degree of a baron to be ransomed as they can agree with their taker.

And as for that article, where the Scots do require to

have such punished as shal lack the cros or token of the realm they be of, we like the same wel; so as if it be agreed upon, your Lordship do give warning thereof in time unto al your soldiers, captains, and others; to the end they may know the penalty, and provide for the remedy thereof, by having each man the cros upon him as is said. We do also think fit, that al chaplains, heralds, trumpeters, and other like officers be so, according to the antient law of arms. All which orders being agreed upon, it shal suffice they be followed and kept by the agreement of the lieutenants or wardens, without any further confirmation.

And thus having written our opinions, with the Queen's Majesties resolutions to the points before touched, her Highnes referreth the ordering of all other things that are to be done for her Majesty's service, and the meeting with the Scots, to be used by your Lordships discretion, in such sort as ye shall think most expedient, according to the authority and commission given you in that behalf. And thus we bid your Lordships right hartily wel to fare. From Westminster, this 24. of September, 1557.

Postscr. Since the writing of these, we have received your letters of the 20. of this month: whereby we perceive as wel that the intelligence of the Scots preparation to set forth is confirmed by the L. Wharton's espial, as also the order that ye have taken for the setting forward of the Queen's Majesties army to meet with the Scots attemptates. And like as we do wel commend your Lordship's good diligence and foresight, so nevertheles doth the Queen's Majesty think good, that giving every man warning to be in a ful and perfect readines, as ye may upon the sudden advance towards, as the Scots doings shal give you cause, ye do notwithstanding foresee, that the army do not assemble and go forward, before ye shal be sure that the Scots do the like: lest, if ye should set forth with the main army before they come forward on their part, ye should consume the victuals of the country without doing of any thing; and so to be fain, for want of provisions, to return back, and spend the

Queen's treasure in vain. Whereunto ye must have special regard.

As for the officers of the army that ye desire may be rated, your Lordship knoweth that we sent you a scedule of the said rates enclosed in our letter of the first of this month. Of the receipt whereof you wrot yourself unto us, and seemed to like the same enough; saving that ye said, there wanted in that book the general of the footmen, the master of the ordinance, and the provost marshal. Which indeed were omitted upon these considerations: first, we thought then, and so think stil, that because the footmen are to be divided into the vaward, rereward, and battel, and so be under several mens charges, there needeth not any general over them. And as for the master of the ordinance, he was left out of our book, for that there was not such officers named in the book sent by you before unto us. Howbeit, seing he is a necessary officer, the Queen's Majesty is now pleased ye shal appoint some fit person to occupy that room, allowing unto him for his entertainment 13sh. 4d. by the day. The provost marshal was by us thought might wel be spared, because there is a knight marshal appointed, who may wel enough discharge that office. And for the men that ye think meet should be allowed in wages unto the treasurer of the army, your Lordship may appoint unto him such a number as you shal by 274 your discretion think convenient.

And because it is considered that the having of men of service about you shal stand you in good sted, the Queen's Majesty knowing the wisdom and good skil of John Brend, esq. in the leading and ordering of footmen, wherein he hath had long experience, hath thought meet to send him presently unto your Lordship, whom ye may use about the ordering of the army, or in such other thing as upon conference with him ye shal think him fit to be employed in. And if ye shall think fit to have any other skilful person sent unto you from hence, her Highnes, upon knowledge thereof from you, will take order for the sending thither out of hand such as shal be fit for that purpose.

M m 2

And to the intent, that if the Scots should come upon the sudden, they may not find the pieces upon the borders unprovided for, the Queen's Majesty requireth your Lordship to write unto the wardens: and take such orders with them, as al the forts, castles, and pieces that be of importance, and stand in danger of the enemy, may be so substantially furnished of men, victuals, munition, ordinance, and all other necessaries, as they may be able to stand upon their guard, and resist the enemy, 'til further rescue may come unto them.

Your loving friends,

Nico. Ebor. Canc. Winchester.

Henry Jernegan.   Jo. Bourne.   Joh. Masone.

E. Waldgrave.   Edm. Peckham.

Number LXXIX.

The Earl of Shrewsbury to the Privy Council; giving account of the retreat of the Scots army from the English borders.

Ubi supra.   IT may please your honourable Lordships to be advertised; Being in continual expectation, and laying daily wait of the Scots entry into England, having our force prepared to defend it, and annoy them in such sort as hath been signified unto your Lordships, and I in readines with one thousand men to have set forwards, and done as the occasion of the enemies proceeding should have required; 275 the Scots, whose enterprize had been much slackned with foul weather, after many consultations, and ful determinations to enter England, being continually pricked forwards thereunto by the Queen and the French, were come the 17. of this instant to Ecford, upon their dry frontiers towards Wark-church: and there, as the intelligence saith, falling into a new consultation, thought, that considering the time of year, the foul weather, and the preparation made for their resistance, they should not be able to do any thing, that might stand with the honor of Scotland.   And herein

sending their expres determination to the Queen of their
resolution, restrained the Earl Huntley of his authority for
that day, because he withstood their opinions. And hereupon encamping that night upon Hawdon-ridg, set forward
next morning, being the 18th, and came neer to Wark,
having brought their ordinance over the Twede, and skirmished before Wark : shewing such likelihood to have given
the approach, that the Englishmen within, looking for the
siege, had rampered up the gates : yet that afternoon they
brake up their camp, and retired back again, and dispersed.

And so their enterprize, begun with great bravery, is
ended with dishonour and shame ; praise be given to God
therefore. Hereupon I have presently dispatched out of
wages al such as were here presently with me ; and mind
to do the like to all the rest, which were last called forth in
this journey, both horsemen and footmen : detaining them
only for a day or two, to se if any service can be done upon
the enemy. But the same thing which was impediment to
the Scots, is like to be let to the doing of any great matter
on our part, both the dark nights, and the short days, and
the high waters, there having this night past fallen a great
rain.

The next point is, to require your Lordships to understand the Queen's Majesties pleasure concerning the number of such garrisons as shall continue this winter, &c.

The charge that the noblemen of Scotland have been
put to this journey, the ill succes, their stoutnes in standing
against the Queen, and the diversity that hath been among
them, may grow to some greater effect than can be yet wel
conjectured. The Earl of Northumberland, the Earl of
Westmerland, Sir Tho. Wharton, Sir James Croft, Sir
Rafe Bulmer, and al the rest of the gentlemen, sent down
from above, and others here, each in their calling, yea, and
al the soldiers, have shewed in this present service a great
good wil, much intelligence, and a patience in doing and
suffering the weather and the want of things.

Please it your Lordships to understand, that the English
upon the frontiers in this mean while have not been idle,

but done divers feats and attemps, as wel in burning such corn and houses as might be relief to the enemies country towards the frontiers, as otherwise. And also my L. Wharton and my L. Evers have burnt and annoyed their neighbours, and in this time have used a great diligence about intelligences, and getting knowledg of the enemies purposes and doings.

---

276   ## Number LXXX.

Cardinal Pole to Queen Mary.

A remembrance of those things that your Highnes's pleasure was I should put in writing, as most convenient, in my poor judgment, to be commoned and spoken of by your Majesty with your Council, called to your presence this afternoon.

Titus, B. 2.
p. 176.
FIRST of al, that your Majesty should put them in remembrance of the charge the King's Highnes gave them at his departing. Which being reduced to certain articles, and put in writing, it seemeth wel, if some of the Lords, for their sudden departure after their charge, had not the same in writing, that it were rehearsed and given unto them, with exhortation to employ al their diligence for the due execution thereof.

And whereas amongst other charges, this was one, that those that be named in the first part counsellors, were all present in the Court: this first your Highnes may require them that they do observe, specially beside for the weight of the matters that be now in hond. The time beside being so short afore the Parliament, to examine them. And that the King's pleasure is, as the matters be proposed in the Council afore the further execution of them, to be enformed thereof, to know his pleasure therein. And amongst other, his Majesty being in expectation to know the utter resolution of the Council touching those matters that be to be entreated in this Parliament. This is that your Majesty looketh to have of them this day, to send with al speed to the King's Highnes.

And whereas for the dilation of the King's coming, your Majesty thought it wel to put in consult, whether it were better therefore to make a dilation and prorogation of the Parliament to Candelmas, being thought by their opinion, that for necessity of money that is to be demanded in the Parliament, and otherwise cannot be provided, the prorogation of that should be much dispendious; your Majesty not disallowing their deliberation, but considering withal the great need of money for to be had for the discharge of the present necessity, which requireth present provision of money; as is for the setting forth of the ships, as wel for the Emperor's passage to Spain as for the King's return; and beside this, for the payment of that is due at Callis, as for your credit with the merchants, approaching the day of 277 payment, and for the debt of Ireland also: of al these it may please your Majesty to know this day of your Council what is done.

And because the most ordinary and just way touching the provision of money to pay your Highnes's debts, is to cal in your own debts; which charge hath been specially committed afore, and is principally considered and renewed in the writing the King's Highness left touching such affairs, that his Council should presently attend unto; where be the names also that have the charge special; therefore your Majesty shal do wel this day to charge them with the same. That with al diligence they attend to the prosecution thereof, giving them al authority that shal be necessary for them to make the most speedy expedition herein: willing them withal, that they never let pas one week, but in the end of the same, at the least, your Majesty may know especially of that is commen in, and what order is taken for the rest.

Also, if it please your Majesty in general for al matters, which be entreated in the Council, which require commission and execution, to give this order, that those that have had commission to execute ony matter, let never pass the week, but they inform the Council what execution is made of their commissions: and that the Council themself should never begin entrance of new matters the second week, but that they have information first what is done in those which were committed to be executed the week afore. I think it should help much to the speedy expedition of al causes. This is my poor advice, remitting al to the godly and prudent judgment of your Majesty.

Number LXXXI.

A sermon preached at the funerals of Queen Mary : by the Bishop of Winchester.

Laudavi mortuos magis quam viventes : sed feliciorem utroque judicavi qui necdum natus est.

Cott. Libr. Vespasian, D. 18. THESE be the words of Solomon in the fourth chapter of the book of the Preacher, called Ecclesiastes. They may be Englished thus; *I can commend the state of the dead above the state of the living; but happier than any of them both is he that was never born.*

The first part containeth a doctrin incredible in the judgment of man : for al men commonly measureth the matter 278 after another sort, coveting rather to live than to dy, rather to have a being in this world than no being.

The second part, *feliciorem utroque judicavi,* &c. is exceeding perillous, tending to paganity, and hath been a principle not among the Christians, but among the heathens and gentils. *Optimum non nasci : best not to be born.* Wherefore it needeth to have a gentle interpretation; else shal we, even from the beginning of the world, controle and slander all the works of God : who, after he had made al creatures, last of al made man; under whose subjection he did put the rest. Now if it had been better men never to have been created, it must follow to be better al the rest also, which were made for man's sake and service, to have been uncreated. So that we shal invert the words of Genesis, and where Moses said, *God saw al that he had made, and it was exceeding good;* we shal say, *God saw al that he had made, and it was naught, in vain, and to small purpose:* because it had been better unmade. Which blasphemy God forefend that it should enter into the heart, or come out of the mouth of a Christian man.

Yet doth Job seem somewhat to maintain on that side, in that he, as one chalenging God, cryeth out, *O Lord! that ever I was born out of my mother's womb. I would I had been strait [conveyed] from birth to burial; from groaning to my grave.* And in another place, *Cursed be the day, in the which the midwife first said, There is a man-child born into the world.* But to resolve this, Right Honorable, in few words, know you that Job, a man of that grace and favour with God, of those gifts of wisdom and patience, knew right wel, that to be born of our parents is not evil; but to be born in the sin and disobedience of our first parents, and thereby in the wrath and displeasure of God, that is evil. Neither desired he so much to be carried from birth to burial, as to have the time of sinning in this wretched world to be cut off and abridged; nor cursed he the day, being the creature of God, but rather sin committed in the day, which sin is of the creation of the Devil.

To make this plain, I wil put this example for a thousand; Christ speaking of Judas said, *Melius erat illi, si natus non fuisset homo ille.* Which seems to maintain the former words of Solomon, *feliciorem utroque,* &c. But consider that Christ had signified before to his disciples, that one of them should betray him, and being demanded whom, said plainly, *He that dippeth his hand in my dish shal betray me.* And strait thereupon inferred, better had it been for that man never to have had a being: not absolutely noting his being, but being such a one as should bewray his Master. Wherof I infer, to have a being is not evil, but to be, as indeed Judas was, a traytor to this Maker, that is evil. To be born in Christ's church, and not to abide therein; to promise, and not to perform; to promise penance here, and not to practise; to hear the truth, and not to believe; to be daily taught, and never to learn; ever to be warned, and never to beware; that is horrible, execrable, cursed, and damnable. I am born into this world to this end, to serve God, and to be saved. I shal be 279 dampned, not because I was born, but because I served not [God.] I come into this world to witnes with the truth, as Christ my master came before me, saying, *Veni in mundum, ut testimonium perhibeam veritati:* but I impugne the truth, and advance falshood. I was regenerate, and by a solemn vow became a member of Christ's catholic church, and have since divided myself from the unity therof, and I am become a member of the new Church of Geneva, or did after lapse to actual and deadly sin: reformed by penance, I am now relapsed again to sin, and dwel stubbornly therin. Mark my end, Right Honorable, and what shal become of me. I shal in the end be dampned everlastingly: not because I was born, or because I was regenerate in Christ's church, or because I did penaunce there; but because I have wilfully departed out of the catholic church, wherin I made my first profession; and because I being relapsed into sin, do impenitently persist therin until my dying day.

Forasmuch as I have hitherto put the example of sin in mine own person, as I might wel do, knowing best in mine own conscience that I am a sinner indeed, I wil put further examples in myself, but ever to your erudition and warning. If I stand here this day in the midst of them that pray, and I pray not, in the midst of them that mourn, and I mourn not, at least ways so far forth as it becometh a Christian man to mourn at the death of them of whose estate nevertheles he hath no doubt, because they departed in the faith of Christ and God: (for so the apostles mourned for the death of Stephen, and the patriarchs at the death of Jacob and Joseph, not doubting of their condition, but serving their own nature and duty of charity.) If I, I say, stand here in the midst of them, that following that example of Judas Maccabæus, who sent 12000 coin to Jerusalem, to be offered for the sins of the dead, do make their obligations here this day at the obsequies of this vertuous and gracious lady, and I in the mean season do mislike their doings, murmuring therat with Judas Iscariot, *Ut quid perditio hæc?* If I,

being ful of infidelity and malice, stand among you, being
so many nobles, or (which is the title and honour that ye
can bear in this world) Christian men. And while you in
time of divine sacrifice, do faithfully and humbly, both in
heart and utter gesture, agnize, reverence, and adore the
same flesh in substance, altho' unvisibly in the sacrament,
which we al shal se in the latter day visible coming in the
firmament; and in the mean season condemn in my heart the
church, and you thus doing, blaspheme so great mystery,
repute the flesh wherby I was redeemed, and the blood of
Christ wherby I was to be sanctified, as a thing common
and pollute; who doubteth but on this case it were better
for me to be out of the church than in it. I do not say absolutely to be out, but in this case rather to be out than in
the church.

Likewise, if ye ask whether is better for me to be born in
this world, and be a rebeller, a murderer, a heretic, a blasphemer, or not to be born at al? In this case I must answer,
better is never to be born: according as Solomon saith, 280
Feliciorem utroque judicavi, &c. leaving ever for a conclusion, that to be born is good, so as we, being regenerate in
water and in the Holy Ghost, do after walk in newnes of life,
and persist in our first profession as members of Christ's catholic church, else not. And therfore of others, which be
fallen from grace and from the church, and be vessels of
ire, and death everlasting, it shal suffice to say, that altho'
better were for them not to be born, yet forasmuch as in
their just punishment the justice of God is to the world set
forth and reveled, it is in a sort necessary so to be, that you,
and al other, knowing the ire and displeasure of God against
his enemies, rebels, and blasphemers, should wholly dedicate yourselves to his obedience, love, and service: thanking God of your creation, of your preservation in this world,
and especially of your redemption by Christ; whom God
the Father hath given unto you, and by him al things. By
whose death it is brought to pas, that corporal death, which
in the beginning was ordained for a pain and punishment, is
now to this good lady, and to al that dyed as she did, a re-

medy and a benefit. And wheras also, death would have been a terrible thing, it is now become most pleasant and acceptable, especially by them that be firmly persuaded another life to be after this, and better than this. Which we must confes to be true, or deny these words of Solomon, *Laudavi mortuos magis quam viventes:* which must be true.

By which words I have occasion given to compare the state of the dead and the living; they being in appearance but two estates; which the church nevertheles hath used to divide into three, whensoever by prayer out of this place it commendeth to God the estates universal. Which I profess to follow.

[*Here he made his prayer for the spiritualty, temporalty, and souls in purgatory.*]

Laudavi mortuos magis, &c. I am driven to compare together two things of their own nature most diverse and contrary, that is to say, life and death, the condition of the living and the condition of the dead. Altho' indeed there is no comparison between them, no similitude, nor possibility to express the felicity of the one, and the misery and calamity of the other. The writers, as wel prophane as ecclesiastical, have wondred to se man so weak and feeble a creature, made subject to so many crosses and calamities, and endeavouring themselves to describe the burden of evils and adversities which man beareth in this world, hath spent their eloquence and invention therabout; and yet were they never able to express the same worthily, and as the thing required. The very same writers, or at the least ways so many of them as were persuaded of the resurrection of the flesh, knowing that corporal death is a passage to a better life, like men standing afar off, and looking after their friends, when they were departed, pronounced of their estate, not by experience, as of worldly adversities which they themselves 281 dayly tasted of, but by credence to God's word, and confidence in his merciful ordinance, that the condition of men departed in God, doth so far in true felicity and joy exceed the condition of the living, as the tongue of man can never suffice to declare, neither the ear to hear, *sed nec in cor hominis ascendit :* concluding, this present life to be ful of miseries, the life to come to be al in joy and happines.

Only this we must remember withal, that two kind of men dyeth : the faithful, the infidel ; the obedient, the rebellious. There are that dyeth under the unity of the church ; there are that dyeth in the sedition of Core. There are that dyeth under the gospel ; there are that dyeth under the Alcoran. As touching the worser sort of these, that is to say, infidels, rebels, and heretics, whom God no more remembreth to relieve with his merits, *quorum non est memor amplius*, because their woful and doleful estate can no otherways be expressed, it shal suffice me to say, and you to know, that they be in pain, in dolour, in ire, in fire, in darknes, and horror : the indignation, the scourge, the vengeance of God, with confusion and damnation everlasting, is powred on them. Neither have they qualification of pain, nor intermission of time, nor hope of end. Oh ! merciful Lord, if this be the condition of men, the end of worldly glory, riches, and vanity, in what case stand we, or whither shal we repair, to take a true view of our condition, but to the words of Solomon, *Feliciorem utroque judicavi qui necdum natus est ?*

Undoubtedly, Right Honourable, it is most true ; neither is there any other end of some, but confusion, death, and darknes. And that without difference, save that only this difference is *potentes potenter*, that is to say, all shal suffer for sin, but *the more mighty men shal suffer more mightily*, the stronger more strongly. I consider that now I speak among them that be mighty : whom, as one ways I reverence, so another ways I wil be bold with them in such things as it behoveth them to hear, and is hurtful for me not to speak.

First, the ministers of Christ's Church, whom the Holy Ghost hath placed there to instruct the flock, and to rule and govern this church which Christ hath purchased with his bloud, *regere Ecclesiam Dei, quam Christus acquisivit in sanguine suo :* they be men of great might, and hath that authority from God which this world cannot give them nor take from them. That that Paul did write to them of Corinth, to assemble together by his assent and authority, altho' he were then corporally absent, saying, *In meo spiritu*, and to deliver to Satan, that is to say, to excommunicate out of the church him that had committed incest with his mother in law: that argueth a mervaillous authority. And likewise, in that *whose sins they remit, are remitted, whose sins they retain, are retained.* But the greater power and authority of the church may be understanded in this, Vid. 1 Cor. *Ecclesia omnes judicat, a nemine judicatur:* i. e. *The* ii. 15. He *church judgeth al men, and is judged of none.* After this that is spi- ritual, judg- sort the church is *potens,* and the ministers thereof *potentes.* eth all things, &c. Who being by God placed, and as the prophet Ezekiel 282 saith, appointed to keep watch and ward upon the walls, and give warning when the enemy cometh, if they se the wolf toward the flock, as at this present, I warn you, the wolves be coming out of Geneva, and other places of Germany, and hath sent their books before, ful of pestilent doctrines, blasphemy, and heresy, to infect the people; if the bishops, I say, and ministers, in this case, should not give warning, neither withstand and resist, but for fear or flattery with the world, forsake their places, and therby give occasion to the wolf to enter, and devour the flock; then should the more mighty be more mightily scourged, and the bloud of the people required at their hands: as it is written, *Sanguinem populi de manu presbyteri requiram.*

Likewise among the temporal estates, there are the princes of the world most mighty and excellent above others. There are the dukes and magistrates, whom whosoever doth not obey, he resisteth the ordinances of God. There are judges to whom the Prince committeth the office of justice; as Trajan the emperor did deliver the sword of justice to his chief officer, with this charge, *Hoc gladio pro me utere, si justa impero, contra me, si injusta:* expresly commanding his own authority and sword of justice to be used against himself, when the equity of the law should so require.

Al these be, as you can consider, mighty. Now, if any of them, be he spiritual or temporal, forsake his place, neg-

lect his office, rule not rightly, judge not justly, counsil not
faithfully; then shal his own judgment be more strait, his
punishment more sharp and fierce, than the punishment of
the poor and simple; and in his chastisement it shal be
proved true, *potentes potenter.*

But hitherto I compare the punishment [between the
strong] and the weak, both being offenders against God,
and both perhaps yet living. The words of Solomon, *Laudavi mortuos magis,* &c. seemeth rather to compare the
estate of the living and the dead, both being in the favour
of God. And altho' of itself there be no doubt nor question
herein among the faithful, yet the love that we have toward
this present life, and the faint faith that we have in the life
to come, hath made a question: and so much the more,
because Solomon in the book of Proverbs hath other words,
as it seemeth, clean contrary, *Melius est canis vivus, quam
leo mortuus :* which is a perillous place, not only preferring
the living before the dead, but preferring the living in a vile
and base estate before the dead, being a far more worthy
creature in man's judgment. For what beast is more vile
than a dog, more worthy than a lion? For such is the sense
of the letter; but far from the meaning of the writer.
Wherfore let us seek the right meaning.

And first, consider, Right Honourable, that the dog, altho' The praise
we use sometimes his name in spight, yet is he of all beasts of a dog.
the most familiar and faithful to man. He is of household
with us, and in our way abroad a true traveiler with his
master; as in the history of young Tobias. He keepeth
watch and ward day and night. He warneth when the 283
enemy cometh: he is ready to do with and for his master.
The history of the poor man in the gospel, whose wounds
the dogs did lick, setteth forth the charity of the beast, in
rebuke to man, who towards his even-christen useth not the
like charity. David the prophet and king, a man of gifts
incomparable, yet compareth himself to a dog. *Quem persequeris, rex Israel? Quem persequeris? Canem unum,
aut culicem unum persequeris?* Of these properties, man,
as ye se, is in the Scriptures sometimes called *canis.* In the

which sense also the prophet calleth the preachers, which are appointed to bark against sin, and barketh not, *Canes mutos, non valentes latrare ; dumb dogs, not able to bark.*

Now are we almost come to the right understanding of these words, *Melior est canis vivus*, &c. that is to say, Better is one lively preacher in the church, that dareth to bark against sin, blasphemy, heresy; better is one lively officer or magistrate in the commonweal, that dareth to speak against injuries, extortions, seditions, rebellions, and other discords, than the dead lion : that is to say, men, perhaps, of great dignity and vocation, who dare not open their mouths and bark ; but suffereth, while al goeth to ruin, to the decay of Christian religion, and the subversion of the public wealth. Hely was Leo, he was a lion of power and authority, as one that governed and judged the people. But in that he dissembled discords, injuries, and extortions, committed especially by his own children, in that he was **The dead lion.** *leo mortuus, a dead lion.* And the plague of God therfore fel upon him. And then like Aaron, who, in the absence of Moses fourty days, condescended, or rather procured that golden calf to be made, wherby idolatry was committed, whatsoever he was at other times or places, yet, for that time and act he was *leo mortuus,* that is to say, a sleeping lion, whom Moses coming from the mount did awake and rebuke, laying to his charge, *quod induxisset in suum populum peccatum maximum.* And therfore, upon Moses de- **The living dog.** claring himself to be *canis vivus,* in punishment of that idolatry, he caused the people to draw their swords one against another. Wherupon exceeding many were slain : I remember not the number now.

Helias was *canis vivus,* when Achab laid to his charge, *Tu conturbas Israel,* he awake with these words, and said, *Ego non conturbo Israel, sed tu, et domus patris tui, qui dereliquisti mandata Domini, et secuti estis Baal :* S. John, that rebuked Herod ; S. Matthew, that rebuked Hircanus for marrying a woman professed a nun ; S. Ambrose, S. Basil, Cyrillus, Amphilochius, and an infinite number more, which in their sermons never spared to rebuke sin; all these were *canes vivi*. Now say I, one living dog, that is to say, one vigilant minister in the church, such as they were, which of good zele did bark against sin and heresy; persecuting that in me, not that that God hath created, but that that the Devil hath planted; one provident governor under the Prince in the commonweal, which shal confer al his studie, travail, and labour, to advaunce the public weal, and not to support sedition and discord; who for himself 284 shal covet nothing inordinately; but when he shal dy, be able truly to write as Ausonius did, *Non auxi, non minui rem;* that is to say, *I have made my revenues no more nor less.* Or be as another was, of whom Herodianus writeth, *Quum omnium plurimum administrasset, erat omnium pauperrimus: He meddled with most matters of al, [and became poorest of al;]* one such, I say, more profiteth Christ's Church, and more advaunceth the commonweal of this country; and therefore is more worthy than ten dreaming dead lions. And the words of Solomon, *Melior est canis vivus,* &c. being thus understood, be not contrary to *Laudavi mortuos,* &c.

So as it is stil left for a most certain ground, that happier is he that in the faith of Christ is departed out of this world, than he that yet liveth in the world. And we being hereof fully persuaded, have no cause to lament, but rather to thank God, and rejoice at the death of them that are so departed, as is now this vertuous and gracious lady, this innocent and unspotted Queen: whose body lyeth there in your lap, whose livery is on your back, whose memory is or ought to be printed in your hearts: whose fame is spred throughout the world, whose praise the stones wil speak, if we do not; and whose soul I verily believe, without prejudice of God's judgment be it spoken, is now in heaven, *ibique sacrificium offert; et pro nobis orat.* And from thence, by means of the glas she looketh in, beholdeth and seeth us: she of herself being too good to tarry any longer among us, *utpote qua dignus non fuit mundus.* Wherfore, I say once again, happier is she now, than when she lived: altho then, in the sight of the world, she was not [at] al unhappy, in the sight of God less.

The praise of the Queen.

She was a king's daughter, she was a king's sister, she was a king's wife : she was a queen, and by the same title a king also. She was a sister to her, that by the like title and right is both king and queen, at this present, of this realm. These be great gifts and benefactions of God ; who in his gifts is ever to be glorified. What she suffered in each of these degrees before and since she came to the crown, I wil not chronicle; only this I say, howsoever it pleased God to will her patience to be exercised in the world, she had in al estates the fear of God in her heart. I verily believe the poorest creature in al this city feared not God more than she did. She had the love, commendation, and admiration of al the world. In this church she maried herself unto this realm, and in token of faith and fidelity did put a ring with a diamond upon her finger; which I understand she never put off after, during her life, whatsoever succes things had : for that is in the hand of God only. She was never unmindful or uncareful of her promise to her realm. She used singular mercy toward offenders. She used much pity and compassion towards the poor and oppressed. She used clemency among her nobles. She restored more noble houses decayed, than ever did prince of this realm, or I pray God ever shal have the like occasion to do hereafter. She re-285 stored to the church such ornaments as in the time of schism were taken away and spoiled. She found the realm poisoned with heresy, and purged it ; and remembring herself to be a member of Christ's Church, refused to write herself *head* thereof. Which title, never no prince, a thousand and five hundred years after Christ, usurped; and was herself by learning able to render a cause why. She could say, that after Zacharias was dead, a Onias the prince

---

a This preacher seems not to be well skilled in Scripture-history. For he mistakes the name of the prince : whose name was not Onias, but Uzziah. And the high priest's name that succeeded Zacharias was Azariah : who withstood the king, when he was going to offer incense. 2 *Chron.* xxvi.

took on him the priest's office, which prospered not with
him, because it was not his vocation, but God struck him
therfore with leprosy in his forehead: and the prophesy
was fulfilled, *Imple facies illorum ignominia*: she could
say, How can I, a woman, be head of the church, who by
Scripture am forbidden to speak in the church? *Mulier
taceat in ecclesia*: except the church shal have a dumb
head? The head of the church must of consequence and
duty preach in the church; and he must offer *sacrificia
pro peccatis mortuorum*. But it is not read, neither in the
Old, neither in the New Testament, that ever women did
sacrifice. These and the like authorities of Scripture she
was able to alledg, why she could not be *caput ecclesiæ*,
and by learning defended the same. Such was her knowledg as wel as vertue: neither ever was there prince on
earth that had more of both.

But altho' she were such a one, yet could she not be immortal. It pleased God, in whose hand the heart and
breath, the life and death, the beginning and end of princes
is, to cal her from this mortal life, of the pleasures therof
(the pleasure she took in the service of God only excepted)
no person, I suppose, took les; so of the troubles and bitter-
nes of the same, none here for his estate taketh more. How
she took her sicknes, and disposed her self against death: Her sick-
how she committed herself to God, and the realm to his ness and
providence: what she did, what she said, how meekly she death.
demanded, and with what reverence she received the sacraments of Christ's church, and especially the sacrament
which Christ hath ordained to be a passeport and safe conduit for a Christian man into the heaven of everlasting
quiet and rest; and therefore called *viaticum*: and after
that, extreme unction, she being, by use of prayer, as expert
to say the psalms without book, as the priest was to read
them therein: how, in the mass-time, at the elevation of the
sacrament, the strength of her body and use of her tongue
being taken away, yet nevertheles she at that instant lifted
up her eyes, *ministros, nuncios devoti cordis*; and in the
benediction of the church, as Jacob blessed his children,

she bowed down her head, and withal yielded a mild and gracious spirit into the hands of her Maker : all this, I say, if it were as pithily expressed, as she godly and devoutly did it, should be to you, as it was to them that saw it, more than ten such sermons. If angels were mortal, I would [rather] liken this her departure to the death of an angel, than of a mortal creature.

286   After this sort dyed this gracious Queen, of whom we may justly say, *Laudavi mortuam magis quam viventem.* And altho' we doubt not of her estate, yet because it is temerity to pronounce of God's secret judgments, or to deny prayer ; to deny [to] one which is due to al ; let us again commend her soul to God, wishing to her, as Tertullian teacheth, *refrigerium et in prima resurrectione consortium.* Which prayer, if it relieve not her, (as one that with God's grace and mercy hath the effect thereof already,) yet shal it help us the rather before God, from whom the prayer of his faithful is never turned back, [or] in vain. And as we for our parts have received worthily detriment and discomfort upon her departing, so let us comfort ourselves in the other sister, whom God hath left, wishing her a prosperous reign in peace and tranquillity, with the blessing which the prophet speaketh of, if it be God's wil, *ut videat filios filiorum et pacem super Israel :* ever confessing, that tho' God hath mercifully provided for them both, yet *Maria optimam partem elegit ;* because it is stil a conclusion, *Laudavi mortuos magis quam viventes.*

And now it only remaineth that we, leaving to speak of these two noble ladies, look and provide for ourselves ; and seing these daily casualties of death, gather our fardles, and put ourselves in a readines [for] what [may happen] by and by. And at this time of the year, [when] it is cold weather and winter, we are taught by Scripture to pray, that we dy not in winter. *Orate ne in hyeme fiat fuga vestra, nec in sabbato.* That is to say, *Pray that ye depart not in winter, nor in the sabbath-day.* Which saying, if it be literally to be taken, in what case is this good lady, which is like now in winter, and this very day, being the shortest day of al the year, to be buried, and creep into the ground. For an answer, understand, Right Honorable, that winter here mentioned consisteth not in cold weather, short days, and long nights, but in cold zeal and affection, and in short devotion towards God, and in cold love and charity towards our neighbours. Pray, therefore, that ye dye not in such a winter, when your charity and devotion shall be cold; which chaunceth at Midsumer as wel as at this time of the year. And touching the other word, *nec in sabbato;* understand [not] therby the sabboth-day of the Jews, which was al in superstition, [but] vacation from good works, with murmuring against the merciful and wonderful works of God. Pray, I say, that ye dye not void of good works, knowing that *qui bona egerint, ibunt in vitam æternam*, &c. neither in rebellion nor murmuring against God and the sacraments of his church, which he daily, by the word of God and the power of men, mercifully and miraculously worked for us.

It followeth, (for I wil touch, but not tary,) *Væ! prægnantibus in illa die;* that is, Woe! to women which shall be great with child, when God shal visit them with death: which words seem hitherto to threaten women dying in child-bed. Among whom, nevertheles, an opinion hath obtained, that to dye *in the bond*, as they cal it, *of our Lady*, and travail of child, hath some furtherance to the favour of God's mercye, in consideration of the travail, pain, and 287 burden wherwith the mother dyeth. And of that opinion am I, and agree with them therin: but the words *Væ! prægnantibus in illo die*, stretcheth as wel to men as to women. For the sense is, Wo! be to him, be he man or woman, that when God shal call him out of this present life shal be found great with child, that is to say, great and puffed up with pride, replenished with wrath, malice, ambition, and covetousnes, that shal have *oculos adulterii plenos*, his eyes ful of concupiscence, his tongue swelling with words of blasphemy, al his mind and body ful of thoughts and actions of sin and disobedience. That man or woman is great with child indeed; and such a child as shal be to the parents everlasting confusion. Esaias writeth, *Væ! genti pecca-trici populo gravi iniquitate*; men or women great with such sinful babes as be spoken of before.

Wherfore to conclude, Right Honorable, let us pray and foresee, that when God shal cal us out of this life, our hearts be not possest with the frost of cold charity and de-votion, neither we be found to keep holiday with the Jews by abstinence from al good works of our own parts, and by the murmuring against Christ and his Church; neither that we be found *prægnantibus in illo die*, but rather lean and lank from such vices; and nevertheles ful and re-plenished [with grace.] *Bonum est gratia stabiliri cor.* Let us pray to God for that grace: let us dedicate ourselves wholly to his service, remaining under his obedience, and within the unity of his Church; within the which none can perish, neither without it be saved. And the day now draw-eth near in the which we are to be visited by corporal death. Let us pray, by voluntary yielding at God's calling to go against him. That we may be worthy through the merits and death of our Saviour Jesus Christ, through faith in him, and obedience to him, to be partakers of everlasting life, joy, and felicity, in the company of his saints, living and lauding him everlastingly. *Cui cum Patre et Spiritu Sancto*, &c.

288

Number LXXXII.

A prayer of the Lady Mary to the Lord Jesu; against the assaults of vices.

E MSS. D.
Sampson.
M. D.

MOST benigne Lord Jesu! Behold me, wretched beggar and most vile sinner, prostrate here before the feet of thy mercy. Behold the wounds, sores, griefs, and vices of my soul, (which, alas! I have brought into the same by sin,) that they may be healed.

Most merciful Lord Jesu! Have pity upon mine infirmi-ties, captivity, and infelicity: by means wherof my miserable soul is pressed down to earthly things, and divided into sundry desires.

Most loving Jesu! I beseech thee for thy great loves sake, which caused thee to deliver thy soul into the hands of sinners to be bound and crucified; and which also did force thee to remain three hours upon the cross, more than the nails either of thy hands or feet had power to do.

For thy charity I humbly desire thee to loose the yoke of my captivity, and to deliver me from al my vices, concupiscence, and evil inclinations, to defend me from al the assaults of mine enemies, and in time of temptation to help me.

Moreover, quench and pluck up by the roots in me al private love, al inordinate motions, passions, and affections, al provokings, readines, and inclinations to pride, wrath, envy, and vain glory, with such other like. For it is in thy power only to deliver me from these things.

Sweet Jesu! Fulfil me with thy grace and most perfect charity. Make me to continue in goodnes, that I may eschew al occasion of sin, strongly overcome temptations, subdue the flesh to the spirit, persecute and banish sin, and obey thy inspiration; escape the deceits and frauds of the Devil, never consent to any sin, nor nourish any thing that should displease thee. But cause me most fervently to thirst for thy honor, laud, and glory, most faithfully to prefer the same, and to give and submit myself wholly to thy wil.

My Lord God, give me grace to cleave to thee only with a clean and pure heart, that I may be unite and knit to thee without separation by a most chaste and fervent love. *Amen.*

Number LXXXIII.

289

A meditation touching adversity, made by my Lady Mary's Grace, 1549.

THIS natural life of ours is but a pilgrimage from this wandring world, and exile from our own country: that is to say, a way from all misery to thee (Lord,) which art our whole felicity. And lest the pleasantnes and commodity of this life should withdraw us from the going to the right and

Ubi supra.

speedy way to thee, thou dost stir and provoke us forward, and as yet ward prick us with thornes, to the intent we should covet a quiet rest, and end of our journey.

Therfore sicknes, weepings, sorrow, mourning, and in conclusion all adversities, be unto us as spurs; with the which we being dull horses, or rather very asses, are forced not to remain long in this transitory way.

Wherfore, Lord, give us grace to forget this way-faring journey, and to remember our proper and true country. And if thou do add a weight of adversity, add therunto strength, that we shal not be overcome with that burden: but having our minds continually erected and lift up to thee, we may be able strongly to bear it.

Lord! al things be thine; therfore do with al things, without any exception, as shal seem convenient to thine unsearchable wisdom. And give us grace never to wil but as thou wilt. So be it.

Number LXXXIV.

A prayer to be read at the hour of death.

supra.   O LORD Jesu! which art the health of al men living, and the everlasting life of them which dye in faith, I, wretched sinner, give and submit myself wholly unto thy most blessed will.

And I being sure that the thing cannot perish which is committed unto thy mercy, willingly now I leave this frail 290 and wicked flesh, in hope of the resurrection; which in better wise shal restore it to me again.

I beseech thee, most merciful Lord Jesus Christ, that thou wilt by thy grace make strong my soul against al temptations; and that thou wilt cover and defend me with the buckler of thy mercy against al the assaults of the Devil.

I se and knowledg that there is in myself no help of salvation, but al my confidence, hope, and trust is in thy most merciful goodnes.

I have no merits nor good works which I may alledge before thee. Of sins and evil works (alas!) I se a great heap;

but through thy mercy I trust to be in the number of them to whom thou wilt not impute their sins; but take and accept me for righteous and just, and to be an inheritor of everlasting life.

Thou, merciful Lord, wert born for my sake. Thou didst suffer both hunger and thirst for my sake. Thou didst preach and teach, thou didst pray and fast for my sake. Thou didst al good works and deeds for my sake. Thou sufferedst most grievous pains and torments for my sake. And, finally, thou gavest thy most precious body to dye, and thy bloud to be shed on the cros for my sake.

Now, most merciful Saviour, let al these things profit me which thou freely hast given me, that hast given thyself for me. Let thy bloud cleanse and wash away the spots and fowlnes of my sins. Let thy righteousnes hide and cover my unrighteousnes. Let the merits of thy passion and bloud be the satisfaction for my sins.

Give me, Lord, thy grace, that my faith and salvation in thy bloud waver not in me, but ever be firm and constant; that the hope of thy mercy and life everlasting never decay in me; that charity wax not cold in me.

Finally, that the weaknes of my flesh be not overcome with the fear of death. Grant me, merciful Father, that when death hath shut up the eyes of my body, yet that the eyes of my soul may stil behold and look upon thee: that when death hath taken away the use of my tongue and speech, yet that my heart may cry and say unto thee, *In manus tuas, Domine, commendo spiritum meum;* that is, O Lord, into thy hand I give and commit my soul: *Domine, Jesu, accipe spiritum meum;* Lord Jesu, receive my soul unto thee. *Amen.*

291   Number LXXXV.

An account of such as were burned for religion in this reign.

MSS. Cecilian.	Year.	Counties.	Number executed.	Places of execution.	
	1555.	London and Middles.	12	Smithfield	9
				Westminster	1
				Uxbridge	2
		Essex	15	Stratford Bowe	2
				Rayley	1
				Hornedon on the Hill	1
				Colchester	2
				Hadley	1
				Ardeley	1
				Rochford	1
				Coxhall	1
				Chelmsford	1
				Maningtree	1
				Harwich	1
				Walden	2
		Hartford	3	Barnet	1
				St. Albons	1
				Ware	1
		Kent	18	Canterbury	15
				Rochester	1
				Dartford	1
				Tunbridg	1
		Sussex	4	Chichester	2
				Lewes	1
				Steyning	1
		Suffolk	3	Bury	1
				Ipswich	1
				Yexford	1
		Norfolk	2	Walsingham	1
				Tetford	1
		Ely Insula	2	Ely	2
		Oxford	2	Oxford	2

Year.	Counties.	Number executed.	Places of execution.	
1555.	Warwick	5	Litchfeld	2
			Coventree	3
	Gloucester	1	Gloucester Civitas	1
	Chester	1	West-chester Civitas	1
	Carmarthen	1	Carmarthen	1
	Pembrook	1	Haverford West	1
	-	1	Cardiff	1
		71		
1556.	London and Middles.	16	Smithfeld	16 292
	Essex	21	Colchester	6
			Stratford Bowe	15
	Kent	7	Canterbury	5
			Rochester	2
	Sussex	10	Lewes	6
			Mayfeld	4
	Suffolk	8	Beckels	3
			Bury	3
			Ipswich	2
	Cambridg	1	Cambridg	1
	Oxon.	1	Oxford	1
	Gloucester	6	Bristol	2
			Glouc. Civitas	2
			Wootton Underhedg	2
	Leycester	2	Leycester	2
	Northt.	1	Northampton	1
	Berk.	3	Newbery	3
	Wiltes.	3	Salisbury	3
	Darby	1	Darby	1
	Guernsey Insula.	3		
		89		
1557.	London and Middles.	14	Smithfeld	10
			Islington	4

Year.	Counties.	Number executed.	Places of execution.	
1557.	Surrey	3	St. George's Felds	3
	Essex	12	Colchester	12
	Kent	24	Canterbury	13
			Wye	2
			Ashford	2
			Maydston	7
	Sussex	27	Lewes	10
			Chichester diocesse elsewhere	17
	Norfolk	5	Norwich	5
	Suffolk	1	Laxfeld	1
	Warwick	1	Lichfeld	1
	Northt.	1	Northampton	1
		88		
1558.	London and Middles.	16	Smithfeld	10
			Brainford	6
	Kent	5	Canterbury	5
	Essex	3	Colchester	3
	Norfolk	3	Norwich	3
	Suffolk	9	Ipsewich	2
			Bury	7
	Southt.	1	Winchester	1
	Gloucest.	2	Bristoll	2
	Devon.	1	Exeter	1
		40		

Annis { 1555——71
         1556——89
         1557——88
         1558——40 }

Total 288, besides those that dyed of famyne in sondry prisons.

A

TABLE

OF

LETTERS, PROCLAMATIONS, SPEECHES, RECORDS, TRACTS, &c.

PRESERVED IN THE FOREGOING CATALOGUE.

in writing, as most convenient, in his judgment, to be commoned and spoken of by her Majesty with her Council, called
to her presence that afternoon.

Number LXXXI. A sermon preached at the funerals of Queen
Mary : by the Bishop of Winchester.

Number LXXXII. A prayer of the Lady Mary's, against the
assaults of vices.

Number LXXXIII. A meditation touching adversity, made by
my Lady Mary's Grace, an. 1549.

Number LXXXIV. A prayer to be read at the hour of death.

Number LXXXV. An account of such as were burned to death
for religion in this reign; specifying the year when, and
place wherein each suffered.

Im TheStory
personalised classic books

"Beautiful gift, lovely finish.
My Niece loves it, so precious!"

Helen R Brumfieldon

⭐⭐⭐⭐⭐

UNIQUE GIFT

FOR KIDS, PARTNERS
AND FRIENDS

Timeless books such as:

Kids

Alice in Wonderland · The Jungle Book · The Wonderful Wizard of Oz
Peter and Wendy · Robin Hood · The Prince and The Pauper
The Railway Children · Treasure Island · A Christmas Carol

Adults

Romeo and Juliet · Dracula

Highly Customizable

Change Book's Title

Replace Character's Names with yours

Upload Photo to inside page!

Add Inscriptions

Visit
Im TheStory.com
and order yours today!

CPSIA information can be obtained
at www.ICGtesting.com
Printed in the USA
BVHW081609220819
556561BV00017B/3670/P